```
HF
5823
K39
1964 (1)
KIRKPATRICK, C A
ADVERTISING
```

Date Due		
DEC 1 8 1974	MAR 3 1 1987	JAN 2 3 1990
APR 1 1 1976		AUG 1 4 1991
NOV 1 1 1976		FEB 1 9 1992
OCT 9 1977		
DEC 1 4 1979		
DEC 1 1 1981		
NOV 2 8 1983		
MAY 1 2 1984		
DEC 1 2 1986		

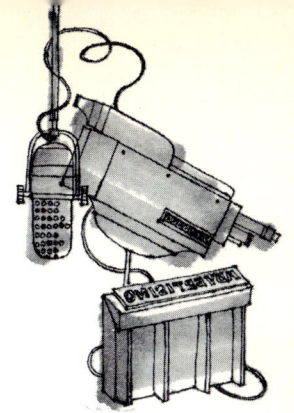

UNDER THE GENERAL EDITORSHIP OF

Taylor W. Meloan, THE UNIVERSITY OF SOUTHERN CALIFORNIA

HOUGHTON MIFFLIN ADVISER IN MARKETING

ADVERTISING

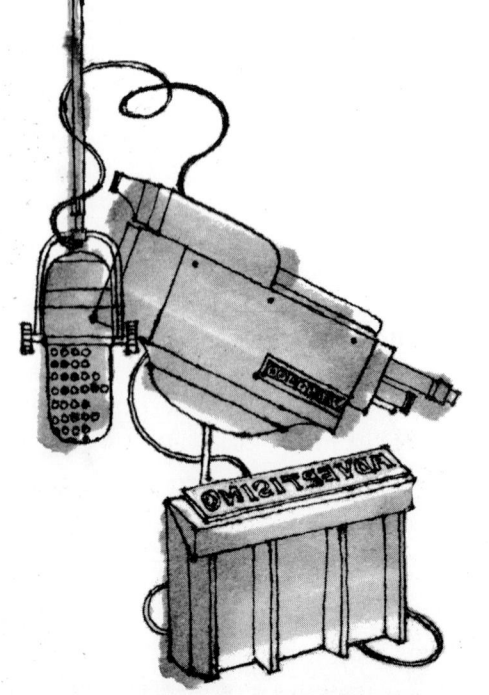

SECOND EDITION

MASS *Communication*
IN *Marketing*

C. A. KIRKPATRICK
University of North Carolina

HOUGHTON MIFFLIN COMPANY · BOSTON
New York · Atlanta · Geneva, Ill. · Dallas · Palo Alto

TO *Molly*

James and

Peter

COPYRIGHT © 1964, 1959 BY C. A. KIRKPATRICK
ALL RIGHTS RESERVED, INCLUDING THE RIGHT TO REPRODUCE
THIS BOOK OR PARTS THEREOF IN ANY FORM.
PRINTED IN THE U.S.A.

General Editor's Introduction

Advertising is an important, sometimes maligned, sometimes overpraised, and often misunderstood function in business and society. The manifold goals of advertising and its role in a marketing communications program need to be understood by tomorrow's professional managers who are now in our colleges and universities. This is equally true of those who will become administrators in the public sector of our economy. For those embarking upon careers in advertising, appreciation of the rationale and strategies behind advertising campaigns, and in-depth knowledge of the operations of advertising institutions, and the characteristics of media are the basic requisites for initial placement and worthwhile contributions to the field.

The second edition of this highly readable text contributes to all of the foregoing objectives, proceeding from analysis of the nature and contributions of advertising to the detailed coverage of media and management of campaigns and the resources to implement them.

TAYLOR W. MELOAN

University of Southern California

Preface

This is the second edition of our textbook about advertising, a subject of relevance to every college student. Some students will go into the world of marketing. Some will go into the communications areas. Some will join the accounting, personnel, finance, and production staffs of firms which advertise. All students will continue to be exposed to advertising. All can benefit from a better understanding of advertising.

Like its predecessor, this edition is primarily concerned with the advertising done by manufacturers. It recognizes advertising as one of three promotional forces sellers use, the other two being personal selling and sales promotion. Sellers buy and use advertising solely on the assumption that their net profit will be greater than otherwise, usually as a result of greater sales volume.

The two chapters comprising Part One are new. They summarize the field of marketing in which advertising operates, of which it is an integral part. Part Two examines the nature of advertising, focusing on its social and economic aspects. The chapter on marketing research in the first edition has been dropped. Part Three deals with identification — brand names, trade-marks, trade characters, and packaging. Part Four, as in the first edition, investigates how advertisements are built, and Part Five contains updated information about advertising media. Advertising management, or Part Six, has been reorganized into a more logical, more teachable sequence. This part now begins with scheduling and ends with evaluation. The final section, Part Seven, treats advertising organizations and institutions. The discussion of the organizations, advertising agencies and advertising departments, has been retained from the first edition. The treatment of the retail advertiser as an advertising institution has also been retained, and new material on the industrial advertiser and the trade advertiser has been added in this second edition.

The debts of the author are great; they are owed to many. Advertisers, representatives of various media, advertising agencies, and research firms have been most generous. Professors Taylor W. Meloan of the University of Southern California and Louis C. Wagner of the University of Washington have made valuable recommendations. Suggestions from users, both teachers and students, have received careful consideration. This edition is better because of the helpful suggestions and the keen criticisms of my colleague, Dr. Rollie Tillman. The author's greatest obligation, however, continues to be to Erma Hughes Kirkpatrick.

C. A. KIRKPATRICK

University of North Carolina

Contents

PART ONE

Marketing Fundamentals for Advertisers   1

Chapter 1   What Ultimate Consumers Buy   3
         2   How Sellers Sell   13

PART TWO

The Background for Advertising   31

Chapter 3   The Nature of Advertising   32
         4   Social and Economic Aspects   48

PART THREE

Identifying the Product   69

Chapter 5   Brand Names, Trade-Marks, and Trade Characters   70
         6   Packaging   93

PART FOUR

Building the Advertisement   107

Chapter 7   Benefits Which Appeal to Buyers   115
         8   Layout   136
         9   Copy   158
        10   Typography, Production, and Color   184

PART FIVE

Media   203

Chapter 11   Newspapers   205
       12   Magazines   219
       13   Television and Radio I   235
       14   Television and Radio II   253

15	Outdoor and Transit	271
16	Point of Purchase	291
17	Direct Mail	308

PART SIX

Advertising Management   325

Chapter 18	Scheduling	327
19	Manufacturers' Consumer Campaigns	345
20	Coordination	357
21	Budgeting	383
22	Evaluation	407

PART SEVEN

Advertising Organizations and Institutions   425

Chapter 23	The Advertising Agency	427
24	The Advertising Department	448
25	Industrial and Trade Advertisers	469
26	The Retail Advertiser	487

Index   509

ADVERTISING

Mass Communication in Marketing

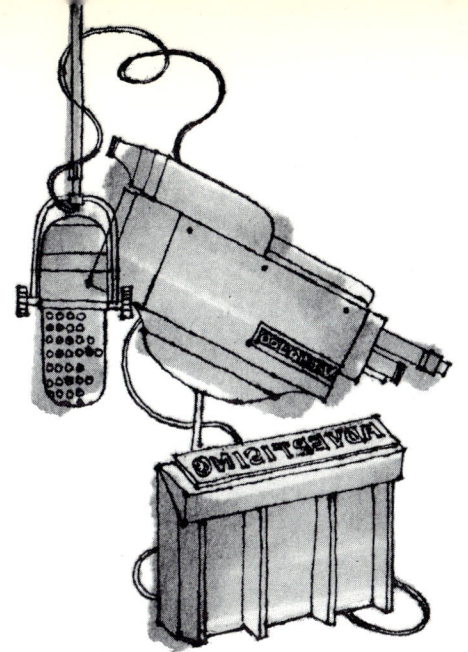

PART ONE

Marketing Fundamentals for Advertisers

Those of us in marketing are greatly concerned with (1) helping to determine the nature and the volume of products and services offered to consumers, (2) influencing prospects to buy those products and services, and (3) placing those products and services in the hands of ultimate consumers. Advertising is one of the methods used by sellers to influence buyers. Because advertising is undeniably a marketing activity, the marketing approach to the study of advertising is the only proper and logical approach.

Look at a hypothetical operating statement. Net sales for this seller, as for any seller, is the basic figure and is expressed as 100%. Of this 100% of sales revenue, 45% goes to cover the cost of the items sold, leaving a gross margin of 55%. This gross margin is then available to provide for three items: profit, general administration, and marketing. Marketing management is allotted 5%. Market stimulation gets 35%: 4 units of personal selling, 2 units of advertising, and 1 unit of sales promotion.

1

Marketing Fundamentals for Advertisers

HYPOTHETICAL OPERATING STATEMENT

Revenue and Gross Margin

Net Sales			100%
Cost of Goods Sold			− 45%
Gross Margin			55%

Gross Margin Breakdown

Profit			5%
General Administration			10%
Marketing			
Market Stimulation			
Personal Selling	20%		
Advertising	10%		
Sales Promotion	5%	35%	
Market Management		5%	40%
			55%

Because the advertising budget is part of the marketing budget, our text begins with a two-chapter section entitled "Marketing Fundamentals for Advertisers." In Chapter 1, we examine the key group in our economy — the ultimate consumer. We must have some understanding of the buying behavior of ultimate consumers and some knowledge of what they buy before we can determine how to reach the consumer through advertising. In Chapter 2, we consider the elements in a seller's promotional mix — Personal Selling, Advertising, Sales Promotion and the Marketing Channel problem manufacturers face. Next, we glance briefly at Publicity and Public Relations, matters closely related to market stimulation, and conclude the section with a consideration of the advertiser's never-ending need for Marketing Research.

Chapter 1

What Ultimate Consumers Buy

The most important buyer in our economy is the ultimate consumer, and the most important type of advertising is that addressed to ultimate consumers. Each consumer tries to exchange his limited and inadequate purchasing power for the assortment of goods and services which will give him the greatest amount of satisfaction. In this process, the consumer decides what *types* or *classes* of products to buy, and then he selects specific *items* or *brands* within those classes. Consumers buy as individuals *and* as members of families and households. This chapter reviews certain features of consumer buying of interest to advertisers.

ULTIMATE CONSUMERS ARE OMNIPOTENT

Consumers with purchasing power constitute a potential market. When motivated to buy, those consumers transform a potential market into a real market in which purchases and sales are made. Each seller designs his marketing program or mix to influence those consumers. Because the buyer is the key to the marketing mix, the seller focuses on him, knowing that a study of buyers is actually a study of demand. The manufacturer who studies the ultimate consumer and then designs and makes a product to suit him is much smarter than the manufacturer who starts with production and then expects the consumer to like and buy what the manufacturer decided to make.

The power of consumers is awesome. Because of his great freedom of choice, the consumer is able to set up his own scale of values and to establish his own goals. He determines which of his wants to satisfy and with what products or services. If enough consumers vote for brand "B" with their dollars, then brand "B" stays on the market and its manufacturer stays in business. Unless enough consumers buy brand "B," the manufacturer must change it so it will attract and capture greater patronage; otherwise, both brand "B" *and* its maker disappear.

The consumer, thus, is a king. He wields life-and-death power over product types and brands, over retailers and manufacturers. True, many consumers are ignorant about needs, product availability, product quality, prices, and sellers.

Marketing Fundamentals for Advertisers

Even so, smart sellers adopt the consumer's point of view; they know that consumers must be satisfied; they are consumer-oriented.

BASIC CONSUMER INFORMATION

If an advertiser is to enjoy the approval and patronage of a substantial number of consumers, if he is to please King Consumer, then he must be informed about *consumer characteristics, buying habits,* and *buying motives.*

Consumer Characteristics

Those consumer characteristics important to a seller depend, of course, upon who the seller is and what he sells. Manufacturers of automobiles, for example, do not need the exact information about consumers that manufacturers of soft drinks need. Despite these differences, we are entitled to assume that many manufacturers need information on these points:

> Number of prospective customers — Age — Sex — Location — Purchasing power — Vocation — Type of dwelling occupied — Education — Family size — Attitude toward manufacturer and his brand — Attitude toward competitors and their brands.

Buying Habits

Because consumers are omnipotent, advertisers must have adequate information about the buying habits of those consumers. Buying habits include the mechanics (the procedures) of buying; they are the *how* of buying. As was true of consumer characteristics, no attempt is made here to list all consumer buying habits of interest to all advertisers. Instead, the following are a few typical questions asked by many advertisers about these habits as they relate to an advertiser's *type* of product:

> When do consumers buy? — Where do they buy? — How much do they buy at a time? — What price do they pay? — What service do they expect when making a purchase? — Where do they get product information? — Does anyone else influence the purchase? — Who actually makes the purchase? — Is buying planned or is it done on impulse?

Buying Motives

Whereas buying habits involve *how* consumers buy, buying motives involve *why* they buy what they do. In a real sense, consumers spend money voluntarily for only one purpose — to get a certain satisfaction or a set of satisfactions. So, the advertiser needs to know *which* satisfactions consumers want and *which* satisfactions they can be induced to buy. This leads to an examination of what satisfactions, advantages, utilities, and benefits the advertiser's products and, indeed, the advertiser himself provide.

Because individuals are complex, consumer motivation is complicated. Motives are classified in various ways. This reflects the fact that a consumer is at the same time both an individual *and* a member of various groups. Instead of remaining

What Ultimate Consumers Buy

constant, consumer motivation is constantly changing in response to several influences. For these and other reasons, consumer motivation will be given more attention later in the text. At this point, it is enough for us to recognize that unless an advertisement promises (and an advertisement essentially is just that — a promise) something buyers want, the advertisement cannot be successful.

Because changes are always going on in consumer characteristics, in buying habits, and in buying motives, advertisers must *become* informed and then *stay* informed in these areas. Otherwise, they may learn in a painful, expensive way just how omnipotent consumers really are.

CONSUMERS BUY PRODUCT-SATISFACTION

The area of *products* (services too, of course, for their sellers) is a most fundamental one for advertisers. We have said earlier and correctly that consumers buy satisfaction. True. But consumers get this satisfaction, they experience and enjoy satisfaction, *only* by using up the utilities or want-satisfying capacities present in goods and services. Most goods and services are selected and bought by individuals who will do the consuming.

Types of Products

The traditional classification of consumer products uses three groupings — *convenience, shopping,* and *specialty.*

1. *Convenience* goods are usually thought of as including such products as cigarettes, chewing gum, soft drinks, candy bars, and magazines. The consumer may purchase these on impulse, or he may plan in advance to make such purchases.

2. *Shopping* goods are what most consumers buy when they purchase furniture, automobiles, appliances, women's ready-to-wear, and houses. In such purchases, quality and price are important considerations.

Just how do convenience goods differ from shopping goods? Although we will have to resort to some qualifications later, these generalizations about *product* differences are sound. The price per unit is low for convenience goods, but high for shopping goods. Thus, each purchase of convenience goods involves a small sum of money, whereas for shopping goods the amount is considerable. Convenience items are more standardized and, hence, more substitutive than are shopping goods. Frequency of repurchase is much higher for convenience products than for shopping products. The presence and the significance of fashion in convenience goods are just about nil, but they can be important in shopping goods. A convenience item is stocked by many, many retailers, a shopping item by a smaller number of dealers.

In addition to these product variations, there are differences involving the *consumer* about which we can generalize. By definition, the consumer's major objective when buying convenience goods is maximum convenience of location in buying; for shopping goods, his or her major objective is maximum value. A consumer's identification and recognition of want are clear and specific as regards convenience products, whereas he is often vague and uncertain about just what he

5

wants in the case of shopping goods. Consumer effort and trouble are at a minimum in the purchase of convenience items, but they often are considerable when shopping goods are involved. Because the potential rewards are small, consumers spend little time examining and comparing convenience products; larger potential rewards justify more comparison of shopping products. The act of buying convenience items can be measured in seconds or minutes, but the buying process for shopping goods often extends over days, even months. Many convenience products but very few shopping products are bought on impulse. Seldom do consumers want information or advice from retail salespersons about convenience goods, but often they want and need guidance and recommendations in the case of shopping goods.

3. *Specialty* goods as a type are not so clear-cut as either convenience or shopping goods, and, at best, each of these types is but a general concept subject to exceptions. Among the products which may well be specialty goods are expensive items in these classifications: perfume, watches, shoes, and men's ready-to-wear. However, a brand of beer, gasoline, headache remedy, or shampoo — all low in price — can be a specialty item. The significant factor in both groups of products is the brand image. Joy perfume, Rolex watches, French Shriner shoes, Hickey-Freeman suits, and Schlitz beer, Gulf gasoline, Bayer aspirin, and Breck shampoo can have such a strong and individual attraction for certain consumers that the brand image in each case places the product in the specialty classification. Certain consumers will not examine competing products when buying those types of product. Indeed, they will go to some trouble to get the brands they esteem so highly.

There is also a patronage version of specialty purchases. Consumers who concentrate their buying in Sears or in A&P stores because of great confidence in those retailers are making purchases of a "specialty" type. The man who buys only Arrow shirts buys a specialty product for brand reasons. The man who buys his shirts only from J. C. Penney stores (Arrow *or* Towncraft, the Penney brand) makes specialty purchases for patronage reasons. The retailer involved does not have to be huge. You may patronize one small bakery rather than another one, thus making its products *specialty* items so far as *you* are concerned.

Every product consumers buy which is not a *specialty* item can be classified as *convenience* or *shopping*.

Qualifications

All consumers do not put the same products into the same classifications. Some consumers shop impulsively only for small items like cigarettes and soft drinks; a few consumers think nothing of buying an expensive suit or watch on impulse. The *same* consumer can, indeed, buy one pair of shoes for shopping reasons, but buy the very next pair for patronage reasons. Then again, an automobile tire can be three types of product to three different buyers. The motorist who checks around and compares buys a shopping good. The motorist who buys only Goodyear tires (*or* Allstate tires) buys a specialty good. The tourist who has both a blowout and plenty of money 1000 miles from home is anxious to make a convenience purchase.

In classifying products, then, we do so in terms of how *most* consumers consider them *most* of the time.

CONSUMERS BUY SELLER-SUPPLIED SERVICES

Whenever a consumer makes a purchase, he, in effect, "buys" an assortment of items, or elements, or components; he "buys" a *group* of utilities. One component part of his omnibus purchase often consists of services sellers supply with merchandise. Sometimes certain of these services are supplied by the manufacturer, others are supplied by the retailer.

Some sellers offer the service of analyzing a buyer's circumstances and needs. The investment counselor or the department store's interior decorators are examples. Some sellers install, inspect, adjust, service, provide accessory equipment for, and train buyers' employees to use the equipment, machines, or appliances they sell. The product guarantee which assures the buyer that the seller will replace, repair, or refund is a service. Credit facilities and delivery are two more services, parking is still another.

In a somewhat different sense, a seller's return privileges, the way he handles complaints and makes adjustments, and what he does about claims and allowances all are part of what his customers buy. The high quality and the comforting competence of a manufacturer's or a retailer's salespersons can be a most valuable service. Even the personal good will and friendship of a seller or a salesman can be a significant consideration.

SELLERS' APPROACHES TO CONSUMER SATISFACTION

Sellers, including all advertisers, are most anxious to offer the product-satisfactions and services consumers want. A seller must constantly question the suitability and the profitability of his product or product line; "what" and "how many" to offer for sale are fundamental questions here.

Advertisers start by recognizing that their products must satisfy consumers' desires. This calls for a recognition of the significance of *merchandising* and for the adoption of the marketing concept. Essentially, this requires a seller to adapt his product to consumers' tastes and then make his brand one that consumers prefer. To be successful here, a seller must be willing to make product changes. His product must at least keep in step with and be the equal of competing products; it must reflect current consumer buying habits and buying motivation. In a sentence, a seller must offer the *right product,* at the *right place,* at the *right time,* with the *right promotion,* at the *right price,* and accompanied by the *right services.*

Even our overly brief reference to products dare not omit reference to *product quality.* A product's quality includes every feature and service which affect that product's capacity to give satisfaction to consumers. Each seller decides what quality of product to offer to buyers. His offering can be of high quality, of low quality, or of medium quality; it can include two of these levels or even all three.

Marketing Fundamentals for Advertisers

Many variables can affect product quality. Size, type, color, appearance, design, shape, raw materials, manufacturing process, workmanship, functional performance (economy, durability, efficiency) — these are examples of determinants of quality.

Two pressures operate in the area of product quality. (1) Consumers expect product quality to be uniform and consistent. The housewife wants the next can of soup or the next bottle of dressing to be just like what she has been buying and using. But (2) the housewife expects, and the manufacturer strives for, quality improvement over time. A rise in quality can, indeed, provide a powerful advertising theme for the manufacturer to use. Sellers often get ideas on how to improve product quality from their own employees (salesmen, production staff, research and development personnel), from prospects and customers, from suppliers, and even from competitors.

CONSUMERS BUY IMAGES

Advertisers must not overlook the role that imagery plays in consumer buying. We noted that the image distinguishes specialty goods from other classifications. Consumers do much more than buy identical products and services from identical sellers. In his buying, a consumer can be greatly influenced by (1) his images of competing *brands,* and (2) his images of competing *sellers*.

Image of the Brand

What are your thoughts and feelings about Pepsi-Cola vs. Coca-Cola — Crest vs. Colgate — Ivory vs. Dial — Gulf vs. Texaco — Ford vs. Chevrolet? What unique group of features and characteristics do you associate with each brand name? What mental pictures of each have become established in your mind?

The brand image is a complex symbol, complex in the same way as is human personality because brand images to you *are* products' personalities. Many consumers consider brand "A" masculine, competing brand "B" feminine. Or they see brand "C" high in prestige and status, competing brand "D" cause for apology or embarrassment because of its "cheapness." Brand "E" appears modern, brand "F" old-fashioned. When celebrating with guests, consumers buy brand "G"; for everyday family consumption, they buy brand "H."

Various factors determine a brand's image. The item's design, color, and package are examples of physical factors. Price, of course, can be a strong influence. The advertising promoting the brand is often a major determinant. Three other factors are: what kinds of consumers buy the brand, what kinds of retailers stock the brand, and what kind of a manufacturer makes the brand.

When a manufacturer's product is quite standardized and his product line quite simplified (cigarettes, gasoline, beer), he may adopt the marketing policy of *product differentiation.* His advertising would stress whatever slight differences he can identify, physical *or* psychological, in the hope of endowing his product with an attractive brand image. The other alternative, of course, is the policy of *market segmentation.* Here the manufacturer sees his total market as consisting of a number of smaller individual markets; he makes and offers different models or designs to each segment of his total market. Where the policy of product differentiation calls for product simplification, the policy of market segmentation leads toward product diversification.

Image of the Seller

When a consumer buys a manufacturer's branded product in a retail store, the consumer *may* be buying primarily because of the identity of either manufacturer *or* retailer; he *must* find the personality of each at least acceptable or he would not make that purchase. Seller image, thus, can involve manufacturers *or* retailers. Both types of seller hope that consumers' images of them will be favorable.

Advertising used by a seller specifically to create the image he desires of himself has been referred to as institutional, corporate, and strategic. This advertising promotes the seller himself, not what he sells. It attempts to build up his reputation, prestige, personality, vitality, and stature. It may stress his policies, research and development, facilities, progressiveness, performance, sense of responsibility, expansion or diversification, personnel, current activities, social contributions, or customer concern. Successful institutional advertising encourages consumers to make more purchases of *specialty* goods.

Institutional advertising is not the only type of advertising that contributes to and helps determine a seller's image. The *brand* advertising a seller does cannot help but give buyers some idea or impression, or some mental picture of the *seller* of the brand even though this type of advertising works primarily to create *brand* image.

CONSUMERS BUY PRICE

Price has to be a basic consideration in practically all consumer decisions to buy or not to buy. Consumers' *desire*-to-buy is unlimited, but consumers' *ability*-to-buy is sorely limited. When a housewife spends a dollar, she hopes to get at least a dollar's worth of utility, and she hopes to look back on her purchase with satisfaction. She realizes that if she spends that dollar for product "A," the dollar will not be available for product "B," and she wants both items. In some product classifications, price is more important to her than it is in other classifications.

As we have seen, the consumer exchanges the amount of money called for on the price tag for an "assortment" of utilities and satisfactions. Several of these already mentioned include physical products, packages, services, and images. The consumer expects price to reflect value and looks on price as one measure of quality. Over time, consumers may become so accustomed to certain prices for some products that these become "customary" prices. The price lines retailers stock and the buying habits of consumers are influenced by these customary prices. At all times, consumers are aware of competitive prices. In situations where brand loyalty is low, a price reduction on brand "A" can do damage to the sales of competing brands "B," "C," and "D."

SELLERS' APPROACHES TO PRICING

In the same way that a seller's products and services must suit the consumers who constitute his market, so also must his prices be satisfactory. The seller's first

What did it cost to add BRYANT QUIETLINE COOLING in this 6-room Jacksonville home?

$700 ☐ $800 ☐ $900 ☐ $1000 ☐

The right answer in this case is $725.

But most home owners would name a higher figure. For people generally believe that air conditioning costs far more than it actually does.

The installation in the 6-room Jacksonville home pictured above (floor area 1288 square feet) was made by a Bryant dealer in the summer of 1962. In simple terms, cooling equipment was added to an adequate forced warm air heating system. And this was done quickly and economically because of the competence of the dealer and the Quietline features built in at the Bryant factory that minimize the complications of installation.

This advertisement is one of a series based on documented air conditioning case histories. In each instance the actual cost to the homeowner was obtained. And the evidence is conclusive that Bryant Quietline cooling can be provided in 6- and 7-room houses at from less than $700 on up to perhaps as much as $1000.

Why these price differentials? The principal reasons are size and design of the house, how well it is insulated or shaded, whether additional wiring or duct work are required and, of course, climatic location.

Your Bryant dealer will gladly tell you how much it will cost to have cool comfort in your home this summer and during the years ahead. And you will probably be pleasantly surprised as was the Jacksonville family on whose experience this $725 case history is based.

Look in the Yellow Pages of the telephone book for your Bryant dealer who represents a company that has specialized in home comfort for more than 50 years. Bryant Manufacturing Company, Indianapolis 7, Indiana.

QUIETLINE AIR CONDITIONING

Prices and costs are major considerations in many buying decisions. (Courtesy: Bryant Manufacturing Company)

What Ultimate Consumers Buy

step toward pricing which will be acceptable to consumers is that of recognizing that, in a very real sense, consumers determine a seller's prices. Consumers exercise this great power by deciding how much they will and will not pay for each seller's product. A second recognition equally necessary is that pricing is an art and not a science; there is no reliable formula to which a seller can turn. Continuing, a seller can set his price too high *or* too low. The higher the price, typically, the greater the gross margin on each unit sold, but also, the greater the consumer's resistance to buying. A seller's objective in pricing is practically always that of maximizing long-term profits. He may think of this as (1) a certain percentage return on sales, (2) a certain percentage return on capital, (3) a specific dollar amount of profit, or (4) a specific share of the market.

Market Minus vs. Cost Plus

The *market minus* approach to pricing is consumer-oriented. It is realistic in that it recognizes demand and supply. Competition is clearly a major factor in the marketplace. One pressure exerted by competition is in the direction of customary, common prices. We have observed that price changes among competing products usually lead to sales volume changes within the product group, often to *price* changes, too.

If competition and custom have contributed to the establishment of a $10 price level for a type of product, a manufacturer might elect to compete at this level and then work backward. Suppose retailers gross 33-⅓%. They pay $6.67 for the item they sell for $10. Suppose wholesalers gross 16-⅔% on *their* selling price. They pay manufacturers $5.56 and then charge retailers $6.67. Our manufacturer, then, would count on $5.56 to cover his costs and his profit. He could, of course, consider making a higher quality version of the product (priced to the consumer at, say, $20) or an economy version (priced to the consumer at $4.95).

If there is no $10 price level about which the market concentrates, our manufacturer's problem is more difficult. He must make rough guesses about sales volume in units at several price levels. This is neither easy nor accurate, but it is his one approach toward attempting to sense consumer demand.

The nature of the *cost plus* approach to pricing is indicated by the term: the seller totals his costs, then he adds an amount equal to the profit he desires, and there he has arrived at his selling price. On the surface, this seems quite simple. You must remember, however, that costs are not always easy to predict; some are not even easy to determine after they have been incurred. There is an element of judgment, even of guess, in most cost figures. If the cost plus adds up to $7.50 and the big market is at $5 *or* at $10, the seller may be in for real trouble.

Low Price vs. Heavy Promotion

Sometimes a manufacturer does not know which course of action will get a more satisfactory consumer reaction: (1) price reductions plus aggressive use of a "lower price" appeal as basic strategy, or (2) budgeting a large sum of money for advertising and other promotion. Strong pressures recommend (2) over (1).

11

Marketing Fundamentals for Advertisers

Competitors can match price cuts immediately; to match advertising activities takes more time. Prices that are very low can produce a low gross margin in dollars, and this limits the amount of money available for market stimulation. Then, effective advertising has a better chance of generating consumer loyalty and steady patronage than does price-cutting. Finally, curtailment of advertising that seems to be weak is easier to achieve than is a restoration of price.

Chapter 2

How Sellers Sell

It is not enough that manufacturers make and retailers stock products consumers like. It is not enough that sellers of services stand ready to supply the kinds of services consumers prefer. A major job, maybe *the* major marketing job, still remains — *selling* those products and services.

This chapter completes our brief, introductory look at marketing and the marketing programs used by sellers. In Chapter 1, we recognized the key role consumers play. We also identified *products* and *prices* as major marketing matters. This chapter contains four new concepts. (1) *Promotional mix*. Each seller considers three ingredients for inclusion in the promotional mix he believes will be most profitable. The three ingredients are personal selling, advertising, and sales promotion. (2) *Marketing channels*. The problem of getting the product from factory to consumer is best seen through the eyes of a manufacturer. He must choose the channel of distribution he believes most suitable. (3) *Publicity* and *public relations*. Selling can be made easier or more difficult by the publicity the seller receives and by the public relations he enjoys. (4) *Marketing research*. No seller should dare discontinue his marketing research even for a brief period of time.

Each seller must decide for himself what combination of elements he will include in his marketing program *and* in what proportions. Each seller wants a program which scores well on *effectiveness* and on *costs;* he wants the least expensive, the most profitable program which will achieve his marketing goals. One industry (cosmetics) may tend toward a pattern quite different from that which is common in another industry (heavy machinery). Even within a single industry, two profitable firms may follow quite different product policies, or different pricing policies, or use different proportions of advertising and personal selling in their promotional mixes, or market their merchandise through different channels of distribution. Whatever a seller does about products, prices, promotion, or channels influences what he does about each of the other three. For example, if a manufacturer begins to make merchandise for Sears or A&P to sell under their own brand names, he probably adds a new channel of distribution, a direct one. He would not, of course, put advertising behind this merchandise. For another example, if

13

Marketing Fundamentals for Advertisers

a manufacturer of industrial products adds a line of consumer products, he certainly might begin to use retailers and advertising for the first time. Or, if another manufacturer abandons his attempts to control the price retailers charge consumers for his product, his product may begin to appear in discount stores.

Seldom if ever can a seller prove that his current marketing program is the best one for him. Why? Because he cannot measure precisely the performance or the contribution of any of the elements in his program. Seldom does a seller go very long without making changes in his program. The design of a marketing program calls for judgment, intuition, and common sense; it, like pricing, is more of an art than a science.

PERSONAL SELLING

What Salesmanship Is

Salesmanship is the *ability* to influence human behavior. It is the *skill* which enables salesmen to persuade buyers to buy. It is the *art* a salesman employs in getting a buyer to see situations as the salesman sees them, to feel about problems as the salesman feels, to do what the salesman recommends that the buyer do about solving those problems. It is the *power* to get a buyer to accept a seller, the seller's product or service, the seller's suggestions.

The principles of personal selling are used to influence attitudes and actions. Because of this fact, salesmanship is useful and is used in many types of circumstances and in many types of relationships. It is difficult to think of any outstanding leader who does not make regular use of the principles of personal selling.

The heart of marketing is the moving of a satisfactory volume of products or services at satisfactory prices, month after month and year after year. To move that volume, more dollars are spent on personal selling than on any other promotional force.

The Job of Selling

A sale-purchase transaction involves (1) a buyer who has a specific need or problem, (2) a product or service which will fill that need or solve that problem, and (3) a salesman who knows how to sell the product to the buyer. The salesman must show the buyer *how,* and must convince the buyer *that,* the buyer will be better off if he buys what the salesman recommends. To be sound, a sale must benefit buyer *and* seller. Unless Buyer B benefits when he buys from Seller S, Buyer B will switch his spending to some other seller.

What a salesman actually does when he makes a sale is to exchange buyer-benefits or buyer-satisfactions for some of the buyer's money. The buyer, in this sense, does *not* buy merchandise or services *as such.* He buys, instead, the benefits or satisfactions, the utilities or advantages he gets from that merchandise or those services.

Service Selling vs. Creative Selling

We are entitled to classify all selling as either *service* selling or *creative* selling. *Service* selling consists of merely serving buyers by supplying them with what they request. The so-called (actually *mis*-called) "salesman" does only what the buyer asks the salesman to do. Much "selling" in retail stores and some selling *to* retailers is no more than this.

Creative selling, on the other hand, is active rather than passive; the salesman initiates and motivates instead of just reacting; he goes on the offensive rather than staying on the defensive. He *sells* in addition to serving. Here are four examples of creative selling: (1) salesman begins to sell a new product just added to his line; (2) salesman makes his first sale to a buyer after earlier, unsuccessful attempts; (3) salesman sells 6 items to a buyer who should buy 6, but intended to buy only 4; and (4) salesman sells a $6 item to a buyer who intended to buy a $4 item.

Creative selling is hard work. It is the hard work of changing buyers' beliefs and habits, of helping buyers make more satisfactory purchases. It calls for much optimism, enthusiasm, and self-confidence. Creative salesmen must be tactful and friendly; they must be good listeners, good actors, good competitors. They delight their customers as well as their sales managers.

Information Salesmen Need

If a creative salesman is to do a good job, he must be well armed with a generous fund of information. Otherwise, he will have difficulty in attempting to change buyers' opinions and buying habits. The salesman who relies on being a "fast talker" usually loses out to a salesman who has much sound information to impart.

Salesmen need information about their *companies*. To many buyers, the salesman *is* his firm. History, size, personnel, and policies are four examples of topics about which most salesmen need to be knowledgeable.

Salesmen need information about the *products* and *services* they sell. If a salesman is to be enthusiastic and poised (and he must), if he is to fit his products and services to buyers' needs (and he must), then he certainly must know what he is selling. Topics include: items in the line; raw materials; manufacturing processes; standards and inspections; related products; physical features, elements, and parts; prices, discounts, and terms.

Above all, salesmen must distinguish between *product-features* and *buyer-benefits*. A *product-feature* is a physical part of a product or a physical fact about it. The padded dashboard on an automobile is an example; so, also, is the self-winding feature of a watch. Because of product-features, products deliver buyer-benefits, sometimes referred to as advantages, utilities, and satisfactions. The padded dashboard provides *safety*, the self-winding feature provides *convenience*.

A salesman must have information about *buyers* before he can expect to make sales to them. Which buyers are of interest to a salesman? Which buyers are entitled to a salesman's time and selling effort? A salesman certainly ought not try to sell his product to a buyer unless that buyer stands a good chance of being satisfied with his purchase. In addition, the buyer certainly must be able to finance his purchase, either on a cash or on a credit basis. Finally, the buyer should certainly have the authority to make the purchase. These three qualifications are basic and almost universal. They separate "prospects" from "suspects." Prospects,

DO YOU HAVE THIS MAN'S BUSINESS PROBLEM?

"How can we fatten our sales volume—without pushing <u>costs</u> up, too?"

Answer: Use Long Distance to extend your sales reach—at minimum sales cost!

Example: Eastern Steel and Metal Company, of West Haven, Conn., makes daily use of Long Distance calls as a supplement to regular selling in the field.

Recently, the firm made a special two-million-pound purchase of steel sheets and coils valued at more than $100,000 and sold it through Long Distance calls to buyers across the nation. Selling costs ran less than 1%.

Many business problems are really communications problems. And they can be solved by effective use of Bell System services: voice... written... or data.

Talk with one of our Communications Consultants. Just call your Bell Telephone Business Office.

BELL TELEPHONE SYSTEM

Solve business problems with communications

Advertising may be used to promote personal selling by telephone. (Courtesy: American Telephone & Telegraph Company)

incidentally, are buyers who should be buying *but are not; customers* are buyers who should be buying *and are.*

Customers die, fail, retire, no longer need what a salesman sells, move away, switch to another seller. They cease to be customers; they quit buying. So, a salesman must always be "prospecting," locating new buyers who qualify as prospects, converting as many as he can into new customers who will replace lost customers.

The Selling Process

As soon as he is adequately informed and as soon as he has selected a worthwhile prospect, the salesman plans the presentation he will make. This presentation should feature the benefits and satisfactions the prospect will enjoy after he buys. The purpose of the presentation is to get the buyer to say "yes" to these questions:

1. Do I really *need* to make a purchase?
2. If so, is this the *product* I should buy?
3. Is this seller a satisfactory *source* from which to buy?
4. Is the *price* he quotes acceptable?
5. Should I go ahead and buy at this *time?*

The salesman will promise satisfactions. He will demonstrate the product's operation if practicable. He will meet and handle objections. If successful, he closes the sale.

SALES MANAGEMENT

One of a sales manager's basic and continuing responsibilities is that of recruiting, selecting, and hiring salesmen. In order to do this satisfactorily, he should have an adequate job analysis and job description for each type of sales job. Common techniques used in the evaluation of applicants include the application form, the physical examination, psychological tests, and interviews.

Another responsibility is that of training. The twin goals of training programs are greater sales volume and lower expense. Training gives salesmen information; training sharpens selling skills. It is vital for new salesmen and helpful to experienced salesmen.

A third responsibility involves the difficult matter of salesmen's compensation. The sales managers must offer a *level* of compensation and an amount of income a salesman can earn during a period of time which are competitive; otherwise, salesmen will leave for greener pastures. And most sales managers try to strike the best balance between incentive and control in their *method* of compensation. Straight commission represents 100% incentive; straight salary represents 100% control. The nature of the selling job determines how much incentive and how much control are needed.

The sales manager's final responsibility to be mentioned here is that of supervision. He must organize his department, direct and control his sales force. Territories, quotas, routing, reports, forecasts, and budgets are involved in supervision.

Marketing Fundamentals for Advertisers

ADVERTISING

Because our entire text is about advertising, this promotional activity will not be treated at this point. What *is* important here is that we see advertising in the context of the total marketing effort. In the promotional mix, advertising must help and be helped by the other ingredients in the mix.

SALES PROMOTION

Personal selling and advertising do not always constitute all of a firm's promotional program or mix. Other promotional activities, classified as *sales promotion*, can be used along with personal selling, or along with advertising, or along with both.

What do a Sales Promotion Manager and his staff do? (1) They perform intra-company jobs for the Advertising Department and for the Sales Department. (2) They are responsible for certain relationships and certain dealings between a manufacturer and the retailers who stock and sell his products. (3) They supervise techniques designed to stimulate buying by ultimate consumers, and they offer services to those consumers.

Intra-Company Services

The Sales Promotion Department does several jobs which make the *Advertising Department's* efforts more productive. For example, a manufacturer often hopes that his retailers will advertise what the manufacturer is advertising at the same time the manufacturer is advertising it. Sales Promotion tries to get this cooperation, urging the retailers to tie their advertising in with the manufacturer's advertising. Or, if a manufacturer designs promotional material such as displays or booklets for use by his retailers, Sales Promotion works to get retailers to use that material. Such use makes the manufacturer's consumer advertising more effective. Sometimes a manufacturer offers to do joint, cooperative advertising with his retailers, sharing the cost of advertisements run by a retailer in his local market. The Sales Promotion Department is logically responsible for such programs.

The *Sales Department,* too, benefits from assignments undertaken by Sales Promotion. Earlier, in the Sales Management section, we noted that the second responsibility of sales managers is to train the firm's salesmen. While this responsibility rests clearly on the shoulders of sales managers, the actual process of training may be assigned to the Sales Promotion Department. Included in many training programs is instruction about the advertising of the salesman's *firm* and about the advertising of the salesman's *retail customers*. Salesmen's portfolios and other visual aids used in making sales presentations may be the responsibility of Sales Promotion. Sometimes the Sales Promotion Department and the Sales Department join in designing programs for the purpose of stimulating company salesmen.

Manufacturer-Retailer Relationships

General Management. One of the many bases on which manufacturers compete is that of relations with their retailers. The typical retailer is small; he does battle

How Sellers Sell

against *mass* retailers (chains, department stores, discounters, mail-order firms, supermarkets) for the patronage of ultimate consumers. In this battle, he welcomes, *he needs,* aid from the manufacturers whose merchandise he handles. And, don't overlook the fact that many manufacturers, too, have a need — they need to have the portion of their sales volumes going through small stores. Because there are many small stores, collectively they represent quite a potential. So both parties, manufacturers as well as retailers, have an interest in achieving good relations.

At any given moment, there are retailers who will accept and benefit from using assistance or advice from a manufacturer's Sales Promotion Department on these problems:

Organization	Buying	Retail salesmanship
Location	Pricing	Sales stimulation
Layout	Personnel Management	Retail advertising
Equipment	Credit and Collection	Store traffic
Stock Control	Records and accounting	Display

Help in solving these managerial problems can be sent with the salesmen who call on retailers. It can be sent by mail. Sometimes a manufacturer holds district clinics for small groups of retailers, making use of talks, classes, movies, conferences, seminars, discussions, or panels.

Point-of-Purchase. This manufacturer-retailer matter usually refers to various types of display promotion of a manufacturer's brand in retail stores. Window displays are an ideal example. A manufacturer's Point-of-Purchase activities *can* be assigned to the Advertising Department, or they *can* be assigned to the Sales Department. More and more, however, Point-of-Purchase is being seen as a manufacturer-retailer matter which should be the responsibility of the Sales Promotion Department. We have a chapter on Point-of-Purchase.

Direct Advertising. There are many, many forms of direct advertising. Some are not really advertising, and few, if any, are personal selling in nature. Thus, the activity seems more appropriate for the sales promotion manager than for either the advertising manager or the sales manager. Much, but not all, of a manufacturer's direct advertising reaches its destination by mail. Examples of promotional literature classed as direct advertising include catalogues a manufacturer sends to his buyers, mailings a manufacturer sends to his retailers, mailings he designs and makes available for his retailers to send to their customers, house organs a manufacturer mails directly to his customers. We have a chapter on direct mail advertising.

Consumer Stimulation and Services

A manufacturer can use *stimulants* and *services* in his attempts to get more consumers to buy his products, to buy more of those products, to remain customers (for a long time, he hopes). Consumer *stimulation* can have a beneficial effect at

WIN! $35,000 IN CASH PRIZES

NAME THE FAMOUS HEINZ TOMATO MAN

1ST PRIZE $10,000 IN CASH

2 SECOND PRIZES EACH $5,000 CASH

15 THIRD PRIZES EACH $1,000 CASH

TIPS TO HELP YOU WIN:

Because the Heinz tomato is the best-tasting in the world, you might well think of such names as "Mr. Aristocrat Tomato," or "Mr. Red Magic," or "Mr. Pedigreed Tomato."

- These names would certainly be appropriate, since over half a century of careful cross-breeding went into the development of this prize strain of tomatoes. But don't send these names in. They're just suggestions to start your own ideas flowing!

- Once you begin thinking of Heinz tomatoes, you'll get lots of even better names. These facts may help you: Heinz tomatoes are grown from pedigreed seeds, planted in the warm fields of the deep South in early spring. When the seedling plants have grown sturdy, they are swiftly transplanted to cool, northern fields, where they mature and bear beautiful glistening-red Heinz tomatoes. These tomatoes are then rushed at flavor peak to nearby Heinz kitchens, where they are made into the world's best-liked ketchup and chili sauce, HEINZ!

FOLLOW THESE SIMPLE RULES:

1. a. Select a name for the famous Heinz Tomato Man, and b. complete this statement in 25 words or less: "I like this name because....................."
2. Use the official entry blank or write your entry on a separate piece of paper. Mail with your name and address, plus a neckband from any package of Heinz Ketchup or Chili Sauce to: Heinz "Name The Tomato Man Contest," P. O. Box 1, Dept. D, Brooklyn 1, N. Y.
3. Entries must be postmarked no later than March 30, 1963, and received by April 10, 1963.
4. Entries of both the name and the reason for selecting same will be judged on the basis of originality, sincerity, human interest and aptness of thought by Advertising Distributors of America, Inc., an independent judging agency. Decision of the judges is final.
5. Submit as many entries as you wish, but be sure that each entry blank is accompanied by a neckband from Heinz Ketchup or Chili Sauce. A separate entry blank or piece of paper, with neckband attached, must be submitted for each entry. Entries must be the original work of contestants submitting them. Only one prizewinner in any family.
6. Contest is subject to all federal, state, and local regulations, and void wherever prohibited or taxed. Any liability for federal, state, or local taxes imposed on a prize received in this contest will be the sole responsibility of the prizewinner.
7. All entries become the property of the H. J. Heinz Co. to use as it sees fit and none will be acknowledged or returned.
8. All persons in the United States and territories may enter, except employees of H. J. Heinz Co., its advertising agencies, Advertising Distributors of America, Inc., and members of their immediate families.
9. Prizes will be awarded as soon as possible after judging is complete, either by person or mail. A list of winners will be sent after June 15, 1963, to entrants requesting same and enclosing a self-addressed, stamped envelope.

FREE GIFT TO EVERY ENTRANT!

- Just for entering this easy contest, Heinz will send you a free package of pedigreed Heinz Red Magic Tomato seeds. Plant them and enjoy extra-delicious Heinz tomatoes fresh from your own garden.

ENTRY BLANK

Mail with one neckband from any bottle of Heinz Ketchup or Chili Sauce to:

HEINZ "NAME THE TOMATO MAN CONTEST"
P. O. BOX 1, DEPT. D, BROOKLYN 1, N. Y.

My name for the Tomato Man is:_____

I like this name because (complete in 25 words or less)

_____
_____
_____
_____

NAME_____
(PLEASE PRINT)
ADDRESS_____
CITY_____ZONE_____STATE_____

Contests and trade characters are sales promotion matters. (Courtesy: H. J. Heinz Co.)

How Sellers Sell

the retail level. Some individual consumers will come to stores partially pre-sold on the brands of certain manufacturers. In addition, and as a consequence, some retailers will feel pressure to stock, maybe even to feature those brands. *Services* are intended to make consumers more frequent buyers and more satisfied users of the products they buy.

Sampling is one type of stimulant. It is often used to introduce a new type of product or to influence the consumer's choice of brand. In sampling operations, a trial of the product is made both convenient and economical for consumers. The manufacturer who samples his product shows his great confidence in it; he assumes that consumers will try it, like it, buy it, and continue to buy it.

A *premium* is a stimulant. It is a bonus, a reward, an inducement which sweetens the seller's offer and makes a purchase more attractive. Trading stamps and coupons can be classified as premiums. So is the merchandise item a consumer gets "free" (upon making a certain purchase) or at a price less than retail market value. Manufacturers use premiums to get their brands bought by more consumers, more often, in greater amounts. Many premiums are heavily publicized by advertising.

Contests are a form of consumer stimulation. They can capture the attention and interest of many persons. They can cause consumers to buy and consume more of a manufacturer's product than would be the case if there were no contest. Contests tantalize by implying that you can get something for nothing.

In addition to consumer stimulation, *consumer services* also are a concern of Sales Promotion. Manufacturers who offer these services do so on the assumption that the better a seller serves his customers, the better customers they will be. Services involved here are largely educational in nature. Information and suggestions can help a consumer (1) buy more wisely and (2) then use the product correctly and care for it properly after purchase. In this way, the consumer gets more for her money and more out of the product.

Consumer services may show how products are made. Factory tours and plant "open houses" do this, as may exhibits at fairs, trade shows, and conventions. The labels and tags a manufacturer puts on his merchandise can be informative and, hence, service-slanted. Incidentally, retail salespersons are often in mind when these labels and tags are being designed. Various types of literature such as folders, leaflets, and diagrams can be part of the service program. Training courses, cooking schools, and fashion shows are possible services. The same is true for product demonstrations, including those in retail stores made by demonstrators who serve as (and appear to be nothing more than) retail salespersons.

MARKETING CHANNELS

If a manufacturer is to sell his merchandise to ultimate consumers, that merchandise obviously must be accessible to consumers. A few manufacturers take their products to consumers, all the way and all by themselves. The Fuller Brush man, almost a part of American folklore, still carries the Fuller Brush Company and its line to the consumer's doorstep. Most manufacturers cannot do this because of the high costs incurred in such distribution or because of the nature of their product line. For example, makers of convenience goods already mentioned (candy bars, beverages, headache remedies) clearly cannot bring their products all the way to you, a consumer. So, most manufacturers depend on the business specialists who make up marketing channels to get their products to consumers. Because they are specialists in performing their tasks, they can usually do so more efficiently than the single manufacturer can.

What is a marketing channel? A marketing channel consists of the persons and firms responsible for the movement of products from their points of origin to their ultimate destinations, from those who make, grow, or extract to those who are the final users or consumers. Some of these firms are *middlemen* — retailers, wholesalers, selling agents, brokers. Other firms supply auxiliary but necessary services such as transportation, insurance, storage, finance. Officially, those who have or take title (legal ownership) to the product constitute the product's channel; other parties, of course, can facilitate or contribute to transfer of title. Physically, the product may pass through that same group of hands or through a different group of hands.

Channel Structure

Two questions face a manufacturer when he designs his channel. (1) Should he use middlemen at the *retail* level, at the *wholesale* level, or at *both* levels? (2) What *types* of retailers and/or wholesalers should he use?

As to *level,* the manufacturer has three basic options. He can use *no* middlemen, distributing his wares direct to the final users or consumers. He can distribute to *retailers,* counting on them to sell to consumers. Or he can sell to *wholesale* middlemen who then will sell to retailers, to industrial buyers, and to other wholesalers.

Some middlemen are called *agent* middlemen because they do not take title to goods being marketed. Prominent are brokers, manufacturers' agents, sales agents, commission houses, and resident buyers. *Merchant* middlemen, on the other hand, do take title. Prominent merchant middlemen in the distribution of consumer goods are wholesalers and retailers; retailers include department stores, mail-order firms, supermarkets, chains, independents, discounters, and variety stores.

A further refinement of types can be illustrated by toothpaste. Should it be available in food stores? variety stores? department stores? discount stores?

The channel structures for consumer products and for industrial products are illustrated in Figures 1 and 2.

Intensity of Distribution

We have just looked at levels and types of middlemen. Now we look at the matter of *intensity. How many* middlemen should there be in the channel? Three degrees of intensity are recognized by manufacturers; two are the extremes, the third is a middle course.

Intensive distribution is the use of *many* middlemen. Sometimes it calls for the use of many *types* of middleman. Soft drinks, razor blades, cigarettes, and chewing

How Sellers Sell

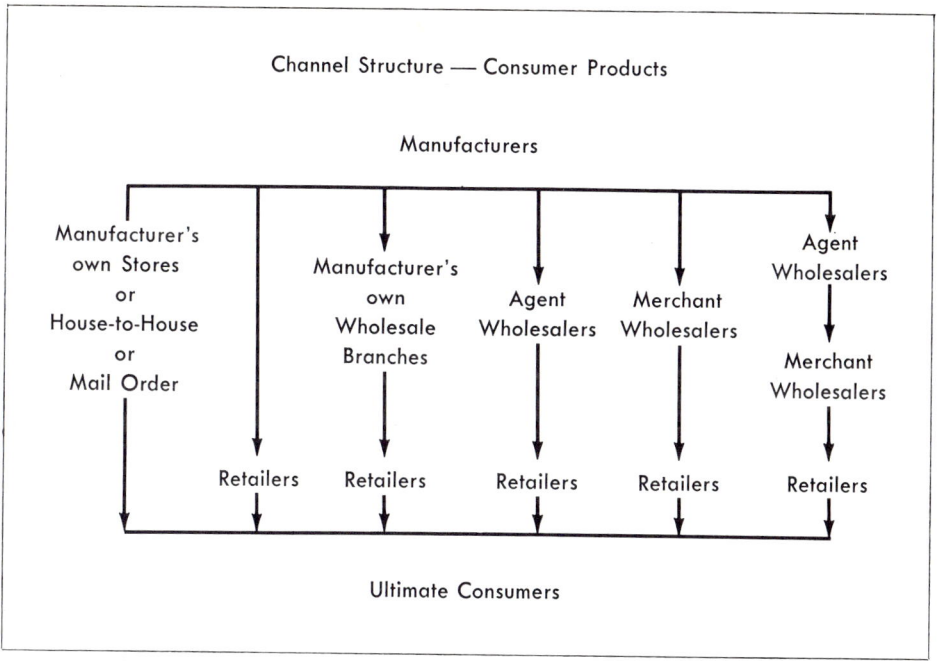

FIGURE 1

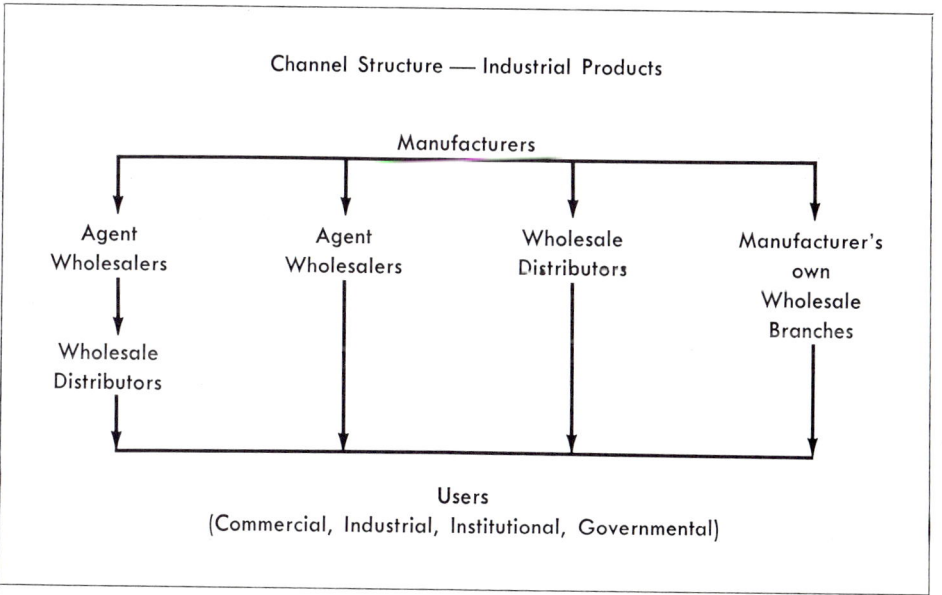

FIGURE 2

Marketing Fundamentals for Advertisers

gum are typical examples. The manufacturer of such products wants those products to be just as close to every prospective user as is practicable. His market consists of many, many consumers. Unit of purchase is small; price per unit is low; consumer purchase is frequent. Retailers enjoy a high stock-turn on a small inventory.

Exclusive distribution is just the reverse of intensive distribution. Literally, this type of channel calls for a manufacturer's product to be available in only *one* store in each city regardless of size of city. Product features and consumer buying habits are quite different from those in intensive distribution. Extremely expensive glassware and pianos are often retailed in this manner. At the wholesale level, manufacturers' agents, food brokers, and an occasional wholesaler enjoy sole selling privileges in their respective areas.

Selective distribution charts a course in between intensive distribution and exclusive distribution. Typical examples are nationally advertised shirts, pens, sterling silverware, shoes, watches, and appliances. Here the manufacturer's product is in fewer than all department stores, fewer than all jewelry stores, fewer than all clothing stores. Selective distribution through retailers often involves fewer than 10,000 stores.

A further refinement within the intensity phase can be illustrated by posing this question: *Which* retailers in San Francisco should handle Rolex watches? *Which* stores in Chicago should stock and sell Parker pens?

What, then, determines intensity of distribution? The sound marketing assumption is that consumer perference dictates retail intensity. If consumers, for example, are not willing to spend much time and effort in shopping and buying chewing gum, then manufacturers of this product must provide for intensive distribution. If consumers will spend time and effort when buying an automobile, distribution can be much more selective. Retail intensity dictates wholesale intensity.

Determinants of Manufacturers' Channels

Each channel entitled to a manufacturer's serious consideration has both attractive and unattractive features. As he analyzes channel possibilities in terms of sales volume, costs, and profits, his thinking concentrates on the *buyers* to whom he will be selling, on his *products,* on *middlemen's operations,* and on *his own circumstances*.

His *buyers* constitute a manufacturer's market, and market attitude and preference constitute the most powerful channel influence. Ultimate consumers and consumer products were treated in Chapter 1. For industrial products, the manufacturer needs to study purchasing agents because they are his buyers. He needs to analyze their buying motives, buying habits, number, geographical location, concentration, and help needed from suppliers.

His *products* help a manufacturer make decisions about channels. Products, too, were classified and treated in Chapter 1. Bulk, weight, perishability, need for servicing by retailer, margin per unit, and importance in buyers' budgets are examples of relevant matters.

Middlemen's operations and features influence a manufacturer's selection of channels. Because his predominant objective is to maximize dollar profits, he immediately compares one possible channel against other possibilities on the bases of potential sales volume, probable cost of using, and possible profit. Prices, discounts, margins, and terms of sale are involved here. Particularly basic in some instances are the selling effort and the degree of cooperation which can be expected from various types of retailer.

Finally, a *manufacturer's own circumstances* can decree that certain channels are realistic and entitled to consideration, but that other channels are simply out of the question and must be ignored. Circumstances include such variables as age, financial strength, size, abilities of management, width of product line, reputation, experience, competition, and intensity of distribution desired. Basic here is the separation of the marketing jobs the *manufacturer assumes* from the marketing jobs he wants to (or must) *transfer to middlemen.* The amount of control a manufacturer wants over his retailers' policies (price, promotion, service) is significant in some cases.

Channel Change

Manufacturers make changes in their marketing channels because changes are always going on in consumer preferences, in the nature of products, in the methods of operation of middlemen, and in manufacturers' own circumstances. No manufacturer can prove that his present channel or channels are the best for him. He may often wonder if he is selling through the wrong types of retailers, or through too few or too many retailers. He knows that seldom is any one channel superior to others on all counts. As a result, he may feel that he should use different channels, for example, in different parts of the country, or for different types of buyer, or for different product lines. Even so, the channel decision is a continuing issue, a fluid and ever changing matter which demands frequent reexamination.

PUBLICITY

Now come two sections which deal with topics which are not marketing matters in a technical sense, but they are too closely tied to a seller's relationship to his prospects and his customers to be omitted. This section is on Publicity; the next is on Public Relations.

What and Where

Publicity is the mention of a manufacturer, or of a retailer, or of either's brand names, or of their products or merchandise, or of their personnel, or of their activities *in the editorial part* of a medium. The media of interest to sellers as far as publicity is concerned are newspapers, magazines, television, and radio. These media are independent and commercial. They carry *editorial* material and *advertising* material. A newspaper's editorial material includes news stories, photographs, feature stories, comics, editorials, cartoons, and such features as weather, serialized fiction, and articles written by "name" columnists. For magazines, editorial material includes articles, stories, features, and photographs. In television and radio, the shows and programs constitute the editorial material.

Publicity vs. Advertising

Advertising is commercial communication; publicity is not commercial. Media charge advertisers for space and time, but media do not bill advertisers for publicity. The advertiser can specify *what* his advertisement shall say and *when* his advertisement shall appear. Thus he can have regular, continuous, even daily advertising if he wants it. For publicity, however, the medium controls the wording and the timing. In advertising, the identity and the purpose of the seller are obvious; publicity is less obvious, less promotional, and is not signed. Consumers credit advertisements to the sponsorship of a seller, but they credit publicity to the sponsorship of an editor. Because of its nature, advertising tends to raise questions, doubts, and defenses in buyers' minds; publicity, on the contrary, tends to enjoy prestige and acceptance because it comes from the editor's office, not from the advertising manager's office.

Forms

News stories are the most common form of publicity. Other forms include reports, announcements, accounts, descriptions, feature stories, letters to the editor, and photographs.

Some publicity is *unplanned*. Here the seller did nothing to bring about the publicity he got; some medium investigated, found a basis for, let's say, a news story, and published or broadcast it.

Some sellers strive for *planned* publicity — favorable, of course. These sellers *create* news, they *arrange* bases for publicity. Planned publicity contains information the seller hopes will be seen by buyers and reacted to by buyers. The reaction the seller usually wants is a favorable attitude toward the seller or what he sells. Planned publicity is a major tool of public relations, the topic of our next major section.

Seller-Media Relations

If a seller wants to maximize the favorable publicity media run about him, he should develop good personal relations with their editors because editors are key individuals. The seller should get acquainted with and earn the respect of editors. How can he do this? By being honest, fair, frank, considerate, sincere, and trustworthy; by not trying to supress *bad* news (unfavorable publicity) and by not asking editors to do so; by refraining from begging, complaining, wasting editors' time, threatening, or trying to apply pressure.

Good relations are encouraged if the seller learns and then respects each editor's criteria for publicity. The publicity item, release, story, or photograph should feature someone or something the editor believes to be of interest to his readers, viewers, or listeners. It should have publication value or broadcast value. Usually

How Sellers Sell

this means that it must be *news*. It must be accurate, complete, well written, easy to read or hear, and in whatever physical form (headings, spacing, number of copies) the editor prefers.

Planning a Publicity Story

Planning for publicity starts with the seller's sharpening his skill in identifying successful bases for publicity stories. He studies each medium to see what *it* accepts, what *its* criteria are. He then works to increase his ability to dream up, to plan, to create successful bases. Such a base provides a subject to write about. This can be a person, an event, a development, an innovation, a period of time.

If the story is a *news* story, it must be *real* news, and the essence of news has not changed since Kipling described it as involved with Who — What — Where — When — How — Why. News is timely and current; it is of interest to many; it is true and accurate; it benefits from being somewhat dramatic, somewhat emotional.

Feature stories need not contain current news, but they, too, must be of real interest. Their 500–1000 words can give readers more color, more depth, more detail than do news stories.

Photographs appear with about one-third of all publicity items accepted and used by media. Study of media and conferences with editors help sellers determine the types of photographs to take and submit. Good illustrations of persons or events are usually characterized by action, color, realism, beauty, or human interest.

PUBLIC RELATIONS

As the term suggests, public relations consists of the relations between, for us, a seller and his "publics." *Fortune* magazine says, "Good public relations is good performance — publicly appreciated." International Harvester offers this, "Public relations is doing the right thing, in the right way, at the right time, and then telling people about it." A cynic has described public relations as arranging in advance to get caught in the act of doing a good deed.

"Publics"

What is a "public"? A group of similar individuals, an assortment of persons having the same interests, problems, circumstances, goals. A seller's "publics" include competitors, employees, educators, government, suppliers, stockholders, media of communication, and, *above all* for us, customers and prospective customers.

Relations

Relations with most "publics" are unavoidable. These relations can help or hurt; the general feeling "publics" have toward a seller and what he sells can also help or hurt. Sellers certainly hope that these groups will understand and approve the sellers' policies, philosophies, and contributions of a social, economic, or educational nature.

Marketing Fundamentals for Advertisers

Public Relations Phases

In phase #1, a seller learns through research what his "publics" think of him. If any unsoundness is present in his operations and is causing unfavorable attitudes, he corrects it. He determines to be right, to do right, to live right, to operate right.

In phase #2, the seller communicates the fact of his rightness to his "publics"; he informs for the purpose of affecting attitudes and influencing actions. He wants to be thought of as being decent, fair, sound, courteous, sensible, trustworthy.

Phase #3 is the reaction or response phase. Adequately informed and favorably impressed, his "publics" give a seller credit for being right; customers and prospective customers cooperate, they give approval and support, they buy. Other "publics" are favorably inclined toward the seller as someone to work for, to invest in, to sell to, to sell against, to publicize, to supervise, to live with, and to know.

These three phases should be thought of and handled as a never-ending cycle. Periodically and honestly, a seller should repeat the question implied in phase #1, he should communicate (phase #2), and he should be alert for "feedback" or response (phase #3).

Public Relations Programs

Achieving good relations with most "publics" demands hard, endless work, but it is well worth the effort. Public relations success demands the planning and then the executing of a complete, long-range program. Only a continuing program will make certain that a seller is understood and accepted, that he deserves and gets the trust and confidence, the good will and respect of his "publics." Only a program insures a seller's being held in great regard and high esteem. Only by adopting a public relations program does a seller acknowledge that public relations is not a specialized activity such as production, nor a specific function such as marketing, nor a smokescreen for defects and deficiencies.

Public Relations vs. Advertising

Public relations is broad; it includes *all* communication between a seller and *all* his "publics." Advertising is one form of communication. So, advertising is one segment of public relations. Indeed, the institutional type of advertising mentioned in Chapter 1 is one of two major tools used by a seller to improve his relations with his "publics." Publicity is the other major tool.

In some firms, the Public Relations Director reports to the Vice President in Charge of Marketing, just as does the Advertising Manager. In a very few firms, the Advertising Manager reports to the Public Relations Director.

MARKETING RESEARCH

What

Marketing research is the application of scientific methods to the solving of marketing problems and the making of marketing decisions. As soon as a marketing problem has been clarified, facts which bear on it are collected. These facts are then organized and combined for study and analysis. Finally, the facts are interpreted and recommendations are made based on these interpretations.

How Sellers Sell

Sellers confront changes every week and every month. Sellers need information before deciding what to do about changes, information that is objective, current, accurate, and adequate. How get this information? Marketing research is the best answer because it provides the best answers.

Why

Marketing research is an aid to management. It is used on the assumption that it helps managers make sounder decisions, select more profitable courses of action, solve problems more correctly. The more information pertaining to a problem an executive has, the sounder should be the action he takes. He decides on an objective, factual basis rather than on a subjective, intuitive basis. The advertising manager, for example, bases his program on facts and on research findings, not on his own reactions, habits, and tastes. His preferences and prejudices, incidentally, are seldom those of his firm's customers and prospective customers.

Marketing research reduces the area of mistakes and errors. It avoids the wasting of time and money in misdirected effort. It reduces the amount of hunch and guesswork in decisions. It helps achieve a large success instead of a small one.

There are, understandably, differences of opinion about what the right decision or the best course of action is. There can even be differences of opinion about the significance or interpretation of facts. But the facts should be known, and there should be agreement on the fact that they are accurate and true.

Sources of Information

1. Much valuable information is recorded in the internal records of most companies. These records should be researched rather than ignored. As an example, sales and profits can be determined for each sales territory and for each customer. In firms with several products or divisions, sales, costs, and profits can be computed for each product and each division. In certain cases, management has come to realize that there is a tremendous amount of marketing data in the firm's own files.

2. Sometimes marketing information of value to a seller has already been compiled and is already available. These secondary sources include, for example, (a) government departments (Commerce, Agriculture), (b) trade associations (National Lumber Manufacturers Association, American Newspaper Publishers Association), (c) business publications (*Advertising Age, Printers' Ink*), and (d) commercial research firms (A. C. Nielsen Company, Market Research Corporation of America).

3. The remaining source is for the company concerned to plan and execute a research project, to do basic, original research.

Typical Research Projects

Here are eighteen examples of research undertaken in the marketing area. Note: the list is illustrative only, not complete.

> A physical comparison of competing products
> Share of market held by each competing brand
> Population trends

Analysis of territorial potentials, sales, and profits
Demand for a new product
Influence of price on sales volume
Feasibility of a manufacturer's controlling resale prices
Setting the price on a new type of product
Features of a good premium offer
Features of a good sampling operation
Extent of retail distribution
Quotas for a manufacturer's retailers
Costs and profits of different distribution channels
Advertising media and scheduling
How much to budget for advertising
Determining the effectiveness of advertising
Sales forecasting
Evaluation of marketing performance

Limitations of Marketing Research

Marketing research is not magic. It is not even the first medicine to be taken when an advertiser feels that all is not well. It certainly is not an exact science; two research methods have been known to come up with different findings, and two researchers have been known to recommend different solutions for the same problem. A thorough research project can consume much time and many dollars and still not give management all the answers desired. Marketing research is an *aid* to management, not a substitute for judgment.

Need for Continuous Research

When does an advertiser need marketing research? *Before, during,* and *after* any advertising. Why? Because change is a market's most changeless feature. New products and new competitors are always appearing in new markets. Every day there are new problems and new solutions, new needs and new opportunities. New research techniques and facilities appear. These changes must be detected promptly, usually through continuous, never-ending research. The *right* answer today may be a *wrong* answer tomorrow.

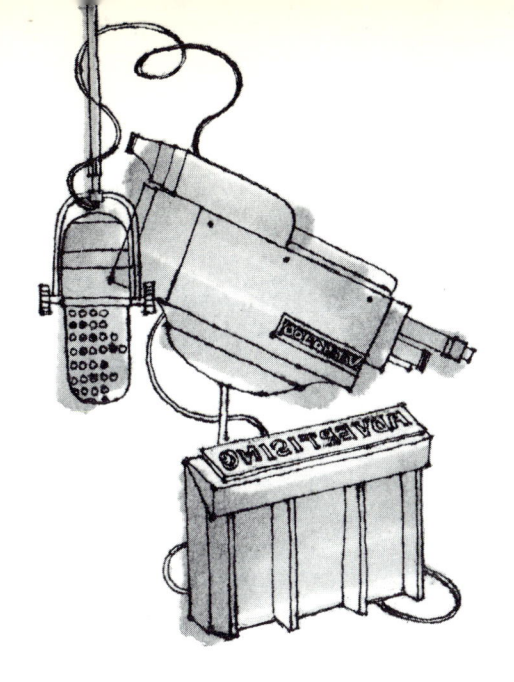

PART TWO

The Background for Advertising

Our first two chapters started by recognizing advertising as a marketing function and as an element, along with personal selling and sales promotion, in the promotional mixes of sellers. The chapters then summarized the various marketing areas of interest to advertisers.

Part II is narrower than Part I. It provides the advertising background necessary for the remainder of the course. The first of two chapters defines and classifies advertising; it describes the composition of the advertising industry; it explains why advertising is used, in situations involving *primary* demand and in situations involving *selective* demand. Circumstances that contribute to advertising success are described.

The part's second chapter consists of five sections. In the first, a hypothetical critic of advertising and a champion of advertising have a go at each other. Many of their observations apply to personal selling as snugly as they do to advertising. Many of the questions they raise do not have simple, clear, provable answers. Section two consists of comments on the debate. In the third section, various guardians or protectors of the consumer are mentioned. Section four is a brief description of the Advertising Council and its operation. A consideration of the Consumer Movement closes the chapter and the part.

Chapter 3

The Nature of Advertising

⌜Advertising is a major industry in the United States today; it is an indispensable activity in our economy.⌝ The role advertising plays continues to increase in significance year after year. The host of new products marketed, the expenses and the risks involved in such launchings, and the high cost of personal selling are among the conditions which are placing a heavy responsibility on the advertising industry. ⌜The United States is an economy with a phenomenal productive capacity and output. ⌜There is a need to find consumers for this output, and advertising plays a vital role in the process of moving the goods from the producer to the consumer. With mass marketing to distribute the output of our mass production, gross national product may well increase to a dramatic degree by 1970. Advertising helps to achieve mass marketing while aiding the consumer in choosing among the almost infinite variety of products offered for his selection.⌝

This book looks at advertising primarily from the manufacturer's point of view; it concerns itself mainly with *national* or *general* advertising. The national advertiser we think about is the manufacturer who sells a limited line of products through retailers.

Several reasons explain why we use the manufacturer's advertising as a base rather than the retailer's advertising. A broader view of advertising may be had from the manufacturer's vantage point because manufacturers as a group use all media, whereas most retailers do not use magazines, network radio, network television, outdoor, or transit advertising. Manufacturers usually sell in many markets and thus confront the variety of problems posed by the differences among the markets in a region or in the entire country. Furthermore, manufacturers have the job of merchandising their advertising to middlemen and of influencing the advertising and selling activities of retailers. The organization and operation of advertising agencies are best studied from the manufacturer's position because retailers make such slender use of agencies. Again, advertising as found in a manufacturer's marketing program is affected by such matters as product planning and channels of distribution; this too argues for looking at advertising through the manufacturer's eyes. Finally, advertising principles should be the core of any first course in advertising, and these principles are most quickly seen and easily grasped by examining advertising at the manufacturer's level.

One facetious definition of advertising reads: "Advertising is a field in which everyone is an expert — it is what everyone knows he could write or do — better, too." We might say that one of the purposes of this book is to show that there is far more to advertising than this definition implies.

WHAT ADVERTISING IS

Advertising is mass *communication* of *information* intended to *persuade* buyers so as to *maximize dollar profits*.

Communication

Advertising communication has several aspects which make it distinctive. It is mass communication, reaching large groups of buyers. Mass communication is demanded by mass production, and it helps make mass production possible. Advertising is non-personal communication in that it is not delivered *by* an actual person, nor is it addressed *to* a specific person although direct mail is sometimes an exception. Advertising is commercial communication because it is used to help assure the advertiser of a long business life with profitable sales. It can be economical because one advertisement may communicate with many buyers, not with just one individual buyer; this makes the cost-per-message low. The communication is speedy, permitting an advertiser to speak to millions of buyers in a matter of a few days or even a few hours. Finally, advertising is identified communication; the advertiser signs his name to his advertisement for the purpose of publicizing his identity.

Information

The information in an advertisement should be of benefit to buyers. It should guide them to a more satisfactory expenditure of their dollars. It should lead them to better solutions for their problems. Otherwise, the advertiser will not get the continued patronage he needs to maximize his long-run profits. This information is clearly within the control of the advertiser.

The advertiser composes his message and then pays according to established rates to have that message delivered. If accepted by a medium, the advertisement appears exactly as and when the advertiser directed. This control belonging to the advertiser is matched by his responsibility. The information in advertising is unquestionably the responsibility of the advertiser. He alone speaks for himself. The advertisement is a matter of record. The advertiser is in no position to claim, "But I was misquoted."

Persuasion

Advertising devoid of persuasion is ineffective. The advertisement that fails to influence anyone, either immediately or in the future, represents a waste of money. Because the advertiser's goal in most of his advertising is greater sales volume, he

The Background for Advertising

first must know what buyers want. Then he translates his product into buyer-satisfaction, building his advertisements somewhat as a salesman builds his presentations. He expects to create favorable attitudes which will lead to favorable actions. The advertiser's hope is to make prospects dissatisfied and to keep customers satisfied. Prospects should be buying his product but are not; so, they are not enjoying the maximum satisfaction possible. Customers are reassured that they did and are doing wisely in buying the advertiser's product.

Profit Maximization

The advertising on which this book is based has but a single, ultimate objective — to contribute the most it can to the maximization of the advertiser's net profit. Indeed, there is very little advertising with any other purpose. Net profit, of course, is the amount by which sales income exceeds costs. A seller influences the net profit figure by influencing either the sales figure, or the expense figure, or both. Most advertising is designed to affect net profits through its direct effects on sales volume and not on costs. There is little oversimplification in the contention that advertising's assignment is to increase sales volume. This increase is expected to be reflected in increased net profit.

TABLE 1.1   TOTAL ANNUAL VOLUME OF ADVERTISING IN THE UNITED STATES, SELECTED YEARS, 1867–1962

(in millions)

1867	$ 50	1950	$ 5,710
1880	200	1951	6,426
1890	360	1952	7,156
1900	542	1953	7,755
1904	821	1954	8,164
1909	1,142	1955	9,194
1915	1,302	1956	9,905
1920	2,935	1957	10,311
1925	3,099	1958	10,145
1930	2,607	1959	11,254
1935	1,690	1960	11,931
1940	2,088	1961	11,845
1945	2,875	1962	12,365

Source: Printers' Ink, **Advertising Guide to Marketing for 1963**, August 30, 1963. Figures for 1962 are estimated.

WHAT ADVERTISING IS NOT

Advertising is not a game. In a game, one side wins, the other loses. When advertising is done properly and profitably, both buyer and seller benefit. Too, the outcome of most games is not a serious, expensive matter; that's why they are games. The results of advertising, on the other hand, are almost always of serious concern.

The Nature of Advertising

Advertising is not a toy. Occasionally, an advertiser appears to be playing with advertising primarily to amuse himself. Few can afford this; moreover, few individuals have the authority to do this. The great majority of advertisers realize that advertising funds come from sales dollars and must be used to increase the number of those sales dollars.

Advertising is not a racket. Only a few advertisements are designed to deceive. A very few advertisers are racketeers. Apart from ethics, dependence on repeat sales insures a high degree of honesty in advertising. Most advertisers act as though every buyer knew the old saying:

> Fool me once, shame on *you;*
> Fool me twice, shame on *me.*

Finally, advertising is not an exact science. The volume of a manufacturer's sales is the result of the play of many factors and many influences. Competitors' decisions, the manufacturer's other promotional activities, changes in prices, products, personnel, or policies — even the weather — can have an important effect on sales volume. These conditions cannot be controlled as a physical scientist must control his experiments. Furthermore, in no two instances are an advertiser's circumstances identical. As a result, the advertiser cannot predict with accuracy what results future advertising will cause. Even more to be deplored, he finds that, after the advertising has been run, he cannot measure with precision what it did for him. Thus, advertising is more of an art than a science.

GROUPS INVOLVED

In product-promoting advertising, five groups are of primary importance: buyers, media, middlemen, advertising agencies, and advertisers.

One type of *buyer* who interests the advertiser is the individual who does not (but should) use the kind of product the advertiser sells. Consumers who do not use electric razors, cigarettes, or deodorants are examples of this classification. These buyers are prospects whom advertisers want to convert into users. A second type is made up of consumers who buy the kind of product, but from the advertiser's competitors. These too are prospects; advertisers want to take them away from their present suppliers. The advertiser's customers are a third type of buyer. Advertisers want to hold these buyers and to increase their purchases. A fourth type consists of those individuals who influence buyers. Sellers of industrial goods are interested in individuals responsible for industrial procurement. Many manufacturers are interested in professional men such as engineers, professors, and dentists who recommend a wide variety of products for others to buy.

Media are the second group involved in advertising. An advertising medium is a commercial vehicle that carries an advertiser's message to his prospects and customers. Eight major media will be examined in our media section: newspapers, magazines, television, radio, outdoor, transit, point-of-purchase, and direct mail.

Middlemen are a third group. Wholesalers and retailers are the two most important types of middlemen, and retailers are entitled to the major attention.

The Background for Advertising

Advertising agencies constitute our fourth classification. To simplify at this point, advertising agencies may be described as the organizations which construct the actual advertisements that consumers see and hear. The primary concern of agencies is the creation of profitable advertising for their clients, the advertisers. Agencies are, however, expanding their scope of operations to include more and more marketing and management activities.

Our fifth and final classification contains the *advertisers* themselves. Of the many types of seller using advertising, two stand out prominently, retailers and manufacturers. Retailers are typically the local merchants who handle the products of many manufacturers in one store or in one store organization; their customers are ultimate consumers who buy for personal or household use. Their advertising is referred to as *local* or *retail* advertising. Examples are the large newspaper advertisements of department stores and food stores.

PRODUCT VERSUS INSTITUTIONAL ADVERTISING

Before looking at reasons which lead manufacturers to advertise, some classification of advertising is necessary. Instead of attempting to include all possible bases of classification, and there are many, two broad and basic groupings will suffice at this point. These two categories are *product* advertising and *institutional* advertising.

Product Advertising

The main purpose of product advertising is to sell merchandise. This type of advertising usually promotes specific, branded products in such a manner as to make the brands seem more desirable. *Direct action* product advertising urges the buyer to take action at once. His immediate response may be ordering the item by mail, or by telephone, or mailing in a coupon. Prompt purchase in a retail store in response to a price reduction would be another example. Much direct action advertising is aimed at current needs of which buyers are aware.

The other version of product advertising is the *indirect action* type. This advertising hopes to increase the buyer's respect for the manufacturer's brand by establishing favorable associations in the buyer's mind. Brand acceptance and approval are built up against a future purchase. Indirect action advertising is a form of long-range promotion, often intended to help create wants in buyers' minds. Most advertising by manufacturers is indirect action, although some advertisements attempt to stimulate both types of action, direct *and* indirect.

Institutional Advertising

While product advertising sells merchandise to buyers, institutional advertising is designed to cultivate good will. Its purpose is to create a frame of mind and to implant feelings favorable to the advertiser's company. Its assignment is to make friends for the institution or organization.

The great bulk of institutional advertising is addressed to buyers and is *patronage* in nature. The manufacturer tells his prospects and his customers about himself,

How are YOU getting to the top?

Are you job-climbing the hard way? Struggling to get ahead. Gaining ground slowly. Always in danger of slipping back.

Or are you getting an up-to-date lift? Riding a method that's sure and sound. Forging ahead of others. Rising to responsible positions by virtue of real ability.

Neither way is easy. Both require time, effort, real determination. But the I.C.S. method is faster because it's powered by *success*. Enrolling with I.C.S. is like being given a hand by the top men in your field.

Behind the 257 I.C.S. Courses, you find recognized authorities, personalized instruction, simplified texts, individual guidance—all you need to prepare for advancement.

Sound good? Then take a moment right now to get all the facts. Mark and mail the coupon below. At no cost and without obligation, you get complete details including three books: (1) Opportunity Handbook for the field of your choice, (2) 36-page pocket guide, "How to Succeed," (3) sample lesson (Math) demonstrating the I.C.S. method. With these, you can plan intelligently how best to get to the top.

For Real Job Security—Get an I. C. S. Diploma!   I. C. S., Scranton 15, Penna.   Accredited Member, National Home Study Council

The goal of this advertisement is direct action, the marking and mailing of the coupon. (Courtesy: International Correspondence Schools)

his policies, and his personnel. He appeals to the patronage motivation of buyers. If successful, he convinces buyers that his operation entitles him to the buyer's dollars. Other institutional advertising is used for *public relations* purposes. Here company management asks advertising to deliver a communication to one of the company's publics. Stockholders, employees, plant cities, and the general public are examples of publics which can be addressed by such advertising. A third type is *public service* advertising. More and more manufacturers are stating publicly their positions and their thinking on issues or problems of current interest. For example, a manufacturer may employ advertising to advocate some course of action involving health, safety, or education. The government uses public service advertising to sell ideas and attitudes about such matters as conservation, saving, and security.

the couple next door...

He's an executive.

She's a housewife.

They're both volunteers in the great fight against cancer.

They help save lives with the message that cancer can be cured—if it is found early and treated promptly and properly. So, they tell their neighbors: "Get an annual health checkup, heed Cancer's Seven Danger Signals."

They're the warm, human link between the cancer patient and the doctor; between the contributor and the research scientist; and between today's disease and tomorrow's hope.

They're two of the more than two million volunteers who are the American Cancer Society.

Wouldn't you like to join them in their unselfish and satisfying work?

AMERICAN CANCER SOCIETY

Most media contribute space or time for public service advertisements such as this. (Courtesy: American Cancer Society)

The Nature of Advertising

WHY ADVERTISING IS USED

By Manufacturers

Manufacturers use advertising for three purposes. One is to create customers for the products they manufacture. Advertisers want to make sales today — and in the future. So, they use advertising to create and to stimulate demand, to open and to expand markets. Manufacturers' physical properties are protected, their key executives are insured; hence it is only natural and consistent that they assure themselves of customers for their goods. As a matter of fact, the contributions of machinery and men are meaningless unless there are markets. A second purpose of advertising is the creation of good will, the primary impact of which is upon sales volume. The third purpose of advertising is to reduce marketing costs, particularly product selling costs. Occasionally, advertising has a specific opportunity to help reduce a production cost, as when public relations advertising is used successfully to reduce absenteeism. All three types just mentioned contribute to more profit, more sales, or both.

In his search for additional sales volume, a manufacturer quickly discovers that there are only three basic sources of more business. One source is the group of individuals who do not now buy the manufacturer's type of product. *Conversion* of some of these non-users into users of the manufacturer's brand enlarges his market. Conversion requires the successful stimulation of primary demand, the demand for a *type* of product in contrast to demand for a *specific brand* of product within a type; advertising used for this purpose is referred to as pioneering or educational advertising. Because this is potentially a large field for many products, competitors sometimes unite in a cooperative effort to stimulate primary demand.

Encroachment is a second technique for increasing sales volume. The job here is to woo and win customers away from competitors through the stimulation of selective demand, the demand for the seller's individual brand. The type of advertising designed to create brand preference is usually called competitive advertising.

Expansion of the purchases of present customers is the only remaining method by which sales volume can be made larger. Various possibilities come to mind. Frequency of use may be stepped up; for example, Dr. Pepper wants you to drink not one but three bottles a day — and then even recommends the hours to you — at 10, at 2, and at 4. Variety of use can be increased for many products. More frequent replacement is encouraged by manufacturers of such products as television sets and toothbrushes. Size of average purchase can be increased; consumers use and serve more generous portions of food and drink if their supplies are large. In somewhat similar fashion, size of average consumption unit can be increased; a *big* glass of fruit juice is the recommended serving. For some products, expansion of market is largely a matter of extension of season; Florida and California *are* delightful in March.

By Consumers

Consumers are interested in and are on a ceaseless search for greater satisfaction of their wants. What is satisfaction? Precisely what the individual consumer wants

The Background for Advertising

from life, be this a matter of beauty, superiority, economy, approval, popularity, power, safety, sex, comfort, convenience, or such. If a consumer is to try a manufacturer's product and then repeat his purchase, the consumer must be convinced that, to maximize his personal satisfaction, he should make a place in his permanent buying pattern for that particular product. The consumer looks to advertising to help increase his satisfaction. What products are available, where, at what prices, and facts about what those products will do to and for buyers are examples of the helpful information consumers expect to find in advertising.

At any one moment a manufacturer's product may be in one of five stages as regards consumer attitude. One unfortunate stage is where the consumer's state of mind is that of ignorance. We fear what we do not know, and, because of this, we are reluctant to buy brands whose names are strange. A second stage is that of consumer recognition; in it the consumer realizes that he has heard of or seen that particular brand at some earlier time but he has not bought it. A third stage is that of consumer acceptance. Here the consumer acts on the suggestion of the manufacturer, of a retailer, or of some individual and makes a trial purchase. If his experiment turns out to be a happy one, the consumer will probably move into stage four, that of consumer preference. This is a most pleasing stage so far as the manufacturer is concerned because consumers in it take the initiative and request the manufacturer's product by name. There is only one stronger indication of the consumer's satisfaction with the brand in question — in stage five, the brand enjoys consumer insistence. Buyers in this fifth position not only ask for the manufacturer's product by name, they insist on getting just that and will accept no substitute. Consumer insistence is the quintessence of loyalty for which manufacturers can strive.

This text supports firmly the contention that the reasons why manufacturers and consumers make use of advertising are not only compatible and complementary, they are mutually essential. If a manufacturer's advertising is to maximize dollar profits for him, then it must help consumers maximize their sums of satisfaction.

OPPORTUNITY TO STIMULATE PRIMARY DEMAND

Primary demand is demand for a *type* or *class* of product or service. It is the demand for rayon or wine, for cigars or leather; it is the demand for truck transportation or insurance, for banking service or advertising. Primary advertising is used in practically all cases to promote primary demand, to increase the buying of a generic product or service, not a specific brand of product or service. Primary advertising hopes to achieve greater demand by (a) converting non-users into users, (b) persuading present users to use larger quantities, and, sometimes, (c) promoting new uses of an established product or service.

Who

Primary advertising is usually done by a *group* of sellers who typically compete against each other. These sellers most often are manufacturers of products or suppliers of services. The National Association of Margarine Manufacturers can

First Edition J & F Suits in long-wearing Columnar Cloth. Cigar Institute of America, Inc.

a cigar dresses up the outer man...

and calms down the inner man!

The purpose of this advertisement is to stimulate primary demand. (Courtesy: Cigar Institute of America, Inc.)

The Background for Advertising

promote the generic product, *margarine,* at the same time that Mazola, Parkay, and Fleischmann's compete among themselves. Or, the Institute of Life Insurance can advertise *life insurance,* aiding the selling efforts of Prudential, Metropolitan, and Northwestern. There is primary advertising in industrial marketing, too. The Gas Appliance Manufacturers Association holds an advertising umbrella over such firms as U.S. Pipe, American Meter Company, and Rockwell Manufacturing Company.

When city A tries to enlarge its retail trading area at the expense of city B, each market may resort to some primary advertising. In the preceding paragraph, we saw manufacturers in an industry working through their trade associations. Here we see retail merchants working through their retail merchants associations.

When states or intra-state organizations (California, New York, Pennsylvania) advertise their tourist or their industrial attractions, they sponsor a type of primary advertising. As for tourism, competitors unite and become allies to get visitors within the specific state's boundaries. Then they become competitors again for the daily expenditures of each visitor.

Sometimes there is a large number of small sellers who make up the advertising group. Individually, each could do very little by advertising; united, the group may be able to do much. Two such groups are the California Prune Advisory Board and the National Cotton Council of America.

In rare instances, a single seller undertakes primary advertising. If he develops a revolutionary new product (at one time, most household appliances were such) and has some "lead time" over future competitors, the seller may even be forced into primary advertising. Or, assume the product is a new industrial material; also assume that its manufacturer does not know (a) how other manufacturers can use it profitably, or (b) which executives in those firms have buying influence. What can he do? Stimulate primary demand. Another example might involve a seller who has a giant share of his industry's total market. He normally would capture a giant portion of any increase in his industry's total volume. Finally, because new individuals become prospects for the first time every day, a dominant firm in an industry (Campbell Soup, for example) may elect to do some continuous stimulation of primary demand.

Factors of Influence

Some individual sellers and some groups of sellers should use primary advertising, others should not. The basis for decision is the question: will advertising increase sales volume enough to increase net profits? That question should be answered in the light of what are believed to be correct answers to the following questions. The more affirmative answers there are, the more correct and accurate they are, the more enthusiastic they are, the better is the opportunity to stimulate primary demand. Assume that the product is *tea.*

Do we know what consumer-desires tea satisfies?

Are these powerful desires?

Can tea compete successfully against whatever non-tea consumers now use to gratify those desires?

Indeed, does tea enjoy some competitive advantage?

The Nature of Advertising

Can strong and specific benefits be promised to tea drinkers?
Can we estimate who, where, and how many prospective tea drinkers there are?
Can we estimate how many of these now drink tea?
Are the attitudes and habits of non-tea drinkers such that we can convert a satisfactory number into consumers?
Is the total market potential for tea, in dollars, large enough to be encouraging?
Is the demand trend *up* for beverages such as tea?
If there are social or economic circumstances which affect tea consumption, are they favorable?
Is gross margin such that it can make possible an adequate advertising fund?
Are able advertising men confident that advertising can expand demand for tea with no cutting of price?
Does the advertising program under consideration have a good chance to contribute to net profit?

OPPORTUNITY TO STIMULATE SELECTIVE DEMAND

The individual seller who markets his branded product or service is mainly concerned with the stimulation of *selective* demand. If his product is *tea* and his brand is *Lipton,* he wants the public to buy much tea, a primary demand matter; but even more, he wants his *Lipton* brand to be the most popular brand. If the total amount of tea bought is represented by a pie chart, he wants the *Lipton* slice to be the largest slice.

Selective demand thus is a portion, a segment, of primary demand. Where primary advertising promoted a type or class of product, selective advertising promotes a brand within that type or class. Primary demand usually involves competition between and among industries, for example, tea vs. coffee. Selective demand involves competition between and among brands, for example, Lipton tea vs. Tender Leaf tea.

The individual seller approaches his advertising decisions much as do sellers interested in the stimulation of primary demand. He thinks in terms of what advertising might do to his *sales revenue* and to his *costs,* both marketing costs *and* production costs. He, as advertisers before him, learns that certain circumstances are more favorable to advertising success than are other circumstances. These can relate to company, to product, to market, and to the promotion program itself.

THE CLIMATE ADVERTISING NEEDS

Like certain plants, advertising does well in some circumstances but poorly in others. This section examines some of the conditions that are necessary to the most satisfactory functioning of advertising.

Company

Advertising thrives best when the sponsoring company is sound, particularly in respect to policies and personnel. Management of such companies is able and enlightened, informed and sympathetic to advertising's objectives. Management understands what advertising should do and what it should not be asked to do; management understands that advertising is cumulative in its effects; management has confidence in advertising, seeing it as a sales- and profit-increasing force; management does not consider advertising to be a panacea. Competent management insists on a thorough and adequate market research program, one which stresses buyers, products, prices, channels, and promotion. Full awareness of the necessity for good public relations, plus an alert and able public relations staff, help provide an atmosphere conducive to profitable advertising.

Product

The first requirement of a product to be advertised is that it possess basic utility, that it provide satisfaction for some consumer want. Next, of course, its price should reflect the quantity and quality of this utility closely enough so as not to be any undue handicap. The physical product and its package should be "right"; a minimum of competitive inferiority and a maximum number of points of competitive superiority are desirable. The more obvious the product's distinctiveness within its product type and the more nearly it is unique, the more advertising can do for it. In reverse manner, the more difficult it is for buyers to identify and evaluate by examination internal qualities of significance, the more effective the advertising can be. Products well identified by excellent brand names, trade marks, and trade characters have greater advertising potentials because of this identification. A final feature of great merit is the presence of strong buying motives, preferably of the emotional type. The satisfaction a product delivers should rank high in the buyer's priority rating of desired satisfactions. Cigarettes, vacation cruises, insurance, perfume, jewelry, and candy are examples of products which can have strong emotional appeal. Advertisements for these products can be based on this emotional appeal. Sugar, scissors, and clothespins are examples of products devoid of strong emotional appeal.

Market

Some markets are more friendly than others toward a manufacturer's advertising. The wider the market, the better the advertiser likes it. If there are masses of prospects and customers, mass communication is clearly needed for reasons of speed and economy. The more responsive the market is to advertising and the greater the potential sales volume, the greater opportunity there is for profitable advertising. Markets characterized by strong primary demand delight the advertiser. The cigarette market is one of stronger primary demand than is the market for smoking tobacco; the same is true of the market for men's low-cut shoes compared with the market for men's high-top shoes. Advertisers want market trends to be favorable rather than unfavorable; advertising does its best job behind a product of growing rather than declining popularity. Even outstanding advertising is sorely handicapped when the product involved is losing or has lost public favor. For example, to try through advertising to put hats on the heads of college men or cigars in their mouths would be ambitious undertakings. In somewhat similar

Product design, packages, and brand names are merchandising matters. (Courtesy: The Proctor & Gamble Company)

The Background for Advertising

fashion, advertisers prefer to advertise in good times rather than bad. While a measure of continuity is essential, advertisers feel that advertising should be heavy when the potential sales response is greatest and light during depressed periods. To supply the market, adequate distribution through middlemen is a requirement. Good products and promotion, attractive margins, and good relations with dealers go far toward getting for a manufacturer the type and number of dealers he needs.

Promotion Program

If a manufacturer's advertising is to be most productive, his entire promotion program, including his advertising, must be constructed intelligently and executed effectively. Activities of the sales department and the sales promotion department constitute most of the rest of the promotion program. It goes without saying that these activities deserve and demand sound management. Furthermore, there should be effective coordination of all promotion. In the specific area of advertising, the need for productive advertisements and imaginative advertising is paramount. In addition, the effort should not be too small if its opportunity to succeed is to be bright. A manufacturer must set the size of his advertising fund at a figure high enough to finance a thorough, well-balanced program. This fund needs able administration. The advertising bought with it needs to be merchandised effectively.

Questions and Problems

1. Advertisers direct their advertising at markets; they sell to and in markets. What are some concepts of a market?
2. How is a seller handicapped when he asks his advertising, all by itself, to cause buyers to buy?
3. "It pays to advertise." *Does* it?
4. Sellers such as telephone companies and electric power companies have little if any direct competition. Why do they advertise?
5. Creative advertising has been defined by one prominent advertiser as advertising that "penetrates, persuades, and propels." Comment.
6. Why was advertising of such little significance prior to 1900?
7. Manufacturers as a group spend more dollars for personal selling than for advertising. Why?
8. A manufacturer's advertising is affected by the advertising of his competitors. Comment.
9. The Republic Sugar Refining Company is a small firm located in Louisiana. Seventy-five per cent of its output is sold to wholesalers and retailers under the Republic brand. The other 25% is sold to industrial users of sugar. Republic does not supply sugar for chain stores to retail under their own labels.
   Price competition in the sugar refining industry is severe; margins are low. Republic's net income last year was considerably less than the average for refineries of comparable size. Currently Republic is operating at 70% capacity.

The Nature of Advertising

Today, as in the past, Republic relies completely on a small sales force and on food brokers to market its sugar. One of the executives thinks the company should begin some consumer advertising. He predicts this would increase Republic's share-of-market and would also use some of its idle capacity.
Do you agree?

10. Suppose the manufacturers of cigars in this country organize a Cigar Manufacturers Trade Association. Suppose further that marketing research finds that the average age of cigar smokers falls in the 35–40-year bracket. The CMTA would like to lower that average-age figure. One approach, obviously, would be to advertise to college students in an effort to get more of them to smoke cigars. How do you feel about this possible course of action?

Chapter 4

Social and Economic Aspects

Marketing costs in this country are high. Their rise has paralleled the rise in our standard of living. The many types of marketing expense help explain why marketing takes 50 to 60 per cent of the dollar the consumer spends for goods and services. The expenses include wholesaling and retailing, buying and selling, transportation and storage, advertising and sales promotion, research and financing, and, present everywhere, the assumption of risks. The geographical distance and the time interval between production and consumption are two more explanations for marketing expenses. Services demanded by the consumer also increase marketing costs, services such as credit, delivery, attention of retail salespersons, returned goods privileges, atmosphere, parking, convenience, and wide assortments from which to choose small units of purchase.

Advertising, the marketing force which helps mass distribution to keep pace with mass production, is the object of much criticism, some justified, some not. One type of critic seems dedicated to the destruction of the American way of life; he sees advertising as an ideal target to attack first. Another type of critic seems most interested in making money by "exposing" something or other — government, management, labor leaders, for example, or college athletics, doctors, or vice. This second type, incidentally, often demands that its books be marketed aggressively — with much advertising. The third type of critic is a respectable fellow. He sees advertising as desirable, even necessary, but in need of some revision. In each of his criticisms there is some truth.

THE GREAT DEBATE

Advertising and the Consumer

Critic: I am delighted, Champion, to correct your thinking about what advertising does to consumers, and I'll deal you a devastating blow at once by calling your attention to *bait* advertising. You know, some advertiser publicizes a low-priced product, he gets prospects in to examine it, then he runs down the advertised item, perhaps disclosing some stipulation not mentioned in his advertisement, and ends by high-pressuring the prospect into buying a high-priced, high-profit product.

Social and Economic Aspects

Some automobile dealers advertise a very low down payment *and* an extremely low weekly payment, but what they don't tell is that you can't have both. Or, they advertise high trade-in allowances but find excuses to whittle down this figure when examining and appraising your car, or point out for the first time that the high trade-in applies only on the seller's highest-priced model. "Factory rebuilt" sewing machines and vacuum cleaners may be advertised at impossibly low prices; if the buyer insists on one, he gets stories about short supply, delayed delivery, no guarantee, and such.

What have you to say, Champion of Advertising?

Champion: Touché. I have no justification whatever for bait advertising. I hope that self-regulation, publicity, and legislation will eliminate it.

Critic: Round one, I assume, is mine by default. Let me open round two by reminding you that consumers are, in large measure, confused and misled by much advertising. We critics argue that many advertisements are false, deceptive, and misleading and that their effect is to compound the consumer's buying difficulties with conflicting, bewildering claims. What is worse, seldom do consumers know when they have been defrauded.

Champion: Very little advertising is misleading intentionally, because advertisers know the consequences. Advertising operates in public; its nature calls attention to itself; it is self-purifying because its sins are obvious and felt immediately. Misleading advertising almost guarantees its own punishment, Critic, because a deceived buyer returneth not to be fleeced anew. The sheer number of products causing confusion is, at the same time, part of our high standard of living.

You mention conflicting claims. Remember that there are basic differences of opinion in religion, medicine, sports, bridge, education, cooking, and economics. Bias is a basic element of our mores — in selling, in politics, in parents' feelings about their offspring, in boy-and-girl situations. And, it's quite easy to move from emphasis into exaggeration. So, don't criticize all advertisers because one takes the short step from enthusiasm to overstatement. There are a few quacks in medicine, a few shysters in law, a few crooks in banking, and some frauds in teaching.

Critic: I am appalled at the amount of advertising in poor taste. Billboards mar the beauty of our natural scenery. Commercials in the broadcast media are too numerous and too long, too blatant and too sensational; they interrupt good music and good drama. Television brings murder, drunkenness, and vulgarity into your living room for your children to see. The functioning of the human body is described with a detailed and graphic accuracy which revolts.

Champion: You are confused, Critic. It is not advertising's job to raise consumers' tastes in entertainment; that is the responsibility of parent, preacher, priest, and professor. Advertising is a *business* activity undertaken for a single purpose — to help maximize dollar profits. Advertisers first *determine* what consumers like and want and then *help gratify* those likes and wants. Incidentally, Critic, just what *is*

The Background for Advertising

good taste? I deem it quite difficult to define what is indecent or objectionable. Taste is an intangible matter, changing as times change. As with values, taste is largely subjective, as a look at the fields of art and music, for example, shows. Furthermore, under our present system, you could not have the good music and good drama you mention without advertising which pays for these programs.

Critic: Well, maybe so, but you cannot deny that much advertising insults the consumer's intelligence. Testimonials and comparative prices are fictitious. Copy is meaningless and irrelevant, information is inadequate. The use of the floating or unfinished comparative irritates. "Blippo gives you more safety — more economy" — more than *what,* Champion?

Champion: Advertisers are not perfect, and advertising has faults. You are right in saying that many advertisements do not give buyers as much information as buyers need. Mass communication, do remember, must speak a language the masses can grasp.

Critic: You've handled yourself fairly well on the last two points — see what you can do with *this* one. I charge that advertising is designed to appeal mainly to a consumer's emotions, urging him to make emotional purchases, even to buy products he should not buy.

Champion: Have a care there, Critic. Don't forget that each consumer is a social, a mental, an economic, a moral, a physical, a religious — yes, even an *emotional* creature. Each of these creatures needs care and nourishment, the emotional one, especially, needing an occasional lift or psychic lark. Who can say, indeed, that a consumer would derive more satisfaction from operatic records than from a box of cigars, or from a book on etiquette than from a piece of costume jewelry. Any girl who wants to be rational can give up cosmetics and trips to the hairdresser — and dates. But is *that* rational? A strong case, Critic, can be made for the argument that only *irrational* consumers strive to make nothing but *rational* purchases.

Critic: Well, we can at least agree that advertising must be criticized for making the consumer unhappy and discontented by causing him to want what he can't afford and by encouraging him to live beyond his means.

Champion: I hate to do this, but you have left yourself wide open. If you are to be complete and consistent, you must tell the consumer not to go to shows or to friends' homes, not to look at magazines, television, or store windows. Last Sunday at church I saw the best-looking suit I've ever seen; I want one like it but don't expect ever to be able to afford it. I'm unhappy. Critic, should I abandon church-going?

Our high standard of living owes much to consumers first made discontented by advertising and then spurred to want and activated to get better products and to

Can Taste Survive in America?

WALTER HOVING
Chairman of the Board
TIFFANY & CO.

Over 120 years ago a Frenchman by the name of Alexis de Tocqueville visited the United States and wrote a remarkable book, "Democracy in America". Among other prophetic observations he predicted the inevitable decline of taste in a democratic society.

In a stratified society such as France had at that time, said de Tocqueville, a fine craftsman has only one set of customers, the aristocracy. They demand the best and the craftsman strives to give it to them. Consequently, quality and taste become his hallmark. This was certainly true during the great periods of the 18th and early 19th centuries in France and England, notably the Regency, Louis XV and Louis XVI styles in France, or the remarkable styles of the brothers Adam, Chippendale, Sheraton, etc., in England.

In a democratic, or as de Tocqueville says, in a fluid society on the other hand, everybody is a potential customer. The demand is not for quality but for cheapness and abundance. For example, the aristocrat who buys a table expects to pass it on to posterity and therefore demands a good one. But the American, says de Tocqueville, who buys a table expects to change his economic and social status shortly, so he buys one that will do for the moment. As the moments succeed one another so do the tables, and the ideal of excellence of quality and taste is lost sight of.

Although I do not agree with M. de Tocqueville's basic premise, it is alarming how accurate his predictions are proving to be in contemporary America, where our ideals of taste and good style are suffering under the onslaught of mass production. From automobiles to teaspoons and from clothes to baby rattles, it is everywhere evident. Although much excellent merchandise is still produced, the general tendency seems to be to cheapen and vulgarize much of the merchandise that is offered by too many of our manufacturers and stores today.

Interestingly enough, the taste of the general public is much better than most manufacturers seem to think, but the public is given fewer and fewer opportunities to choose between the "good" and the "bad". Most of the time they have to choose between the "bad" and the "even worse". Something should be done and, I believe, can be done to improve the situation.

For example, seven years ago when the present management took over at Tiffany's we decided to do something about it in our field and here is what we did. First of all we set very high standards for ourselves in taste and design. And let me emphasize that these were our own standards. They were not based on surveys of what the public liked or didn't like. Such surveys, I think, are just plain nonsense because the public doesn't want to lead in this matter, they want to follow.

Then we went through all our stocks and separated the sheep from the goats and held a gigantic clearance sale which startled New York. This was the first clearance sale Tiffany's had had in over 100 years, and it really cleared the decks and gave us room to follow our new policies.

Next we gathered around us good designers and stylists who were able to understand our new point of view and could be instrumental in creating the kind of merchandise that would measure up to our higher standards.

Then we began redesigning our jewelry, china, glass, silverware and other merchandise. And don't think this concerned itself solely with jewelry over $100,000 or china plates at $100 each. Not by any means. We were just as careful to have taste reflected in things that sold as low as five and ten dollars. The rules of taste, we believe, have nothing to do with price. A low priced article can be just as attractive as a high priced one if it is properly designed.

We lost a good deal of business in the beginning, but we decided that under no circumstances would we pander to so-called popular tastes. We would rather lose the business than do so. When you take a position like this you can't be weak-kneed about it.

But soon instead of losing business we began to gain, and now seven years later we can look back and say that the policy has been extraordinarily successful. The volume of business has increased substantially and the earnings per share have more than tripled. So here you have a concrete demonstration that selling taste, style and quality is not just an impractical dream but can be made to pay off right now in the twentieth century.

But more important to us is that we feel we are doing our bit to educate young people to raise their **own** standards to a higher level. Even the youngest bride can now come in to Tiffany's and be sure that the Christmas or wedding present she selects will be attractive no matter how undeveloped her own taste may be.

We are convinced that in spite of M. de Tocqueville's thesis a democratic society **can** achieve high standards of taste. Even though the demands of the twentieth century are vastly different from those of the eighteenth and although obviously mass production poses different disciplines from handcrafting, there is no reason, in our judgement, why **standards** of taste cannot be just as high as any that existed in the great periods of the past.

I suggest, therefore, that you come in to Tiffany's and see for yourself the results of these higher twentieth century standards the next time you are in New York. You will find it a stimulating and rewarding experience.

A well-known retailer buys advertising space to discuss the general level of public taste. (Courtesy: Tiffany & Co.)

The Background for Advertising

achieve a higher plane of living. Luxuries of today, seen and wanted by the masses, become necessities tomorrow, taken for granted. Living has become easier, safer, more enjoyable, more convenient, more comfortable.

Critic: Well, I've saved until last my most serious indictment of advertising for what it does to consumers. Here it is: You must admit that advertising is making stereotypes of consumers. Uniformity is the order of the day. There is an "organization man" model everywhere you look — in business, in government, in college teaching, even in the clergy. The fact that the "Joneses" are the common pattern for consumers (and I guess sometimes I *do* mean common), and the further fact that everyone today runs in a pack, copying and agreeing with the Joneses, must be charged to advertising. Thanks to advertising you and I must say, "Individuality is dead — long live blind conformity!"

Champion: The conformity you impute to advertising is only a figment of your distorted imagination. Why so? *Because the Joneses won't stand still!* And they don't stand still because new products and improved products are presented to them every year — through advertising. While *you* are catching up with the Joneses, *they* are climbing farther up on the living-standard ladder. Annual increases in the number, the types, and the availability of consumer products widen the range of consumer choice. Once upon a time, all refrigerators were white and all automobiles were black. Today you can choose from 17 models of one of the "low priced three" automobiles, and the color combinations run much higher than that figure.

Actually, advertising *will not let* consumers conform. It spurs manufacturers to make new and better products, and it spurs consumers to want new, better, and even more products. The conclusion is unavoidable that advertising can thrive only if there are differences among products and differences among the preferences, values, and satisfactions of consumers. Above all others, the United States consumer can do much to assert himself and to gratify his own personal ambitions. It is he who gets good products at low prices. It is he who has the time and the money to pursue his own individual cultural, intellectual, religious, civic, and social interests.

Critic, in respect to housing, recreation, travel, and hobbies, for examples, who is the more standardized, the typical consumer in the United States — or the typical consumer in Asia, South America, or Africa?

Advertising and Products

Critic: If advertising sold products which are no worse than inferior, I'd be disturbed but not depressed. Because it sells so many *worthless* products — of no real value — my blood pressure soars.

Champion: Advertising may sell an inferior product *once*. The vast majority of sellers, probably well over 90 per cent of them, must have repeat patronage from their customers if the sellers are to stay in business, and repeat buying demands that

CREATIVE CODE

American Association of Advertising Agencies

The members of the American Association of Advertising Agencies recognize:

1. That advertising bears a dual responsibility in the American economic system and way of life.

To the public it is a primary way of knowing about the goods and services which are the products of American free enterprise, goods and services which can be freely chosen to suit the desires and needs of the individual. The public is entitled to expect that advertising will be reliable in content and honest in presentation.

To the advertiser it is a primary way of persuading people to buy his goods or services, within the framework of a highly competitive economic system. He is entitled to regard advertising as a dynamic means of building his business and his profits.

2. That advertising enjoys a particularly intimate relationship to the American family. It enters the home as an integral part of television and radio programs, to speak to the individual and often to the entire family. It shares the pages of favorite newspapers and magazines. It presents itself to travelers and to readers of the daily mails. In all these forms, it bears a special responsibility to respect the tastes and self-interest of the public.

3. That advertising is directed to sizable groups or to the public at large, which is made up of many interests and many tastes. As is the case with all public enterprises, ranging from sports to education and even to religion, it is almost impossible to speak without finding someone in disagreement. Nonetheless, advertising people recognize their obligation to operate within the traditional American limitations: to serve the interests of the majority and to respect the rights of the minority.

Therefore we, the members of the American Association of Advertising Agencies, in addition to supporting and obeying the laws and legal regulations pertaining to advertising, undertake to extend and broaden the application of high ethical standards. Specifically, we will not knowingly produce advertising which contains:

a. False or misleading statements or exaggerations, visual or verbal.

b. Testimonials which do not reflect the real choice of a competent witness.

c. Price claims which are misleading.

d. Comparisons which unfairly disparage a competitive product or service.

e. Claims insufficiently supported, or which distort the true meaning or practicable application of statements made by professional or scientific authority.

f. Statements, suggestions or pictures offensive to public decency.

We recognize that there are areas which are subject to honestly different interpretations and judgment. Taste is subjective and may even vary from time to time as well as from individual to individual. Frequency of seeing or hearing advertising messages will necessarily vary greatly from person to person.

However, we agree not to recommend to an advertiser and to discourage the use of advertising which is in poor or questionable taste or which is deliberately irritating through content, presentation or excessive repetition.

Clear and willful violations of this Code shall be referred to the Board of Directors of the American Association of Advertising Agencies for appropriate action, including possible annulment of membership as provided in Article IV, Section 5, of the Constitution and By-Laws.

Conscientious adherence to the letter and the spirit of this Code will strengthen advertising and the free enterprise system of which it is part. *Adopted April 26, 1962*

Endorsed by

Advertising Association of the West, Advertising Federation of America, Agricultural Publishers Association, Associated Business Publications, Association of Industrial Advertisers, Association of National Advertisers, Magazine Publishers Association, National Business Publications, Newspaper Advertising Executives Association, Radio Code Review Board (National Association of Broadcasters), Station Representatives Association, TV Code Review Board (NAB)

Advertising agencies have an interest in proper as well as profitable advertising. (Courtesy: American Association of Advertising Agencies)

The Background for Advertising

the product satisfy the buyer. By advertising his branded merchandise, a manufacturer does more than *admit* paternity — he *boasts* proudly about it. Because his identity is known, the consumer can vote against him when making subsequent purchases. And remember, Critic, a product you loathe, a product you consider worthless, that same product may be loved by millions to whom it gives real satisfaction.

Come to think of it, Critic, you are 180 degrees off course. Advertising works for product superiority, not product inferiority. The influence of advertising is for standardized products of uniform quality, month after month and market after market. They *must* be, for the advertiser's reputation is at stake. As his volume increases, he can finance better research, inspection, and control. The result? Outstanding values, as the copywriters say.

Critic: I disagree. Advertising not only sells many inferior products, it also emphasizes *insignificant* details, it stresses *minor* differences, it encourages *unimportant* product changes.

Champion: A series of minor improvements, year after year, can result in a vastly improved product in a relatively short period of time.

Advertising and Manufacturers' Costs

Critic: You were brave but naïve, Champion, to allow this topic on the agenda. Everybody knows that the manufacturer who advertises has higher costs than the manufacturer who does not. His selling prices, consequently, must be higher. Indeed, I venture to suggest that the sales volume of most advertisers would *rise* if they abandoned advertising and reduced their prices by the amount of their advertising expense.

Champion: You both sadden and infuriate me, Critic, with that comment. I'll try to be more sympathetic than scornful. Because a manufacturer has two basic assignments, the *making* of goods and then the *selling* of those goods, let's look at production costs and then at promotion costs.

Although the result is neither automatic nor inevitable, mass production *can* reduce *cost-to-make*. Logic and experience seem clear — greater sales volume from advertising usually effects economies in production. The interest and the intent of the advertiser are to use advertising to help market enough merchandise, month by month, to permit the most profitable volume of production. The manufacturer wants to reach this optimum production rate and then stabilize there. Better buying, cheaper transportation and storage, greater specialization of labor, more efficient machinery, and more effective utilization of physical plant and personnel are features of this optimum production rate and contribute to lower manufacturing costs.

Listen, Friend Critic, you read this morning that a certain manufacturer has just spent $5,000,000 modernizing his production facilities. The consumers of the products made in that factory must, you know, pay that bill over the life of those facilities. Shouldn't you scream and beat your breast about *that* expenditure?

Social and Economic Aspects

As for *promotion* costs, let's recall that a manufacturer has three marketing activities to choose from when building his promotion program, namely, personal selling, advertising, and sales promotion. He assumes a new and an additional expense item when he begins to advertise. But, effective advertising can work to reduce the cost of personal selling which is, by far, the largest promotion expense for most manufacturers. How? Advertising reduces buyers' resistance by pre-selling them. Salesmen make more and more successful calls, thereby using their time more productively. Both the salesman's morale and his presentations are strengthened. Better salesmen and better middlemen are attracted to manufacturers who advertise. Large-scale economies per unit of product, similar to those found in production costs, are possible for marketing costs; if marketing 1,000,000 units of product costs $300,000, marketing 2,000,000 need not cost $600,000.

But, the advertiser's objective is not the lowest possible *promotion* cost per unit; his goal is still the maximization of dollar profits. This means that the manufacturer will increase the promotion cost per unit of product if the larger sales volume resulting reduces the *production* cost per unit by a greater amount.

Advertising and Consumer Prices

Critic: You admitted, Champion, that advertising is one more marketing expense. Since this is true, I hope you will display both grace and consistency by agreeing that advertising raises consumer prices and then operates to hold those prices high. If you concur that advertising makes for price rigidity and retards price competition, we can move on to the last topic on our agenda. OK?

Champion: No, *no,* NO! Your statement is guilty of oversimplification. Let's recognize that advertising can raise consumer prices, it can leave consumer prices unchanged, or it can reduce them. Does advertising raise consumer prices? Some does, intentionally. A manufacturer may take $5 worth of physical necktie, add $5 worth of prestige, envy, exclusiveness, and impression value through advertising, and sell the tie to consumers for $10. In this instance advertising creates $5 worth of utility, and the consumer pays for it if he buys that tie. He, of course, does not *have* to buy that tie. Advertising can raise prices in a second, an *unintentional* manner; ineffective or mismanaged advertising forces up the seller's prices. In a third and final manner, advertising can raise consumer prices if the manufacturer makes vigorous and extensive use of advertising to develop a market for a new type of product while it is in the primary or pioneering stage.

In the short run, Critic, price competition among advertised brands may be discouraged. In the long run, advertising works in the direction of lower prices. There is pressure from non-advertised products of the same type, from private brands of the same type, and from substitute or alternative types of product. No advertiser has been known to ignore price competition for any considerable period of time.

The key issue, Critic, is not whether advertising adds to the cost of the product — the key issue is whether advertising makes the consumer pay more for the same amount of satisfaction. And, incidentally, your assumption that a manufacturer's sales volume would rise if advertising were abandoned and prices reduced by the

The Background for Advertising

cost of advertising is subject to serious doubt. Consider a soft drink with an advertising cost of $\frac{1}{50}$ of a cent, a can of soup whose advertising cost is $\frac{1}{20}$ of a cent, or a cake of soap and a breakfast food, each supporting an advertising cost of $\frac{3}{10}$ of a cent. Care to comment, Critic?

Critic: You are unfair.

Advertising and the Economy

Critic: You've stalled long enough, Champion, hoping to avoid, no doubt, an examination of what advertising does to and in our economy — a topic hardly to your liking. But, ready or not, here I come. I charge that advertising encourages the growth of a few, large companies in an industry. Look at the cigarette industry, the appliance industry, and, above all, the automobile industry. Advertising has let giants develop in each of these areas, giants so large and in such control of the market that no newcomer can break in because he can't match the size of the advertising efforts in those fields. This concentration of production in the hands of a few large advertisers results in restricted output and in high prices.

Champion: How you do love, Critic, to put cart before horse. The competitive system we have in this country is the *cause* of advertising, *not the result* of it. We had it before advertising, and we would continue to have it if all advertising were outlawed. Please, do remember your economics! If a quasi-monopolist raises prices, he invites competition — and he invites his customers to find substitute products. If his sales increase sharply, he invites retaliation by his competitors who are determined to checkmate then reverse that encroachment. Before an entrepreneur could start the manufacture of automobiles, there are such matters as capital, patents, management, and a dealer organization, just to mention a few. Advertising is just *one* factor involved in starting a new business. A small meat packer in a city of 100,000 can spend just as many promotion dollars in that market as can Swift and he can capture a larger share of that market — by advertising.

Critic: My next charge is that most advertising is an economic waste, having no effect other than to switch some customers from Able soap to Baker soap, and other customers from Baker to Able.

Champion: I thought you just said that advertising promotes monopoly. Now you are saying that advertising creates a multiplicity of brands. Do you feel well?

Critic: Do respect my title. Critics don't have to be consistent, you know. Dare you deny that competitive advertising wastes our resources and asks the consumer to foot the bill?

Champion: There is some waste in advertising, mainly because it is not a science and because sometimes sound decisions and recommendations of able specialists are overruled by those who sign the checks. This economic waste argument of yours

Social and Economic Aspects

assumes a fixed market — one that can neither contract nor expand. How could that be the case — either for one product or all products? What you call competitive advertising makes the industry's market, the total market, larger. Too, product quality benefits from the effects of competitive advertising. If advertising is uneconomical just because of its basic character, then so is *all* selling.

Just between you and me, Critic, I must admit I *like* for Baker to try to take me away from Able, and then for Able to try to woo and win me back. It's fun. And I don't *stay* switched, you know, unless I'm benefited.

Critic: All right, be irrational if you want to about Baker and Able, but *not* about the terrible control advertising has over the business cycle. Manufacturers spend lavishly in good times, then they cut advertising back drastically when times are bad. Give in?

Champion: Of course not. Several influences are much stronger than is advertising in determining the volume of consumer buying. The consumer's ability to pay is one, and his outlook is another. Price movements are another significant influence. The fear of higher prices and the fear of future shortages are both much more powerful in causing purchases than advertising is. As with monopolies, business cycles were with us, going up and down, long before advertising was a force of any consequence. All I agree to is that advertising may help increase the distance between peak and trough.

Critic: Before I go, do grant that advertisers control our media, exerting considerable influence over editorial policy and decisions.

Champion: You are mistaken. Editors guard their independence zealously against any influence of advertisers. And, they have achieved a high degree of editorial independence. A good publisher risks the confidence of his readers (his most cherished asset) if he lets advertisers control his policies. If he relaxes his control in favor of advertisers, circulation falls, and advertisers quit using that medium.

Critic: All right, all right, but now let me refer to the shameful allocation, to the wicked waste, of our national resources. The way our economy functions now, there is a scandalous imbalance between the Private Sector and the Public Sector. Many of the dollars spent in advertising do nothing but manipulate materially minded consumers to buy products and services they otherwise would not want. That advertising *and* those purchases represent social waste. Because of this waste, the Public Sector — parks, hospitals, slum clearance, highways, schools — is neglected. You agree?

Champion: Recent and continuing improvement have given us the best highways, housing, and hospitals in the world. Don't overlook that! And if the public actually wants more and better, why don't voters elect senators and representatives who will

The Background for Advertising

see that the public *gets* more and better ones? Now about that use (*abuse* to you) of resources. Do you want the public to allocate its resources, or do you want this done by some intellectual genius in Washington? If some socially slanted, sophisticated Solomon were allowed to commandeer one-half of the amount spent annually for advertising and to spend it as *he* dictated, what do you think would happen to corporate *and* personal earnings and taxes? How do you buy highways and hospitals? With taxes, of course. And where do taxes come from? Taxes come from earnings and profits, and earnings and profits come from sales.

COMMENTS ON THE GREAT DEBATE

What conclusions are to be drawn from the debate? What comments are in order? Here are some assumptions and claims worth a bit of thought.

Consumers

Psychic satisfaction is a real utility. Psychological values are as real and as needed as are physical values. Consumers, indeed, spend more money, time, and concern for "nominal" utilities than for "basic" utilities. Advertising can add utility to a product, so it can add to that product's value. Remember, value is a subjective, individual matter.

Advertising does not dictate consumers' values or tastes. Our freedom of consumer choice allows each consumer to determine *his own* scale of values and to buy what gives *him* satisfaction. Advertisers know better than to try to subvert consumers' value judgments. Unless advertising is compatible with consumer values, it will not be accepted by consumers and, therefore, it will not influence them. Whether you approve or disapprove, our consumers are materialistic; they are strongly attracted to possessions, services, experiences, and luxuries. They get their craving for high-level consumption and a high *material* standard of living from family, friends, and school, maybe even a bit from church. They do *not* get their values from advertising. And when intellectuals damn advertising for being in low taste, they are actually criticizing the consumer, his family, and his friends for having low taste.

Some advertising makes for better informed buyers and better buying. Some advertisements, of course, communicate nothing of interest and help to buyers. Sometimes the conflicting claims of competitors only puzzle and perplex. Sometimes, though, housewives *do* learn about products, product uses, care, and prices from some advertisements. Ask any housewife how she would like to shop department stores or food stores, without advertising.

Our standard of living is high. Our consumer is the best fed, best dressed, best housed, best informed, best entertained, and best transported in the world. He enjoys greater material welfare, in greater numbers, than his counterpart in any other type of economy. Advertising is an integral part of that economy.

Communication benefits from advertising. Newspapers and magazines, television and radio provide news, information, entertainment, relaxation, and music quite economically. Each media makes some contribution to education and culture.

Products, Costs, and Prices

The net effect of advertising on products seems to be favorable. Advertising deserves some credit for the continuous appearance of more and better products. It encourages sellers to compete on a *product* basis.

There is no proof of what advertising does to sellers' costs. Most probably, advertising lowers total costs for some, increases total costs for others. It seems reasonable to assume that advertising can help reduce per-unit production costs for certain manufacturers. It seems equally reasonable to assume that advertising replaces more expensive promotion (usually personal selling) for certain sellers. Consider, however, a manufacturer who wants to increase his sales from 100% to 125%. It is certainly possible that the amount of additional advertising necessary to achieve the 125% level may raise total costs so high that the 100% level is more profitable.

There is no proof of what advertising does to the level of consumer prices. The buyer of advertised products pays for their advertising. Our marketing costs are high, and advertising is one of these costs. *But,* marketing costs are high because of our type of competitive economy, not because of advertising.

No one can prove that advertised products cost more, the same, or less than non-advertised products of the same quality. An advertised product can cost more if its manufacturer incurred heavy expenses for product research, market research, and for market development only to see "free riders" appear in the form of non-advertised competition and private brand competition. Interestingly, to one who believes that advertising can add value to a product, the concept of an "advertised product vs. a non-advertised product *of the same quality*" may be unrealistic.

Advertising has made consumer prices more rigid. Some sellers advertise their brands in the hope of making *specialty* goods of them. These sellers want to achieve such a degree of brand loyalty that customers will be so addicted to those brands that the customers will not be lured away to competing brands which sell at lower prices.

Advertising does retard price competition. This may, but certainly need not, work to the consumer's disadvantage. Consumer prices consist of cost to make and cost to market. The main interest of both seller and buyer is in (a) lower prices for the same quality or (b) better quality for the same prices. If discontinuing advertising would cause either of these without reducing sales, most sellers would abandon advertising.

The lowering of prices is not the only course of action beneficial to consumers. If, as a result of advertising, a manufacturer is able to effect a net reduction in manufacturing-costs-plus-marketing-costs per unit of product, these savings may go for wages and salaries, dividends, better products, better consumer service, stronger financial position for the company, expansion, modernization, research, wider margins for middlemen, promotion, or lower prices. The two most important influences in determining the disposition of the savings are competition and the motivation of the seller.

The Economy

Advertising is a part of, and is in harmony with, our present competitive, free enterprise system. Just what products and services shall be placed on the market

The Background for Advertising

can be decreed by cartels, or by the state, or by consumers. Many of those who would abolish advertising must want the government to determine what and how much shall be manufactured and at what price it shall be sold. Social and economic progress demand that the consumer decide. Abolish advertising because it is wasteful and competitive? Then abolish competition. One cannot be consistent and (a) condemn advertising as wasteful and uneconomical, yet, at the same time, (b) favor personal selling and private competition. Advertising must remain unless our basic economic philosophy, structure, and operation are to be replaced.

Advertising encourages an expanding economy. Buying and producing go hand-in-hand. If we want to make products on a mass production scale, we must have also buying and consumption on a large scale; otherwise, production will have to be cut back. It is difficult to imagine how today's volume of consumer products could be marketed without effective consumer advertising. Some mass production giants have, of course, become huge and dominant in certain industries. They are so big, powerful, and entrenched that they probably discourage the appearance of small, new, competitive firms.

Much advertising is defensive in nature. Manufacturer Loggs must advertise because competing manufacturer Koggs started to advertise. Loggs' decision to advertise was made *for* him, not *by* him. Few of the critics who deplore Loggs' advertising as competitive have been known to criticize Loggs should he have retaliated by enlarging his sales force.

Advertising can be an efficient selling tool. The right of sellers in a free market to use advertising needs no defense. In an economy of the free enterprise type, a seller is entitled to design his own promotional mix, to include advertising if he wants to do so. He is entitled to promote his wares as *he* thinks best rather than be told by Washington how he can and cannot promote them. Matching the consumer's freedom of choice is the seller's freedom to try to influence that choice — through advertising, a communication technique which serves many sellers quite well.

GUARDIANS OF THE CONSUMER

The Consumer Herself

It is proper and not strange to mention the consumer herself as the first line of defense against sellers whose advertising is unethical. The American housewife is not easily duped; indeed, she is sharp and shrewd in buying. She is, on balance, not a badly informed buyer. Seldom does she buy a product, or from a seller, a second time if the first purchase was in response to dishonest advertising. Her most effective weapon? *Her power to decide not to buy.* She may even take the trouble of telling the seller why he lost her patronage.

The Advertiser Himself

Does it pay a seller to be honest? Can he survive, let alone prosper, if he carries high principles with him into the market place? Is unethical advertising bound to be unprofitable? Advertising that offends, irritates, or deceives does the seller no good, in the middle run as well as in the long run. False advertising results in customers taking their business to other sellers. Every realistic advertiser knows that misleading advertising can put him out of business, rather quickly, too. A manufacturer's product must satisfy, must live up to the claims made for it, or the manufacturer stores up future grief for himself. An aroused and hostile group of consumers is something no manufacturer wants.

The consumer is not the only possible source of punishment for the dishonest advertiser; his competitors, too, are a force which must be considered. When a seller brings discredit and condemnation down on his own head, he does a disservice to the group of which he is a member; in one sense, he asks this group to take corrective action. Competitors can bring pressure on the seller who needs to mend his ways; their interest in his conduct is obvious, their incentive is powerful, their tactics are numerous.

The Advertising Agency

Because advertiser and advertising agency share so many interests in common, because their reactions to the same stimuli are so often identical, it is understandable for an advertising agency to favor ethical, effective advertising. The advertising agency respects the consumer because that individual, as already mentioned, determines which product, which advertisers, and which advertising she will favor. It is the agency's responsibility to advise clients against running any advertising to which consumers in quantity will object. If the agency is to hold its present clients and attract additional ones, its best policy is to be known as the creator of sound advertising.

The Advertising Medium

Just as advertisers and advertising agencies want to maximize dollar profits by pleasing their customers and selling to them, time after time, so also does the advertising medium. Two groups of customers support advertising media: readers, listeners, and viewers constitute the circulation type of customer — advertisers are the other group. Media want to carry honest, acceptable advertising. Their standards force them to refuse millions of dollars worth of proffered advertising each year. Otherwise, *Good Housekeeping* could not make this consumer guaranty:

> If any product or any service is not as advertised herein, it will, upon request and verification of complaint, be replaced or the money paid therefor refunded. Good Housekeeping has satisfied itself that all products and services offered in this issue are good products and services.

A lowering of standards would drive away some of a medium's readers, listeners, or viewers — circulation would deteriorate in quality as well as quantity — advertisers would switch their advertising to other media. The result? Shrinkage of both types of revenue.

The *New York Times* has long been known as a newspaper which exercises a strict censorship over the advertising it accepts. Here are some examples:[1]

---
[1] This material was sent to the author by Mr. J. W. Gannon of the *New York Times*.

The Background for Advertising

Carpet advertisement
    As offered: "Never before have you been able to buy such a beautiful carpet at such a low price."
    As changed: "Never before have we been able to offer such a beautiful carpet."

Financial Advisory Service
    As offered: ". . . where phenomenal profits are made repeatedly in just such bargains as these."
    As changed: ". . . where unusual opportunities for the alert investor have been uncovered."

Underwear
    As offered: "Naughty . . . but so nice to your figure."
    As changed: "Paris inspired . . . but so nice to your figure."

The Advertising Trade Paper

There are several publications edited for the advertising business. Included within this group of trade papers are *Advertising Age, Advertising & Sales Promotion, Industrial Marketing, Printers' Ink,* and *Sales Management.* These and other trade papers run editorials and feature articles in support of honest, helpful advertising and against abuses. Probably the best known contribution from this source is the Printers' Ink Model Statute, a suggested piece of state legislation to curtail fraudulent and misleading advertising by making false or misleading advertising a misdemeanor. Here is the text of this statute:

> Any person, firm, corporation, or association, who with intent to sell or in any wise dispose of merchandise, securities, service, or anything offered by such person, firm, corporation, or association, directly or indirectly, to the public for sale or distribution, or with intent to increase the consumption thereof, or to induce the public in any manner to enter into any obligation relating thereto, or to acquire title thereto, or an interest therein, makes, publishes, disseminates, circulates, or places before the public, or causes, directly or indirectly, to be made, published, disseminated, circulated or placed before the public, in this state, in a newspaper or other publication, or in the form of a book, notice, handbill, poster, bill, circular, pamphlet, or letter, or in any other way, an advertisement of any sort regarding merchandise, securities, service, or anything so offered to the public, which advertisement contains assertions, representation, or statement of fact which is untrue, deceptive or misleading shall be guilty of a misdemeanor.

Advertising Organizations

We have seen that advertisers, advertising agencies, and media promote, singly, sound advertising. Group action, too, is found in each of these areas. There are Advertising Clubs in scores of cities, each club usually affiliated with a number of other clubs in such organizations as the Advertising Association of the West or the Advertising Federation of America. The former works, for example, to promote better advertising and to increase consumer confidence in advertising as an aid to buying. The Advertising Federation of America links together sixteen national asso-

How do you measure confidence?

By what happens.

Over 10 million women readers of Good Housekeeping (including 763,000 more young readers since last year) reach trustingly for products they see in this magazine. The reason is simple and unique:

Good Housekeeping is the *only* magazine that guarantees the performance of every product advertised between its covers. *Guarantees.**

Good Housekeeping
Magazine and Institute

Above NMS June '61 - Jan. '62 data copyrighted 1962
by A. C. Nielsen Company and reprinted with permission.

Magazines own no asset more valuable than the trust and confidence of their readers. (Courtesy: Good Housekeeping)

The Background for Advertising

ciations, over one hundred local advertising clubs, and over eleven hundred companies, advertisers, agencies, media, suppliers, and such. Its activities center around these five objectives:

1. To explain advertising to the public
2. To raise continually higher the standards of truth and good taste in advertising
3. To help make advertising more effective for business and more useful to the public
4. To help protect advertising against harmful restrictions and possible taxation
5. To encourage further improvement in education and training for men and women in advertising or preparing for advertising

In the agency field, there is the American Association of Advertising Agencies, a horizontal organization active in advancing the cause of advertising as a whole.

In the media field, there is a trade association for each of the major media. The American Newspaper Publishers Association and the National Association of Broadcasters, to mention two, are groups whose objectives, among others, include the adoption and observance of codes of good advertising.

The Better Business Bureau operates in many localities and on the national level, too, in the consumer's interests. At the retail level, the bureaus work primarily to prevent and to eliminate unethical advertising, keeping watch on a retailer's competitors for him. On the national level, the Better Business Bureau aims to build standards of fair dealing and fair competition. It serves as a self-regulatory agency to protect consumers against unfair practices. It helps make customers better buyers of merchandise.

Federal Government

In addition to state laws, notably of the Printers' Ink Model Statute type, and to some municipal ordinances against false and misleading advertising, more protection is found at the national level. Various branches of the federal government are active in preventing sellers from using advertising in an improper manner. One such

Conservation and protection are typical of the causes promoted by the Advertising Council. (Courtesy: Advertising Council, Inc.)

Social and Economic Aspects

agency is the Federal Trade Commission. Because it is the foe of unfair or deceptive trade practices, the commission works to stamp out advertising that is untrue or misleading. For example, it is the commission's responsibility to see that there is no misleading advertising of food, drug, or cosmetic products. A continuing activity of the FTC is the scrutinizing of advertisements for the purpose of spotting any whose claims cannot be supported.

Specialized protection is provided by other federal units. The Food and Drug Administration keeps an eye on the packages and labels used for foods, drugs, curative devices, and cosmetics. The Federal Alcohol Administration takes a keen interest in the copy claims made in advertising for alcoholic beverages. The Securities and Exchange Commission has authority over the advertising of securities in interstate commerce. The Post Office department prohibits the use of the mails for sending false or fraudulent advertising. The broadcast media report to the Federal Communication Commission.

THE ADVERTISING COUNCIL

In January of 1942 the War Advertising Council was formed to enlist the forces of advertising in the winning of World War II. The broad purpose of this organization was to help inform the public about vital wartime programs and then to get individual citizens to cooperate. Business and the advertising industry donated over one billion dollars worth of advertising time and space to persuade citizens to help solve more than one hundred and fifty homefront problems. Examples of these problems were: using V-mail, giving blood, starting victory gardens, saving tin, and reducing absenteeism.

Today the successor organization is known as the Advertising Council, a nonprofit organization founded and supported by business to conduct public service advertising campaigns telling the public how individuals can help with important national problems. Time and space are donated by advertisers and by media, advertisements are created without charge by advertising agencies, and all three, advertisers, media, and advertising agencies, pay the Council's operating expenses. Timely national causes given advertising support by the Council include: better schools, civil defense, savings bonds, Red Cross, registering and voting, increasing the number of nurses, winning friends for freedom overseas, reduction of traffic accidents, and conservation of natural resources.

THE CONSUMER MOVEMENT

Origin and Composition

The publication in 1927 of a book entitled *Your Money's Worth* is generally regarded as marking the start of a development referred to as the Consumer Movement.[2] The theme of the book, briefly, was that the consumer came nowhere close to getting his money's worth when buying goods and services for his own use. When

[2] S. Chase and F. J. Schlink, *Your Money's Worth* (New York: The Macmillan Co., 1927).

viewed in context, the book is seen to have appeared at an interesting point in time. The number and the complexity of consumer goods on the market had been increasing at a spirited rate. Prices had been rising. A most severe depression was not far ahead. Individuals were wondering if high pressure selling and unethical advertising were making suckers of consumers. *Your Money's Worth* was followed immediately by a succession of "exposé" books which pictured the consumer as a prey or a pawn in our marketing process — as a human guinea pig.

The Consumer Movement is most difficult to define or even describe because of its heterogeneous nature. It includes books and lobbying, organizations and events, meetings and a type of retailing institution, courses in schools and laws, labels on packages, and an attitude toward marketing, particularly the promotional phases, which reflects suspicion at least, undying hostility in the extreme. Perhaps one can defend the summary observation that the Consumer Movement carries on activities designed to help consumers in the purchase, use, and care of consumer goods. Among the organizations participating are the American Association of University Women, National Consumer-Retailer Council, General Federation of Women's Clubs, National League of Women Voters, and American Home Economics Association.

Objectives

The twin aims of the Consumer Movement are the (a) sounder buying and (b) more efficient use and care of products and services by consumers. The reasoning is that if consumers dispose of their dollar incomes more wisely, their real incomes will increase, and they will enjoy a higher standard of living. The movement places much stress on the education and the protection of the consumer in respect to the manufacturing and the marketing of consumer goods. *What* to buy is the dominant concern but *whether* to buy and *when* are not ignored. Specific goals are better retail selling, truthful and objective advertising, informative labeling, and product standardization.

Activities

Among the varied activities found in the Consumer Movement, some are clearly *educational* in character. Courses which prepare individuals to be better consumers are offered both at the high school and the college levels. Attention is given to this matter in such areas as home economics, business administration, and the social sciences. The discussion groups and speeches at some of the meetings of the organizations mentioned are largely educational in design. At such sessions various consumer problems are examined.

Other activities have to do with *legislation*. Whenever consumer problems become political issues, organizations interested in consumer welfare can be counted on to make their stands known and their influence felt. Federal legislation and operation were referred to earlier in this chapter. Two pieces of legislation which were not mentioned, dealing with the labeling of wool products and fur products, are examples of legislation favored by consumer groups. Some voices in the Consumer Movement speak in favor of product standardization and mandatory grade labeling.

Social and Economic Aspects

Consumer-financed *testing services* are a phase of the movement. Three of these are Consumers' Research, Consumers' Union, and Intermountain Consumers' Services. These are non-profit organizations whose main purpose is to tell consumers the truth about products and services they will be buying. The organizations test products, rate them, and report ratings with reasons therefor to subscribers in periodic bulletins. Ratings are Recommended, Intermediate, Not recommended — or Best Buy, Acceptable, Not Acceptable. The testing services do some testing themselves, they rely on technical consultants and advisers, and they employ outside laboratories.

Despite their integrity and independence, their high purposes, and their dedicated staffs, these testing services suffer from real handicaps. The proliferation of new products joins the modest size of the services' budgets to make their undertakings most difficult. There are understandable doubts about size of sample, size of staff, and amount of know-how in the area of testing. Physical features only are considered, fashion features are largely ignored. And, horror of horror, when a consumer finds the services' ratings of a specific brand in disagreement, and this has happened, rather than have him guess which he can believe, one may well wonder if the consumer should become an addict of — yes, of advertising.

The Consumer Movement also has been instrumental in the establishment of *consumer cooperatives,* especially in the food field. These substitutes for regular retail stores permit a group of consumers to provide its own retailing facilities on a non-profit basis and, thereby, to avoid contributing to a merchant's profit. Advocates claim higher quality and lower net prices as advantages of consumer cooperatives. Even so, this form of do-it-yourself retailing has never attained any significance in this country. Because our housewives are relatively well-to-do they can prefer and afford retail services. Furthermore, they are mobile, not bound together by strong ties, not very loyal to their retail suppliers, impatient, and often disappointed at the size of refunds from the cooperatives. Above all, they love to shop — in efficient supermarkets.

Conclusions

It seems fair to conclude that the Consumer Movement has made a modest contribution to consumer welfare. Business has come to realize that the movement must be recognized rather than ignored or captured. There has been some curbing influence on overstatements in advertising; some housewives are better informed buyers than they were formerly; there is more product testing; some labels are more informative.

The movement is neither localized nor centralized. No director heads a single, unified organization of consumers. The nature of the consumer himself or herself could easily be the reason for this. Mr. Consumer thinks of himself primarily as a manufacturer, a merchant, a coach, a professor, or an accountant — not as a consumer. He is more inclined to attempt to raise his standard of living through increasing his *dollar* income than his *real* income. To himself, he is a producer, an earner of income rather than a consumer. Mrs. Consumer is the *wholesaler's* wife, the *banker's* wife, or the *salesman's* wife. She has, in addition, precious little time

The Background for Advertising

during which she can assume her role as a consumer. Her consumer bonds are not nearly so strong as her other bonds. In significant numbers she is alert enough to realize that some criticisms of advertising emanating from the Consumer Movement have been as extreme, as inaccurate, as irrational, and as exaggerated as the worst advertising the movement condemns.

Questions and Problems

1. Does advertising influence consumers, or do consumers influence advertising? Explain.
2. Does the total amount of money being spent for advertising reflect the state of our national economy?
3. Should the sellers who make up an industry (beverages, automobiles, airlines) be prohibited from spending more than a certain maximum amount each year in advertising?
4. Why are so many of the so-called "intellectuals" so hostile toward and critical of advertising?
5. If advertising were outlawed overnight, what would be the effects on consumers?
6. Why is more advertising directed to buyers' emotions than to buyers' reason?
7. How can a consumer use advertising so as to make more intelligent purchases?
8. Comment on a federal tax on advertising.
9. What might be the effects of a manufacturer's using too much advertising for his product?
10. The copy of a retail "bait" ad includes these claims: "Genuine Superba sewing machines. Electric. Late models. Rebuilt and good as new. Biggest bargain ever. Friday only. Price? Just $9.95." What might the retailer do if you went to the store and asked about these machines?

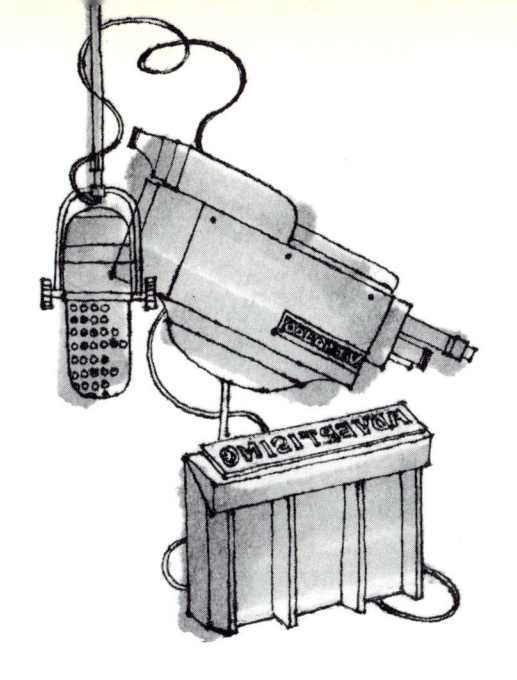

PART THREE

Identifying the Product

Two parts have been covered, one on marketing fundamentals and one on the background against which advertising operates. This third part deals with identification. Its first chapter treats brand names, trade-marks, and trade characters; its other chapter treats packages. As was true of the first two parts, this part on identification does not take up any advertising matters of a technical nature. Instead, it is concerned with matters which demand research and decisions before the seller builds his first advertisement. Brand names, trade-marks, and packages are merchandising (product) matters; trade characters belong in the province of sales promotion.

Chapter 5

Brand Names, Trade-Marks, and Trade Characters

BASIC INFORMATION

What

The term "trade-mark" is the official, legal designation for brand names and trade-marks because the law defines a trade-mark as a word, name, symbol, or device — or a combination of these. When a manufacturer identifies his merchandise, he can use a brand name, or he can use both a brand name and a trade-mark; in the former instance, his brand name is also his trade-mark. Legally, then, the term "trade-mark" is broader than the term "brand name" because trade-marks include brand names, while the brand name may be one version of trade-marks. Even so, a distinction may be made between the two in our thinking. Let us think of brand names as being *words,* and let us consider trade-marks to be *symbols* or *devices.* In the automobile field, how many brand names (makes) do you know? How many trade-marks (symbols or devices)?

Brand names and trade-marks are used both by manufacturers and by middlemen. Manufacturers' brands are often referred to as *national* brands; the brands of middlemen are known as *private* or *distributor* brands.

Examples of manufacturers' brands:

    Arm and Hammer baking soda (Church and Dwight Company)
    Rumford baking powder (Rumford Company)
    Swans Down cake flour (General Foods Corporation)
    Cream of Wheat cereal (Cream of Wheat Corporation)
    Edgeworth tobacco (Larus & Brother Company)

Examples of distributors' brands:

    Harmony House pillows (Sears, Roebuck and Company)
    Ann Page gelatin (The Great Atlantic and Pacific Tea Company)

Brand Names, Trade-Marks, and Trade Characters

Kroger grapefruit juice (Kroger Company)
Nu-Treat margarine (Colonial Stores Incorporated)
Young Cosmopolitans clothes (Best & Company)

Brand names must not be confused with *trade names*. Where brand name refers to product, trade name refers to company. The name of the firm, the official style of the company, as it is sometimes called, is its trade name. The ten names just listed in parentheses are trade names.

The brand name can come from the trade name:

Dunlop tires (Dunlop Tire and Rubber Corporation)
Florsheim shoes (Florsheim Shoe Company)
Caterpillar earthmoving equipment (Caterpillar Tractor Company)
Lane cedar chests (Lane Company)
Master padlocks (Master Lock Company)

Or, the brand name can be quite different:

Norelco shavers (North American Philips Company)
Bufferin pain reliever (Bristol-Myers)
Weldwood paneling (U.S. Plywood Corporation)
Wrinkl-Shed fabrics (Dan River Mills)
Absorbine, Jr. remedy (W. F. Young, Inc.)

In addition to its many brand names, Procter & Gamble has a company trade-mark. It is shown below together with acceptable variations. (Courtesy: The Procter & Gamble Company)

71

Identifying the Product

Uses by Sellers

The typical seller of advertised goods wants his products to be easily and quickly identifiable through the two senses of sight and hearing. Where the item is identified primarily by its brand name, and these cases are in the majority, then the brand name in the form of a word or phrase can be stressed by the seller. Where visual identification is important, the seller can feature trade-marks in the form of symbols, designs, pictures, forms, or insignia because of their high memory value.

The manufacturer today has several specific objectives in mind when he identifies his goods with brand names and trade-marks. He hopes to achieve greater stability of sales volume and greater stability of price through transforming his product, to the maximum degree possible, into a specialty good, one with particular and individual appeal for buyers. He hopes for greater control of the marketing of his goods and for a reduction in the substitution attempted by retailers. He wants to protect himself from unfair competition and from being associated with inferior products. The addition of new products will be easier. Demand creation through appeals to selective buying motives becomes possible.

Uses by Consumers

Consumers used trade-marks originally to identify the maker or the source of specific goods; today, consumers are almost exclusively interested in the identification of *products* rather than the makers of those products. Witness the success of so many private brands — the manufacturers of which are completely anonymous. In her initial purchase, the consumer can buy what she wants; in subsequent buying,

Parker says of its trade-mark, "The new Parker corporate symbol consists of two capital P's, back to back, with a vertical Arrow shaft. The double P stands, of course, for Parker Pen's initials. Symmetrical and powerful, the stylized representation suggests the balance, scope and corporate character of the largest writing instrument company in the world." (Courtesy: The Parker Pen Company)

Brand Names, Trade-Marks, and Trade Characters

she can buy the brand again, or she can avoid it. She leans heavily on brands when buying products about which she can tell little and about which she is largely ignorant — watches, appliances, and drug products. Her shopping is more convenient as well as safer.

Consumers may look on the brand name as a symbol of product quality, of a product's characteristics and features, and as a symbol of the satisfactions products supply. Brand names can place the responsibility for product quality. They can connote the reputation of the manufacturer, and they may communicate a mental image of the product.

Importance

A manufacturer must put time, money, and effort behind a new brand name if he is to establish it firmly in the market. Just imagine, for example, what is needed to launch a new brand of toothpaste nationally. The newly chosen brand name can help in an advertising way — or it can hurt; it can make the advertising and sale of the product easier — or more difficult. Weak brand names demand stronger promotion. Self-service is growing. The number of brands, likewise, is increasing. Advertising costs are rising. Competition among products is intensified. Now, against these background facts, recognize this most basic truth: *manufacturers do not intend to change their brand names or trade-marks — ever.* Because they are selected for indefinite, even permanent use as identification tags, the original selection is a most serious step. For years the Pure Oil Company sold its tires under the brand name Yale, then changed to Pure. For years the Coca-Cola Company discouraged the public from calling for a "Coke," then had to cooperate with the inevitable by registering the one-word name as a trade-mark. A proprietary medicine used to be called Baume Analgesique Bengue. Today? Ben-Gay. There is no difficulty in imagining how long, demanding, and costly these changes were.

If a brand name is selected wisely and promoted effectively it can become a valuable piece of property. It can, indeed, become its owner's largest asset. At one time, the California Packing Corporation, owners of the Del Monte brand name, also owned the right to use the brand name Sunkist on canned and dried fruit, whereas the Sunkist Growers, Inc., had the right to the brand name's use on fresh fruit. When concentrated orange juice came on the market, the Sunkist Growers, Inc., naturally wanted to pack and market a *Sunkist* version, but they did not have the right to do so. As a solution Sunkist Growers, Inc., paid $1,250,000 to the California Packing Corporation for the right to use the brand name *Sunkist* on canned citrus juice, particularly orange concentrate.

TYPES OF BRAND NAMES

Personal Name

The personal brand name can be that of the *founder* of the company. An individual's attraction to — his affection for — his own name urges him to give his name to the product he sells. See examples on page 74.

73

Identifying the Product

    Dr. Scholl (foot powder)   Firestone (tires)
    Hershey (chocolate)   Lydia E. Pinkham (compound)
    Gerber (baby food)   Cannon (towels)

The name can be that of a deceased *historical person,* one whose record and fame seem fixed. There is comfort in knowing that the reputation of this famous person is unlikely to be tarnished. Examples:

    Ben Franklin (pencils)   Prince Albert (tobacco)
    Lincoln (fabrics)   Martha Washington (cosmetics)
    Betsy Ross (bread)   Robert Burns (cigars)

Fictional names serve as brand names, as these indicate:

    Jack Frost (sugar)   Little Bo Peep (ammonia)
    Jack and Jill (cat food)   Old Black Joe (fertilizer)
    Macbeth (glassware)   Hiawatha (thread)

Finally, personal names can come from *mythology:*

    Ajax (cleanser)   Pandora (lingerie)
    Apollo (candy)   Trojan (blankets)
    Atlas (tires)   Venus (pencils)

Company Name

An established and respected company name can be a valuable source of a brand name. This is the most common source, incidentally, of names for industrial products. These brand names are part of company names:

    Gulf (gasoline)   Daisy (guns)
    Vagabond (trailers)   Universal (matches)
    Grip-Tite (bases for bowls) Philco (radios)
    Green Spot (orangeade)   Lord Jeff (sweaters)

If the advertiser prefers to use this source but modify or improvise a bit, several variation patterns are available. For example:

    Esso (petroleum products)   B.C. (headache remedy)
    Nabisco (cookies)   L & M (cigarettes)
    Scotkins (napkins)   Duco (cement)
    Scotties (tissues)   GMC (trucks)

Dictionary Word

The dictionary is a prolific source of brand names. The fact that the words are known helps counterbalance their lack of distinctiveness. The word or words can be chosen in an arbitrary manner; or, they can be meaningful, often some familiar object noted for a certain specific quality appropriate and complimentary to the product. Here are some more or less arbitrary names:

Brand Names, Trade-Marks, and Trade Characters

Arrow (shirts)
Carnation (milk)
Lotus (crystal)

Bicycle (playing cards)
Congress (playing cards)
Carnival (soda straws)

More meaningful are these dictionary names:

Nix (deodorant)
Talon (zipper)
Bull Dog (tape)

Joy (perfume)
Holiday (lounges)
Dash (dog food)

Foreign Word

A somewhat overly simplified characterization of foreign words as brand names is that their prestige value is matched by their difficulty of pronunciation. How many of these can you pronounce correctly and confidently?

Aalborg Aquavit (beverages)
L'Aiglon (dresses)
Tovarisch (vodka)
Bien Jolie (corsets)

Antonio y Cleopatra (cigars)
Yucatan (chewing gum)
Richelieu (jewelry)
Vol de Nuit (perfume)

Coined Name

There are advantages and disadvantages to an advertiser's coining his own brand name, the outstanding advantage being just that — such a name is his own. It can be tailored to fit his circumstances. The right to the exclusive use of it can be more easily established and defended than is the case with certain other types of brand names. On the minus side are the difficulty of coining an outstanding name and the expense of implanting it in the minds of consumers. In addition, if the name is too complicated, the public may not "get" the connotation of the name because few people will bother to break the name down into its parts; few consumers will grasp the meaning to the point of being able to play the name back when asked about it. Once established, the descriptive quality of many coined names becomes insignificant. Do you know of a housewife disturbed because her stove is named Frigidaire — or her refrigerator Hotpoint?

One technique of coining a brand name is that of *combination*. Here are some:

Nine Lives (cat food)
Linen Finish (serviettes)
Spic and Span (cleanser)

Evergreen (toilet tissue)
Mobilaire (air conditioning)
Cordspun (fabrics)

In the other direction there are brand names coined by *shortening* some word. Samples:

Rel (for head colds)
M-Ten (meat tenderizer)
Iso-Vis (motor oil)

Cops (copper cleaner)
Jif (peanut butter)
Jax (beer)

Misspelling is a third route to a coined brand name. *Toni*, incidentally, is an adaptation of *tony*, meaning swank.

Identifying the Product

  Ha-dees (auto heaters)   Pi-Do (piecrust mix)
  Kan-Kil (insecticides)   Kool-Aid (drink flavors)
  Hold-E-Zee (screwdrivers)   My-T Fine (desserts)
  Toni (home permanents)   Sucaryl (non-caloric sweetener)

 Then if he prefers, the advertiser can coin a unique word which is utterly and completely *meaningless*. These are exclusive — they are expensive.

  Kodak (cameras)   Hep (insect killer; oven cleaner)
  Drax (fabric finish)   Ipana (toothpaste)
  Marfak (lubricant)   Rit (dyes)

 A fifth method of coining a brand name is to attach an *affix* to some related word; the affix can be either a prefix or a suffix.

Prefix	*Suffix*
Neolite (shoe soles)	Fluffo (shortening)
O-Cedar (mops)	Playtex (baby pants)
Anti-Colic (nursers)	Drano (drain opener)
Co-jamas (misses' pajamas)	Foamex (foamed lastex)
Du-Lite (paint)	Samsonite (luggage)

 The sixth possibility in coined names is one composed of *letters,* or *numbers,* or a combination of the two. A significant fact about this type of brand name is that the name A-1 is used for these products: bleach, flour, macaroni, metal polish, beer, sauce, and soap. Some examples of coined names are:

Letters	*Numbers*	*Letters and Numbers*
RPM (motor oil)	8:30 (perfume)	X-2R (sheets)
TNT (pop corn)	"21" (perfume)	No. 5 (perfume)
ZBT (baby powder)	500 (ale)	V-8 (vegetable juice)
SKF (ball bearings)	76 (ale)	B-43 (food supplement)
O.K. (baking powder)	76 (gasoline)	C-7 (lettuce)

Licensed Names

 Should an advertiser not find the brand name he wants in the areas of personal names, company name, dictionary words, foreign terms, or coined names, there is still one more possibility. He may *license* the use of a brand name owned by someone else. Some small companies see this course of action as permitting them to compete against the brands of large competitors. Sometimes package and label, each with sales power, are part of the arrangement. Fewer promotional dollars will be needed because other sellers, too, are publicizing the brand name. Above all, there will be little pioneering needed and little delay because the name is established — now. Disadvantages of licensing the use of a brand name are the licensing fee and the fact that the name is owned and shared by others. These brand names have been available on a licensing basis:

  Mickey Mouse (cookies)   Chessie (scarves)
  Fruit of the Loom (shirts)   Donald Duck (juices)

Brand Names, Trade-Marks, and Trade Characters

GENERAL CONSIDERATIONS

Before mentioning the specific features or values advertisers want in their brand names and trade-marks, a few general comments are in order. One observation is that several forces or barriers may make difficult the job of selection. If the name or mark is already in use, it may be denied to an advertiser. If a name or mark cannot be protected legally, its selection could be most unwise. If two of the characteristics the advertiser would like to incorporate into the brand name are hostile to each other, even mutually exclusive, then this contradiction may result in a compromise.

A primary requirement is that brand names and trade-marks be placed on the product, on the product's container, on labels or tags attached to the product, or on displays associated with the product. Neither should injure the product in performance or appearance. The advertiser wants the identification symbols, both names and marks, to accompany the product all the way to the consumer and to remain and identify during the consumer's use of the product. Liquids, foods, and soap offer particular challenges in this respect. How would *you* brand or mark a cake of soap, for example, so that its identity is unquestionable as long as any of the cake remains? This is only *one* of the advertiser's requirements.

Another general hope of the advertiser is for adaptability and versatility. The two broadcast media, television and radio, immediately come to mind. Television intensifies all features of brand names and trade-marks, recommending that they be pleasing to see as well as to hear. The nature of radio argues for names and marks which can be described easily and clearly in just a few words, capable of being recognized by sound alone. Both identification devices should perform satisfactorily on all sizes of package and in all sizes of advertisement, in color and in black-and-white, in small size and when blown up, indoors and outside, and on all printing surfaces. If there are silhouette possibilities, three dimensional possibilities, or animation possibilities for television, so much the better since television advertising thrives on these qualities.

Good brand names and trade-marks are economical. The simplest economy is that of physical application to product. Another type of economy is that provided by names and marks which will not result in litigation. But, the economy of greatest concern to the greatest number of advertisers relates to the cost of getting the name or mark established and accepted in the market. Consumers must become acquainted with each type of identification. Both must be impressed on consumers' minds until they are known. Brand names and trade-marks which are simple and unified rather than complicated in sound and in appearance are preferable. They are the ones most likely to achieve speed, ease, and certainty of recognition.

DESIRABLE CHARACTERISTICS — BRAND NAMES AND TRADE-MARKS

Distinctive

Because the main purpose of brand names and trade-marks is to identify and distinguish, distinctiveness is a most desirable quality. Distinctive names and

Identifying the Product

marks are attention compelling, they have interest, impact, and memory value, they possess individuality. When they are unique, graphic or even startling possibilities are present, especially in television and radio. Striking design or strong pictorial illustration adds memory value to trade-marks. These brand names rank high in distinctiveness:

> Hex (mothproofing material) Chux (disposable diapers)
> Stopette (deodorant) Yes (cleansing tissues)
> Jello (gelatin products) Trix (cereal)
> Uneeda (crackers) Air-Wick (room deodorizer)

Appropriate

Brand names and trade-marks must be suited to markets, buyers, and, most important of all, products. For products sold in foreign as well as in domestic markets, personal names often work out nicely. Women consumers are attracted to feminine names and marks, and men to masculine ones. Both forms of identification need to be in harmony with the nature of the products they identify. Suitable brand names are:

> Johnson & Murphy (shoes) Pard (dog food)
> Evening in Paris (perfume) Discreet (deodorant)
> Mrs. Filbert's (sandwich spread) Flexible Flyer (sleds)

Suggestive

Well-chosen brand names and trade-marks often have a suggestive quality which is beneficial. Suggestiveness can, by arousing interest, enhance the performance of the seller's advertising and can contribute to the marketing success of his product. A brand name can suggest the product itself, or the product's quality, or some benefit, feature, or characteristic of the product. It can suggest what the product is for, or what it will do. It can suggest that the product will fill a human need or want. Examples:

> Kools (cigarettes) Mum (deodorant)
> Gleem (toothpaste) Accordorfold (doors)
> Halo (shampoo) Beautyrest (mattresses)
> Endurance (house paints) Zerex (antifreeze)

DESIRABLE CHARACTERISTICS — BRAND NAMES

Easy to Master

Brand names should be easy to read, write, spell, recognize, and remember. A brand name is defective if more than one pronunciation of it is likely; some consumers will not risk the embarrassment of mispronouncing a brand name even when they are alone, dealing with an unknown salesperson, and in a strange market. When how-to-pronounce-it instructions are included in an advertisement the advertiser is indicating that his brand name is not all it should be. For example, *du Maurier* (cigarettes) instructs advertising readers to say *de-more-ee-ay*. Hinde-

Brand Names, Trade-Marks, and Trade Characters

Dauch (trade name) says in its advertising, "Hinde rhymes with Find; Dauch is pronounced Dowk." Just how *do* you pronounce *Dowk?* Contrast Lux and Ritz with these:

    Bacardi (rum)   Sunoco (gasolines)
    Pall Mall (cigarettes)   Kreuger (beer)
    Girard Perregaux (watches)   Lycoborol (heat powder)
    Izod (shirts)   Grand Prix (perfume)

Short

Consumers like short brand names, seven letters in length or less. Many call for *Luckies,* not *Lucky Strike;* they order a *Coke,* not a *Coca-Cola;* they refer to a *Chevrolet* as a *Chevy;* to them, *Budweiser* has become *Bud.* Brevity aids the advertiser in his effort to achieve simplicity and unity in brand name. This is an important consideration for products bought by almost everybody. Brevity permits bold display, especially on small products and packages. For heavy users of outdoor electric signs, short names mean lower costs of construction and operation. Short names include:

        Duz (cleaner)   Nips (antacid)
        His (after shave lotion)   Orbit (gum)
        Flit (insecticide)   Now (dessert)
        Par (soap)   Lug (heels)

Family Suitability

When a manufacturer makes a family of products rather than just a single product, he can adopt individual, separate brand names for each — or, he can group all his products under a blanket or family brand name. General Motors, Ford, and Chrysler follow the individual name policy, as do Lever Brothers, Procter and Gamble, and Colgate-Palmolive. A single family brand is preferred by Gerber, Heinz, Westinghouse, Elizabeth Arden, and Johnson & Johnson.

The blanket brand facilitates institutional advertising. It permits the transfer of consumer good will from one product to others within the family. Harmonious and unified advertisements which include two or more products are easily constructed. Blanket brands banish the problem of what to name products added to the line, and, as has been indicated, naming a new product entails various risks. Too, the launching of a new product may be made easier and more economical because its relationship to established products is obvious. Some time ago, some consumers thought *Congoleum* products and *Nairn* products were made by two manufacturers; so the company replaced these names with the single brand name, *Gold Seal.* Another company, the manufacturer of a pop-up automatic toaster named *Toastmaster,* added electric water heaters to its line. Did it name these *Heatmaster?* No! It named them *Toastmaster.*

There are, however, influences which recommend individual rather than blanket branding. If one member of the family of products incurs the wrath and boycott of consumers, the other members, too, suffer. Sometimes the products are so unrelated as not to benefit significantly from common identification — sometimes

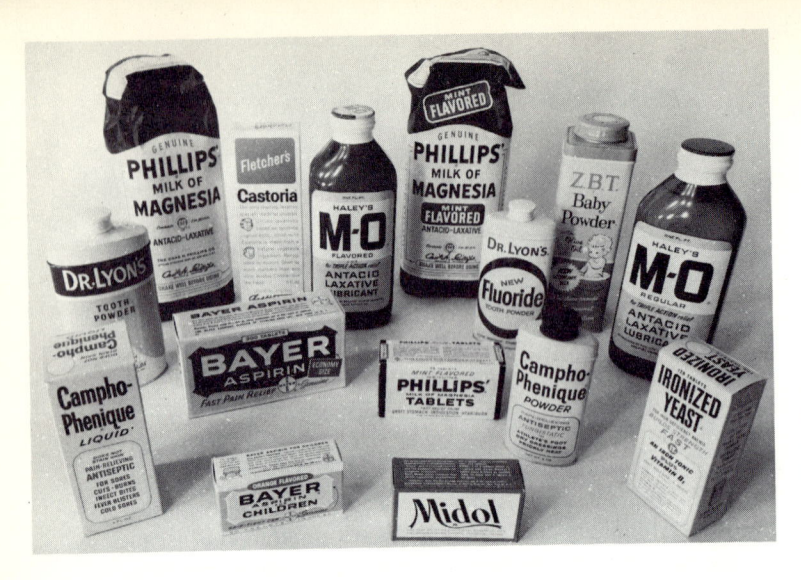

Sterling Drug gives its products individual brand names. (Courtesy: Sterling Drug, Inc.)

one line could be handicapped if given another product's name. The meat packers, for example, would hardly give the same brand name to their foods for plants and to their foods for humans. When the makers of *Kleenex* added toilet tissue, they branded it *Delsey*. Keen-Kutter was fine for edged tools — but then the company added hammers and retained the same brand name. Individual brands permit greater product individuality and the greater concentration of consumer attention on each one. Individual brands can easily encourage and achieve the more aggressive selling of each, and the result of this can be a greater total promotion effort.

UNDESIRABLE CHARACTERISTICS — BRAND NAMES AND TRADE-MARKS

Commonplace

Brand names and trade-marks should avoid being commonplace. Such identification is flat and dull because it is overused, and difficult to protect because it is not distinctive. It fails to be functional, causing confusion in consumers' minds instead of certainty.

In the area of brand names, there is far too much use of these:

Royal	General
Standard	Magic
National	Golden
Champion	Universal

A register of brands contains these:

Big Ben (clocks)	Big Jess (work clothes)
Big Fellow (peas)	Big Joe (flour)
Big Hunk (candy bar)	Big Red (dog food)
Big Jack (soap)	Big Stinky (fly traps)

Commonplace designs in the trade-mark field include the circle, square, star, cross, diamond, and triangle.

Brand Names, Trade-Marks, and Trade Characters

Negative Connotation

If a brand name or a trade-mark is guilty of negative connotation, its effect on sales can be unfortunate. For example, if the pronunciation of the brand name sounds like some vulgar or obscene word in a foreign language, then individuals of that extraction may be offended. More broadly, if there is any unpleasant or disagreeable association possible in consumers' minds, then the name or mark is defective. Students have described these as risky on this score:

Brand Names	*Trade-Marks*
Dr. Sweat (root beer)	Turtles (candy)
Kaffee Hag (coffee)	Black Horse (ale)
Griesedich (beer)	Gargoyle (lubricants)
Fairy (soap)	
Clabber Girl (baking powder)	
Le Gout (seasoning)	

Confusing Similarity

Brand names and trade-marks are defective both in a promotional sense and in a legal sense when they are too similar to other brand names and trade-marks. In promotion, as elsewhere, imitation is the sincerest form of flattery; in law, imitation shades into infringement. A manufacturer who named his products *Plomb* later had to drop this name and replace it because the courts ruled that it infringed on the established brand name, *Plumb*. Another manufacturer, not Eastman, was denied the use of the name *Kodak* for cigarette lighters he planned to produce. *Peaks* and *Alps* as names for candy bars have been held to infringe on *Mounds*, just as *Jazz-Sea* was decreed too like *Jantzen*. A deodorant originally named *Nay* was hurriedly renamed *Theme* when another deodorant called *Ney* was discovered. In checking for similarity, the advertiser usually searches first through the trade-marks (brand names) registered with the United States Patent Office; then he may or may not check any listings of unregistered trade-marks. Some trade associations, some trade papers, and the trade-mark bureau of the United States Printing and Lithograph Company maintain such files.

Belabored Names and Marks

Sometimes the advertiser strains too hard in creating his brand name or his trade-mark. Such identification often seems too clever; it often seems just senseless.

Alcoa's recently adopted trade-mark is abstract, simple, compact. "A" stands for Alcoa and for aluminum. (Courtesy: Alcoa Aluminum Company of America)

Identifying the Product

The advertiser can take a related word and spell it backwards, as in *Serutan*. He can rely on expression and inflection, as in Odorono (Odor? Oh *No!*). He can be cute or coy, as in *Hadacol,* or obscure, as in *Drene*. There are persons who think these brand names too belabored:

One Pull (corsets)	C-Far (field glasses)
Dum Dum (paints)	Hands Up (hand cosmetics)
Happy (seasoning salt)	Hi-There (panties)
U-Bet (syrups)	Doo-Tee (nursery seats)
Goo-Goo (candy bars)	I-C-U (metal polish)
My Wife's (pancake syrup)	Deb You (hosiery)

Trade-marks are belabored when they baffle consumers, when they are meaningless and of abstract design, and when they place too much dependence on color.

Misrepresentation

Advertisers must not allow their brand names or trade-marks to deceive consumers about the origin, raw materials, ingredients, manufacturing processes, or features of merchandise. One example will suffice here: The United States Shoe Company made and sold *Red Cross* shoes for more than fifty years. Then the Federal Trade Commission stepped in and ordered the company to stop using that brand name because it might imply some sponsorship by the American National Red Cross. So, the name *Gold Cross* appeared on the packages and in the advertisements with this statement: "The same fine foot-wear known as *Red Cross* shoes for over 50 years." But the company continued its fight against the FTC ruling and finally won. The name now? You guessed it — the *Red Cross* shoe, formerly the *Gold Cross* shoe, before that *Red Cross* shoe. The company agreed to include this disclaimer in its promotion, "This product has no connection whatever with the American National Red Cross."

Current Fashion

Styles in current favor are risky in that they make an identification mark, chosen for permanent use, appear "dated" when the styles lose their popularity. Hemlines and waistlines are up this year — down next year. Beards were once in fashion — now they are not. The White Rock girl Psyche who thrilled her viewers in 1893 has had to change her vital statistics noticeably to stay in favor. Unless the advertiser is willing to bring a contemporary trade-mark up to date periodically, his best best is to choose from the *distant* past. General Motors did this when they selected Napoleon's coach as the Fisher Body trade-mark.

GENERIC BRAND NAMES

Advertisers want their brand names to become universally known and preferred, but they do *not* want their brand names to become generic. Why? A generic name is public property, part of the common language, available legally for use by anyone. A brand name has become generic when the public refers to that *type* or

Advertisements such as this prevent brand names from becoming generic. (Courtesy: The Coca-Cola Company)

class of product by the manufacturer's brand name. These are generic terms which once were brand names: lanolin, milk of magnesia, celluloid, escalator, malted milk, cellophane, aspirin, shredded wheat, linoleum, percale, and kerosene. Brand names in some danger of becoming generic are: Coke, Deepfreeze, Kleenex, Formica, Kodak, and Frigidaire. The tragedy of a brand name becoming generic is the loss to the owner — loss of time, dollars, and effort spent establishing the name, only to lose the rights to its exclusive use.

The Technical and Education Advisor of Du Pont wrote this about cellophane:[1]

As you probably know, one of Du Pont's most highly prized trade-marks — the word cellophane — was lost to us through misuse of the word in such a way that the courts ruled it had become a generic term and no longer referred specifically to our product. As a result, any manufacturer of transparent cellulose film may now use it. One of the sins of omission leading to this loss of a valuable asset was our failure to call the attention of those mis-using the Du Pont trade-mark to the fact that they had done so.

Ever since then, as you can imagine, we have striven to do this, even though we recognize very well that those to whom we write may feel that our correction is a carping one and that it might even smack of ingratitude. Actually, this is not the case at all. There is nothing personal or critical in it. We are merely taking a step that is legally necessary to protect something of value.

How can a manufacturer prevent a brand name from becoming generic? The first step is to see that the public has a descriptive word or phrase for the *type* of product. See examples on page 84.

[1] Quoted by permission from a letter by George R. Seidel, Technical and Education Advisor.

Identifying the Product

Q-Tips *cotton swabs*
Vaseline *petroleum jelly*
Prestone *antifreeze*
Band-Aid *adhesive bandages*
Audimeter *electric recorder*
Deepfreeze *home freezer*

A second step is to indicate plainly that the brand name is legally a trade-mark and is being so used. Placing it in quotation marks or in italics, capitalizing it, coloring it, or executing it in distinctive lettering or art work are possible techniques. Still another tactic is to designate the brand name as a registered trade-mark, perhaps with the phrase "Reg. U.S. Pat. Off." or with the simple symbol ®. Some protection is afforded by placing the name on two or more products or product lines.

A third step is to protest any and all misuse of the brand name. The market must be policed vigorously. Improper use should be called to the offender's attention promptly. Cooperation can be solicited in advertising. A final resort is to take legal action.

THE LANHAM ACT

The legal aspects of trade-marks, including brand names, are many, complicated, and not always certain. It was intended that the Lanham Act, which became effective in 1947, would clarify trade-mark legislation as well as liberalize and strengthen it. The act gave trade-mark owners more protection than they had enjoyed formerly; it made registration so attractive that it is virtually mandatory for trade-marks used in interstate commerce.

Trade-Mark Rights Under Common Law

Rights in a trade-mark begin and are obtained by a seller's starting to use it; from the first moment of use, those rights exist. Seniority is the basic issue — not registration; common law protects the seller against infringement and unfair competition if the seller can prove seniority of adoption and use even when the trade-mark is not registered. These rights are preserved by continuous use of the trade-mark; consistent use continues the seller's rights to the exclusive use of the mark. Of course, the seller is well advised to make a record of his adoption, his first use of, and his first advertising of the trade-mark.

Registration

The Lanham Act makes most attractive the registration of trade-marks in the United States Patent Office even though registration does not create legal rights, but, instead, makes them a matter of record. Failure to register, indeed, need not hurt existing and established rights.

Of the two registers provided, the Principal Register and the Supplemental Register, the former is the more important. After a trade-mark has been in continuous use and registered on the Principal Register for five years, there is little chance of challenging the seller's right to it or of having the registration cancelled. If, during that five-year period, the seller's claim is not contested successfully, then, with some specified exceptions, his trade-mark acquires the status of incontestability, which means that the seller gets the permanent right to use the trade-mark for his

Brand Names, Trade-Marks, and Trade Characters

class of product. The seller can lose this right only by abandonment(two years of non-use, unexplained, is legal evidence of abandonment), or by condoning the use of the trade-mark by others instead of taking legal action when infringement or appropriation starts, or by allowing the brand name to become generic.

Registration on the Principal Register is "constructive notice" to all of the seller's claims to ownership. No one else can start using his trade-mark and later plead ignorance of the seller's claim. The registration certificate can become conclusive evidence of the registrant's exclusive right to use the mark.

"Secondary Meaning" Principle

One of the liberalizing features of the Lanham Act has to do with the use of surnames, descriptive names, and geographic names as brand names. Prior to the passage of the act, a brand name basically descriptive, or mainly geographic, or primarily a surname could be adopted, of course, but not registered, making protection difficult. The doctrine of "secondary meaning" permits some surnames, some descriptive names, and some geographic names to be eligible for registration and, consequently, for trade-mark protection. A seller can register on the Principal Register a surname, a descriptive name, or a geographic name if it has acquired "secondary meaning" as a brand name. The key question is: Is the brand name distinctive of the seller's product — does the public relate the brand name to a specific seller? *Parker* pens and *Stetson* hats, *Wearever* utensils and *RealSilk* hosiery, *Paris* garters and *Elgin* watches are examples.

Other Marks

The Lanham Act provided for the registration of three additional types of marks. *Service* marks can be registered by such sellers of services as banks, transportation companies, insurance companies, and hotels. *Certification* marks such as the seal of the Underwriters Laboratories, or the Good Housekeeping guaranty seal can now be registered. *Collective* marks are eligible, marks such as the AAA of the American Automobile Association, or a union label, or the mark of a cooperative such as Sunkist Growers, Inc.

Supplemental Register

Two important services are provided by the Supplemental Register. First, it is available to manufacturers who cannot qualify for the Principal Register but must have some form of United States registration before being able to register their trade-marks abroad. Second, this register accepts types of identification ineligible for the Principal Register. These include entire packages, configuration of goods, labels, slogans, names of trade characters, novel use of color, and distinctive sound effects. The National Broadcasting Company's station break chimes, *bong, bing, bong,* was the first of these sound effects to be registered.

TRADE CHARACTERS

An advertiser has three main choices when he embarks on the search for a trade character. First, he can examine the entire range of animate beings in the hope of

The popularity and appeal of a trade character may be transferred to a variety of consumer products. (Courtesy: The Chesapeake and Ohio Railroad)

finding something appropriate. In such an examination, he will explore the worlds of humans, animals, birds and fowls, fish, and insects. A second option is to touch some inanimate object with the magic wand that bestows personality and animation on whatever it touches. The advertiser's product is a possibility, as is some trademark feature which up to now has been both immobile and mute. Third, the advertiser can locate some personality that already has an established following and can buy the services of that particular personality as his trade character. The owners of Little Lulu, Donald Duck, and Li'l Abner have all sold their services as trade characters.

As for features and characteristics, the trade character may be masculine or feminine, or, indeed, rather sexless. It is a personality in its own right, with the power to walk, act, and talk. It may be a product of whimsey; it may represent at least a tame attempt at humor.

How They are Used

Trade characters join brand names and trade-marks as an identification device. Whenever the consumer sees or hears the character, an association forms in the consumer's mind that relates the trade character to its manufacturer or product. If displayed by retailers, the trade character identifies where the consumer can buy the product in question, and, should it be an element of the package, the trade character would identify the actual physical product of the advertiser.

As an example of this first use there is the personality created by the G. M. Basford Company, an advertising agency, to add a distinctive individuality to a client whose company name was "National Starch Products." Identification is

Brand Names, Trade-Marks, and Trade Characters

usually low, or at least a problem, where "National" is the key word; there are so many of them. The trade character the agency designed is a nameless, impish moppet with big round eyes and a triangle for a nose. The agency's Mr. J. C. Snape writes:

> We created this type of trade character so that we would have a spokesman for National. One that would have the universal appeal of a child and a doll, rather than one with distinctive human resemblance that might antagonize readers by being the type of person they dislike. Too, by having a child/doll character we felt that we had a device that would permit us to speak naively and broadly about National products without 'talking down' to the reader.
>
> We have not decided upon a name. At present we see no need for one.

A very common use of the trade character is to symbolize a product's virtues. An outstanding example is the Tough Guy of the Hastings Manufacturing Company. In 1937 the company launched a new product, the Hastings Steel-Vent piston ring. This ring controlled oil because it was tough enough to stop oil pumping, yet it was gentle on cylinder walls. Nothing was more natural for the Hastings company than to adopt the slogan, "Tough — But Oh So Gentle," and the trade character, the Tough Guy, to put across the outstanding features of the Hastings piston ring. Now the Tough Guy is so well known that he typifies the company and its products to thousands of repairmen and jobbers; he also obtains high readership for the company's advertising.

Another use of the trade character is to personify a consumer-enemy or a consumer-problem that the advertiser's product or service will combat. Such a trade character is *Wicked Willie Weevil,* property of the U.S. Industrial Chemicals Company Division of the National Distillers Products Corporation. *Wicked Willie Weevil* promotes Pyrenone Grain Protectant and Pyrenone Wheat Protectant which are insecticides that are used to prevent insect damage to stored grains including corn, oats, rye, rice, barley, wheat, and other small grains. The communication

"DOODLES"

"Doodles," friendly and humorous, sells for Parker in various ways. (Courtesy: The Parker Pen Company)

Identifying the Product

from the company's advertising agency, once again the G. M. Basford Company, continues:

> *Wicked Willie Weevil* is a caricature of an actual weevil. The drill, used for Willie's nose, is symbolic of the holes eaten in grain by weevils. His 'Carpetbagger' type of dress, complete with gold watch chain, was chosen because weevil damage is confined largely to the southern states just as the carpetbagger devastation was largely a southern problem.

The advertiser's messages can be delivered by his trade character in all major media. Television, of course, immediately comes to mind. It is quite possible for the trade character to express certain opinions or to make statements that would seem out of place if voiced by the advertiser himself. The fact that he has a trade character means that the advertiser has more variety available in telling his story. Mr. George C. Frank, Assistant to the President, writes that the Erie Railroad uses its trade character "Smiley" to make more effective certain advertising:

> 'Smiley' is not used in national advertising as a symbol of the Erie, but he is used extensively in our on-line advertising — that is, in our newspaper advertising to 120 towns along the Erie right of way. He makes what might be a rather self-interested message human and warm. Advertisements of this kind can be quite deadly and very hard to obtain readership, but we know from our studies that 'Smiley' brings a certain something that makes people stop and read. In that sense alone he is invaluable to Erie as part of the advertising message.

If the advertiser is selling something that is a bit dull or certainly less than exciting, then he may ask a trade character to perk up or enliven his selling. Services and technical products are clearly in need of such help. The Union Wire Rope Corporation does not claim its products to be hair-raising or spine-tingling — nor even spectacular in the way many other products are. To do something about this, the company adopted as a trade character a man fashioned of rope and named *Tuffy*. Mr. Ray G. Noble, Assistant Vice President, has this to say about *Tuffy:*

> Since using this *Tuffy* Trade Character, it has proved to be especially valuable in the field of advertising our product. I believe we can safely say that the entire field of rope users throughout the United States knows by now that *Tuffy* means high quality Union Wire Rope.

One of the oddest and most interesting uses of a trade character is that made by a company that formerly was named the Minnesota Valley Canning Company. Its legally official name now — the Green Giant Company. A letter from their Mr. Jack Mullowney reads in part:

> Up to about eighteen months ago our Company was known as the Minnesota Valley Canning Company. The great bulk of the consuming public did not know the name of our Company, but they did know our *Green Giant*. The grocery trade often referred to us as 'The Green Giant people,' 'The Green Giant Canners,' etc. Consumers often addressed letters simply 'The Green Giant.' It was necessary for consumers to obtain the name of Le Sueur from either a label or from an advertise-

Betty Crocker's "image" has been changed twice since 1936. In 1955, she was given more maturity and warmth. More recently, she was given a smile. (Courtesy: General Mills, Inc.)

ment. On our labels and in our ads, Le Sueur and Minnesota Valley Canning Company were printed together and as a single unit, but very often consumers would ignore our corporate name and write:

'The Green Giant
Le Sueur, Minnesota'

We recognized this growing demand to call ourselves 'Green Giant,' and because our operations were no longer confined to the valley of the Minnesota River, we changed our corporate name to Green Giant Company. It is the story of a trade character's 'taking over' a company.

One trade character owes her existence to the uncertainty as to how the company's brand name should be pronounced. Sue Shard was created to teach consumers how to pronounce the product's name, Suchard. Some buyers called for "Such-ard," while some said "Suck-ard"; too many buyers were, of course, calling for "Hershey" or other brands where there was no embarrassing risk of mispronunciation. So, the company's first step was to print on the candy bar and on its carton, "Say Soo Shard." As it worked out, this message was neither large nor dramatic, and, as a result, "Soo" was replaced by "Sue." Mr. B. G. Forrest, Vice President, wrote (on a letterhead that pictures Sue in the lower left corner):

> We started using our 'Sue Shard' for advertising purposes in the fall of 1946. She was a Powers model, and we made quite a few pictures of her at that time. We used her extensively in our advertising during the years 1946, 1947 and 1948. We still use her to some extent in our advertising but most particularly on our various packing supplies.

Sometimes the trade character can supply the advertiser with an interesting, effective advertising theme or continuity. At one time, for example, Elsie the Borden Cow had a new son, and an entire advertising effort was devoted to running a contest to select a name for him.

Novelty items can result from trade characters. The Green Giant Company has, on occasion, offered a four-foot rag doll version of its Green Giant for two labels and $3.50.

89

Identifying the Product

Finally, trade characters can personalize the manufacturer and his product, endowing them with warmth and friendly concern. Betty Crocker personalizes her company; Hot Dan the Mustard Man personalizes his product. Incidentally, Betty Crocker provides housewives with a contact in the huge General Mills organization — someone to whom they can write. In somewhat similar fashion, a trade character could be the mouthpiece for the manufacturer who sends advice and suggestions to his wholesalers and retailers.

Procter and Gamble's "Mr. Clean"

When the Procter and Gamble Company was asked about their "Mr. Clean," here is what they said:

> Who is Mr. Clean? Mr. Clean is the brand name and the visual representation of the all-purpose liquid household cleaner, manufactured and distributed by The Procter & Gamble Company, Cincinnati, Ohio. Mr. Clean, the personality, has appeared in all of the brand's advertising since its introduction in 1958. He is a muscular cleaning man attired in white sailor's working clothes, characterized by his clean-shaven head and a gold earring in his left ear. He is portrayed as the housewife's friend, ready and willing to help with the dull, thankless task of housecleaning. He is a friendly, helpful, engaging personality, the kind of person welcome in any house.

Mr. Clean is a success both as a brand name and as a trade character. (Courtesy: The Procter & Gamble Company)

Copyright: The Procter & Gamble Company.

Brand Names, Trade-Marks, and Trade Characters

How and why was he born? Procter & Gamble and its advertising agency, Tatham-Laird, Inc., were faced with the problem of launching a new all-purpose liquid cleaner in a highly competitive market. Therefore, the agency's major task was to identify in a distinctive manner this all-purpose liquid cleaner as a product that would do more cleaning . . . faster and easier than any other type of cleaning product, powder or liquid.

The agency started its search for a name by pursuing the premise that simplicity is often the key to emphasis. In this case it proved to be true. The absolute champion in a given field may be known simply as Mr. Golf or Mr. Baseball, as is the case with Arnold Palmer and Stan Musial, respectively. Therefore, the champion in the cleaner field could logically be called "Mr. Clean."

Mr. Clean's physical appearance went through several stages of development, but finally he emerged as a muscular, immaculately clad cleaning man with an earring . . . "the all-time champ at all kinds of cleaning, Mr. Clean himself."

How is he used in advertising? In our introductory advertising, we engaged in a delightful bit of fantasy. That such a character as Mr. Clean really existed and could be purchased for a nominal sum at the grocery store was, of course, pure make-believe. As with Santa Claus, nobody could seriously believe there was a Mr. Clean . . . but wouldn't it be fun if there were . . . ? Not only did we ask the public to pretend with us that Mr. Clean existed, but that "Grandmothers Love . . . Babies Love . . . Mothers Love . . . Brides Love . . . Dads Love . . . Dogs Love . . . *Any* Mrs. Loves Mr. Clean."

If, in view of the tremendous impact of this introductory advertising, the public was unwilling to play this game with us, we could safely assume the brand would become just another cleaner in an already crowded market.

Evidence is that the public was willing and eager to accept our fantasy and the Mr. Clean concept helped establish a successful business.

How does Mr. Clean differ from other trademarks? Every manufacturer who employs a trademark or a trade character will defend it on the basis that it makes his product stand apart from its competition, and enables the consumer to identify the product quickly and accurately. We attribute these advantages to Mr. Clean . . . and much more. He is more than a symbol printed on a package, or added as an afterthought at the end of a commercial. Mr. Clean is an integral part of the brand's advertising. He is a cleaning man ready and willing to help solve the problems of housecleaning. He is the product "come alive."

Questions and Problems

1. A college football team may personify its nickname and have an Indian, a Deacon, or a Cavalier perform at games. Is such a personality a trade character?
2. Compare brand names with personal names.
3. What are some conditions or developments which put pressure on a seller to change a brand name?
4. How are private brands and national brands alike?
5. A single manufacturer uses a family brand name *and* individual brand names. Comment.

Identifying the Product

6. When is company name more important than brand name?
7. What are the advantages and disadvantages of using different brand names on product lines of different quality?
8. Should a manufacturer of electric razors design a trade character who dramatizes a product-virtue rather than one who personifies a consumer-enemy?
9. A manufacturer has for years used a bulldog as his trade-mark. Argue that he should begin using the bulldog as a trade character.
10. Picture a major petroleum company such as Gulf, Texaco, or Humble; assume its name to be Monarch. Certain marketing executives of Monarch have been impressed with the success of various trade characters. Their interest was made known to all top management of Monarch and to Monarch's advertising agency. As a result, company and agency decided to explore the possibility of Monarch's sponsoring a trade character. If sponsored, the trade character would be introduced the following year when the company planned to market a new premium motor fuel.

The advertising agency recommended a tough and evil, dirty and repulsive, hobo-type character named Dirty Dan Carbon. The new and improved motor fuel would be the deadly enemy of Dirty Dan; it would help prevent and help rid motors of carbon. Clearly, Dirty Dan could be adapted to many promotional uses, roles, and situations.

What is your reaction to the agency's recommendation?

Chapter 6

Packaging

Interest and activity in the field of packaging have never been greater. Aerosol cans, squeeze bottles, and collapsible tubes contain more products than ever before. Aluminum foil, clear film wrappings, and plastic containers are in wide use. Increasingly, food products are being packaged in "mix-in" containers, "bake-in" containers, and in "boil-in-the-bag" containers. Soluble premeasured packets, cutting edges, spray tops, and pour spouts reflect package competition and improvement. Fewer packages are glued or stapled shut, and more packages are perforated or offer pull-tapes. Why? Consumer preferences. So, let's start by looking at what is expected of packages.

PACKAGE QUALITIES

Protection

The most important assignment given to a package is that of protecting its *contents;* unless the product reaches the consumer in good condition, nothing else the package does matters. Products must not be allowed to spill, leak, or evaporate — to spoil, discolor, or lose flavor. There must be no damage or breakage, no contamination, adulteration, or physical deterioration. Various products can be affected adversely by weather, atmosphere, temperature, shock, light, moisture, and the passage of time. Protection starts at the factory, moves to the point of purchase in the retail store, and then continues in the home. Proper packaging can protect the *consumer* against such hazards as leaky cartons and cut fingers.

Identification

The package joins the brand name, the trade-mark, and the trade character in sharing the responsibility for identifying a manufacturer's product. In the store, the need is for ready and certain recognition so that consumers can identify the type of product in the package (peaches, coffee, toothpaste) and distinguish one brand from competing brands (Del Monte, Maxwell House, Crest). Another need is for high visibility and extreme legibility — at toe level as well as at eye

Identifying the Product

level, from a distance of several feet, and from more than one direction. If a manufacturer of a family of products so desires, he can, through the use of shape, color, and design, ask his packages to identify the other members of the family. Mistaken identity must be prevented in the home as well as in the store.

Sales Appeal

It is the duty of the package to make a positive and significant contribution to the sale of the product. This is essentially a matter of consumer appeal because consumers dictate which products are to be stocked by retailers. Packages which rate well on appeal are eye-catching and provocative, capturing the buyer's attention and arousing her interest. Attractive appearance helps sales by helping convert non-users of that type of product into consumers, and by helping woo consumers away from competitors. Excellence in respect to the package's functional performance aids in these two endeavors and also can encourage greater consumption among established customers. Good packaging, thus, promotes both impulse buying *and* repeat, planned purchases.

Economy

A fourth attribute of outstanding packages is economy. The cost of the package must, of course, be included in the consumer price, and for certain products, the proportion is high. Ink, adhesives, cosmetics, drugs, and motor oil are products whose packaging accounts for not less than one-third of the manufacturer's selling price. Whether the manufacturer buys his packages or makes them, he wants economy. Identifying them, packing them, handling them, shipping them, storing them, selling them — all must be reasonable in cost. Two other expenses, those of complaints and returned goods, should not be increased because of the product's package.

WHAT MANUFACTURERS WANT

The manufacturer's package must do a job at the point of purchase, the retail store, and then do another job at the point of use, the home. It is quite possible for a package to do this first job satisfactorily, to get displayed effectively, picked up, examined, and bought — but then be used infrequently in the home because of faulty design. A second general consideration is that of legality, of conforming to federal, state, and local legislation. For example, the Federal Food, Drug, and Cosmetic Act declares that foods, drugs, and cosmetics shall be deemed to be misbranded if the container is so made, formed, or filled as to be misleading.

As regards the four qualities desired in a package, nothing need be added here about *protection*. As for *identification,* the manufacturer's main concern is to design a package with unmistakable identity no matter how it is dropped or placed on shelf, counter, or floor by retailers. Bags of sugar are a good example of a package which can be found stacked or just piled in all possible positions.

Most manufacturers are keenly interested in the third feature, *sales appeal.* They want their packages to look like good sellers which deserve full support when being

Packaging

considered by retailers. They want their packages to look well in all advertising media to be used. They want packages with high attraction and interest value, able to provoke and intrigue shoppers, successful in stimulating impulse purchases. A hard fact of life is that the *retailer* controls the position, shelf space, height, and display of a manufacturer's merchandise; the manufacturer controls only the package. The manufacturer must rely on it to reach out, get the attention of shoppers, convey a feeling of quality, and invite the shopper's confidence — immediately.

As for *economy,* the typical manufacturer wants inexpensive materials which will protect, identify, and sell satisfactorily. He thinks particularly of assembly-line filling and of packing with automatic machinery. He strives for the minimum in weight and bulk so as to hold down shipping and handling costs.

WHAT RETAILERS WANT

You have no trouble guessing that the retailer wants to stock the packages consumers want.

He wants, furthermore, protective packages — against vermin and insects, against fading when displayed in a sunny window. Because soiled and shopworn packages cause markdowns, he wants packages sturdy enough to resist damage from being handled by shoppers. If age and freshness are significant, the retailer wants the package to be coded in a manner easy to read.

In addition to the identification matters already referred to, retailers like packages difficult to "mis-face" when being placed on shelves by careless employees. This consideration, plus the fact that more and more products are being placed on shelves with an *end* showing rather than a side, recommends that no panel or surface of a package be left unidentified. The brand name should be visible from every angle. In self service operation, prices should be clearly identifiable to checkers at the cash registers.

As for sales appeal, retailers are, of course, interested in the aspects mentioned already. Display and appearance are key matters, especially when many units of the same product are stacked on or with each other. Because today's food shopper makes most of her buying decisions *in the store,* food store merchants favor packages which stimulate the impulse to buy. They also like selling copy which is helpful to retail salespeople as well as to shoppers.

Economy in packaging has various meanings to retailers. It means maximum shelf life, for example, and a minimum of returned goods and complaints. It means economical handling, sorting, pricing, selling, weighing, and wrapping. Sometimes it means that wrapping is unnecessary. It means safe stacking without a costly separator of paper or cardboard between layers of packages. This consideration recommends packages with flat tops and flat bottoms — it faults packages which are unstable, pyramidal, or peaked. Expense is avoided if package size fits the retailer's present shelves and equipment. Merchants with self-service operation hope a package will discourage pilferage.

Identifying the Product

WHAT CONSUMERS WANT

In a somewhat chronological sequence, one of the first concerns of consumers is to be able to *identify* packages. If shopping is done in rushed or distracting circumstances, identification in the store is a serious matter. Once home, the consumer wants clear and complete identification on the dispensing or using container after any outside container has been thrown away. The medicine cabinet, the kitchen shelf, and the frozen food compartment are three areas where certain and instant identification is essential.

The consumer's interest then shifts to *inspection*. The use of window-front packages, clear plastic, cellophane, and glass is explained in large degree by the shopper's insistence on being able to see and examine products easily and readily. Metal, cardboard, and paper make inspection more difficult if not impossible. Some packages permit product visibility only; others permit product accessibility.

After a typical purchase, the next major consideration involves the *opening* of the package, and the consumer's wish here is for ease, convenience, and speed. The sardine can, the anchor top with no ledge or shoulder to pry against, the metal strip with key, the pry-off lids which get so mutilated in removal as to be utterly unusable again, the glued tops of cardboard packages which must be cut or pried open or slit, the "press here along dotted line" packages which are hard on fingernails *and* tempers — these the housewife loathes. Her preferences: the opening tape, perforated lids, tops which screw off or snap open, and cans which are easily opened with wall-type can openers.

Once the package is open, then comes the matter of *use,* a consideration which can take many forms. If the item purchased is to be a gift, then the package should exude prestige. If the product is to be handled by the consumer, then the dispensing or using package should be convenient and comfortable to use. Economical use calls for a shampoo bottle so grooved that the danger of its slipping from wet hands is minimized, for a peanut butter can from which all the contents can be extracted, and for cottage cheese in a package shaped to make maximum use of the limited space in a refrigerator. Packages must be functional; cold cereals, catsup, and cake flour need protection until the contents are all used, by all users, under all conditions of normally rough usage. Some food and beverage containers must be so attractive that consumers will not hesitate to put them on the table when the family is eating, and it is a fact that more consumers than will admit to it serve milk from a bottle or carton on the table. Consumers spend much money for built-in convenience. They buy pour spouts, brush caps, squeeze bottles, spray cans, applicator tops, pre-measured amounts in fractional packages, margarine and butter in pats or at least with measuring marks, short wide jars easy to spoon from, caps which serve as measuring caps, waxed paper and foil in boxes with cutting edges, and jelly in collapsible tubes.

Consumer interest in opening is matched by similar interest in *closing*. Packages must be easy to reseal effectively, and lids must fit snugly when put back on glass containers. Closures must work quickly, surely, and conveniently until all of the contents are consumed.

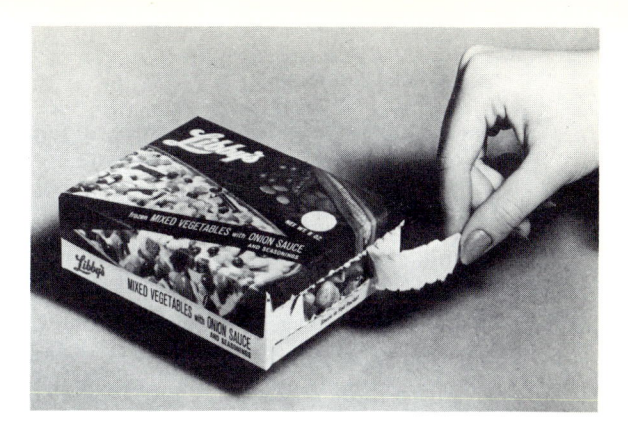

Housewives prefer packages which are easy to open. (Courtesy: Container Corporation of America)

For some products there can be a somewhat serious problem of *disposal*. There are two large offenders on this score, one of which is the outside container, usually a box or a carton. The other is the bottle on which there is a deposit. Because retailers as well as consumers dislike bottle deposits, we find such substitutes as cardboard, metal, and throw-away glass containers.

DEPARTMENTAL INTEREST IN PACKAGING

Just who in a manufacturing organization should have something to say about the company's packages? No one can deny the *sales* department some voice, perhaps the dominant voice, in packaging decisions. It seems only fair to let the persons who must sell the product influence its package; those are the persons who are or should be in close touch with consumer motives and habits, with trade attitudes, and with the relationship between packaging and pricing. The *president* of the company seems entitled to be heard from on packaging matters. Because he deals with the physical handling of the package, is interested in costs, and is affected by package changes, the *production* manager has a right to take part in packaging discussions and decisions. The *advertising* staff has an interest in package design and appearance, in how the package reproduces in the various media, and in the possibility of finding an advertising theme in some package feature. *Sales promotion* thinks in terms of retail preferences and consumer attitudes, of coupons and box tops. The *purchasing* department is concerned with cost and supply, *research* with materials, tests, and specifications, and the *legal* department with requirements and infringement. Many companies have a packaging committee from the areas mentioned which is responsible for packaging policy and practice. Outside parties interested in packaging include package designers, package producers, product engineers and consultants, advertising agencies, marketing research firms, commercial laboratories, and suppliers of packaging materials.

SUGGESTIONS ABOUT DESIGN

The surfaces of a package should be used in such a manner that the total or over-all performance of that package is maximized. The typical rectangular package has four panels and two ends. The front or display panel usually stresses the pictorial and excludes almost all copy because the principal assignment given this

Identifying the Product

panel is to catch the shopper's eye and attract favorable attention. The back panel and the two side panels are the consumer's panels. They may contain identification, selling copy, price, directions, ingredients, illustrations of how the product may be used, recipes, and whatever information is required by law. The ends may be used for brand identification or a brief selling message, perhaps a slogan; the bottom is the weakest of the six panels insofar as copy is concerned. It is not uncommon for a single package to have one panel designed especially for drug store use and another for supermarket use. Sometimes a manufacturer uses the same front and side panels but then has a group of different back panels, perhaps five or six of them; there is merit in this practice, both in the store and in the home.

Strong, positive brand identification is a "must," with the brand name the single most important sales building element. Trade-marks, slogans, trade characters, color, illustrations, and layout are also used to help make identification instantaneous and certain on all six panels. Side panels sometimes continue the design on the front panel because the package is often seen first from an angle.

Simple, uncluttered layout is best. Orderly arrangement, the generous and effective use of white space, and modern, clean patterns make for the total effect desired. The cans and multi-paks of as plebeian a product as beer have been given a "high style" treatment to appeal to housewives shopping in food stores.

Conditions under which the product will be retailed and bought or not bought by consumers have considerable influence on design. The package must have sales appeal and look attractive from any angle, position, or direction — at ankle level or above eye level. The packages of all but the one lowest priced product in each class must help fight that one competitor who enjoys a competitive advantage with his lowest price. As for the shopper, there are millions of women who, because of carelessness or pride, do not wear their glasses when shopping even though they should. Will these consumers identify a certain manufacturer's product and read all about its advantages? Not if there's a chance that difficulty of reading might lead to embarrassment.

Efforts to keep the company's advertising and its packages related and in character with each other are worth making. When shopping, consumers should be able to spot the packages they have seen or heard advertised. As mentioned, brand name, trade-mark, and other common units can identify package with advertisement; picturing or describing the package in the advertisement accomplishes the same purpose. Packages should cash in on the company's advertising by dramatizing and illustrating the advertising message. Because six-pak containers of beverages can be changed frequently, those of some companies reproduce the artwork from the company's current advertising. Above all, the package must not be a disappointment to consumers who have seen it in advertisements.

COPY ON PACKAGES

Several types of copy appear on packages; one type about which there is no option is that required by law. Mandatory information as required by the Federal Food, Drug, and Cosmetic Act includes such items as these:

Packaging

Common name of product
Name and address of manufacturer or distributor on two or more panels
Common names of ingredients
Capacity in terms of weight, measure, or number
Listing of any artificial preservative or flavoring
Warning against the use of the product in an amount or for a length of time that may endanger health
Directions for proper use

Basic data about the product, in addition to common name of product, brand name, and name and address of manufacturer, are to be found on most packages. In this group are such items as quantity, description of contents, how made, ingredients, quality or grade, and information about manufacturing. In the ready-to-wear field, shoppers have indicated interest in price, size, color, style, texture, quality, shrinkage, color fastness, washability, and utility.

Copy which is best described as *selling* copy is placed on many packages. Product features are stressed, uses and benefits are emphasized, and the service the product will give is described. Seals of approval and guarantees are part of selling copy, as are recommendations of other products made by the manufacturer. Selling copy is often written with the retail salesperson as well as the consumer in mind.

Some packages need to carry directions about product uses and sometimes instructions about the proper care of the product. Such directions need to be simple and clear, easy to read, and easily understood by the most limited consumer. Instructions need to be exact and specific, often in 1-2-3 style. Words can be teamed with illustrations to emphasize whatever is important in an effort to prevent any unhappiness on the part of consumers. There is pressure to hold down the wordage of directions even though brevity can be bought only at the price of detail. A different color may be used for directions.

A most controversial question involving the inclusion or omission of *price* crops up at three points in this text. Should prices be placed on products? In advertisements? In window displays? The general conviction held here is that prices *should* be displayed in all three — that omission puts the seller on the defensive much more so and more often than does inclusion. In self-service operations, of course, there is little option. Placing a white price spot on the top of the package reduces the scrawling clerks might do across the front panel. As for gift packages, price information must be removable completely, without a trace, and with no damage to the product or package.

SOME PACKAGING DECISIONS

Size

One of the first questions which must be answered relates to package size. For many products, of course, size is a factor about which little can be done. Consumer preference is a major influence — consumers do or do not care for packages of fifty cigarettes, they do or do not prefer to open one large bottle rather than four or five

Identifying the Product

small ones, they do or do not demand smaller packages of food products because of limited storage space. Distribution channels are an influence in that variety stores, for example, have strong convictions and policies about prices, and a product's price, of course, determines how much of it there is to be packaged. Price lines and pricing ranges are closely allied factors, because the question of whether to have a giant tube of toothpaste is similar in some respects to the question of whether to make a small tube for variety stores. When supermarkets decide to offer candy at 29 cents, they have, in effect, determined size of package. Shifts in the business cycle can cause shifts in package size when custom argues against a change in price. Competition is an influence, permitting a seller to plan an entire promotion on the basis of his being the first of his group to offer a new size; competitors can get together, too, and work through their trade association for standardization of sizes. Taxes and legal requirements affect size. The same is true of available packaging machinery. The attitude of the federal government is a consideration; some time ago Washington favored beer containers of 7, 12, 16, 32, and 64 ounce capacity and opposed the 6, 8, 10, 11, 24, 25.6, and 38.4 ounce sizes. Some manufacturers of premium products package a one-fifth gallon to compete price-wise with other manufacturers' quarts, or 5-ounce items to compete with 6-ounce items.

Materials

The more common packaging materials are metal, glass, wood, paper, cardboard, plastic, cloth, and cellophane. The nature of the product and its needs must be considered, as must the conditions under which the product is used. Availability, possible shortages, and cost are major matters. The relative sales appeals of the various possibilities must be weighed; in one such instance, the increased sales of ice cream justified fully a switch to transparent plastic containers. Occasionally, pressure from competition or from consumers results in a manufacturer's packaging the same product in two materials — jar and tube, for example. Sellers of each material point with pride to many advantages they claim for their respective offerings. Those promoting the use of the collapsible metal tube boast that it is safe, is light in weight, keeps out air and light, shrinks as the contents are used, dispenses the contents satisfactorily, poses no disposal problem, protects the contents, is sanitary and durable, and tells the amount of the contents still inside. Du Pont cellophane "shows what it protects — protects what it shows."

Color

Color of package can be an asset or a handicap in that it can help or hurt sales. Consumer reaction, then, has much to say about what colors a package should wear. Do housewives expect sugar to be put in *white* packages? Do they prefer face powder in *blue* boxes rather than *green*? Do they feel that both blue *and* green packages look larger and less heavy than *black* packages of the same size? Type of product, quality of product, and conditions of display cannot be ignored. For a manufacturer of more than one type of product, colors can be used to identify sizes, models, flavors, and qualities. For a more extensive treatment of color, look ahead to the discussion preceding the colored illustrations in this book.

Packaging

Shape

Shape, perhaps, offers a manufacturer a narrower range of choice than do size, materials, and color. Custom almost decrees that baking powder cans be round, the laws of physics do not permit square light bulbs no matter how much such bulbs would delight decorators, and equally fixed is the shape of most products to be packaged. The package is asked to be both attractive and convenient as regards shape. Neither retailers nor consumers care for shapes which are unstable, which do not stack nicely, which are awkward. A perfume bottle should look like a perfume bottle, not like a catsup bottle.

Dual Use Packages

A dual use package is one which has a secondary usefulness after its contents have been consumed. Drinking glasses, boxes of jewelry or cigarettes, diaper pails, waste baskets, toys and cutouts for children, refrigerator dishes, cloth from flour and feed sacks — these are examples. The plus of the dual use package is its greater appeal, especially when the secondary use relates to the product it contains. The outstanding minus is the greater cost. Another possible minus is the danger of a housewife's switching brands rather than buying one more of the same brand and then throwing away the drinking glass, let us say, because she has already accumulated all the cheese-spread-drinking-glasses she needs. Some consumers are embarrassed when caught in the act of using a package for its secondary use. Other consumers react unfavorably if the secondary utility makes the package cost too much — or *look* as though it costs too much.

Combination Packages

Combination or multiple packages can be of several types. The simplest packages two or more of the same item together or puts together two different sizes or styles. A slight variation would be the inclusion of a premium of some sort. A second possibility is the assortment — five or six kinds of soups, cake mixes, beverages, spices, or baby food. A third possibility is the ensemble of complementary products, shave cream, lotion, and powder; frankfurters and rolls; spaghetti and sauce. Combination packages are used to introduce new products, to increase the unit of sale, to make a bid for gift buying, to spur impulse buying, to provide more consumer convenience, and to supply retailers with larger display units.

Family Resemblance

The issue of whether a manufacturer's packages should be designed to look alike is similar in many respects to the question in Chapter 5 about individual brand names versus blanket brand names. The advocates of resemblance stress the prestige of the line, cross promotion, harmonious appearance in the store and in the home, and the ease of adding new products. Within family resemblance, of course, there must be some package individuality for identification in buying and using. Persons opposed to resemblance feel that retailers are inclined to favor and feature individualized packages. They fear resemblance between products of different qualities. They see each package as losing its own personality. They wonder whether the

Family resemblance in packaging. Note how the design provides visibility. (Courtesy: Container Corporation of America)

amount of space occupied by a group of look-alike packages may cause the retailer to ask himself if he is playing favorites — if his buying is too concentrated. Color, layout, shape, and typography are among the devices used to achieve family resemblance among packages.

Gift Packages

Some manufacturers package part of their merchandise in gift packages for such occasions as Valentine Day, Mother's Day, and Christmas. Consumers are attracted by gift packages, and retailers get behind them so as not to be caught with a heavy stock of Valentine boxed candy, for example, on February 15. Gift packages can be completely different from the regular package. For the completely different gift packages which do not sell during the special season, some manufacturers accept returns, and some retailers sell the packages at cut prices, often to employees and friends. In order to reduce the loss due to the non-sale of special packages, some producers use a gift wrapper, band, or sleeve slipped over the regular package, and, if that unit remains unsold, the wrapper can be removed and discarded after the special day.

Package Change

There comes a time in the life of just about every package when an overhaul job is indicated. When sales slump, when the package begins to look "dated," when competitors modernize their packages, when a manufacturer decides to enter a new market (electric shavers and the feminine market or deodorants and the masculine market), when a product formerly white begins to be made in four separate colors, when new materials or new processes widen the range of the manufacturer's packaging choices, when two companies merge — these may call for package change. The purpose in almost 100 per cent of the cases is *to increase sales*.

Because *any* package change will be puzzling to some users of the product, and because any change causes some immediate increase in expenses, and because retailers are inconvenienced thereby, changes must not be made too often. When they *are* made, the overwhelming recommendation is for doing the complete change in one step. Single step change maximizes the interest and impact which accompany and follow change. The boldness, the decisiveness of the all-in-one change stimulates consumers, retailers, and the manufacturer's own salesmen. Often the change supplies the advertising agency with a theme for a campaign. In practically every change, some identification features or elements should be carried over and retained in the new package for the sake of continuity.

The execution of a package change calls for superb timing. There must be a minimum of "out of stock" time on the part of retailers. What about old stock? Keeping the manufacturer's salesforce and middlemen informed during the planning of the change is most helpful. Sometimes heavy stocks in some stores can be transferred to other stores in an equalization move.

GRADE LABELING VERSUS INFORMATIVE LABELING

When manufacturers are considering what to tell consumers from the surfaces of their packages, a fundamental question involves the difference between informative labeling and grade labeling. Informative labeling tells the consumer in the manufacturer's own words what the consumer wants to know or needs to know about the product. There *is* room for selling copy within the area of informative labeling.

Grade labeling uses some designations or systems (A-B-C, or 1-2-3, or First-Second-Third) to indicate the comparative quality, performance, utility, and desirability of products. An individual seller, either manufacturer or retailer, can use grade labeling for his merchandise and some, of course, do. Advocates of grade labeling, however, almost to a man have in mind *compulsory* grade labeling — for all consumer products in interstate commerce — according to standards established by the federal government — with grading done by federal employees. Those advocates want to have *grade*-marks added to *trade*-marks.

Advantages Claimed

Several arguments are advanced by those who swear by grade labeling. One is that grade labeling enables the consumer to compare and judge products easily, quickly, and accurately, the result being that the consumer does a better job of buying. Informative labels, it is held, are biased. Because they do not use the same terms, informative labels do not communicate to consumers in a single, standardized manner. Is the top grade *fancy* or *choice* — is it *select* or *prime?* Another point made is that many products and their packages are too small physically to hold the information essential for most satisfactory purchase and consumption. The simplicity and clarity of grade labeling are stressed; even an ignorant, inexpert individual understands how it works. And, in case you are concerned about advertising, there is still plenty of room for the makers of superior A-grade products (in contrast to *minimum* A-grade products) to advertise their higher quality.

Disadvantages Claimed

Those who swear *at* grade labeling usually lead off by observing that different consumers buy the same product for different reasons and for different uses; thus, they assign different weights to the same product features or characteristics. A

Identifying the Product

single set of standards, then, is not universally accepted in any one market, much less nationwide. A second point is that many decisions would be arbitrary in setting up standards to measure the usefulness or desirability of *each grade*. What flavor is B — and what C? Which aroma is A — and which B? Is it fair for 89 to be B and both 91 and 99 A? What about personal tastes not measurable by physical testing?

Some opponents fear what they think grade labeling will do to products. They see it discouraging product improvement because, they believe, pressure will develop for standardized products at the lowest points within each grade. Revision of standards upward could become a most difficult and resisted move. Inertia would oppose product change — yet products are changing constantly. What can be done when a manufacturer of a product graded A brings out a model much superior to his present one? Are both Cadillac and Chevrolet eligible for A rating? What about the A product which deteriorates to grade B while on the retailer's shelf?

Then there is the argument that the integrity of the grading process would be difficult to protect. There's the recognition that the administration, continuous inspection, operation, and enforcement of the program would be costly. There is the whisper that the whole idea is socialistic and contrary to our concept of free enterprise.

Opponents also observe that few products other than foods and drugs are suitable for grade labeling — that houses, consumer services, and fashion goods, for example, defy grade labeling. And, as food and drug products already are closely supervised, there really seems to be no need for grade labeling.

PACKAGE INSERTS

Package inserts can take many forms. They can be leaflets, samples, folders, decals, booklets, coupons, pictures, premiums, or mailing cards, to mention a few possibilities. As the term suggests, they are usually placed inside the package, sometimes inside the outer container, sometimes inside the dispensing or using container. Originally used to make a better, tighter fit between product and package, the package insert now is assigned promotion duties, and copy for the insert is properly the responsibility of the Sales Promotion department.

Advantages

The merits of the package insert are numerous. They are economical to manufacture, to enclose, and to deliver; indeed, the physical distribution of the insert usually costs the advertiser nothing. The insert is a most versatile item. It enjoys a minimum of waste circulation. Its circulation, furthermore, is of high quality because it tells its story to a customer who bought the product not long ago and it often tells the story just when that customer is ready to use the product.

Problems

There is some risk of damage to certain types of inserts in the consumer's opening of the package. There is the problem of the consumer's not noticing or even of

Packaging

his ignoring the insert. The small size of some inserts is a handicap. Finally, no insert can be included which will impair the quality of any product it touches, nor must the consumer *think* that it does.

Uses

Samples of some uses of package inserts are:

Recipes	Directions for use of product
List of product benefits	Offer or request testimonials
Description of other products of seller	Explanation of seller's guarantee or service policy
Announcement of contest	
List of product uses	Information about company
Explanation of recent changes in product, package, or price	Warning insert to tell of low supply
	Invitation to radio or TV show
Samples or premiums	Offer of literature
Coupons	Offer of samples or premiums
Thank you note	Items for children to collect and exchange

Questions and Problems

1. Draft a check list in the form of questions which manufacturers could use when analyzing and evaluating a proposed modernization of a product's package.
2. If you asked a representative group of housewives what features they want in packages, what might they tell you?
3. List some causes of package change.
4. Comment on the cost of a product's package.
5. Comment on the sales power of dual-use packages.
6. How does nature of product affect design of the package?
7. A manufacturer makes sweaters and swimsuits. Should his packages look alike? Comment.
8. Housewives deliberately go to food stores to make certain planned and specific purchases. While there, they often make certain unplanned, impulse-type purchases; good packaging can encourage this type of purchase. List some products which might rank high on a list of impulse-bought items.
9. A manufacturer's shirts of the same size and type retail for $3.95, $4.95, and $6.95. A mail-order firm offers the same size of automobile tire at $21.89, $16.84, and $13.74. Do you see a relationship to grade labeling?
10. A food manufacturer decides to launch a high-price, high-quality line of food specialties. These are to come from all over the world, and each item is to be of the highest quality. Fruits, soups, seafoods, and desserts are typical of the delicacies to be in the line. Prestige products of this sort have small market potential and low turnover; consequently, they need high markups and outstanding packaging. What features should the manufacturer incorporate into the packages of this luxury line?

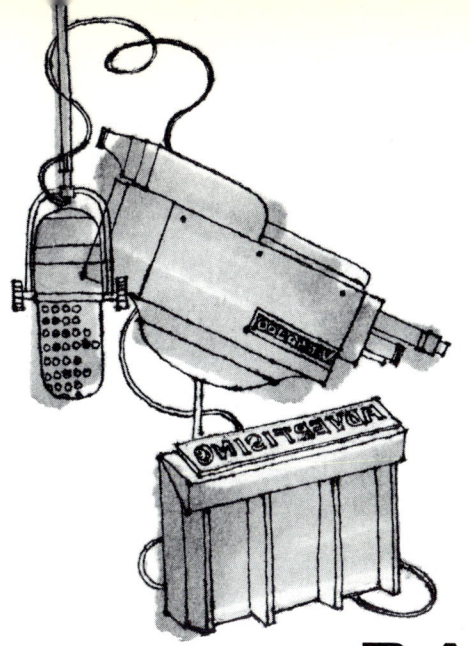

PART FOUR

Building the Advertisement

Now that we have looked at marketing fundamentals, at background for advertising, and at product identification, we are ready to take up the building of an advertisement. So it is appropriate that this overview deal with *communication*. Unless an advertisement communicates, it cannot succeed.

THE COMMUNICATION PROCESS

Communicators are persons or firms which have something they want to say to certain other persons or firms. Their communication starts with an idea, a concept, or a thought which is the essence or substance of the communicator's message. The communicator translates this message into symbolic forms (words, illustrations, and such) and sends it to the individuals he wants to reach. These individuals, the communicator hopes, will receive the symbols and from them reconstruct in their minds the original idea and message of the communicator. Furthermore, the communicator hopes these individuals will react favorably to his message. Communication, thus, consists in large part of sending, receiving, and responding. Whether or

Building the Advertisement

not it succeeds in achieving a transfer of meaning depends on the encoding job the sender does and on the decoding job the receiver does.

Communication Symbols

Words are the most familiar tool or type of symbol employed by communicators; the use of words is the normal way of communicating, the first method communicators consider. *Spoken* words are influenced by the quality and volume of voice, tone, pitch, speed of delivery, and the timing of pauses. When the speaker can be seen, his facial expressions, gestures, movement, manner, and appearance are elements in his communicating. In the use of *written* words, choice of words and composition of phrases and sentences are important. Color, typography, and the use of white space are other considerations.

Illustrations are used to communicate. Everyone has heard the old claim that "one picture is worth a thousand words"; interestingly, this concept had to be expressed in the scorned symbol — in seven of them. Illustrations are generally divided into two classifications, photographs and drawings.

Numbers are a third type of symbol communicators use. Just about all numbers are clear and finite; they are commonly used to denote sizes and prices, quantities and values.

Forms and *shapes* can communicate. They can be abstract, or they can be the well known triangle, star, circle, spiral, and rectangle.

Finally, *sound, sound effects,* even *silence* are communication symbols.

Communicators' Objectives

The purposes of communicators are numerous and varied. Here are some examples:

To buy	To teach	To clarify	To compliment
To sell	To learn	To confuse	To criticize
To inform	To send information to buyers		To cause
To misinform	To get information from buyers		To prevent
To reveal	To affirm		To feature sellers
To conceal	To deny		To feature buyers

To influence, persuade, motivate, or actuate

One-Way vs. Two-Way Communication

In *one*-way communication, as the term suggests, the sender tells or reports, informs or suggests. The flow is one-directional; the sender feeds material to the receiver.

In *two*-way communication, there is an exchange of ideas, information, or convictions; there is a sharing of concepts. In contrast to one-way communication, we now see action *and* reaction, stimulus *and* response, feeding *and* feedback. Here the sender sends and receives back, the receiver receives and sends.

Building the Advertisement

ADVERTISING AS COMMUNICATION

Advertisers are sellers of goods or services who choose to include advertising, a form of mass communication, in their promotional mixes. These sellers elect to *communicate* to customers and prospective customers — to the buyers who constitute their markets — *through advertising*. A major responsibility on the advertiser is to know all he should about those buyers, including, of course, what his product or service will do for them. Another responsibility which a seller must meet before he advertises involves doing everything he can both to deserve and get the trust and confidence of buyers. A buyer is not inclined to read, to listen to, or to accept an advertiser's promises and recommendations unless the buyer trusts the advertiser. The same buyer is more likely to believe the same communication from an advertiser he considers trustworthy than from an advertiser he considers questionable.

Advertising as communication will now be considered in five sections: Objectives, Construction, Transmittal, Reception, and Response.

Objectives

Every advertisement should have an objective; every advertising effort or program should have an objective; and these objectives should be just as specific as possible. As he works toward the establishing of specific goals, the advertiser finds himself refining and clarifying his thoughts. This is desirable because the clearer his message is to him, the better chance he has of making it clear to buyers; only clear negatives make clear photographs.

What does an advertiser want his advertisements to do? (A) Sometimes *attitudes* are involved. In certain cases, the advertiser wants buyers to receive and approve an idea, to begin to accept a certain assumption or hold a certain conviction, to adopt a certain attitude. For example, the idea might be that of heating a house with electricity. In the case of opinionated buyers, the advertiser wants to change the attitude of buyers who assume that houses should be heated with oil or gas, or to strengthen and reinforce the attitude of buyers who are already sold on electricity. (B) Sometimes, *action* is involved. The advertiser may, for example, want prospective buyers to request literature from an electrical manufacturer, or to register for a prize at local electrical appliance stores.

There are occasions when an advertiser must try to gain a short-run, intermediate goal in order to gain his long-run, ultimate goal. For example, his advertising may have to interest buyers and inform them if, later, his advertising is to convert prospective customers into actual customers. Care should be taken to see that immediate goals are compatible with ultimate goals. For example, a retailer noted for his high quality, high prices, and high prestige could not justify his running a bargain-type, clearance-type advertisement no matter how overstocked he is at the moment.

Construction

What an advertiser actually communicates to buyers is a message. The heart of an advertising message is an idea, and the form of the message is a promise of some

Building the Advertisement

satisfaction buyers want. The selection of the idea on which to build the message is a most important step. Why? Advertising simply will not work unless it promises buyers something buyers want or can be persuaded to want. Most advertising that is read is read in the hope of reward.

Encoding. Once the advertiser has selected the right idea and promise to communicate, his next job is that of composing the communication, of expressing the idea and promise in symbols. This is the process of *encoding*.

Symbols available to advertisers are those already listed as used by communicators: words, illustrations, numbers, forms and shapes, sounds and sound effects. If the buyer is actually to read the substance of what the advertiser wrote, if the buyer is actually to hear the essence of what the advertiser said, the encoding must be done with great skill.

Symbols must be *suitable*. They must be appropriate for the advertiser's objective and for the medium of transition (newspapers, television); they must be in character with the advertiser himself and with the product or service he is advertising. Above all, they must be suitable as regards the buyers the advertiser wants to reach. They must be symbols the buyers know, use, prefer, familiar symbols with meaning and relevance to those buyers. They must be suitable by being clear and simple, neither irritating by "talking down" nor disgusting by "talking up."

Symbols must be *harmonious*. Within each advertisement, symbols must blend; words and illustrations, color, layout, and type, all must be in harmony.

Problem of Meaning. We dare not omit reference to semantics and meaning. Semantics is the science which deals with the meaning, uses, and effects of words. As has been implied, genuine communication takes place only if the meaning of the message *to the buyer* is the same as the meaning of the message *to the advertiser*. If the two meanings are identical, there is understanding, otherwise, misunderstanding.

In an effort to achieve a transfer of meaning, some advertisers intentionally build communications of words which can be understood by the least educated segment of the buyer-group addressed. Other advertisers take the calculated risk of using a few longer, less common words in order to give their advertisements verve or élan.

Bulk, length, or volume of message bears on this matter of meaning. If the amount is excessive, the large quantity discourages or even repels buyers, reducing the amount of buyer-understanding and buyer-acceptance. Because so many buyers know so little about the subjects of so many advertisements, many advertisers try to observe the limit of *only one idea* per advertisement.

Transmittal

Sellers pay advertising media to deliver sellers' advertising. These vehicles or carriers are independent and commercial; major ones are newspapers, magazines, television, radio, outdoor, and transit. Car cards, incidentally, are the major form of transit advertising.

Building the Advertisement

Two concepts are involved here. First, there is the advertiser's market. This is the group of buyers he wants his advertising communication to reach. Second, there is the concept of a medium's circulation. Each advertiser would prefer that his message be delivered to every buyer who is a customer, a prospective customer, or a buying influence. Obviously, there is little or no reason for the advertiser to want anyone else to get the message; other individuals would do him little or no additional good. One feature of the ideal medium, therefore, is a circulation which consists of everyone the advertiser wants to reach, and no one else.

After checking out the circulation/market matter, the advertiser asks about the suitability and probable effectiveness of various media as regards his product, his objectives, his message. These he weighs in the light of costs.

Very briefly, we note that there are *space* media consisting of newspapers, magazines, outdoor, and transit. There is a *time* medium, radio. Television is a *space-and-time* medium. The features of these six will be examined in our section on media.

Reception

Reception is the translating, the unscrambling phase of the communication process. Here it is that buyers *decode* what the advertiser encoded when he was constructing his advertising message. That is, decoding *can* take place as the advertiser planned and hoped. Three considerations are critical at this point; one involves *attention,* one involves *meaning,* the third involves *acceptance.*

Internal Difficulties in Getting Attention. Many personal matters bid for a buyer's *attention.* If a buyer is in deep thought about clothes, money, travel, assignments, guilt, games, examinations, social activities, automobiles, he cannot be receiving much of an advertising communication. Insufficiency of time forces you and all other buyers to be selective, *highly* selective, about what you read and watch and listen to, because no buyer can attend to all the advertising aimed at him or her. Buyer-attention has great influence over buyer-action because buyer-attention selects the stimuli to which the buyer exposes himself. As soon as one matter captures a buyer's attention, the other matters clamoring for that same attention fade.

A buyer's emotional state can block attention. Because logic and proved facts are not enough, because logic and facts can be subordinated to feeling and sentiment, smart advertisers try to reach buyers' emotions. In attending, then in learning, and finally in remembering, emotions play a significant role. There is much truth in the claims that we do not question what we want to hear, that we do not hear what we do not want to hear.

At the moment an advertising communication reaches a buyer, he is always in *some* frame of mind; he always has *some* feelings, hopes, fears, and concerns of the moment; he is already in *some* mood. In addition, some buyers hate the advertiser, others love him; some have never heard of his brand, others have used it with complete satisfaction for years. No advertiser knows how many buyers are in each of how many groups at the moment his advertising message reaches them. So an advertiser may use the first stage or phase of his advertisement (headlines, illustrations,

Building the Advertisement

sound effects) in an effort to pre-condition the total buyer group, to unify their moods and frames of mind, to prepare buyers, to encourage certain specific expectations.

External Difficulties in Getting Attention. The advertiser finds himself plagued by external competition as he attempts to capture buyers' attention. Noises, movement, and, occasionally, odors may have effective hold of that attention, or they may intrude and interrupt when the advertiser does have control. Defects in printing or in broadcasting reduce buyers' attention. Red lights, sirens, and traffic conditions affect a motorist's attention. A magazine advertisement may lose out to a television commercial, to a cartoon in the magazine, even to another advertisement in the magazine.

The Problem of Meaning. Our second critical consideration involves *meaning*. It is the advertiser's intent that buyers get the same meaning when decoding an advertising message that the advertiser encoded into the message. Success depends, of course, on whether the buyer interprets the symbols which constitute the advertisement as did the advertiser. So many, many symbols are subject to personal, individual interpretation. Suppose a voice over the radio says to you, "Picture a parent and child seated on a bench in the park." What did *you* "see"? A father and son? A father and daughter? A mother and daughter? A mother and son?

The Problem of Acceptance. Seeing and hearing are not enough. Even grasping and understanding the advertiser's message are not enough. There is not enough to satisfy the advertiser until the buyer *believes* and *accepts* what the advertiser communicated.

A buyer is the product of his own heredity, environment, and experience. He has his own unique assortment of wants and fears, habits and frustrations, prejudices and loyalties, anxieties and goals, dislikes and values. All these considerations, and others, too, influence what a buyer approves and accepts; they influence the two matters of greatest interest to advertisers — the buyer's attitudes and actions.

If the correct meaning of an advertising message is to be accepted, the meaning must be within the buyer's experience and capabilities, within his personal worlds, both physical and mental. The meaning must be relevant to the buyer's desires and compatible with his experience, circumstances, and convictions. It must be in line with his likes and dislikes, with his assumptions and feelings. It must not ask the buyer to be inconsistent with or to violate his own set of values. Words and illustrations must be realistic, believable, true to life. The advertiser should promise no more than the buyer believes the product or service should deliver; the advertiser should firmly avoid exaggeration, extreme claims, and sly distortion of fact. Truth is true only to the extent that buyers understand *and accept*.

Response

Advertising is *commercial* communication; it is a promotional expense a seller elects to incur. The advertiser expects to recover his advertising costs as a result of

Building the Advertisement

the additional sales volume caused by his advertising. He expects his net profit in dollars to be greater than it otherwise would be, greater because he decided to spend some money in advertising. So advertising is asked, is expected to stimulate buyers to respond, to react favorably toward the advertiser. Indeed, advertising which gets no favorable reaction from buyers represents waste for the most part. The seller's profit figure would have been better off without it.

Three Steps Toward Response. Briefly, let's review the three steps which precede response.

1. The buyer must give attention to the advertisement and receive it. Remember, if the message is incompatible with his opinions and assumptions, if the message is uninteresting or promises no reward, then the buyer avoids or rejects it.

2. The buyer must understand the advertiser's message and its meaning. Once again, remember that many factors influence what a buyer perceives.

3. The buyer must believe and agree with the substance of the message. He identifies the advertiser as a friend who understands the buyer, as one who wants to help the buyer to greater personal satisfaction. He finds himself becoming personally involved in the advertiser's promises. He begins to feel the need to do something. Both as an individual and as a member of various groups, he considers the course of action recommended by the advertiser as realistic, appropriate, and acceptable. He is now ready to respond.

The Buyer's Reaction. An advertisement is not nearly so much a seller's saying something as it is a stimulus which gets a buyer to do the advertiser's wish. As was implied in the section on Objectives, buyers can make advertisers happy in two ways. (A) A buyer can adopt a new attitude, one favorable toward the advertiser; he can replace a hostile attitude with a friendly attitude; or he can renew, reaffirm, and reinforce a favorable attitude already held. All three versions of attitude-response encourage subsequent purchases. (B) A buyer can do something physical, he can take overt action favorable toward the advertiser. Making a telephone call, mailing a coupon, or scheduling on his calendar a visit to a retail store are examples.

Reaction by the buyer can extend over quite a period of time. He can start by becoming vaguely conscious of the advertiser or his brand. Because the advertiser is given only a limited amount of attention, he is able to convey only a limited amount of information. As the advertiser continues to talk, in advertisement after advertisement, about the buyer's problems and fears, his goals and dreams, the buyer shows a degree of interest. The buyer gives the messages more thought because he has become a bit curious about the advertiser's intent. Feelings of personal identification, involvement, and need begin to develop. The buyer gives the advertiser's suggestion serious thought, consideration, and evaluation; he wonders just how he would make out *if* he did what the advertiser recommends. In an approval of the advertiser's proposal, the buyer decides to do the advertiser's request. The buyer acts, often on a limited scale if that is possible. In a "happy ending," the buyer replaces any limited commitment with unqualified indefinite cooperation and patronage.

Building the Advertisement

Do remember that advertising is *mass* communication. The mass consists of a group of buyers, a number of individuals. Each is just that, an individual. There are, to be sure, similarities which tend to unify the group. The big unifier is the fact that all are prospective customers of the advertiser. In similar fashion, however, there are differences among the buyers. What does this mean? It means that thousands of consumers can read the same magazine advertisement or see the same television commercial, but not all respond in the same way. Response to the advertiser's suggestion can range all the way from hostile irritation to instant and enthusiastic compliance.

Chapter 7

Benefits Which Appeal to Buyers

Having looked at marketing fundamentals, at the background for advertising and at the advertiser's identification devices, we are now ready to find out how an advertisement is built. Four chapters comprise this section. In the first, we investigate the heart of every advertisement — the benefits promised to buyers of the advertised product. The second chapter of the four deals with the advertisement's illustration and layout; the third takes up copy and copy writing; the final chapter of the four sees the copy set in type and the advertisement printed, perhaps in color.

The successful advertisement gets the attention of the individuals it hopes to influence, makes those individuals want to read the copy, and then makes them want the product advertised. Success depends on how effective the advertisement is in getting attention, arousing interest, stimulating desire, achieving conviction, and then inducing action — all on the part of buyers.

PART I — THE ROLE OF BENEFITS

An Advertisement's Goals

Attention. The first goal of an advertisement is that of stopping or alerting the maximum number of prospects. Who is a prospect? Anyone who will benefit (or at least has a strong probability of benefiting) from buying the product or service being advertised. The advertiser's great eagerness for the attention of all prospects should be matched by his small interest in the attention of non-prospects. Advertisers of girdles stand to benefit little or none from masculine readership; advertising of very expensive homes cannot benefit consumers who cannot afford them — nor benefit from their readership. So, the attention sought is that of *prospects,* not of everybody.

An advertisement easy to understand makes each prospect feel that he is being addressed almost personally. This result is best achieved by presenting a beneficial, powerful, distinctive idea so that the prospect grasps it at a glance. Such an outstanding idea is necessary because of the intense competition for consumers' attention and time. The typical consumer does not read more than half a dozen adver-

Building the Advertisement

tisements in a magazine, nor does he spend over ten or twelve minutes on his daily newspaper. The instantaneous impact and stopping power must be great in order to get the consumer to decide to notice an advertisement.

Attention has quality as well as quantity. Because these characteristics are, by nature, hostile toward each other, few advertisements attract large amounts of both. Since the mere getting of consumer attention is not a difficult problem, advertisers are often tempted to use universal attention-getters or even freak attention-getters so as to score high on quantity. Such tactics are harmful when the attention-getting devices are not relevant; they distract consumers. Knowing this, smart *food* advertisers, for example, build their advertisements to show and tell about *food*.

Interest. Having attracted the attention of the maximum number of prospects, the advertisement's next goal is to convert as much of that attention as possible into interest. It is obvious that interest itself is a type of attention. If the first goal is thought of as eye or visual attention, the second goal, interest, can be thought of as mental or emotional attention. The only true and ultimate interest of concern to advertisers is the consumer's interest in what the advertised product will do to and for him. In some instances, certain advertisers must first attract consumers' attention to wants, problems, or situations of general human appeal so as to achieve readership, but, as quickly as possible, they then transform *this* type of interest into the basic type just mentioned.

When does a prospect begin to be interested? When he begins to relate in his own thinking his personal needs and the advertised product. His interest becomes serious when he adds to these two considerations a third, the product's price. To arouse this serious interest, an advertisement must be built around matters of interest to buyers — of vital interest, if possible. Men are interested in sports and automobiles; women are interested in food and housekeeping; both groups are interested in family, people, and news. All consumers have hopes and problems, possessions and accomplishments. All are interested in getting what they want; all are interested in themselves.

Desire. Most advertisements make a serious attempt to gain this third goal, consumer desire. From the prospect's point of view, this stage is the one in which he begins to want the product, to think of the product as perhaps *the* answer to one of his needs or wants. Often an advertisement will either establish a need or want, or remind the consumer of one, before recommending the advertised product as the answer.

Desire is fanned by promises of benefits and advantages. In choosing the satisfactions to promise, the wise advertiser is guided by the *prospects'* desires — not by the advertiser's own desires, nor by what he *thinks* prospects desire, nor by what he thinks prospects *should* desire.

Conviction. In the conviction phase, the prospect accepts the seller's recommendations, he admits he should buy, he decides to buy. The prospect concludes that the seller's promises of satisfaction are well founded and, hence, trustworthy; he reassures himself of his own ability to benefit from a purchase. The price of the product appears less than the amount of satisfaction the product will deliver. The seller has proved his claims, thereby making the prospect confident of his decision.

Only the direct-action advertisements must work seriously at attaining this goal of conviction; they, of course, have no option but to attempt to get both conviction and the fifth goal, action. Few indirect-action advertisements undertake to do the entire job of conviction; instead, they rely on salesmen and personal selling for a healthy bit of assistance.

Action. Although all advertisements want, in some sense, a response by the prospect, only the direct-action ones want reaction that is overt, immediate, and specific. Eventually, the only action satisfactory to advertisers is a purchase. Most indirect-action advertisements will settle at the moment of reading for a favorable mental or emotional reaction.

Product Features Versus Buyer Benefits

Product Features. Persons who build profitable advertisements know and respect the basic differences between product features and buyer benefits. Product features are elements or qualities (a) of a product or (b) of the seller's proposition which can contribute to consumer satisfaction. The (a) group consists of what the product *is* or *has* — raw materials, manufacturing processes, workmanship, grades, colors, models, sizes, special ingredients, patented parts, the product's package — even the product's price. The (b) group consists of what the seller does or offers — credit, delivery, service, or guarantee.

Advertisers are continuously in search of *unique* product features because of the resulting competitive advantages. But, sad to state, there just aren't many such features. Both product research and buyer research are employed in the hopes of discovering important product features.

The most common use of product feature material is that of support or proof for the benefits promised and the advantages claimed. Indeed, there seems to be no excuse for mentioning any product feature which fails to translate into some type of consumer satisfaction. To stress a product feature as a complete or adequate reason for buying is seldom an effective tactic.

Buyer Benefits. What buyers are really interested in, what they actually buy, are not product features; *buyers buy benefits.* (Don't *you?*) Buyer benefits are the satisfactions a product delivers. They stem from what the product delivers. They stem from what the product or the seller does for the buyer or gives to the buyer. Any particular buyer benefit may be available from any brand or from any seller — or only from one specific brand or one individual seller.

The difference between product features and buyer benefits and the relationship between them is of great importance. *Benefits* are advantages, gains, or utilities which satisfy human desires — they are what buyers buy. Benefits originate in, come from, and are possible only because of product *features.* Benefits are the effects of features; features are the causes of benefits. Because a pair of shoes is made as it is, the shoes deliver to the buyer the satisfactions of appearance, comfort,

How to hold down a neat white collar job. It's a snap!

It's a Tabber-Snap, to be exact—Arrow's ingenious, quick-closing, sure-closing way to fasten down a neat tab collar. And that's just the beginning. Arrow has done a neat job all the way on this Paddock Club shirt. Consider the fabric: a silky-smooth broadcloth made of the finest long-staple cotton.

Note the appearance. Precise Arrow tailoring follows natural lines for perfect fit. And the Paddock Club will always stay that way. Reason? It's "Sanforized" labeled. You don't have to be a big spender to pick up this tab. It's only $0. Also available in colors, stripes and checks. Arrow silk tie, $0.00.

Wherever you go 🏹 you look better in —*ARROW*—

Good appearance is promised here with a somewhat light touch. (Courtesy: The Arrow Company)

and economy. Because of its construction and features, an automobile delivers pride, protection, pleasure, economy, utility, and comfort.

For the builder of an advertisement to be careless in his handling of product features and buyer benefits is a gross, inexcusable mistake. If he fails to separate one group from the other, if he uses features and benefits interchangeably, his guilt is great. Confused thinking about features and benefits instead of clear thinking explains one of the wastes in current advertising, namely the stressing of product features as such. It is a fact, of course, that the features of a few selected products rate high in consumer interest. This is true of the new automobile models, of fashion apparel, and, to a degree, of home appliances and some food products. For the great majority of consumer products, however, product features are weak in getting the attention, readership, and purchases of consumers. The most basic rule there is in all advertising is that the consumer is not interested in products or in sellers — he is interested only in what products and sellers will do *for him*.

Consumer Motivation

Nature of Motivation. A consumer's motivation is the mechanism which controls his behavior, including his buying. Motivation is the key to behavior, the explanation of why consumers spend their dollars as they do. Motivation includes those influences, attitudes, and considerations which determine consumer choice and cause consumer action. Motivation is reflected in an inside urge, an inadequacy which asks for corrective steps, an emptiness which demands to be filled, a problem which asks a solution. The consumer wants — then satisfies that want.

Motivation is an individual matter. Each consumer, selfish and self-centered, sets up his own goals and values, his own targets and aspirations. Each decides, subject to his limitations, what he wants from life and then pays life's prices for those particular satisfactions. Almost any student can be the best dancer or the best bridge player in his group — if he will pay the price. More students than do would make straight A's — if the price were not so high. Each consumer determines which benefits and advantages he wants to enjoy personally, then he reads those advertisements and buys those products which promise those chosen satisfactions. The skeptical, selfish questions each consumer hurls at advertisements and sellers are: "What will your product do for *me?* What do *I* get out of the deal?"

Motivation and Buying. His motivation sends each consumer off on a shopping search for whatever assortment of satisfactions he has decided are desirable. All voluntary purchases are made solely in response to this motivation. Directed purchases as, for example, that of a textbook required in a certain course, are not, of course, subject to this control. Any time a consumer buys product "A" for $5, he automatically implies (a) that he sees more personal satisfaction in "A" than in "B," or "D," each costing $5, and (b) that he prefers product "A" in his possession rather than the $5. Each consumer decides for himself the types and amounts of satisfaction each product delivers. Advertisers seek to identify those causes of this consumer's decision to buy "A" *which they can influence.* Advertisers gain their objectives by helping consumers gain theirs.

Building the Advertisement

Logical reasons even when presented skillfully seldom stimulate the consumer's urge to buy. The consumer is, after all, a strange and challenging person. He prefers to be contented rather than logical, he prefers products which make him look and feel good rather than products whose purchase he can defend coldly, scientifically, objectively, unemotionally. The consumer rationalizes certain of his purchases, justifying them on grounds other than those which actually caused the purchases. Many of today's purchases are made mainly because of habit; what influences led to the initial buying decision have been long forgotten. Advertisers hope, understandably, that first purchases will be happy experiences, that the gratification enjoyed will recommend that the consumer repeat the experience, that a buying habit will become established.

Motivation is complex. The typical consumer prefers to live in a state of psychological equilibrium, but he finds this equilibrium threatened and even upset by various types of influence, some internal and some external. For example, these influences can be physiological, psychological, social, cultural, spiritual, moral, political, or economic. Influences from these areas can disturb a consumer's equilibrium, causing drives or tensions. Advertising is one of these influences. Every drive is related to other drives; some drives clash with and compete against other drives. The consumer acts to relieve or reduce his most insistent tensions. The advertiser hopes, of course, that the action engaged in will be a purchase of the advertiser's product.

The consumer carries around at all times a "self image," idealized, of course. When he contemplates buying, the consumer feels inclined to buy products, brands, and services which are in harmony with his image of himself; he wants his purchases to qualify for *self* approval.

Variations in Motivation. The advertiser's undertaking is complicated by the fact that motivation varies from consumer to consumer and even, from time to time, within the same individual. Consumers differ in training and experience, in capabilities, education, and personality. These differences affect motivation. Environment of a geographical, social, or cultural sort is a variable. Then, consumers differ in respect to the intensity or strength of various motives and to the combinations of motives which are responsible for so many purchases.

The motivation pattern within a single individual is subject to change. As his age increases, the consumer sees certain motives decline in influence while others become more urgent. Season of year and stage of businss cycle are a pair of influences; at Christmas time gift buying joins buying for personal consumption, and when times get bad, economy and durability may replace approval and pride. Change in a person's marital or family status usually effects changes in his motivation. Immediate circumstances, perhaps involving need, or health, or purchasing power, can change drastically and quickly.

Social Groups and Stratification

The consumer is more than an individual seeking self approval. He is also a member of various small groups, and he is included in whatever social class he happens to be in. He wants to be noticed and accepted in good standing. He wants group and class approval in addition to self approval.

Groups. The typical consumer has family, friends, neighbors, and associates. He may well belong to a number of organizations — religious, professional, fraternal, social, business, civic, or athletic. His attitudes are influenced by these small groups, and his attitudes, as we have noted, are of great interest to advertisers.

Social Classes. Most sociological studies of consumers stratify consumers into five ranks or levels. In looking from top to bottom, one cannot escape an implication of status, of superior and inferior, of upper and lower. The top class is often termed the "upper" class and contains "old" families with wealth, certain business and professional folks, and a high proportion of college graduates. Next is the "upper-middle" or semi-upper class. Here again are many college graduates, also small business men and certain professional men. Third is the "lower-middle" group. Many of these are high school graduates, some are blue-collar workers, some are self-employed, some are small merchants. Fourth is the "upper-lower" or working class. This level is made up of clerical workers and skilled wage earners; it is by far the largest of the five groups. Some of these in the fourth class are high school graduates. The fifth and bottom position is occupied by the "lower-lower" group. Here are the unskilled workers who must spend just about all they make for basic necessities. Grammar school education is common.

What determines which social level one occupies? Financial ability to buy is one important influence, but no longer is it thought to be the *sole* determinant. Amount of income and the source of that income are two phases of ability to buy. Occupation is another important influence. Education, too, is a significant influence. Three other determinants sometimes mentioned are type of dwelling occupied, neighborhood, and number of generations of United States ancestry.

Effects on Buying Behavior. Small groups and social classes affect consumers' buying decisions through their effects on consumers' views, opinions, and tastes. The consumer feels pressure to identify himself with the attitudes and the values of his groups and of his class. He feels pressure to conform. He accepts and adopts group and class judgments about how to reduce his tensions; purchases are one approach to the reduction of tensions.

The typical consumer tends to save and to spend the same portions of disposable personal income as does his group. His group has arrived at what it considers the most desirable compromise between its desire for many products and services and its desire for many dollars. Our consumer tends to adopt this group ratio as his personal ratio. Then, when spending the dollars he elects to spend, the consumer feels the influence of his class in deciding *what* to buy and what *not* to buy, which *stores* to patronize and which *not* to patronize. Interestingly, he feels "right" or "correct" with certain products as possessions and "wrong" with others. The price he pays must not be too high for his class nor too low. The consumer feels at home in some stores but clearly out of place, a stranger, an intruder, in others.

Building the Advertisement

Income alone was once thought to dictate social status and to determine buying patterns and decisions. More recently sellers are recognizing that consumer income changes more quickly than do consumer buying habits, that sometimes social status can be a stronger influence than is income. A young medical doctor may earn the same amount of money as a truck driver, but their buying patterns will not be identical. Assistant professors do not buy what carpenters buy, even when they earn as much.

Within any one of the five social classes, then, consumers tend to have the same goals, hopes, attitudes, preferences, and customs. Because their values are the same, persons in each class tend to be alike in respect to taste, and because taste is identical, buying behavior and buying decisions tend to be uniform.

Basic And Acquired Wants

Consumer wants may be separated and classified according to whether they are basic or acquired. Basic wants are almost completely universal within our society; they tend to get more uniform treatment from all individuals than do acquired wants. Basic wants include personal and physical needs, and most of them are either in constant operation or else recur frequently. There is not unanimous agreement as to how many wants are basic. Some claim that there is only one — to keep living as long and as happily as possible. Some believe there are four — shelter and sustenance, sex, security, and superiority. A longer list, more helpful to builders of advertisements, is this:

Food and drink	Sex
Comfort	Safety from pain, fear, danger
Approval	Superiority over others
Welfare of loved ones	Survival
Mastery over obstacles	Play and pleasure

Acquired wants are those we have learned to value and develop. They are secondary wants. A glance at the list below will show that they are not as clearly defined concepts as are the basic wants:

Economy	Convenience
Information	Quality
Cleanliness	Dependability
Efficiency	Beauty
Profit	Fashion
Curiosity	Durability

Many advertisers can present their products as answers to these wants. These advertisers may then feel that their advertising, if it is well done, will be of interest to many consumers, especially if the appeal is made to the basic, more universal, wants. However, an advertiser must not accept lists such as these as more than guideposts or check lists. For each product, consumer research must be carried on to determine the feature of that specific product which is of greatest interest to consumers.

Emotional Versus Rational Motivation

Once it was thought that each purchase made by consumers was either emotional *or* rational in nature, that it was irrational, unstudied, and impulsive, or planned, well thought out, weighed in advance. This older school of thought classified as "emotionally motivated" purchases made for such reasons as pride, sensual satisfaction, fear, curiosity, or sociability. Classified as "rationally motivated" were purchases made for such reasons as durability, efficiency, economy, dependability, or accuracy. Emotional appeals were also known as "short circuit" and "human interest" appeals, rational appeals as "long circuit" and "reason why" appeals.

A more up-to-date, more realistic assumption seems to be that consumers make very few purchases which are 100% emotional *or* 100% rational. These mutually exclusive extremes have been replaced by a scale which ranges from *quite emotional* to *quite sensible*. One quick glance at the emotional-rational dichotomy points up the difficulty of separating the irrational from the rational. If we claim that emotional buying is that in which emotions, feelings, and sentiment are present, then all buying is emotional. If, however, we claim that rational buying is that done to maximize pleasure and satisfaction and to minimize pain and dissatisfaction, then all buying is rational. Just what *is* an emotional purchase, a rational purchase? Is the purchase of a home, an automobile, a college education, a ring, or a suit *all* one or the other?

Because many a purchase is made for emotional-*plus*-rational reasons, we note many an advertisement built to appeal to both types. Such an advertisement can hit hard at an emotional attitude or emotional motive, but then offer proof, logical and objective, to convince and reassure the consumer that the advertiser's recommended course of action will result in consumer satisfaction.

Our conclusion? Let's say that the consumer studies, thinks about, weighs, and analyzes *some* purchases more than other purchases. In most instances, the consumer wants his or her purchases to *appear* to have been made rationally.

Primary Versus Selective Considerations

A seller's potential market can be divided simply into (a) consumers who should use that *type* of product (piano, insurance, electric shaver) but do not, and (b) consumers who should and do. A pioneering job is necessary for the first group because, before one of them buys a brand "BBB" electric shaver, for example, he must earlier have decided to make an almost revolutionary change — to begin shaving with electricity. Because primary promotion and benefits have to do with the kind of class or type of product which is bought, they are often undertaken and supported by trade associations. Primary promotion stresses *what*.

As for the group of consumers already buying the seller's type of product, the indicated job is a selective or competitive one. Where primary promotion stressed *what,* selective promotion stresses *which*. In most situations, *which* is a matter of brands — the Schick electric shaver versus the Norelco electric shaver; occasionally, *which* is a matter of *source, which* manufacturer or *which* retailer. Selective benefits are of little influence or even interest to a consumer until he has been impressed favorably by the primary benefits involved.

Building the Advertisement

Product Versus Patronage Benefits

In Chapter 3 we divided advertising into two broad and basic groupings: product advertising and institutional advertising. Product advertising, we noted, promotes specific, branded products while institutional advertising is designed to cultivate good will. Most institutional advertising is patronage in nature; the advertiser tries to convince buyers that his operation entitles him to the buyer's dollars. Similarly, the advertiser may choose between emphasizing *product benefits* which are the satisfactions enjoyed from the consumption of a specific, branded product or *patronage benefits* which are the satisfactions resulting from the consumer's buying from the specific seller.

These are typical product benefits: design, color, size, package, raw materials, workmanship, patented features. These are typical patronage benefits: merchandise assortment, quality, low prices, location, services, integrity, courtesy.

Positive Versus Negative Appeals

Benefits can be expressed either in a *positive* manner or in a *negative* manner, as experiences and sensations which consumers *want* — or *want to avoid*. The positive approach pictures what the consumer wants to be or have; it describes the attainment of goals inviting and pleasant, the enjoyment of satisfactions sought.

Or, the same basic idea, the same basic benefit, can be presented from the opposite direction. The appeal here is to fear, the negative version of positive benefits. Instead of presenting safety, the advertiser presents fear of danger; instead of comfort, he presents fear of discomfort; instead of pleasure, he presents fear of pain. Instead of stressing what the consumer wants, the negative approach features what the consumer wants to get rid of or avoid. It points up such unpleasantness as loss, risk, embarrassment, mistakes, worries, dangers, and drudgery.

What can be said of the use of negative appeals? Fear is, in itself, a powerful drive. The negative approach can be quite effective in establishing need when the consumer is totally unaware of the fact that he has a problem or suffers from a condition needing correction. If the product is somewhat distasteful, or if the greatest benefit is one of avoidance or correction, then a case can be made for the negative appeal. Graphic, arresting, and vivid, negative appeals can rank high in memory value and distinctiveness.

On the other side of the ledger is the danger that fear, the basis of negative appeals, is often less stimulating to action than is a positive appeal. Another danger is that negative appeals can easily discourage reading interest in the advertisement, much less buying interest in the product. If too depressing or distasteful, a strong negative appeal can cause consumers to refuse to accept the advertiser's message. If the negative appeal is presented in such a manner as to cause consumers to feel scolded or criticized, the resulting irritation, guilt, and general uncertainty can work to the advertiser's harm. Ill will and unpleasant associations are definite possibilities.

The strongest point in favor of positive rather than negative appeals is the consumer's natural and strong preference to identify himself with and to be a part of desirable situations rather than undesirable ones. Positive appeals show what con-

HOW MANY ACRES DOES IT COST TO DIE?

Over the years, your brains and sweat have built a farm. Soil, equipment, and skill have created a productive operation whose yield is good to see. Probably you sit back, now and then, and take pride and comfort from the thought that your family will inherit a thriving concern.

But will they? Can you be sure?

We ask these questions because here at Prudential we've put our sincere efforts into the job of helping farmers *preserve* what they have built. We've found that before the heirs get anything, the bills eat up 20-30% and sometimes up to 50% of the average estate. Money is needed to pay estate and inheritance taxes, property and income taxes, executor's fee, probate costs, the mortgage and other debts. Often there is not enough cash in the estate to pay these bills. When this happens, the choice assets—or part of the farm itself—may have to be sold to raise the needed money within the law's time limit.

Your Prudential Agent can show you the steps to take *now* to provide the money to pay these bills *for* the estate—not *from* the estate—so you can pass along the *whole* farm to your heirs.

Showing you these steps is just one of the jobs your Prudential Agent is equipped to do. He's well trained in all aspects of life insurance, particularly as they relate to farmers. He knows your problems, and he's interested in helping you. Welcome him when he calls.

THE **PRUDENTIAL** INSURANCE COMPANY OF AMERICA
This advertisement appears in FARM JOURNAL and SUCCESSFUL FARMING

The concepts of money, death, and expenses are combined to make a strong appeal. (Courtesy: The Prudential Insurance Company of America)

Building the Advertisement

sumers want to be — not what they are. Few of us enjoy being shown and told what we are. We prefer to think of ourselves as strong rather than weak, as successes rather than failures, as beautiful and alluring rather than ugly and undesirable. The chic, the attractive are more to our liking than the drab, the dowdy. From the very start, positive appeals keep the consumer's attention directed to the satisfaction the consumer wants; the result is a simpler advertisement easier to understand.

There is no single conclusion about positive and negative appeals. Some advertisers have done exceedingly well using negative appeals, proving that the negative can be used to excellent advantage. The negative seems to be of greater potential effect where consumers need to correct, to replace, to cure, or to relieve rather than where the need is to prevent or to avoid. A negative appeal need not result in an advertisement which is 100 per cent negative. The negative illustration may be counterbalanced by the positive headline, or vice versa. The before-and-after format includes both negative and positive values. Advertisers themselves vote overwhelmingly for positive appeals. They feel that, in the majority of cases, the positive is liked better, is remembered longer, and is more effective or appropriate than the negative.

Selecting the Benefits

Reduced to its essentials, an advertisement is the presentation of one or more benefits or advantages which are enjoyed by those who buy and consume the advertised product. How does the builder of an advertisement select the benefit or benefits on which to base his advertisement? Two techniques are mentioned at this point — the check list of consumer wants, and market research. A third possibility, motivation research, is considered in the second part of this chapter.

Check List of Consumer Wants. Step one on this approach calls for the advertiser to get a list of all satisfactions desired by consumers — satisfactions which can be found in and delivered by the advertiser's product. This list can be built from scratch by the advertiser, or it can be derived by getting a general list of universal wants and then striking from that list those satisfactions which the advertiser's product is incapable of providing. This want list needs to be broken down into sub-divisions. To list *economy* is not nearly so helpful as to specify *economical to buy, economical to operate, economical to service, economical to dispose of,* and so forth. Step two checks the various strong points of the product against the list with the objective in mind of pairing up product features with buyer benefits. The advertiser is particularly interested in how *universal* and how *strong* are the wants which pair with his product's most outstanding features.

The check list of consumer wants approach is well worth making. It is speedy, inexpensive, convenient to follow, and challenging. The habit of thinking analytically within the buyer area and the product area before starting an advertisement is one worth acquiring. There are, of course, complications and inadequacies. The listing process provides nothing quantitative, no order of magnitude; this is unfortunate in the case of a product which delivers two or three significant types of satisfaction. Different consumers feel differently about their problems and possible solutions to them; some buy product "C" for one reason, some for another, and some for two or more reasons. No list of wants supplies the information about buyers needed by advertisers nor is it a substitute for common sense and judgment.

Marketing Research. Whereas the check list approach to the selection of advertising benefits is a desk or office type of process, the market research approach calls for field work. Ideally, the advertiser would set up a sample of prospects and then do market research surveys. Equally ideal would be a thorough and complete study of what *prospects* think — which leads them not to buy, and of what *customers* think — leading them to buy. Such a study would ask consumers about *types* of products as well as *brands*. The benefits which seem most attractive and persuasive may be pretested, if the advertiser wants to and can, before final selections are made.

Potentially, market research is much to be preferred over the check list as an approach to the choosing of benefits to stress. Where complete, sound research is out of the question, and this is often the case, the check list is always practicable.

How Many Benefits to Use

One of the problems in the selection of benefits involves the number of benefits the advertiser should present. One possibility is to select a single benefit and feature only it in all the advertisements comprising that particular campaign. A second possibility is to feature only one benefit in each advertisement but to include several benefits during the life of the campaign. A third possibility is to include two or more benefits in any one advertisement.

One Benefit. The practice of building an advertisement around a single benefit has much merit. It is sound in the same sense that unity and simplicity are sound. It is easier for an advertiser to establish *one* claim and get it accepted than *several* claims. The consumer's ability to grasp a complicated message is limited, and his inclination to study a message until he understands it is slight indeed. The consumer, furthermore, *is* inclined to take one step on his own — if he believes brand "A" is superior on *one* significant score, he is inclined to believe "A" better in an over-all way.

Two or More Benefits. There are several pressures on an advertiser to include two or more appeals in a single advertisement. Consumer Brown finds in the advertiser's product *one* type of satisfaction — Consumer Jones finds a different type of satisfaction in the same item. Or, Brown uses the product for one purpose whereas Jones puts the same product to an entirely different use. Or, Brown and Jones, having different goals and obeying dissimilar motivation patterns, react to different stimuli; the strength of motive differs — between the two individuals. Or, each individual, Brown and Jones, is motivated by his own combination of benefits or in search of his own combination of satisfactions when contemplating the purchase of the advertiser's product. Or, an emotional or human interest benefit may be included to get Brown and Jones to read — then a rational appeal is present in

Building the Advertisement

order to get them to buy; consumers expect rewards for reading *and* rewards for buying. Finally, many manufacturers must remember that their advertisements are read by, and stimulate or fail to stimulate, *dealers* in addition to *consumers*.

Rationalization. The widespread indulgence in rationalizing by consumers explains to some extent the number of advertisements containing two or more benefits. The consumer is constantly concerned with protecting his privacy and his pride; he is continuously dreaming up excuses for his attitudes and respectable reasons for his behavior. He is reluctant to admit that advertising affects him, preferring to think of himself as the world's most controlled and rational buyer. He may buy for frivolous or even base cause — but needs logical, decent, proper reasons to offer to those who question his purchase or even to himself.

If the advertiser's most effective appeal is clearly emotional and of doubtful respectability socially, he may combine with it a rational type of benefit. The illustrations, for instance, may appeal to lusts, vanities, or desires of which the consumer cannot be proud, picturing emotional, sensuous satisfaction. But, the copywriters will write to the consumer's reason, realizing that emotional behavior delights in rational support. Sometimes the rational material is included for its *conviction* value. Often it pictures *economy*.

Summary. Many advertisements include more than one benefit. Most of these feature prominently a big or main benefit and put less emphasis on one or more minor benefits. This represents a conscious compromise because the advertisement's general appeal is broadened at the cost of less force back of a single benefit; the shotgun has been chosen over the rifle. In multi-benefit advertisements, the total number of benefits to be included must be limited drastically and firmly. To qualify for possible inclusion, any benefit, including the minor ones, must have considerable strength. Even when presenting two or more benefits, an advertisement should try to leave the consumer with but a single impression — one of the desirability of the product. Progress is made toward this objective if the included benefits mesh and harmonize with each other in expressing the advertiser's message.

Comments About Benefits

Without doubt, the most significant comment which can be made about benefits is that consumers do not buy products or services — they buy psychological satisfaction. Consumers exchange their dollars for specific values, advantages, utilities. So, this first comment is that he who builds advertisements simply *must* appeal to the self-interest of selfish, self-centered individuals. He must translate his product or service into the answer to a strong, basic, universal human want. When any seller approaches any buyer, the buyer's immediate reaction is the inquiry, "What's in it for me?" That buyer never reduces his hoard of dollars except to gain personal gratification, even should he empty his purse in a beggar's cup.

The benefit should be a big sales idea; it should be the most important feature in all promotional advertising. Small, short advertisements are, of course, often of a reminder type and contain no specific benefit or sales idea. If the big sales idea turns out not to have been very big, the advertisement will fail, because this sales idea is what the advertiser counts on to stimulate and exercise consumer buying motives. The best big sales idea is the promise of a powerful benefit — one which appeals to buyers. It is a simple idea so that consumers can grasp it certainly, painlessly, and instantly. It is a specific idea and not abstract or general.

The consumer to whom the advertiser wants to sell should be allowed to control the choice of the benefits to be featured. These benefits should be satisfactions consumers want or, in some instances, satisfactions they can be taught to want. The imitation of competitors' claims and promises is a course of action to be rejected adamantly. Great advertising is different advertising, not copycat advertising. The advertiser's own hunch or conviction can be equally disastrous. The fisherman fills his creel by offering fish what *they* want — not what the *fisherman* thinks is good.

Most advertisers are definitely interested in two groups of buyers — the prospect group and the customer group. Selection of benefits to emphasize must be made in the light of this fact. Incidentally, a higher proportion of the *owners* of brand "A" read the advertisements of brand "A" than of the *prospects* for brand "A." Advertisers of products which are quickly consumed must give special recognition to their customers in selecting the benefits to stress.

Finally, because advertising is directed toward groups of individuals, because it is mass communication, any benefit selected will fail to stimulate some consumers. The advertiser knows in advance that even the best sales idea will interest and appeal to less than 100 per cent of his total potential market. Unlike the salesman, the advertiser cannot tailor his message to each individual buyer.

PART II — MOTIVATION RESEARCH

One of the outstanding marketing developments of recent times was the interest which developed during the 1950's in *motivation research,* a phase of marketing research. Because the subject matter deals with why consumers feel and act as they do, motivation research makes an appropriate second section in this chapter on benefits.

Background

The term *motivation research* is a misnomer. Both *motivation analysis* and *psychological research* are more accurate designations. In practically every instance, the person who uses the term motivation research (or its initials MR) is referring to research which uses certain psychological techniques or procedures. *All consumer research is motivation research,* yet seldom indeed is the term *motivation research* used to refer to all research in the area of consumer motivation. The mistake made was that of giving an activity the name of the activity's objective. Actually, in common usage, *motivation research* consists of certain tools and techniques used to identify and evaluate the motivation back of consumers' purchases. The tools and techniques are largely from the fields of psychology, psychiatry, sociology, and anthropology.

Building the Advertisement

Consumers don't always like what they say they like — they don't always do what they say they do. Consumers' attitudes and actions are not always as consumers report them. Some consumers don't tell the truth about the automobiles they buy, the magazines they read, the beer they drink, and the food they do and do not buy.

Consumer motivation is *most* complex. Most consumers know but little about their own motivation, and they understand even less. Few consumers know what they want in a conscious, consistent, continuing way, and even fewer know why.

Three psychological areas are involved. In one, the consumer knows why he feels as he does and why he acts as he does — and will supply this information when asked about it. The direct, question-and-answer approach is satisfactory in exploring this area and in establishing these facts. In a second area, the consumer also knows what his attitudes and opinions are — but he refuses to divulge this information. To talk or even to think about this motivation is most unpleasant and painful because the nature of the motivation does not show the consumer in a favorable light. He is reluctant to admit that he smokes cigars, for example, to increase his feeling of masculinity, or that he bought the make of automobile he did mainly to have a more expensive one than some friend had. In a third area there are forces and pressures in operation of which the consumer is unaware — forces and pressures which affect attitudes and actions. Because he is ignorant of the nature and functioning of these hidden influences, the consumer obviously cannot report on them or reveal anything about them *directly*.

As was mentioned, the direct, question-and-answer approach is effective in the first area; this approach does not work in the second and third areas. In the second area, the consumer *will* not discuss — he may even not admit — his motives. He finds that the truth damages his picture and his opinion of himself. To reveal his motivation is intolerable because it is neither respectable to himself nor acceptable to society. In the third area, the consumer *cannot* give accurate answers to direct questions about his feelings and behavior because his motivation is not known to him. He cannot report on the attitudes in this area which cause purchases because he does not know what these attitudes are.

Against this background, the advertiser needs to know what consumers really want, and what they can be persuaded to want. He needs to know the consumer motives, feelings, and attitudes which he can make use of in selling his product. He needs to know what causes purchases. Why do consumers buy what and as they do? Why do they *think* they buy as they do? Why do they *say* they buy as they do? In a word, the advertiser needs to know why consumers act and react as they do.

The nature of the issues involved can be indicated by these questions which refer to actual motivation research studies:

Do cigarettes help a person concentrate on his job?
Does the consumer want his disinfectant to be colored and to have a mild sting?
Do housewives want suds in their dishpans?
Does the buyer choose the Cadillac because he wants to get his money's worth?
Are lazy, spendthrift women the ones who buy instant coffee?
Is chewing gum good for boredom? Tensions? Anger?

Benefits Which Appeal to Buyers

Do housewives feel that they shirk their responsibilities when they buy and serve easy-to-fix, precooked foods?

Regarding the last question, for example, take a cake mix whose advertising has been stressing *economy* or *speed of preparation*. The facts may be that housewives are reluctant to buy a cake mix because using a mix makes housewives feel guilty. Why? To serve cakes made from mixes may imply that the housewife is a poor cake baker, is lazy, does not love her family, does not run her kitchen efficiently — even that she lacks individuality. Deep inside she may feel that she should work as hard and as long as her husband, that she is shirking her responsibility as a wife and mother unless she "slaves" in the kitchen, that the cakes she serves should be *hers* rather than mixes out of a box.

Once these facts have been established, the advertiser may well shift his emphasis. Instead of economy or speed of preparation, he may switch to such benefits as *approval* or *praise*. He can even leave some ingredient out of the product (egg, flavoring), ask the housewife to add, and then reassure the housewife that she truly *is* something she wants badly to be, namely, *creative*.

What Motivation Research Is

A review of the features of traditional or conventional research gives us a pattern against which to contrast motivation research. Traditional research stresses the quantitative; it features numerical information; it asks who, what, where; it is greatly concerned with *how many*. To get such data, traditional research sets up a sample of the population as scientifically as possible. Then, for personal interviewers, ordinary individuals are selected and given some training in how to interview. These interviewers question the persons in the sample, using a questionnaire that is largely fixed and not to be adapted. Answers are desired in a form such as will permit a tabulation of the findings. While conventional research seems more concerned with the actions of consumers than with the motivation back of those actions, it seems both unfair and inaccurate to refer to this type of research as mere "nose counting."

Motivation research is interested in discovering the real explanations for consumers' attitudes and actions. The big question it asks is, "Why?". Motivation research does not accept consumers' answers to direct questioning about why they bought what they did. It is more interested in non-statistical matters than in data which will tabulate neatly. It is particularly concerned with motivation which consumers *will not* knowingly reveal, or *cannot* consciously reveal. In its search for the psychological and social explanations of consumer actions, motivation research deals with consumer's desires and values, beliefs and emotions, prejudices and images. Advertisers' interest in motivation research stems from their interest in learning more about the deep, hidden behavior which relates to buying decisions — in learning more about consumer reactions to various stimuli.

Techniques

The techniques used in motivation research fall into two groups. Depth interviews constitute one group; projective techniques constitute the other. Projective techniques include stimulus pictures, free word association, sentence completion, and group interviews. In both groups of techniques, the preference is for the indirect approach over the direct approach used in conventional research. The objective of both groups is a more complete understanding of consumer drives, attitudes, and actions — a more accurate grasp of what determines consumer decisions and choices. The findings in each group must be interpreted by experts.

Depth Interviews. The depth interview is non-directive and relatively unstructured. It is informal and narrative, not standardized as is the conventional interview. The questions are open-end, with no answers suggested. The interview usually lasts an hour or two but can extend over a much longer period of time. At the conclusion of the interview, the interviewer leaves with hunches, hints, and intuitions. After 50 to 200 interviews, trends may emerge.

The idea of the depth interview is to get the consumer to talk and talk freely. The interviewer tries to get on the consumer's side, to get in mental and emotional step with him, to appear to the consumer as a sympathetic, understanding friend. The interviewer makes a minimum contribution to the conversation. The approach is indirect, oblique, subtle. The interviewer's hope is to find in the large mass of consumer comments significant keys to consumer motivation.

Stimulus Pictures. In these tests, the consumer is shown a picture or a series of pictures and is asked to respond. The pictures are intentionally vague or incomplete; several interpretations are possible. The consumer is asked to interpret the picture, to tell a story about it, or to suggest an ending for it. For example, each of a series of pictures may show several persons; the consumer is asked to tell who they are, what their backgrounds are, what they are doing, saying, and thinking, and, finally, the outcome of the situation. Or, a picture may show two individuals one of whom has just made a comment or asked a question which is in a balloon coming from that individual's mouth; the consumer is asked to write the reply for the other individual to make.

Word Association and Sentence Completion. In free word association the researcher speaks the key or stimulus word and the consumer is asked to answer with the first word to come to mind. Sentence completion is exactly what the term implies.

Group Interviews. Motivation research makes some use of group interviews. Six to twelve consumers are brought together and asked to comment on some topic or issue.

Comments About Projective Methods. Projective techniques are designed so that they do not quite make sense in the form presented to the consumer; they are incomplete; something is missing. The consumer is confronted with a word, a sentence, a picture, or a problem which is *intentionally* ambiguous. The question posed to the consumer is, "What does this suggest to *you?*

The researcher knows the elements present in the test — what the test itself consists of and contains. He knows what data or information he has after the consumer has completed the test; he has no difficulty in identifying what the consumer contributed. In supplying whatever was missing from the test, in adding whatever seemed needed to make sense out of the test, the consumer projects himself — his feelings, his personality, his needs into his responses and into his answers. As he describes, explains, and narrates, the consumer supplies information, *in code* as it were, which he either would not supply, or could not supply to direct questioning. If the consumer were to read a complete transcript of his answers, he would be just as much in the dark about their real implications as when a doctor tells him his blood pressure figures. There are no "correct" answers or "school solutions" to projective tests. The consumer, consequently, supplies basic information and reveals hidden feelings without difficulty, discomfort, or embarrassment.

Three Features of Motivation Research

Motivation research is far less concerned with statistically sound samples than is traditional research. For example, only a relatively small number of depth interviews is made in the typical research project. The willingness or unwillingness of a specific individual to cooperate, furthermore, sometimes determines whether or not he or she is included in the sample. This does not work in favor of sound samples. Some of those most enthusiastic about motivation research claim that their findings are so universal that there is no reason to be concerned with the stability or the representativeness of the sample. Motivation researchers are not in unanimous agreement about how many consumers should be included in a sample nor about how those should be selected.

Motivation research is characterized by a lack of precision — by the unavoidable presence of possible variations. For example, in depth interviews, the influence of interviewer bias cannot be eliminated, nor are the moods of the consumers interviewed identical. Because the consumer wanders and rambles, any classification and tabulation, even any comparison, of the information obtained from consumers are most difficult. The time and the place of interviews and tests are under less than complete control. Some consumers refuse to project themselves into the information they give to psychologists. Then there is the problem of interpretation. Data and information are subject to the personal, subjective interpretation of the researcher. Two interpreters with the same data can come to different conclusions, or one interpreter can hold one conclusion today but arrive at a different conclusion at a later date. Because each interpreter reflects his own attitudes and beliefs, three social scientists shown the same basic data can come up with three different interpretations — findings as well as recommendations.

The social scientists engaged in motivation research are, themselves, a heterogeneous group. Psychology and psychiatry are interested in the consumer as an *individual;* sociology and anthropology are interested in *groups* of persons. Psychiatry does not speak the same language as does sociology, nor psychology as anthropology. None of the four is fluent in the world of marketing. So, communication is difficult among the social scientists, and between them and marketers.

Building the Advertisement

Conclusions About Motivation Research

Motivation research must be recognized for what it actually is — just one type or form of *marketing* research. Motivation research, furthermore, is not the only approach to learning about consumer motivation; data obtained by traditional, direct research can throw light on the *why* of consumer buying. It is the advertiser's responsibility to select that research method which will do the best job on his specific problem at hand. As with other types of research, motivation research is no substitute either for managerial judgment or for other types of research. Above all, motivation research is not a panacea for all advertising and marketing problems.

Advertisers need both types of information — information on *how many* as supplied by conventional research, *and* information on *why* as supplied by motivation research and, to some extent, by regular consumer surveys. An advertiser needs a list of motives which relate to his product, motives listed in order of magnitude of influence on buyers. Sometimes the advertiser uses conventional research to get a picture of *what* is happening — then engages in psychological procedures to determine *why*. So, the goal of motivation research is a desirable one, and the activities themselves are a valuable addition and supplement to the older statistical research activities.

The samples used by motivation research should be as soundly constructed as those in conventional research. They should be of adequate size, and they should be typical of the entire group under investigation.

The qualitative findings of motivation research need to be quantified — they need to be counted and measured — they must be expressed as proportions or percentages of the entire population. Advertisers have to know the *relative* importance of motives in the total situations before they can defend the basing of decisions on them. Advertisers have to know more than just the identity of hidden drives — they need to know how influential those drives are in the reading, listening, viewing, and buying of consumers. Traditional research can be used to quantify motivation research.

Motivation research started out studying generic products — cigarettes, chewing gum, instant coffee. Findings, consequently, were broad and general. Each advertiser, of course, is concerned about and needs information about his *brand* of product and those brands which compete against it.

Motivation research, to be sound, must be the product of sound interviewers and sound interpreters who use sound techniques. Interviewers need to be able and honest. Only trained scientists are qualified to analyse and interpret motivation research data. The greater understanding these scientists have of marketing research, the better. Soundness of technique is equally essential. There *are* problems — technical problems — in transferring techniques from the social sciences and applying them to marketing problems. If the tests are to measure what they are supposed to measure, then it must have been established that the methods found effective in *clinical* conditions are also effective when applied to *masses* of individuals.

The need for studying why consumers think and act as they do has been recognized for a long time. The techniques called motivation research have been used by social scientists for a long time. In marketing, these techniques are an extension of established, well-known marketing research practices. Motivation research is not *good* or *bad* — there is good motivation research, and bad. Good motivation research makes a most valuable contribution to advertisers' attempts to learn more about the attitudes and actions of consumers. Often this contribution is the discovery of ideas, suspicions, opinions, and hypotheses which can then be researched in a conventional manner.

Questions and Problems

1. What does the college man *really* buy when he buys suits, slacks, sport coats, jackets, and sweaters?
2. List some of the benefits promised by candidates for political office.
3. Should the benefit of *economy* be included in all ads in some manner?
4. Today, umbrellas are more popular with college men than before. Why?
5. What reasons can you suggest against the use of negative appeals?
6. Why is sex appeal used so widely to advertise "un-sexy" products?
7. "The advertiser can imitate — or innovate." Comment.
8. Comment on whether ads for children's products should be built to appeal to children or to their parents.
9. Should automobile manufacturers stress benefits to women as well as benefits to men?
10. The Republic National Bank, chartered in the 1930's, is a $600,000,000 bank. It conducts a general banking (18 services) and trust business. Fifty offices in 10 cities provide statewide service to 150,000 depositors.

    The banking industry in the state in which Republic operates is quite competitive. This keen competition is reflected in a sizable volume of aggressive advertising. Bank advertising, once formal and dignified, has shifted to a more friendly style. It is now trying to humanize both the bank and the banker. Republic's consumer advertising appears in newspapers, outdoor, radio, transit, and TV. Direct mail and a few magazines are used in promoting Republic's services to business and industry.

    Advertising plans for next year are now being made. Suggest benefits Republic might stress in next year's advertising.

Chapter 8

Layout

This chapter is written almost exclusively about the two publication media — newspapers and magazines; and, within these two, only one type of advertisement is considered — the display advertisement. There can be, of course, considerable translation of these principles and techniques over to the transportation and outdoor media. Limited application is possible in point-of-purchase materials and in direct mail. Television can make only slender use of this chapter, and radio can adapt it not at all.

THE VISUALIZATION STEP

The study of the subject of layout starts with an understanding of *visualization,* a word which has two meanings. In its narrow sense, visualization refers to what shall be portrayed in an advertising illustration. Should the product be included? Should persons be shown admiring or using the product? Should the illustration be an abstract drawing or a symbol? The broader view, which we shall use, sees visualization to be the process of determining which elements or units an advertisement should contain. Should the advertisement be illustrated? Should a coupon be included? What about the trade mark or the trade character? Should there be one illustration, or several? What should be illustrated? Clearly, the first concept of visualization is included in the second. What an advertising illustration should portray cannot be determined intelligently without knowing what the other component parts of the advertisement are to be.

Elements

The elements, units, or masses (these terms are synonymous in this chapter) of which advertisements are made include the following four: *headings,* consisting of headlines and subheads; *illustrations; body copy* or blocks of copy; and the *logotype* or display symbol, also referred to as the signature, slug, or nameplate. The logotype can feature the brand name or the firm name; it is often a base supporting the rest of the advertisement, but sometimes it is placed in the headings or even in the copy block. If an advertisement contains no logotype, identification

Layout

may be built in by including an illustration of the product or by putting the brand name in the headline or in the illustration. The design of the logotype, unlike that of the trade mark, may be changed.

In addition to these more-or-less standard four, there are other elements of a layout available to the visualizer. Examples are trade marks, trade characters, coupons, packages, prices, and seals of approval. Of a slightly different nature is white space. Most display advertisements make a positive rather than a neutral use of white space.

Visualizing

An idea or a mental image about how an advertisement might look marks the start of visualization. Here the visualizer imagines what units or masses should go into the advertisement. He pictures in his mind the items which should be included. He dreams of how to give graphic definition to his idea. He explores the various combinations by which to communicate a message and an impression.

Next, the physical is called on to express the mental. Visualizing actually starts when the layout artist's pencil sketches on paper the first version of a future advertisement.

Influences

Various factors influence the visualizer. Typographical matters include the paper on which the advertisement will be printed, the printing process to be used, the art work, and the typography. Scheduling matters include the medium to be used, the advertisement, the relationship of the advertisement to other advertisements of the seller, and the scheduled date of appearance. Factors connected with the advertisement itself include its classification, its objective, its appeal, the product to be featured, and the amount of copy. The advertiser himself is an influence through the operation of his preferences and prejudices. He wants his advertisements to be distinctive from those of his competitors; he wants freshness, variety, and a change of pace from his own recent advertising. An all-pervasive influence is the necessity for the visualization to do the best job possible for the advertiser in communicating and influencing.

THE LAYOUT STEP

Nature of Layout

Visualization cannot be done in any realistic sense without some reference to layout. One cannot imagine the elements which should comprise an advertisement without speculating, simultaneously, about their physical relationships to each other. And when the visualizer does put pencil to paper in an exploratory, tentative way, he cannot postpone experimenting in layout. So, visualization merges into layout, and the final version of visualization becomes the final layout. Even though the same person does both visualization and layout, and, indeed, appears to do them in a single step, the two jobs are basically different in nature.

Building the Advertisement

Layout is arrangement. Layout assigns positions to each unit or mass in the advertisement. Layout decrees which elements shall be important and those which are of less significance by the space it gives to each. Where that space is and how much there is of it separates the featured units from those receiving less prominence. Thus, a layout is a plan, a diagram, a blueprint. It differs from the earlier visualizations in that it is more specific, more complete, more polished, and sounder. It displays what visualization decided the advertisement should contain. If visualization is thought of as telling *what,* then layout's job is to say *where.*

Layout Types

For our purposes, layouts can be classified into three types, the first of which is the *thumbnail.* These are small sketches done in the experimental stage. They are miniatures which indicate the elements to be included and their arrangement, but they omit detail. Many may be done before one is accepted.

A second type is the *rough,* also referred to as the *visual.* Roughs are the same size as the future advertisement but are still early drafts done quickly. They contain most of the features of the proposed advertisement. Illustrations are roughed in, and headings are lettered in hastily; copy blocks are represented by horizontal parallel lines; a logotype is included. Because roughs indicate accurately the spacing and the design of the subject matter, they are quite useful for early analysis, discussion, and criticism. As with the thumbnails, many roughs may be executed before one is selected.

The third type, the *comprehensive,* is a further refinement of the rough. It is more carefully done and more complete. Type may be pasted in where there formerly were parallel lines, and artwork may replace roughed in illustrations. Photostats of the trade mark or logotype may be included. In its most elaborate version, the comprehensive looks strikingly similar to the final advertisement.

Groups Concerned

Demands are made of layout by advertisers, by advertising agencies, and by those engaged in the physical production of advertising. The advertiser asks layout to make the maximum contribution of which it is capable to securing the attention of all prospects. He asks layout to secure, in addition, the maximum of readership by those prospects. He expects layout to help put across his message quickly by making that message easy to see and easy to grasp. The advertiser hopes layout will direct prospects immediately to the start of the message and then will control the path of the reader's eye all the way through to the end of the advertisement.

Advertising agencies employ layout to help achieve the most effective organization and presentation of the client's message. Agencies expect layout to help tell advertising stories most effectively. In the planning stage, agencies execute and discard layouts until confident that the client can be shown the survivors. The client sees how his advertisements might look — and then can suggest to the advertising agency whatever revisions he thinks will serve to improve them.

Layouts are working drawings to printers, engravers, and others who actually produce advertising. To those individuals, layouts serve as instructions and guides to the physical production of advertisements.

Layout Characteristics Desired

Just as there was no magic formula for writing copy, neither is there one for laying out advertisements. There are, nevertheless, several common characteristics found in effective layouts. One of these is *structural soundness*. The effective layout is obviously well built; its composition is streamlined and clean. Its arrangement is orderly and logical. There is no suggestion of hurried, careless, or defective construction.

Another feature typical of well laid out advertising is an *invitation* asking all prospects into the advertisement — to see the illustration, to grasp the meaning of the headline, to read the copy, and to identify the advertiser and his product. Inviting advertisements may go so far as to be striking in their determination to stop all prospects. They should avoid, of course, irrelevant tactics to get attention and readership because such techniques call the reader's attention to the layout itself, and that is not desirable. Tricks, stunts, and novelty do not make for sound invitations because they are based on curiosity, a weak appeal. Stimulating, interesting advertisements which do not imitate other layouts invite readership and get it.

Attractiveness, too, is a desirable characteristic of layouts. Harmony and stimulation, interest and charm are examples of values which, when incorporated into advertising, contribute to effectiveness. Just as for individuals, advertisements that are pleasing to look at are the ones which *are* looked at favorably.

A final characteristic of effective layouts is their *simplicity*. Such layouts are direct and straight-forward, they are easily understood, they are marked by an absence of clutter, crowdedness, and confusion. The significance of each unit is recognized immediately. Because they are constructed simply, such layouts are forceful; their impact is strong.

A glance at these four characteristics of structural soundness, invitation, attractiveness and simplicity which make for good advertisements reminds us of the basic purpose of advertising layout. This purpose is to help do the job wanted done by the advertiser. Layout contributes by helping capture the attention of prospects, by helping maximize their reading of the advertisement, and by helping encourage favorable response. It is *not* the basic purpose of layout to win a prize or an award for the art director who laid out the advertisement.

THE DEVELOPMENT OF A SPECIFIC ADVERTISEMENT

The group of illustrations following this discussion shows how the art work was developed for an advertisement for the Massachusetts Mutual Life Insurance Company. A description, from their advertising agency, of how this advertisement was created and developed reads as follows:

Building the Advertisement

In describing all of the steps involved in creating this advertisement, we must go back to the inception of the Massachusetts Mutual campaign.[1] For, as with the advertising of many products and services, we do not think in terms of a single advertisement, but within the framework of a long-range campaign.

When we originally designed this campaign, we set out to accomplish a very specific goal. We wanted to distinguish Massachusetts Mutual from all other life insurance companies, to point out its unique personality. We wanted to make the Massachusetts Mutual name synonymous with attributes of friendliness, helpfulness, all the characteristics of a person you would like to know.

To help create this image visually, we decided upon an illustration technique that would portray simple, human-interest situations, highlighting emotional experiences which would be identifiable with the personal experiences of prospective buyers of life insurance. Copy was designed to carry out this approach, to appeal simply and directly to the readers' emotions. Within this long-term format, then, the advertisement illustrated on the following pages, promoting the sale of mortgage life insurance, was prepared.

Our first problem was to dramatize this type of story, to capture the interest of our reader audience. Several illustration suggestions were detailed and considered with rough copy written for each to help the copy and art group determine which illustration idea would enable us to get across best the importance of mortgage insurance to young home owners with growing families. Some of these ideas were:

A. Adding room to house — small boy about 8 intently hammering into upright beam — father, mother, and workman looking on, admiring the boy's industry.
Copy lead in: that one small nail placed strategically can make all the difference in the world. . . .

B. Father laying plastic tile floor in recreation room. He and young son taking a break, sipping soda pop, but father looks tired, is mopping his brow with handkerchief.
Copy lead in: even if you're not a "do-it-yourself" man, you put so much of yourself into your house — your family's home. . . .

C. Family planting small tree in front of house, Mother is holding tree straight while young father and 5-year-old boy shovel dirt onto roots. Boy "helps" by scooping dirt with small shovel. Hose, with water on, lying on ground.
Copy lead in: roots are for trees, and families, too. . . .

After intra-agency discussion — involving the copywriter, copy group supervisor, art director, art supervisor, and the account executive — it was decided to submit the tree-planting idea to the client as our recommendation for creative rendition. Massachusetts Mutual's advertising manager approved the illustrative recommendation and the general copy approach, giving us clearance to proceed. At this point our ideas were introduced to the artist, Norman Rockwell, and final art was then ordered.

[1] The illustrations are reproduced by the courtesy of Massachusetts Mutual Life Insurance Company. Information was furnished by the J. Walter Thompson Company.

This rough layout, done by J. Walter Thompson art director for copy group consideration, was the first step in the creation of the advertisement.

The original art was this drawing by Norman Rockwell.

This was the mechanical or final layout.

This final proof shows exactly how the advertisement looked when it appeared in magazines.

Roots are for trees . . . for families, too. And what better way to establish those roots than by making certain your family will always have a home of their own even if something should happen to you.

Massachusetts Mutual can help give you this peace of mind — and more besides — through a convenient Mortgage Retirement Plan. Not only will it assure your family a debt-free home . . . it can also help you pay off the mortgage sooner . . . give you a constantly increasing reserve and a monthly income during the years after you've paid the mortgage.

Protection for family roots costs so little and means so much to homeowners. If you don't have it, you need it. Talk it over with a Massachusetts Mutual man, or call our General Agent listed under Massachusetts Mutual in the phone book.

Massachusetts Mutual
LIFE INSURANCE COMPANY
SPRINGFIELD, MASSACHUSETTS
The Policyholders' Company

Layout

While Mr. Rockwell was preparing the final art for the advertisement, copy was written. The first piece of copy, in this instance, was very close to the final form.

As soon as the Rockwell art was received, the account executive took both copy and finished art, along with a comprehensive layout of the combined elements, to the client for final approval by the advertising manager and the company's marketing executives.

Coincidentally with the production of the advertisement, Massachusetts Mutual's promotion staff developed and produced various promotion materials for use by the company's agents. These included brochures, tying in with the advertisement, direct mail letters, and cards; plus a coordinated direct mail plan to build interest among the Massachusetts Mutual field force, itself, for the mortgage insurance promotion.

WEIGHT IN LAYOUT

There are two well-known approaches to the problem of attracting attention to an advertisement. One, the *interest* approach, makes use of the nature of the advertiser's message to help achieve attention, relying largely on the appeal selected and the benefits promised. The importance of this approach was pointed out in Chapter 7. The other approach is *mechanical* and can involve external techniques as well as internal ones. Placing an advertisement in a preferred position, for example, perhaps on the back cover of a magazine, is an external technique for maximizing attention. Increasing the size of the advertisement is another.

Internal techniques of attracting attention are the ones of concern to us here because they are the ones related to layout. The elements within an advertisement which capture readers' attention have, obviously, what may be called *attraction value*. They have the power to secure notice. And, in the area of layout, this value or power constitutes weight. One unit or mass which makes twice as strong a bid for a reader's attention as does another unit or mass must be considered as weighing twice as much as the second.

What factors, then, are basic in this concept of weight? *Size* is a simple and obvious method of attracting more attention. For instance, the coupon in an advertisement may be enlarged. When the size of an element is increased, its attention-compelling power — and its weight — is increased. Elephants in a circus parade are an example of weight through size. *Shape* is another factor. Circles weight more in the reader's mind than do squares or rectangles of the same area. Irregular shapes weigh even more than circles of the same area. You are well aware of the attention-capturing power of pleasing shapes. Readers look for and at *color*. Any mass in color weighs more than the same mass in black-and-white. Color's counterpart in black-and-white advertising is the degree of blackness. Finally, *distance* from the optical center is a factor in weight.

OPTICAL CENTER

The optical center of the space an advertisement will occupy is the point which the reader's eye designates as the center of the area. The eye chooses it as the first,

Building the Advertisement

the natural spot on which to rest or fall when the area is completely blank — delineated only by the four lines which bound it. The advertisement's balance rests on this optical center. Readers accept as center the *vertical* line which divides the area into left and right halves; it is the *horizontal* dividing line they push up to an area about 10 per cent above the physical center.

The optical center is a factor in layout because it is the position of greatest attention value. Often an advertisement's headline is placed in the optical center. Either price or product or both can be featured there. The main illustration or at least the most dramatic element in it is placed there frequently. Not all advertisements make specific and obvious use of the optical center, but it is there available if its use is desirable.

The central spot of the optical center has been described as the point on which the advertisement hangs. So, it is to this spot, as well as to each other, that size, shape, and color must be related. Thus, we come to the fourth factor, *distance*, in our concept of weight. Arranging and adjusting these four variables so as to achieve good balance is a matter of trial, error, and practice.

REQUISITES OF GOOD LAYOUT

Advertisements need to be well arranged because most persons have a sense of what is good design. It is true that the layout artist must work within the objectives and the instructions of the advertiser; the layout artist must consider more than just artistry and his own personal preferences. Perhaps the most obvious example here is of the layout artist's being told that the advertisement must contain a coupon. Another truth, of course, is that good design cannot be achieved or guaranteed by the use of formulas. Those who lay out advertisements must develop a feeling of what is right and a sense of what is good taste.

Even a brief examination of a magazine reveals that some advertisements are much more successful than others in achieving good feeling tone. Some contain ill-assorted, unrelated elements in composition which can be nothing but discordant or, indeed, repelling. In other advertisements, the variables of size, shape, color, and distance have been put together in harmonious combinations that cause favorable reactions because they are pleasant. These advertisements are pleasing to look at; their layouts are logical and effective because they observe the principles of *unity, contrast, proportion, movement,* and *balance.* These fundamentals are universal and permanent features of good design.

Unity

What and Why. In the preceding chapter, unity of thought or message was pictured as a prerequisite for effective copy. This chapter describes unity of design or appearance as a prerequisite for effective layout. What is unity in layout? Unity is one-ness. It is the characteristic which makes an advertisement cohesive. It is the quality which merges several units into a single, unified whole. A person is sometimes described as well dressed if you cannot remember specifically what she was wearing. In similar fashion, an advertisement is well laid out if none

Layout

of its elements calls unusual attention to itself. Here is a test that is simple but sound: If the removal of any element from the advertisement fails to destroy the advertisement's composition, if this omission fails to make the advertisement appear incomplete or inadequate, then the layout was not unified. And, it must be observed, the absence of unity is a most common weakness in layout.

Unity ties the parts of an advertisement together and fuses them into a whole. The result is an orderly, compact, logical appearance. There is harmony because there is integration. Unification helps get, hold, and concentrate the attention of prospects; it makes more probable and more speedy the prospect's comprehension of the advertiser's message. Above all, the unified advertisement makes (and leaves the reader with) a *single* impression, which, if strong, should have a good chance of causing the one reaction most desired by the advertiser.

How Unity is Achieved. Sound visualization is the best assurance of unified advertisements. Visualizing is the stage in which restrictions can be laid down about the total number of units the advertisement shall contain. Here, too, the number of display elements can be controlled; if the number seems large, it can be reduced. The visualizer, by including only one dominant mass, can prevent a fight between two masses for the reader's attention. Eliminating those elements which contribute nothing to advertising performance makes for simplicity, which contributes to unity.

There are mechanical steps, too, which lead toward unity. Borders help hold an advertisement together even though the border consists of white space. Units can overlap; a rectangle, for example, can hold together two ovals or circles. Two or three small units can be attached to a central unit. Elements, especially if related, can be grouped closely, or, in a less subtle manner, rules, brackets, and base lines can be used. Elements can be placed in a panel; they can be lined up flush with an actual or even an invisible vertical line.

Certain mistakes must be avoided if unity is to be achieved. Fences and lines must not separate the area into subdivisions, because partitions such as these split the advertisement and can even give it the appearance of having been glued together. Cluttered, jumbled layouts tend to confuse and to repel readers; unnecessary elements, particularly ornaments and decorations, are not to be allowed. The other extreme, too much looseness or scattering, is equally fatal to unity. Irrelevance is an enemy of unity; the artificial, the tricky, and the novel demand careful handling. Too much contrast reduces unity. Elements which do not harmonize with each other are bad because they permit the reader to leave the advertisement thinking about layout instead of about the product's desirability.

Contrast

What and Why. Contrast is difference. It is present in a group of elements when those elements are not alike.

The skillful inclusion of contrast strengthens an advertisement in several ways. Contrast increases both the number of readers attracted and the amount of reading they do. Good contrast adds to the distinctiveness of an advertisement, permitting

Building the Advertisement

it to be in greater contrast to ordinary advertisements and, hence, to compete more successfully against them. Harmonious contrast makes a favorable impression because it is lively and varied. The tension inherent in contrast provides interest and combats monotony. Because equal emphasis results in no emphasis, contrast contributes to layout by making important masses stand out and by subordinating the less important.

How Contrast is Achieved. Contrast can be achieved in every unit advertisements contain. *Size,* of course, can provide contrast. The area occupied by the one dominant unit can be greater than that occupied by any other unit. Short units can combine with tall, and wide copy blocks can be included with narrow ones. Even within the illustration one may see, for example, a tiny secretary sitting on a giant-sized chair, or small figures of retailer and customer looking at huge swatches of broadloom.

Contrast can be a function of *shape*. Because a circle is the complement of a square, the two together provide harmonious contrast, perhaps in the form of a circular illustration and a rectangular copy block. Triangular masses afford another shape choice. Silhouettes are in sharp contrast to square finish illustrations.

Color or tone offers another area for contrast. The conflict of red against blue is familiar. In black-and-white, white may shade into light gray, then into dark gray, and finally into black. There is dramatic isolation in picturing individuals against a dark or even black background. In a checkerboard pattern, illustrations are usually in the dark squares and copy in the light ones.

Contrast may also be achieved through *direction*. Vertical contrasts with horizontal, and left with right. For example, the long axis of each rectangle in an advertisement should not run in the same direction.

Proportion

What and Why. Good layout demands good proportion in two areas. The first has to do with the shape of the advertisement itself. Here the reader's eye notes how the width of the advertisement looks in relationship to its height, and that eye recognizes satisfactory or normal ratios. The second area has to do with the manner in which the advertisement's space is divided. In this second area, the reader's eye notes the relationships of mass to mass, and of mass to the whole. Internal proportion is a matter of space subdivisions — of the dimensions of the units in the layout. The three basic forms involved are the circle, the square, and the triangle.

Nicely proportioned layouts are pleasing to look at because they possess harmony and order. They are optically interesting and, hence, they attract readership. Their combinations of sizes, shapes, and tones are pleasant to the eye and to the aesthetic sense of the viewer. They give each element the importance it deserves.

How Proportion is Achieved. The one great rule for achieving pleasant proportions is to avoid areas the dimensions of which are obvious. If mathematical relationships between areas or lines are recognized immediately by the reader to be 1 to 1, for example, or 2 to 1, proportion is not good. Arithmetic division of a space into halves, thirds, or quarters is uninteresting. Whenever subdivisions are seen quickly to be equal, they strike the reader as mechanical and uniform, flat and dull.

Unequal divisions are more interesting than equal ones. Their beauty stems from their subtlety. Instead of the square, whose equality of dimensions is readily apparent, layout artists prefer the rectangle. The ratio of 5-to-8 is a favorite, being referred to by some as the "Golden Section." Other favored proportions are the 2 to 5 and the 3 to 5, preferably with the long axis vertical rather than horizontal. The classic division of a vertical rectangle is in the proportions of 3-to-12-to-4.

To the great rule of using unequal divisions can be added a minor suggestion or two. Proportion should be arranged in such a manner as to avoid too many prominent masses or units. This is best done by giving heroic size to one unit so as to direct attention to it. Subdivisions which are too uniform have a mechanical appearance which suggests monotony; that extreme degree of uniformity is undesirable. Unrelated sizes and shapes are bad proportion because they detract from the unity each layout needs.

White Space. White space is the area not occupied by any mass or element. It is an integral and inevitable factor in proportion. The layout artist should fashion and employ white space at the time that the more obvious units — illustrations, headings, copy blocks, and logotype — are being designed.

There are many uses of white space. It can make an advertisement more attractive and less formidable by preventing a crowded appearance or a composition that seems too tight. Roads of white space, rather wide, make an advertisement of many parts less discouraging to the reader. Because it cannot avoid having shape, white space can influence (and is influenced by) the shapes of the various masses in the layout; this means that it has control possibilities in respect to directing the reader's attention. Isolation can be a product of white space; its contrast value is a mechanical way of getting attention and of giving emphasis. White space allows any important element, such as an indented paragraph, to be featured. White space may be an aid to unity in that it permits groupings and provides borders; it can, however, destroy unity if incorrectly used. Picture captions need white space, especially where each of a series of pictures has its own caption. White space implies luxury. It activates the entire arrangement by supplying elbow room, breathing space, and freedom.

Movement

What and Why. If an advertisement is to appear dynamic rather than static, its layout must contain movement. This is the feature which incorporates action and rhythm into layouts. It provides a visual type of flow and sequence. It endows the advertisement with follow-through, with coherence. Actual motion is found in such media as television, point of purchase, and outdoor; pictured motion can be found in illustrations. Here, however, we are concerned with the motion or movement built into layouts. Such motion usually flows left to right, and from top to bottom.

Building the Advertisement

The contribution of movement to layout is a major one. Motion helps keep balance from looking stiff by giving a natural sweep and grace to an advertisement. Attractiveness and interest are increased because of the injection of life and action. Movement gets the reader to spend more time inside the advertisement by supplying a logical sequence to follow — by conducting the reader on a tour of the layout in the order the advertiser prefers. Movement maps out for the reader an easy, clearly marked, inviting visual path to follow in somewhat the same manner as a marked route on a road map aids the tourist. To the extent that movement guides the reader's eye, it reduces the number of elements the reader misses or neglects.

Gaze Motion. One way to build movement into layouts is through the use of *gaze motion*. Someone animate, human or animal, looks at an object so as to influence the reader's attention and guide the reader's look in the desired direction.

There are two versions of gaze motion. In one, the object is the reader himself because someone is looking directly out of the advertisement intent on stopping readers and capturing their attention. The principle here is well-known. We often sense that we are being stared at, and, as a result, we feel pressure to look to see who is doing the staring. An example immediately at hand is that of the student writing a letter in class — until he or she can no longer postpone looking up at the instructor whose gaze is bearing down on that one student.

In the other version of gaze motion someone in the advertisement gazes at one of the units in the layout, one the advertiser wants the reader, too, to notice. Here again is a well-known principle. We feel a strong urge to look at what other persons are looking at; curiosity makes us want to know what it is that attracted the other person's attention. See a crowd peering up into the sky, or at a high spot on a tall building, or into the window of a store, or at a fight in the stands at a football game — and, if you can restrain yourself from looking, then you can eat one, just one, salted almond.

Structural Motion. Another way to build movement into layout is through the use of *structural motion*. The principle involved here is that the reader's attention is inclined to follow lines of direction and patterns of movement incorporated into an advertisement by mechanical means.

Many specific devices are employed to provide structural motion. Arrows and pointed fingers are among the most obvious, pointing to units of the advertisement the reader should notice. Lines of direction can be curving lines, diagonal lines or just a person walking in a certain direction. Spirals, overlaps, numbers, numbered flags, a series of small pictures, pyramidal shapes or other angles, a string of dots — these can supply structural motion.

In addition to devices, there are techniques which impart this type of motion. The repetition of an object helps create a pattern of interest; the repeated item can be a shape, a color, the trade mark, price, or a paragraph marker. The first word of each paragraph may be underlined. The shading of tone or color can be structural motion. Movement can be achieved by building the layout along the lines of

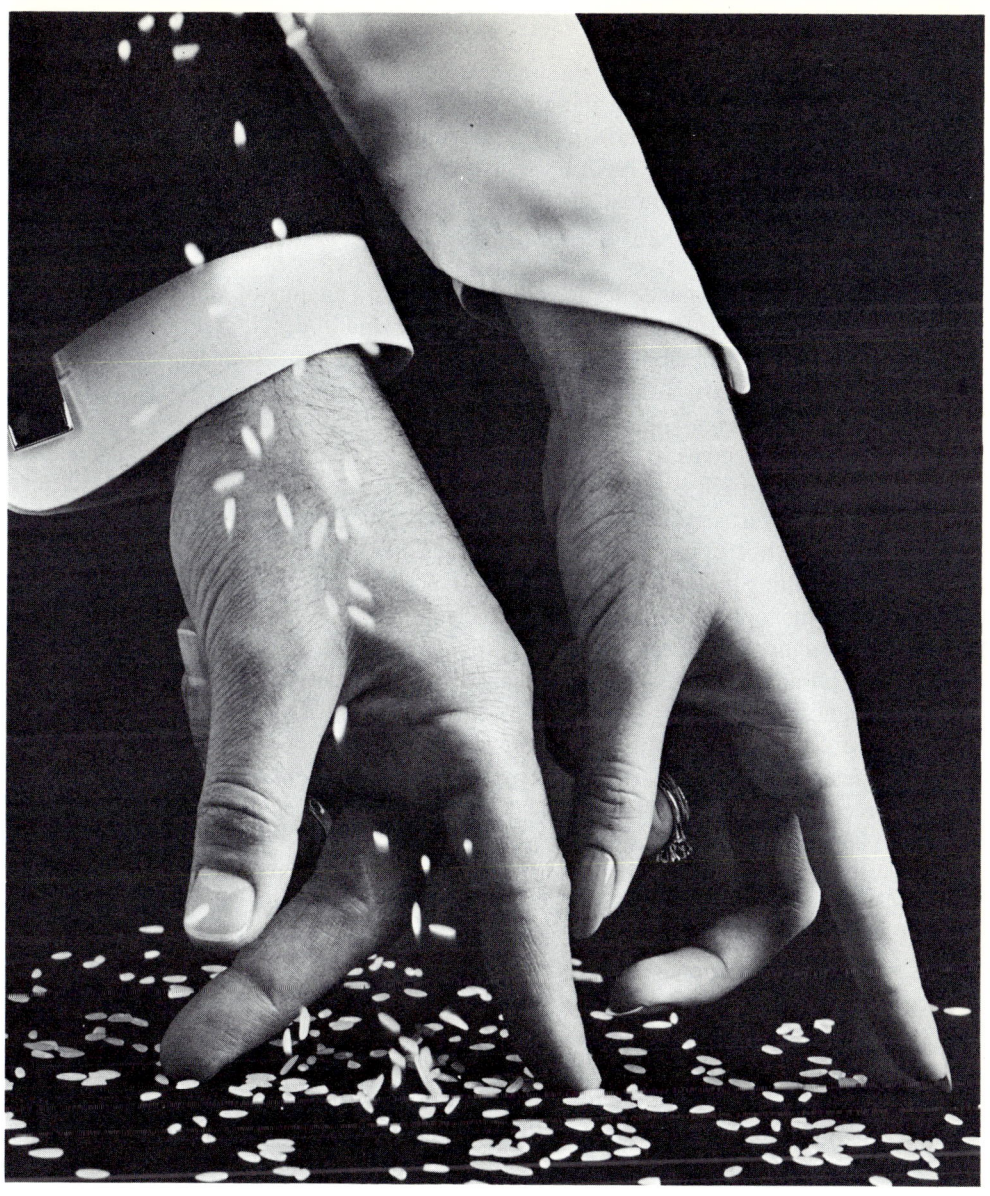

And happily ever after, let your fingers do the walking! Let the Yellow Pages help you furnish your new home... find any product or service! Read the ads for information on product features, brand names, store locations and hours. Before you march down the aisle of any store... **shop the Yellow Pages way!**

Few readers miss the structural motion in this advertisement. (Courtesy: American Telephone & Telegraph Company)

Building the Advertisement

certain letters of the alphabet; examples are S, J, Z, C, V, and O. The continuity strip as a technique of telling the advertiser's story leads eyes and attention to the next section — to learn what's next. Staggering the units down and across from the top achieves structural motion. In a somewhat more subtle manner the shapes and the directional placement of the units or masses themselves produce motion.

Balance

What and Why. Balance in an advertisement is a matter of weight distribution. Balance involves the location of sizes, shapes, and tones in relationship to the optical center. It is obvious that balance has two basic dimensions, left versus right and top versus bottom. Left versus right is by far the more important; each of these two halves must weigh approximately the same. True, the top and the bottom must not be so unbalanced as to disturb readers, but the fine degree of balance demanded between left and right is *not* essential between top and bottom.

When an advertisement is in balance, its masses appear to be settled in respect to each other, not tipping over, and to belong naturally where they are. There is stability resulting from weights being in balance, and there is equilibrium with respect to the optical center. The see-saw principle is observed — the more an element weighs, the closer it must be to the vertical center line. A picture or headline off-center to the left can be balanced by a logotype or a coupon off-center to the right.

Layouts should be balanced because balance is essential to sound composition. In balanced layouts, the various units asking for the reader's attention are in a state of attractive equality. The layouts are pleasing to look at because they obey a basic law of nature — that of equilibrium. Readers know, automatically and instantly, if an advertisement is not in balance. The absence of balance calls the reader's attention to that fact, although he may not realize what is disturbing him, and distracts him from the advertiser's message. In the balanced advertisement, no element draws attention so far to the left or the right as to make the advertisement seem unstable.

Formal Balance. The simplest and quickest way to insure that the left and the right halves of an advertisement weigh the same is to resort to *formal* balance. In this type of balance, all masses in the left half are duplicated in the right half in corresponding positions. Each half, left and right, contains half of each element because each element is centered and balanced on the central vertical axis. Since left half masses are matched in the right half, since each half contains literally what the other half contains, the two halves *must* weigh the same. This formal balance is the result of symmetry. When the layout is folded vertically down the middle, each element in the left half coincides with its exact counterpart in the right half. If there are only slight differences between the halves, then the advertisement is, perhaps, 85 or 90 per cent formal in balance.

The perfect symmetry, the unmistakable equipoise of formal balance endows an advertisement with certain qualities and connotations. There is a feeling of quality and refinement. There are implications of dignity and restraint, of formality and

Balance

The New Yorker has found that it serves both its readers and its advertisers more effectively if it tries to maintain an intelligent balance* between editorial and advertising pages and an interesting variety in both.

*A publishing principle which has guided The New Yorker for thirty-two years.

The New Yorker Magazine appropriately uses formal balance in this advertisement emphasizing its attempt to maintain balance between editorial and advertising pages. (Courtesy: The New Yorker Magazine)

reserve. There are undertones of conservatism and security — of stability, strength, and solidarity. These qualities suggest formal balance for institutional, financial, and professional use; they make it acceptable where prospects are few or prices are high. Banks, for example, tend to use formal balance in their advertisements.

But sometimes there are prices the advertiser may have to pay when he uses formally balanced layouts. His advertisements may seem cold instead of warm and inviting, aloof instead of friendly. Their primness may deny the advertisements any charm, and their uniformity may rule out sparkle. In the extreme, the layouts appear static and lifeless — even dull because they are so obviously tidy and respectable.

Informal Balance. Balance without symmetry, the off-center arrangement which achieves equilibrium without the centered balance found in formal balance, is *informal* in character. Formal balance places two boys of equal weight the same distance from the center of a see-saw. Informal balance places a small boy far from the center of the same see-saw and a big boy near the center. In a layout, the central spot in the optical center is still the fulcrum around which the advertisement's masses balance. But here, in contrast to formal balance, the left half units are unlike the right half units in shape and tone; individually, they are unequal to the right half units in size and weight. All units attract attention just strongly enough to bring the entire layout into pleasing equilibrium. Informal balance is optical, not physical; visual, not mechanical; subtle, not obvious. The left and right halves weigh the same, but they do not duplicate each other.

Building the Advertisement

The great charm of informal balance results from the hidden yet pleasant nature of the equilibrium. The unevenness of the patterns allows them to be unusual and original, forceful and dynamic, active and vigorous. In extreme instances, one finds surprise, daring, even excitement in these layouts. Interesting space divisions contrast with the identical sub-areas of formal balance. The lively, contemporary appearance fits today's pace and mood.

There is some slight risk in the use of informal balance not run when using formal balance. The layout artist must develop a sense of balance because there are no scales or formulas here; hence, balance is not foolproof. Sometimes readers do not see in an advertisement the equipoise the artist saw.

THE USE OF ILLUSTRATIONS

There *are* times when illustrations should be omitted from advertisements — but not many. It is true that illustrations, like every other element, must justify their inclusion, but it is equally true that justification is seldom difficult. The United States consumer is used to illustrations, she is an expert at getting their meaning, she both expects and looks for them. Historically, illustrations and not letters were the first form of written communication, and, currently, they constitute a universal language. The popularity of the "picture" magazines is at an all-time high; similar popularity is enjoyed by "picture" advertisements.

Why

The advertiser's purpose in giving his message pictorial expression is the same as it is when he includes any other element in a layout — to help his advertisement do a better job. The illustration is a powerful influence in shaping the character, the personality, and the tone of its advertisement. It is not uncommon for an advertiser to portray prestige and atmosphere in an illustration on the assumption that the class shown in the picture imputes class to his product and to him. In other instances, certain concepts (safety or faith) and certain objects (a horse race or a baby) simply defy communication by words; the inadequacy of language is compensated for by the use of pictures. In somewhat similar fashion, dramatization can be achieved with words, but any attempt to approach the dramatic action found in salesmen's demonstrations demands illustrations. Other values which can be built into advertisements by illustrations are description, suggestion, emphasis, and memory. As a final example, the illustrations often hold a campaign together by serving as a visual thread of continuity.

Illustrations do things to buyers as well as to advertisements. Pictures or drawings can be selected which will arrest and capture the initial attention of those individuals the advertiser wants to reach. Illustrations and headlines are about 75 per cent responsible for stopping prospects and getting their attention. A well-chosen illustration helps convert *visual* attention into *personal* attention, inducing people to read the copy by making them want to know more. Following through, the same illustration kindles the reader's interest in the product, helps make the reader want the product, and often contains proof of the claims found in the headline or in the

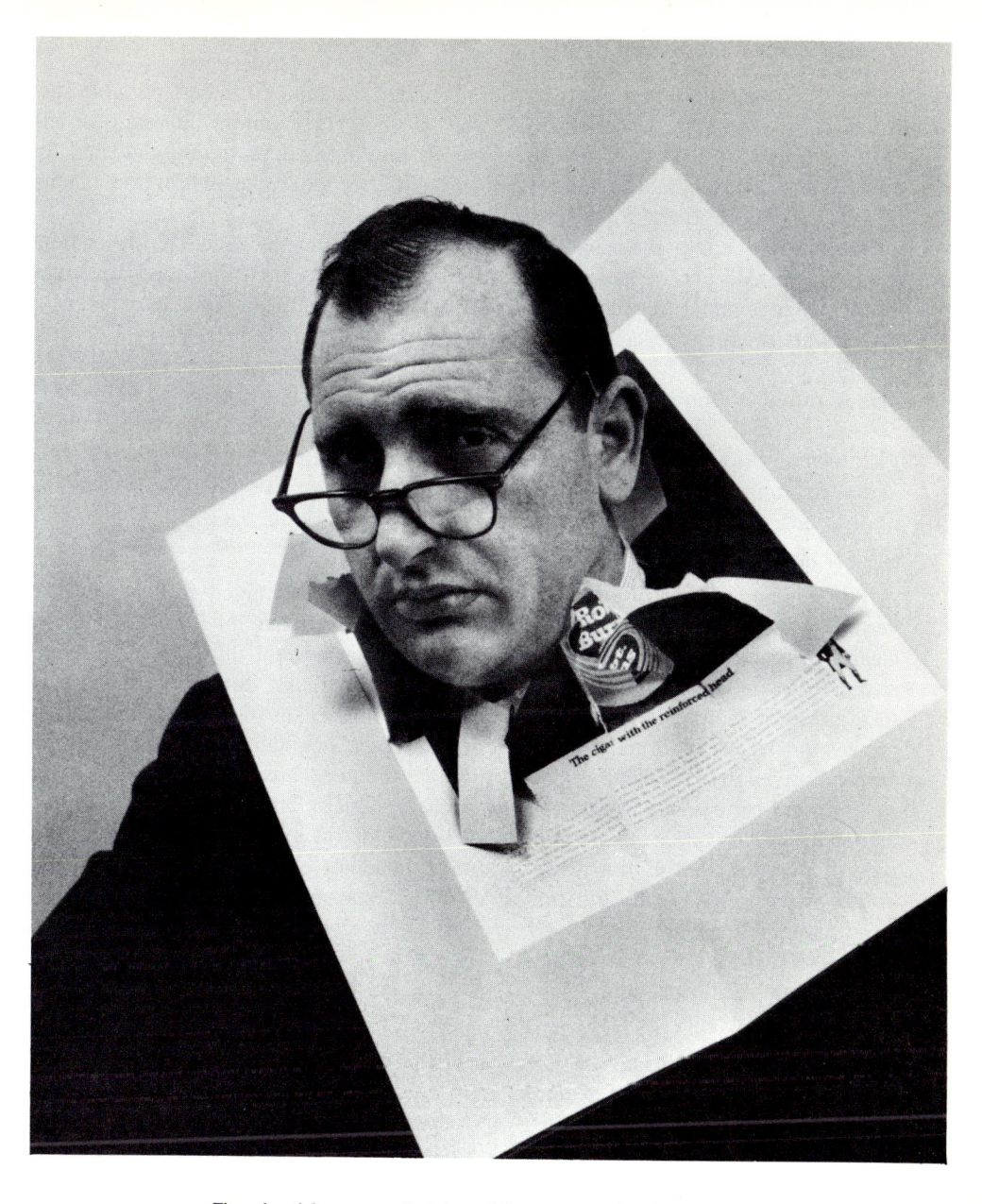

**The advertising agency that doesn't have an occasional disagreement with the client is simply not presenting new, different, or adventuresome advertising ideas.
At Young & Rubicam we wear our bruises like badges.**

This house advertisement for an advertising agency is interesting because of its illustration. (Courtesy: Young & Rubicam)

Building the Advertisement

body copy. Another contribution is that of giving the reader the best possible substitute for the product itself, namely, a picture of it. In addition, illustrations help the reader identify the product, its package, its brand name, its trade mark, and the advertiser's trade character. They show what the product can do for the reader, how he should use it, and the results of his using it.

The reader's comprehension of an advertisement may be aided if illustrations are included. Because consumers are visual minded, they find illustrated advertisements easier to understand than those not illustrated. Pictures may help explain the text and are often clearer and more detailed in conveying an impression of a product than are words alone. Imagine the job of announcing in an advertisement the new models of an automobile — without being allowed to use illustrations! The reader's perception of the advertisement's message is hastened by the right illustrations. Pictures and drawings help make a point quickly and help put the advertiser's story across for immediate understanding. Wordage is less than it would be without illustrations. Above all, illustrations need not be *read* — only *seen*.

Number and Size

The number of illustrations in an advertisement is determined by what the advertiser wants to accomplish through illustration. One dominant illustration seems clearly desirable; it usually gets more attention than several illustrations of equal size. Alone or with subordinate illustrations, the dominant illustration is superior to a group of pictures with no center of attention. Because a single large picture implies quality, most formally balanced advertisements contain one illustration only. Small illustrations can lighten up and ventilate the copy area, can add interest and motion, and can show various features of the product. The amount of space in a layout to give to one or more illustrations depends on such considerations as the type of product, the objects to be pictured, the other elements in the layout, the size of the advertisement, and the advertiser's aims. Most advertisements need a large, dominant illustration. Many advertisements give two-thirds of the space to illustrations, some give as much as 90 per cent, with a line of copy above, surprinted on, or below the illustration.

What to Picture

Several factors influence the selection of the objects to be pictured in an advertisement's illustration. For example, the purpose of the advertiser is a significant consideration. The scheduled date of the advertisement's appearance can be a major influence, particularly if that date is close, for example, to Christmas, Halloween, or Valentine Day. The nature of what is being advertised helps determine the content of the illustration. For instance, a manufacturer of certain personal products would be guilty of intolerably poor taste in showing his products in his advertising. Or, the sellers of such services as insurance and advertising have no tangible product to display. A final example of influential factors involves the person to whom the message is addressed. Research has determined, for example, that men are attracted by illustrations of other men, men and women, mechanical products, and sports scenes. Women favor illustrations of other women, clothes, food, children, and domestic situations. Both men and women are inclined to notice

Layout

illustrations of animals and natural scenery. The choice of what to picture is broad.

The *product* is perhaps the first object to think of illustrating. One possibility, of course, is to show the product or its package alone. This is simple and clear to the reader because the product is what he will be buying in a physical sense. Often appearance or identification are justifications for presenting the product or its package alone. Mail-order advertising practically demands this technique. Or, the product can be shown against an impressive background for the purpose of implying product quality. For example, an automobile can be shown parked in front of a mansion, or silverware can be shown on linen with china and crystal. A slightly different version is to picture one of the product's parts, or some detail of the product; these can be enlarged for emphasis or for clarity if desired. Showing how the product is constructed, and showing it ready for (or actually in) operation are other options.

Probably the most popular type of illustration shows the product being used by one or more persons. Activity and motion are assets easily included in such illustrations; they show that the product works, and works to the obvious delight of the users. It is difficult to quarrel with those who believe that showing cereal being eaten and enjoyed is superior to showing the cereal in its package, that an appliance being used is more effective than one seen in a dealer's store, and that a coat on a person is more persuasive than the same coat on a hanger. If he wants to, the advertiser can use this type of illustration to demonstrate how his products work or how they should be used.

The question of including the product is followed by the question of including *persons,* a matter referred to in the preceding paragraph. Persons add much human interest and attraction power because readers, being persons, are more interested in other persons than in mere products. The product alone or even in a setting ranks low in interest value. Individuals in action, individuals showing pleasure over the product, individuals doing things to or with, in or on the product have attention-compelling power. Of course, each advertiser must determine for himself whether or not to include persons.

Photographs Versus Art

If an advertisement is to be illustrated, a basic choice must be made between using photographs or art. True, it *is* possible for the use of photographs to be out of the question, or, indeed, impossible. Past happenings which were not photographed certainly cannot be photographed now; similarly, pictures cannot be taken now of future events. In some circumstances, photographs could possibly be made, but considerations involving distance, time, cost, or authorization may dictate otherwise. The typical situation, however, is one in which the advertiser or the layout artist can use either the one technique or the other.

Photographs have several assets. Because they are accurate, they invite belief; because they are realistic and authentic, the evidence or proof inherent in photographs ranks high in conviction value. Photographs record a moment in time, showing persons and objects exactly as they were at that split second. If case histories or testimonials are the copy format for a series of advertisements, the photograph

Building the Advertisement

recommends itself as the preferred type of illustration. Finally, in the vast majority of circumstances, photographs can be obtained easily, quickly, and economically.

Art does certain jobs better than photographs do. Art is superior in creating atmosphere and in conveying impressions. It allows more style, more distinctiveness, and more vigor to be built into the illustration. Art permits greater emphasis on and glorification of the product than does the photograph. Construction details of machines and appliances can be better pictured by art. Diagrams, particularly, make points understandable through the use of simplicity and clarity of detail. In addition, the artist enjoys greater control than does the photographer because he can get the exact expressions, positions — even the personalities and the moods he wants. He does not have to search for just the right models — he can create the individuals he needs.

Suggestions About Illustrations

A most essential quality of outstanding illustrations is their relevancy. If the advertiser insists that this characteristic be present in his illustrations, he will automatically avoid mistakes seen far too often. His illustrations will be selected to stop and influence his *prospects* — not everybody. He will disapprove illustrations which do nothing more than attract attention, because he knows that attention just for its own sake is weak. He will screen ruthlessly the gag type of illustration, knowing that these can easily be too "clever," so much so, in fact, that they can be dangerous. Some mistakes from the area of the gag type illustration are: Illustrations are seen turned upside down or on their sides. Pictures look one way right side up, but portray another object when turned upside down. Or, a manufacturer of industrial stacking racks displays a pretty girl in a swim suit — with the headline "Well Stacked." Irrelevant or inappropriate humor that does not harmonize with the rest of the advertisement has a difficult job in directing the reader's serious attention to the product being advertised. Illustrations that are freakish, repelling, or repulsive seldom do well for the advertiser. It is the suitable, helpful, pertinent illustration that gets the reader's *patronage* in addition to his *attention*.

The outstanding illustration is grasped instantly and accepted easily. The meaning of such illustrations is plain and clear at first glance. This feature is not present in pictures which possess only curiosity value. When the illustration is too complicated or involved, too abstract or sophisticated, this characteristic is missing. Then there must be acceptance or belief as well as understanding. Credible pictures appear normal, natural, and unposed. They do not promise more than the product can deliver, nor do they ask the reader to accept what, to him, seems impossible.

Illustrations must be sound in a technical sense. Faces should not be looking *out* of the advertisement, thereby encouraging the reader to do likewise. There should be no suggestion of cheapness in the quality of the illustration; saving pennies here can cost dollars. Just as each advertisement needs a single dominant focal point, so does each illustration, too. All "bugs" should be screened — a pair of dice should "seven out," a cow should be milked and a horse mounted in the correct manner, a weightlifter's knees should be locked when he is doing the two-arm military press. The middle, upper middle, and top areas of an advertisement give an illustration maximum visibility, whereas the bottom area ranks lowest.

If the product is new or improved, if it needs to be seen to be appreciated, or if identification is necessary, the inclusion of the product is logical; there is less reason for this inclusion if the product is unchanged and well known. A personal picture of the advertiser and a picture of his factory are most difficult to justify. In all cases, the illustration must be tied to the headline and to the body copy. Pictures are *means* — not *ends*. Because the reader is interested mainly in results, in what the product will do *for him,* he should leave an advertisement thinking not about the illustration — but about his need for and the desirability of the advertised product.

Questions and Problems

1. Where else, besides in ads, can unity be found with contrast?
2. There are well-known clichés in advertising copy. Are there clichés in advertising art?
3. What dangers are present when an advertiser "presents his product in a setting" for the illustration?
4. List some effective ways of obtaining distinction in layout.
5. What can be done with layout to attract attention to small ads?
6. What are some uses of white space in advertising?
7. Why are illustrations used showing objects other than the seller's product?
8. Why do some ads make no particular use of their optical centers?
9. How do you account for as many formally balanced ads as you see?
10. The Metropolitan Mutual Life Insurance Company is a large, national firm. Founded in 1885, it has grown into one of the 10 largest life insurance companies and has agencies in all 50 states. Its slogan is "Let Metropolitan Mutual Protect Your family.

    Metropolitan Mutual is a consistent advertiser, spending most of its advertising budget in magazines and TV. The firm's attitude toward advertising is healthy, and its advertising staff is able. Because of the nature of life insurance, Metropolitan Mutual's ads must recognize, refer to, and present a concept of *the future.* Children's education, death of the major earner, and retirement are examples of needs for which insurance is recommended.

    Assume you work in the firm's advertising department and have been asked to come up with some techniques for *picturing the future* in Metropolitan Mutual's advertising.

Chapter 9

Copy

The word *copy* has many meanings. Sometimes it refers to the text or body copy of an advertisement — the words printed in the smaller size of type. Sometimes it refers to the text plus the headings — the body copy plus headlines and subheads. Sometimes it is used so broadly as to include all typographical matter in the advertisement — the text plus the headings plus all other printed elements such as picture captions, slogans, brand names, trade marks, prices, and logotypes. A logotype is the advertiser's name or signature in prominent and distinctive lettering. A final and even broader use lets the word copy refer to the entire advertisement, including illustrations. In this chapter, we think of copy as the reading matter, the words and figures, in an advertisement. We are particularly concerned with words, sentences, paragraphs, subheads, and headlines.

Very few advertisements omit copy; very, *very* few can defend such an omission. Why? Copy is the essence, the heart, the core of an advertisement. Copy shoulders the main responsibility for influencing buyers; it determines whether or not an advertisement produces the desired reaction.

BACKGROUND INFORMATION FOR COPYWRITERS

The background needed for copywriting breaks down into four areas, namely, *buyers, products, channels,* and *promotion.* As for *buyers,* the copywriter needs to have in mind a clear, detailed picture of the person who should buy the product about which copy is to be written. This person is a present customer of the advertiser, or a present customer of a competitor of the advertiser, or a non-user of the advertiser's type of product. Essential buyer information includes buyer characteristics (age, sex, income, and such), buying habits, and buying motives. There is a danger that successful copywriters may lose personal touch with the great mass market of typical consumers. Some copywriters, particularly those in the upper income brackets, adjust for this tendency by reading the comics, talking to many consumers in the lower income brackets, sitting in the bleachers, and viewing the most popular movies and television shows.

In the *product* area, copywriters need to know all the facts about the product and its manufacturer which will be helpful. As was pointed out in the preceding chapter, the most important data about products are the benefits they provide in the uses to which consumers put them. Copywriters, of all persons, must be clear about the difference between benefits and product features, features which explain why the product can deliver benefits. The competitive standing of the product is necessary information; copywriters have an understandable interest in the product's competitive superiority, and, to complete the picture, they cannot ignore the plus points and the minus points of competing products and their promotion. If the copywriter himself has tried the product and found it good, so much the better.

Channels of distribution are not a subject of paramount concern to most copywriters. A general grasp of the advertiser's policies, procedures, and distribution is usually sufficient background information.

As for *promotion,* copywriters have a slender interest in personal selling, a bit more interest in sales promotion, and a great interest in advertising. Copy is usually written for one advertisement of a series, suggesting that, in most instances, the copywriter know the purpose of the campaign, its theme, the benefit or benefits it features, and the relationship of the advertisement being planned to the other advertisements in the campaign. The purpose of the advertisement — just exactly what the reader is to do — must be clear. The medium in which the copy will appear must be identified so that copy will fit the medium harmoniously. While the copywriter is not expected to be an expert on layout, he finds a working knowledge of the subject most essential; also valuable is the ability to work and get along with artists and illustrators.

Copywriters need to be able to write copy which will help buyers do a better buying job. Such copy helps to market merchandise by stimulating buying, by making consumers want the product. Important considerations here are (a) what to say, or the substance of the message, and (b) how to say it, or the style of the message. Above all, outstanding copywriters remember to write to a *buyer,* to a buyer not interested in advertising; they guard against writing to please themselves, their wives, their bosses, their associates, or other advertising people. They correctly rank performance over praise, customers over compliments, actions over awards. They know that if the reader's reaction is "What an ad!" — then the advertisement was a failure.

COPYWRITING AND RESEARCH

Every now and then one sees references to friction between copywriters and marketing researchers. The situation usually described pictures the copywriter as suspicious and resentful as regards the use of research findings. He feels in a strait jacket when told that, because of information gathered by research, he must do this and not do that. Ideally, copy and research operate in an atmosphere of cooperation rather than hostility. Copy must lean on and use research, all marketing research including copy research, for *facts.* Research, furthermore, checks on the effectiveness of copy, and copy, of course, can be improved only if one knows the

Building the Advertisement

response to advertising run earlier. Research cannot build advertisements nor write copy. The construction of outstanding advertising and the writing of outstanding copy are arts which cannot be reduced to formulas. Exceptional advertising copy demands copywriters with imagination and even a bit of inspiration. Sound, profitable advertisements produced by straight thinking, careful analysis, and organization are, however, much more numerous than the exceptional advertisements which spring from inspiration. The ingenious copywriter who looks on research as a source of information, neither as a competitor nor as a restraint, can produce effective copy even though he is limited in imagination.

THE ROLE OF COPY PRINCIPLES

What Principles Are

This whole chapter, of necessity, is essentially a collection of copy principles. Just what are copy principles? They are general rules for writing effective, productive copy; they are guides which relate to copy techniques. Copy principles identify the ideas and practices which, after much usage, have been found effective and successful. There is an element of universality in principles — most of them apply to services as well as products, to radio as well as magazines, to retail copy as well as manufacturer's copy.

Principles emerge from experimentation. A particular procedure or course of action is tried, and then the reaction is studied. Conclusions are reached — the tactic is or is not worth repeating, or, the execution should be modified in a certain manner. Inquiries, coupons, other traceable returns, research — these are used to discover whether or not the copy as finally run proved to be successful. A follow-up to find how the tactic made out and what the results were is absolutely essential to the development of principles.

As with *most* generalizations, copy principles apply to *most* advertisements. There are exceptions to most, perhaps to all, principles. Indeed, one can argue well that the only true rule in advertising is that there are *no* hard-and-fast, never-to-be-violated rules.

Use of Principles

Copywriters observe copy principles on the assumption and with the expectation that the resulting advertisements will enjoy a better-than-average performance. Principles throw light on the issues and problems confronting copywriters. Decisions made with full knowledge of the principles which apply are usually safer and sounder because of that knowledge. Developed out of trial and error, principles summarize the tactics, the elements, the techniques which turned out to be productive and profitable in the past. It is logical to believe that, if followed *now,* those same principles will reduce greatly the chances of failure.

As was true with research, principles are no substitute for common sense and judgment. In addition to research and principles, copywriters still need talent and imagination, inventiveness and ingenuity. The writing of effective copy is largely the art of the *application* of copy principles.

Crystal Owls • Height 5" • $70 each

Wise counselors recommend a visit to Steuben Glass to
choose Christmas presents of brilliant crystal.

STEUBEN GLASS
FIFTH AVENUE AT 56th STREET • NEW YORK 22, N.Y.

The market for Steuben items is such that formally balanced advertisements can be defended. Note the inclusion of price. (Courtesy: Steuben Glass)

Building the Advertisement

What happens when copy principles are ignored and violated? The chances are that the copywriter who flouts established principles will either (a) turn out some of the most outstanding, extraordinary copy of the decade, real Hall of Fame material, or (b) be the author of some of the most disappointing, ineffectual advertising ever run. Horse racing supplies a good analogy. The bettor who bets two dollars on the *favorite* in each of seven races *to show* will probably leave the races with a dollar or two in his pocket. The bettor who places a single bet during the afternoon, fourteen dollars, on the one *longest shot* that day *to win,* either leaves the races with a pocket full of money — or broke. It is worth emphasizing that most often he leaves broke.

THE BUYING DECISIONS

Because advertising is used to help sell products and services, a glance at the buying steps is worth taking. The buyer makes five decisions in the affirmative in making a purchase. So long as any one is missing, he does not buy; when he has said "yes" to all five, a purchase results. These five decisions relate to *need, product, source, price,* and *time.*

Need

The consumer does not buy until he becomes dissatisfied with his current state of affairs and unhappy with his present conditions. He must acquire the feeling that he lacks something useful and desirable, that his satisfactions are not as great as they could be. Until he wants to have or be more, he is not close to buying; the buying operation cannot start until there is an awareness and admission of *need.*

Product

As mentioned in Chapter 7, consumers do not buy services nor physical products as such; they buy the satisfactions and gratifications which result from the consumption of those services and products. They buy benefits, not features. Only when the consumer begins to see in the service or product the answer to his need does he begin to be a prospective purchaser.

Source

It is obvious that a buyer must feel that a seller is a satisfactory source of the item to be bought, else he would not seriously consider buying from that seller. Buyers do not have to be wildly enthusiastic fans of the seller, but they must find him acceptable to do business with — they must approve of him in that sense and to that degree. Source is usually a matter of *which manufacturer* or *which retailer;* it involves such issues as reputation, prestige, location, and policies. Institutional advertising, you recall, sells *sources* to consumers.

Price

No service or product is bought voluntarily unless the consumer believes it worth its price. Price joins source, then, in having to qualify as acceptable. Price is closely related to two other decisions, *need* and *product,* because the consumer relates price

Copy

to the urgency of his need and to the gratification he anticipates from consumption of the product.

Time

Finally, the consumer must agree that he should act *now* on his first four buying decisions. He must decide to make *and then make* the purchase, without delay. This final affirmative which triggers the purchase is often a critical step, sometimes a fearful one. Seldom can the consumer feel completely confident of the correctness of his selection.

COPY OBJECTIVES

All of the advertisements of interest to us should try for a favorable reaction or response of some specific sort; in other words, there should be an assignment given each advertisement. Eventually, advertising should result in more purchases by consumers — in greater sales volume for the advertiser. Product advertising affects sales by promoting the product, institutional advertising affects sales by promoting the advertiser. Very few advertisements, however, either those of manufacturers or retailers, hope to make immediate sales all by themselves.

A copywriter is expected to write copy which will influence the attitudes and actions of buyers. Until he knows what consumer response to the advertisement is desired, he is not ready to start drafting an advertising message which will register, be remembered, and persuade. The copywriter cannot know what to write until he knows what he wants the reader to do. At some future date, someone will have to try to determine how effective or productive the copy was. This can be attempted only against the job the copy was assigned. Copy goals should be as specific as possible. Seldom should one advertisement be asked to produce a maximum number of inquiries *and* a maximum number of purchases; seldom should one advertisement be asked to get both direct and indirect reaction.

Direct Action Objectives

A majority of retail advertisements but only a minority of manufacturers' advertisements are intended to cause a direct reaction. The immediate response desired to most retail advertisements is a visit to the advertising store. Mail-order advertisements, of course, hope to produce purchases, purchases which can be made in a few minutes by means of telephone calls or letters from the consumers. Inquiries are a form of direct reaction; these, like purchases, can be made of manufacturers or of retailers; they usually amount to the consumer's examining, or learning more about, the product advertised. A coupon may be included in advertisements soliciting inquiries. Quite similar to inquiries are consumers' requests for samples, premiums, and contest entry blanks. The mildest form of direct reaction is for the consumer to investigate, to analyze his situation or circumstances.

Indirect Action Objectives

Most product advertising done by manufacturers and most institutional advertising of all advertisers have indirect goals. They try to cause a psychological re-

163

Examine the Famous FORBES
STOCK MARKET COURSE
FREE for 10 Days in Your Own Home
*Either Return Course Without Obligation or
Keep It and Pay Only $1.83 Per Lesson!*

NEWLY REVISED

WHEN THE FORBES Stock Market Course was first conceived we thought it would have limited appeal to sophisticated investors so we only prepared a small number, sent each lesson out separately and had to charge $100 to cover the expensive initial preparation and high handling costs. We soon discovered that the "average" investor wanted and *needed* the Course even more than the experienced investor.

HOW WE REDUCED THE PRICE—BUT ENHANCED THE VALUE

Instead of mailing 15 individual Lessons, we consolidated the entire Course into one handsome binder holding all 15 Lessons. This, combined with the economies of "mass" production, enabled us to greatly reduce costs. As we reduced the price we were able to make the Course available to more and more investors at more attractive prices. NOW, the same Forbes Stock Market Course (but updated and expanded to meet today's needs) is available to Forbes readers for only $27.50—$1.83 per Lesson... a clear saving of $72.50! And ... by getting all 15 Lessons at one time, each student can set his own pace. The fast student needn't be held back by the slow ones. Furthermore, after you have completed the 15 Lessons you may ask any question about the material in the Course which is not absolutely clear to you.

PRACTICAL "LEARNING BY DOING" COURSE

This unique Course represents the ambitious pooling of the entire Forbes organization's know-how, experience and resources. No expense has been spared, no effort too great to prepare the soundest Stock Market Course *the average investor could utilize.* The now famous Forbes Course is practical—it is based on "learning by doing." At the end of each lesson you'll find a self-testing "Quiz" so you can check your own progress. You'll also find specific "Exercises" at the conclusion of most lessons to help you put into practice what you have just learned.

A WEALTH OF MATERIAL AT A NOMINAL PRICE

Read the partial list of what the Course covers in the panel at the left. Then, decide to replace "hit-or-miss" investment methods with the proven techniques that have worked for others—can work for you—in this famous 15 Lesson Course. After completing the Course, you'll be grateful you took this important step to stock market knowledge.

What you discover in a single lesson and apply to your investments could be a turning point in your future ... could set in motion a chain of many successful transactions.

15 PROFIT-PACKED LESSONS
Partial Contents

1. **Capital Building Through Stock Trading.** Principles Followed by Successful Investors. How to Set Up a Sound Investment Program.
2. **How to Select Stocks for Profit.** Investing vs. Trading. 9 Yardsticks for Investing. How to Select Stocks for Trading Profits.
3. **How to Make Money in Bear Markets.** What to Do If You Get Caught in the Break. Gold Stocks In a Bear Market. How Short Selling Works. A Safe Method of Short Selling. Use of Credit in Short Selling.
4. **Interpreting the Market Action.** How to "Read" the Market. 4 Technical Market Indicators. How to Detect Shift from Bear to Bull Market. How to Detect Start of a Bull Market. Signals to Watch. How to Tell Start of Vigorous Bear Cycle from Modest Recovery.
5. **Reading Market Patterns.** Current Value of Charts. Charting Methods. How to Detect "Trading Markets."
6. **How Securities Markets Function.** What Your Broker Does. Kinds of Stock Orders and How to Use Them.
7. **Common Stocks—Factors Affecting Their Prices.** Outstanding Characteristics of Bull and Bear Markets. Market Trends and the Business Cycle.
8. **Preferred Stocks and Bonds**—Their Advantages and Limitations. Five Guide Posts on Buying Preferred Shares. When to Buy Bonds. Using Bond Market as Stock Barometer.
9. **Protecting Yourself Against Bear Markets.** Signs Heralding Approaching End of a Bull Market.
10. **Sources of Investment Information.** What Investment Services Offer. How to Use Investment Manuals and Source Books. How to Read an Annual Report. Business and Economic Reports.
11. **Reading the Financial Page.** 9 Important Items to Look For.
12. **Dividends and Rights.** Types of Dividends. Calculating Value of Rights. Best Time to Exercise or Sell.
13. **Dollar-Cost Averaging.** How it Works, with Examples. Advantages and Disadvantages.
14. **The Professional Wisdom of Wall Street.** Twenty-Six Wall Street Axioms. Nine Golden Rules of Wall Street. Investors Stk. Analysis Guide.
15. **Symposium of Stk. Mkt. Inquiries.**

PLUS . . . Specific "Exercises" to Help You Put Into Practice What You Learn In Each Lesson.

Mail Coupon Today—10 Days Free Examination

FORBES Inc.
70 Fifth Avenue, New York, N. Y. 10011

Please enroll me in the original $100 FORBES STOCK MARKET COURSE which covers 15 Lessons. Permanent Binder and valuable Supplementary Material. I understand that all Material is copyrighted for the confidential use of enrolled students only, and that I can examine the Course for 10 days free. After this period I will return it without obligation or remit only $27.50 (plus postage and handling). Add $1.10 on N.Y.C. orders.

☐ Check here if you enclose $27.50 to save $1 postage and handling costs.
(Money-back in 10 days if not completely satisfied)

Name...
(Please Print)
Address..
City.................... Zone...... State...........

Example of long copy used to stimulate direct action. (Courtesy: Forbes, Inc.)

sponse. They hope to establish favorable attitudes and associations in the minds of buyers who are neutral or hostile, ignorant or misinformed. As for his customers, the advertiser hopes they will reaffirm their faith and confidence in the advertiser's company and product. The advertiser wants these customers to renew their intention to continue buying the advertiser's product when next in the market or when that product is next on the market. This is a matter of brand loyalty. Indirect action copy is designed to implant the brand name or company name in consumers' thinking and to get consumers to understand, to accept, and to agree with the advertiser's promises.

THE COPY FORMAT

An important line separates the nature of the advertising message from the technique or pattern chosen to present that message. The big sales idea is *what* the advertiser communicates; *how* or by what copy format he elects to transmit that idea is another issue. Sometimes this difference is expressed as the contrast between *substance* and *style,* sometimes as the contrast between *matter* and *manner*. An unfortunate choice of copy format can rob a strong sales idea of power and effectiveness.

The copy format is how the copy story shall be told. This concept is also known as *copy slant* and *copy angle*. In the conventional advertisement there is a dominant picture, a headline, some text or body copy, and a logotype. The conventional copy format in such an advertisement is a straightforward, direct presentation of buyer benefits and reasons for buying. Other possibilities include the following:

First Person	The speaker or first person can be one of many personalities. The product can be personified, for example. Someone connected with the advertising company, even up to and including the president, may deliver the story.
Dialogue	Doctor and patient, user and non-user of the product, parent and child, husband and wife, salesman and buyer, and two personalities connected with the product's TV show have all been used effectively.
Cartoon	One illustration shows one or more individuals in a situation intended to be somewhat humorous.
Strips	In one version, the *continuity* strip, a story or plot develops through a series of illustrations. Humor may or may not be attempted. In a different version, referred to as *picture-and-caption,* each individual illustration is independent of the others; there is no story tying them together.
Trade Character	In some advertisements, the message comes from the mouth of the advertiser's trade character.
Verse	Some rhymes, songs, and jingles rate high in memory value.

Building the Advertisement

Question-and-Answer   This format is particularly effective for new types of products and for long copy.
Recipes   A favorite for food copy.
Testimonials   Although sometimes abused, the testimonial continues to be one of the most effective ways of presenting an advertising message. Testifiers seem to be of three types: the expert; the person prominent in the world of sports, stage, screen, or society; and the "ordinary, everyday Joe."
Editorial   Here the copy and even the entire advertisement looks very much like the editorial features in the same medium. This copy format can often be found in the *Reader's Digest, Time,* and the *New Yorker.* Reading notices in newspapers are another example.
Sponsored Column   Certain individuals put together several small advertisements and combine them into a sponsored column. The advertising messages come ostensibly from the mouth of the sponsor.

HEADLINES

A headline is a word or phrase printed in large letters and implying, in effect, that just below (occasionally to one side) is an advertising message. *Picture captions* name, describe, or explain illustrations; captions are *not* headlines nor should they be asked to serve as such.

The headline is generally agreed to be the most important single copy element in the typical advertisement. It is the most read of all copy elements. Some advertising men believe that 50 to 75 per cent of the performance of an advertisement must be credited to the headline. Headline plus illustration assume almost the complete job of getting initial readership. The longer the copy, the more important is the headline. Each advertisement should contain a headline unless there are most unusual and strong justifications for its omission. Even then, its *functions* cannot be omitted. Copywriters usually write the headline before writing the text, but not always. It is not unusual for 100 to be written before one is selected, nor for the rest of the copy to be written in less time than was needed to perfect the headline. Good headline words are *you, wanted, new, now, announcing, how, which, who, this, these, easy, success, secret, advice, opportunity,* and *free.* Consumers will pay almost any price to get something "free."

Jobs of Headlines

The first of these jobs assigned to headlines is to make contact with buyers whom the advertiser wants to influence. While it is true that the illustration is of great assistance, and even the layout is of some help, the headline bears much of the responsibility for getting the attention of prospects and customers, for breaking into their streams of thought, for appealing to them. It is not the headline's job to try

A&F Co
"THE GREATEST SPORTING GOODS STORE IN THE WORLD"

Coverts are stirring

The coverts stir and your dog is as eager as you to flush the birds. Enjoy this golden moment fully. Come to us for the best in guns and gear.

Webley & Scott Shotguns Product of a famous English firm of gunsmiths, who build completely in their own factory. Supplied in 12- and 16-gauge; and, this fall for the first time, in 20-gauge. 2¾" chambers; 26" to 30" barrels; automatic ejectors; box-lock action. Selected walnut stock, straight or half pistol grip, with silver nameplate. Borings from full choke to cylinder $295.00

Shell Tote This handy bag of strong, thick cowhide is designed for carrying shells to skeet and trap club or a field shoot. Holds 8 boxes (200) shotgun shells $10.50

V.C. Gun Case This light, compact case of hand-sewn English russet leather, is suited perfectly to fine shotguns. Lined with billiard cloth; leather straps and reinforced corners of leather, sliding brass lock.
Double Barrel, Over and Under,
  Automatic $70.00
Gun with extra barrel . . $80.00

This company is one of few advertisers who can defend the use of the word "coverts" in a headline. (Courtesy: Abercrombie & Fitch Co.)

Abercrombie & Fitch
New York — 360 MADISON AVENUE   *Chicago* — VL&A — 9 NO. WABASH

Building the Advertisement

for the attention of *everybody;* it *is* its job to try for the attention of *every prospective customer.*

The second job for the headline is to induce buyers to read the text or body copy. The buyer's attention to the headline must be converted into an interest in learning more about what is implied in the headline. Readers use advertising headlines in the same manner as they use news headlines — to help them decide whether or not the message or story below should be read.

The third job, to deliver a short but complete selling message, is not assigned to very many headlines. To summarize the advertising message in the headline is not difficult to do. And, it is certainly true that some readers will read only the headline and no more of the copy. If, however, the essence of the story is revealed in the headline, some readers who could have been induced to read the text will not read it. The advertisement does poorly on the second job because it succeeds in doing the third job. Advertising people do not agree on whether or not a brief but complete sales point should be made in the headline. Probably more headlines make the mistake of telling too much than that of telling too little. These headlines are brief but complete selling messages:

> LIFE gives you the largest *able-to-buy* audience of any weekly or bi-weekly magazine
> Frigidaire washing action gets clothes 38% cleaner
> *LEXOL* preserves leather
> Pepsi-Cola refreshes without filling
> Ex-Lax helps your child toward his normal regularity . . . gently . . . overnight!
> General Electric *Thinline* Air Conditioner has no unsightly overhang — inside or out

Headline Types

There are two worthwhile bases on which to classify headlines, *content* and *form,* with overlapping, of course, between these groups. As for content, there are four main types, *identification, boast, news,* and *benefit.*

Identification headlines are most frequently nothing more than the brand name of the product; price may or may not be included. In other cases, the headline consists of the advertiser's name or, occasionally, his slogan. This is a weak type of headline because it assumes that the product is of great interest — that consumers are most anxious to learn more about it. Unless this is the case, and seldom is it, then the chances of the text's being read are not good. These brand names have served as headlines:

> Champion (spark plugs)   Arpege (perfume)
> Courvoisier (cognac)   Kohler (plumbing fixtures)
> Marlboro (cigarettes)   Cadillac (automobiles)

Boast headlines feature the product or the advertiser in sweeping, extravagant claims. These claims are often so general as to make the headline extremely ineffec-

Copy

tive. The bragging, boastful nature of the message reveals that the advertiser thinks too highly and too much about himself, too condescendingly and too little about the consumer. Examples:

>Easiest way to sew ever invented
>Best-tasting cigarette you ever smoked!
>The best value in sleep at *any* price
>The world's best tie . . . regardless of price
>Sensational new cigarette!
>Greatest spinning reel ever made!

Because consumers want to know the latest, to keep current on what is happening, and to stay abreast of what's new, they are attracted to *news* headlines. The news in the headline can relate to the product, its packaging, its price, its uses, its users, or to the advertiser. A complete selling message can easily be built into a news type headline. Examples:

New Victor Automatic Calculator saves you costly man-hours
New Kodak camera gives you the kind of travel movies people usually *pay* to see!
Sensible new approach to weight control

Benefit headlines are powerful and effective because they promise the consumer the realization of his hopes and success in his ambitions. They imply that there *is* a way — perhaps even quick and painless — to get something he wants; they offer a solution to a problem; they indicate that the text below shows the consumer how to gain one of the objectives. Like news headlines, these too can be complete selling messages. In respect to quality of content, benefit headlines outrank the other three types. Examples:

>Free! Be our guest at breakfast 24 times!
>Kraft gives you sliced Swiss cheese with the *freshcut* taste!
>Guaranteed to go thru ice, mud or snow or we pay the tow
>Enjoy year-round fun with the C.I.T. plan

The second basis on which we classify headlines is that of *form*. Once again, four types are considered, *question, command, curiosity,* and *selective*.

A headline can be phrased as a *question*. When the question calls for a "yes" or a "no" as the answer, it is quite restrictive and, as a consequence, can easily fail to attract the readership of many persons who are prospects. For an extreme example, the question "Were You Born In 1945?" seems entirely too restrictive ever to be used; for prospects born in other years, there is no implied reward for reading. Much more effective is the question for which the answer can be found in the advertisement — questions which ask what's wrong in the illustration, which pictured individual is famous and which is the look-alike, or which mistakes *you* make. Examples:

>How well do you know your heart?
>So you want *really fine* shoes?

How much do you know about Money?

This little True-False test might prove profitable—try it.

1. "Never keep all your money in one place. It's wiser to spread it around, with your checking account in one place, your wife's in another, and your savings still somewhere else."

   True ( ) or *False* ( )

2. "Never get too confidential with a banker. Your finances are your own business and the less he knows about them, the better."

   True ( ) or *False* ( )

3. "You're better off never borrowing any money."

   True ( ) or *False* ( )

4. "If you do have to borrow, and it's for several different purposes (home loan, auto loan, personal loan, etc.), never do all your borrowing from the same place."

   True ( ) or *False* ( )

The Answers?

You probably recognized that if you answered "TRUE" to any one of these statements, you're *wrong*. They're all FALSE, and here's why:

1. If you spread your accounts all over town, you're not as likely to become an important customer at any *one* place. With both a savings and checking account working for you at one and the same Full Service commercial bank, you have the edge when it comes to asking for a loan to buy a car, take a trip or even start a business. (Full Service banks make *all* types of loans, you know, and usually at lower rates.)

2. The more your bank knows about you, the more it can help you grow financially — through counsel, through credit references, and (most important) through *loans*. That's why Full Service commercial banks are in business.

3. Borrowing money is *not* naughty, your forefathers to the contrary. In fact, it's financially foolish not to borrow if you can *invest* the borrowed money to make more money. A bank loan is often a shrewder move than dipping into your savings.

4. By doing all your borrowing — and all your other banking business — with a Full Service commercial bank, you will earn special treatment that can result in a more advantageous loan.

How do you "get started" with a Full Service bank?

Pick a Full Service bank near your home or office. (Unlike many financial institutions, a Full Service bank is one that offers checking accounts, savings accounts, all types of loans, etc.)

Open both a checking *and* a savings account, and try to keep them active and growing. (While you're there, get to know some of the bank officers and ask them to help you prepare a Personal Financial Statement.) Then, from time to time, borrow a little money for some legitimate purpose.

Summing up, it appears that if there's any secret to "knowing about money," it's simply to get to know your banker *before* you need him and then use him for all he's worth. A responsible relationship with a Full Service commercial bank is the best financial and personal reference you can have. Why not get started now?

Your Full Service Commercial Bank

COPYRIGHT 1962/FOUNDATION FOR COMMERCIAL BANKS/PHILA. 1, PA.

Both challenge and curiosity value are in this questioning headline. (Courtesy: Foundation for Commercial Banks)

Copy

>Which of these homes expresses the real *you?*
>Have perspiration stains ever ruined your dress?
>Where *do* your taxes go?
>How would *you* pay a big unexpected hospital bill?

Another headline form is the *command*. The difficulty of building a buyer benefit into a command headline and the difficulty of including a reason for buying help explain why command type headlines are seen so infrequently. A less significant explanation is the danger of causing some irritation and some resentment on the part of consumers. If the headline is to be a command, it should try to tell consumers to do what they already want to do. Examples:

>Give them the protection of Hartford Group Insurance!
>Spark up mealtimes with California wines!
>Save now on Chase & Sanborn
>Seal it with "SCOTCH" brand . . . it'll *stay* sealed!
>Don't blow your top!
>Don't do it yourself!

A third possibility in respect to form is the *curiosity* headline. Sometimes the copywriter tries for provocation, hoping that consumers will see the headline as a game to play, a sporting proposition, something to decipher. Sometimes the headline is a single word, incomplete fragment, sometimes a blind statement which makes no sense in itself, sometimes an intriguing question which fires the consumer's imagi-

An example of the use of humor in advertising. (Courtesy: The Philadelphia Bulletin)

In Philadelphia nearly everybody reads The Bulletin
(Evening and Sunday)

Building the Advertisement

nation and challenges him to read more. Sometimes, of course, these headlines are much less puzzling and much more meaningful when related to the advertisement's illustration or to the product being advertised. Curiosity headlines are devoid of any direct selling value, and, in addition, they appeal to a weak motive, curiosity. Their effectiveness is increased when they are tied in with buyer benefits, news, or the product involved. Examples:

> The year the camel got its nose in the army's tent
> With his feet in ice water
> What does your handwriting reveal about you?
> How General Electric got the "HOSE SNAKES" off the floor
> Tabula rasa
> A hair is a tree

Selective headlines are our fourth form. The great merit of selective headlines is their power to alert the group the advertiser wants to influence, letting non-prospects continue on their ways. Selective headlines involve a serious compromise; the more selective they are, the *fewer* readers will be attracted — but the *higher* their quality. Just like the "yes-no" question headline, the overly selective headline lets too many prospects stay away from reading. Why should an unmarried coed read about a cosmetic product if the lead word in the headline is "mothers?" At the other extreme, the copywriter should seldom if ever try to write a headline *everybody* will read. Examples:

> For weight watchers . . . low calorie D-Zerta Pudding
> TEEN AGERS! Get results from new Dorothy Gray SCRUB KIT
> To every lady-in-waiting
> Man! What a shampoo for men!
> Going to Europe?
> To a future *engineer*

Headline Suggestions

Physically, headlines should be as short as possible. A generous range to suggest to copywriters is 3 to 14 words, with strong recommendation of the 4 to 8 segment. Brief headlines are necessary because of the reader's brief span of attention. Content, however, is more important than the exact number of words. Regardless of specific length, the headline must be one which the reader grasps instantly. Because newspapers get a rapid and short reading whereas magazines are read more leisurely, headlines in magazines can be longer than in newspapers. Type size should be large enough to contrast effectively with text type. Reading is invited by surrounding the headline with an adequate amount of white space and by limiting the headline to one line of medium length or to two short lines.

As for substance, the safest rule is to express the big sales idea, the heart of the message, in the headline. The place of honor definitely belongs to the buyer, not to the product nor to the advertiser nor to the advertisement. If at all possible, self-interest should be obvious in it; news, too, is a valuable element. Above all, there should be a strong implication that reading the text will be to the buyer's ad-

This is silly.

Some men still come home from a hard day's work and then have to wash or dry dishes.

Some women with far more important things to do, still have to stop after every breakfast, lunch and dinner and waste their time hand-washing dishes.

This is silly.

An automatic dishwasher saves more time and work than a clothes washer. Contributes more to your leisure than a stereo set. Costs one tenth of what you spend on a new car. Gives the whole family more time for fun together.

Really?

Yes. Our KitchenAid Dishwashers are so effective, you don't even have to rinse off the dishes first. Our unique drying system is safe even for plasticware and fine china.

Are KitchenAid owners happy with them?

Over half the dishwashers we sell are bought on their recommendation. No wonder: KitchenAid has the best service record in the business. That figures. We have a dishwasher history dating back 77 years. And we also make most of the dishwashing equipment for fine hotels, restaurants and hospitals.

So take off that apron and relax. Get an automatic dishwasher.

And before you choose one be sure to look at KitchenAid and compare it feature for feature. KitchenAid also offers you the widest choice of models.

Interested? Send for free booklet: "KitchenAid Dishwasher Comparison Chart". KitchenAid Home Dishwasher Division, Dept. KSI-3, The Hobart Manufacturing Company, Troy, Ohio.

KitchenAid®
DISHWASHERS

This advertisement illustrates the use of a blind headline. (Courtesy: The Hobart Manufacturing Co.)

Building the Advertisement

vantage. The substance of the headline should be in harmony and agreement with both the illustration and the first or lead paragraph of the text.

As for technical construction, the outstanding headlines are usually written in the second person for vigor and in the present tense, not the future tense, for strength. They are active, not passive; they include colorful, lively verbs. They make interesting reading because they are cheerful and optimistic, simple and specific, vivid and provocative. Their directness and their relevancy contribute to their clarity.

Young copywriters are often inclined to make the mistake in writing headlines of assuming that the cute headline, the clever headline, the pun, or the gag will do the job the advertiser hopes to do. The type of headline which does nothing but shock or startle, for example, the one reading, "Don't Read This," is another choice impossible to defend. The blind, irrelevant headline which depends completely on curiosity value may delight its author, but seldom will it excite consumers enough to induce their reading of the text. Vague claims, broad generalizations, obvious truisms, and wild boasts are additional mistakes to be avoided. Headlines which only entertain or amuse call attention to themselves and not to the product, thereby insuring failure.

No rule can be laid down about whether brand names should or should not appear in headlines. Few can quarrel with the contention that when either brand name or company name *is* included in a headline, it tends to reduce the reading of the text because that headline was made more selective by the inclusion. If the product and its brand name are almost universally known in the market, inclusion of brand name can be justified. If there are no news values to build into the headline, once again, inclusion of the brand name can be defended. If, however, the product is new or the message is newsworthy, omission seems wiser. If either the logotype or the package is featured prominently, the brand name can usually be omitted safely. Whenever included, either brand name or company name must justify its presence in a headline.

SUBHEADS

Subheads are secondary headlines, subordinate to the main headline. As for type size, subheads are smaller than headlines but larger than the text.

Those subheads placed immediately under main headlines usually continue and expand the thought of the main headline, developing, amplifying, or, perhaps, qualifying it. They increase the interest value of the advertisement and thereby strengthen the advertiser's bid for readers. Those subheads scattered about in the text ventilate it; they identify the subject or topic of their respective copy units; they summarize the advertiser's sales points throughout the text. They, too, can make a bid for readership by featuring secondary benefits and by making the text easier to read.

TEXT OR BODY COPY

Purpose

The text or body copy of an advertisement is the element asked to get the prospect to do what the advertiser wants done. The illustration and headline captured

Copy

the attention of a number of prospects, and the headline generated enough interest to induce a considerable portion of those prospects to start reading the text. The responsibility of the text, the assignment given it, is to cause the reader to react as the advertiser hopes. The text, more so than any other element, influences and persuades — or fails to do so.

In Chapter 7 the full range of goals which an advertisement may seek was defined: attention, interest, desire, conviction, and action. Whereas a salesman can and usually must try for all five, the typical advertisement will settle for less, for attention, interest, and desire. Action to a salesman means purchase; action to an advertisement is practically always less than an immediate purchase.

The text or body copy makes claims of advantages to buyers and promises benefits to them. It paints word pictures of satisfactions to be had. It explains and emphasizes reasons for buying, stressing *how* and *why*. It develops the advertiser's message and makes it believable. It offers proof of claims. It attempts to get the consumer-reaction desired by telling a fully adequate story, detailed and specific, and by spelling out the facts the buyers need or want.

The Big Sales Idea

The basic core, the central thought, the essential message of an advertisement should be a big sales idea. This sales idea is the benefit selected for featuring and any unusual twist given it. The best ideas are those which promise satisfaction, telling buyers "what's in it for *them.*" The text of an advertisement is organized around this big sales idea; the idea serves as a point of focus. Because it is concentrated on this one concept, the text can be powerful and intense. The emphatic nature, the impact of the idea make for greater clarity and understanding.

The big sales idea needs to be expressed in just about every important element in the advertisement. It should be obvious in the illustration, the headline, the lead or first paragraph, the text, and in the closing paragraph. It is, thus, announced at the beginning, enlarged on in the text, and repeated in the ending of the advertisement, often in the form of a specific phrase or slogan. Such repetition insures a greater grasp of the idea, deeper penetration, and more memory value. If not the campaign theme, and it may well be, the big sales idea must be in harmony with that theme.

Organization

The procedure of organizing the text or body copy starts with a clear picture of the reader to whom the copy is being written. Next, the copywriter needs to know what specific reaction is desired from that reader. Then comes the organizing step — the building of a presentation, paragraph by paragraph, which will get that reaction from as many readers as possible.

The most effective organization is one designed from the reader's point of view. Ideas are put in proper sequence: copy elements are put in proper sequence; there is orderly arrangement and flow in each area. There is unity and a logical thread of continuity in good organization. Because ideas are developed properly, the text holds together; the reading sequence is clear.

Building the Advertisement

Although it is obvious that no single outline can fit many situations, here is a standard pattern which can sometimes be used, sometimes be modified:

1. Recognize a buyer-problem or a buyer-desire. This recognition is usually made in the headline so as to get maximum attention of prospects. The problem or desire should be true to life and present in the prospects' own experience.

2. Recommend the product being advertised as the best solution or best answer to the problem or desire. The emphasis here is on the product *as a solution* — not on the product itself. The problem or desire is still the major consideration.

3. Promise benefits and advantages. Spell out in adequate detail and in attractive terms the satisfaction to be had.

4. Personalize these benefits and advantages if possible. Reassure the reader that the satisfactions to be had are available *to him,* that he will benefit *personally,* that the satisfactions are designed for *his* situation and for *his* circumstances. Specific information is especially helpful here.

5. Offer proof for the advantages claimed and the benefits promised.

6. Ask for action. Be absolutely and completely clear to the reader about what he is to do. Tell him *where* the product can be found and its *price* if those bits of information are appropriate. If there is a particular reason why the reader should act *now,* include it.

Lead Paragraph

The lead or first paragraph of the text is the most important paragraph; its influence is great in a reader's decision to read or not read the second, third, and fourth paragraphs. It is true that some advertisements use a number of independent, one-paragraph copy blocks, some advertisements prefer a layout so divided that their body copy, too, is not a sequence of paragraphs, and still other advertisements contain only a single paragraph of text. Even so, many advertisements do and will continue to contain lead paragraphs, their most important paragraphs.

The lead paragraph should develop from and continue the thought of the headline, enlarging on it and amplifying it. By following up the headline idea, by expressing the same point in other words, the paragraph gives emphasis to what the headline said. The lead paragraph can well afford to limit itself to backing up the headline's basic concept — there are other paragraphs for other uses. The very first sentence should begin to transfer *reading* interest into *product* interest. This is best attempted by appealing from the start to the reader's self-interest — by offering a solution to a problem or by suggesting an answer to a need or want. Seldom is the lead paragraph the place to comment on product features. Here are two examples of lead paragraphs which support their headlines:

Only the O-Cedar Sponge Mop has the "wonder-working angle"

"Wonder-working angle" is an O-Cedar *exclusive* that gets floors cleaner — faster! The sponge hugs flat to the floor . . . scrubs out the most stubborn dirt . . . picks up far more water yet squeezes out drier. You can actually damp mop an entire floor in just *minutes.*

The Outer Banks — where the ghosts of early America still walk

Off the Carolina coast, where Cape Hatteras points seaward, is a thin ribbon of islands called the Outer Banks. This lonely, windswept stretch has always been wild and primitive. Yet it has known some of the great names of history . . . Sir Francis Drake . . . Blackbeard the pirate . . . Virginia Dare, the first English child born in America . . . Orville and Wilbur Wright, who made the first airplane flight at nearby Kitty Hawk.

Occasionally, the headline and the lead paragraph do *not* stress benefits or news about products. In these exceptional cases, the explanation can usually be found in the standardized, physically identical nature of the product — a nature which makes the product of low interest to consumers. The answer for these situations may be to build human interest material or humor into headline and lead paragraph — even into illustrations — to attract the readership of a worthwhile number of prospects and then shift the reader's interest over to the product.

The better lead paragraphs are short and to the point. Some run not more than twenty words in length, many contain less than fifty words. Three sentences which average fourteen or fifteen words in length can make up an outstanding paragraph. A good lead paragraph moves out at full speed from the very first word.

Interior Paragraphs

The lead paragraph may be separated by some interior text from the closing paragraph. Interior paragraphs flow on from the lead paragraph, developing the advertising message and expanding it. The more common sequence is to lead with buyer benefits and then to support them with product features; this is the effect-back-to-cause pattern. Only when the advertiser's product is generally recognized to be the best in its classification or when it enjoys great buyer-interest is the copywriter entitled to consider seriously the cause-back-to-effect sequence — product feature back to buyer benefit.

Interior paragraphs deal largely with benefits promised and proof to back up those promises. *Benefits* have been referred to many times in this chapter; they are the advantages, the gratifications, the satisfactions wanted by the consumer which the advertised product will supply. In presenting these, the copywriter recognizes the consumer's point of view, stressing what the consumer wants to hear rather than what the advertiser wants to say. This prevents a presentation of the product just as a product — what it *is* and *has;* this insures a presentation which, instead, concentrates on the consumer. The headline benefit will certainly be repeated and amplified. Other benefits, too, may be included. A contrast will be made between how the consumer is now and how he will be, between what he wants and what he wants to change or avoid. The promises of benefits are expected to transfer the consumer's interest in the product into interest in buying the product.

Proof is needed in many advertisements, in perhaps *most* of them, if the consumer is to accept and believe the promises of benefits and the other claims made. And remember, the typical consumer is both wary and skeptical. Direct action copy, strongly competitive copy, and industrial copy are three types of advertising in which much proof is found. Conversely, indirect action copy, consumer copy, and announcement copy are three types requiring less proof. Here are some of the more common types of proof:

Building the Advertisement

Construction evidence
Product feature
Performance
Tests the advertiser ran
Tests the consumer can run
Tests by research firms
Case history

Product's rank in the market
Guarantee
Testimonial
Endorsement
Trial offer
Demonstration offer
Sample

Closing the Text

Just as most presentations of salesmen include an attempt to close a sale, similarly, most advertisements should include a specific bid for the reader reaction desired. The close may be a sentence or a short paragraph. It can range from subtle suggestion and indirect implication to the unmistakable command which uses words such as *do, go, act, telephone, try, use* and *ask*. In all cases, the copy should be specific and clear about the response wanted. This response, furthermore, should be made as easy and convenient as possible for the consumer.

The reaction desired to *indirect action* copy is a matter of consumer attitudes. Pleasant impressions and favorable mental associations involve the product, sometimes the advertiser, occasionally the retail dealer handling the product. For long text, the closing paragraph may be a summary. In every instance, the closing words should repeat the big sales idea on which the advertising message is based. Some verbatim repetition of key words or phrases may be desirable in this restatement of the basic idea. Implications, invitations, suggestions, and even gentle commands are appropriate. These closing paragraphs are from indirect action advertisements:

So, a word of warning when you get brakes relined: Demand quality lining. It stops better, wears longer. Stay away from the cut-rate places. Know your servicemen. Know your lining. If it is Bendix Eclipse, it's top quality.

The people of Union Carbide are constantly at work on new and improved alloys to make better metal products for all of us.

Direct action copy wants a behavior type of response, usually an *inquiry* or a *purchase*. The close in this type of advertising needs to be as clear about what the advertiser will do as about what the reader is asked to do. It needs to be stronger and, often, longer than the closes in indirect action copy; a short suggestion is clearly inadequate. A coupon may be part of the closing attempt. Because the reader must be quite moved and impressed before he goes into action, a powerful reason for acting *now* is effective. Sometimes a time limit is placed on the advertiser's offer, or the supply is limited, or a price rise is imminent, or a reward or premium of some sort is offered as an inducement for acting at once. Easy terms of purchase may be available. Guarantees and trial offers may be made a part of the offer for the purpose of reassuring readers. Here are two closing paragraphs from direct action advertisements:

Learn how DICTABELT and Dictaphone TIME-MASTER can help *you* communicate faster, easier and better. Call your local Dictaphone office, or write

Dictaphone Dept. E, 420 Lexington Ave., N.Y. 17, N.Y. Ask about our rental plan, too.

Send the coupon and receive, by mail and without charge, a booklet which tells about Phoenix Mutual Plans. Similar plans are available for women — and for Employee Pension Programs. Don't put it off. Send for your copy now.

Various elements or units are seen sometimes below the text or body copy. There may be a list of the advertiser's other products, or a list of some of the advertiser's retail dealers. Sometimes the reader is given an invitation to and information about the advertiser's radio or television shows. Sometimes the element is a slogan or a trade mark. In many advertisements the bottom element is the logotype identifying the advertiser.

LENGTH OF TEXT

What is *long* copy? How much is *short*? How much text or body copy should an advertisement contain? What are the merits of long copy, and of short copy?

No breakpoints have ever been established which classify copy according to length. A rough grouping defines short copy as that containing fewer than 100 words, and long copy as running in excess of 200 words. Of course, 1,000 words written in an interesting, easily grasped, pleasing style can seem short, whereas 100 dull and difficult words can seem quite long. Length, then, matters not — so long as the consumer is interested enough to keep reading. *What* an advertisement says and *how* it says it are more important than *how long* the copy runs. The concept of good copy versus weak copy is much more valuable than the long versus short contrast.

Various factors influence copy length. One, of course, is the intent of the advertiser; he may be wanting to do a reminder job, or to qualify for a certain low rate, or to explain a new contest. The nature of the product message is a major determinant; vacation tours demand more copy than chewing gum. The nature of the medium is another factor; broadcast codes include provisions about length, and a poster, obviously, cannot accommodate the quantity of copy which can be handled on a car card or in a magazine. The prospect's need for information is a factor; purchasing agents usually must have considerably more information about industrial products than individuals need about consumer products.

The merits of short copy are obvious. It is more inviting and less discouraging to prospective readers. It saves the reader's time and effort. It gets read by more individuals; readership falls off sharply, for example, as length increases from a few words up to 100 words. Finally, short copy may be less expensive.

Long copy, too, has merits. If illustrations and brief copy will not do the advertiser's job, then long copy is essential, especially for new, strange, or complicated products. A completely adequate story often demands a large volume of body copy. If there must be much reason-why material and proof, short copy is out of the question. If human interest material, humor, or drama is needed to attract readership, there is pressure for considerable copy.

Building the Advertisement

Our conclusion is that copy *must* be long enough to do the job assigned to it; it *need not* be any longer. As the King said gravely in the trial scene in *Alice in Wonderland,* "Begin at the beginning and go on til you come to the end; then stop." The copywriter should say what ought to be said and should use no more than the volume of copy needed, but he should not start off determined solely to write either a long or a short advertisement. Long copy can be acceptable and even attractive through the proper use of generous space size, white space, subheads, large type size, short lines, and short paragraphs. Brevity at the price of sales power is a poor choice.

SOME COPY CONSIDERATIONS

Information

Before an advertisement can influence and actuate, it must stop and inform. Basically, the reader wants to know what the product is, what it costs, and, above all, what it does to and for him. Two background facts are well worth remembering. One, the typical consumer actually knows very little about the product and its capacity to provide satisfaction. Two, the consumer is not going to study, to strain, to work hard in order to understand the advertiser's message. These two facts recommend that every advertisement be full enough of information to tell the exact story the advertiser wants to tell *and* full enough so that the consumer will not have to do any inferring or assuming. A normal reading of the copy should leave no unanswered questions and no inaccurate ideas in the reader's thinking. Never should the reader be expected to check any past or future advertisements to get essential information. Adequacy is the rule here just as it was for length of copy.

Interest

Unless consumers find copy interesting, they will not read it. Until the advertiser captures the consumer's mind and gets the consumer to thinking about the product as a possible purchase, the advertiser has not made much progress. Consumers are readers before they are buyers, and great numbers of them leave the advertising message literally at the end of every sentence unless the copy is good reading — pleasant, enjoyable, even entertaining. Copy that is dull, boring, and monotonously like competitor's copy is passed over in favor of copy that is unusual, fresh, and sparkling.

Certain matters are more interesting than others. Women are interested in clothes, food, family, and home. Men are interested in income, earning ability, sports, and mechanical products. Sexy copy and illustrations appeal to few women and do not excite buying desire in many men.

The consumer's greatest, most intense, most permanent interest is, of course, in himself. He is the king to whom the advertiser must pay homage. He has little time and less inclination to read about how good a product is or how grand the advertiser is. He *does* find interesting copy which tells how much the product and the advertiser will do for him — sometimes so interesting that he finds the copy easier to read than to ignore. Copy that ties in with the personal experience of the consumer, that helps him with his problems, that shows him how to get what he wants, is interesting copy.

Believability

We have just recognized that if copy is to be *read,* it must be *interesting.* We now observe that if copy is to *influence,* it must be believed.

The consumer's emotions and feelings have much to say about what that consumer believes because belief is an individual, a personal matter, resting more on emotion than on reason. The consumer's background and experience are strong influences. If the consumer has information which contradicts the advertising claims, he has trouble accepting the claims. If he has had experiences incompatible with those claims, he is inclined not to believe. Consumers tend to believe what they want to believe — about how to become beautiful, or healthy, or wealthy, for example. They tend to believe what others believe, friends, authorities, even "everybody."

Interestingly, truth is not enough. There are cases on record of consumers' refusing to believe that products had undergone and survived certain extremely demanding tests — when they actually had. There are more cases of consumers' accepting and believing untrue copy. Of course the claims, promises, and statements should be true. In addition, the big sales idea must strike the consumer as fitting, suitable and plausible, in harmony with his own experience. Belief is greater when the satisfaction promised ties in to a basic, genuine consumer desire; such promises are easy to believe. A course of moderation, one which allows only reasonable and sensible promises, one which keeps claims within the consumer's everyday, normal experience invites belief. Understatement can be more powerful than overstatement in achieving belief.

Disbelief is greatly encouraged by gross exaggeration and the wanton use of superlatives. Claims that are vague and general instead of specific and factual invite rejection. Copy that is insincere, extravagant, or excessively competitive is accepted by few consumers as truthful. Phrases that are meaningless and phrases that are not understood obviously cannot be believed. Omissions of proof of promises, the proof mentioned a few pages back, can be responsible for the consumer's unwillingness or inability to believe.

Persuasion

To be successful, copy must persuade; to be persuasive, copy must, most of all, be *sincere,* a quality most difficult to simulate. When the advertising message is honest and frank, when it is characterized by restraint and simplicity, when its tone is friendly and warm, then readers are inclined to go along with the advertiser's suggestions. Persuasive copy reflects the advertiser's genuine concern for the reader and the interest the advertiser feels in helping the reader enjoy greater success in his undertakings. A straightforward, direct, obvious approach to helping the reader maximize his satisfactions is usually more effective than an oblique, circuitous approach.

Memory Value

Product identification is a most serious matter for advertisers. Advertising message identification is a difficult problem of the same sort. Copywriters can easily become discouraged or even depressed upon learning how many consumers do not

Building the Advertisement

know what advertising story is being told currently by and about brand "A" or brand "B."

Memorable copy starts with the selection of a powerful sales idea; weak ideas just do not register, penetrate, and stick. Building on a *single* idea, not two or three, makes for greater memory value because one grasps and retains a single idea more often and more successfully than several ideas. A completely clear presentation is a prerequisite for memorable copy; what the reader fails to understand, he fails to remember. A distinctive presentation results in the story's being remembered longer than otherwise, because the sameness of copycat copy and copycat format tend to make sponsor identity vague, uncertain, or even anonymous. A final suggestion is that the big sales idea, the featured promise, be repeated several times within the advertisement; restatement is as difficult to overdo as it is effective.

Price

When should prices be included in advertisements? Pressure to include prices originates in the reader's desire to know the price, his inability to consider intelligently and seriously the product as a possible purchase while still ignorant of price, and in the fact that no element in making a buyer's decision is more significant than price. Omission of price makes the figure a mystery, an irritating mystery to some. Most retailers have no option — they *must* include price.

Unavoidable differences in retail prices exert strong pressure on many manufacturers to omit prices from their advertising. The price of a product can vary from region to region, from market to market, even from retailer to retailer within a market. Transportation, taxes, installation, and the accessories selected are examples of the causes of price variation. In the case of a very high price, the advertiser may prefer to give a salesman an opportunity to build up the product's value in the prospect's mind before revealing the product's price. When the price is low, widely known, and identical with competitor's prices, there is less reason for its inclusion.

The generalization indicated seems to be that prices should be included unless there is extremely strong justification for omitting them. Many advertisers who do not quote prices because of price variation could quote *approximate* price, such as "about $15." When prices *are* included, they should be close to what the consumer must pay; they should not be "bait" prices.

Questions and Problems

1. Advertising copywriters, unlike salesmen, cannot check with buyers to see that the copy message was received and understood. Suggest some buyer-questions the answers to which should be built into the copy of most ads.
2. A manufacturer of canned and frozen soups is wondering if his advertising for next year should be of a *humorous* type, or not. Comment.
3. If you were to draft eight rules for copywriters to observe when writing headlines, what would they be?
4. Every now and then advertisers include "Your money back if you're not satisfied" offers in their ads. How risky is this?

Copy

5. Argue that prices should be omitted from manufacturers' ads.
6. What may result when an ad does not contain enough copy?
7. When should the hidden or buried offer be used rather than the featured offer?
8. Compare the use of headlines in ads with their use in news stories.
9. A manufacturer offers a product sample in his ads. How can he hold down the requests of children and other non-prospects?
10. For the past ten years, Jim Johnson, 29 years of age, has been a salesman for the King firm which makes men's clothing. Jim works on the West Coast; he lines up new retail accounts, and he services his active accounts. Jim is an avid reader and analyzer of King's advertising and of the advertising run by King's competitors. He can usually find time to talk advertising with his retailers.

Jim is a good salesman. His company is good. But, for five years Jim has been restless. He thinks he would enjoy and be good at writing promotional material, including advertising, addressed to ultimate consumers. The last time Jim was at the home office attending a sales conference, he asked the King advertising manager to be considered for the next writing vacancy. Comment.

Chapter 10

Typography, Production, and Color

This chapter consists of three sections: one treats *typography,* one treats *production,* one treats *color. Typography* involves the selecting and arranging of type faces and sizes. *Production* puts the advertisement into printed form. *Color* raises the question of whether the advertisement should be done in black-and-white, or in color.

TYPOGRAPHY

Anatomy of Type

Face. A type face is a designer's interpretation of a basic form; it is the shape, the proportions, and the design of the letter or figure you see printed. Each type face has its own name, usually that of its designer, and no two faces look exactly alike. The type face in which this book is printed is Times Roman. Type faces differ in the same way that the handwriting of individuals differs. All lower case or small letters have a center body, and eleven have either ascenders (b, d, f, h, k, l) or descenders (g, j, p, q, y). Upper case or capital letters are of uniform height, and one has a descender, the *Q*. Some type faces have longer ascenders and descenders, proportionally, than do others. In any one size, lower case letters without ascenders or descenders are of equal depth; they do vary in width, as a glance at *m* and *i* shows.

The type face rests securely on top of a *shoulder* or base. The face does not occupy all of the shoulder area but, instead, allows enough of the top and bottom of the shoulder to extend above and below the face so that a letter with a descender will not touch a letter with an ascender in the next line below.

Some but not all type faces have *serifs.* These are short little bars, flourishes, or lines found at the ends of the main strokes or lines of letters. Serifs were added originally so that letters chiseled in stone would look more finished.

Family. A widely known type face, for example, bears the name Caledonia. The Caledonia *family* consists of the *alphabets, weights,* and *widths* in which Caledonia can be had. As for alphabets, popular faces are usually available in lower and upper case letters, small capitals, italic lower case, and italic capitals. Weight is determined

184

by thickness of line. Most faces in common usage have two or more weights, often four, sometimes even more; a quartet frequently found consists of lightface, medium, boldface, and extra bold. Adjustment of weight permits color control, variety, and emphasis. Width has to do with the lateral space occupied by a type face. The condensed version has a face narrower than the regular version, and, so, requires less width; the extended version is wider and must have more horizontal room than the regular.

Type Measurement

There are three basic measurements in the area of type: the *point,* the *pica,* and the *agate line.*

Type faces are measured vertically in terms of *points.* As there are 72 points to an inch, a single point is about the thickness of a calling card. Point size measures the shoulder on which the face rests rather than the face itself. In 36-point size, the type face of the *h* and the *j* are closer to one-half inch in length, clearly, than are the *a* and the *e.* You recall, too, that some faces have longer ascenders and descenders than do other faces, but it is the body on which the face rests which determines size. Type of interest to advertisers ranges from 6-point to 72-point and can usually be had in these sizes: 6, 8, 10, 12, 14, 18, 24, 30, 36, 42, 48, 54, 60, and 72. Body type, used for setting the main text of the advertisement's copy, is usually 14-point or smaller; display type, used mainly in headlines, is usually 18-point or larger. Most editorial matter in newspapers is set in 8-point size; most textbooks are printed in 10-, 11-, or 12-point type.

The *pica* is a linear measurement 12-points or $\frac{1}{6}$ of an inch long. Width of column and length of type line are usually measured in terms of picas.

The *agate line* is $\frac{1}{14}$ of an inch deep and one column wide. Much space in newspapers and some space in magazines are ordered and priced in terms of agate lines.

Type Groups

A type *group* consists of families having the same general features and somewhat similar faces. Families may be combined into three groups, the *roman,* the *gothic,* and third, a *miscellaneous* group.

Roman. This group derives its name from the letters carved on stone in Rome during the days when Rome ruled the world. Probably the most famous Roman letters are at the base of Trajan's Column, erected in A.D. 114 in Trajan's Forum in Rome. The lines forming Roman letters are not of the same width — part of the letter is thick, part is thin. The letters are simple combinations of curves, angles, and serifs.

The Roman group traditionally has been subdivided into *Oldstyle* and *Modern,* terms which refer to design rather than to dates. A comparison of the two shows that, in *Oldstyle* faces, there is less contrast between the thick and thin strokes. The axis of round letters is diagonal, and the letters are free and flowing, soft and warm. Serifs are diagonal or oblique, somewhat blunt, and round off into the stem of the letter. The *Modern* faces show a pronounced difference between the thick and thin

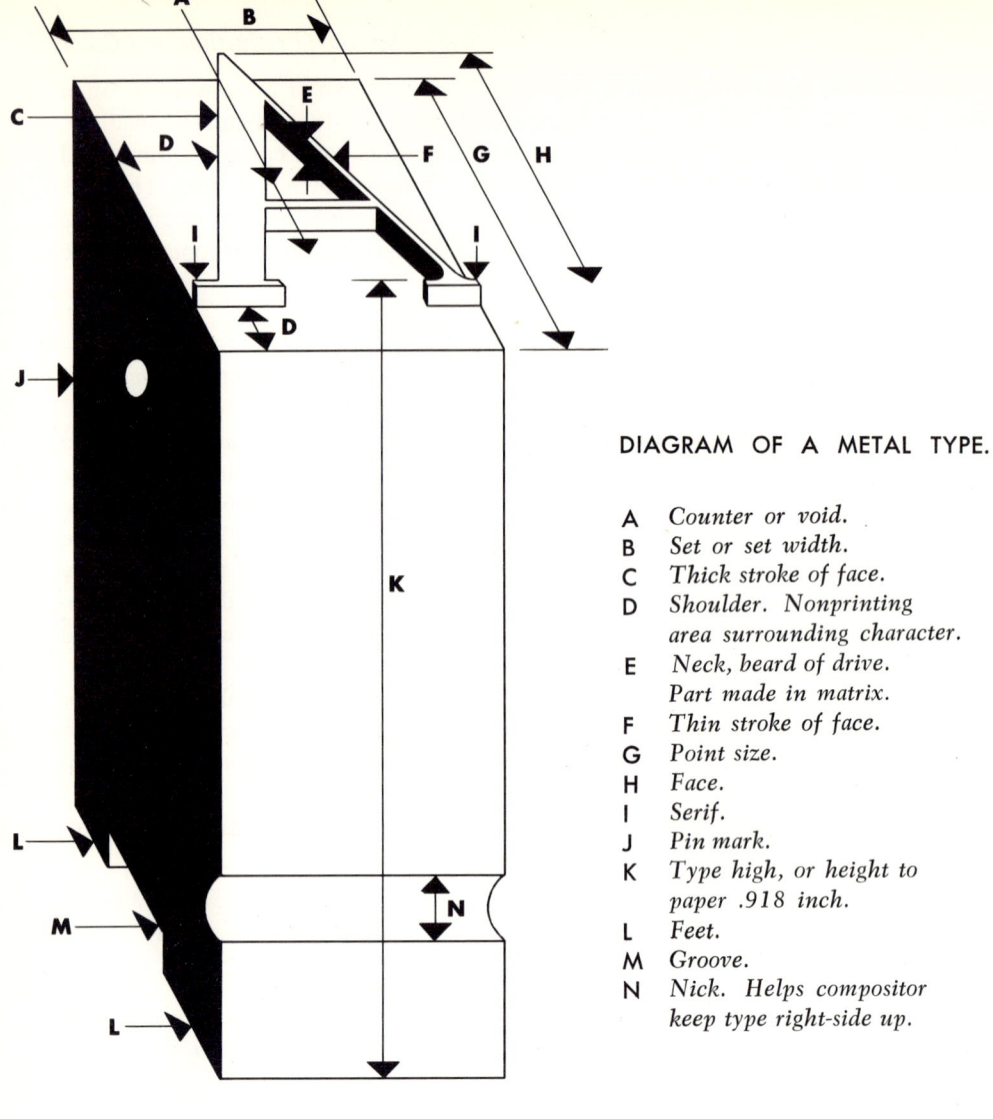

DIAGRAM OF A METAL TYPE.

A   Counter or void.
B   Set or set width.
C   Thick stroke of face.
D   Shoulder. Nonprinting area surrounding character.
E   Neck, beard of drive. Part made in matrix.
F   Thin stroke of face.
G   Point size.
H   Face.
I   Serif.
J   Pin mark.
K   Type high, or height to paper .918 inch.
L   Feet.
M   Groove.
N   Nick. Helps compositor keep type right-side up.

From Westvaco Inspirations; Artist, Bradbury Thompson. (Courtesy: West Virginia Pulp and Paper Company)

strokes, the serifs are delicate and horizontal, straight and flat. In contrast to Oldstyle, Modern Roman is darker in tone, its shape is of greater regularity, and its curves are more precise. Modern Roman gives a sharp, steel-cut impression. Caslon is an example of Oldstyle, Bodoni of Modern

The Roman group contains a majority of the type faces and is used for almost all books, newspapers, and magazines. Its greatest asset, legibility, stems from its design and from its long, wide usage. The type children learn to read is Roman. Another asset is the range of variety possible within a single family. Because of its irregular contours, Roman is more readable than Gothic, the next group to be con-

This line of type is Futura Book

This line of type is Futura Medium

This line of type is Futura Demi

This line of type is Futura Bold

This line of type is Futura Extra Bold

An example of variations in weight.

This line of type is Extra Condensed Gothic

This line of type is Regular Gothic

This line of type is Extended Gothic

An example of variations in width.

ABCDEFGHIJKLMNOPQRSTUVWXYZ
abcdefghijklmnopqrstuvwxyz
ABCDEFGHIJKLMNOPQRSTUVWXYZ
ABCDEFGHIJKLMNOPQRSTUVWXYZ
abcdefghijklmnopqrstuvwxyz
,.:;?!(|) * " - — & $ fi fl ff ffi ffl

1234567890   *1234567890*

A complete font in 11 point Caledonia.

Building the Advertisement

sidered. This comparative advantage explains why Roman is used for type masses and is the most popular design for display use.

Gothic. Gothic refers to *block* type faces. It is skeletonized Roman of square or block design and is constructed of lines of the same thickness. Angles are uniform; curves are normally arcs or segments of a circle. Gothic does not usually have serifs. Many letters are composed of straight lines and circles; the *o* is a circle, the *d* is a straight line plus one-half a circle, the *t* is a straight line plus a crossbar. Gothic is modern and crisp, clean and geometric. It is better for display than for body copy.

Miscellaneous — Text, Script, and Cursive. There are many groups of type faces other than Roman and Gothic. Some are termed contemporary, some decorative, some ornamental, others antique. Three which are of some importance, although less used than Roman or Gothic, are Text, Script, and Cursive.

Text, also referred to as Old English, is of ecclesiastical parentage in that it was the handwriting used by monks when copying religious manuscripts with wide-pointed reed pens. Today it connotes reverence and antiquity. When in masses, Text is most difficult to read. Newspapers which select it as their name style would not dare use it for news items or editorials. Banks and insurance companies, too, sometimes choose Text for their name style. Because of its low readability, Text is restricted mainly to display use, to decorative initials, and to formal announcements.

Script, a pattern designed to simulate handwriting, is an adaptation of the italic form. A personal — even a familiar — atmosphere can be achieved with script. Script is graceful, fragile, delicate, and ornate. Because Script, like Text, is less legible than Roman and Gothic, it is most useful in display headings and as a spot of variety or contrast. In Script, all lower case letters are connected; if these letters do not touch each other, then the type is called *Cursive.*

Italics. Aldus Manutius, a Venetian printer, designed the first italics in 1501. Italics are *not* a separate type group, but, instead, are a version available in many Roman and in some Gothic faces. Italic letters are not vertical; they slant so as to resemble handwriting. As one version, italics have the same style and design, serifs and strokes as do their vertical counterparts; they are sloping adaptations of and companions for these vertical versions.

The flowing lines, the curves, the slender contour, the delicate expression of italics recommend it for display lines addressed to feminine readers and for subheads. Other uses are for emphasis, contrast, motion, and decorative value.

Selection of Type Face

Influences. Many influences may guide the advertiser in his selection of type faces. Among the strongest are these:

Nature of product	Impression desired by advertiser
Type of buyer to be influenced	Medium to carry the advertisement
Appeal to be stressed	Size of advertisement
Nature of art work	Amount of copy
Recent and current choices of faces	

Text   Old English

         Goudy Text

                           Bodoni

                Roman   Caslon   *Brush*

                           Garamond

                                 Script and   *Typo Script*
                                 Cursive

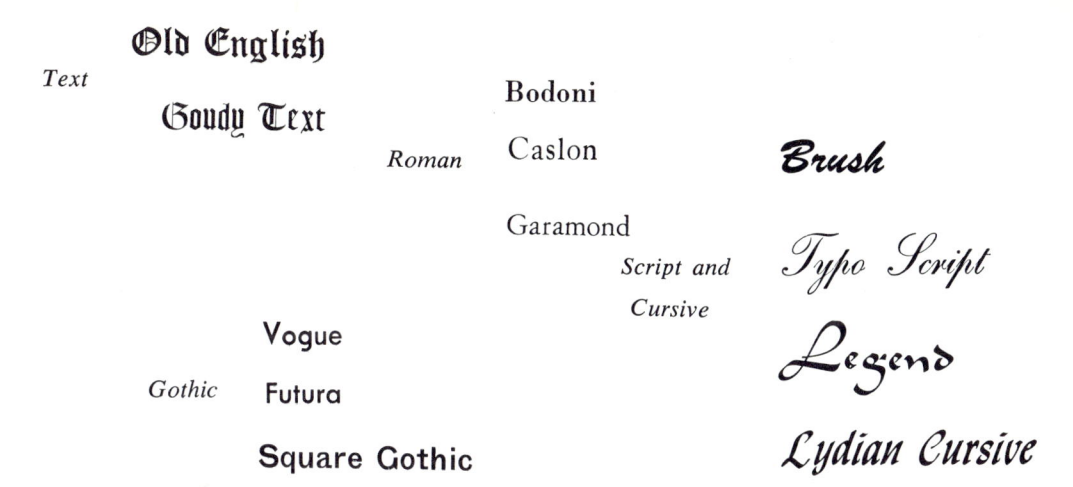

                 Vogue   *Legend*

Gothic   Futura

            Square Gothic   *Lydian Cursive*

Different type faces and groups.

Qualities Desired. By far and away the most essential quality of type is *readability*. The purpose of type is to communicate and to influence, and this objective can be attained only if the advertising message is read. How can readability be assured? The design of the face is one major consideration because some faces are more legible than others. The second major matter is familiarity. As has been noted, Roman faces are used in practically all body copy, and they are the most widely used group for display headings. Most body copy, indeed, is set in less than a dozen Roman faces. These two considerations, design and familiarity, recommend a standard, round, readable Roman face. Type popularity waxes and wanes but, for body copy, one could seldom be criticized seriously if his choice is Baskerville, Bodoni, Bookman, Caledonia, Caslon, Century Schoolbook, Cheltenham, Garamond, or Times Roman.

A second quality desired in type is *appropriateness*. Some faces bespeak dignity, others informality; some are plainly masculine, others feminine; some endow an advertisement with snob appeal, others with bargain appeal. The wise advertiser insists on a type face in keeping with his product, his message, and his objective because such a face will create a more unified advertisement. Tractors and perfume need different atmospheres; so do clearance advertisements and prestige advertisements.

Finally, *attractiveness* is wanted. An advertiser wants his message to enjoy competitive advantages over competing messages, to be superior to them. Distinctive type faces add to the appearance of advertisements by making them more pleasing, thereby making a stronger bid for readership. As with layout, the reader should not be conscious of type as such.

Handlettering. If available faces seem somewhat less than adequate, then handlettering by a commercial artist may be indicated. Headlines and logotypes are often handlettered, and script sometimes is. Among the values of handlettering are emphasis, contrast, attention, individuality, variety, and range of choice.

Building the Advertisement

Suggestions About Typography

Size of Type and Length of Line. A major factor in the legibility of copy is the type size and length of line in which the copy is set. While type can be too large or too small, the greater danger is that of its being too small. Is there a guide to size? Perhaps the only generalization permitted is that type should be large enough for easy reading. Small type in long lines and large type in short lines make for difficult reading. Minimum size range for body copy in most advertisements is 10- to 12-point. Increasing the type size, however, does *not* insure an increase in sales volume. As for length of line, the advertiser should beware of both long lines which are discouraging and tiring and short lines which are choppy and make heavy demands on the reader's concentration and patience. Effort should be made to break lines at points which make for the greatest speed and ease of understanding rather than at awkward, senseless points.

Number of Faces. Twin rules here are to limit severely the number of type faces included in a single advertisement and to combine faces with care. In many advertisements, just one face provides all the variety and emphasis needed as well as typographical simplicity and safety. In other cases, one face is used for headings and another for body copy. Any combining should be done by someone with a knowledge of typography, and if more than two faces are to be included in the same advertisement, the decisions should be made by an expert typographer. Type faces have personalities just as individuals do; because some are formal and others friendly, some powerful but others delicate, faces in combination can complement each other — or they can clash with each other.

Variety. When the appearance of large masses of type is one of monotonous sameness, readership is discouraged. This mistake can be avoided by the injection of variety into the advertisement's typography. Several elements can be varied for the purpose of making the typography lively enough to invite reading. The first to consider, naturally, is design of face; one family may supply this, or, more than one family may be used. A second variable, also referred to earlier, is size of type. A third element is weight of type, and a fourth is width of type; lightface and boldface, condensed and extended have already been mentioned. Decoration, emphasis, and spacing are other areas with potential for variety. Regardless of *how* variety is obtained, it should be in good taste, balanced and orderly, not overdone, and harmonious.

Headings. Display lines should harmonize with the text material. When they are not handlettered, headlines most often are set in the boldface of the body family, or of some harmonizing face. Headlines in script can usually be defended in advertisements addressed to women; those in all capitals may seem distant and cold. Headings may be in color as well as in boldface.

Long headlines can be made more attractive by changing the face, size, or family of type. Breaking them down, too, into four- or five-word phrases helps. Long headlines are more difficult to read if arranged vertically in one- or two-word lengths,

ONE MINUTE TO PLAY ... JUST SIXTY SECONDS. A LOT CAN HAPPEN TO CHANGE THE SCORE .... IT'S THAT WAY WITH A COMMERCIAL, TOO. IN ONE SHORT MINUTE, IT MUST GRIP THE VIEWERS ... GIVE THEM AN INTERESTING SALES STORY ... MAKE THEM WANT WHAT YOU'VE GOT TO SELL .... WHAT WE LIKE TO DO IS TO LEAVE THE SPECTATORS CHEERING. BUT MORE IMPORTANT, TO HANG UP SCORES FOR OUR CLIENTS IN SALES AND PROFITS.
N. W. AYER & SON, INC.   THE COMMERCIAL IS THE PAYOFF.

Few advertisements use typewriter type faces. Even fewer use all capitals. (Courtesy: N. W. Ayer & Son, Inc.)

Building the Advertisement

or if they curl or wander around. The space between headline and text should be at least equal to the space between the lines of the headline.

Emphasis. Typography has an obligation to emphasize the most important parts of the advertiser's message. Many are the techniques to incorporate emphasis into an advertisement through typography, emphasis which highlights illustrations, headings, package, price, coupon, logotype, words, sentences, and paragraphs. Size, capitals, italics, other type faces, boldface, color, handlettering, script, letterspacing, circles, boxes, underlining, decoration, contrast, isolation, intensity, and motion are all methods for emphasis. Because emphasis is easily overdone, and because if every unit is emphasized there is *no* emphasis, caution and restraint are recommended. Not many elements should be emphasized; not many different techniques should be used in one advertisement; not many techniques should be used to emphasize any one element. It is almost always a mistake to let typography call attention to itself.

Spacing. The discussion of layout in the last chapter gave attention to the spacing of elements within an advertisement. Typography, too, is concerned with spacing and is, indeed, affected by layout, but its concern is with spacing between words, lines, and paragraphs.

Words can, of course, be too close together or too far apart, either extreme reducing the legibility of the copy. If words are too close, they run together and confuse the reader. Lines of type in capitals demand more space between words than do the same lines in lower case. Certain type faces, too, must have more white space between words than other faces. If the spacing is too wide, the reader again must work to get the meaning of the words. Wide spacing is dangerous for another reason — it permits "rivers of white" to appear. These reduce readability by interrupting the rhythm of the reading process and by distracting the reader. They also hurt the appearance of an advertisement by making it spotty.

Space between lines is a matter of *leading,* pronounced "ledding," and of this, too, there can be more or less than there should be. In leading, thin strips of metal are inserted between lines of type to provide white space which separates the lines. The amount of leading is expressed in points, widely used leading being 1-point and

An example of display type in three point sizes.

This is 18 point Garamond.

This is 24 point Garamond.

This is 36 point Garamond.

Typography, Production, and Color

2-point. When lines of type are separated by no leading, they are described as having been set solid. Type can be set safely without leading because type is so designed that there is a thin separation of white space between lines of type even when set solid. You will recall from the discussion of type anatomy that point size includes the shoulder, which is blank space in that it does not print. Too much leading lets lines fall apart, too little leading affects appearance and legibility adversely. There is no formula which indicates the proper amount. Faces with short ascenders and descenders, and faces with unusually small lower case letters usually require more leading than other faces do.

Paragraphs should be short, especially the first one, and should be separated properly. They must hang together but not too closely together. Where there is much copy, several paragraphs can be grouped under each of several subheads, thus breaking the copy up and ventilating it with display lines. Interest can be added by varying the length of paragraphs, using greater than normal indentation, changing the width of one or two paragraphs, making steps of them, or staggering them back and forth.

PRODUCTION — ENGRAVINGS

Line Engravings

This type of engraving, also called a line cut, is a printing plate that reproduces copy which is in one tone of black or in any color that reproduces black. It duplicates the lines and solids in art work. The printing surface is an assortment of lines and solid areas — the rest has been etched away. The reader's eye can separate the copy into separate lines and separate solid areas. Most line engravings are zinc; the better ones, costing more, are copper. Two or more colors can be printed by this process provided each color has its own separate copy and its own separate plate.

Line engravings are speedy, simple, and economical to make. They print satisfactorialy on almost any paper. Bold, even startling effects in black are possible. Such facts help explain why line cuts are the most popular form of engraving. On the minus side, line engravings can be made only from drawings which have sharp contrasts and clean delineation. Illustrations reproduce in solid blacks and whites and not in any gray or middle (or half) tones. Photographs, color paintings, and wash drawings cannot be reproduced by line engravings.

An example of leading.

The size of the type in this paragraph is 10 point. It is set solid, that is, there is no leading or space between the lines of type. Note the cramped appearance of this paragraph which means it would be difficult to read long amounts of copy set in this manner. The type face is Garamond.

The size of the type in this paragraph is 10 point. It has 3 point leading, that is, thin strips of metal have been inserted between the lines of type. Note the increase in legibility compared to the example at the left, especially apparent if this were longer copy. The type face is Garamond.

Building the Advertisement

Below: A simple line cut. Right: Dramatic effects may be achieved through the use of line cuts.

Halftone Engravings

A halftone is an engraving used to reproduce photographs, color paintings, and wash drawings. The wash drawing, incidentally, is an assortment of gray tones; it is one of the most widely used types of advertising illustration. The name halftone is appropriate because the engraving cannot contain all degrees of tone — the nature of the halftone does not permit pure whites or pure blacks to be printed. The reason for this is that the art work is transferred to the metal printing plate, usually copper, not directly but *through a screen,* breaking the art work down into an assortment of small dots of different sizes too small to show individually. Only by using a screen can designs with tonal gradations in between black and white be reproduced and printed with those gradations retained.

A photograph, for example, is composed of both lines and tones. The lines pose no problem because a line engraving will reproduce them. The tones, however, cannot be reproduced intact; they must be reduced to separated, broken lines — dots — which can be inked. The basic difference between the line cut and the halftone is this reduction of tones to dots. Where line cuts print from lines and solid areas, halftones print from dots.

The screen is the key element in the making of halftone engravings. It is a mesh similar to a window screen, having two sets of fine, parallel lines at right angles to

Typography, Production, and Color

each other. Halftones are referred to by their screens as, for example, a 100-line screen; this screen has 100 parallel lines to the inch in each direction; thus, a square inch of 100-line screen contains 10,000 dots. The finer the screen, the finer the detail in the printing. The quality of paper used in newspapers calls for screens of 55 to 85 lines. Magazines normally take screens of 100 to 133 lines. Widely used screens are 55, 65, 85, 100, 110, 120, and 133. The 133-line screen is the finest commonly used for commercial work.

Halftone screens in general use.

55 Line Screen

For national advertising in newspapers

65 Line Screen

For editorial use in newspapers

85 Line Screen

For commercial printers on paper similar to newsprint

100 Line Screen

For textbooks, on machine-finished paper

120 Line Screen

For national magazine advertising and dull coated papers

133 Line Screen

For high-grade commercial printing on coated paper

Building the Advertisement

Ben Day

A process was developed by Benjamin Day which gives line plates, either black-and-white or color, some of the tonal appearance and life of a halftone. The procedure adds a shaded background or screening of tones and lines to line engravings — backgrounds which were not in the original art work. Scores of patterns are available including fine straight lines, wavy lines, crossed lines, stippled effects, dots of various sizes, herringbone designs, and grains. Ben Day contributes by providing a variety of shadows, shading, and tone which reduces the harshness of line drawings. Because it is applied mechanically, sometimes to the negative but usually to the engraving plate before etching, it is more uniform and economical than drawing by hand.

PRODUCTION — PRINTING PROCESSES

Relief

Letterpress, one form of relief, prints most of our newspapers, many magazines, and much direct mail. Relief printing is done from a *raised* surface. It gets its name from the fact that the printing surface stands out *in relief.* The surface which will print the type or the design is above the level of the plate to which it is attached; the letters and lines are raised — the plate recessed. Only the printing surface receives ink from inking rollers which pass over it, then it comes in contact with the paper, and deposits its ink onto the paper. Printing by a rubber stamp after contact with an ink pad or by your fingertips in fingerprinting are examples of relief printing. Relief printing is the oldest, most common technique. The process is speedy, its results are clear and sharp, and it is economical for short runs.

Lithography

Lithography is printing from a *flat* surface. The image area and the non-printing area are on the same plane, an arrangement possible because grease attracts grease and water repels grease. The special metal printing plate has a finely grained surface which will accept and retain water *or* grease. The copy or design to be printed is placed on the plate, usually by photography, with a greasy substance which sensitizes the copy area so that it has an affinity for oily ink. Then a water roller is applied. Water is refused by the design area because it was sensitized but is received by and adheres to the non-design area, conditioning the non-design area so that it will refuse oily ink. Next, an ink charged roller passes across the plate, inking only the design area which then can transfer the design to paper.

Direct lithography involves the transfer of copy from sensitized parts of the smooth, flat plate to paper. Indirect lithography or *offset* involves the transfer of copy from plate to a rubber blanketed roller and then to paper. Much more use is made of offset than of direct lithography. In comparison with relief printing, offset is sometimes less expensive, being economical for long runs because the presses can run at high speed.

Gravure

Gravure or intaglio printing is done from a *depressed* surface. It is, thus, the

Typography, Production, and Color

reverse of relief printing. The subject matter or design is incised into the printing plate, depressed below the level of the plate. The surface of the plate is inked, filling the sunken design, and then is wiped clean by a blade. In the printing process, the ink from the subsurface design is transferred to paper. Eyes or fingertips can identify the raised printing this process does on calling cards and invitations.

Gravure printing produces deep, rich effects and excellent gradation of tone. It is economical for long press runs, and it is speedy. Even so, it is the least used of the three printing processes, mainly because it is so time-consuming and because

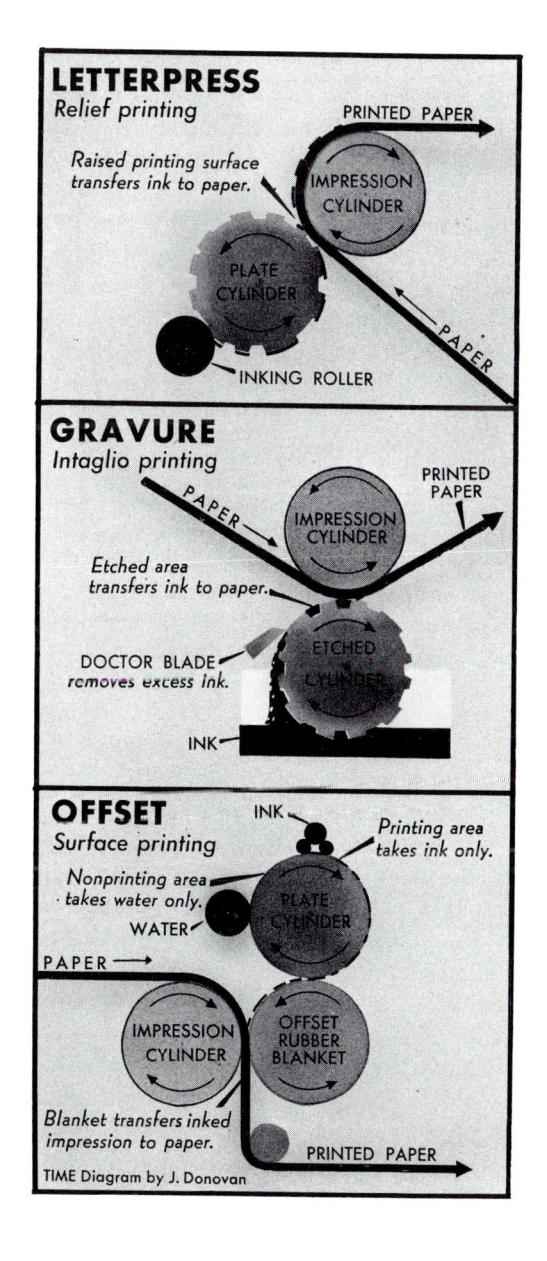

These diagrams picture the basic operations of three printing processes. (Courtesy: TIME)

197

Building the Advertisement

its high preparation costs prohibit its use for small quantities. In addition, the process does not reproduce detailed copy too satisfactorily.

COLOR

Color is a vital and increasingly significant element in our pattern of consumption and living. Indeed, it may play a larger role than we realize, for color influences the behavior of individuals as workers and as buyers through its effects on the emotions. We may feel cooler in a blue room than in a room whose predominant color is orange. Because of color, we buy certain products in volume and emphatically reject others.

Each year more products appear in color, many of which had previously offered the buyer no choice whatsoever in this respect. And, since color is of growing importance, it is only natural that we note more color in advertising. It is because of this growth and prominence of color advertising that this section has been included to treat the nature and use of advertising in color. Although the topic of color is at home in a dozen or so chapters in this text, it has seemed logical to centralize its study in this section and to show, by means of a color-insert section, how some of its uses actually apply. The last five pages of the insert reproduce some color advertisements, each selected to illustrate major uses of color in advertising. Although a brief caption accompanies each advertisement, the layout, copy, and typography of each advertisement should be discussed and its effectiveness evaluated; the student should look for the answers to such questions as:

1. Why, in addition to reasons given in the caption, was color used in this advertisement rather than black and white?
2. What do the specific colors used contribute to the advertisement? Could you suggest others that might have been used as effectively, or more so?
3. If you had to do essentially this advertisement in black and white, what changes in layout, copy, or typography would you want to make?

Qualities or Attributes of Color

When the layman speaks of color he uses such terms as sky-blue, cocoa brown, peach, or rust to indicate the different colors. These terms are picturesque and often very effective from a psychological point of view. The advertiser may do well to use them in his communications with the public, but for the planning of his products and their advertisements he needs something less vague and indefinite. To meet this need for a way to describe accurately a color, several color systems have been devised. The two major systems in use are that developed by Albert H. Munsell and that of Wilhelm Ostwald. We shall give an indication of the nature of these systems without delving into their complexities or differentiating between the two. Further discussion belongs to the field of color theory.

Color has three qualities or attributes. They are *hue, value,* and *chroma* or intensity. *Hue* is the quality by which we distinguish one color from another. It is the quality which distinguishes red from green, blue from yellow, and so on. The color wheel on page 1 of the color insert shows twenty-four hues. These are full

1

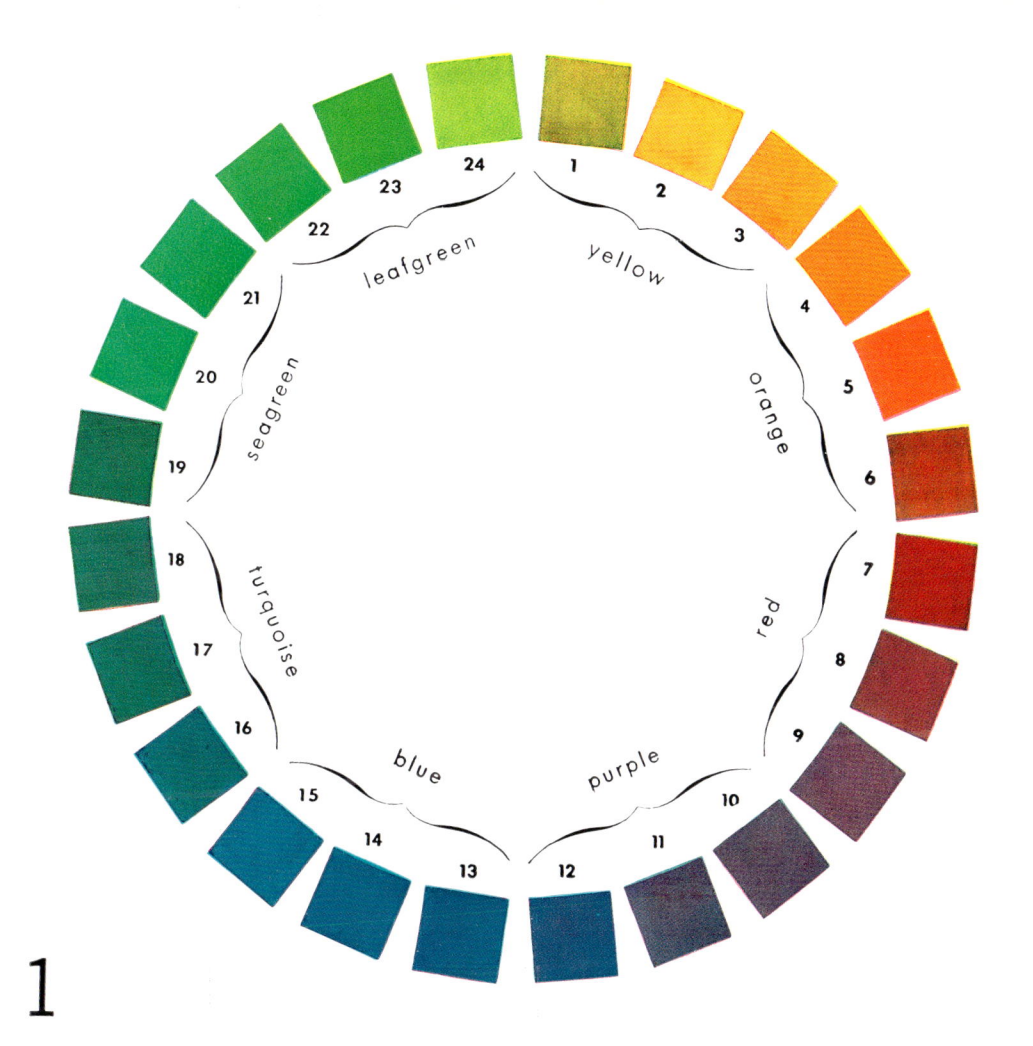

ABOVE: A color wheel illustrating differences in hue, the quality by which we distinguish one color from another. RIGHT: This value scale shows the range of values achieved by adding white. FAR RIGHT: Changes in chroma or intensity are achieved by adding values of gray to a hue. (From Basic Color by Egbert Jacobson. Copyright 1948, Paul Theobald and Company, Chicago, Illinois.)

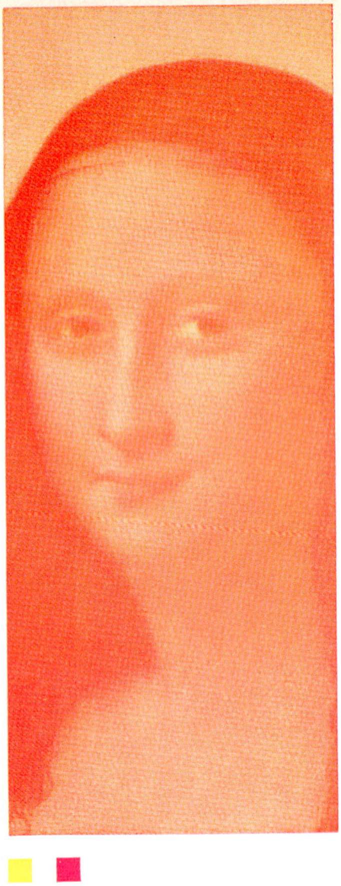

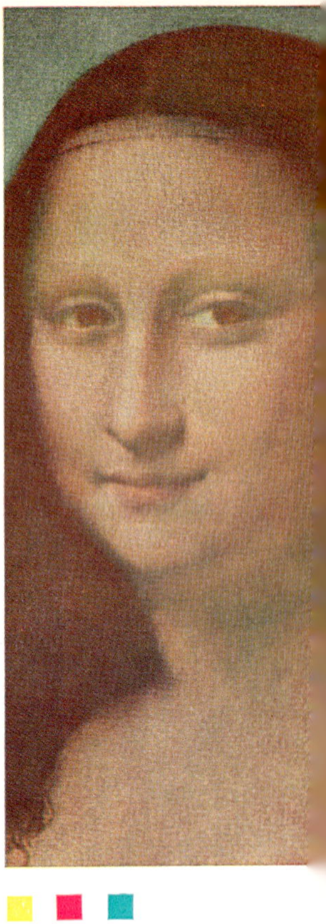

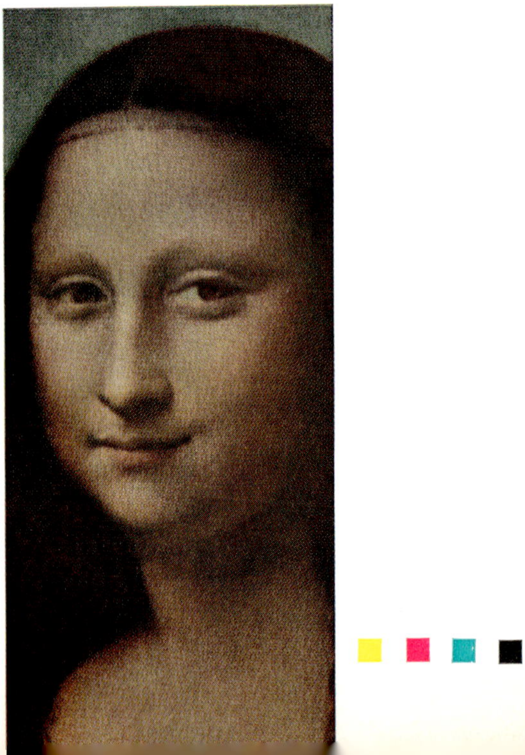

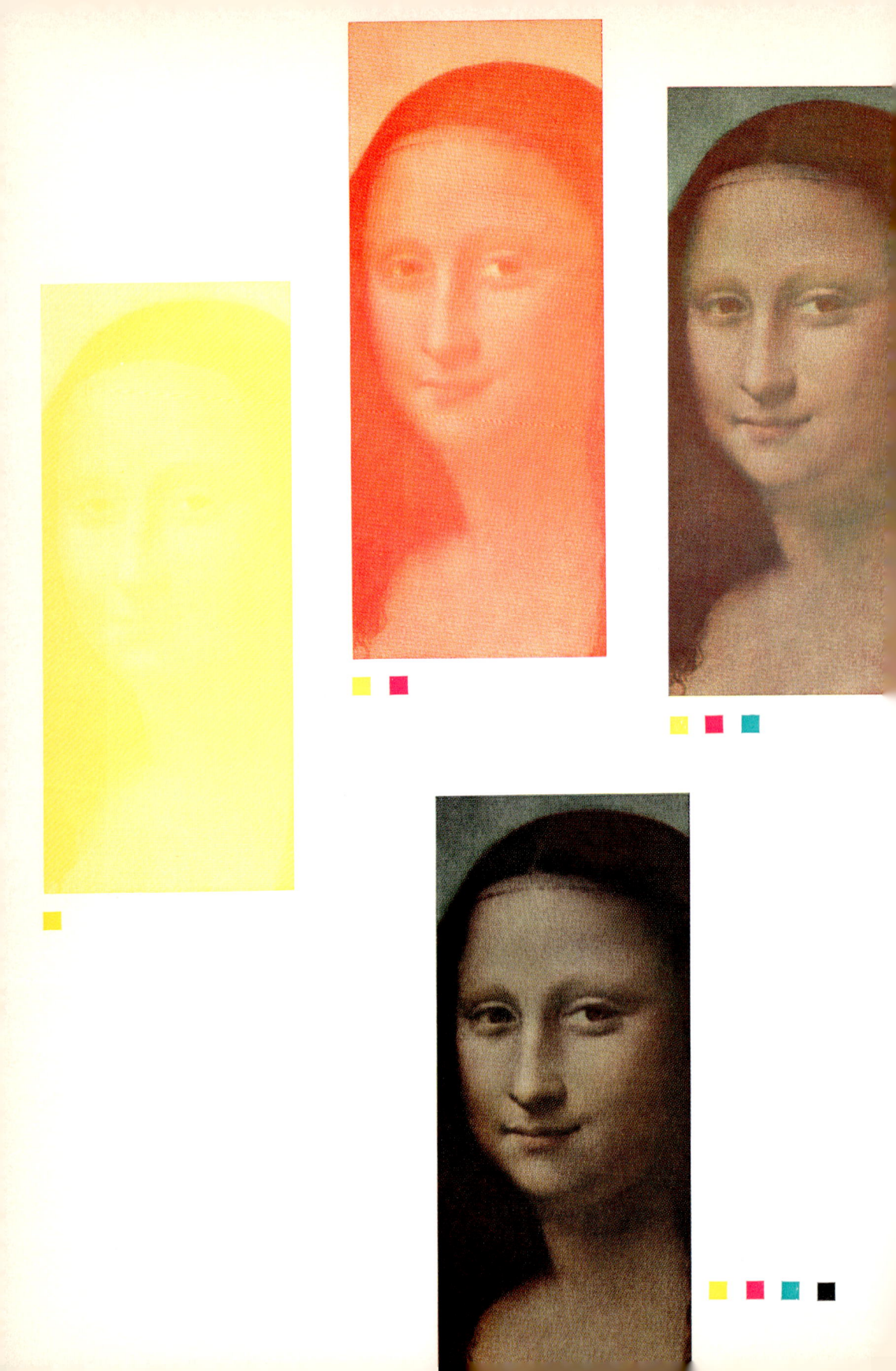

(From The Treasury of Art Masterpieces edited by Thomas Craven. Copyright © by Simon and Schuster Inc. Adapted by Bradbury Thompson for Westvaco Inspirations, West Virginia Pulp and Paper Company).

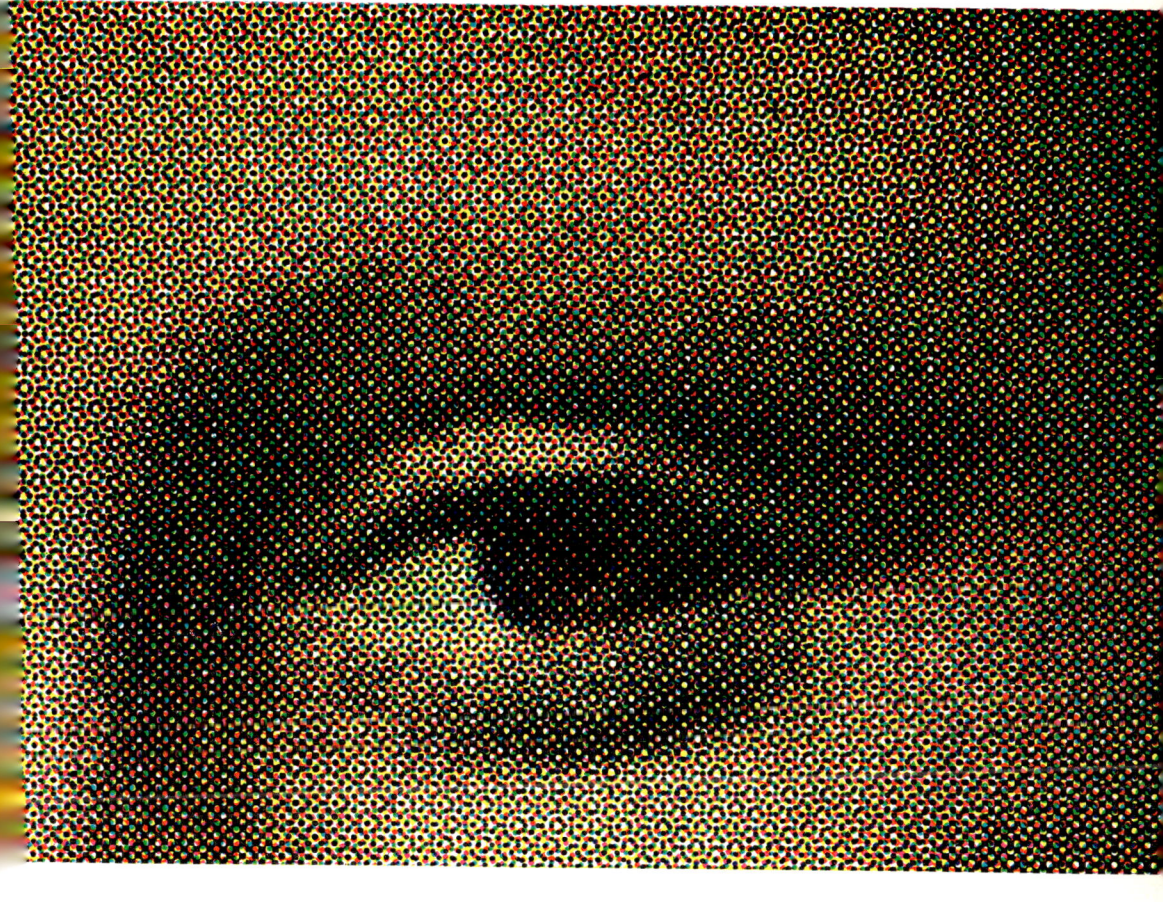

3 ABOVE: An enlarged detail of a 4-color process halftone.

2 OPPOSITE PAGE: An illustration of 4-color progressive proofs. In this instance, first the yellow plate, then with the red added, then with blue, and lastly combined with black to achieve the final result.

From Hamilton—the only watches run electrically

Electricity gives them uncanny accuracy. No winding, no twist of the wrist needed. A tiny power cell inside does the work. Rugged, practical watches, Hamilton Electrics have fewer parts (no mainspring!). Your Hamilton Jeweler now has the new Anniversary series celebrating the first birthday of the world's only electric watch. (Top to bottom) Victor, $89.50; Pacer, $125; Titan, $95. Hamilton Watch Company, Lancaster, Pennsylvania.

HAMILTON
CREATOR OF THE WORLD'S FIRST ELECTRIC WATCH

4   Color joins design to help attract attention to this advertisement. Does this use of color serve to suggest that these watches run electrically? Has structural motion been used to advantage? (Courtesy Hamilton Watch Company)

Salter—actual size

Miniature—actual size

You get a better shake with Morton Salters & Miniatures

Family eating is a little less work and a lot more fun when you use handy Morton Salters and Morton Miniatures. These ready-filled shakers of salt won't break or spill. There's nothing to clean or refill. Salters and Miniatures are ideal for barbecues, picnics, parties—anywhere food is served. Salters come three to a carton. Miniatures come six to a tray. Pick up a couple of packages today.

5 Although the red watermelon has both appetite and attention values, the major function of color here is to identify two of the advertiser's packages. Could salt be advertised as effectively in black and white? (Courtesy Morton Salt Company)

6 Here color is used to create an atmosphere of prestige and quality; that this is a luxury product for women is expressed as much by the color used as by the typography and copy. (Courtesy W. A. Sheaffer Pen Company)

7 The cool blue background contrasts with the warm colors of the frankfurters to stimulate the reader's appetite for this product, especially as it is shown in use. Why are most magazine food advertisements in color? (Courtesy George A. Hormel Company)

PARTY FRANKS. Hormel *all-meat* Frankfurts are slit, stuffed with cheese, wrapped with lean, flavory Hormel Bacon. Brief broiling... then wonderful eating!

HORMEL is the word for frankfurts (all meat!)

HORMEL Geo. A. Hormel & Co., Austin, Minn.

New!

Motor Oil with Thermostatic Action

Adjusts automatically to protect your engine at every temperature!

Your car's engine soars through daily temperature changes of more than 100°! That's why you need the thermostatic motor oil— X-100® Premium.

Starting: Engine's cold. Quick starts call for a light, easy-flowing oil. X-100 Premium acts as a *light oil*.

'Round town: Your engine warms up slowly during short trips. X-100 Premium acts as a *medium-grade oil*.

On the turnpike: X-100 Premium adjusts once more... acts as a *heavy oil* that resists thinning out under heat of highway speeds.

It's 3 Grades of Motor Oil in One

FOR STARTING COLD
FOR RUNNING WARM
FOR RUNNING HOT

For the finest engine care, switch to X-100 Premium

---

8   Color is used here to dramatize a product feature — three grades of motor oil in one. How has color been employed to achieve unity and to suggest temperatures? (Courtesy Shell Oil Company)

Typography, Production, and Color

colors and theoretically are free from any sensation of whiteness or blackness. *Value* is the degree of lightness or darkness of a color. It is the quality which differentiates a dark red from a light red. The illustration on the first page of the color insert shows a value scale ranging from light to dark. The value of a color is seen by comparing it with the grays of the value scale. *Chroma* or intensity refers to color strength. Chroma varies from a neutral gray to the strongest obtainable chroma of any hue at the various value levels. A triangle such as the one on the first page of the color insert could be made for each of the hues in the color wheel.

Thus, when the advertiser or artist wants to describe a color accurately, he gives the number or letter of the hue as found in the color wheel, the value of the hue with numbers ranging in the steps shown from black to white, and the number or letters indicating chroma or intensity.

Color Reproduction

In printing, yellow, red, and blue are the three primary colors. They are basic colors because they can be combined so as to produce almost any hue desired; neither yellow, red, nor blue can be produced by combining any other colors. Although not a color in the technical sense, black is referred to as one of the colors in the 4-color process. It is usually used for an advertisement's body copy due to its high degree of legibility. Black is also used to provide strength of detail, depth, emphasis, contrast, and richness. It helps reproduce natural tints and shades of gray.

Both line cuts and halftones can be used to reproduce copy in color. For line cuts, each color must have its own separate copy and its own separate printing plate. For halftones, the advertiser can use black plus one color, black plus two colors, or the full 4-color process. In 4-color reproduction, the artwork is photographed four separate times, each time through a different filter, because four halftones are necessary, each made from its own negative. This process is illustrated on the second page of the color insert.

A 4-color illustration printed from these four plates consists of many tiny dots — yellow, red, blue, and black dots — which appear to merge and blend together so as to reproduce the original copy. Dots of each color are interspersed among dots of the three other colors, as illustrated on page 3 of the color insert. These dots, because they appear to merge, can be used to reproduce photographs and other continuous-tone illustrations which could not otherwise be used in letterpress printing.

Psychology of Color

Some persons, when depressed, say that they are "blue." Sometimes persons are described as being "green" with envy or "black" with rage. When one feels "in the pink," he may want to go out and paint the town "red." Colors, thus, have certain emotional associations. Because of their association with fire and the sun, red, orange, and yellow are warm colors. Because of their association with the sea and the sky, blue, violet, and green are cool colors. By injecting suggestion and symbolism into advertisements, color can be a powerful psychological tool.

Building the Advertisement

Research findings do not agree about the influence of colors on buyers. It is risky to forecast the effects of any contemplated color scheme, and, here again, market research is needed. Nevertheless, here are some values or implications of certain colors:

Yellow: Cheerfulness, dishonesty, youth, light, hate, cowardice, joyousness, optimism, spring, brightness.
Red: Action, life, blood, fire, heat, passion, danger, power, loyalty, bravery, anger, excitement.
Blue: Coldness, serenity, depression, melancholy, truth, purity, formality, depth, restraint.
Orange: Harvest, fall, middle life, tastiness, abundance, fire, attention, action.
Green: Immaturity, youth, spring, nature, envy, greed, jealousy, cheapness, ignorance.
Violet: Dignity, royalty, sorrow, despair, richness.
White: Cleanliness, fear, purity, sickness, virginity.
Black: Mystery, strength, mourning, heaviness.

Checks on the color preferences of buyers do not agree. However, it is interesting to see what a fairly typical one looks like:

Infants	*Children*	*College students*	*Adults*
Red	Blue	Blue	Blue
Blue	Red	Red	Red
White	Yellow	Green	Green
Green	Green	Yellow	Violet
Brown	White	Orange	Orange

Uses of Color

Prominent among the uses advertisers make of color are these:

To attract buyers' attention. More buyers observe advertisements in color than in black and white.

To stimulate the interest and to whet the desire of buyers. Food products, for example, can often be given eye appeal and be made mouth-watering with color.

To help buyers identify product, brand name, and trade-mark.

To help buyers identify successive advertisements. Color frames, background, and decoration may be used for this purpose.

To provide emphasis through the use of two colors which contrast greatly in respect to value. Charts, product features, and various copy elements may be the objects of such emphasis.

To illustrate, interpret, and prove, often in a powerful manner, the buyer benefit(s) promised in the body copy.

To contribute to structural motion. Features in color such as initial letters, flags, or numbers can constitute effective structural motion, guiding the reader's attention.

To endow an advertisement with quality or prestige, or to inject a certain mood or atmosphere into an illustration.

To relate body copy to the illustration or to the headline through the repetition of a color.

To show the structure, design, or installation of a product.

Media and Color

For some years now the use of R.O.P. color advertising, black plus one color as well as full-color, has been growing in *newspapers*. R.O.P. stands for "run of paper" and refers to advertisements placed anywhere in the issue the newspaper publisher chooses to place them. The advertiser's other option, of course, is to stipulate that his advertisement appear on a specific page — the sports page, perhaps, or the society page. Preferred position stipulated in this manner usually costs the advertiser more than R.O.P. position.

Newspapers charge a premium for color advertising. This extra price is not the only factor an advertiser considers when deciding whether or not to use color. He would like color reproduction to be of higher quality and more dependable. He wishes color were available from all newspapers. He wishes newspapers would make firm commitments to run color advertisements on the specific days he prefers; he is not happy when a newspaper insists, as some do, on a three-day leeway when scheduling color advertisements.

Magazines quote their basic, lowest rates for black-and-white advertising. Black plus one color costs more. Black plus three colors (4-color process) costs even more. Some magazines accept color advertising of no smaller size than half-page; some drop this minimum to quarter-page size. Like newspapers, magazines set up earlier closing dates for color advertisements than for black-and-white advertisements. The closing date is the date by which the advertisement must be in the publisher's hands if it is to be included in a certain issue of the publication. Magazines, particularly general consumer magazines, carry much color advertising.

Television is a natural medium for color. The number of shows and the number of commercials in color can be expected to increase. Eventually, television may be used for direct merchandising; the consumer could buy from his living room after seeing products displayed by color television.

In the *outdoor* medium, color is the rule for posters, painted displays, and electric spectaculars. Color combinations which rank high in legibility are black on yellow, green on white, red on white, and blue on white.

Most advertisements in the *transit* medium are in color. For car cards, as for outdoor posters, there is no additional space cost for color. *Point-of-purchase* items are usually in color. There is also wide use of color in *direct mail*. Paper, copy, order forms, the mailing envelope, and mail-order catalogues are examples of items often in color.

Limitations of Color

As regards some advertisements, color may be unavailable, unnecessary, or undesirable. If his advertising fund is quite limited, the advertiser may have no real choice except to run black-and-white advertisements. If he plans to run an advertisement all in type, he is under strong pressure to make the type black. If color will not do more of a job than black and white, there's little point in using it.

The persuasion or influence value of an advertisement may be of more importance than its attention value. If color does nothing but increase attention an advertisement gets, then color is probably not worth its added cost. Furthermore, it seems

Building the Advertisement

reasonable to assume that color makes more conspicuous the defects of an advertisement inherently weak.

Color advertising costs more than black-and-white (artwork, plates, some space), and it requires more preparation time. Because it costs more, it influences the number of advertisements a seller can run with the same number of dollars. Color influences size of advertisement, and size is a great influence on number. If a seller decides to replace a black-and-white advertisement in his schedule with one in full color, he must cut back somewhere if additional dollars are not to be had.

Finally, color is less unusual than it once was. The great volume of advertising in color sets the stage for a smart advertiser to do an outstanding job with black-and-white. In certain consumer magazines a black-and-white advertisement has a great chance of standing out.

Do these limitations outweigh the advantages? There is no pat answer. Each advertiser must consider his own product, problems, circumstances, goals, dollars, and media. As best he can, he and he alone must search to determine whether or not the increase in cost is equaled by a correspondent increase in advertising effectiveness.

Questions and Problems

1. A canner of tomatoes substitutes pictures of round, red tomatoes for the o's in the word "tomato." What are other examples of typographical novelty?
2. A manufacturer of typewriters is wondering if his magazine ads should be set in typewriter type. Comment.
3. What jobs can color do in an ad?
4. List some factors which determine the readability of copy.
5. Explain the use of more than one type face in an ad.
6. What pressures urge the use of color in a manufacturer's ads?
7. How may the advertising message affect the ad's typography?
8. Why is hand-lettering used?
9. What can one say for black-plus-one-color as against the four-color process?
10. The American Paper Products Corporation is a large, diversified producer. Among its products are kraft board, newsprint, book paper, bond paper, towel paper, wrapping paper, and multiwall shipping sacks.

    For many years, American had mailed a Christmas card to a long list which included customers, prospective customers, suppliers, advertising media, stockholders, and others. Early one year, the advertising manager of American suggested that the mailing be a Christmas prayer set in Goudy Text, an unfamiliar, difficult-to-read type face. When the advertising manager showed what he had in mind, top management thought well of the idea. Reaction was so favorable, indeed, that the firm decided to run the Christmas prayer as a one-time ad in a December issue of a leading advertising trade paper. The prayer over the firm's name made up the entire ad. Comment.

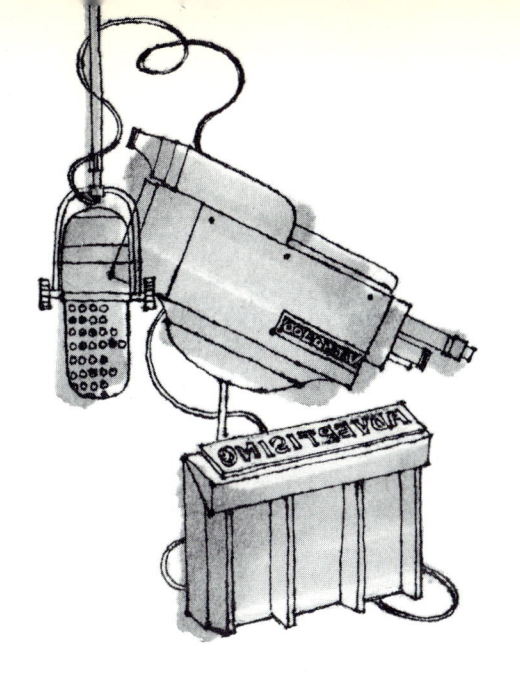

PART FIVE

Media

In the preceding section, we saw how advertisements are designed and built. Once an advertisement has been finished, the next step is to communicate to buyers, to transmit or transport the advertiser's message to his prospective customers, to get his message seen or heard by the persons he wants to influence. So, we are ready now to look at the means by which advertisers expose their advertisements to buyers. We are ready to examine advertising media — the vehicles which carry advertisements to buyers.

The next seven chapters deal with the major media from which advertisers buy space or time. The ones we take up are these: newspapers, magazines, television, radio, outdoor, transit, point-of-purchase, and direct mail.

Which one or which ones should an advertiser pay to deliver his advertising message? It all depends. The nature of the *product or service* he sells is one basic consideration. Another influence is the nature of the *market* (buyers with needs and dollars) he wants to reach. Still another major factor is the nature of his *message*, his promise of satisfaction, and the response he wants to his message. A fourth consideration combines the *characteristics and circulation* of the various media. Here the advertiser wants a high degree of identity between (a) the buyer group

Media

he wants to reach and (b) the audience each medium reaches. Last, but far from least, is the basic matter of *cost*.

Each advertiser hopes to reach his market effectively and economically. He wants his promotion strategy to be sound in the same way that he hopes for soundness in his product strategy, his channel strategy, and his pricing strategy. Media strategy, of course, is a part of advertising strategy, which is a part of promotion strategy. No advertiser can prove that any one media mix or program is "best." What seems best for one product may be totally inappropriate for another product, and what seems best this year will probably need revising next year.

Media decisions are difficult. The programs or media combinations available to most advertisers are quite numerous. Designing a media mix is a challenging undertaking which demands much information, imagination, and judgment.

Chapter 11

Newspapers

Newspapers, the first medium for us to study, have for years been first among media on the basis of advertising revenue. Of the total amount of money spent each year in advertising, the newspaper share is about 30%. Monday-Saturday daily papers have a combined circulation of about 60,000,000, are read by well over 100,000,000 consumers, and reach 90% of U.S. families. Afternoon papers (circulation 35,000,000) outnumbering morning papers (circulation 25,000,000) approximately 1,500 to 300. About 550 Sunday newspapers have a circulation close to 50,000,000. About 6,000 weekly newspapers have a circulation of some 30,000,000.

Newspapers have two sources of income, *advertising revenue* and *circulation revenue*. The number of dollars received from the sale of advertising space accounts for one-half to three-fourths of total revenue; single copy sales and the subscription sales account for the circulation revenue. This relationship between the two types of revenue is not matched by the ratio of advertising content to editorial content. Advertising occupies from 50 to 60 per cent of the space in newspapers.

There are two sizes of newspaper. The *standard* page for years was 8 columns across and about 300 lines (21" or 22") deep — approximating 2,400 lines to the page. The column is about 2 inches in width. Some newspapers of standard size have gone to 9 columns from 8. The *tabloid* page is 5 columns across and about 200 lines (14") deep — approximating 1,000 lines to a page. Tabloid columns, like standard columns, are about 2 inches in width.

CLASSIFICATION

Morning Newspapers

The morning paper has several characteristics of interest to advertisers. It is more masculine than feminine, featuring sports, business and finance, and news. It has time to report on events and happenings, and to check facts and figures for completeness and correctness. Its circulation can cover a wide area because there are several hours of travel time available to it between midnight and breakfast time;

Media

manufacturers can benefit from just about all of this circulation — retailers stand to benefit very little from copies sold outside the retail trading area of the city of publication. The morning paper has a large street sale, many copies of which are read on the way to work and never return with the reader to his residence. In the case of metropolitan markets, many readers do their reading while traveling *toward* the location of the newspaper's retail advertisers; just the reverse is true for the city's afternoon newspapers read by homeward-bound commuters. The reader of the morning paper can respond to an advertisement *on that same day*.

Afternoon Newspapers

The afternoon newspaper is much that the morning paper is not. It is more feminine than masculine. It circulates closer to home, having less time during which to travel from the point of publication; this means a minimum of waste circulation for retailers. Being more numerous than the morning newspapers, the afternoon papers are often found to be the *only* daily in smaller markets; typically, a town's first daily newspaper to be established is an afternoon paper rather than a morning paper. The afternoon paper is handicapped in the collecting and reporting of late news by its hour of appearance. In an attempt partially to compensate, it makes a noticeable effort to entertain its readers with comics, puzzles, and other regular

A newspaper's reading life is short — for morning and evening papers — for women and men. (Courtesy: Richmond Times-Dispatch)

Research Department
RICHMOND TIMES-DISPATCH
RICHMOND NEWS LEADER
Virginia 1958

Data based on a mail survey of 2,004 adult readers of the evening News Leader and the morning Times-Dispatch.

AT WHAT HOUR IS A DAILY PAPER READ?

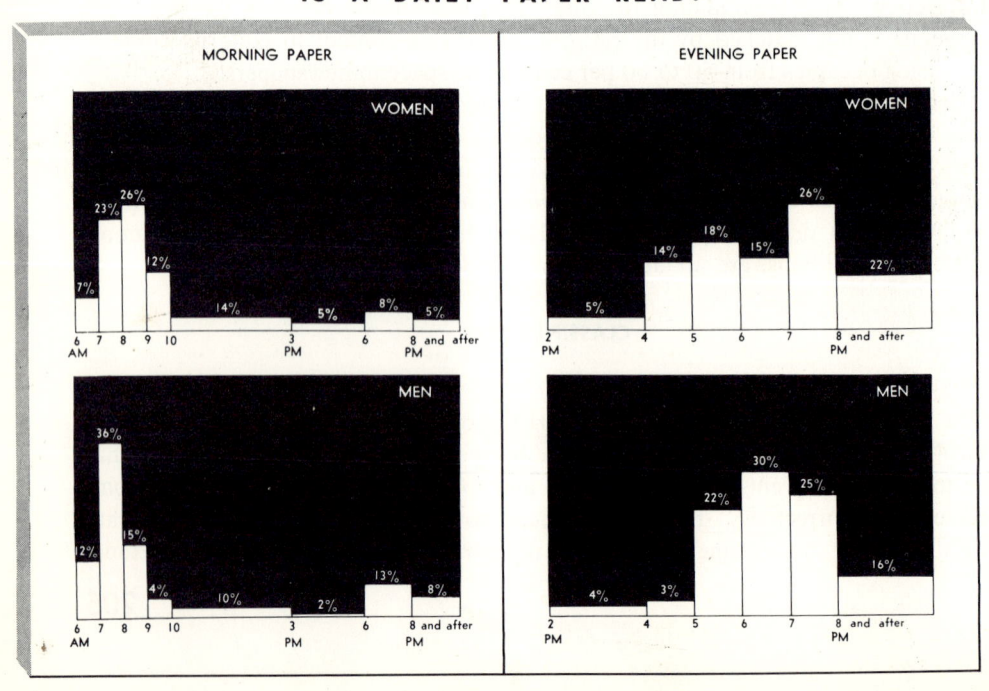

MORNING PAPER — WOMEN

Hour	%
6 AM	7%
7	23%
8	26%
9	12%
10	14%
3 PM	5%
6 PM	8%
8 and after PM	5%

MORNING PAPER — MEN

Hour	%
6 AM	12%
7	36%
8	15%
9	4%
10	10%
3 PM	2%
6 PM	13%
8 and after PM	8%

EVENING PAPER — WOMEN

Hour	%
2 PM	5%
4	14%
5	18%
6	15%
7	26%
8 and after PM	22%

EVENING PAPER — MEN

Hour	%
2 PM	4%
4	3%
5	22%
6	30%
7	25%
8 and after PM	16%

features. A high percentage of the copies of an afternoon paper is delivered to readers' residences by carrier boys, and much is made of this home-delivered feature. Papers point out that more of the family is together in the late afternoon and evening than is true earlier in the day; afternoon papers also claim that the individual readers are relaxed and receptive, that they can read slowly and fully.

Sunday Newspapers

Certain of the features of the afternoon paper are also characteristic of Sunday papers — intensified. The family is at home and has more reading time at its disposal on Sunday than on any other day of the week. The Sunday paper gets into the home. The result is thorough readership, longer and more leisurely reading, and reading by various members of the family. Many daily newspapers do not publish on Sunday, releasing their week-day readers — even forcing them to become customers and readers of some other paper on Sunday. Being sectionalized, most Sunday papers give strong editorial support and background to various classes of advertising; they also give several persons the opportunity to read the paper systematically yet simultaneously. These favorable circumstances are most appropriate because the Sunday issue is huge and formidable, requiring many hours should one be curious or brash enough to undertake to read every word. The reader needs more time because there are more advertisements as well as more news stories.

The comic strips of Monday-through-Saturday may become an entire section, in color, on Sunday. These comic sections get high readership — from adults as well as youngsters, from well-educated consumers in all income groups. Most of the comic supplements are open to advertisers.

Non-Daily Newspapers

Small communities, either independent towns or suburban communities, often support a small, less-than-daily newspaper. Patronized mainly by local advertisers, these publications enjoy quite thorough and careful reading and even a longer life than is true of daily newspapers. By comparison with larger, daily newspapers, the non-dailies charge high prices per reader for their advertising space.

Shopping Newspapers

The shopping newspaper is really not a newspaper; these publications are almost completely full of advertising, containing no news such as is the stock in trade of newspapers, and containing very little editorial matter of other types. They appear once a week, usually on Thursday afternoon. Their circulation is described as *controlled,* meaning that the copies are distributed free to a group of readers selected by the publisher. In an ideal operation, the publisher place a copy of his shopping newspaper at the front doors of all residential quarters in his market during Thursday afternoon. The gigantic nature of this undertaking poses a serious distribution problem. Shopping newspapers are found in our larger markets; some are independent, some are published on a cooperative basis by the local retailers; their rates are somewhat lower than the rates of the local newspapers.

Media

FEATURES OF THE MEDIUM

An outstanding accomplishment of the newspaper is its *intensive coverage of its market* — of the city in which the paper is published and that city's retail trading area. This coverage is so thorough and complete that it is sometimes described as saturation. There is a daily newspaper in every market of significance. Over 90 per cent of the families in this country can be reached through the newspaper medium. For the typical family, the newspaper is the first periodical taken and the last given up; for many families, it is the *only* periodical bought. Because it is clearly a mass type of medium, newspapers enjoy a low cost per unit of circulation.

Of all the media we study, only the newspaper has as its primary objective and responsibility the *delivery of news*. This job must be done satisfactorily if the paper is to survive. Every issue must be *new* — every issue must be *news*. Because the papers appear daily in all sizable markets so as to disseminate fresh and interesting information to their readers, they permit a seller to advertise with a high degree of frequency. In addition, sellers can tie the content of their advertising to the news contained in the editorial columns of the paper, thereby making their advertisements timely — *newsvertising,* as it were. Storms, wrecks, and rescues are examples of unscheduled happenings to which advertising can be tied. Bowl games, elections, Mother's Day, and championship fights are news developments on which advertisers can schedule in advance.

The newspaper's *appeal is broad and diversified,* aimed at all ages, races, income groups, classes, and vocations. This is essential because the paper reaches all types of consumer. Of course, in markets with two or more morning papers or two or more afternoon papers, each newspaper edits its contents or, in marketing terms, plans its product for whatever segment of the market it aims to capture. Something is included for each member of the family, and many features appeal to more than one member. Whether an individual's interests run to agriculture, society, finance, food, sports, or news, there are features, pages, or even sections devoted to that subject. In contrast to magazines, the newspaper is edited for everybody in its locality — and for no one else. No wonder its close bond with its readers makes it a strong local influence in civic and social as well as in personal matters.

The newspaper is, generally, *a local medium,* local in origin, in coverage, and in interest. Each is tailored to suit its own market. Because it is a local medium, advertisers can localize their copy so as to reflect local conditions, problems, and prices. Manufacturers with selective distribution can, in their advertisements, name their local retail dealers — a difficult feat in some other media. Manufacturers with exclusive distribution can run their advertisements over their retailers' names. Geographic selectivity permits the manufacturer to advertise in certain markets and to do no advertising in other markets. He can tell the same story at the best times in various sections of the country — or he can tell different stories simultaneously all across the country, east to west or north to south. Seasonal promotions and sectional promotions, thus, are easily scheduled in newspapers. The small manufacturer can be a big, heavy advertiser in certain areas merely by limiting the number of markets in which he advertises.

Newspapers

The newspaper is the traditional *shopping guide of housewives.* They consult newspaper advertisements in planning their shopping and lean heavily on this advertising for information about grocery products and department store items. Consumer response to newspaper advertising is quick; buying follows closely after the reading which tells where the item can be bought and, often, at what price. Retailers like to see manufacturers' advertisements in *their,* the retailers', medium. Their favorable reaction makes it easier to attain the cooperation and tie-ins manufacturers desire.

The *scheduling* of newspaper advertisements by advertisers is much more satisfactory than scheduling in certain other media, magazines and outdoor, for example. Because closing dates and hours are late, an advertiser can start or stop his advertising on very short notice. Emergency communications of a newsworthy nature are possible, as are last-minute changes in copy.

The features mentioned up to this point have, in the main, been favorable ones. Are there any unfavorable, negative characteristics? The physical newspaper has a very short life. The time spent by the reader in reading it amounts to only a few minutes, and, because nothing is so dull and dead as yesterday's newspaper, few copies are filed for future reference. Not only is the reading brief, often it is also rushed and hurried. Then, newspapers suffer by comparison with magazines on the score of reproduction. The quality of their paper and the speed of printing make for less than outstanding appearance and limit the detail and display potentialities of the medium. Finally, there is little or no selectivity possible for the paper as a whole within its market; advertisers wanting to reach segments of the market with special interests find the job most difficult. This same feature results in much waste circulation for sellers of high-priced products. An interesting discussion can be based on the question of whether or not the manufacturers of the most expensive automobiles made in this country should use newspaper advertising.

TYPES OF ADVERTISING

Of the many possible classifications of newspaper advertising, the one which seems most suitable for our purposes consists of five groupings: general display, retail display, classified display, and reading notice. Display advertisements account for the great majority of advertising dollars the newspapers receive and of the advertising lines they run. The headlines, subheads, prices, and advertisers' signatures in display advertising use type sizes larger than the sizes used for the body copy. Illustrations, too, are a common feature of display advertisements. The typical full-page advertisement run by a department store is an example of display advertising.

General Display

This class of advertising is also referred to as national and even sometimes as *foreign.* It is signed and paid for by a national or sectional advertiser, either (a) a manufacturer of branded products (food, gasoline, soap, tobacco) who sells to and through retail merchants, or (b) a seller of services (railroads, utilities, insurance,

Media

hotels). General display advertisements are scattered throughout most of the newspaper; they are not grouped together under headings as are the "want ads" in the classified section. General advertising is smaller than retail advertising in dollar volume and accounts for an even smaller portion of newspaper linage. Most general advertisements are built by advertising agencies. They stress *what type* of product to buy and *which brand.*

Few newspapers can afford to have their own sales force out in the field selling space to general advertisers. So, almost every paper employs a publisher's representative to do this selling job, to act as a substitute for the salesmen it does not employ. These newspaper representatives call on advertisers and on advertising agencies, selling advertising space for and in a number of non-competing newspapers. Some representatives work on a commission arrangement with their newspapers, perhaps 10%, while others are paid a flat fee.

Retail Display

All display advertising not classified as general is considered to be *retail* and is sometimes referred to as *local.* Retail advertising is done by hometown firms, by retail stores and local sellers of services. These advertisements are addressed to the ultimate consumer, are signed by the retailer, and stress *where* to buy. They constitute two-thirds to three-fourths of total advertising revenue. Retailers, incidentally, spend more dollars in newspaper advertising than in any other medium.

Classified[1]

Classified advertisements are often referred to as "want ads." They are small and one-column wide. They consist of solid lines of small type of a single type face; 5½-point and 6-point are the most common type sizes. Widely used type faces include Corona, Regal, Spartan, Ideal, and Vogue. Their topography is uniform. They contain no headlines, no illustrations, no logotypes, no white space. Copy should be featured by clarity and brevity, by truthfulness and simplicity, by the absence of over-used words and the avoidance of extreme abbreviation. Inclusion of price is clearly desirable in certain advertisements. Classified advertisers, as other advertisers, should promise some specific satisfaction to buyers and should provide some simple method by which buyers can get in touch with advertisers.

These advertisements are usually placed on certain pages well toward the back of of the paper. The name for this type of advertising stems from the newspaper practice of classifying these small advertisements in special columns under descriptive headings which relate to products, services, needs, or the aim of the advertiser. Here are examples of headings:

100–199	Real Estate
200–299	Rentals
300–399	Employment
400–499	Business Opportunities

[1] The author is indebted to Dr. J. D. Landes, Dean, School of Business Administration, Lamar State College of Technology, for most of the information on Classified and Classified Display advertising.

500–599   Financial
600–699   Miscellaneous
700–799   Automotive
800–899   Announcements

Sub-classes for one of these may well look like this:

500   Stocks, Bonds, Investments
505   Mortgages, Contracts
510   Real Estate Loans
515   Wanted to Borrow
520   State Regulated Lenders
525   Money to Loan
530   Automobile Loans

Classified advertisements serve the newspapers which carry them *and* the general public of sellers and buyers who use them. The primary service to *newspapers* takes the form of revenue. For many newspapers, the ratio of classified advertising revenue to total revenue (all advertising revenue plus all circulation revenue) ranges between 20% and 30%. For some papers, it is even more than 30%. A second service to newspapers is a favorable influence on the number of copies a newspaper sells. As for *sellers and buyers,* the classified columns serve as a public "trading post." Advertisers find whatever they seek, and buyers find bargains. Both groups and others, too, find human interest in the advertisements.

Classified Display

As its designation implies, advertising of this type is a combination of classified and display advertising — not in 50–50 ratio, but with a greater resemblance to the classified. Larger in size than classified advertisements, classified display makes limited use of such display features as heavy borders, illustrations, cuts, typographical variety, ornaments, layout, and white space.

These advertisements are commonly grouped at the beginning or at the end of the classified section, or at both. Occasionally, some are seen at the top or bottom of classified columns. Items advertised include automobiles, appliances, real estate, and loans.

Reading Notices

Advertisements which look remarkably like news stories are called *reading notices*. Some newspapers accept this particular copy format — some do not. The headline is intended to have some news value or quality, any illustration resembles those the newspaper uses for its editorial features, and the body copy is set in the same type the paper uses for its news items or in a face that is quite similar. Reading notices are more expensive per line than display or classified advertising. Each advertisement must be marked with "adv." or the full word "advertisement" so that readers will not mistake it for editorial matter.

Media

CIRCULATION

Media sell circulation, and circulation is a group of individuals — a market for goods and services. Media, thus, deliver markets to advertisers, and markets support media. The circulation of just about all medium and large-sized newspapers is audited by an outside, independent organization, the Audit Bureau of Circulations. So as to let advertisers know how many copies of a given newspaper are sold where, the ABC requires publishers to break down their circulation into:

City Zone: This is the area within the corporate limits of the city, plus adjoining and continuing areas which overflow the city proper and are in no significant way different from it.

Trading Zone: This zone surrounds and extends further out than the city zone. It is the retail trading area whose trading center is the city itself. Its residents normally make a trip to the city when in need of shopping goods.

All Other: Copies of the paper not sold in the city zone nor in the trading zone make up this third classification.

Newspaper Facts

Number of Dailies	Combined Circulation
1,761	59,261,000
Morning Papers	Circulation
312	24,094,000
Evening Papers	Circulation
1,458	35,167,000
Sunday Papers	Circulation
558	48,216,000
Weekly Papers	Circulation
6,300	30,000,000

Basic data about newspapers. (*Courtesy:* Advertising Age)

RATE STRUCTURE

Newspaper rates are quoted for (a) an agate line or (b) a column inch. Many small newspapers quote only in terms of the column inch; most large newspapers quote only in terms of the agate line; middle-size newspapers frequently quote general rates in terms of lines but retail rates in terms of column inches. There is no formula which will tell a publisher what his rates should be. Of the influences which do determine rates, circulation, of course, is the most basic. Other influences include competition, local income level, public acceptance of the newspaper (also termed reader preference for the paper), and, of course, cost-and-profit considerations.

General Versus Retail

A prominent feature of newspaper rates is the differential between general rates and retail rates. The amount by which general rates are higher than retail rates varies from publisher to publisher, and this variation is wide. Even so, within this admittedly broad range, a general rate that is 60 per cent higher on weekdays and 75 per cent higher on Sundays than the retail rate is not the least bit unusual.

Why are there higher prices for manufacturers' advertisements than for retailers' advertisements? General advertising is commissionable — retail advertising is not; this means that the general rate figures can be and usually are reduced by the commissions the newspaper grants to advertising agencies and to the newspaper representative who sells space to general advertisers. Another explanation is that there is no waste circulation for general advertisers, whereas local advertisers stand to benefit very little if at all from the sale of copies of the newspaper outside the newspaper's retail trading area. Retailers, furthermore, buy more advertising space — more regularly — and for it pay more dollars than do manufacturers; the principle of quantity discounts argues for lower prices for retailers. The advertising of some of these retailers, incidentally, is newsworthy enough to be a favorable influence on the newspaper's circulation. A further justification for the differential rests on the fact that the general advertiser is an expensive type of customer; selling space to him and to his advertising agency is costly, and he demands and gets more merchandising and research service from the newspaper than does the great majority of local advertisers.

Each newspaper decides which advertisers are entitled to its local rates and which must pay the higher general rates. Some manufacturers get their retail dealers to place advertising so as to qualify for the lower local rates.

Discounts

Newspaper rates can be *flat,* or they can be set on a *sliding scale.* When rates are flat, the advertiser can qualify for no discounts regardless of the volume or the frequency of his advertisements; he pays the full amount. The sliding scale type of rate structure does offer discounts to advertisers. Here the *open* or one-time rate is the highest rate; discounts reducing this figure can be earned by an advertiser who (a) uses not less than specified amounts of space every day, every other day, every week, and every month during a time period, usually one year, or (b) uses not less than specified numbers of advertisements. Volume and frequency, thus, are the two bases for discounts.

General advertisers and their advertising agencies strongly prefer bulk or volume discounts based on total linage or total dollars spent during a 12-month period. These two groups are not enthusiastic over frequency or continuity discounts, discounts based on minimum sizes of advertisements and minimum numbers of advertisements run during a 12-month period. In addition, these advertisers and their agencies would like to see a single discount pattern or structure develop, gain approval and acceptance, and be adopted by all newspapers. This resentment of frequency discounts stems from the conviction that frequency discounts are hostile to, that they reduce, advertising flexibility.

Media

Most local rates are open rates, that is, subject to discounts. General rates, once largely flat, are now more and more subject to volume and frequency discounts. Typically and traditionally, general rates (but not local rates) have been subject to a 15 per cent commission to advertising agencies.

Color

For some years now the use of R.O.P. (run of paper) color advertising has been growing. Color reproduction is increasing in quality, and ways of decreasing the price premium are being developed. Availability increases. R.O.P. color is now available in about 450 markets which account for 80% of daily newspaper circulation. Color linage may account for 25%–30% of all newspaper advertising linage before 1970.

Combination Rates

In some markets, a morning newspaper and an afternoon newspaper are owned by the same publisher. In such cases, there may be an *optional* combination rate — or a *forced* combination rate. In the latter instance, an advertiser must buy the same space in both papers, must run the same copy, and must observe whatever time limit the publisher has put into effect about how soon the second advertisement must appear. Some publishers, for example, require that the second advertisement follow the first one immediately — this afternoon's (the first) advertisement must be followed by tomorrow morning's (the second) advertisement. Other publishers may allow as much as a three-day lag between the two advertisements. An advertiser may have strong feelings about the mandatory or forced combination rate. He may have what he considers to be an excellent reason for wanting to use just the morning paper — or just the afternoon paper. He may feel that the duplication of readership is, for him, undesirable and unprofitable. Above all, he may feel that he is being forced to buy a package deal — a sort of job lot assortment in which one of the papers cannot stand on its own feet.

POSITION

There are certain positions in most advertising media which are superior to and hence preferred over certain other positions in the same media. Although position in a newspaper is not a major determinant of the readership an advertisement gets nor of the effectiveness of an advertisement, it is still important. An advertiser has two alternatives in respect to position in newspapers. He can buy space on a R.O.P. basis, paying no premium for preferred position and relying on the publisher to place the advertisement in a spot satisfactory to the advertiser; most advertisers do just this. Or, the advertiser can specify that his advertisement occupy a preferred position — a matter of (a) section or page, or (b) location on the page, or both.

As for section or page, our first observation is that little or no advertising is seen on the first or the editorial page of most newspapers. The desirability and the appropriateness of certain sections of the Sunday newspaper (business and finance, society, book review, sports) for certain advertisers has already been suggested.

Newspapers

As for page, there are two preferred types. One type is superior to R.O.P. because of its number and location in the newspaper; pages 2, 3, 4, and 5 are better for general advertising than are most other pages, and the same is true of the back page.

TABLE 11.1   READING BY SECTIONS

A section of a newspaper is any group of pages carrying news and advertising which are folded separately as one part of the newspaper. The following figures show that there is little variation in the readership of the first and second sections of a newspaper.*

* This study has not measured a sufficient number of issues with 3 or 4 sections to enable it to report on them.

	MEN High	MEN Median	WOMEN High	WOMEN Median
Any for Section I	100%	99%	100%	99%
Any for Section I exclusive of first page	100	97	100	99
Any for Section II	100	99	100	99
Any for Section II exclusive of first page	100	98	100	99

Source: "138-Study Summary," **The Continuing Study of Newspaper Reading** (New York: Advertising Research Foundation).

TABLE 11.2   READING BY TYPE OF PAGE

Forget the special pages such as sports, food, and society, and consider only the pages with general news and advertising. You will note that, on the average, nearly two-thirds of the men readers and nearly three-quarters of the women readers read one or more items or advertisements on such pages. (Headline reading is not counted.)

	# of Pages	MEN Median Reading	WOMEN Median Reading
All Pages	4404	60%	70%
Front Pages	136	98	97
(General News Pages (with advertising	2075	64	73
Women's & Food Pages	211	20	72
Society Pages	208	35	81
Sports Pages	328	68	27
Comic Pages	153	84	83

Source: "138-Study Summary," **The Continuing Study of Newspaper Reading** (New York: Advertising Research Foundation).

Media

Important news stories which don't quite make page 1 often start on pages 2 and 3. The other type bases its claim to superiority on the nature of its editorial content, just as is true of the sections of the Sunday newspaper. The farm page, the entertainment page, and the food page are examples of positions which can increase the effectiveness of the advertising of certain sellers.

TABLE 11.3 READING BY TYPES OF CONTENT

Per Cent of Those Interviewed Who Read Any	MEN Studies #1–138 High	Median	WOMEN Studies #1–138 High	Median
Editorials	77%	43%	63%	27%
Editorial Page Items	96	83	96	79
Comics	96	81	94	78
Financial News	53	28	45	10
Radio Programs or News	76	40	83	50
Society News or Pictures	88	36	98	83
Sports News or Pictures	95	76	82	34
Display Advertising	97	80	100	95
National Advertising	92	54	90	60
Local Advertising	94	74	99	94
Department Store Advertising	75	39	99	85
Classified Advertising	69	39	83	45
Amusement Advertising	66	43	78	59

Source: "138-Study Summary," **The Continuing Study of Newspaper Reading** (New York: Advertising Research Foundation).

Just as there are preferred sections and pages, so are there preferred spots or positions on the page. Generally speaking, advertising benefits from nearness to editorial matter because some glances and some attention will drift or ricochet to the advertisement from that reading matter. *Next to reading matter* (touching reading matter on one vertical side), and *following reading matter* are the kinds of proximity desired. In standard-sized papers, advertisers like to be above the center (horizontal) fold, and they like even more to be at the top of the column. The visibility is greater here — there are fewer advertisements here — news stories start here at the top of the page. *Full* position adds strength to an advertisement of less than page size; when an advertisement has editorial material along each vertical side and there is no advertising above it, it is said to enjoy full position. Two other definitions of full position are: (a) advertising space not touched by other advertisements, and (b) top of page and next to reading. Full page advertisements are not thought of as occupying full position. An island position (top of column, reading matter on all three sides) is excellent but rare. And, of course, a buried position (surrounded on all four sides by advertising) is shunned.

COST COMPARISONS

Within each medium there are many choices available to the advertiser — many newspapers, many magazines, many broadcast stations from which he can select the ones to use. Comparison, of course, must precede selection, but when he begins to compare, the advertiser is confronted by differences between any two newspapers or television stations. Immediately the advertiser recognizes his need for a yardstick — a common denominator — a formula which will help him compare the costs of various individual media, newspapers, for example, with different circulations and with different rates.

The measurement used to compare newspaper costs is the *milline rate*. This rate is an imaginary, artificial rate in the sense that advertisers are not billed in terms of it; they are billed in terms of the actual line rate or the actual column inch rate. The milline rate is completely firm and realistic in that it is the cost of sending one agate line of advertising to 1,000,000 readers.

Here is the formula for the milline rate:

$$\frac{\text{Line rate} \times 1{,}000{,}000}{\text{circulation}}$$

Suppose a newspaper has a line rate of $2.00 and a circulation of 571,000. Substituting:

$$\frac{\$2 \times 1{,}000{,}000}{571{,}000} = \frac{\$2{,}000{,}000}{571{,}000} = \$3.50 \text{ milline rate}$$

Now let's look at a smaller paper, one with a line rate of $ .12 and a circulation of 23,000. Substituting:

$$\frac{\$ .12 \times 1{,}000{,}000}{23{,}000} = \frac{\$120{,}000}{23{,}000} = \$5.22 \text{ milline rate}$$

Most newspapers quote two milline rates. The *maximil* is computed at the highest, one-time rate and is, consequently, the maximum milline rate. The *minimil* is computed at the lowest rate the advertiser can qualify for — the basic rate less the greatest discount he can earn; this is the minimum milline rate. If the rate is flat, then the maximil and the minimil are, of course, identical. Only a glance at milline rates is needed to discover that the highest milline rates are to be found among the smallest papers in small towns. The typical milline rate goes up as circulation goes down, and vice versa.

Even among papers of roughly comparable size, papers which compete directly with each other in the same market, some milline rates are higher than others. For example, the *New York Times* has a milline rate higher than that of the *New York News*. It is true, certainly, that the *News* is a tabloid paper, but the difference in milline rates still demands explanation. In general, the defense of a low figure is based on the claim that the newspaper is edited for and reaches the great mass market of readers; low milline rates and huge circulations usually go together. The

Media

defense of a high milline rate can be based on the type of reader the newspaper has (greater purchasing power, superior social standing, greater influence, more responsive) or on features of the newspaper itself (excellent mechanical reproduction, prestige of editorial content, absence of any local newspaper competition).

Questions and Problems

1. Comment on day of appearance for newspaper ads.
2. Compare preferred positions in Sunday newspapers with preferred positions in weekday newspapers.
3. Why are newspapers bought outside their respective retail trading areas?
4. Why do manufacturers advertise in small non-daily newspapers whose readers read large-city dailies?
5. Why is there more retail advertising than general advertising in newspapers?
6. How does the basic nature of newspapers influence the ads they carry?
7. List some types of selectivity available to newspaper advertisers.
8. What forms of non-advertising competition confront the retailer who advertises in the Sunday newspaper?
9. Comment on sponsored advertising columns as found in newspapers.
10. Comment on the placement or positioning of ads by a newspaper.

Chapter 12

Magazines

Magazines, our second publication medium, are available in great variety. Most are published once a month or once a week. Many monthly magazines appear during the month preceding the month of issue(the December *McCall's* can be bought on November 21), and many weekly magazines appear several days before the date of issue (*Life* is dated Monday but is issued the preceding Thursday). There is the pocket size (*Reader's Digest*), the standard size (*National Geographic*), the flat size (*Time*), and the large size (*Life*). As for type of reader, the editorial content of some is designed to appeal to consumers, the content of others appeals to business readers, and the editorial features of still other magazines attract farm readers.

BASIC CLASSIFICATION

General Consumer Magazines

Many magazines are edited for the general consumer, their content of articles, fiction, and special features being such as to appeal to the general reader. These magazines are bought and read for both information and entertainment by consumers who have common interests and higher than average incomes. When one of these general consumer magazines has a circulation of several million, it is sometimes referred to as a "mass" magazine. *Reader's Digest, Life,* and *Look* are examples. Magazines with smaller circulations are termed "class." Their smaller circulations reflect a higher degree of selectivity than is present in the larger magazines, selectivity which, of course, results in an advertising cost per unit of circulation higher than that for the more general consumer magazines. *The New Yorker, Bride's Magazine,* and *The Woman Bowler* are "class" magazines. The so-called "shelter" magazines (*Better Homes & Gardens, The American Home*) have changed from "class" to "mass" and carry a significant volume of advertising. The distinction between "mass" and "class" magazines is not a clear one; because *all* magazines constitute a class-type of medium, *each* magazine enjoys a certain type and amount of "class."

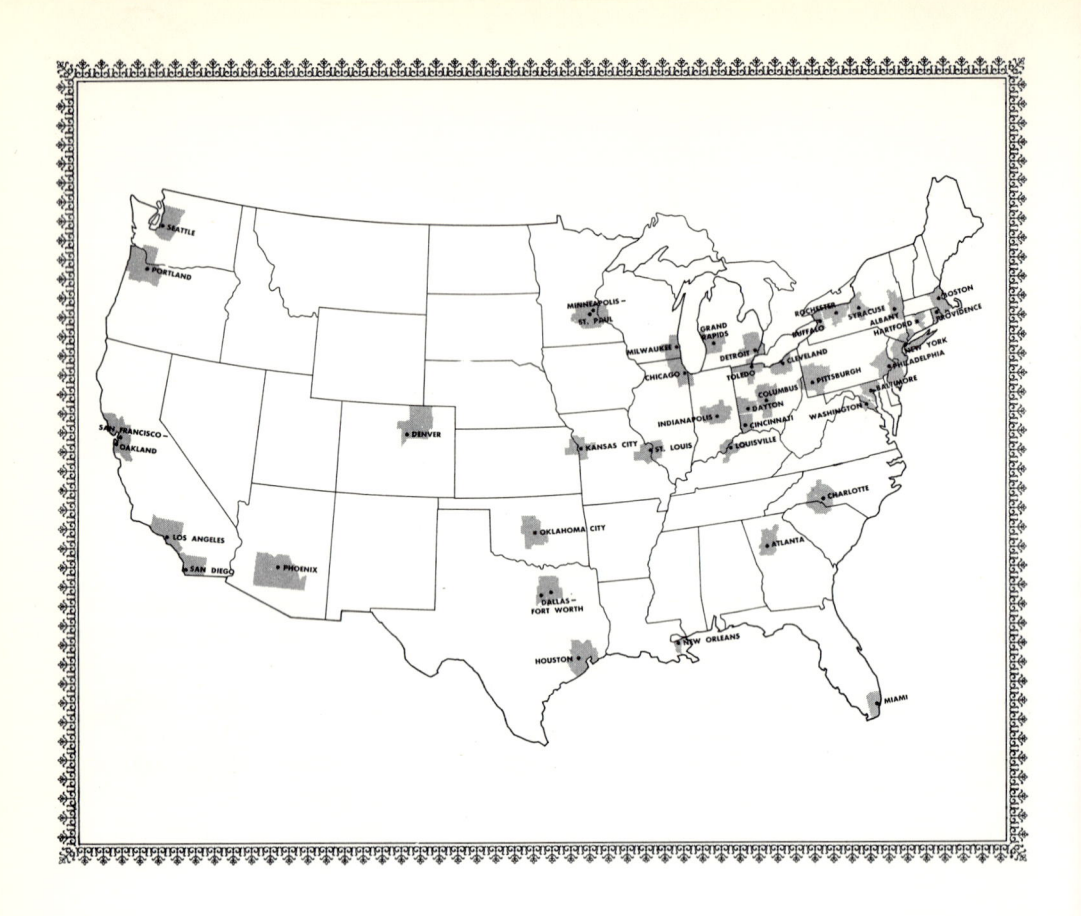

These are America's 40 primary markets for quality merchandise

Forty primary markets account for anywhere from two-thirds to virtually all of the potential U.S. sales of quality goods and services.

These forty markets have been defined, analyzed and indexed in a new study prepared by The New Yorker. Entitled "The Primary Markets for Quality Merchandise," the study has three major uses:

1. To assist in marketing decisions of a company selling a quality product.
2. To furnish a method for comparing sales performances with market potentials.
3. To provide the background of a marketing plan for new or improved products, domestic or imported.

To receive a copy of this marketing study, write Stuart N. Spizer, Director of Research, The New Yorker.

THE NEW YORKER, No. 25 West 43rd Street, New York 36, New York. Other Advertising Offices: Chicago, San Francisco, Los Angeles, Atlanta, London

This magazine is proud of the taste and income — and of the purchases — of its readers. © The New Yorker Magazine, Inc.)

Women's Magazines

Although there are various types of magazines edited for women (screen and romance, for example, or fashion and beauty), the one of greatest interest to us is the women's service magazine. *Good Housekeeping* and *McCall's* illustrate this type. Editorial features about family, home, and housekeeping are aimed at the millions of housewives who do much household buying and who influence many other purchases. Today's woman can have many interests and activities because of the amounts of time and money at her disposal. The women's service type of magazine is one of her sources of fiction, of information about fashion, and of help about her personal and family problems.

One type of women's service magazine is distributed in certain retail stores. *Woman's Day,* for example, is available in some supermarkets; *Everywoman's Family Circle* is on sale in other food stores. These magazines must be bought single copy only — they do not accept subscriptions. The price of these magazines to the consumer is low, reflecting (a) the low cost of distributing the issues to the stores and (b) the absence of any expense for selling subscriptions to the magazines. Products other than foods may be advertised in magazines sponsored by food stores.

Business Magazines

These publications are characterized by their high selectivity, their small circulations, their intimate knowledge of their readers, their low dollar rates per page, and their rational content. Because most of the advertisements promise some version of the same benefit, *increased profits from greater sales or reduced costs,* they enjoy high readership. Many subscriptions are paid for out of company funds; each copy is often routed around among several company employees for examination. *Horizontal* magazines are edited for *one* type of reader in *many* industries (*Modern Packaging, Purchasing, Sales Management*); a *vertical* magazine is edited for *many* readers within a *single* industry or area (*Aviation Week, Automotive News, Pulp and Paper*).

Trade magazines or papers are one subdivision of business magazines. These publications deal mainly with the marketing operations and problems of middlemen. Advertisers in trade papers feature products for wholesalers and retailers to use such as cash registers and scales, or products for them to buy for resale. *Wholesale Grocer News* and *Progressive Grocer* are examples of trade magazines.

Another subdivision of business magazines is made up of *industrial* magazines, vertical publications which do for industries what trade magazines do for commerce and distribution. The intent of industrial magazines is to help producers produce more. *Textile World* and *Iron Age* are examples.

Institutional magazines, a third type of business magazines, do for institutions what trade papers do for mercantile firms. *Hospital Management* and *Hotel Management* are institutional magazines.

A fourth group within the business magazine area, the *professional* magazine, is edited for a specialized or technical group of readers. Some advertisers in these periodicals want to sell *to* the readers, other advertisers want to sell *through* them.

Media

Engineering News-Record is edited for and read by engineers and contractors, *Architectural Record* for and by architects and engineers.

A fifth and final group of business magazines is *executive* in character. These publications are edited for individuals with administrative and managerial responsibilities of a serious nature, for the so-called "top management" reader. Essentially horizontal, these magazines are represented by such periodicals as *Business Week* and *Fortune*.

Agricultural Magazines

This general type of magazine is edited for rural consumers, featuring matters which relate to farms and farm families. It may be general (*The Nation's Agriculture, The Progressive Farmer*), or it may be specialized (*Breeder's Gazette, Michigan Farm News*). The relatively large number of specialized publications is readily understandable — Mississippi's crops differ from Minnesota's, and citrus problems are not identical with wheat problems.

Miscellaneous Magazines

In addition to the major classifications just listed, there are other types of magazines. Examples of this miscellaneous group are the religious, the fraternal, the educational, the comic, and the military service magazines.

NEWSPAPER MAGAZINES

Newspaper magazines occupy a unique position in the media field because of their dual character. Even though they appear once a week as a newspaper supplement, their style and format — their over-all nature — are those of a magazine. Containing fiction and articles, pictures and features, these publications are actually Sunday magazines which hitchhike a free ride with Sunday newspapers. The newspaper magazine is not deliberately and specifically bought by readers, it is placed in readers' hands at no extra cost; it is sold to consumers separately from the newspaper of which it is one section. The growth of newspaper magazines in circulation and their growth as carriers of advertising have been quite impressive.

There are two types of newspaper magazines. The *syndicated* type (*Parade, This Week, Family Weekly*), is edited and printed by a publishing company which then makes the magazine available in finished form to noncompeting newspapers throughout the country. The newspaper buys an adequate quantity of the supplement, inserts one into each Sunday copy, and sells the paper to its readers. The *individual* type (*New York Times Magazine, Atlantic Journal-Constitution Magazine, Louisville Courier-Journal Sunday Magazine*) is edited and published locally by the newspaper distributing it. Both types prefer a 850-line page, 5 columns by 170 lines.

Advertisers are interested in and influenced by several features of these publications. Newspaper magazines reach the same consumers who read the newspapers; thus they enjoy their newspapers' intensive coverage and heavy impact in each market. They enjoy a longer life than does the newspaper which carries them. They are more national in flavor than local. Since their appearance, both their physical

Magazines

and editorial quality have risen. Reproduction-wise, the supplements are of higher quality than the newspapers they accompany but of lower quality than many general consumer magazines.

FEATURES OF THE MEDIUM

Merits

Among their various assets, magazines are probably proudest of their *selectivity*. Each magazine is edited to please and to serve a specific group — even the general consumer magazine is read by consumers whose tastes and interests are common, at least roughly. Selectivity of reader is achieved through the editor's control of editorial content (fiction, articles, features, and illustrations); and, once a homogeneous group of readers has been established, then advertising selectivity becomes possible — each advertiser can determine for himself whether that particular group of readers should be advertised to in the magazine's advertising pages. Whether the key factor is age, sex, purchasing power, interests, religion, or vocation, there is a magazine edited for almost any homogeneous group an advertiser might want to reach.

Magazines boast of the *types of individuals* who read magazines as contrasted with non-readers. The magazine reader is considerably younger and better educated than is the non-reader. The reader's family is larger, the head of the family has a better job, the family has more money, and the general influence of the family is greater than for non-reading families. Magazines provide thorough coverage of the upper income groups; the families which spend the most for the basic classifications of goods and services also spend the most for magazines.

Reader confidence is a magazine asset. With the possible exception of some gift subscriptions, a magazine is bought and read only by individuals who believe in it, who consider it an authority, who accept its editorial features and its advertising. The authority of the printed word is prominent in the thinking of many persons. All magazines screen the advertisements offered them, and some go so far as to vouch for the products whose advertising they accept.

Magazines are proud of their *national coverage*. Most magazines circulate all over the country, and magazines as a medium reach over 80 per cent of our homes. Circulation does a good job of paralleling the public's purchasing power and, at the same time, of achieving fairly even readership in city, town, and rural communities. A manufacturer's advertising story is told uniformly and simultaneously all across the nation. Magazines are one of few media able to follow a consumer to whatever section of the country he or she may go.

Long life, particularly in contrast to the short life of newspapers, is a plus feature of the medium. Because few magazines feature *news,* few get out-of-date quickly, and this explains why so many issues remain in the home at least until the next issue comes out, or even longer. It would be interesting to know, for example, how many back issues there are of the *National Geographic* filed away in the homes of readers. Because it is not discarded quickly, a magazine can be, and is, picked up and read several times. Because the consumer can choose his time of reading, his

Magazine Advertising IMPACT Means Business!

It all adds up to the fact that it's the *total impact* of magazines... their ability to break through the advertising sound barrier in so many different ways... that makes them such a strong selling tool in every local community, for every one of the people you sell to.

So, when you can, tell the *whole* story of your company's magazine promotion. Because magazine advertising *impact* is more than a catchword—it's the *key* word to remember when you're telling dealers why and how magazines work. In fact, the word *impact* is a ready-made checklist for you—like this:

I **Influence**—Magazines set our national tastes in how we dress... eat... furnish our homes... how we get around, what we do.

M **Market selectivity**—Magazines select the people your company wants to reach... its best customers and prospects ... the bigger families with larger incomes... the families who do more buying.

P **Product presentation**—Magazines give your company's advertising the right time and place to put across its <u>full</u> story. You get more attention... and more action.

A **Audience receptivity**—Magazines stimulate desires for products and services of all kinds because they tell convincingly not only <u>what</u>... but <u>why</u>, and <u>how</u>.

C **Coverage**—Magazines are read in better than eight out of every ten homes across the nation. Powerful coverage in every local community.

T **Traffic-building**—Magazines offer more opportunities for local promotions than any other mass medium. They channel customers right to the sales outlet.

You'll think of a lot of ways to use your company's magazine advertising in your calls—as a source of facts and sales points—as a sales portfolio for demonstrating the advantages of your product or service—and, above all, as a powerful promotion force that's bound to pay off for the people you sell to because it makes sales. That's the big reason why eight out of every ten national companies use magazine advertising year in and year out...in ever-increasing numbers, with ever-growing dollar investments.

Magazines stress these six features when promoting the magazine medium. (Courtesy: Magazine Advertising Bureau)

frame of mind can be relaxed and receptive; he can be attracted and interested by advertising; he will read longer advertisements than when he is reading newspapers. Magazines can get thorough readership; they can be read and then re-read.

A magazine's *editorial features* may contribute to the effectiveness of the advertising it contains. Articles and, to a degree, even fiction can relate to, explain, and encourage the purchase of certain products and services. The favorable atmosphere created by the editorial content blesses the advertisements with greater sales power.

Another magazine advantage is that of *prestige,* both with consumers and with retailers. Consumers are favorably impressed with the high quality paper, the reproduction of art work, especially in color, and with the excellence of over-all appearance. They like the detailed, realistic, true-to-life illustrations of product and package. They know that good writers and good artists have produced editorial material which is outstanding in its power to inform, to relax, to recreate, and to entertain. They realize that consumers all over the country read about and know, buy and use, the products they see advertised in magazines. Retailers are keenly aware of these consumer attitudes and actions; in addition, retailers know full well that substantial magazine advertising campaigns cannot be bought by small manufacturers.

More recently, a more *imaginative use of space* has added to the flexibility and elasticity of magazine advertising. When readers open a magazine, they may find multi-page inserts or aluminum foil; recipe books, catalogs, or guide books which can be detached and kept for reference; and, if the magazine was bought from a newsstand, it just might contain a sample of some product. *Life* offers these special space units:

    Three-page inside front cover gatefold
    Front cover and "page one" double gatefold
    Single gatefold
    Double gatefold
    Single accordion gatefold
    Double accordion gatefold
    Dutch doors
    Venetian doors
    French doors
    Small size multi-page section
    Small size pages on card stock

Limitations

A serious limitation imposed on advertisers by magazines has to do with *time.* Getting ready for a sizable use of magazine advertising usually must start months before the appearance of the first advertisement. Indeed, magazine advertising in color is one of the most difficult advertising commitments to revise or amend. The artwork, for example, may easily require weeks, and the engravers may need the same amount of time to make color plates. Then the magazine must produce two or three or four million copies of an issue, a printing job which cannot be finished in just a day or two. Once printed, many of these copies must be distributed to over

Media

100,000 newsstands in all fifty states, and, at the same time, the remaining copies must be mailed so that newsstands and subscribers get their copies *on the same day*. Since weekly magazines simply must not be late, almost split-second scheduling is demanded. One can understand, therefore, why a weekly magazine may set its closing date for 4-color advertisements seven weeks preceding the date of issue. After the closing date, the magazine accepts no more advertising, allows no changes in advertisements already accepted, and permits no cancellations. All of this means that magazine copy cannot be up-to-the-minute in reflecting recent events, cannot be current or newsworthy to the degree, for instance, that newspaper copy can. This time limitation urges the advertiser to run *safe* copy, to avoid being vulnerable to unhappy vagaries of fate and coincidence. An example of an unhappy experience was a beer advertisement containing the testimonial of a prominent person — the advertisement appeared in magazines only a few days after the testifier had a fatal heart attack.

There are three or four limitations in addition to that of time. The advertiser can communicate with his buyers only infrequently, especially when contrasted with television and radio, and even when contrasted with newspapers. The cost of mechanical preparation can run into big figures. Finally, for magazines which do not publish regional editions, national distribution, already described as a merit, is also a limitation. For example, few manufacturers with less than national distribution can use magazine advertising profitably. Furthermore, regional differences in product, market, price, preferences, and temperature restrict the copywriter. There can be little sectional or regional flavor in the copy.

CIRCULATION

A magazine's circulation consists of the individuals who buy it and read it. Circulation can be built by excellent editing, by putting together a good magazine, and then by doing an effective, sound marketing job. A quicker, less desirable route to increased circulation is through the cutting of price and the use of high pressure promotion tactics, involving, perhaps, combination offers or premiums. Price reductions and pressure selling reduce the quality of the magazine's circulation regardless of their effect on its quantity.

Primary Versus Secondary Circulation

A magazine's *primary* circulation is the number of copies it gets paid for, the number of copies readers buy. Most magazines have this figure audited by an outside firm (Audit Bureau of Circulations, Business Publications Audit of Circulation), and the figure for consumer magazines is often referred to as "net paid ABC circulation." Primary circulation is of high quality because of the high degree of reader interest it reflects. Multiple readership of a magazine by members of the family buying it is also of high quality.

Secondary circulation is also referred to as pass-along-circulation and as readership. It is the total number of persons who read the copies of an issue of a magazine over and above the primary circulation figure. Because secondary circulation is not audited, its magnitude can only be estimated. When a consumer reads a magazine passed on to him by a neighbor or friend, or when a man looks through a barber shop's magazine while getting a haircut, each is a unit of secondary circulation. At the same time that advertisers want secondary circulation because they benefit from it, they recognize that its quality is generally lower than that of primary circulation. The pass-along reader either lacks interest in the magazine, or he lacks the money with which to buy it. Either of these circumstances may classify the person as a second class prospect.

Subscription Versus Single Copy

Magazines with a high proportion of subscription sales to single copy or newsstand sales (business, news, and farm magazines, for example) stress their relatively even circulation throughout the year, their steady readership, and their ability to "define" their audience. They credit their readers with enough interest in the magazines and with enough dollars to buy a year's supply at a time. And they claim, correctly, that five or six dollars is a fair-sized single purchase. In an aside, they observe that, although newsstands do serve urban markets, what about the non-urban consumers, particularly the suburbanites.

Magazines with a high proportion of single copy sales (movie, romance, radio, television, mechanics, and science magazines, for example) speak with feeling about proved vitality and sustained reader interest, pointing out, correctly, that any reader of theirs can cast a vote of "no confidence" in the magazine just as soon as the next issue comes out — by not buying it. This option is not available to subscribers. Magazines with large single copy sales remind advertisers that the reader's trip to the newsstand is an extra trip, sometimes even inconvenient, and that the single copy prices for a year's issues total more than a subscription costs; these are presented as proof of great reader attraction.

Publishers of general consumer magazines have been promoting subscription sales more vigorously than single copy sales. A predominance of subscription sales assures the publisher that a large, steady volume of circulation will be included in his rate base. This is particularly desirable and comforting when costs are rising continuously, and the magazine must get more money from its only sources, advertisers and readers. There is no "right" ratio of subscription circulation to single copy circulation; for magazines as a group, subscription volume is greater than single copy volume.

Guaranteed Versus Delivered

A magazine makes a firm commitment to its advertisers to sell not less than a specific, publicized number of copies of each issue. This fact, incidentally, is indicative of the small amount of seasonal fluctuation in magazine circulation. This guaranteed figure is approximately the greatest volume the magazine feels confident of achieving, issue after issue. It is safely, but closely, under the audited figure for number of copies sold which, of course, is the delivered figure. If a magazine guarantees a circulation of 2,000,000 copies but sells only 1,900,000 each advertiser gets a rebate of 5 per cent. If the same magazine grows to 2,500,000 and feels

Media

confidently that this figure can be maintained, then it raises its guarantee to 2,300,000 or 2,400,000 *and* raises its advertising rates.

Individual Versus Bulk

When a reader of a magazine buys from a newsstand or when he buys a subscription, his purchase is of an *individual* nature; he acted singly and of his own volition. When an instructor forces the students in one of his classes to take a semester subscription to a magazine by paying their money to whichever one of their group the students elect treasurer, who then places a single order for 40, 50, or 60 copies of each issue which come to the treasurer in a single bundle, those copies constitute a *bulk* sale. Because some of the students would not have bought if the purchase had just been suggested rather than required, their quality as readers may be lower than that of readers who buy the magazine individually. Advertisers strongly prefer a unit of individual circulation over a unit of bulk circulation.

Total Versus Partial

In the late 1950's, two significant innovations took place in the magazine medium involving circulation. (1) Certain magazines began to offer advertisers the opportunity to buy *regional* (less than national) coverage. Prior to this change, an advertiser bought the entire circulation of a magazine, or he stayed out of it entirely. *Life, Look, Esquire, Reader's Digest, Better Homes,* and *Time* are some of the publications which began to sell advertising space in regional or sectional editions in addition, of course, to space in each one's national edition. Some magazines observed state lines when setting up their zones or regions. Others adopted marketing areas as their regional units — marketing areas which ignore state lines. One magazine delineated 4 regions; another set up 52 zones for our 50 states. Editorial content is usually identical in all editions making a *regional* copy of the magazine nothing more nor less than the national edition (editorial material and national advertisements) plus its own regional advertisements. Some magazines stipulate that regional advertisements be full page only. Advertising in regional editions ranges from 15% to 90% more expensive (see Cost Comparison section on pages 233 and 234) than in the national edition.

(2) The second innovation involves intensity of advertising in that some magazines began to allow advertisers to buy less than 100% of the magazine's national circulation. For example, a magazine with a national circulation of 6,000,000 might permit an advertiser to buy 2,000,000 or 4,000,000. His advertisement then would be in ⅓ or ⅔ of the total circulation. If the advertiser so desired, he obviously could run advertisement "A" in ⅓, advertisement "B" in a second ⅓, and advertisement "C" in the remaining ⅓. A simpler pattern, called the "alternate copy split run," schedules advertisement "A" for ½ and advertisement "B" for the other ½ of a magazine's total circulation. One magazine went so far as to offer to place advertisement "A" in newsstand copies and advertisement "B" in subscription copies.

Sectional or zone advertising quickly became popular. Regional marketers and/or regional brands were able to enjoy the power and authority, the prestige and impact,

Beginning January...
8 Regional Editions
in Good Housekeeping

(Effective issue of January, 1963. Seven regions currently available. See listing.)

MARKET REGIONS:

1. **NEW ENGLAND:** Maine, New Hampshire, Vermont, Massachusetts, Rhode Island and Connecticut
2. **MID-ATLANTIC:** New York, Pennsylvania, New Jersey, Delaware, Maryland, District of Columbia
3. **EAST CENTRAL:** Michigan, Ohio, Indiana, West Virginia, Kentucky
4. **WEST CENTRAL:** Montana, Wyoming, Colorado, North Dakota, South Dakota, Nebraska, Kansas, Minnesota, Iowa, Missouri
5. **CENTRAL:** Wisconsin, Illinois
6. **SOUTH EASTERN:** Alabama, Florida, Georgia, Mississippi, North Carolina, South Carolina, Tennessee, Virginia
7. **SOUTH WESTERN:** Arkansas, Louisiana, New Mexico, Oklahoma and Texas
8. **PACIFIC:** Washington, Oregon, Idaho, Nevada, Utah, Arizona, California, Alaska and Hawaii

RATES

MARKET	CIRCULATION (ABC 12/31/61)	BLACK AND WHITE PAGE	BLACK AND WHITE DOUBLE COLUMN OR 1/2 PAGE HORIZONTAL	TWO COLOR PAGE	TWO COLOR DOUBLE COLUMN OR 1/2 PAGE HORIZONTAL	FOUR COLOR PAGE	FOUR COLOR DOUBLE COLUMN OR 1/2 PAGE HORIZONTAL
#1	331,000	$1,750	$1,170	$1,900	$1,250	$2,160	$1,430
#2	1,160,000	5,640	3,780	6,130	4,040	6,960	4,590
#3	758,000	3,780	2,530	4,110	2,710	4,670	3,080
#4	412,000	2,140	1,430	2,330	1,540	2,650	1,750
#5	529,000	2,680	1,800	2,910	1,920	3,310	2,180
#6	551,000	2,800	1,880	3,060	2,020	3,480	2,290
#7	387,000	2,030	1,360	2,210	1,460	2,510	1,650
#8	752,000	3,750	2,510	4,070	2,690	4,630	3,050

REGIONAL DISCOUNTS

a) Combinations of 2 or more regions earn a 5% discount.
b) Advertisers buying all 8 regions earn an additional 5% discount over all other discounts.
c) Effective with the January 1963 issue, regional linage is applicable to and eligible for national volume discounts. Supplements rate card #34.

For complete details on Good Housekeeping's flexible "Match-A-Market" coverage, see your Good Housekeeping representative.

Good Housekeeping
MAGAZINE AND INSTITUTE

Good Housekeeping Guarantees: IF PRODUCT OR PERFORMANCE DEFECTIVE, REPLACEMENT OR REFUND TO CONSUMER

Typical example of how certain magazines have broken down what once was one national edition into several regional editions. (Courtesy: Good Housekeeping)

Media

of the magazine medium. Advertising copy could stress sectional interest, and illustrations could be selected to match each area's tastes. Additional promotion could be scheduled in areas where sales were high, *or* low. Regional testing in magazines became possible, testing of products or advertising. The same manufacturer could advertise different products in different areas, an important consideration for seasonal products. Aggressive promotion by competitors in certain sections of the country could be met with heavier magazine advertising in those sections. Region-by-region introduction of new products could enjoy the support of magazine advertising. Finally, many manufacturers could list their retail dealers satisfactorily in regional advertisements.

RATE STRUCTURE

Magazines, like newspapers, sell circulation; their advertising rates are determined largely by the quality and the quantity of their readers. Costs, too, are an influence affecting advertising rates. For a number of years after World War II the expenses of magazines rose steadily — costs of paper, of printing, of editorial contents, of physical distribution, of selling space, and of promoting circulation. The pressure of these rising costs forced up advertising rates (which account for over half of the revenue of magazines), cover prices (single copy prices), and subscription prices. Although there is only slight seasonal variation in the circulation of magazines and no seasonal differences in advertising rates, there is considerable difference among the months as regards advertising volume. Magazines take in the greatest number of advertising dollars in May, October, and November. January is a low month ("consumers have no money left — Christmas, you know"); July and August also are low months ("consumers are off on vacations, and, anyway, they just don't read magazines in the summer").

Unit of Sale

Magazine space is sold (a) by agate line, and (b) by page or fractional page as determined by each magazine. Typically, all interior (non-cover) black-and-white pages in a given magazine cost the same; also, two one-half pages usually cost more than one page. A listing of *standard* units often looks like this:

1 page	1 column
½ page (vertical)	⅛ column
½ page (horizontal)	agate line
¼ page	

Some magazines offer advertisers *junior* units. These have editorial material above and along one side. Here is a typical listing of junior units:

1 page	½ page	1 column

A standard page in *Holiday* or in *McCall's* contains 680 lines; a junior page in each contains 429 lines.

MARKETING MEETING

MARKETING DIRECTOR: *"How can we be sure?"*

PRESIDENT: *"We can't. But we owe it to ourselves to investigate every approach."*

No company today can ignore the exciting changes taking place in the American marketplace.

Witness the phenomenal rise in high school and college attendance. Consider its effect on occupation . . . on income . . . on buying habits.

Education changes people's tastes. They become more curious . . . more critical . . . more discerning.

They *read* more.

They are reading *magazines* more. (Circulations are at an all-time high.)

This spiraling reader interest—combined with the unique magazine advantages of flexibility, selectivity, believability—has brought new efficiency to an already dynamic medium.

Have *you* examined magazines, recently?

You won't be first to discover that they are the growth advertising medium of the 60's.

Can you afford to be last?

MAGAZINES MAKE THINGS HAPPEN!

Advertisement run by magazines to sell magazines as a type of advertising medium. (Courtesy: Magazine Advertising Bureau)

Media

A magazine's four covers are a special type of space. The outside front cover of consumer magazines is seldom offered to advertisers, serving somewhat as the magazine's own advertisement. Some business magazines, however, do make at least a portion of their outside front covers available for advertising. The second cover (inside front), the third cover (inside back), and the fourth cover (outside back) usually carry advertising and are sold only as page units; often their advertisements must be 4-color. It is not uncommon for the outside back cover, the most expensive advertising page, to cost about twice as much as an interior black-and-white page, nor for the second and third covers to be priced at one figure — about 80 per cent as much as the fourth cover. A few magazines charge no more for the inside covers than for other interior pages.

Discounts

If a magazine offers no discounts to advertisers, its rates are referred to as *flat*. Otherwise, a magazine sets its rates on a sliding scale, making the advertiser's cost depend on the *volume* and/or the *frequency* of his advertising. Some magazines base their discounts on the amount of space the advertiser uses within a specified period of time; others base discounts on number of dollars spent instead of amount of space used; still others base the discounts on how frequently the advertisements appear. Monthly magazines may offer a lower rate for 6 advertisements during a year and a still lower rate for 12 advertisements; weekly magazines may have successively lower rates for 13, 26, 39, and 52 appearances during a 12-month period.

In addition to volume and frequency discounts, most magazines offer a 15 per cent commission to recognized advertising agencies, and many offer a 2 per cent cash discount.

Color

The basic, lowest rates charged by a magazine are for black-and-white advertisements. Black plus one color costs more — black plus three colors (4-color process) costs even more in most magazines. Some magazines allow advertisers to use color in one-half page or even one-quarter page space.

Bleed

Advertisements which print over the margin to the very edge of the paper, thereby doing away with the borders, are called *bleed* advertisements. The design, the elements comprising the advertisement, continues to the edge of the page, causing the ink to "bleed" when the paper is cut. Junior space units can bleed across the bottom and along one side. Some magazines make no extra charge for bleed advertisements. However, premiums of 10, 15, and 20 per cent are not unusual. For this extra charge the advertiser gets greater attention value and impact because of the larger area his advertisement occupies, because of the striking appearance of bleed advertisements, and because of the distinctiveness of a technique used by a minority of advertisers. Bleed advertisements are seen by more readers and are read by more readers than is true of non-bleed advertisements.

232

Preferred Positions

The fact that the second, third, and fourth covers are preferred positions has already been observed. The center spread is a preferred position for a 2-page advertisement on facing pages. Because these two facing pages in the center of many magazines are a continuous sheet of paper, there is no problem of alignment in layout, and, in addition, these pages are more likely to be seen than most other pages. The first advertising page following the main editorial section ("Campbell Soup page") is a preferred page. Other better-than-average pages are the one opposite the lead editorial feature, the one facing the table of contents, the one opposite the index of advertisers, and the one opposite a popular and regular cartoon. The first page and the last page are also preferred positions. Instead of making a premium charge for these preferred positions, a more common policy is for a magazine (a) to sell these good spots only for cycle occupancy (an advertiser would agree to take page 1 every fourth issue, for example) or (b) to assign them on a priority basis to the magazine's best advertising customers.

Inserts

If an advertiser wants to be quite distinctive and is willing to pay a premium, he can choose not to use the regular magazine paper stock but, instead, to use an insert. In so doing, he gets one or more pages printed and then forwards this advertisement to the magazine for insertion. Usually the insert is of heavier weight than the ordinary magazine page, of a different finish, of a different color, or even of a different material.

For the premium he pays, the advertiser can choose whatever stock, color, ink, and printing process he prefers. He can turn out a better job because he can put as much time and as many dollars into the project as he prefers. He benefits because inserts stand out, they contrast with the other advertisements; their impact can be vivid and dramatic. If the paper stock is decidedly different in a physical sense, the magazine tends to open there. With only minor changes, inserts can be converted into blotters, calendars, folders, counter displays, package inserts, or mailing cards.

COST COMPARISONS

In the previous chapter, we saw advertisers checking the milline rates of newspapers in an attempt to make the soundest selections of newspapers. When those same advertisers analyze magazines, the common denominator they use is *cost per page per thousand*. The two figures needed in order to compute cost per page per thousand are the cost of a black-and-white page and the net paid circulation of the magazine. Suppose a certain magazine charges $30,000 for a black-and-white page at a time when its net paid circulation is 6,000,000. If this circulation figure is divided into the page cost and multiplied by 1,000, the cost per page per thousand is seen to be $5.

Cost per page per thousand figures are useful in comparing the cost of advertising in various magazines. As was true with milline rates, the cost per page per thousand

Media

figures do not tell how many prospects or even how many readers will read the seller's advertisement.

Why are some cost per page per thousand figures so much higher than others? If a magazine has a large size page (*Look, Life*), it seems entitled to a higher price than is a magazine which sells advertisers a small size page (*Reader's Digest*). The greater the selectivity of the magazine, perhaps in purchasing power, perhaps in the interests of its readers, the more defensible is a high figure. *Town & Country,* for example, has a cost per page per thousand about five times as high as does *Life; Ski's* figure is more than four times as high as is *Look's*. Excellence of editorial content and a high degree of reader loyalty are two other justifications for a high cost per page per thousand.

Because of the fierce competition among magazines, it is only natural that each seeks some basis for comparison on which that particular magazine ranks first. So, we see a magazine boasting about the amount of time its readers spend with it — per copy or per page. Another magazine brags that its cost per *4-color* page per thousand is lower than that of competitors. Various types of readership leadership have been discovered. The total readership audience is one version, number of readers per dollar is another. Other types of leadership claimed are reader belief and confidence in the magazine and in its advertising, number of readers per copy, and readership by the entire family. Circulation per dollar is another basis of comparison as are the number of pages of advertising carried and the number of dollars of advertising revenue. A final basis for comparison is the number of times the typical reader picks up the magazine and reads in it.

Questions and Problems

1. Just what are you supposed to think when you see merchandise in stores tagged "As advertised in LIFE"?
2. Many magazines are edited for the general adult female, but few are edited for the general adult male. Why?
3. Compare the reading a magazine gets with the reading a newspaper gets.
4. What are some disadvantages of multi-page ads in consumer magazines?
5. What limitations are imposed an advertisers by the basic nature of magazines?
6. What sorts of information can be found on a magazine rate card?
7. What forms of selectivity are found in the magazine medium?
8. Comment on a manufacturer's running the same ad simultaneously in several magazines.
9. A manufacturer of fine watches (defined as a watch which retails for more than $60) does not now advertise in magazines. Suggest reasons why the magazine medium *is* appropriate for his advertising.
10. When you graduate, assume you go to work for *The Progressive Farmer* as a salesman of advertising space. Some of your sales calls will be on manufacturers of farm equipment and on their advertising agencies. How should you prepare for those calls? What should you take to those individuals?

Chapter 13

Television and Radio I

We have just studied newspapers and magazines, publication media which have obvious similarities and obvious differences. Now we take up our second pair of media — the broadcast media of television and radio; they too have many similarities yet certain basic differences. From the time radio became a commercial medium in the 1920's until the end of the 1940–49 decade it was the most glamorous of advertising vehicles. Radio was drama, showmanship, comedy, and big-name talent from stage and screen. With the start of the 1950–59 decade, radio's star began to wane as television's star began to wax. Today, television is a much more important national advertising medium than is radio. Indeed, the 100 largest advertisers spend more in television than in newspapers, magazines, outdoor, and business papers combined. Prominent in this group are manufacturers of food, grocery items, drugs, automobiles, cosmetics, cigarettes, and household cleaners.

Because of their many points of similarity, television and radio confront the instructor with a problem, the problem of just how the two media should be treated. Their degree of similarity argues against a separate examination of each, but their amount of dissimilarity prohibits a combined, single treatment. This text presents what the author's students for years have preferred — a point-by-point treatment of the dominant of the two, television, followed by whatever comments, if any, are needed about radio. Our approach is to take up a feature or element of television (circulation, programs, commercials, etc.) and then, before moving to the next element, to make any comments indicated about radio. Although the radio sections will sometimes remind the reader of some similarity, the radio material more often will point out respects in which radio differs from television.

COMPOSITION AND CLASSIFICATION (TV)

Stations and Networks

Television stations broadcast their picture (video) by means of amplitude modulation (AM) and their sound (audio) by means of frequency modulation (FM). Because video transmission demands more power than the transmission of audio,

Media

a station's AM power is greater than its FM power. Television sound or audio travels from the transmission tower to the horizon and no farther. Thus, the height of the antenna above the average terrain is a matter of significance; FM signals received in a straight line, unreflected, are preferred by listeners because the signals are clear, strong, and clean. Television stations cover satisfactorily a distance of fifty or sixty miles from their transmission towers. In addition to the commercial stations there are some educational, non-commercial stations.

Nowadays, almost all of our commercial television stations have *network* ties — to the American Broadcasting Company, the Columbia Broadcasting System, or the National Broadcasting Company. Each of these three has a basic chain or network of over 150 stations. Networks permit the broadcast of the same show at the same time over many stations. The interconnected stations comprising a network are connected either by coaxial cables or by microwave relay stations, stations which operate as broadcast boosters to pull television FM waves back before they go off into space. Noninterconnected stations telecast taped shows sent out by the network. There are regional networks as well as national ones. The networks and the individual stations promote their mutual interests through their trade association, the National Association of Broadcasters.

Types of Advertising

Television advertising is classified into three groups. *Network,* as the term suggests, is that which originates in one station and is broadcast simultaneously over a group of stations. For all except the originating station, the program comes from another station.

Spot advertising originates in the studio of (or is originated by) the station broadcasting the program. The typical advertiser is a national or at least a regional seller; he is not a local advertiser. A television representative sells spot advertising for his list of stations just as a newspaper representative sells space in the newspapers on his list. The advertiser buys his stations one by one, "spotting" his promotion in those markets and over those stations he needs. The word *spot* is used in a geographic sense.

Local television advertising is that bought by local advertisers. When a regional seller buys time from just one station, however, his purchase is also put in this classification.

COMPOSITION AND CLASSIFICATION (RADIO)

AM vs. FM

Standard broadcasting for radio is AM (amplitude modulation), and AM stations outnumber FM (frequency modulation) stations about 4 to 1. AM stations have two coverage areas. In the primary coverage area, reception is excellent and regular; in the secondary coverage area, the quality of reception varies from time to time and all the way from excellent to unsatisfactory. AM radio waves travel farther at night than during the day.

Television and Radio I

FM broadcasting has several interesting characteristics. There is less static and less noise; there is no fading. The tonal range is wide, and the high fidelity gives a more realistic sound to the spoken word and to music than is true of AM. The FM coverage area is quite stable because the FM waves, unlike AM waves, travel no farther at night than during the day. As was mentioned in respect to television audio, the FM signal is limited to the "line of sight" — a distance of about fifty to sixty miles.

Stations and Networks

Some radio stations are referred to as *clear channel* stations. This term refers to a powerful station (50,000 watts) which has virtually exclusive use of its frequency and serves a wide area free from interference from other stations. Clear channel stations typically serve many markets; they encounter little or no reception difficulties in their secondary coverage areas.

Regional stations are authorized to use up to 5,000 watts of power; thus they serve a smaller area than do the 50,000 watt clear channel stations. Regional stations usually cover several markets, but they are limited some by interference. The regional station often shares its frequency with other stations somewhat distant geographically which use the same spot on the radio dial.

Local stations use up to 250 watts of power, they are quite restricted by interference from other stations, and many throughout the country operate on the same frequency. These are essentially community stations, each serving its own local market.

Station coverage map for television (WNAC-TV) and for radio (WNAC). Courtesy: WNAC and WNAC-TV, Boston, Massachusetts)

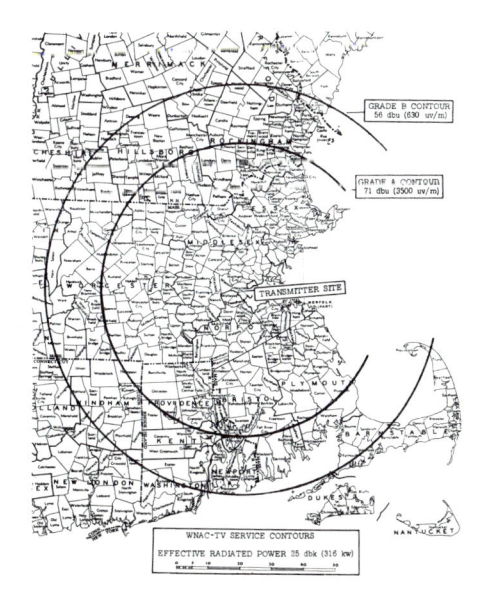

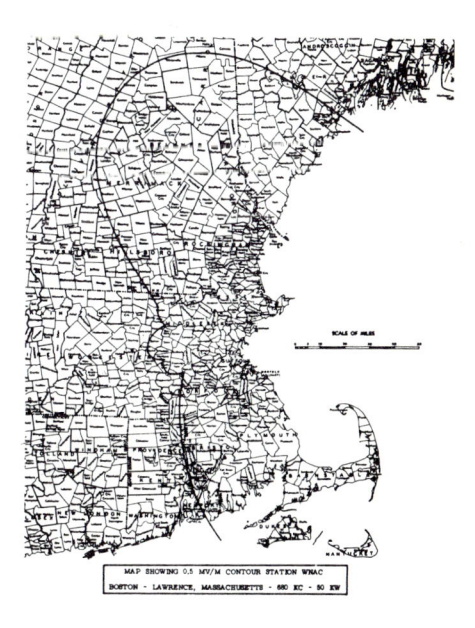

Media

For television, network advertising is largest in dollar revenue, followed by spot and then by local. For radio, local advertising leads, followed by spot and then by network.

FEATURES OF THE MEDIUM (TV)

Industry Features

Television makes full use of *visual and auditory communication* simultaneously. It combines radio, movies, and theater; it uses sight, sound, motion, and color. Television is the only major medium in which the advertiser's products can be demonstrated — by a salesman — realistically. Because the salesman on television can describe and explain as he demonstrates a product, his presentation is the next best form of promotion to personal selling. And, the commercial does not compete directly during its broadcast seconds with any editorial material or with any other commercial. As for sound, the medium offers the advertiser the opportunity to use the human voice in the presentation of his selling story and, in addition, even, for teaching consumers how to pronounce his brand name. Motion and color add showmanship, entertain at the same time that they advertise, present trade characters to the public, and implant package identification. Color and television, indeed, seem to have been made for each other. Color, for example, can help induce moods, serve as proof of benefits promised, can be used to stimulate appetite appeals, or is available to do *any* of the advertising jobs only color can do. The identity of the seller sponsoring the advertising can be established in viewers' minds more certainly and more satisfactorily than is the case in most other media.

Television is a *mass* medium. Because 90 per cent of all homes have television receivers, the medium can reach almost all income groups in all sections of the country. The number of homes having two or more sets is relatively small but growing. Being a mass medium and supplying entertainment and recreation to the typical household for about five hours a day, television is a social, cultural, and educational force of major significance. Its responsibility to the general public is reflected in the fact that the Federal Communications Commission licenses the stations to operate, assigns wave lengths, sets station power and hours, and attempts to see that programming is in the public interest.

For advertisers who sponsor their own programs, television stations, unlike newspapers and magazines, *do not supply editorial accompaniment.* Newspapers contain news stories and comic strips, and magazines contain stories and articles no matter how many advertisements they carry — no matter whose these advertisements are. The advertisers had no responsibility for the collection of those editorial features nor any authority to choose or edit them. In television, however, the advertiser who decides to sponsor his own program buys merely time, nothing more, from the station. He must then decide how to use that time; he must choose what type of program to broadcast. In addition to time costs, the advertiser pays talent costs, production costs, and any expense he incurs in publicizing his program. The consumer does not pay directly for the entertainment which sugar-coats the television commercials; he does pay out of his pocket for his newspapers and his magazines. It is quite difficult for a consumer to tell in advance whether he will like the editorial material (the program) the advertiser will broadcast. By the time he knows whether or not he likes the program, it's usually too late for him to salvage much from time he considers wasted.

There are some *handicaps* from which the television advertising message suffers. Because the message is not physical, the consumer cannot feel it with her hands nor take it to the market with her, nor refer back to it later. The message is a fleeting one; it evaporates; it must be caught on the fly if at all. Quality of reception can be unsatisfactory for the commercials or, indeed, for the program itself, reducing the audience for the commercials. The message must be brief; unless live programs are accurately timed and executed, closing commercials may have to be condensed even further or, in some instances, omitted completely.

Television as an advertising medium offers the seller several *types of selectivity*. He can select his markets in which to advertise and the individual station or stations to use in each. He can select day of week and time of day to advertise. He can choose from a wide range of program types. He can buy the amount of time he thinks he needs, and he can schedule these time units as frequently as he thinks wise. He can localize his promotion just as he could in newspapers.

There are, of course, some *time problems* in television. One of these results from the country's four different time zones. This time zone problem is a difficult one because the composition of the television audience changes as the clock runs. The nature of the problem is clear when one remembers that 7 P.M. arrives in New York at the same moment that 4 P.M. arrives in California. The minimum amount of difficulty is present when an advertiser sponsors a network program which is limited to two adjacent time zones. Audience dissimilarity is least if the show is broadcast at 7 P.M. in New York and at 6 P.M. in Chicago, for example. There are few advertisers and few products which can defend the broadcasting of any single program in New York city at 7 P.M. and at 4 P.M. in Los Angeles. One answer is to record or tape all programs; this permits the advertiser to broadcast the same show at the same hour in each market. An allied problem is that of daylight saving; its solution is the same as for the time zone problem. A third problem plagues the television industry and lends itself to no simple solution. This problem is the limited amount of top quality broadcast time. There are just three hours and no more between 7:30 P.M. and 10:30 P.M.

Consumer Features

Television chased radio out of the living room. The first black-and-white sets consigned radio to other rooms, and the first color sets subsequently demoted black-and-white receivers to less important rooms. Five out of six television sets are in living rooms with the few remaining sets in bedrooms, dens, and dining rooms.

As for *use,* the peak audience is in the evening. Viewing is relatively light from breakfast time until about 2 P.M. but starts increasing then and continues to increase until 9:30 P.M. Unlike a magazine, a television set can accommodate a group of individuals all at the same time. Viewing does, however, normally require all or almost all of the individual's attention. No doubt a few housewives turn on tele-

Media

vision and listen only — just as to radio. Most housewives have discovered few household jobs or activities which can be combined satisfactorily with television viewing *and* listening. The consumer's use of his television set is habit forming. The frequency of many of the shows and their format encourage consumer interest, consumer loyalty, and consumer involvement.

When contrasted with newspapers and magazines, television is seen to be a much more *personal medium*. Because real persons are seen on the screen and real voices are heard within the confines of the consumer's home, television advertising is much more intimate than that in the publication media. It is more persuasive and immediate; for live shows, the consumer feels that he is participating in them as they occur. Because television personalities are both strangers and guests in the consumer's living room, they should be well behaved and even well mannered.

FEATURES OF THE MEDIUM (RADIO)

Industry Features

The most unusual feature of radio as an advertising medium is the fact that it is the *only non-visual medium*. All others communicate to the consumer through his or her sense of sight; radio alone uses time instead of space and the ear but not the eye. This feature is seen to be a handicap when one remembers that a person's sense of hearing is one of his *minor* senses — that a person receives over three-fourths of his impressions and information through his sense of sight. So, radio is not the most effective medium for portraying fashion or product features, nor for transmitting certain descriptions or explanations, nor for broadcasting variety shows.

For many years radio's coverage of United States homes has been that of almost complete *saturation*. Over 98 per cent of our homes have radio receivers, and the great majority has more than one set. Most households can tune in many stations. Expansion for the industry is quite a challenge in the light of home saturation — and the fact that more than twenty-four hours cannot be packed into a single day. Some stations, true, can ask for more hours of operation or for more power. Every station can strive for greater individual popularity. All stations can hope for a larger population, more homes, and for more dollars of consumer income.

In contrast to television, *radio shows are simpler and less costly to produce*. The producer does not have to worry about the age or the appearance of actors on radio. Actors need not memorize their lines — they can use scripts. An actor can even play more than one role. Settings and costumes and make-up are nonessentials. There is no need for camera work which, at best, is complicated. There is less need for rehearsal. Plans can be changed more easily as well as later.

Consumer Features

Seen through the eyes of consumers, radio is a most *ubiquitous communicator*. There are many more sets than households. Since television dethroned radio in the living room, more and more radios are found in the kitchen, the bedroom, and even the dining room. The easy mobility of radio within the home permits the consumer to listen wherever he or she prefers. Portable radios can accompany consumers everywhere, millions of radios reach them in public places, tens of millions of automobile radios speak to consumers in transit.

Radio makes *modest demands of listeners.* Motorists drive and listen. Barbers cut hair and customers get haircuts while listening. In contrast to television, the housewife can listen while engaged in other activities because radio does not demand 100 per cent of her attention. There is nothing for her to look at; there is nothing for her to read. Time after time, research has reported that housewives like radio because they "can do other things while listening." The fact that a consumer can do something else while listening is both a plus point and a minus point so far as the advertiser is concerned.

The consumer's *use of radio* is interesting. Peak use is in the morning and is of such magnitude that radio competes fairly satisfactorily against television throughout most of the forenoon. In the afternoon television begins to assert itself. Housewives ask radio to supply a feeling of companionship and some relief from the monotony of housework. Consumers as a group look to radio for entertainment and information. For the typical individual, the time spent each day listening to radio is less than the amount of time spent watching television. Even so, millions of consumers listen to radio if only from habit. Consumers can usually find radio programs tailored to the basic activities in which consumers engage during the day. Better than any other medium, including television, radio can accompany the individual as he awakens, as he gets up and dresses, as he eats his breakfast, as he drives his automobile to work, as he does his work, as he drives home, and as he goes to sleep.

The Role of Radio

The appearance of television as a commercial medium about 1950 signaled the start of a decline in the amount of radio listening during the day. Radio's problem was clear — to retain an audience against the competition of television, especially in the evening. Even in television homes there are about two hours of radio listening each day. Radio does an excellent job in the area of news. Having no "publication dates," it is the most appropriate advertising medium for communicating emergency, flash-type bulletins and reports instantly. It is broadcasting more news than formerly, not just news more often.

Radio does an excellent job sending music to listeners, particularly orchestra music. For most people, few sights on television are as completely dull and quickly tiring to watch as are symphony concerts.

Radio, of course, does well what can be done with the spoken word. All the warmth, the persuasiveness, the understanding, and the memorability of the human voice are available; the same holds for the impact and the effectiveness of sound effects. Conversation, discussion, and interviews can be relaxed. Because the listener cannot see either the radio performers or their settings, he can imagine them, identify himself with them, and become involved precisely as he prefers. This is impossible for television.

When television became the family medium, radio became the individual medium. Once a medium of general audiences, radio is now a medium of more specialized audiences; it is a more selective medium than it was before television. Among the

Media

specialized groups for whom programs are designed are the hobby groups, the teenage market, the male consumer, farmers, racial groups, and motorists going to work between 7 A.M. and 9 A.M. and returning home between 5 P.M .and 7 P.M.

Competition from and with television has caused some changes in radio. Once a national or regional medium, radio is today primarily a local medium. Its customer group is dominated by local advertisers and by manufacturers who make spot use of the medium, especially manufacturers of low-priced consumer products. When television took away radio's variety shows because it can do them better, radio began to emphasize news, weather, music, and sports — programs which many consumers prefer to hear rather than to see. The popularity of Hi-Fi sets attests to the existence of a sizable market for non-visual music. Radio cut its charges for time and talent. It began to stress daytime potentials. It reminded advertisers that its flexibility was greater than that of television. It began to design and to promote summer programs for summertime products.

AUDIENCE MEASUREMENT IN TELEVISION AND RADIO

There are audited figures available to advertisers telling how many copies a newspaper or a magazine sells. Measurement in the two broadcast media, however, is a far more difficult problem. Engineers can determine how far from its point of broadcast a station's signal is strong enough to give satisfactory reception. Stations get audience mail, indicating where viewers and listeners live. But, the big four among the measurement techniques are the coincidental telephone call, the automatic recorder, the personal interview, and the diary.

Coincidental Telephone Calls

Telephone calls are made to homes during the actual broadcast to discover which programs are being seen or heard at the moment of the call. The interrogator first

Radio Sets in Working Order

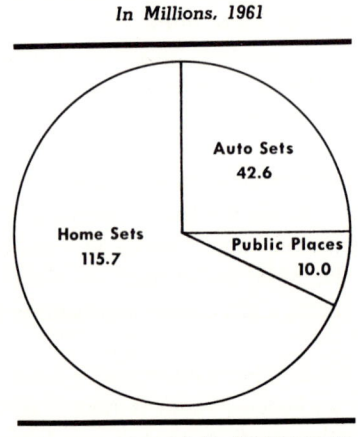

In Millions, 1961

Auto Sets
42.6

Home Sets
115.7

Public Places
10.0

Source: Radio Advertising Bureau estimates

242

asks whether anyone was looking at television or listening to the radio when the telephone rang. If the answer is affirmative, he then asks what the program is and over what station it is being broadcast. Whenever he wants to, the interrogator can add supplementary questions. For example, he can ask the consumer to name the product advertised on the program or to report how many men, women, and children are looking or listening.

Advantages. The telephone call is an economical method of doing research. No memory factor is involved because the consumer is asked about what he is doing at that moment. The technique allows the researcher to check on the consumer's awareness of product being advertised and of sponsor of the program. It measures what the advertiser wants measured in that it reflects actual viewing and listening. Above all, the coincidental telephone call is speedy — ratings can be had the next day.

Disadvantages. A major defect of this technique is the automatic exclusion of non-telephone households. The method is workable only between the hours of 8 A.M. and 10 P.M. Because it checks on viewing or listening as of one moment, it reflects average audience and that only to the show itself, not to the commercials. The number of questions must be kept low. One person speaks for the entire family, or one person speaks for his or her receiver. Each respondent must decide according to his own standards and judgment the minimum amount of attention to classify him as a viewer or listener; this is especially a problem in radio. The technique omits out-of-home viewing and listening.

The Automatic Recorder

This electronic device, of which the best known is the Audimeter of the A. C. Nielsen Company, is attached to a television or a radio set. The unit contains a film which automatically records any use of the set during a two-week period, showing date and hour when the set is on and to what station. By the end of the two weeks, the consumer receives an empty film cartridge from the company, inserts it in place of the now full film, and sends it to the company for decoding and inclusion in the total viewing or listening pattern. Audimeters have been designed which record the use of *all* television or radio receivers in the sample homes. Nielsen contributes toward maintenance service on the receivers in his sample homes and gives a small reward for mailing films in promptly.

Advantages. The automatic recorder provides a complete record of the sets in use 24 hours a day and 365 days a year. Accuracy is based on the operation of a machine, not the operation of an individual's memory. The recorder shows the number of sets in use minute-by-minute for the entire program, changes that take place during the program, and what the sample does about further looking or listening at the end of each program. There is a record of whether the commercials are tuned out or off. Because any type of household (telephone or non-telephone, urban or rural) can be included, the sample can be sound statistically and data can be expanded into a circulation figure of total sets-in-use.

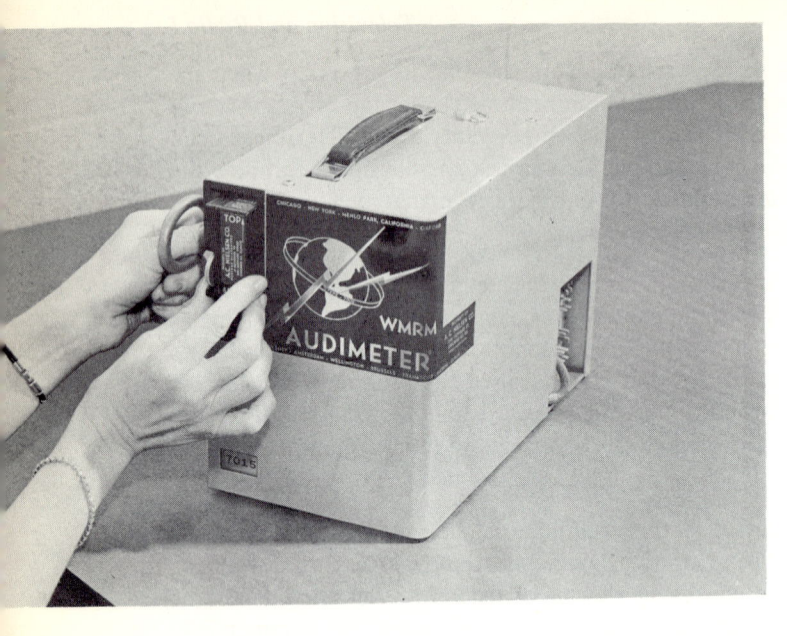

The Audimeter, an electronic device developed by the A. C. Nielsen Company, makes a minute-by-minute film record of the usage of each radio and television set in the home. It identifies the stations received and the time each station is tuned in and out. (Courtesy: A. C. Nielsen Company)

Disadvantages. The most serious criticism voiced about the automatic recorder is that it records *tuning — not looking and listening.* Although a receiver may be on and the film, of course, recording that fact, no consumer need be paying any attention to the broadcast, no consumer need be in the room with the receiver during the commercials, indeed, no consumer even need be in the house. A set left on accidentally when the inhabitants go to work is credited to the station to which it was last tuned even though no one saw or heard it from, say, 7:30 A.M. to 5:30 P.M. There are some mechanical failures among the recorders. There is no check on sponsor identification nor on brand identity. The technique is fairly expensive.

Instantaneous Recording. There is an instantaneous version of the automatic recorder. This is a large electric panel board which is connected by wires to a sample of local television sets; the sample might be 100 sets in some markets, 250 sets in larger markets. The board is so designed that it can tell how many of the sets constituting the sample are on and tuned to each of the local stations.

The Personal Interview

In this technique, researchers ring doorbells and ask consumers about their use of their receivers. The interviewers show consumers a recent program schedule or roster and get consumers to check those programs watched. The use of a list of programs makes this an aided recall type of research. Morning programs are checked the same day, evening programs are checked the following day.

Advantages. The plus features of the roster recall technique are essentially the plus factors of face-to-face interviewing.

Disadvantages. This is an urban technique which must exclude the rural portion of the broadcast audience. There is a question about how accurate the consumer's memory is and another about whether his desire to "look good," to impress the interviewer, will influence his answers. As with the coincidental telephone calls, one person speaks for the family.

The Diary

Consumers are asked to keep a record of all their looking and listening — in the home and elsewhere, too. Diary forms are supplied members of the sample. Rewards are paid to induce consumers to keep accurate records and to mail them promptly.

Advantages. An advantage of the diary is its low cost. In addition, this technique is similar to that of the personal interview and the automatic recorder in that consumer information is available which cannot be obtained through telephone calls.

Disadvantages. The accuracy of the diary depends on the accuracy of the person who keeps it. Consumers forget, they make errors in recording, they are guilty of omissions. Some neglect posting until the time comes for the diary to be returned, causing a last-minute, frantic catching up. There is some question as to whether or not a segment of the total population exists which will not log its listening and looking. Again, one person reports for the family and there is no check on exposure to the commercials.

Latest development in automatic recording devices is the Nielsen Instantaneous Audimeter. Television receivers in the survey household are connected directly to the central station equipment (shown right) by telephone lines. In this way, Nielsen has an immediate minute-by-minute record of the television tuning in the sample, which means ratings are available at the moment of the telecast. The Nielsen Instantaneous Audimeter Service is currently operated in the metropolitan New York television market. (Courtesy: A. C. Nielsen Company)

The Recordimeter, an electrical device developed by the A. C. Nielsen Company, reminds cooperators to record station tuning in the Audilog. It verifies the accuracy and completeness of the Audilog entries for each set in the home by automatically recording total daily minutes of usage. (Courtesy: A. C. Nielsen Company)

CIRCULATION (TV)

Having looked at the techniques used to measure radio and television broadcast audiences, what comments are in order about television circulation? Unlike the newspaper and magazine media, television must base its circulation figure on a sample; it must take what the sample shows and expand those data; it must project; it must extend the sample pattern to the total population from which the sample was taken. There is a complete count of copies sold for newspapers and magazines; not so, not possible, for television. In television there is no such guaranteed circulation as we found in magazines; in television there is no such audited circulation as we found in newspapers. When an advertiser buys thirty minutes of time from a television station, he is actually buying the *opportunity to develop* circulation for his advertising.

In general, there are two basic elements in television circulation, the population of the country and the number of television receivers. As for circulation or audience for a specific broadcast, there are many influences. These include type of program, hour of broadcast, station broadcasting the show, competing shows broadcast at the same hour in the same market, number of receivers in the station's coverage area, population of the coverage area, promotion given the program by the advertiser and the station, weather, and season of year.

Basic Aspects

Potential audience is the total number of individuals who can be reached by all the television sets in a station's coverage area or geographical area. Most of these sets are in homes, but many are in clubs, hotels, restaurants, airports, motels, bars, and the like.

Actual audience is circulation — the number of individuals who see or hear the advertiser's program or his commercials. You recall that for telephone calls, for face-to-face interviews, and for diaries, each individual must decide what constitutes viewing.

Ratings express the percentage of homes viewing a specific show. They measure relative program popularity and are based on the total sample. Ratings vary from market to market.

Share of audience is obtained by dividing a program's individual rating by the total number of sets in use during the broadcast of the program. For example, let us assume that coincidental telephone calls are our technique and that 100 calls are made. If 50 individuals say they were viewing at the time of the call, then the sets-in-use figure is 50 per cent. Assume that 20 of the 50 say they are watching show "A." Twenty divided by 100, the number of calls made, equals 20 per cent and this is the rating of show "A." This same 20 divided by 50 (number of sets in use) gives us the share of audience for show "A" — 40 per cent.

Advertisers and Television Circulation

The various measurement techniques used in the television medium do not agree in respect to the popularity of television shows or the number of persons reached by those shows. This fact is a cause of confusion and even doubt about the soundness of all techniques. There are questions but no generally accepted answers relative to the basic accuracy of one method over another. There is the question of whether or not the various research firms are measuring the same variable. There are questions about the soundness of the samples. The samples used are relatively small, and their patterns are expanded to reflect the behavior of very large populations. It is also a fact that all the measurements are only approximations. Informed persons in the television industry recognize that good judgment is, of course, essential; that measurements can only narrow the area within which common sense and sound decisions operate; that measurements are most useful as guides, not as absolutes; and that measurements require expert handling.

A serious matter is the fact that all the measurements concentrate on the program or show; only the automatic recorder reports whether or not the commercials were received, and even it does not tell how many persons, *if any,* paid attention to, understood, and reacted favorably to the commercials. Yet, it is the commercial rather than the show which "sells" the product. Popularity of show can be high and the advertiser's audience can be large, but, if a significant portion of the audience misses the commercials or if the commercials are ineffective, then advertising performance can easily be so low as to make the advertising effort too expensive to continue. Any attempt to measure consumer intentness and enthusiasm as regards program commercials or, even more difficult, for announcements, would be a most formidable undertaking.

Advertisers, their advertising agencies, producers of shows, talent, stations, and the networks are all vitally interested in television circulation — for shows and for commercials. Advertisers, for example, want answers to such questions as these:

How many prospects are there for my product?
How many persons watch my show?
Just who are these individuals?
What are their characteristics?
Do they constitute a high quality audience for my advertising?

Media

How many of them see my commercials?
How many different individuals are reached by my commercials during a four-week period?
How many of these are prospects for my product?
What effects do my commercials have on my prospects?

In 1963, much interest developed in the measurement of television and radio audiences. Congressional hearings uncovered some unfavorable, disturbing facts about the rating services. Samples seemed quite small and somewhat out-of-date, claims of accuracy seemed excessive, and the handling of data in some cases seemed most questionable. Just about this same time, individual advertisers spoke up in favor of "guaranteed" audiences, claiming that television, certainly, should guarantee an advertiser that a specific minimum number of consumers would view a series should the advertiser sponsor it. A leading trade paper predicted that some form of guaranteed circulation by television networks was inevitable. Because audience size cannot be guaranteed unless audience size can be measured, the obvious need was for accurate, recognized, and accepted measurement techniques. This called for (1) standards for the rating services and their measurements, and (2) a periodic audit of the rating services.

CIRCULATION (RADIO)

The same four measurement techniques mentioned earlier are used in radio as well as in television. Somewhat peculiar to radio is the difficult problem of measuring out-of-home circulation or listening.

As we have said there are millions of sets in such places as barber shops, hotel lobbies, taverns, stores, clubs, restaurants, schools, and hospitals. There are millions of portable radios which go with consumers to beaches and parks, on picnics and vacations. There are radios in barns. As the prices dropped on the sensitive transistor radios, this audience increased rapidly.

Then there are the automobile radios. They serve a tremendous potential audience which certainly becomes a real audience during driving-to-work and driving-home hours. Personal interviews, diaries, and questionnaires put under windshield wipers of parked cars have all been used to learn more about this circulation.

RATE STRUCTURE (TV)

In the study of our first two media, newspapers and magazines, we saw that what these advertising media sell to advertisers is circulation. Equally clear was the fact that circulation is the basic determinant of the advertising rates quoted by newspapers and magazines. The bases and the principles of rate-setting are the same for television as they are for the publication media. The two most important considerations are *quantity* and *quality* of circulation. For example, when a manufacturer buys announcements on a participation program, that is, one designed and controlled by the station or the network and used by non-competitive advertisers who buy commercials on it, he expects to pay in line with the size of audience that program enjoys and in line with the quality of those viewers. Or, if the manufacturer buys a thirty-minute time period for his own sponsored show, he expects to pay in line with the number of consumers the station can reach, the financial ability-to-buy of those consumers, and the consumers' need for his product.

Unit of Sale

There are several units of time offered for sale by television networks and stations. The largest common unit *for programs* is sixty minutes. Then come the one-half hour, the fifteen-minute, the ten-minute, and the five-minute period. As for *announcements,* there is the one-minute commercial; 20-, 30-, and 40-second commercials; the ten-second I.D. (the few seconds used by a station to identify its call letters); and some announcements of even less than ten seconds in length.

Discounts

Most networks and stations offer various forms of discounts to advertisers. A quantity-type discount is found in the lower cost-per-minute prices for the larger time units. For example, one half-hour may cost 60 per cent of the hour figure — not 50 per cent; similarly, one quarter-hour may cost 40 per cent of the hour figure — not 25 per cent. Another type of discount is based on the number of time units bought during a given period. Discount cycles of 13 times, 26 times, and 52 times are common. One station, for instance, quotes different prices for these frequencies: 1 to 12; 13 to 25; 26 to 51; 52 to 103; 104 to 155; 156 to 259; and 260 and over. Another version of this discount is the Package Plan for one-minute announcements, twenty-second station breaks, and ten-second I.D.'s. Five to nine per week, for example, cost more individually than ten or more per week. Some broadcasters offer summer discounts to stimulate business during what is the slowest quarter of the year.

Daytime Versus Nighttime Rates

The broadcast day contains some high-potential hours and some whose potential is not as high. Accordingly, an hour at one time can and does cost more or less than it costs at another time. A four-way grouping with rate differentials might look like this:

"A" time   7:00 P.M.–10:30 P.M. All days   100 per cent rate
"B" time   6:00 P.M.– 7:00 P.M. Weekdays   67 per cent rate
           1:00 P.M.– 7:00 P.M. Sundays
"C" time   9:00 A.M.– 6:00 P.M. All days   50 per cent rate
           10:30 P.M.–12:00 M. All days
"D" time   12:00 M. – 9:00 A.M. All days   34 per cent rate

The general rule is that nighttime is the most costly time because there is little of it, because the quantity of circulation is greatest then, and because of the relatively high quality of this circulation for the vast majority of advertisers. Daytime costs

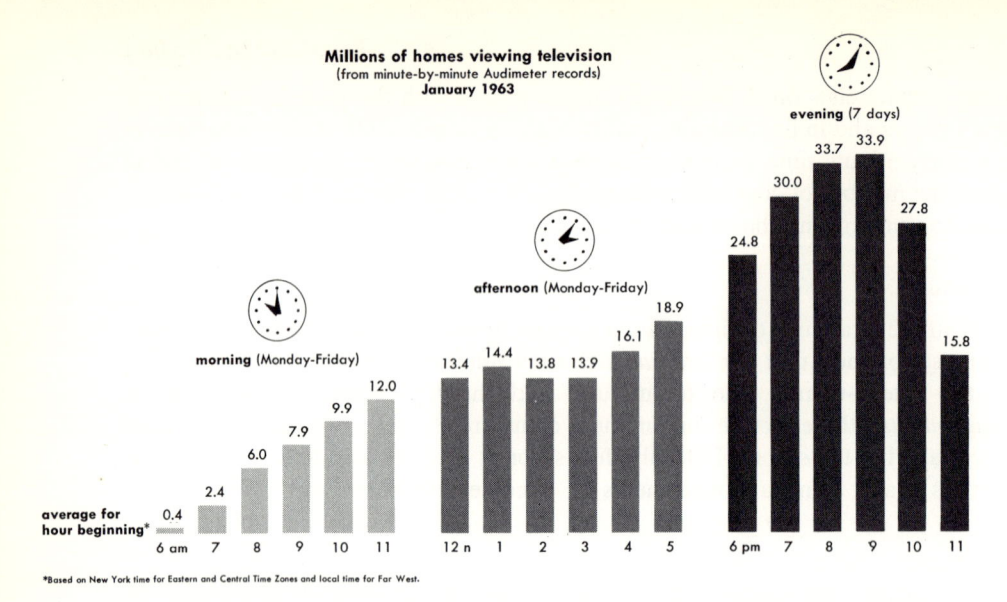

Millions of homes viewing television
(from minute-by-minute Audimeter records)
January 1963

morning (Monday-Friday): average for hour beginning* — 6 am 0.4, 7 2.4, 8 6.0, 9 7.9, 10 9.9, 11 12.0

afternoon (Monday-Friday): 12 n 13.4, 1 14.4, 2 13.8, 3 13.9, 4 16.1, 5 18.9

evening (7 days): 6 pm 24.8, 7 30.0, 8 33.7, 9 33.9, 10 27.8, 11 15.8

*Based on New York time for Eastern and Central Time Zones and local time for Far West.

There is more television viewing in the afternoon than in the morning, and more at night than in the afternoon. (Source: A. C. Nielsen Company)

less, and late nighttime costs still less. A point which must be emphasized, however, is that each station must tailor its own rates to its own locality and to its own circumstances. Audience potential, both quantitatively and qualitatively, is the key consideration in the setting of station rates.

General Versus Retail

Some but not all television stations follow the newspaper practice of offering lower rates to retail advertisers. When this is done, the retail rate may range from 50 per cent to 80 per cent of the general rate.

Cost Comparison

The most common calculation used for comparing costs in television is the cost-per-1000-homes-reached-per-commercial-minute. One commercial minute (a 60-second commercial) during *evening* hours may cost about $40,000. If this advertisement is received in 10,000,000 homes, then cost per 1000 homes is $4. This cost figure for *daytime* television is about one-half the nighttime figure; audiences are smaller, and the time is more difficult to sell.

Cost-per-1000-homes-per-commercial-minute does not provide the information most advertisers would prefer, namely, the number of prospects reached by the commercials and how many seconds of commercial reached the typical viewer-prospect. Advertisers would certainly prefer the base which is the undeniable unit of all advertising circulation — the individual consumer.

Rate Card Information

That information on rate cards which is of greatest interest to advertisers consists, as you guessed, of rate information — time charges, discounts, and terms of sale.

Television and Radio I

Advertisers are also interested in talent and production costs, but they seldom find specific answers to these questions on rate cards.

In addition, however, rate cards contain information of a general character. They identify the station's call letters, they reveal its ownership and location, they list its personnel, and they tell when the current rates went into effect. Power, frequency and channel, antenna height expressed in numbers of feet above terrain, and the type of time on which the station operates (Eastern Standard, Pacific) are additional items of information. Rate cards summarize the station's policies about programs, products unacceptable for advertising, commercials, contracts, and commissions on sales. Advertisers and advertising agencies can get all this information from the stations' rate cards, or they can consult the television edition of the *Standard Rate and Data Service*.

RATE STRUCTURE (RADIO)

If a seller wants to sponsor a radio program, he can buy the same units of time he found available in television. As for commercials, too, his choices are about the same with one possible difference — the time range may be a bit wider in radio. For example, one advertiser called attention to himself by using a *three-word* announcement. Six-, eight-, and ten-second commercials occur despite an effort to standardize short announcements at eight seconds and sixteen words. Stations charge the same for twenty-second transcribed announcements as for thirty-five to forty-five words live — the same for one-minute transcriptions as for 125 words live. Various "packages" of commercials (12, 21, 28, 35) are offered by most stations.

TOP TEN LOCAL RADIO ADVERTISERS

Local Business Category	% of Total Local Revenue Category Represents	% of Stations with Revenue From Category	Avg. % of Local Revenue Category Represents to Stations with This Business
Auto Dealers	9.4%	97.8%	10.9%
New Car Dealers	6.9	91.2	7.4
Used Car Dealers	2.5	68.3	3.5
Supermarkets	6.1	92.5	8.3
Chain Supermarkets	3.8	74.6	4.9
Independent Supermarkets	2.3	64.9	3.4
Appliance Stores	4.8	88.7	5.2
Department Stores	4.6	87.1	5.2
Furniture Stores	4.6	90.0	4.8
Banks	4.1	88.1	4.6
Soft Drink Bottlers	3.7	82.1	4.4
Movie Houses	2.9	85.9	4.0
Four-Wall	2.0	79.9	2.4
Drive-In	.9	51.4	1.6
Tires, Batteries, Access.	2.9	83.1	3.4
Savings & Loan Assn.	2.7	73.7	3.6

Source: Radio Advertising Bureau

Media

The discount pattern approximates that of television. One station quotes these for broadcasts during a year:

Number of broadcasts	Discount
13	5 per cent
26	10 per cent
52	15 per cent
100	20 per cent
200	30 per cent
300 and over	40 per cent

Another station packages announcements in these quantities:

Number of announcements	Discount
7 per week	5 per cent
14 per week	10 per cent
21 per week	15 per cent
28 per week	20 per cent

Originally, evening hours and evening announcements in radio were priced at twice the daytime figures. Then television came along and attracted the lion's share of the evening audience, reducing the circulation potential of radio and forcing a reduction in evening rates. Generally, the premium on nighttime disappeared, leaving radio with a single rate. Premium rates for some daytime hours, those for which listening is heavy, are not unknown.

Questions and Problems

1. Why is there disagreement among the various services which rate TV shows and measure TV audiences?
2. What jobs can a trade character do well in radio?
3. What are some of the problems remote pick-ups pose in TV?
4. Why have convenience goods been so successfully advertised over radio?
5. What are some advantages radio enjoys over TV?
6. What are some ways in which radio differs from newspapers as an advertising medium?
7. Will TV eventually destroy radio as an advertising medium?
8. List some of TV's limitations as an advertising medium.
9. In what ways is radio a selective medium?
10. In what ways is TV a flexible medium?

Chapter 14

Television and Radio II

SPOT (TV)

Broadcasting falls into two classifications, it is either *spot* or else it is *network*. Any advertising not network must be spot. In the case of spot broadcasts, the program originates in (or is originated by) the station broadcasting it; the program is not imported from another station. When buying spot broadcasting, the advertiser purchases time from one or more stations individually, one by one, market by market; he deals directly with the station or with its representative.

The word *spot* can be thought of as referring to a spot on a map, to a single market in which a seller decides to use some broadcast advertising. Thus, spot broadcasting is broadcasting which has been spotted or localized. The term spot broadcasting does not apply just to announcements. Spot broadcasting includes the eight-second announcement *and* the two- or three-hour show broadcast over a single station. A manufacturer is using spot advertising when he buys a taped program and then has it broadcast by a group of stations on the best days and at the best hours he can obtain from the stations individually.

Advantages of Spot

Manufacturers of such products as soap, food, tobacco, beverages, drugs, and cosmetics have discovered that spot advertising is attractive on several counts. Spot is *selective*. It permits the advertiser to choose the markets in which his advertising should be run and to exclude other markets. There is selectivity of program, even to the extent of sponsoring a different one in each market if the advertiser so prefers. The advertiser selects within each market that station which will do the best job for him; the station of a particular network is not the most desirable station in some markets. The advertiser can attempt to schedule his programs for the best days and the best hours in each market. Finally, spot offers the advertiser the opportunity to choose which of his products he will promote in each market and which benefit to promise buyers.

In addition to being selective, spot television is *flexible*. The advertiser can adjust the intensity of his advertising effort in each market to his current needs in

Media

that market. When the need is for announcements, he can buy them; when the need develops for programs, he can switch to them. The volume of broadcast time is a flexible element as is the frequency of his advertising messages. Whatever degree of saturation seems best can be had. The amount of money to spend in each market and the length of the advertising period in each can be increased or decreased as conditions change.

In contrast to network, spot permits considerable *localization* of a manufacturer's television advertising. Manufacturers have local problems; some solutions are available only in individual markets. Shows and talent, commercials and benefits can be tailored to each market. Boston's problems and preferences differ from those of New Orleans; neither Boston nor New Orleans is just like Los Angeles or Detroit.

Spot television is a *versatile* advertising medium. It is appropriate for seasonal services and products such as anti-freeze. It is appropriate for sectional products such as sun tan lotion, or for a new product which is being launched on a market by market basis. Spot television is good for supporting or supplementary use, particularly in problem markets. Finally, it is suitable for testing use.

Disadvantages of Spot

Spot lacks the glamour and prestige of network television. Time sold by stations individually (small unit of purchase) comes at a higher price than time bought on networks (quantity purchase). The process of buying spot time is time consuming, complicated, and detailed; this adds to its cost. Finally, supervision and control of many individual broadcasts is obviously more difficult than when the advertiser sponsors a single program on network.

SPOT (RADIO)

Little need be added on spot broadcasting in the medium of radio. Many radio stations sell announcements in specific and pre-determined quantities per week. An advertiser, for example, may buy ten, or one hundred, or three hundred, depending on the degree of saturation he needs. The stations then do the scheduling (days and hours) of the number of announcements bought.

NETWORK (TV)

Broadcasting that is not spot must, of course, be network. Here a single program originates in a central studio and is sent to the stations comprising the network. The program is broadcast simultaneously by this group of stations in their respective markets. Some of the stations are owned and operated by the networks, some are independently owned. Within an organization (ABC, CBS, NBC), there may be a *basic* network or group of stations and one or more *supplementary* groups of stations. When compared with the first two media we studied, network has similarities to the national editions of magazines whereas spot has similarities to newspapers.

Advantages of Network

Some of the advantages of network were suggested in listing the disadvantages of spot because some of the strong points of one are weak points of the other. Networks may have first claim on the best broadcast hours of their stations. Advertising undertakings which should have network programs are often of such size that for them the advertiser can, or even must, buy top talent. Such shows rank high with consumers in respect to prestige and glamour. Such shows often get an enviable amount of publicity. Such shows can be merchandised to the manufacturer's salesmen and to his trade easily and effectively.

The combination price is lower than the total of prices when time is bought separately from individual stations. And, even though the amount often seems and is huge, the advertising can be economical and profitable for manufacturers whose distribution pattern fits the network pattern.

Network advertising has a simplicity of administration not true of spot advertising. There is only a single show to be built; it reaches many markets simultaneously; its control is, by contrast to spot, simple. Because only a single transaction is involved, network purchases mean less time spent in negotiation and in time buying.

Disadvantages of Network

Several disadvantages of network have been suggested. Certain stations in each network are relatively weak and do not cover their respective markets effectively. For certain advertisers, for those which do not have any or adequate distribution in certain markets, some stations of a network are wasteful. Time differences from east to west and seasonal differences between north and south present problems. Network commitments often must run into many months and many dollars. Shows cannot be tailored to suit consumer preference in each market. This limitation is seen in its true perspective when one studies the market-by-market ratings of a particular show and sees that it may be six or seven times as popular in its most-liked market as it is in its least-liked market.

Brand or product protection is not exactly a disadvantage of network television, but it is a problem serious enough to deserve mention at this point. During daytime hours, manufacturers like to have their commercials separated from commercials advertising competing brands by fifteen minutes, both before and after. Lux, for example, would hardly like to see its closing commercial followed, after a station break, by the opening commercial of an Ivory show; the same is true of Ford and Chevrolet, or Camel and Chesterfield. During evening hours, the isolation desired grows from fifteen to thirty minutes. To grant the protection wanted is not easy. Shows with alternate-week sponsors compound the problem by mentioning the two sponsoring products by brand name during some portion of each show. Another complication develops when the manufacturer of a large family of products (Procter & Gamble, General Foods) wishes to advertise a number of his products during a series. Still another complication arises when a manufacturer does not want certain other *types* of products, non-competitive products, mind you, to be advertised close to his commercials. Some manufacturers of food products demand

Media

protection from any commercials for deodorants, for example; even two different types of products which fight the common cold find proximity irritating.

THE TELEVISION PROGRAM

The television advertiser has a wide choice as regards the program to sponsor. He may choose a taped show, or a studio production, or a remote pick-up such as a parade, a political convention, or a sports event. Remote pick-ups can be intense and exciting; their realism and sense of participation delight the viewer; their avoidance of studio expense delights the sponsor. Another choice for the advertiser to make is between a regular show, one of a series, and the special, or spectacular. Still another choice, in some ways the most basic, involves program format or type. Among the better known and widely used types are these:

Variety	Quiz	Comedy
Audience participation	Music	Drama
Mystery	Sports	News
Panel	Special event	Western

Participation Programs

A popular type of television vehicle for a seller's commercials is the *participation program*. This is a show designed, controlled, and publicized by a station or by a network. Time and talent costs are paid by a group of non-competitive advertisers in return for participating announcements. Each advertiser supplies only his own commercials; he has no control in the building of the show nor any responsibility for building its audience.

The advertiser's commercials on a participation program do not have their own exclusive show. Some are scheduled for station breaks on those shows which run thirty minutes or longer. Others are scheduled to be broadcast during the show. For network shows of middle or long length, a seller may buy *one segment* of the show and sponsor it.

Participation shows are popular with advertisers because this type of show permits the advertiser to limit or even to minimize both his investment and his risks. There is, of course, the problem or even the absence of sponsor identification. Furthermore, it is the advertiser's responsibility to make certain that the show he buys time on suits his particular product or service and that his fellow-sponsors are acceptable.

Control of Program Design

Since there is no editor to put together the editorial content of television programs, editors such as those in the newspaper and magazine fields, the question arises as to who will design the programs advertisers sponsor. The preceding section on participating programs pointed out that both stations and networks build "magazine" type programs and sell participating announcements on them. These programs are described as "magazine format" in nature because the network or the station designs the editorial content, sells and accepts sellers' advertisements, and places them as appropriately as possible, just as magazines do. When the station or the network controls its programs, what it sells to an advertiser actually is *time* — commercial time. In contrast, when an advertiser sponsors his own show, he buys two types of time from the station or network — program time *and* commercial time. Only when the station or network controls the programming can the medium sell any type of "guaranteed" circulation to advertisers. In such instances, should the advertiser's commercials not reach the guaranteed minimum audience, additional commercials would be broadcast without charge until the minimum circulation is reached.

Much television programming during day-time hours is of the "magazine concept" or participation type. There is a distinct possibility that more night-time programming will adopt this same pattern.

Taped versus Live Shows

Another of the choices for the advertiser to make is that between using a taped show or a live show. There are two basic types of taped shows. In one instance, a show is broadcast live in one market but is sent simultaneously to other markets and recorded there on tape for broadcast at a later hour. In the second instance, and our concern at the moment is with this, a show (or more usually a *series* of shows) is studio produced and taped, not broadcast at the time of production, for future use by an advertiser. Somewhat similar is the advertiser's broadcast of films originally made for the movies.

One great virtue of taped shows is that they can be broadcast again and again. Because television is an insatiable medium, requiring an enormous amount of material, the rerun of programs is most natural. Another great virtue is high technical quality; a well taped show can seldom be distinguished from a live show. The performance is controlled, actions are repeated until they suit the director, there are no ad libs. Thus, the performance can avoid missed lines and cues, accidents, bad camera angles, and other errors of humans or defects of machines.

Live shows are costly to produce. When not taped for repeat use, their cost cannot be spread over a number of appearances. But the live shows can have something the taped shows cannot have — immediacy. Viewers know that they are seeing a performance just as it occurs, not as it was taped a long time ago. The currency, the spontaneity of the action gives viewers the feeling of being in a theater. Whereas taped shows worship the formula approach, live shows can and do attempt the new, the untried, the original. They can offer freshness. They can offer showmanship.

Selecting the Program

The start toward profitable selection is to recall the purpose of the program. The basic assignment given to the program is to capture the looking and the listening of the maximum number of the advertiser's prospects and customers. A second assignment is to supply an appropriate and helpful vehicle for the advertiser's commercials, a vehicle which will help prepare those prospects and customers for the advertising messages. A third assignment given the program is to stimulate

Media

viewer loyalty and to encourage regular viewing. Finally, the advertiser hopes that his show will become known as just that — *his* show; he hopes that his identity as sponsor will be established quickly, economically, surely, and widely.

What factors influence an advertiser as he approaches the task of choosing a program to sponsor? Certainly he must consider the amount of money he expects to spend in television and the amount of time he expects to buy. A most basic element here is length of show and its frequency of broadcast. Another consideration is the nature of the advertiser's product or service. Program and product should suit each other; their association should be an harmonious one. Some viewers, for instance, feel that commercials for beauty products and preparations are not completely at home on crime shows. The availability of talent is another factor to be considered. The personality of the station carrying the broadcast is sometimes an important matter in spot broadcasting. The nature of the shows with which the advertisers will be competing is an influence, often a powerful one. In network broadcasting there is the problem already mentioned of sectional preferences which often lead to a wide range in market-to-market ratings. Finally, the impact of the program on the advertiser's salesmen and dealers is not to be ignored.

We have listed the common types of program — quiz, music, comedy, western, variety, and the like. At any one moment, one of these is the most "popular" type; it gets the highest ratings; it is the type most imitated. A sad observation is that most imitations are weak *inherently* in addition to their being weak because they are imitations. Popularity tends to go in cycles. One season, the comedians are on top. Next season, the quiz shows take over first place, only to be replaced before long by the westerns. But, sooner or later, comedy again reigns — until replaced by, perhaps, variety shows. One attraction of the variety show, incidentally, is its potential appeal to almost *everybody;* this feature is not unnoticed by advertisers who feel that they *must* reach a large number of consumers in order to justify a program with a large price tag.

Changing the Program

The medium of television has been described as insatiable. It is. In similar fashion, the typical viewer is insatiable — for freshness, for innovation, for variety, for change. To a degree, *all* performers on television seem very real in consumers' living rooms and very wearing. So, the typical television program does not stay on the air long without some change intended as a hypodermic to perk up drooping interest. The consumer's desire for change and the advertiser's desire for the popular program type of the moment lead to much switching of programs and to much redoing of program format.

Cost of Program

For most advertisers who sponsor them, television programs run into large figures. A single broadcast costing the advertiser $1,000,000 is not unknown. First of all, the seller buys broadcast time; this is usually the major item in the total cost, but for some advertisers and for some shows it is less than one-half of that total. Then the seller must buy the program or the show itself; top talent comes high.

Television and Radio II

There are, of course, the commercials — little shows in their own right and often quite expensive. Both for the program itself and for the commercials there are many expenses. Both must be produced, and that means materials, facilities, and personnel. Rehearsals are time consuming, but scripts cannot be used; action, including facial expressions, must be right. Costumes and make-up, scenery and settings, sound and sight effects — all cost. Sometimes special studio facilities must be constructed. Photography is always expensive. Finally, the advertiser seldom dares count on his program's acquiring an adequate audience all on its own; so, he advertises his advertising. All of these costs add up to many dollars. No wonder most advertisers select for sponsorships shows which they think will make a bid for many viewers.

Amount of Advertising Allowed on Sponsored TV Programs

Length of Pgm. (in Minutes)	5:00	10:00	15:00	20:00	25:00	30:00	35:00	40:00	45:00	50:00	55:00	60:00
"AA" and "A" Time	1:00	2:00	2:30	2:40	2:50	3:00	3:30	4:00	4:30	5:00	5:30	6:00
All Other Time	1:15	2:10	3:00	3:30	4:00	4:15	4:45	5:15	5:45	6:10	6:35	7:00
Length of Pgm. (in Minutes)	65:00	70:00	75:00	80:00	85:00	90:00	95:00	100:00	105:00	110:00	115:00	120:00
"AA" and "A" Time	6:30	7:00	7:30	8:00	8:30	9:00	9:30	10:00	10:30	11:00	11:30	12:00
All Other Time	7:35	8:10	8:45	9:20	9:55	10:30	11:05	11:40	12:15	12:50	13:25	14:00

(*Courtesy:* Advertising Age)

Types of Sponsorship

The television series with a single sponsor is not common; it costs too much. Instead, there is *alternate-week* sponsorship, and there is *co-sponsorship*.

When a series has *alternate-week sponsors,* each of the two advertisers pays the full cost *every other week* and gets full use of all commercial time that week. This cuts the cost in half or, stated a bit differently, it is a technique for buying one-half of an advertising vehicle. This type of sponsorship involves two problems. One, sponsor identification is more troublesome and difficult. Two, each sponsor has a voice in the operation.

In the *co-sponsor* arrangement, two non-competing advertisers share the cost and the commercial time *on each show* in the series. A variant on this arrangement would be for a manufacturer of two products, two makes, or two brands to co-sponsor within his own company. One pattern of co-sponsorship is for advertiser "A" to get two minutes of commercial time and advertiser "B" to get one minute of commercial time *this* week. Next week, "B" gets two minutes and "A" gets one minute. Co-sponsorship makes great demands of advertising commercials. Sponsor identification and joint management are the same problems they were in alternate-week sponsorship.

Media

THE RADIO PROGRAM

Many of the comments about television programs apply equally to radio programs. The magazine pattern type of participation program has in large measure replaced the programs sponsored by individual manufacturers. News and music are popular formats. As was indicated, radio shows are less complicated, demand less planning and rehearsal, can get along with fewer and less able actors and even with lower quality writing, and, of course, cost advertisers considerably less than do television shows.

SCHEDULING IN TELEVISION AND RADIO

Programs versus Announcements

A comparison of programs with announcements reveals some specific advantages of the former not enjoyed by announcements. For the advertiser using a *program*, both he, the sponsor, and his product have their own show with which to be associated. Furthermore, each sponsor can, within certain limits, either build or buy exactly the show he feels will be most effective for him. Thus the advertiser has greater control over the type of consumer constituting the audience for his broadcast. Builders of participation programs, by way of contrast, must keep in mind various types of sponsor when designing the show; these sponsors, you recall, are non-competitive. There is impact, there is prestige attaching to programs which announcements cannot have; the television special which runs for 60 minutes or longer affects the advertiser's public, his sales force, and his wholesalers and retailers in a manner impossible with announcements. Finally, the sponsor of a program has something to say about the editorial material which precedes immediately his commercial or follows his commercial, or both. Such control can be used to good advantage.

Announcements have their particular advantages. They are excellent for reminder use, for helping to maintain current advertising momentum, for making single, brief selling points. Being simpler, they require less management and less handling than do programs. They can be used in such limited volume as to require considerably fewer dollars, too. Announcements cost less per consumer impression than do programs. They can be scheduled with great frequency. A saturation schedule running throughout the day and evening reaches a great number of buyers.

Selection of Station

In all markets having more than one broadcast station, there is the question of which the advertiser should use. In theory, the advertiser can use *one* station, or *all* stations, or some number in between those two extremes. There are more radio stations to choose from than there are television stations.

Advertisers are interested in a station's programming; the programs it broadcasts reveal much about the character of the station and the competence of its personnel. Station reputation is also reflected by its network affiliation and by its standards for programs and commercials. Station popularity, largely dependent on programming, is a matter of concern. The station's power is of interest because power affects the geographical area covered, and that determines the number and type of consumers reached by that station. Availability of time and availability of talent or of the proper program help guide the advertiser in his selection of station. The advertiser has great interest in the programs which would be adjacent to his and in the programs over other stations which would be competing against his program for viewers or hearers. The adjacent program which leads or precedes his program can do much to help or hurt, depending on the size and on the mood of the audience which it passes on to our advertiser. Rates and discounts are no small consideration. The cooperation and the merchandising services a station offers are other influences.

Selection of Day and Hour

Day of week and hour of day are important choices because they influence both the size and the composition of the advertiser's potential audience; because of this fact, they influence his costs. Before noon, and even up until about 3 P.M., the dominant personality in the broadcast audience is the housewife. From 3 P.M. until 6 P.M. are the children's hours. Between 6 P.M. and 8 P.M., adults *and* children look and listen; from 8 P.M. on, broadcast audiences are mainly adults.

The Summer Decision

Consumers spend less time and less attention looking at television and listening to radio during the summer months than in the other seasons. The peaks for viewing and listening come in the winter season, from December to March. Spring and fall see only a slight decline from the winter's highs. Summer is the low season, even for shows which run on unchanged month after month throughout the year. For television, July is the low month of the low season. Wholly apart from consumers' broadcast habits but completely synchronized is the determination of some performers to take off a quarter of the year — in order to stay on the air for a greater number of years and to enjoy more what they earn during the three quarters of relatively heavy looking and listening. Briefly, the big problem is this: what should the advertiser who is on the air during fall, winter, and spring do during the summer.

One obvious course of action is to go off the air completely for thirteen weeks in the summer. If an advertiser has a good time slot and relinquishes it for the summer, he may not be successful in his attempt to reoccupy that time period when fall comes. In addition, starting up again after an absence, even an absence of only thirteen weeks, can be a more difficult undertaking than the advertiser anticipated. A second course of action open to sponsors of certain shows is to continue the same shows through fall, winter, spring, and summer. News broadcasts are an example of this type of show. A third possibility is for the advertiser to pick up a live summer replacement, one less expensive than his regular program, one probably wanting to become the regular program of some sponsor. The typical summer replacement is of lower quality and effectiveness than the regular program it replaces. It has, furthermore, less time in which to develop a steady, loyal audience. A fourth possible course of action is to repeat the more popular shows of the past thirty-nine weeks.

Media

THE TELEVISION COMMERCIAL

Classifications

The sellers' advertising messages, the commercials, can be classified in several ways. One is to make a class of the commercials which are *part of programs* sponsored by advertisers and to make another class of *announcements* which, you recall, do not have their own programs. This second group can be further divided into station breaks, announcements on participating programs, and I.D.'s.

A second procedure divides television commercials into (a) *live,* (b) *taped,* and (c) *those which combine* both live elements and taped elements.

Still a third classification designates commercials as *billboards, regular,* or *I.D.'s.* A billboard is the opening or closing section of a television show; typically it consists of fanfare, the name of the show, the name of the star(s) of the show, and the name of the sponsoring company or brand. Billboards use program time, not station break time. Regular commercials are interior commercials broadcast between the time that the program actually starts and the end of the show.

The I.D. is the last type in our third classification. On the hour, on the half-hour, and on the quarter-hour, television stations reserve time for their own use. A common disposition of ten seconds is for the use of the station in identifying itself, which it is required to do periodically. I.D.'s are brief commercials broadcast within this ten-second unit of time. I.D.'s can follow one of several patterns. Some consist of eight seconds of video and six seconds of audio, with the station using the remainder for identifying itself. Or, the video may run the full ten seconds and the audio seven seconds, limiting the station to three seconds of oral identification only. Sometimes this ten-second I.D. shares visual identification with the station.

Because the I.D. is in a difficult position, its job is difficult. It is usually preceded by a closing commercial and by a station break. It is usually followed by a billboard or an opening commercial. So, its competition is rugged. Other handicaps are the brevity of the communication, the absence of any program connection, and the fact that I.D.'s have little or no prestige with consumers or with retailers. But the I.D. has plus points, too. Best of all, its price is low. Impact can be packed into it. There *are* excellent and, hence, desirable locations for I.D.'s between popular programs. Finally, commitments can be canceled on short notice.

Formats

In the chapter on *copy,* format was described as *how* the advertiser tells his story, and several formats widely used in newspapers and magazines were mentioned. In television, too, there are several choices open to advertisers.

One of the simpler possibilities is for the advertiser to use audio only. Here an off-screen voice delivers the commercials, perhaps while a ball game or a fight continues. The great handicap of this technique is the failure to use one of television's greatest features — the ability to communicate to the consumer through his sense of sight. If audio alone will do a satisfactory job, maybe the advertiser should be using radio instead of television.

Television and Radio II

A second method, also a simple one, is the use of video only. Once again, a written advertising message can be superimposed while the ball game or the fight continues. This method suffers from the absence of words spoken by a human voice and from the absence of advertising sound effects.

Third, one or more slides can be projected onto the screen, and the advertising message can be delivered by an unseen announcer. Description, explanation, and illustration are all present — but no motion and no live persons.

A fourth format calls for a demonstration of the product accompanied by description and explanation from an announcer, seen or unseen. There is a wide range of choice and possibilities within this format. And, one is forced to the conclusion that the omission of product demonstration from television advertising is most difficult to justify.

A fifth format is dramatization. The commercial is in the form of a story or playlet with a plot. Two or more persons or personalities use action and dialogue to generate human interest. Sometimes the announcer gets a happy consumer to give a testimonial for the product advertised.

Animation is the final format to be mentioned here. Animation uses drawn personalities such as Donald Duck, puppets, cartoon animals, and trade characters instead of real-life persons. The process of creating and producing an animated commercial is expensive. Furthermore, some consumers prefer real-life persons to drawings; they find real persons more convincing than cartoon persons. In addition, there is greater opportunity to demonstrate and to dramatize the product when real-life persons are used. Experience has shown, however, that some make-believe salesmen such as kittens or dragons can do an effective job. Another virtue of the animated commercial is that it lasts and can be used again and again.

Building the Commercial

The *importance of the commercial* must not be underestimated nor forgotten. Television shows, no matter how outstanding and no matter how large their audiences, do not sell the sponsor's product; only the commercials can do that. So, the need for commercials which will reach prospects and influence them favorably is continuing, universal, and undeniable.

Basically, and briefly, the commercial joins all other advertising copy in its *need of a big sales idea* as a base. Big sales ideas in television are the same as in publication media — they are buyer benefits. Most of the copy qualities which are sound for *readers* (believability, sincerity, good taste, etc.) are equally sound for *viewer-listeners* who, after all, do some reading on TV screens.

Commercials must *get the buyer's attention immediately*. The first two or three seconds are for the commercial what the headline is for the publication advertisement. During that brief moment and often with the deliberate use of a certain amount of noise and provocation, the advertiser must from the very start imply to the consumer that the commercial just beginning is interesting, beneficial and entertaining. The consumer has little idea during those first two or three seconds of just what the advertiser is going to do or of just how he proposes to do it. If the

Media

commercial's opening is too mild, the result is no registration — and no sales power; if it is too aggressive, the result is no viewing — and no sales power.

Commercials need *unity* because unity permits simplicity and simplicity is essential. Constructing the commercial on a single big sales idea helps insure unity. Having the video *and* the audio communicate the same idea at the same time contributes to unity. Building each commercial on a program as a complete, self-contained, independent unit is most desirable. Any overuse of gadgets is a threat to unity; this danger is great because of the wide choice of sound effects and photographic tricks. Probably the greatest damage done to unity is from including too many pictures, too many product details, and too many ideas; excesses here so crowd and clutter up a commercial that unity is impossible.

Commercials need to be *clear*. Recommended procedure is to plan the video first and then fit it to the audio. Each should communicate clearly. There should be no question as to who the sponsor (company or brand name) is, as to what the product or package looks like, or as to what the consumer is to do. The sequence of the commercial should be the most logical, the easiest to grasp, that can be devised. Repetition throughout and then restatement at the end improve clarity.

Harmony is a feature of successful commercials. There must be harmony between the type of show and the type of product being advertised. The commercial and its show must match each other emotionally and psychologically. The commercial must fit the buyers it intends to influence; its setting must strike those individuals as appropriate, authentic, and realistic. When an on-screen announcer delivers a commercial, he and the product and the message must blend together in a complementary, harmonious manner; the announcer's sex and type must be right; he or she must not be identified with a competing brand. Finally, the advertiser hopes that his commercial will be in harmony with what is to be broadcast immediately before and immediately after the commercial.

Some Questions About Commercials

One of the early questions to be decided by sponsors of programs involves the *amount of commercial time* to be scheduled. There is pressure on the advertiser to use the maximum number of minutes and seconds for which he can get clearance. A general rule is that until 6 P.M., 15 per cent of a program can be used for commercials; after 6 P.M., 10 per cent. However, five-minute newscasts have been known to include these:

Opening billboard	20 seconds
Main commercial	60 seconds
Second commercial	15 seconds
Closing billboard	20 seconds

The code of the television industry states that "in accordance with good telecast advertising practices, the time standards for advertising copy are as follows:"[2]

[2] NAB, *The Television Code*. (Washington: NAB, 7th edition, May 1962, pp. 18, 19).

XIV. Time Standards for Advertising

1. Prime Time

   Definition: A continuous period of not less than three hours of each broadcast day within the station's highest rate time periods. Commercial material for both individually sponsored and participation programs within any 30-minute period of prime time may not exceed 4 minutes plus total station break time in the aggregate of 70 seconds.

   Commercial material in prime time includes billboards, public service announcements, promotional announcements for other programs as well as commercial copy.

2. Non-Prime Time

   Definition: All time other than prime time. Commercial material for both individually sponsored and participation programs within any 30-minute time period in nonprime time may exceed 6 minutes plus station break time. Commercial material for all other periods of time shall not exceed this ratio, except that individual programs of 5-minutes duration may include commercial material not in excess of 1 minute 15 seconds and individual programs of 10-minutes duration may include commercial material not in excess of 2 minutes 10 seconds.

   Not more than three announcements shall be scheduled consecutively.

   Commercial material in non-prime time does not include public service announcements, promotional announcements for other programs, and opening and closing "billboards" which give program or sponsor identification.

Another question, one obviously related to the first one, involves the *placement of the commercials* within the sponsor's time period. Here the advertiser must first break his total commercial time down into individual commercials, and then he must schedule them within his program. What is the best division of three minutes of commercial time on a thirty-minute show? Should a thirty-minute show have two ten-second billboards plus three other commercials? Is a thirty-sixty-thirty breakdown the best one possible for two commercial minutes? These questions must be answered by each advertiser. Some advertisers whose shows are suitable place the opening and closing commercials just inside the show itself, hoping thereby to arouse some interest before the opening one and to hold the viewer through the closing commercial by withholding the end of the show. Certainly interior commercials must be placed with care. They should occupy "logical" spots if there are such. Their settings should be the most helpful possible. They should be placed so as to do a minimum of damage and disruption to the show.

A third question asks *whether or not the commercials should be integrated*. An integrated commercial is a part of the show; it matches the mood, the style, and the nature of the show; it may be executed by the leading members of the cast, preferably including the star. Some in television, including some entertainers, feel strongly that entertainers should be asked only to entertain — not to try to sell the sponsor's merchandise. Some star entertainers are also star salesmen, others are not. If the star cannot or will not deliver an effective commercial, then the advertiser's

Media

only choice is to build commercials outstanding enough to hold his viewers. A compromise is to integrate *one* commercial of two or three.

A fourth and final question returns to a matter mentioned briefly in the section on circulation. There the point was made that the audience for commercials is *not* the audience for the show. The question here is, *just how effective are commercials* and how can they be made even more effective. Two measurements, then, are needed — one of the quantity and quality of the audience the commercial reaches and the other one of the response or reaction of that audience to the commercial. How many individuals leave the room when commercials start? How many cut off the commercial *mentally* and begin to converse or do something else? How helpful is the show in putting viewers in a responsive frame of mind? Are the transitions from show to commercial and then back to show smooth? At what point does a commercial's effectiveness begin to decline? How much sooner do the advertiser and his advertising agency tire of a commercial than consumers tire of it? These questions point up the problem of determining the effectiveness of commercials.

THE RADIO COMMERCIAL

Types

Radio commercials, like those in television, are station breaks, or they are on participation programs, or they are part of a program sponsored by a specific advertiser. They are delivered live, or they are transcribed.

Most radio commercials are straight, delivered most often by one announcer but occasionally by two. Another format is the human interest skit. Often a little drama involving two persons points up a consumer problem, and then it is followed by a third voice, that of the announcer, recommending the advertised product as the solution. Music and other sound effects may be included in this second format. Third, there are integrated commercials in radio just as in television.

A format famous in radio is the singing commercial or jingle. These have attention power and are particularly well suited for spot announcements. They can be so catchy that consumers actually enjoy them; listeners sing along at home with the ones they like especially well; listeners even write in to radio stations requesting their favorites. Singing commercials have good memory value, they can be used for months and months, they sugarcoat the "hard" sell.

There are, to be sure, some negative aspects to the singing commercial. They cost more than straight commercials. They can easily be low in sales power; both quantity and quality of this element may be less than in other formats. In some, the singing detracts; in others, it distracts. Always, the singing is irrelevant and therefore a gimmick, and gimmicks are tricky.

If the singing commercial is to be used, the melody should be simple. By all means, care must be taken to see that the brand name and the buyer benefit will be heard clearly. Selling value is essential, maybe in the form of a straight selling message delivered in the regular voice of an announcer at the conclusion of the jingle.

Television and Radio II

Length of Commercials

The radio industry has its own code and each station has its own regulations and practices as to the ratio of commercial time to total time. The proportions in the table are typical of large stations.

MAXIMUM COMMERCIAL TIME
(minutes and seconds)

Length of Program	News Day and Evening	Programs Before 6 p.m.	Programs After 6 p.m.
5:00	1:00	1:15	1:00
10:00	1:45	2:10	2:00
15:00	2:15	3:00	2:30
25:00		4:00	2:50
30:00		4:15	3:00
60:00		7:00	6:00

Suggestions

Those who create radio commercials can follow no more basic rule than that of writing for the ear — not for the eye *and* the ear. Remember, the consumer *hears* the commercial copy, he does not see it. Because he is unable to see anything, he must be spared the need for anything visual; he must be able to grasp the advertiser's message and to understand it solely through oral communication. Repetition of key names, numbers, and words helps to make up for the non-physical, non-visual character of the message. Sound effects, too, may help; they include bells, clocks, whistles, foghorns, bugle calls, animal noises, news tickers, and fire sirens.

As a form of writing, the radio commercial ranks close to the top in its need for careful composition. The writing must be simple because it is not seen; in addition, we have observed that the audience is a mass audience and that this mass audience listens with considerably less than 100 per cent attention. Hence, simplicity of style is imperative. The short, clear sentence is the type radio demands. As a matter of fact, writing need not be limited in form to complete sentences; incomplete sentences, isolated expressions, and fragmentary remarks can be quite effective. The use of idioms and contractions, even the use of the ungrammatical, can make the message sound more conversational. Words should be chosen in the light of how they sound, not how they look. Certain pairs of words sound confusingly alike; chief and cheap, smell and swell, breadth and breath, price and prize are examples. Personal words should be included generously.

Listeners want to be respected and not offended by radio advertisers. Many consumers, it must be recognized, are somewhat hostile to all radio advertising; many are convinced (or at least they assume) that commercials are too numerous, too insistent, too repetitious, too silly, or even too repugnant. Probably most consumers think commercials are longer than they really are. When you add to this consumer attitude the fact that the spoken word is quite direct and personal, that it offends

Media

more quickly and easily than the written word, the avoidance of questionable writing is seen to be mandatory.

What about radio commercials created in a manner intended to irritate the listener? That the neutral type of commercial is handicapped seems undeniable; it does not register effectively in the listener's mind nor is it well remembered. A certain evaporation, furthermore, seems to take place in the consumer's memory between his hearing an irritating commercial and his next purchase; he may remember the brand name when next in the market to buy, but he may not remember much or any of the irritation he felt earlier when listening to the commercial. There is no question but that certain radio commercials with intentional irritation value have done very well and that irritation is safer in radio than in television. Perhaps the suggestion in order is that irritation value can be effective but must be handled most carefully. It must not be so extreme as to hurt the advertiser.

No commercial on radio is any better than its delivery. Emphasis, emotion, persuasion, and conviction must be in the announcer's voice as well as in the written copy. The announcer should sound like an ally, a friend of the listener. His delivery needs to be relaxed and informal, friendly and conversational, easy and personal. Advertisers hope for correct pronunciation and clear expression; they hope their commercials will sound spoken and not read. Even though an announcer can read 160 to 175 words per minute, a safe rate of 120 is preferred.

MERCHANDISING THE BROADCAST SHOW

In order to get the maximum performance from each dollar he spends in broadcast advertising, particularly in television, the manufacturer usually is wise to merchandise his advertising. You recall that the phrase "merchandising the advertising" refers to a manufacturer's informing the public, his salesmen, and his dealers about his advertising and stimulating their enthusiasm about it. Because the need for an effective merchandising job varies in direct proportion to the amount of money spent in the medium, sponsors of the more expensive programs are, naturally, the advertisers most anxious to do a successful merchandising job. These advertisers get some help from broadcast stations; the stations have a most intimate interest in the audiences for the shows they broadcast and in the support and cooperation given those shows by local retailers.

There are several objectives of merchandising the broadcast shows. One is to insure that the maximum number of prospects obtainable will see or hear the show and its commercials, will like what they see and hear, and will become regular viewers and listeners. Another is to make certain that the manufacturer's sales force is fully informed of advertising plans and programs well in advance of their taking place; it is the hope and intent of the manufacturer that salesmen's knowledge and enthusiasm concerning the company's advertising will be reflected in greater performance by those salesmen. A third objective is to see that the trade, particularly the retailers handling the advertised product, know about the promotion and are impressed by it. When this third goal is achieved, retailers will often and in number support the manufacturer's product with one or more of the three types of support

Television and Radio II

retailers can give — display at the point of purchase, their own advertising, and personal selling.

How does a manufacturer merchandise his broadcast shows to his consumer prospects, to his salesmen, and to his dealers? One possibility is for him to buy local television, radio, or newspaper advertising in the broadcast markets for the sole and specific purpose of advertising his shows. Another possibility is for the manufacturer to mention his broadcast program in his national advertising, including cross plugs on any other television or radio show the manufacturer sponsors. Package inserts are still another possibility. To reach wholesalers and retailers, the manufacturer may run advertisements in trade papers or use direct mail to tell the story of his program; he may even be able to get a news story included in trade papers if his program is spectacular or unusual enough to have publicity value.

The broadcast stations can contribute to the merchandising effort by plugging the show over their own facilities and in their local advertisements. In addition, station personnel can work with local retailers.

The manufacturer's salesmen get the advertising story from company personnel and, perhaps, from representatives of the company's advertising agency. Sales meetings are appropriate settings for this purpose. A star from the program may be scheduled to appear briefly at these sales meetings. If the broadcast program is expensive enough, material on it can be prepared for inclusion in the salesman's portfolio.

Questions and Problems

1. Contrast the informal, free-comment, extemporaneous type of broadcast commercial with the written-and-read-as-written type.
2. Some consumers discontinue TV viewing for the duration of the commercials. How can their number be reduced?
3. Comment on the use of commercial broadcast announcements rather than of broadcast shows.
4. What techniques are used to build an audience for a series of TV shows?
5. What are some of the considerations which determine whether radio advertising is profitable?
6. Should a manufacturer advertise his TV shows?
7. Comment on the seasonal use of TV by advertisers.
8. Comment on the selection of hour of day for a TV show.
9. What is good about studio audiences for TV shows?
10. Greeting cards and fine watches are two products with much seasonal variation in annual sales volume. December may account for 50% in the case of greeting cards, 20% for the watches. Mother's Day, Father's Day, Valentine's Day, and Easter may produce 25% for greeting cards. April, May, and June produce 25% of watch sales.

Media

When manufacturers of greeting cards and fine watches consider the use of TV, they naturally try to contrast the desirability of co-sponsoring a weekly series against the desirability of sole sponsorship of five or six "specials" during the season. This type of show is one of a kind, has unusual interest, is irregularly scheduled, is usually broadcast between 8 and 11 P.M., forces some regular program(s) off the air, features well-known stars, and runs from one to two hours. Comment on this sponsorship decision.

Chapter 15

Outdoor and Transit

PART I — OUTDOOR

The importance of outdoor advertising has been increasing during recent years. There have been increases both in population and in the number of automobiles, in automobile travel for business and for pleasure. The growth of our suburbs, the decentralization of our retail structure, and our shorter work week have resulted in more consumer exposure to outdoor advertising than ever before.

Outdoor advertising takes many forms, three of which we consider. *Posters* comprise the print classification; *painted bulletins* and *painted walls* comprise the painted display classification; *spectaculars* comprise the electric classification. Spectaculars, painted displays, and 24-sheet posters (the most important size), account for over 95 per cent of the outdoor advertising volume controlled and serviced by established outdoor advertising plants.

The basic unit making up the outdoor advertising industry is the outdoor advertising plant. These are not factories. Instead, the term *plant* refers to the physical properties of the local outdoor advertising company. A plant's most valuable asset, by far, consists of the positions or sites on which it has advertising structures — panels for posters, bulletins and walls for painted advertisements, and the framework and illumination which, at night, become electric spectaculars.

Posters

24-Sheet and 30-Sheet Posters. The poster frame or panel for the 24-sheet poster is 12 feet high by 25 feet wide, a standard size uniform throughout the country. The poster itself is $8\frac{2}{3}$ feet high by $19\frac{1}{2}$ feet wide. In the middle 1950's some 30-sheet posters with a copy area $9\frac{7}{12}$ feet high by $21\frac{7}{12}$ feet wide appeared on these same panels. The 25 per cent increase in size was made possible by reducing on all four sides the border surrounding the poster. The 30-sheet poster delivers the same circulation as would a 24-sheet poster on the same panel but its production cost averages about 25 per cent greater than for 24-sheet posters. Each advertiser must decide whether the added emphasis, readership, impact, and memory

Media

value of the 30-sheet size are enough to justify the added cost. Panels are located on well-traveled streets and roads, in neighborhood retail centers, and on downtown sites where traffic is high. *Regular* panels are not lighted and, consequently, enjoy circulation about twelve hours a day, roughly from 6 A.M. to 6 P.M. *Illuminated* panels, being lighted, work approximately eighteen hours a day, from about 6 A.M. to 12 P.M.

The 24-sheet posters consist of sheets of paper which are printed and then pasted onto the metal panel. Once these posters were made up of 24 sheets, but now that figure is usually 10 or 12. Most posters are lithographed. They reflect an increased use of slick, glossy paper, of beaded plastic which produces a luminous effect when struck by automobile headlights, and of daylight fluorescent inks. The bright glow, the brilliance, and the radiance of some of these inks are such that, under some daylight conditions, colors become so intense they seem illuminated. National advertisers change their posters at 30-day intervals, local advertisers less often. Each advertiser buys his posters, pays for their production, and supplies them to the outdoor advertising plant operator.

3-Sheet Posters. These small posters, vertical whereas the 24- and 30-sheet posters are horizontal, are 82 inches high by 41 inches wide. Used mainly to influence pedestrian traffic, they are usually seen in congested areas, on corner walls, or on the sides of retail stores. The 3-sheet posters hope to do a reminder job and to encourage impulsive buying decisions, often by showing the product.

Painted Displays

Painted Bulletins. Bulletins are constructed of sheet metal or of wood. Some of the metal ones consist of removable sections which can be taken down, painted indoors, and then returned to duty. Their sizes are not standardized; usually larger than posters, many run from 12 to 18 feet high and from 40 to 72 feet wide. The outdoor advertising industry, however, is encouraging the acceptance and adoption of these sizes:

Standard Highway Bulletin	13′ × 41′ 8″
Deluxe Urban Bulletin	13′ 4″ × 46′ 10″
Standard Streamliner Bulletin	15′ × 46′

Bulletins are seen in cities, in suburbs, in highway locations, and along railroads. Particularly suitable are downtown locations where traffic is heavy and locations on the main highway approaches to cities. Like posters, some bulletins are illuminated, some not. The illuminated ones usually are painted three times a year (original job plus two repaints), the unilluminated ones twice. Painting is by hand, and copy can be changed with each paint job.

Embellishments of various sorts are used to dress up certain bulletins, to decorate them, to give them individuality. The frame itself can be designed in a shape other than the usual rectangle. A clock, a thermometer, or action devices can be built into the bulletin. Paints are available which give luminous, radiant effects, doing for bulletins somewhat the same job fluorescent inks do for posters. Reflec-

Outdoor and Transit

tive sheeting and buttons as well as plastic beads can produce an impressive appearance in color when lighted by automobile headlights. Innovations in illumination make possible striking and unusual variations. Cut-outs have been designed to extend beyond the four sides of the bulletin, and some even extend in front and behind to add a third dimension. Plastic or plywood cut-outs can present the product, the package, the trade mark, or the trade character. Another type of cut-out features the brand name in neon letters. For variety, cut-outs may be rotated every 30, 60, or 90 days among good locations within a market or among several markets.

Some plant operators make a *rotary plan* available to advertisers. Suppose rotary locations are available in six zones of a city. The advertiser might arrange for a bulletin in one zone for January and February. Then this could move to a second zone for March and April, the bulletin being removed from one frame and installed in another frame. The advertiser can select whatever number of bulletins seems most desirable; he can also select the frequency of change, the common intervals being 30, 60, and 90 days.

Painted Walls. Displays on the sides of buildings are known as painted walls. The surface can be brick or wood, the location can be downtown or neighborhood. Painted walls vary in size and shape depending on the space available. They are generally repainted every six or twelve months.

Spectaculars

Spectaculars are the types of electric signs which have helped make Broadway "The Great White Way" for the 1,500,000 persons who, it is estimated, visit the Times Square area each day. Size is determined by location, and, while there *are* some small ones, the word *spectacular* usually brings to mind an advertisement much larger than posters or painted bulletins. Such spectaculars are elaborate in their use of color, motion, and action; their animation is both varied and striking. Position and visibility are quite important in the location of spectaculars. Because a spectacular is expensive and is primarily a night display, only sites with heavy night traffic can stand the high costs involved. Each spectacular is designed for a specific advertiser; its heart is an ingenious idea presented in a unique and dramatic manner.

Times Square is famous for its spectaculars. The versatile BOAC display consists of a panel of 4104 closely set lamps. (Courtesy: Douglas Leigh, Inc.)

Media

Features of the Medium

Outdoor advertising is interesting on several counts. It is the oldest of the media we study. Being immobile or fixed, it cannot go to consumers, they must come to it. Consumers do not seek outdoor advertisements, they do not handle them, they do not buy nor own them. Outdoor advertising demands little of the consumer's time and reading effort. This is a *mass* medium with a huge circulation; it speaks to everybody. There is very little an advertiser can do about limiting or selecting the type of consumer who will be exposed to his advertisement. Among the prominent *national* users of outdoor advertising are the automotive, beverage, food, and confection industries. *Local* users include banks, department stores, hotels and motor courts, bakeries, laundries, dairies, utilities, and amusements.

This medium is colorful; the advertisements are large, making for boldness, impact, and drama. The advertising story is delivered not indoors but out of the house, close to retail stores. By speaking to the right consumers at the right times and in the right places, a timeliness is achieved which is impossible for any other medium except the point-of-purchase medium. The medium is adaptable in that the manufacturer can select which markets to advertise in, the volume of advertising to use in each, and, in some instances, even the sites to occupy. The manufacturer can adapt his outdoor advertising to his own individual distribution pattern and to his competitive circumstances in each market.

There are limitations, too, in the medium. Because copy must be extremely brief, the medium is not a natural for most new products, for all long-copy products, for pioneering products. It is a "reminder" medium. So, even though it is a major medium for a few advertisers, its more common roles are those of support for other media and of added promotion in markets needing it. Outdoor advertisements get keen competition from a wide range of distractions — from sun, sky, buildings, people, automobiles, and consumer preoccupations. There is no editorial matter to attract consumers as is found in newspapers and magazines, television and radio. While it is an all-year medium, there is some shrinkage of circulation during winter months. The prominence of the medium, its great asset from an advertising point of view, makes it a handy whipping boy. There have, of course, been some instances of abuse and poor taste which have caused criticism, hostile legislation, and a public relations problem. The two criticisms most often heard are that outdoor advertising (1) detracts from the beauties of nature, and (2) distracts drivers, causing a safety hazard. Outdoor structures are barred from some of the new expressways and turnpikes even though the outdoor advertising industry claims that accidents on these highways would be reduced if there were more to relieve monotony, such as some outdoor advertisements.

Posters. Poster advertising can be of heavy intensity or light, the coverage can be national or neighborhood, the time period can be one month or twelve. There is much repetition of the same story; one consumer sees the same poster day after day and the same message on poster after poster. This high frequency of impressions makes for greater penetration. Of the three forms of outdoor advertising, posters can do the best job of intercepting consumers on their way to stores. Posters have

Posters and painted bulletins are the pride of the outdoor medium; signs are not. (Courtesy: Outdoor Advertising, Inc.)

a good effect on local retailers, encouraging their support and cooperation. Posters lend themselves well to vertical cooperative advertising and to the identification of local retailers. Automobile, petroleum, food, and beverage advertisers have used the repetition feature of poster advertising successfully to establish brand name familiarity, package identification, and product prestige.

Painted Displays. Painted advertising differs from printed advertising in several respects. Coverage is more selective because the advertiser selects each position individually. The larger size available makes for greater impact. Because they are placed only in outstanding locations, painted bulletins can dominate from key sites on travel routes and from the most visible spots downtown. Because they are hand painted, the advertiser can get exactly what he wants, changing copy from display to display if he prefers. Because copy changes are infrequent, there is an institutional flavor in the painted advertising of such firms as banks and hotels.

Spectaculars. Without any question, spectaculars are the showmanship version of outdoor advertising. Conspicuous and fascinating, they capture consumers' attention and make a vivid impression on consumers' memories. Bubbling liquids, waterfalls, cups of steaming coffee, and smoke rings enjoy word-of-mouth publicity all over the country. Because of their elaborate construction and their high cost, copy changes are usually less often than once a year. Manufacturers of impulse goods of universal demand such as drug products, tobacco products, and beverages use spectaculars effectively to establish the identities of brand names, trade characters, trade marks, slogans, and packages.

Media

Rate Structure — Posters

Showings. Imagine a man who wants to become an outdoor advertising plant operator; imagine, further, that he decides to go into business in a market where, until now, there has been no outdoor advertising. The outdoor advertising plant operator's first step is to get control of all the desirable positions he can, leasing most of them, perhaps buying a few. The next step is that of classifying the sites into poster locations and paint locations. (Let us assume the market is too small for spectaculars.) Our plant operator then builds his structures, his panels and his frames, on these locations. Then the market must be divided into zones because our operator must have poster panels in each section of the market in line with the nature and the volume of the traffic in each. The 24-sheet poster panels are separated into the regular group and the illuminated group, the latter consisting of locations where the traffic from 6 P.M. to 12 P.M. is heavy enough to justify lights.

The plant operator is now ready to group his 24-sheet poster panels into *showings,* the unit in which 24-sheet poster advertising is bought and sold. How does he set up showings? He follows systematic, standardized methods which determine coverage requirements for his market. He studies traffic patterns, counts circulation, and analyzes his locations in an effort to determine how many posters are needed to do an effective advertising job. He gives considerable weight to size of population. Finally, he decides on the number of poster panels for each intensity he will make available to advertisers.

No. 100 Showings. Suppose our plant operator wound up with 400 panels, 200 regular and 200 illuminated. Suppose, further, that the plant operator determines that an appropriately distributed group of 10 regular and 10 illuminated posters constitutes a No. 100 showing. Our operator, then, has 20 of the No. 100 showings to offer to advertisers.

A No. 100 showing is the standard for thorough coverage of a market; it gives completely adequate representation throughout the market. Its panels are so distributed that the number of consumers exposed to the posted advertising message is approximately equal to the population of the market. The number of posters in a No. 100 showing can vary all the way from one in a small town to over one hundred in a large city. Each of our operator's 20 showings is equal to the other 19 in number of panels, circulation, price, effectiveness, and advertising power. Each contains excellent, good, average, and fair locations. Each is equally desirable from the

24- and 30-sheet posters are appropriate for beverages such as Teem. (Courtesy: Outdoor Advertising, Inc.)

point of view of the typical advertiser who is interested in market coverage and not in specific locations. Food advertisers, of course, hope for locations near food stores; at least one oil company prefers locations *not* close to its service stations, feeling that the stations themselves do a promotion job in their immediate areas. Each plant usually includes some "singles" which can be used by local advertisers of a neighborhood type.

Other Showings. A No. 50 showing joins the No. 100 showing to make up the most popular pair of intensities. The No. 50 showing contains about one-half as many posters as the No. 100 showing and is approximately one-half as effective. In some markets a No. 25 showing is available. There are also 3-sheet posters sold in groups tailored to fit each advertiser's needs.

Some advertisers have used No. 50 showings in what is called the *pyramid* technique. Here the advertiser buys 4 No. 50 showings *to be posted at 5-day intervals*. Intensity, thus, is stepped up during a 15-day period from that of a No. 50 showing to that of a No. 200 showing. On occasion, an advertiser has been known to continue this pyramiding until he achieves a "saturation" intensity from a No. 400 showing.

Rate Data. Each plant operator sets the prices on his posters, being guided by volume and quality of circulation. His price entitles the advertiser to space for 30 days and the servicing of that space; it does not include the poster itself which the advertiser must supply. Generally speaking, there are no quantity or frequency discounts, and there is only one rate, not a national rate and a local rate. A discount to recognized advertising agencies of 16⅔ per cent is usual. Nationwide, the cost approximates 15 cents per 1,000 Net Advertising Circulation for 24-sheet posters.

Rate Structure — Displays and Spectaculars

Displays are bought on an individual basis for one-, two-, or three-year periods. Three-year contracts for new displays and one-year contracts for existing ones are not uncommon. Painted displays are claimed by some in advertising to be the most economical form of advertising.

Spectaculars, too, are bought on an individual basis, but the contracts range from three to ten years in length. The advertiser pays construction and installation costs, then he pays a monthly rental that ranges from $2,500 to $25,000.

For displays and for spectaculars, there may be a quantity discount of 5%–10% for each year after the first.

Circulation

The large circulation of outdoor advertising permits almost complete coverage of all age, income, occupation, and education groups. Various studies have come up with such findings as these:[1]

[1] These figures typify the information collected by and available from the Traffic Audit Bureau.

Media

80% of the persons 10 years of age and older are outdoors some part of every day. 84% of the men and 68% of the women go outdoors daily.
98% go outdoors during the standard posting period of 30 days.
75% are outdoors every day of the week.

Gross circulation is determined by counting the pedestrians and the persons in vehicles who pass the outdoor advertisement. This figure is then reduced to *effective* circulation — the number of consumers who travel *toward the advertisement* and, hence, have a reasonable physical opportunity to see it. Because only those persons moving toward the advertisement have a good chance to see it, gross circulation is reduced to:

50% of the pedestrian traffic
50% of the automobile and truck passengers
25% of the bus and streetcar passengers

The third and final step in measuring circulation is to convert effective circulation into Net Advertising Circulation by considering *space position value*. The basic question here is this: how effectively do a plant's structures dominate the traffic to which they are exposed? How well do the positions communicate to their circulation? Each plant is given an average, single figure here, a multiplier which includes and ranges down from 100 per cent. Space position value is determined by these factors:

Length of approach or the distance for which the consumer has a clear view of the advertisement.
Speed of traffic.
Angle of panel to traffic. Head-on and angled advertisements are much superior to parallel structures.
Number of other advertisements on the same site or nearby. Zero, of course, is the best score here.
Distance the advertisement is off to the side of the line of travel.

If effective circulation is 12,000 and the space position value for the plant is .8, then the Net Advertising Circulation or N.A.C. is 9,600.

Copy

No medium surpasses outdoor in its need for a single, basic sales idea — an arresting, powerful idea. It must be a simple idea so that the consumer will grasp it in a very few seconds. It must be a strong idea because of the brevity of the copy. It must be an emotional idea because the medium is not one suited to a rational approach. It must be a warm, human idea of almost universal appeal. Sometimes the advertiser adapts the idea he is using in other media, the theme from his other advertising. Of all media, outdoor can probably do more with a humorous treatment or twist than any other. If the idea has possibilities of continuous use, month after month in a succession of posters, so much the better.

Copy based on this idea needs to be direct, emphatic, and short. One must recognize that an automobile traveling at sixty miles per hour gives passengers less than three seconds to *read* and *grasp* an advertisement 250 feet away. While copy ranges from zero to fifteen in wordage, the copywriter is well urged to think of putting across five words in five seconds. Copy that is bold and obvious in its clarity helps make the identification of the product and the registration of the message immediate, certain, and easy.

Design

Outdoor advertisements consist of a few elements chosen from a small number of possibilities. *Three* is standard for the number of elements to include; more than three give a crowded, cluttered impression; more than three create a layout problem for the artist because they create a consumer problem of grasping or understanding. Fewer than three can seldom do an effective advertising job. In an effort to hold the number down to three, two or three small units can sometimes be combined into a single unit. What can the three elements be? Copy, of course, is usually one; the others can come from a group consisting of illustration, brand name, product, package, trade mark, trade character, and slogan. Some posters provide space for a retail strip or imprint across the bottom.

The paramount rule in outdoor design is that of simplicity. There must be only one point of dominant interest if the message is to be read quickly and grasped quickly by a consumer who may be distant and who is usually in motion. Layout must be informal, unsymmetrical — even striking enough to cause surprise. The elements included should differ in size, shape, weight, and color; an apple, a banana, and a pear are better than three pears in a row. All non-essential details are better omitted because they distract. Harmony, sound composition, and snug integration are most desirable. In this respect, the bulletins with dimensions in a ratio of 1 to 3 pose a more difficult layout problem than the posters with their approximately 1 to 2 ratio.

Because outdoor is more an art medium than a copy medium, seldom should the advertiser rely solely on words. There should be one illustration, bold, dynamic, graphic, and no secondary illustrations. The illustrations should be realistic and true to the product. The meaning of the illustration should be obvious at a glance and at a distance. Seldom should a person be standing at full length; a close up, head, head and shoulders, or even a reclining figure are better because they give an impression of greater size. Inanimate objects, including even the product in use, are generally inferior to animals, children, pretty girls, and human interest situations. Color in illustration makes for greater visibility, emphasis, realism, and identification.

As for lettering, the rule is that of legibility. Simple, clean block lettering with good spacing and good color contrasts is usually quite readable from various distances. Lettering that is fancy, novel, too condensed, too thin or too thick, and letters which vary greatly in weight or coloring are risky. The most legible color combinations for posters are these:

       1. Black on yellow
       2. Green on white

Media

    3. Red on white
    4. Blue on white
    5. White on blue

PART II — TRANSIT

Transit advertising is found in and on the vehicles and stations which make up our public transit systems. The three basic types are:

    Car cards — placed inside street cars, buses, subways, elevated, and suburban trains.

    Bus posters — large signs placed on the outside of street cars and buses. This group includes the transit spectacular about which more will be said later.

    Station posters — various sized posters found in and about subway, elevated, and suburban train stations.

Car cards are displayed in the vehicles of just about every public transportation system, telling their stories to passengers. The great bulk of car cards is seen in cities of 25,000 and over. Approximately 70,000 vehicles carry cards in about 500 city and suburban markets. Bus posters can be had in nearly all of the 500 markets; they tell their stories to riders, motorists, and pedestrians. Station posters deliver their messages from the facilities of rapid transit and suburban railroads in New York City, Chicago, Boston, and Philadelphia to riders of public transportation. The display period for car cards, bus posters, and station posters is one month.

Transit advertising amounts to about $23,000,000 annually. Its small size is caused by the limitation of physical space. There is just so much room in which to place car cards, bus posters, and station posters — and no more. There are just so many car cards a passenger can see from where he sits or stands — and no more. (While this is true, advertisers can turn the lack of space to advantage in standing out above the competition.) So, the medium is usually more appropriate in a *supporting* role than for use as an advertiser's sole or major medium. Small size is no significant hardship as regards the range of advertisers who use the medium successfully. Almost any and all types of advertiser of consumer goods, local, regional, and national, are among its customers. About 65% of transit advertising is regional or local, about 35% is national.

Inside Space

As was mentioned, car cards are displayed on interior surfaces of buses and street cars; they are seen in the cars of elevated, subway, and suburban trains; they are available in certain ferries. The basic unit of time for car-card exposure is one month. This means that the advertiser has an opportunity to change his cards every month. Most advertisers, however, prefer to replace them on a two-month rather than a one-month schedule. Local advertisers change cards less often than national advertisers, and the fewer cards an advertiser uses, the less often he replaces them.

    Position. Most car cards occupy space in racks over the side windows of buses, street cars, subway cars, and elevated trains. The cards back against a curved sur-

A king-size bus poster. (Courtesy: Transit-Advertising Association)

face in such a manner that, being above the heads of seated passengers, the lower part of the card gets more attention than does the upper part. In addition to side positions, car-card space is available over the doors and at the ends of some vehicles. The effective area of the most popular size of side card, the 11 by 28 inches card, includes about six seats. Such a card can be seen and read by passengers sitting three seats forward and three seats back, and by riders standing in the aisle in this area.

No specific positions are guaranteed to an advertiser using regular car cards. This circumstance is no cause for concern in respect to the side cards in subway, elevated, and suburban trains because these positions are of about equal quality. There is no significant difference in potential effectiveness among the positions themselves. Then, to equalize whatever slight differences there are in position values, each advertiser's cards are placed in the vehicles at random; this assures each advertiser of a balanced assortment of spaces. Advertisers using two cards to the car in the New York subways can count on the cards in each pair to be placed on opposite sides of the car and approximately one-half car length apart.

Position in buses is a bit different. Here the cards *forward* and *right* enjoy an advantage. Riders face front, they disembark at the front, and they sit toward the front when passengers are few. The right side is superior to the left side because passengers prefer what they see out of the right side windows rather than to look out the left windows at approaching traffic.

Size. The standard racks which hold side cards in buses and train cars are 11 inches high. Side cards are available in the following sizes:

> 11 inches by 14 inches
> 11 inches by 21 inches
> 11 inches by 28 inches
> 11 inches by 42 inches
> 11 inches by 56 inches
> 11 inches by 84 inches
> 11 inches by 212 inches

End cards, sometimes referred to as bulkhead cards, are 22 inches by 21 inches; over-the-door cards are 16 inches by 44 inches. The special center position in New

Media

York subway cars is 11 inches by 21 inches. In addition, many cities have two other types of cards — the flat bulkheads, situated behind the driver's seat, and the curved "cineramic" frames spotted at intervals along the vehicle. Both are 22″ × 21″.

Rates. Advertisers use car cards in three standard intensities usually referred to as *service* or *run*. The top intensity is full service or full run and calls for a card in every vehicle. Medium intensity is obtained with half service or half run — a card in every other vehicle. This half service is the intensity used by most advertisers. Quarter service or quarter run produces the lowest intensity because it places a card in every fourth vehicle.

Car-card rates are based on twelve months of continuous use by the advertiser. To this base or low rate, charges are added for shorter time units. These premiums average:

> For 6 to 11 months use — 5 per cent
> For 3 to 5 months use — 10 per cent
> For 1 to 2 months use — 20 to 30 per cent

The factors determining the cost of car-card advertising to any advertiser are identifiable without difficulty. The *size* of his card is one fundamental element. Allied to size is the manner of *position*. Bulkhead and over-the-door cards, for example, are special position cards as well as cards of special size — so they take special rates. The *period of time* for which the advertiser buys space is a factor mentioned in the preceding paragraph. The *intensity of service,* similarly, is an obvious factor. Finally, the *number of riders* has a most direct influence on the rates quoted for the cards.

Outside Space

Bus posters are the large signs on the outside of buses and street cars. They occupy space on the front, the sides, and the back of vehicles. In a very real sense, bus posters are closer kin to outdoor advertisements than to car cards and station posters. Because they are exposed to the weather, the physical displays must be durable. Most are made of waterproofed cardboard, composition board, or aluminum. Some make use of reflectorized elements or luminous paint. The outside lights of the vehicle may be made to work for the advertiser, with the STOP light getting particular attention.

Size   The Transit-Advertising Association has adopted these standard sizes for outside space:

> 30″ × 44″ (King-Size)
> 21″ × 44″ (Traveling Display)
> 11″ × 42″ (Front End Display)
> 21″ × 72″ (Rear End Display)
> 7½″ × 60″ (Read End Display)

This formerly green San Diego bus was repainted in Pacific Air Lines colors: red, white, and blue. (Courtesy: Pacific Air Lines)

Rates. Bus posters are sold on a unit basis. The advertiser pays according to the number of spaces he rents. In some markets quotations are by the month, in others they are by the week. Sometimes the displays are grouped and sold by showings — intensive, representative, and minimum. Quantity discounts may apply.

King-Size Bus Posters. An interesting version of the bus poster is the king-size bus poster. Here the advertiser may buy a complete paint job on a bus, transforming the entire vehicle into his ad. Or, on a more modest scale, the advertiser may take only the side of a bus and have his ad painted directly on it, usually by hand. Some of these advertising spaces are 3 feet high by 18 feet wide, or even 4 feet high by 20 feet wide. More can be done in the way of elaborate display on the street side of a bus because exit doors break up the design area on the curb side. Position which approximates eye-level places the advertiser's message within close range of pedestrians, automobile riders, and transit riders. Some advertisers incorporate a regular traveling display frame as an element of the total design. Special copy, seasonal, for example, may be placed in this frame.

Station Posters

Station posters are on subways and elevated platforms; they are both in and on stations and terminals. They are available in New York City, Chicago, Boston, and Philadelphia. The station poster is a first cousin of the car card — and of the outdoor poster. Its larger size gives it certain points of superiority over the car card. It adapts the techniques and features found in outdoor posters. A monthly change of copy is possible as is true of both car cards and outdoor posters.

Size. In New York, Boston, and Philadelphia, sizes of station posters are uniform. They are:

1-sheet	46 inches high by 30 inches wide
2-sheet	46 inches high by 60 inches wide
3-sheet	84 inches high by 42 inches wide

In Chicago, six sizes are available.

283

Standard sizes for airport and station posters are one, two, and three sheets. (Courtesy: Transportation Displays, Inc.)

Rates. Station posters are sold in units (25, 50, 75, or 100) or by showings. The advertising company selling the space for the transit system determines the number of posters needed to cover the market, which stations shall be included, and how many posters shall be included at each station. These showings are designated as *representative* because, in the company's opinion, each such showing covers the market adequately. Double the representative showing and you have an *intensive* showing; halve it and you have a *minimum* showing. Size of poster joins intensity of showing to determine the cost to the advertiser.

Circulation

In respect to circulation, car cards and station posters can be grouped together as they are seen by practically the same individuals. Indeed, no separate studies have been made of station posters, so no specific data are available on them. Because traveling displays communicate to riders *and* to non-riders, their circulation must be considered separately.

Car Cards. Every rider in a carded vehicle is one unit of circulation. Thus, car-card circulation equals the total number of passengers, including revenue passengers, pay and non-pay transfers, free passengers, and school tickets. From twenty to twenty-five billion passengers ride each year. Riders who cannot see and those who cannot read are units of circulation.

Since the standard display period for car cards is one month, gross circulation is expressed as the number of passengers riding during a month. The figure is usually an average for six months and is expressed, "Monthly rides, 6 months average."

Advertisers are interested in refining this total circulation figure so as to get at some concept of effective circulation. This smaller, more meaningful figure consists of riders who read a certain car card. Physical circumstances place a top limit on effective circulation by limiting a passenger's ability to see and read.

Outdoor and Transit

Traveling Displays. In contrast to car cards and station posters, traveling displays reach a large audience of riders *and* non-riders. For years, the medium attempted to measure circulation by hand clocking. Now a motion picture camera is mounted in a window of the bus just over the king size poster to record the number of individuals exposed to traveling displays. All types of urban and suburban neighborhood are covered by traveling displays — residential, shopping, office, and industrial.

Characteristics of Riders. A rider is a person 15 years or older who rides in a transit vehicle at least once a month. One study showed that 80 per cent of the basic population are riders, specifically, 76 per cent of all men, 84 per cent of all women, and 81 per cent of all housewives. A majority of city consumers, 63 per cent of all men and 59 per cent of all women, ride regularly (four or more times a week) in public transportation vehicles.

There is little variation in the percentage of riders found in each of the four rental groups which were established to indicate economic level. More than three-quarters of the consumers in each group are riders.

Length of ride ranges from 20 to 30 minutes. It is not surprising that length of ride varies directly with size of city.

Car Card Cost. As we have seen, every medium has its own basic measure of the cost of its circulation. For car cards, this figure is expressed as *cost per thousand riders*. To compute this figure, the monthly rate for full service for an 11 by 28 inches card is divided by the average number of monthly rides in thousands. For example, assume full service for this size card costs $1,700 a month, and circulation totals 28,969,041. Dividing $1,700 by 28,969 gives a cost of approximately 6 cents per thousand riders. For the country as a whole, cost per thousand runs about 5 cents.

Features of the Medium

Ready-Made Audience. One of the unusual characteristics of transportation advertising is the ready-made nature of the circulation. Transportation advertising is a by-product, an unrelated activity of public transportation. It is an unessential activity in that the buses and cars would run and passengers would ride if there were no advertisements. The seller of transportation advertising translates this fact into a bargain for advertisers by pointing out that public service commissions take little notice of advertising revenue when setting the fares passengers will pay. Furthermore, the transit company does not have to spend dollars and effort in getting and holding an audience for advertisers to address. This argues for lower advertising rates than otherwise would have to be charged. Advertisers, too, particularly those using the broadcast media, welcome with pleasure the ready-made nature of the audience.

Purchase-and-Sale Features. Some transit systems handle their own space selling problems by dealing directly with advertisers and advertising agencies. Most systems lease their advertising space to an independent transportation advertising company

Production and Mechanical Specifications

Transit advertising is a national, regional and local advertising medium that utilizes space for display advertisements on the inside or outside of buses, streetcars, subway and commuter trains. Transit advertising, available in every major market in the United States, is offered by more than 70,000 vehicles.

TYPES OF SPACE AVAILABLE

In general, space is designated as Inside or Outside Display. Each type of display offers a selection of sizes, as follows:

INSIDE SPACE . . . Advertisements within the transit vehicle are displayed along each side and in special positions. All inside advertising is referred to as "Car Card Advertising."

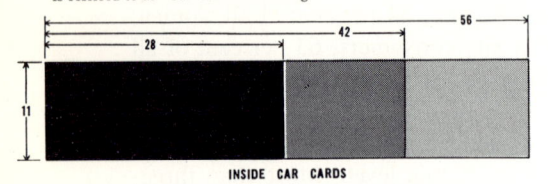

INSIDE CAR CARDS

SIDE CARDS are a standard 11 inches high. The lengths of these cards vary, but the most common are 28, 42 and 56 inches.

SPECIAL POSITION CARDS are available. Sizes and locations vary according to the construction of the transit vehicle.

OUTSIDE SPACE . . . Outside display units are available on the sides, front and rear of vehicles. Bus posters are displayed in three sizes of standardized frames on the side of vehicles. These standardized sizes are:

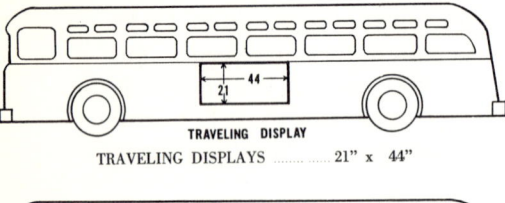

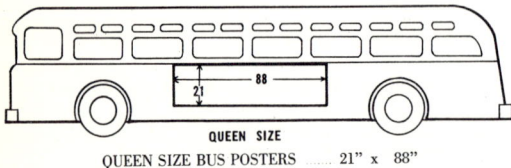

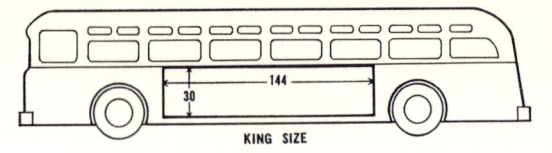

TRAVELING DISPLAY
TRAVELING DISPLAYS .... 21" x 44"

QUEEN SIZE
QUEEN SIZE BUS POSTERS .... 21" x 88"

KING SIZE
KING SIZE BUS POSTERS .... 30" x 144"

The front-end and rear-end spaces vary in size according to the construction of the vehicle. The most common size is the 11 inch by 42 inch front-end space and the 21 inch by 72 inch or 7½ inch by 60 inch rear space. Other special types of outside display units may also be developed in cooperation with local transit advertising companies.

HOW TO BUY TRANSIT ADVERTISING

Rates are based on monthly showings, with discounts generally granted for 3, 6 and 12 month contracts. An order form for transit advertising, containing terms and conditions, has been developed by and is available from the American Association of Advertising Agencies and the National Association of Transit Advertising.

CAR CARDS, inside vehicles, are sold by full, half and quarter showings. OUTSIDE DISPLAYS are generally sold on a unit basis. Because the physical characteristics of markets vary, the local transit company should be consulted for recommendations on minimum, representative and intensive showings.

PRODUCTION INFORMATION

Both car cards and outside display advertisements are provided by the advertiser and should be shipped to the proper location several days in advance of the desired showing.

CAR CARDS should be printed on four or five-ply stock, with the grain running horizontally. Any reproduction process may be used. Cards are held in place on the top and bottom by flanges in the car card racks and on the sides by steel springs. A margin of at least ½ inch should be maintained on all sides.

KING SIZE POSTERS and QUEEN SIZE POSTERS should be produced on 70 or 80 pound waterproof opaque outdoor poster paper. Posters are bonded to ⅛ inch Masonite or Duron panels, supplied by the transit company, which are held in place on all sides by a frame. A margin of 1½ inches should be allowed on all four sides to allow for space covered by the frame. Any reproduction process may be used.

OUTSIDE TRAVELING DISPLAYS, and front and rear-end posters should be produced on at least 10-ply waterproof stock, with the grain running horizontally, and varnished after printing. A margin of at least one inch should be allowed on all four sides to allow for space covered by frame. Any reproduction process may be used.

GENERAL INFORMATION

In most markets there are some restrictions on transit advertising, many of these resulting from local ordinances. Contact the local transit company for details.

Additional information about transit advertising is available from the advertising company in each market or from the NATA. Copies of *Media/scope's* "Media Buyers' Check List" for buying transit advertising are available from Media/scope, 5201 Old Orchard Road, Skokie, Illinois.

Inside and outside display space in the transit medium. (Courtesy: Transit-Advertising Association)

which then markets the space. These independent transportation advertising companies are usually regional or national in scope of operation. It is the advertiser's responsibility to have car cards, station posters, and traveling displays in the transit company's hands ten days prior to the showing date. The physical job of carding the vehicles is included in the rates quoted advertisers. Practically all systems and companies quote a 15 per cent commission to recognized advertising agencies. A very few offer a 2 per cent cash discount. In most markets, a single rate is charged both national and local advertisers.

Outdoor and Transit

Limited Advertising Competition. There are definite limits on the amounts of space suitable for car cards, station posters, and traveling displays. In similar fashion, there are size limitations in all three. The number of cards in a vehicle is not only limited — the figure is known. The range for typical buses, for example, is from fifteen to twenty-five cards. These limitations act as equalizing forces, matching large and small advertisers more evenly than they are matched, for example, in television or magazines. The small advertiser is less handicapped because the larger advertiser cannot dominate the medium.

Favorable Reading Conditions. Travel conditions are favorable to high readership of car cards. The riders have been described with considerable accuracy as a "captive" audience. Most passengers consider their trips boring and distasteful, neither exciting nor pleasant. There are not many activities in which a rider can engage. Not over one rider in six has reading matter with him, and even these few do not read their material all the time they are in transit. Riders can't remove the advertisements, nor do they remove themselves until they reach their stops; they cannot turn the advertising off, nor turn the page. When you remember the frequency of riding and the length of trip, you must credit the medium with large measures of absorption and comprehension, of penetration and remembrance.

Urban Medium. Transit advertisements speak to city consumers, mainly in markets of 25,000 population and over. Coverage of the suburbs does not change the fundamentally urban character of the medium. It covers its urban market both extensively and intensively. There is continuous exposure to large groups of people, twenty-four hours a day in the larger markets. Market-by-market selectivity, of course, is available.

Mass Medium. There is little selectivity in transit advertising insofar as type of passenger is concerned. Both sexes and, except in smaller markets, all income groups are reached. In medium and small size markets, the advertising facilities of the entire transit system are sold as a unit. In metropolitan markets, certain lines or areas can be bought individually, permitting some geographical selectivity.

Repetition Value. The audience for car cards and station posters is of a constant, continuous type. There is much regular riding from home to work and back. During the thirty-day period, about two-thirds of all riders make at least eight round trips. The long exposure period plus this volume of repeat riding cause transit advertising to rank high in repetition value.

Out of the House. A simple separation classifies advertising media into two groups, those which communicate to the consumer *in* his or her house, and those which speak to him or her *out* of the house. Transit advertising, obviously, is in the second group. Consumers must go to it; it cannot go to them. A significant proportion of riders are on their way to shop. They and all other riders are close to points of sale, and that means that many are close to the buying act. Consumers

Media

out of their homes are much closer to buying in three important respects, physically, financially, and emotionally, than are consumers indoors.

30 Day Reach and Repetition #100 Showing		
	Reach	Repetition
SAN FRANCISCO	98%	25 times
OAKLAND	95	19
MINNEAPOLIS	91	13.5
ST. PAUL	95	17
HOUSTON	95	18
NORFOLK-PORTSMOUTH	99	33
SPOKANE	99	29
GREENVILLE	97	21
WATERLOO	97	21
LIMA	98	24
RENO	95	18
POCATELLO	99	32.5
GULFPORT	87	18
AUSTIN	95	18.5
N. PLATTE	89	12.5
AVERAGE	94%	21 times

These figures show how much of a market's population is reached and how often by a #100 showing during a 30-day period. (Courtesy: Advertising Age*)*

The "Take One" Feature. Some advertisers use car cards to offer printed materials of various types to passengers. A replaceable pad of twenty-five to fifty perforated business reply cards is one version. When mailed to the advertiser these serve as requests for samples or literature or as leads for the advertiser's salesmen. Leaflets for the passengers to read are another version. Still a third consists of coupons which can be mailed to the advertiser or taken to retail dealers. These materials may be stapled or wired to the car card; the back of a pad may be inserted into a slit in the card; they may be placed in a cardboard pocket on the card. The advertiser must pay a premium for using the "take one" feature, both for production and for servicing. There is no effective way to screen the curious and the destructive. Personal loan companies and insurance companies are among the heavy users of this feature.

Users and Uses. Certain products and certain services seem to advertise in the transit medium with considerable benefit. Impulse items with mass appeal and low price, which means that volume and frequency of purchase are high, are prominent among the users. Modest price, however, is not a prerequisite to advertising success, because car cards can be used to help sell high-priced products. National advertisers use the medium for gum, beverages, cosmetics, confections, food store products, and drug store products. Local advertisers include banks, savings and loan associations, cleaners, laundries, and a merchant group of which the retailers of furniture, clothing, home furnishings, and jewelry are members.

Outdoor and Transit

Copy Considerations

The word copy in this heading is used in its broad sense, for layout and typography, too, will be mentioned. Although most of the comments relate to car cards, much of the thinking is largely applicable and adaptable to station posters and to traveling displays.

Copy length. The amount of copy that can be placed successfully on an 11 by 28 inches card is not a difficult problem if one remembers that legibility, not reading time, sets the maximum limit. In an earlier section the typical ride was described as lasting 20 to 30 minutes. A passenger can do quite a bit of reading in that relatively long period of time. So there is no reason at all for car cards to be considered "baby" posters and built accordingly. Instead of being a miniature poster, a car card is much more similar in nature to a magazine advertisement. Copy must be brief in the outdoor medium; it need not be brief on car cards. Twenty-five words of copy, unthinkable on a 24-sheet poster, is a sound, rule-of-thumb maximum, but up to fifty words can be included without impairing the chances of accumulating a satisfactory audience.

Copy Features. Copy for the transit medium should be written with two facts in mind. First, there is little selectivity of readers; riders are everybody, of all types. Second, transit advertising plays its best role when used as a supplementary medium. These two conditions argue for simple copy and for the use of "reminder" copy. As little copy flexibility is possible, the medium attracts and does well for copy that needs little change. A most appropriate goal of an advertiser is to establish the identity of his brand name, his trade mark, or his package with riders. Cards with headlines attract more readers than those without headlines. Headlines should be strong, often including the brand name.

Layout. Simplicity is as desirable in layout as in copy. Unnecessary detail is to be omitted, and a crowded appearance is well avoided. Elements commonly found in transit advertisements include copy, illustration, product, package, brand name, and trade mark. Unlike newspaper and magazine advertisements, a car card's optical center is in the *lower* two-thirds of the space. Typically, a curved car card is seen from below by a seated rider, at an angle and from a distance. In these circumstances, the focal point of attention is nearer the bottom of the card than the top. This fact makes the footline position more powerful than the headline position. The curvature of cards which conform to the curved surface of the vehicle's roof makes the top of the card the most difficult area for reading. Often a subhead is placed in this top area, leading into the copy. Human interest illustrations are effective. The "pretty girl" type of illustration gets a larger audience of both men *and* women than any other type. While an illustration of the product or the package is a desirable element, such an illustration seems to do better if the product or package is not allowed to dominate but, instead, is subordinated to other features.

Media

Typography. Transit advertising is excellent for color. Various advertisers use color for such purposes as package identification, human interest, attention value, or appetite appeal. The full-color process gets somewhat larger audiences. Color in the headline may help build larger audiences. There is no additional space cost for the use of color. As for type, simple Gothic lettering is best because tricky lettering, serifs, and thin scripts are not appropriate in this medium in which observation of the cards is often from some distance away, from a variety of angles, and under changing conditions of illumination. Typography benefits by being bold and emphatic. Small size type works against maximum legibility.

Questions and Problems

1. What types of competition does a car card encounter in its bid for passengers' attention?
2. Are bus riders returning home a lower quality circulation than bus riders going to the city?
3. Comment on an advertiser's choice between painted bulletins and electric spectaculars.
4. List some features of a good outdoor ad.
5. What are some aspects of *timing* in outdoor advertising?
6. What differences are there between downtown outdoor advertising sites and highway sites?
7. A salesman for transit advertising is told by a prospective advertiser that "Nobody reads car cards!" What should the salesman do?
8. What are some characteristics of the circulation found in the transit medium?
9. Should prices be quoted on car cards?
10. The Dixie Stores corporation is a regional chain of food supermarkets located in the Southeastern states. The sales of its 450 units approximate $450,000,000 annually. The firm's management read with interest the experience of a distributor of a line of frozen foods in a distant city. This distributor had taken a practically unknown brand of frozen foods, advertised it modestly but unconventionally *only with car cards,* saw its sales increase by 600% in 2 years and its share-of-market reach 35%. Two Dixie executives favor an institutional advertising campaign which would use only car cards in the major markets where Dixie had stores. Evaluate this idea.

Chapter 16

Point of Purchase

The point-of-purchase advertising medium is known by several other names such as *dealer helps, dealer aids, dealer displays, merchandising,* and *point-of-sale materials.* The designation *point of purchase* seems best for our use; it places the emphasis on the buyer rather than on the seller, and, even more to the point, the industry itself selected as the name of its trade association the *Point of Purchase Advertising Institute.* Although the medium is not nearly so cleanly delineated as the six others we have studied, it consists in the main of advertising materials located at, on, or in retail stores; an ideal example is the retail window display. Despite their retail location, the vast majority of these materials are produced and supplied by manufacturers.

The point-of-purchase medium has been increasing in importance for some time. More new types of products have been appearing each year, and, in addition, the growth in the number of brands on the market, manufacturers' and middlemen's, has been great. At the same time, there has been less and less personal selling in retail stores. Part of this decrease represents a decline in the quality of salesmanship practiced at the retail level, part reflects a shift to self-service retailing. Also at the same time there has been an increase in the volume of impulse buying done by consumers. Regardless of how effective an advertising message the manufacturer delivered to consumers or to retailers in such media as newspapers, magazines, television, radio, outdoor, and transportation, there is need for a final word to the consumer while he or she is shopping. The point-of-purchase medium makes it possible for the manufacturer to speak to consumers who are actually making buying decisions in the market place.

CLASSIFICATION

There are several possible bases on which to classify point-of-purchase materials, one of which separates *exterior* items from *interior* items. Service stations are a type of retail business which makes much use of exterior items — signs, banners, pennants, and displays, for example. Interior items are found in store windows, on counters and shelves, on or hanging from the ceiling or the walls, and on the floor.

Media

Another classification groups *temporary* materials together and sets them apart from the more *permanent* ones. Most point-of-purchase items are temporary — counter cards, dummy packages, cut-outs, shelf strips, and streamers. Of a more permanent nature are exterior store identification signs, barometers, clocks, thermometers, and floor cabinets and merchandisers; even calendars and racks stay in use a fairly long time.

Still another classification is based on the materials of which the items are made. The most widely used materials are *cardboard, metal, plastics,* and *wood;* other materials used are cloth, glass, and acetate.

Ten of the most popular point-of-purchase items are:

>Magazine advertisement reprints
>Easel-backed cards
>Window banners and streamers
>Decals on windows, doors, and mirrors
>Wall posters
>Racks of wire, metal, and wood
>Plaques
>Merchandise displays on counters and floor
>Display shipping cartons
>Exhibition displays

A special type of item used by a few manufacturers is the traveling or itinerant display. Usually a window or floor display, this form of point-of-purchase advertising is routed around among a manufacturer's better retail dealers. Each of these retailers is allowed to exhibit the display for some such period as one week, ten days, or two weeks, and then he sends it on to the next store on the list. Because these are expensive to manufacture, they must have a life span measured in months rather than days. They must not be closely identified with the news of the day; they are especially suitable for anniversary use — for a manufacturer celebrating his one hundredth year of operation, for example. Selection of retailer, booking, and routing are basic problems.

FEATURES OF THE MEDIUM

One of the basic differences between the point-of-purchase medium and the other media already examined involves *circulation*. Because there are different types of materials in different locations, there are several different circulations involved. For none of these circulations are there audited or even total figures because techniques of measurement have not been developed which will determine those figures satisfactorily. Exterior circulation, the sidewalk traffic enjoyed by window displays, is both high quality (consumers shopping away from and out of their homes) and low quality (workers passing on their way to work). Should a manufacturer send out 4,000 window displays to retailers handling his product, the quantitative circulation they get is determined by the number of stores installing the item, the length of the installation periods, and the amount of sidewalk traffic.

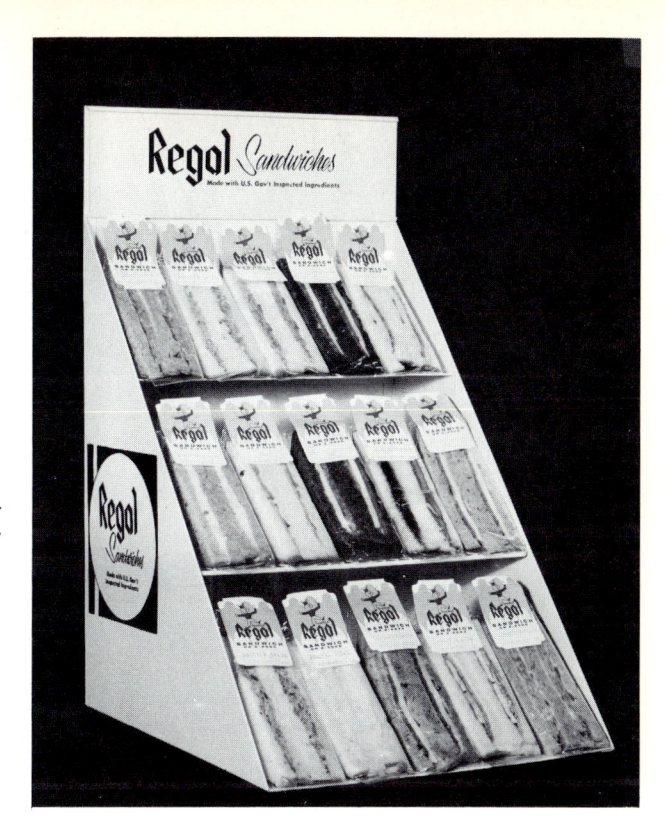

A counter display container. (Courtesy: Point-of-Purchase Advertising Institute)

Point-of-purchase advertising exerts a strong influence in the direction of *impulse purchases* and *replacement purchases.* A housewife, for example, sees a new mix on display in a food store; she buys one package even though she had not intended to make that particular purchase. Or, a display of sugar reminds her that her stock of that item is dangerously low — so she replenishes it. The strength of the buying stimulus stems to a degree from the nearness of consumer to the actual product, and from the fact that the consumer is very close to buying physically, emotionally, and financially. No other medium enjoys such a combination of time, place, and atmosphere; at no other time are merchandise, money, and mood so cooperative and harmonious.

The designer of point-of-purchase advertising must sell *two* buyers. First, he must impress the retailer with the excellence, the effectiveness of the point-of-purchase item itself; otherwise the item, no matter how good it is, will not be used. The second selling job, of course, is done on the individual shopper; she must react favorably to the advertising for it to be successful. Each retailer has his own ideas of effective and ineffective materials. For many of the point-of-purchase items in his store, the retailer can judge the results, perhaps even observe the benefits which accrue to him from the influence of the items.

There are two serious distribution problems in the medium. One consists of the physical distribution of the materials from manufacturer to, perhaps, thousands of retailers. Various techniques for effecting this distribution will be mentioned in a later section of this chapter. The other problem is posed by the amount of

Packages of the product spell the brand names in this window display. (Courtesy: P. Lorillard)

difference among the manufacturer's retail dealers. In a bit of oversimplification, these retailers are better than average merchants or less than average merchants. The range, the difference is so great as to recommend (often it dictates) that different point-of-purchase materials be sent to each group. This result is logical even though to some it may seem odd. The manufacturer's best customers, the more able retailers, get the manufacturer's best materials, while his small customers whose need is greater get less help in that they get fewer, smaller items. A possible variation is for the manufacturer (a) to separate the smaller retailers into those with considerable promise and those whose future shows little or no change for the better, then (b) to supply a better assortment of materials to the more promising group.

Both manufacturer and retailer cash in handsomely from the same outstanding point-of-purchase advertising. The manufacturer's advertising in other media is made more effective when its essential message is repeated just before a buyer makes a purchase. This repetition is particularly beneficial when the product is a new one. Point-of-purchase advertising does not have to be remembered. In cases where the retailer ties in any of his other promotion to that of the manufacturer, the manufacturer's message gets additional support. As for the typical retailer, he could not dream of buying or producing point-of-purchase materials as good as those he gets free from manufacturers; he simply could not match this free material in variety, in quality, or in quantity. Many small retailers in large markets feel that the other media are totally inappropriate because their large circulations (and high costs) represent too much waste. For these retailers, point of purchase is just about the sole advertising medium, and for manufacturers who supply superior items, these retailers can feel a great amount of good will.

Advertisers are interested in the selectivity to be had in each medium. Because there are literally scores of items and materials within the medium, few other media if, indeed, any one at all can match point of purchase in the wide range of selection available. In addition to nature of item, the advertiser enjoys geographic selectivity. He can select the sections of the country to include and those to exclude; he can select markets in the same manner; he can include and exclude even down to the sections of a city. One other form of selectivity relates to the retail store in which his point-of-purchase advertising will be placed. Here some manufacturers can choose the type or types of store (drug, food, clothing) and then the individual stores within each type selected. In certain instances, a manufacturer's decisions about selectivity add a cumulative feature to his advertising; this results when several or many retailers in the same market display the same point-of-purchase item at the same time.

For the temporary materials, a retailer is faced by a change interval problem. How long shall he leave a display in a window, on a counter, or on the floor? The typical retail merchant has many products in stock, he would like to expose many of them to his customers and prospective customers, he knows that his customers expect or even insist on frequent changes in displays. There is no single rule for the merchant to follow, no formula for him to use. He is justified, perhaps, in thinking of one week or two as the time period which he will lengthen or shorten as circumstances recommend. A large store with many windows gives the retailer the option of staggering the days when windows are changed, thus offering some new window displays to window shoppers just about every day. Manufacturers hope that at least some of their window display items impress some retailers so favorably that, when removed from the windows, the items will either be used as floor, wall, or counter displays or be scheduled for a second use at some future date.

A final important feature of the medium is the keen and increasing competition for the good display spots in stores. In grocery stores, for example, certain manufacturers benefit noticeably if their point-of-purchase materials are near the bread shelves, or the refrigerated fixtures, or the coffee, or near such staples as flour and sugar. Space close to the prescription counter in drug stores, and space close to the elevators and the wrapping desks in department stores are eagerly sought by manufacturers for their displays. The windows, of course, of practically all stores are preferred locations; the same holds for space near the checkout point and near the cash register. Because there is more floor traffic in the front of a store than in the back, spots near the front door or even in the front area of the store are better than average in effectiveness. The end of an aisle is a good location, as is space close to the manufacturer's products. Eye-level height is preferred to lower or higher positions. The desirable spots vary not only from manufacturer to manufac-

Media

turer and from store to store, they vary also from season to season and, to a degree, even from day to day.

USES OF THE MEDIUM

By Manufacturers

In general, a manufacturer wants his point-of-purchase advertising to affect and influence consumers exactly as does, he hopes, the manufacturer's other promotion. This medium permits the manufacturer to make his last bid for the shopper's preference and money before that shopper buys. This last bid usually stresses product display and identification; it reminds the shopper of the manufacturer's earlier advertising in other media; it undertakes to move the manufacturer's merchandise the "last three feet." By influencing the consumer to make a purchase, the medium helps make all the manufacturer's other advertising, all his personal selling, and all his other sales-promoting activities more productive.

Manufacturers hope to influence retailers, too. They use the medium to help in getting retailers to stock new products; this is particularly true when the manufac-

A food store display featuring complementary products. Note prominence of prices. (Courtesy: H. J. Heinz Company)

turer and his promotion fund are so small that any other local advertising, newspaper or broadcast, for example, would be too expensive. Good point-of-purchase materials help increase the size of retail orders, help introduce special offers, and help the retailer "trade up" some of his customers. Manufacturers who supply outstanding materials automatically make a strong bid for retail good will and support.

By Retailers

Retailers use the point-of-purchase medium to get the attention of prospects and then to urge those prospects to buy promptly, then and there. The nature of the medium makes it superior to other media in respect to power to induce an immediate purchase. Exterior items and window displays attempt to influence, even to control, sidewalk traffic by converting part of it into floor traffic. They are to keep passers-by from passing by. Interior displays other than window displays try for a sale. Some dispense the product from wall, shelf, counter, floor, or cabinet, usually the regular, standard product, occasionally a sample. Some ask the shopper to examine the product, others explain or demonstrate a product use or a buyer benefit. Some recommend an impulse purchase, some a reminder or replacement purchase, some a combination purchase of related products. Some serve as sources of product information and selling information for retail salespeople. Almost all attempt to convert "eyers" into buyers.

By Consumers

Point of purchase joins other consumer advertising in supplying helpful information to consumers, information about problems, solutions, and satisfactions. It can answer certain consumer questions; it can contribute to speedier shopping. We have already mentioned its service of a reminder nature.

ESSENTIALS OF GOOD DISPLAY

Many of the ideas and principles from the chapters on copy, layout, and typography are as valid and as applicable in the point-of-purchase medium as in such media as newspapers and magazines. The comments in this section, accordingly, are brief.

Point-of-purchase advertising must be built around and on a *big sales idea,* one whose attention power is great enough to arrest shoppers. One idea is preferable to several and, if appropriate, it should be the same one featured currently in the seller's advertising in other media. If it is the same, more customers will grasp the idea at a glance.

Copy should be simple, short, and direct, and this will not be possible to achieve if the item is assigned too big a job or too many jobs; an easy yet costly mistake is to attempt too much; a brief story told clearly and quickly is indicated. Type should be legible for a distance of ten to fifteen feet, and the most important copy should be placed high enough so that it will not be masked if products are massed about the base of the display.

Informal bin-type container which encourages examination by customers without fear of disrupting display. (Courtesy: Gibraltar Corrugated Paper Company, Inc.)

Should price be included, especially in window displays? In the vast majority of instances, they should be included. It seems correct to conclude that only a very few, extremely exclusive shops may be able to justify the absence of prices from their window displays. Perhaps it is true that prices are a secondary or even quite minor consideration for the patrons of such retail establishments. Indeed, one can claim that the inclusion of prices would reduce the prestige of such stores. For practically all stores, however, there is no consideration more prominent in a consumer's decision to buy or not to buy than is price of product. In a very real sense, one cannot contemplate seriously the purchase of a product unless one knows its price. A window shopper has two main choices after looking at a window display which does not include price. She can enter the store and inquire about price; or, she can walk on, wondering if the merchant omitted price because he fears that shoppers will consider the price high. The second course of action certainly seems the more probable choice. Without doubt, more merchants omit prices from their windows than can defend their omissions.

As for *design,* a point-of-purchase display should be bold and distinctive, enough of a stopper to reach out and grab shoppers at once. Shoppers should discover in a split second the type of product being promoted and the brand name.

Point-of-Purchase

The unity and simplicity, the balance and proportion desired are the same mentioned in earlier chapters. A focal point of interest and a limit on the number of elements included contribute to the performance of window displays.

Retailers have a definite preference for certain *features* in point-of-purchase materials. Motion and light are the two favorites. Sound has been incorporated into certain displays so as to increase their effectiveness. A talking trade character, for example, may deliver a sales message to shoppers continuously, or when turned on manually by a shopper, or when its electric eye or beam is actuated by the approach of a shopper. Some displays waft a fragrance out over the adjacent area; others, to complete the appeal to all senses, offer something for the shopper to taste. Three-dimensional items and items which show the product in use are well liked. Incidentally, retailers are enthusiastic about lighting, motion, and sound *only if they work*.

There are *merchandise displays* to be seen on store floors, on store counters, and in bins or baskets of various types. This is a most effective form of display because consumers like to see, feel, handle and examine products while considering their purchase. If consumers are to buy from displays, the most important quality to build into these displays of actual merchandise is informality. The design should not be so perfect that the consumer will be reluctant to remove or even move one or more units. The jumbled, mass display or at least one with a starter gap to imply that it has been bought from is greatly superior to the formal, balanced display. Price should be displayed on all sides — price for a multi-unit purchase if possible.

METHODS OF DISTRIBUTION

Point-of-purchase advertising is unlike any other medium in that it confronts the manufacturer with a distribution problem. The issue is: how shall the manufacturer get his window displays, for example, into the hands and into the windows of the greatest number of retailers. Several techniques are used by various manufacturers.

The most popular method of distribution is for the manufacturer to ship the material direct to the retailer for installation by the retailer himself. The assumption or at least the hope here is that the shipment reaches the retailer at the most favorable time, that it will be opened and examined at once, that the retailer will be so favorably impressed with the items that he will install them promptly, and then that the materials will be left on display for a satisfactory length of time. A variation on this technique which is appropriate for and used by some manufacturers is for field personnel of the manufacturer to deliver and install the items. In most cases these field men are regular salesmen; only a few manufacturers can afford to have staffs of display men out in the field. Asking a salesman to install point-of-purchase advertising is understandable from his company's point of view; there is control over the man, and this control can be used to obtain greater control over the medium. Some salesmen, particularly those on commission, resent being asked to do any non-selling jobs; this, too, is understandable.

This award-winning store display was originally an advertisement. (Courtesy: New England Confectionery Company)

A few companies ask their salesmen to deliver point-of-purchase materials, but they do not expect the men to do any installation. Some companies employ commercial installation firms to handle the physical distribution and installation of at least certain company materials, usually the more expensive, more complicated items. This method is costly, but it is easily possible for the large number of installations resulting to justify the cost. Sometimes a manufacturer will send the advertising material to his wholesalers and expect them to carry on from that point. This method does not assure the manufacturer of the largest number of installations. Finally, some materials are included in the shipping cases with the merchandise. This method, obviously, results in so much waste that it is feasible only for inexpensive display items. Two merits of this method are "free" distribution and timeliness — when he sees what may look like an impossible quantity of merchandise to sell, the retailer may be inclined to install some point-of-purchase advertising to help.

SELECTION OF POINT-OF-PURCHASE MATERIALS BY RETAILERS

At any given moment, a retailer has a fixed (and usually inadequate) amount of space, he has a large number of products in stock, and his sales, turnover, and profit figures could and should be better. In thinking of how to maximize dollar sales and dollar profits, he thinks of his square feet of selling and display space, of how to use this space so that each square foot makes its maximum contribution possible to net profit. All the while, there is considerable competition both for the more desirable merchandise spots and for the more desirable display spots in his store. There is also a continuous stream of point-of-purchase advertising materials coming in from various manufacturers — material free and in such abundance that the retailer discards a goodly amount of it unused. Against this background, how does the retailer decide which materials to use and which not to use?

The *merchandise* involved has much to do with the retailer's choices. For example, if the product is new or is being stocked for the first time, its point-of-purchase advertising has a better than average chance of being used. If the product is unusually profitable, its mark-up recommends the installation of its advertising materials. Somewhat strangely, fast-moving products *and* slow-moving products are naturals for support by point-of-purchase advertising. A product with a high impulse purchase potential is a favorite. Unless his stock of a product is adequate, a retailer would seldom be inclined to promote it with point-of-purchase advertising.

The *point-of-purchase material itself* has much to do with the retailer's choices. Size, for example, is a major matter for obvious reasons; an item can be too small for use as well as too large. Quality is a major consideration; the retailer must find the item attractive in appearance and effective in its influence on shoppers. Certain items will not be used unless they are sturdy in construction and dependable in operation. The physical shipment should be easy to open, and the item itself should be easy to assemble, to install, and to clean. Materials which do suggestion selling, which promote other and related products invite the retailer's favor. Materials which are functional in that they perform a service for the retailer are often welcome. Protective counter mats, change wells into which the cashier can put change, kick plates for doors, and such signs as "Please Pay When Served" are examples.

The *relations between the retailer and manufacturer* can be of influence. If the product is franchised, if the retailer has an exclusive agency, then he naturally will be more inclined to grant the requests of the particular manufacturer whose product and materials are involved. If the manufacturer's salesman is a favorite of the retailer, that salesman can get more cooperation and concessions from the retailer than can a salesman whose relations with the retailer are less cordial. If a retailer is impressed with a manufacturer's national advertising, or, better yet, if he rates the manufacturer as an outstanding source of merchandising aid, the retailer often uses that manufacturer's material rather than the material of someone else.

Retailers want point-of-purchase advertising that is *suitable* for their use. They want materials which fit into their plans and are appropriate in the light of their retail promotion programs. Particularly do retailers want promotion force to put behind seasonal products and into seasonal promotions. Retailers do not consider it suitable for a manufacturer to bundle together and mail in a single package the entire assortment of the manufacturer's point-of-purchase materials for the coming season.

PAYMENT TO AND BY MANUFACTURERS

Most dealings between retailers and manufacturers involving point-of-purchase advertising *do not* call for any payment of any sort. The items are placed in the retailer's hands at no cost for the items themselves or for their transportation. Two-thirds of the manufacturers supplying these aids to retailers make no charge whatever; one-third charge occasionally. Of the items charged for, few are completely self-liquidating; retailers are asked to pay only a part of the cost.

Media

Why do manufacturers sometimes make a charge? If the item in question is semi-permanent in nature, if it is a furniture-and-fixtures item as much as it is a point-of-purchase item, if it is an expensive item — then it is logical and proper for the retailer to defray at least part of the cost. Large store signs which overhang the sidewalk, clocks, display cabinets, and elaborate floor dispensers are examples. In the case of traveling displays, the modest charge sometimes made is a subtle bid for greater care in handling and greater retail support. The dollars paid by retailers to manufacturers reduce the cost of the materials and also reduce waste in the medium; if the retailer *pays* for it, he is more apt to *use* it. Sometimes the price is not quoted in terms of dollars but, instead, in terms of the retailer's order of merchandise. Here the manufacturer decides what minimum order a retailer must buy in order to get an outstanding point-of-purchase item — free; the item is a bonus that sweetens the deal. In designing these deals, the manufacturer must take care to offer a really excellent item and not to overload his retailers. Charging for materials demands more record-keeping by the manufacturer. Some retailers,

Store displays often are tied to a manufacturer's other promotional activities. They often repeat his advertising messages from other media. (Courtesy: H. J. Heinz Company)

furthermore, refuse to pay for materials which involve cost when, at the same time, they throw away free materials unused.

Some retailers are in a strategic position, having excellent spots desired by many manufacturers. Where this is the case, it is understandable if the retailer expects and gets some sort of reward or remuneration from occupants of those spots. Payment to the retailer may be in dollars, in free goods, or in services.

WASTE IN THE MEDIUM

As has been indicated, not all the window displays and counter displays a manufacturer buys wind up in windows and on counters. It is probable that the volume unused for various reasons runs about 20 to 25 per cent of the total produced. For certain items, the figure is well in excess of 50 per cent. This waste can run into many dollars when one remembers that a window display costing $4 is not at all uncommon.

How can a manufacturer determine the proportion of his advertising retailers use and the proportion which is a total waste? Unfortunately, he cannot, at least with any degree of precision. One possibility is for the manufacturer to ask his salesmen to report on the use of his point-of-purchase offerings; or, he may ask wholesalers' salesmen to make this check. He can telephone a small sample of his retailers and ask about the matter; or, he can send business reply cards to a sample, asking retailers to indicate their use of certain displays. Free goods are sometimes offered for a snapshot of an installed display, or contests can be run for snapshots of the best displays. If the manufacturer turns the installation job over to a commercial installation firm, he gets from that firm a report of the number of installations. Acutely needed is a more accurate, practicable method of measuring the used and the unused portions of material produced for retail use.

Waste Reduction Involving Point-of-Purchase Materials

The first attack on waste in the medium properly involves the materials the manufacturer buys. The pressing need is for greater concern with quality; until quality has been raised to at least the minimum level acceptable, there should be less concern with, even a reduction in, quantity. One method of raising the quality of much point-of-purchase advertising is to tie it in with the manufacturer's advertising in other media, a tie-in achieved by transferring certain elements from the other advertising (colors, illustration, or, certainly, the big sales idea) to point-of-purchase use. An outdoor poster, for example, or a car card can be reduced in size and made into a counter display card. Quality is raised by giving displays a retail look, by toning down the manufacturer's name and featuring the retailer's name. Retailers give a higher rating and better positions to displays which sell several products rather than just one; they like ensemble displays built about such themes as vacations, back-to-school promotions, gardening, spring house-cleaning, or picnics. A final comment is that the quality of some display material is, occasionally, too high; if the maximum installation period probable is one week, the display should be designed to last a week — not a month.

Media

Waste Reduction Involving Retailers

There are several steps a manufacturer can take toward waste reduction which involve his retailers. The first of these steps is clear; it is more consideration of the merchandising needs of retailers. Materials should be designed in the light of the problems, the physical facilities, and the preferences of the manufacturer's retail customers. For many a manufacturer this demands a classifying of his dealers, possibly by type of retail business, possibly by size of customer, possibly by section of country. There is need for greater recognition of the differences between drug stores and food stores, between a manufacturer's largest retail accounts and his smallest ones, between New York, North Carolina, and Nevada retailers. Whatever the classifications, each group should receive the items it needs, suitable and appropriate items which fit into the merchandising plans of each store in the group. And, no store should be sent more material than it can use.

Some manufacturers insist that no point-of-purchase advertising be sent to a retailer unless the retailer has made a specific request for it. They are convinced that this is a worthwhile step in the reduction of unused materials. These manufacturers inform the retailer about their offerings mainly through their salesmen, through direct mail, and through advertisements in trade papers; information includes what is available, suggestions about use of the items, specifications such as amount of space the item requires, how the retailer can place an order, and, of course, why he should get and use the materials. Ease of ordering is essential.

The more the retailer knows about specific aids, the greater is the chance of his using them. He likes to learn from copy on the outside of the shipping container or package just what is inside — the nature of the item, its size, what it looks like when installed, the recommended display dates, and instructions for installation.

Waste Reduction by Manufacturers

Some of the manufacturer's responsibilities for reducing waste in his handling of his point-of-purchase advertising program are simple. He must, for instance, avoid ordering quantities which are too large. He must work for a more selective placement of his materials, seeking quality here just as in the materials themselves. He must notify retailers well in advance about the availability and the shipment of materials, particularly the more expensive, more elaborate materials. This notification should go to the proper person, and then the shipment itself should reach that person in plenty of time.

Some waste will be eliminated if the advertiser invites and then analyzes the attitudes, the preferences, and the advice of certain groups. The firms manufacturing the materials which constitute the medium have experience which makes their opinions and recommendations worthwhile. These companies not only have creative staffs which can make sound suggestions, they also have a keen and obvious interest in the use of more and more effective point-of-purchase advertising. It is only natural that advertisers lean heavily on the manufacturers of displays, for example, in reaching decisions about the quality of displays to use and the prices to pay for them. The advertiser's middlemen, particularly his retailers, are a group whose advice is helpful. After all, the retailer is the one who approves and installs an item or turns thumbs down on it. A third group from whom the advertiser can get valuable information consists of his own company's salesforce.

A manufacturer is obligated to educate and train his salesmen as well as to interrogate them. He benefits from teaching them about the desirability of, indeed, the necessity for, strong support at the point of purchase. Many salesmen resent being asked by their companies to do any job which the salesmen may think of as being non-selling in character. These salesmen need to realize that whatever they do in the way of selling *for* the retailer helps them greatly in selling *to* the retailer, and the point-of-purchase advertising of their companies can do a selling job for retailers. If the point-of-purchase program is explained and sold to salesmen, item by item and feature by feature, then salesmen can compete more successfully for the preferred retail locations because they can justify more convincingly their requests for these locations. Some salesmen are expected to be handy with foil, paper, tape, scissors, hammer, and tacks. The salesman's supervisor must check to see that he discharges his responsibilities, whatever they be, in respect to his company's point-of-purchase advertising.

Pre-testing, one more approach to the reduction of waste, can be employed to get an idea of the stopping power, the selling power, and the over-all suitability of proposed advertising pieces. A manufacturer can set up a panel of retailers in test markets and work with them in pre-testing various items. If the manufacturer's salesman knows that an item has been actually installed and tested in a store under normal conditions and found effective, he can recommend it convincingly to retailers because he has proof of its power to increase traffic, sales, and profit. If the retailer is asked to pay $50 to $100 for some item such as a floor merchandiser, he will request proof of performance — and he is entitled to it.

MANAGEMENT OF THE MEDIUM

Because of its nature, point-of-purchase advertising must be classified as a sales promotion activity rather than as advertising. In Chapter 20 where coordination is discussed, the position is taken that the sales promotion manager rather than the advertising manager is responsible for this medium. Yet the truth is that many an advertising manager is in charge of his company's point-of-purchase advertising and, in other companies, the sales manager is in charge of the medium. The explanation is simple: many, *many* companies do not have a separate sales promotion department and manager, and quite a few companies do not have advertising departments. Because of these facts of company organization, it is not surprising that the advertising manager is the dominant executive in the planning, selecting, and buying of point-of-purchase materials — for *all* sizes of companies. The two most common locations for the dollars which pay for point-of-purchase are within the sales promotion budget and within the advertising budget. The larger the company, the more probable is the assignment of its point-of-purchase advertising to a sales promotion manager. By contrast, in the smaller companies, the role and significance of this medium are greater relative to the other media used.

Media

Productive use of the medium calls for a program, well planned in advance, rather than for just some displays. Management needs to give adequate thought to the group or groups of retailers to whom the company will offer aids, the specific items comprising the line of offerings, how many displays a year shall be ordered and in what quantities, the best schedule of the use of the aids, and from whom they should be bought. A basic consideration of design is the degree of versatility desirable in the items. Sometimes an item should be so flexible and multi-purpose that *any* retailer can use it. In other instances, the item should be highly tailored for one specific type of store.

Timing needs to be both adequate and synchronized. Planning should take place, in certain situations, about six months before the scheduled installation date, designing four or five months in advance, production should lead by two or three months, and physical distribution should get the advertising into dealers' hands one month before use. One large food chain, incidentally, plans its in-store displays four to six months in advance; and, some retailers want to know of any big project three months in advance. As for synchronization, company salesmen and retailers need to know early what consumer advertising the company will be running in other media. This information must be supplied in detail. The sales department must see that wholesalers and retailers are adequately stocked with merchandise prior to any promotion. Time must be budgeted during which the point-of-purchase program will be explained and sold to salesmen and dealers.

The involvement of company salesmen demands skillful management. Most displays which are installed for rather than by retailers are installed by manufacturers' salesmen. No company employee has so much influence on what retailers do in this medium as does the salesman. The outstanding salesman is enthusiastic about his program. He uses point-of-purchase to sell his company and his merchandise to retailers. He gets good shelf position and as many facings as he can for that merchandise so as to increase the performance of his point-of-purchase materials. He persuades the retailer to integrate his, the retailer's, selling and promotion efforts with the manufacturer's promotion. He gets the retailer to use the material, to use it properly, and to leave it up as long as possible. The salesman carefully avoids any neglect of the medium or any belittling of it to dealers; he does not plaster a store with material without permission. Obviously, the sales manager, the sales promotion manager, and the advertising manager must work in close cooperation to maximize the effectiveness of the medium.

More and more, manufacturers are calling on their advertising agencies to help plan, design, and even buy certain point-of-purchase items. More and more advertising agencies are becoming active in this form of advertising. Agencies have discovered that they cannot ignore the medium nor remain indifferent to it. Point-of-purchase can easily influence the getting of clients, the holding of clients, and the performance of clients' advertising in other media.

Questions and Problems

1. What inducements might a manufacturer offer a retailer to get P-O-P support from that retailer?
2. Retail food stores dispose of much P-O-P material without ever using it. Suggest features that may be present in the P-O-P items they *do* use.
3. What factors influence the number of items a retailer will include in a window display?
4. What are some disadvantages of animated displays?
5. What differences do you see between window displays and outdoor posters?
6. List some major problems a manufacturer confronts when he begins to use P-O-P advertising.
7. What are some characteristics of a good window display?
8. What are some common objectives of P-O-P advertising?
9. How can a manufacturer try to determine how much of his P-O-P material is used?
10. General Mills, Gillette, Jantzen, and 3M's are typical of a group of manufacturers with a common P-O-P problem. Each sells its products through many retailers. Each buys P-O-P materials for its retailers. Some of these materials can be thought of as "A" in quality, some as "B." The "A" materials are for the manufacturer's better retailers, the "B" materials are for the manufacturer's average retailers. How should one of these manufacturers go about separating his better retailers from his average retailers?

Chapter 17

Direct Mail

In the preceding chapter we took up an advertising medium which was quite different in many respects from the first six media studied. Direct mail now joins point-of-purchase as another medium with basic differences from the first six, as another medium which many companies assign to the sales promotion manager rather than to the advertising manager. The sales promotion manager uses all sorts of direct advertising in promoting sales to and through wholesalers and retailers. He knows more about direct advertising than any other company official because of the great volume of direct-mail advertising addressed to or to be used by his company's middlemen. Prerequisite to a study of direct-mail advertising is a clear understanding of just what *direct advertising, mail-order selling,* and *direct-mail advertising* are.

DIRECT ADVERTISING

Direct advertising consists of written, printed, or processed advertising messages delivered directly to buyers selected by the advertisers. The advertising goes direct from the seller to the buyer without making use of any media such as newspapers or television. Some direct advertising goes by mail. Of the rest, some is delivered by salesmen of the manufacturer or the retailer; some is on retail counters available to customers, and some is enclosed in the packages or bundles of those customers; some is placed in or on automobiles, given to passersby on the sidewalk, or distributed door to door.

MAIL-ORDER SELLING

Mail-order selling is not an advertising medium but, instead, is a method of marketing products and services. The seller undertakes to do the entire selling job *by mail;* he makes use of no middlemen, no salesmen, no personal selling. There are some mail-order sellers who use only direct-mail advertising, and there are some who use other media, alone or in combination with direct-mail advertising.

Direct Mail

DIRECT-MAIL ADVERTISING

That volume of direct advertising sent by mail is referred to as direct-mail advertising; the advertising medium is a *mail* medium and is *direct*. Available since the establishment of the postal service in 1775, direct-mail advertising is the most used, the most important form of direct advertising. Direct-mail advertising items often are cards, booklets, or folders, for example. Reference to direct-mail advertising is usually to materials designed solely by or for the advertiser, produced in some quantity, and distributed directly by mail to a group of individuals chosen by the advertiser. A typical mailing can be thought of as consisting of an outside envelope, a letter, a folder, a reply form, and a postage-paid return envelope. Although it can do a complete advertising job, direct-mail advertising in the vast majority of instances is used along with other media; its primary purpose is to support the efforts of salesmen so as to help them sell more.

Our interest is in direct-mail advertising, not in the broader area of direct advertising nor in the specialized operation of mail-order selling. All types and levels of business firms use direct-mail advertising; just about all advertisers, regardless of size of advertising fund, use it.

Postal classes are a fundamental consideration in direct-mail advertising. First class is for matter wholly or partly handwritten, for typewritten material, and for carbon copies of these, sealed or unsealed. First class mail enjoys prestige, is speedy, gets good attention because personal and business letters go that way, may get the mailing past an executive's secretary, and is returned or forwarded at no extra charge. Its negative aspect is that it is expensive.

Second class postage is for newspapers and magazines, and fourth class consists of parcel post. Third class is for items not first class or second class which weigh eight ounces or less. The advertiser's almost only choice, then, is between third class and first class. Comparing these, one finds that third class mail is slower, less impressive, unsealed so that it can be inspected — and less expensive. Third class is usually put in post office boxes after the first class mail, and its volume is lighter. One attempt is made to deliver third class mail; if it fails, the mailing is destroyed unless return postage has been guaranteed.

FORMS OF DIRECT-MAIL ADVERTISING

Mailing Cards

The most popular card is the government's postal card which can be had in single or double form. If the advertiser does not like the single card, he can design and use his own private mailing card, or post card. If the advertiser does not care for the double card, he can produce his own business reply card, enclose it in his mailing, and then pay the postage when the reply card is returned. Cards are used to carry brief messages, to acknowledge orders, to announce or "lead" the next mailing (a more elaborate, expensive one), to tease the addressee, to remind him or her, to make an offer, to answer an inquiry, and to help bring a mailing list up-to-date. Cards can be put into the mails quickly and at low cost. They are

Media

convenient to handle and read. Their space is limited, their message is not confidential, and their physical appearance is not impressive.

Letters

While the letter is often sent out in an envelope by itself, a letter accompanied by one or more additional items is probably the most widely used type of mailing. Indeed, the letter contributes much to the success of such items as catalogs and booklets because the letter is the most important element in its mailing. Letters can be sent first class and made to look like personal correspondence, or they can go third class, form letters which look like form letters.

Letters have many advantages. They are close to personal selling, being the most personal form of direct-mail advertising. They are the most popular form found in this medium, and their adaptability explains why they are used for more purposes than any other form. Letters are quite effective in getting immediate action; they are speedy and economical for getting replies. Few mail-order sellers could continue to operate if denied the use of letters.

Outside Envelopes

The outside or mailing envelope in which the advertiser sends his material is usually a standard envelope addressed on the front. Window envelopes cost more, but relieve the advertiser of the addressing job. The outside envelope may bid for

When top and bottom are folded, this becomes a mailing. Space for the address is on the reverse side. (Courtesy: The Prudential Insurance Company of America)

attention in several ways. It can be colored; illustrations and copy, perhaps "teaser" in nature, can be put on it; sometimes seals or stickers are attached. Whatever identification the sender chooses to display should go in the upper left corner, not on the back. Typed addresses are preferred to the use of handwriting, plates, or addressed labels.

Circulars and Leaflets

Of direct-mail advertising forms, circulars and leaflets are the least expensive per unit and, next to outdoor posters, they are the oldest type of advertising. These small sheets, printed on one side or both, can feature color and illustrations. They may be mailed alone, or they may accompany letters, invoices, or statements. Popular with mail-order sellers, circulars and leaflets can expand the information contained in a letter, amplifying the details buyers need. They are particularly helpful in listing product specifications, in emphasizing a product's features, and in featuring other products of the advertiser. Circulars and leaflets are versatile; they are inexpensive to produce and to mail, traveling free in many instances. One drawback is that they reduce the personal quality of any letter they accompany.

Folders

The folder is an adult leaflet or a booklet without binding. It is less personal than a letter but more personal than a booklet. It can be folded several times in several ways; one panel or surface can be a reply card already addressed. Much variety is possible in size, color, and shape. Next in usage to letters, folders are appropriate in telling an impersonal sales story. They can be mailed alone or not, mailed in an envelope or not, used singly or in a series. They can be designed so that they ask to be read and acted on at once, or they can aim to build good will. Folders are both versatile and inexpensive.

Booklets

Booklets run more than four pages in length. They are usually mailed in envelopes, often in response to requests prompted by the offer of the booklet in other media. They are designed for thorough reading and study, often with the hope that buyers will keep them and refer to them over a period of time. Where the folder is inadequate, where much copy and many illustrations are needed, where the subject requires much space and an extremely clear presentation, the booklet is indicated. Booklets contain helpful reference information which answers buyers' questions; they tell about products and their features; they tell the stories behind products. The designer of a booklet has a wide range of choice — about length, covers, colors, cost, and illustrations.

The more elite booklets are called *brochures*. They are glamorous and impressive, even elaborate and pretentious. Brochures offer the advertiser unlimited opportunities to create a prestige mailing item.

Self-mailers

The self-mailer is not a distinctive form of direct-mail advertising in the same sense as is a card or a booklet. Self-mailers, instead, are any items which do not

HOW MUCH IS IT COSTING YOU TO BE 64% WRONG?

A recent study has shown that 64% of the calls made by industrial salesmen were made *on the wrong man*. The sales time waste factor in your business may be higher, or lower, than this. Whatever it is, consider what professionally planned direct mail could do to improve sales performance and reduce selling costs.

When sales leads are developed by direct mail, using pre-qualified lists, you can see how much better the chances are of calling on the *right* man. Every response received is a self-selected prospect — a person with current active interest.

If you have a waste factor in the calls your salesmen are making, look to us for a time and profit conservation program. We've been a working partner with sales management for over 42 years.

DICKIE-RAYMOND
SALES PROMOTION COUNSEL – DIRECT MAIL ADVERTISING
NEW YORK: 225 PARK AVENUE – MU 6-2280
BOSTON: D-R BUILDING, COLUMBIA PARK, BOSTON 1 – AV 8-1234

PROVE IT!

Is your management asking for more positive proof of results from advertising? Most are.

That's one beauty of promotion and advertising through direct mail. You can measure it in terms of response. In sales leads. In conversion of leads into sales. In increased business traceable to leads from sales promotion. Or in readership. Used as an adjunct to general media, direct mail makes *all* your advertising work better.

For top results you need experienced professional counsel like Dickie-Raymond. None better. Ask for booklet "Meet Dickie-Raymond" that describes this service.

DICKIE-RAYMOND
SALES PROMOTION COUNSEL – DIRECT MAIL ADVERTISING
NEW YORK: 225 PARK AVENUE – MU 6-2280
BOSTON: DR BUILDING, COLUMBIA PARK, BOSTON 1 – AV 8-1234

These ads promote the services of an advertising agency which specializes in direct mail. (Courtesy: Dickie-Raymond)

require outside mailing envelopes. A folded *card,* a folded *circular,* or a *folder* can have its fold secured by a pasted tab or by a stamp. Because self-mailers do not use envelopes, they can be of any size the advertiser prefers. Because they go third class, they are economical. Although satisfactory for certain types of announcements and for other non-prestige communications, self-mailers have a narrow range of acceptability. To executives, they imply a long list, an impersonal story, an emphasis on economy, and low quality.

Broadsides

A broadside is a giant circular — an enlarged folder which can be mailed in an envelope but usually is sent as a self-mailer, saving the costs of envelope, insertion, and sealing. The address goes directly on the self-mailer or on a label which is then pasted on. There is no limit to the size of broadsides; while most are not over 17 by 22 inches, advertisers use some 19 by 25 inches or even 25 by 28 inches. Named for their stopping power, broadsides make such a forceful impression and have such a powerful impact that they have been referred to as "spectaculars in print." Broadsides are excellent attention getters. They are appropriate to open or to end a series of mailings. Huge illustrations, bold headlines, a minimum of copy, and large type all make for quick and easy reading of a long pictorialized story. Seldom sent to consumers, most broadsides are aimed at wholesalers and retailers; some are designed to be displayed in retail stores.

Catalogues

One way to place information about products and prices into buyers' hands is through the use of catalogues. Because they are expensive, catalogues are expected to enjoy long lives. The mailing of the more costly ones may be announced in advance, perhaps with a mailing card. Most catalogues benefit greatly from an accompanying letter which introduces and explains them. Business buyers prefer catalogues of a size which files conveniently; if the catalogue is long, business buyers hope it will contain an index so that information can be located easily and quickly.

House Organs

Some advertisers publish a company magazine more-or-less regularly either for customers and prospective ones or for retailers and wholesalers. These external house organs are sent at no cost to the addressee. They carry no advertising except the advertiser's. Editors of house organs feature articles, stories, jokes, cartoons, names, and pictures; editors try to entertain as well as to influence. Expensive, house organs are good for building good will and prestige.

Gifts

Gifts such as pencils, memo books, blotters, calendars, and ash trays are often sent by mail. Because the intent is to obligate the buyer so that he will buy, these gifts need to be both attractive and useful.

FEATURES OF THE MEDIUM

Advantages

For the first and only time, we see an advertising medium *controlled exclusively by the advertiser.* So long as he observes post-office regulations, the advertiser can do whatever he pleases. Instead of using a "common carrier" type of medium, the advertiser creates his own. This control embraces the circulation as well as the advertising. Instead of accepting and communicating with a magazine's readers, for example, a fixed group which he cannot change, the seller using direct-mail advertising chooses the group to make up his circulation.

Mailings are addressed to the buyer usually *by his own name* and are *delivered directly* to him. This permits mailing pieces to get into the best places, into the hands of most-difficult-to-see individuals. Business executives (many, *many* of whom open all their own mail) can be reached at their offices or at their homes. It is quite probable that consumers receive less direct-mail advertising and give it better reading than is popularly supposed.

There are *few distractions* competing for the reader's attention at the moment he opens his mail. Because the advertisement and the medium are the same, there is no other element bidding for notice. There is no competition with other advertisements nor rivalry with editorial matter.

Direct-mail advertising is the most *flexible, adjustable,* and *adaptable* of all media. The seller can send out one mailing or mail over a period of years. We have already seen that many forms offer variety in color, design, size, and style; novelty can be had by shaping the item like a bottle, a safe, or a barrel and by using cut-outs, pop-ups, odd folds, and swatches. Cost per mailing can range upward from a postal card to as high as the advertiser cares to go; literally, no advertising fund is too small for some direct-mail advertising. The advertiser can cover part of a city — or the entire country. He can mail to ten persons — or to tens of thousands, he can send each addressee one mailing or many, and he can schedule the many according to whatever frequency seems best. Independent of publication dates, he can put out a rush mailing in a matter of hours if necessary. Experimentation in the medium is easy because the advertiser can start, change, or stop quickly.

Selectivity is an outstanding characteristic of this medium. Because the advertiser hand-picks his circulation, he can hold waste circulation down to a minimum, and this, of course, means economy. Specific coverage of definite markets poses no difficulty whether the advertiser wants to reach one hundred millionaires or one hundred advertising instructors.

Direct-mail advertising is *personal* advertising. It is the closest substitute for personal selling in that it can be tailored and individualized. In no other medium can the advertiser address his buyers by name; in no other medium can the advertising message be private, personal, and confidential.

Advertisers can *measure the performance* of direct-mail advertising satisfactorily. Results can be checked by measuring the response to a mailing, and this can be done because the identity of the addressee is known.

Limitations

Essentially a class medium, direct-mail advertising has a *high cost per unit of circulation*. This demands that its market be delineated sharply and recommends it more strongly for communicating with middlemen, professional groups, and purchasing agents than with consumers. Each manufacturer must determine for himself, usually by trial and error, whether or not he can send direct-mail advertising profitably to individual consumers. An automobile manufacturer may well discover, for instance, that the medium is excellent for recommending authorized dealer service to motorists owning three- or four-year-old automobiles of his make.

Direct-mail advertising which has not been requested suffers to some extent from *low reader interest*. Such mailings have an unfavorable reputation and are sometimes referred to as "junk" mail. The result is that some pieces never get to the addressee, that those which do reach him or her are easily ignored, that they must make a favorable impression literally in a matter of seconds, and that much is thrown away immediately.

The absence of editorial accompaniment was listed as an advantage in that such material cannot distract the reader if it is not present. The other side of this coin is a limitation — the advertisement *gets no assistance* from editorial material. This confronts the designer of direct-mail advertising with a great challenge, making him wistful on occasions, no doubt, for a job in television.

USES OF DIRECT-MAIL ADVERTISING

Manufacturers use direct mail to transmit non-advertising messages, too. Direct mail is appropriate, for example, to acknowledge payments, to handle complaints,

Macy's sent this 8-page (standard newspaper size) mailing to its customers. (Courtesy: Macy's)

Macy's Private Sale of FASCINATING HOUSEWARES

at all 6 Macy's Stores 6 days...
JANUARY 27 THROUGH FEBRUARY 1

★ Macy's 6% cash policy on pricing its goods: We endeavor, with reasonable exceptions which include goods price-controlled by the manufacturer, to save our customers at least 6% for cash

and to improve employee morale. These activities are desirable, of course, but they are not advertising. Letters to stimulate salesmen can be sent to company salesmen, to distributors' salesmen, and even to some retailers' salesmen but, once again, these are not advertising communications. If we limit our thinking to *direct-mail advertising,* we see that it is used (a) to sell products and (b) to help promote sales by improving the salesman's performance and by increasing his productivity.

To Sell Products

Some direct-mail advertising is asked to sell goods and services without the help of any other marketing force. We have seen that mail-order selling does just this. Some sellers use direct-mail advertising to reach buyers and areas not covered by their salesmen. Some sellers use this type of advertising to get customers to send in orders in between salesmen's calls. The inclusion in the mailing of order blanks and business reply envelopes or business reply order cards makes buying easier. Students, incidentally, often use direct-mail advertising to sell themselves to future employers.

Media

To Promote Sales

The greater volume of direct-mail advertising is sales promotional in character, recommending that the activity be assigned to the sales promotion department rather than to the advertising department. This direct-mail advertising makes personal selling more effective. The advertising is used to get leads for salesmen to follow up, and it paves the way for those contacts; direct-mail advertising, the "handshake ahead of the meeting," can make salesmen's calls much more effective. New salesmen and new products can be introduced to buyers in this manner, informing and pre-selling those buyers to the end that interviews will be more numerous, shorter, and more successful. Mailings can be used to follow up a salesman's calls, to welcome new customers and first orders, and to keep in touch with buyers between calls. Mailings are suitable for creating, building, and holding good will. They help both to secure new customers and to reactivate dormant accounts.

The use of direct-mail advertising to acquaint wholesalers and, especially, retailers with the company promotion program is well known. Its use in advertising to the public is less well known but is quite provocative. The basic question is this: which sellers can use this medium profitably in advertising to the ultimate consumer? In other words, for which sellers can the plus features of the medium counterbalance the high unit cost? The amount of patronage which the seller has the opportunity of attracting is, no doubt, the major factor involved. For example, the price of an automobile recommends that product for consideration. Or, motorists' purchases of service station products might be large enough to justify mailings to motorists by the petroleum marketers. Further experimentation seems indicated in order to maximize the use of the medium for profitable manufacturer-to-consumer advertising.

Because direct-mail advertising can be controlled so closely, it is often used as a research technique to identify the most effective advertising and sales promotional activities and elements. The medium is used to test ideas and markets, to discover which benefit of several has the greatest appeal, to determine what product should be offered as a premium. It can be used to collect names for a mailing list and then it can be used to help keep that list current.

CIRCULATION — THE MAILING LIST

The list of names to which the advertiser sends his mailings bears the major responsibility for the success of the advertising. Indeed, in the entire operation of planning and preparing direct-mail advertising, the most important single consideration is the mailing list. The best appeal, the best offer, the best mailing, the best timing — these are wasted and cannot be profitable if mailings are sent to the wrong persons.

The ideal list is a *complete* roster or inventory of the individuals whom the advertiser wants to influence; in most instances those individuals are persons who should and can buy the item being advertised. Completeness calls for the inclusion of each name just once; there should be no more duplication of a name than omission of it. The second requirement of the ideal list is that it be *accurate*. To be accurate, the list must be current or up-to-date. Initials must be right, names must be spelled correctly, and any job titles of addressees must be accurate. The third feature of the ideal list is that it be *subdivided* in whatever manner is indicated. Not all lists need to be broken down into groups or classifications, but most lists do if the advertiser is to benefit to the maximum degree possible from the selectivity of his most selective medium. One possible breakdown separates addressees into prospects, inactive customers, and active customers; this last group can be subdivided by amount of purchases if that is worthwhile. Other bases for subdivisions are credit rating, sex, urban versus rural, geographical region or state, line of business, and, of course, the alphabet.

Sources of Lists

One of the best lists for most advertisers is their *customer* list — cash customers and credit customers, former customers and present customers. Few customers buy all they could from any one seller, and customers of seller A are prospects of seller B.

Groups which can be reached without the advertiser's having to know the names of the addressees include *boxholders* on rural free delivery routes, *occupants* of specific street addresses where there is city delivery, and *post-office box holders*.

Mailing lists can be compiled from individual *responses* to the seller's advertising. Names on coupons come to mind immediately as an example of this. Both publication media, newspapers and magazines, and both broadcast media, television and radio, are used to invite responses.

A simple way to get a mailing list is through *purchase* of the list itself or of its use. In both instances, cost varies with the quality of the list; quality can be a matter of selectivity, of difficulty in compiling the list, of correctness, of completeness, or of basic quality of the names. Purchase is more common for lists of business firms than for lists of consumers. Brokers act as rental agents for list owners; the rental cost averages $20 to $25 per 1,000 names with the broker getting a 20 per cent commission. Magazine publishers, for example, might go through list brokers and rent their circulation lists to book clubs for direct-mail advertising use. Exchanging names with a non-competitor is one version of purchasing a list.

Public records are a source of mailing lists. Government employees often compile lists from records relating to taxes, building permits, or automobile licenses.

Many lists come from *directories,* among those commonly used being city, telephone, trade, credit rating, and college directories. Professional rosters and membership lists are similar as sources of names.

A manufacturer's *salesmen* and his *dealers* are valuable sources of names which should be added to the manufacturer's lists. Retail dealers can identify the individual consumers in their respective communities to whom the manufacturer should send mailings.

Miscellaneous sources include convention registrations, news items in newspapers (engagements, incorporations, etc.), names clipped by clipping bureaus, contest entries, and, for retailers, delivery records, C.O.D. sales, and alteration tickets.

Media

Keeping Lists Accurate

Mailing lists get out-of-date for various reasons. Names themselves change — a girl marries, two firms merge, the holder of a specific position changes. Both individuals and companies change their addresses; both die and disappear. The circumstances, needs, or status of an individual can change in such a direction as to remove that individual from the advertiser's prospect group. A normal annual change in mailing lists of 15 to 20 per cent can soar well above the 50 per cent mark in wartime.

What can the advertiser do to correct for these changes? Addressees can be asked to notify the advertiser promptly of change in address. A double postal card or a double mailing card can be sent to each addressee asking (a) about the correctness of the address and (b) whether the addressee wants to continue getting the advertiser's mailings. Some companies ask their salesmen to help keep lists current and correct; many companies can prove to their salesmen that accurate mailing lists benefit salesmen enough to be worth some attention and care from the sales force. Occasionally, a company will send each salesman a copy of the mailing list for his territory, claiming that the list is complete and current, thus challenging the salesman to spot any corrections or any dropping and adding needed. A few companies assign to some office worker the responsibility for scanning business papers to spot changes in companies, addresses, and personnel.

The post office can contribute to the accuracy of mailing lists. If there is a return address on the mailing, and there certainly should be, undeliverable first class mail will be returned to the sender. If return postage is guaranteed, any mailing which cannot be delivered will be returned. The postal authorities can be authorized to forward the mailing, or to return the mailing, or to forward the mailing and then report back to the advertiser. Each local post office has a list-checking service which will do just that at reasonable cost for a list of local addresses.

The problem of duplication is essentially one of accuracy. Users of large quantities of direct-mail advertising frequently rent lists from a variety of owners. On these rented lists there will be some names which are already on the advertiser's *customer* list; there is duplication.

Cross-checking to avoid duplication effects a saving on the number of mailings sent. Company prestige and customer respect are protected; by avoiding the appearance of carelessness, waste, and ignorance, the advertiser also avoids unfavorable reaction by his customers. Companies which do not cross-check rented lists recognize these benefits, but they feel that the process of cross-checking is far too costly to justify it. So, many of this group of advertisers enclose a small printed statement of apology to customers in all such mailings rather than cross-check for duplication.

SUGGESTIONS ABOUT LETTERS

Because the most important form of direct-mail advertising is the *letter,* and because many of the letters we write could be improved, a few comments about letters and letter writing seem justified. The writing of an advertising letter is the writing of advertising copy, and all that was said in Chapters 7 and 9 about benefits and copywriting applies here. Indeed, the principles of layout and typography in Chapters 8 and 10 also are generally sound in designing advertising letters. So, the following thoughts are intended to be in addition to the ideas expressed in the earlier chapters rather than a repetition of them.

The Salutation

The opening of the letter can be a personalized *fill-in* (Mr. Smith's name and address or at least "Dear Mr. Smith"), a *headline* ("Here is good news for motorists"), or an impersonal salutation ("Dear Friend"). When the personalized fill-in is used in processed letters, there is a problem in matching the blackness of the fill-in with the blackness of the body of the letter. This attempt to match is made for reasons of appearance, not with any intent of fooling the addressee into thinking he was sent an individually typed letter. One way to solve the problem of matching is to avoid it — to type the fill-in in another color. Letters with filled-in salutation should be dated, do cost more, and look more personal. Some letter writers, incidentally, think that addressing a stranger as "Dear" is both unrealistic and even nonsensical.

A headline can be a most effective start for a letter just as for an advertisement for newspapers or magazines. Benefits or news can be built into a headline of two or three lines of three or four words each. The longer the headline is, the less general and more specific it can be. Fill-ins and pressure to include a date are both avoided by the use of headlines *or* impersonal salutations.

The Body

The body of the letter should emphasize just one basic idea, and the idea needs quick introduction. The copy can come to the point immediately in the headline if one is used or, if the salutation is filled in, the basic idea can be presented in the first sentence or two. Prompt revelation of the advertiser's message permits the reader to make a speedy yet intelligent decision about whether or not to read the letter. Courtesy and good will can show in the first few words of the letter. Often these words make a definite promise of benefit; often they are phrased as a question which the reader must answer in the affirmative.

Letters vary widely in length. Magazine publishers have been quite successful with letters running twenty-five or thirty words in length; they have also done very well with four- and five-page letters. Because mail-order sellers must include full descriptions of what they are selling *and* much written salesmanship, their letters average longer than do sales promotional letters. If much proof is necessary, longer letters result. Regardless of length of letter, short paragraphs are preferred because they make the letter more attractive physically and easier to read. The first line of each can be indented, or be overhung, or set flush with the other lines. Key paragraphs can be set in shorter lines and centered. For long letters, skillfully integrated subheads get more thorough readership by more readers. Subheads, display lines, and entire paragraphs can be printed in a second color for emphasis.

Media

White space is used for the same purposes in letters as in newspaper and magazine advertisements.

Trite phrases and stereotyped expressions impair seriously the effectiveness of letters. In no instances should these or similar phrases be used:

at your earliest convenience	in reply to your favor
attached hereto	permit me to state
enclosed herewith	please be advised
enclosed please find	we beg to remain
hand you herewith	thanking you in advance

Instead of the stiff, cold impression given by such phrases, the advertiser wants his letter to strike the reader as warm and human, sincere and natural. Otherwise, the advertiser is using the most personalized of advertising media but not sending a personalized, conversational communication. Letters need more than just the *resemblance* to personal correspondence — they also need its *friendliness* and *informality*.

The Closing

The closing section of the letter usually summarizes the advertiser's message and contains a strong urge to action; few letters can afford to aim for nothing more concrete than prestige or good will. An entire paragraph may be used to ask for reader reaction, and it may include such strong inciters as special offers or time limits on the offer. A signature, even if facsimile, increases the effectiveness of the letter; often the signature should be that of a high executive in the company, perhaps the president.

Formula — Or Not?

Our copy chapter indicated that formulas cannot create profitable advertising copy; that same truth applies to direct-mail advertising letters, too. Here, as with other types of copy, formulas are restrictive, they cramp the style of the outstanding copy writer, and they tend to feature the mechanical approach to copywriting over the creative approach. A formula which is successful for A does not necessarily work for B, nor need it work again for A if used for some different purpose or, indeed, for the same purpose. If, however, some sort of a pattern is desired, here is one possibility for mail-order selling:

1. Know exactly what the writer wants the letter to accomplish. Then, tap a center of interest and establish a point of contact with the reader by offering an important benefit or the answer to a reader problem in the headline or lead paragraph.

2. Enlarge upon the benefit or solution, describing and explaining its important features and its essential details. Give the reader all the information he needs, building into this fund of facts answers to the more common objections which arise in readers' minds. Be specific in telling the reader what the product will do *for him,* what *he* will get when he makes the purchase.

Direct Mail

3. Include a generous amount of proof for the claims and promises made in step 2. Money-back guarantees, testimonials, endorsements, and case histories are particularly convincing in advertising letters.

4. Be forceful and obvious in asking the reader to do what you want him to do. Rephrase the strongest benefit so as to show (a) what satisfactions will result from a purchase *and* (b) what inaction and delay will cost.

5. Make action by the reader easy. Tell him exactly and clearly what to do and how to do it. If possible, avoid confronting the reader with several choices, even going so far as to recommend the quantity to buy.

Letterheads, Gadgets, and Postscripts

Letterheads deserve more attention than they get. Advertisers need more than one, and they need to revise and modernize them occasionally. Quality of paper joins quality of printing as a matter of significance. Essential information (who, what, where), attention value, eye appeal, and good design are essentials. Color is a possibility. Some advertising communications can be sent on sheets headed "Memo" or "Special Bulletin." When a letter gets no response, some advertisers send, as a follow-up, a carbon — made at the time of the original typing just for this possible need; across the top of such a carbon the advertiser may or may not choose to handwrite, "You must not have received our letter."

Gadgets are used by some advertisers, are not used by others. The most common type of gadget is a well-known item, and it is usually secured to the letter with cellophane tape, or by a staple, or with glue of some sort, or put in a cellophane bag. Among the widely used gadgets are:

Buttons	Mirrors
Coins	Pins
Dice	Poker chips
Feathers	Ribbons
Keys	Rubber bands

Odd folds, pop-ups, and cut-outs are kin to gadgets, as are scented letters and letterheads with some of the edge of the paper burned. What's good about gadgets? They are good stoppers, getting attention and, perhaps, interest; they can add showmanship and even realism to the letter. On the other side of the ledger, gadgets add to the cost of the letter, they may be so clever that they distract, and, if they are made of glass or have points or edges, they can be dangerous. In all cases, gadgets are to be subordinated to, and snugly integrated into, the advertising message.

Postscripts are seen in many direct-mail advertising letters. The space occupied by a postscript has unusual attention value because of its nearness to what many readers look at first, the writer's signature; consequently, postscripts get high readership. The postscript can present a testimonial; it can consist of the advertiser's slogan; it may restate the major buyer benefit. Sometimes the postscript is handwritten for added warmth and effectiveness.

Media

TECHNIQUES

Some sellers use direct-mail advertising in a *continuous* manner. For example, department stores may enclose some advertising material with customers' monthly statements, or advertising media may send steady streams of mailings at more-or-less regular intervals to advertisers who are customers or prospective customers. Such continuous programs are indefinite in length, running for years in some instances. Seldom does the advertiser expect or request any specific, direct action from addressees; instead, his hopes are to keep in touch, to stay remembered, to build good will. A group of mailings can be devoted to a single subject and obviously similar in format — or each can have its own subject and design. Textbook publishers mail to professors on a *continuous* basis; so do those who administer "college alumni giving" programs.

The *wear out* technique is followed mainly by the mail-order sellers. For example, a mail-order seller selects for promotion to a list of consumers a product with a modest price and with small probability of repeat purchases. The number of mailings planned is indefinite, and each one differs to a degree from the one it follows. The advertiser hopes that each mailing to the group makes a sale, but he is satisfied if the total effort pays for itself and returns some profit. The cost and the performance of each mailing are watched closely, the "well is pumped until dry," mailings are discontinued on that product when the number of purchases is so small as to cause a loss. At that point, the mail-order seller may or may not start advertising another product to the same list of names.

A third technique follows a *campaign* pattern. Mail-order sellers often use this technique when selling high priced specialty products with repeat possibilities. The campaign, completely designed before the first mailing is made, consists of a specific number of mailing pieces. Each piece has its own goal or assignment; each is a complete unit which does not depend on any other unit in the series. As soon as an addressee takes the action desired by the advertiser (a purchase, for example, or a request for a salesman to call), he is sent no more mailings. The number of mailings ranges from two to ten or even more, with four a common figure. The intervals between mailings usually vary, but, if he chooses, the advertiser can use a single interval throughout the series. Popular intervals include ten days, two weeks, three weeks, and one month. In a five-unit series, the first and second and then the second and third may be separated by one week, the fourth mailing may follow one month later, and the final piece may be mailed one month after the fourth.

TIMING

No single schedule is ideal for all users of direct-mail advertising because scheduling is an individual problem. Trial and error provide the only sound approach to proper timing and, as is true in so many other areas, an advertiser's most effective schedule *this* time may be less than that *next* time. Do remember while reading this section that exceptions can probably be found for every generalization made.

Direct Mail

As for *month of year,* most advertisers spend more heavily in January, February, March, April, May, September, October, and November than in June, July, and August. December, the low month in total dollar volume, is a bad month for most advertisers but an excellent month for a few.

What about *week of month?* The first few days and the last few days of the month are avoided by many advertisers, leaving the tenth-to-the-twenty-fifth as the preferred period. As more and more retailers send out monthly statements all during the entire month instead of only at the month's end, there will be less congestion in mail boxes around the first of the month.

Choice of *days of week* for addressees to receive mailings goes to Tuesday, Wednesday, and Thursday with most advertisers trying to avoid Monday, Friday, and Saturday. Pay day is a good day for the advertiser's mailing to arrive; the day after a holiday, the day on which some big news breaks, and the day the rent is due are examples of bad days. First class mail, incidentally, can be scheduled in respect to delivery day much more satisfactorily than can third class mail.

Time of day sometimes permits the advertiser a choice. If local mail is posted, for example, about 8 A.M., it may reach the addressee soon after lunch when that person is more relaxed, more optimistic, and less hurried. First class mail is usually received in the first mail — third class in a later mail.

TESTING

Direct-mail advertisers, particularly the large mail-order sellers, test just about everything and keep detailed records of the performance of each mailing. Keys of various sorts can be used to identify the mailing which the addressee is reacting to or answering. For example, the business reply card in mailing A can be addressed to Room 345, Trust Building — the one in mailing B to Room 346, Trust Building. Or, different street numbers can be used, or A. B. Carlson can be the man to write to in one mailing — A. C. Carlson in another. An even simpler key is to put a different letter or number inconspicuously in the corner of the reply form.

In the area of postage, advertisers check:

    Air mail versus first class
    First class versus third class
    Regular stamps versus commemorative stamps
    Metered postage versus permit postage
    Business reply cards versus business reply envelopes

Other variables on which tests are run include:

    Suitability of mailing lists
    Geographic area to cover
    Composition of the mailing
    Offer to make to addressees
    Copy and color possibilities
    Method of reproducing the copy

Media

Number and timing of mailings
Use of home addresses of executives

Questions and Problems

1. Compare direct mail advertising with package inserts.
2. In what ways is direct mail advertising like personal selling?
3. Can you think of words which probably are quite effective in direct mail advertising?
4. On pages 320–1, a pattern or outline is suggested for mail-order selling. How might this pattern be adapted for use by a college senior applying for a job?
5. What problems does the advertiser confront in direct mail that he does not face in other media?
6. What are some handicaps of direct mail as an advertising medium?
7. Comment on the procedure of getting mailing lists through list brokers.
8. What can advertisers do about letters which obviously are form letters?
9. What can be said about the seasonal use of direct mail advertising?
10. Textbook publishers could send mailings to a professor's home address, or to his school address. Comment.

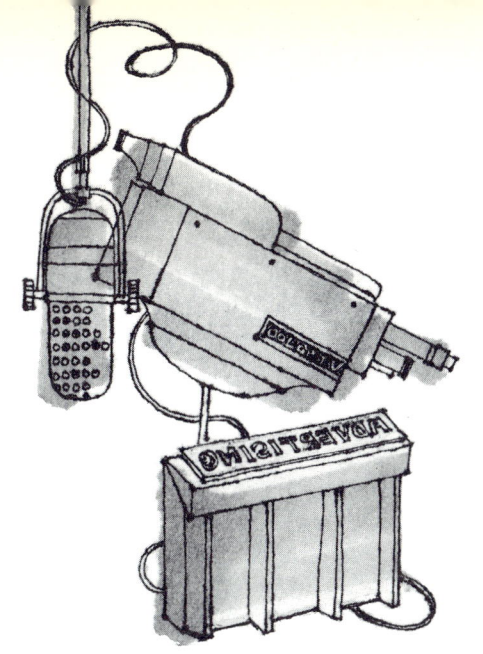

PART SIX

Advertising Management

We have just finished a study of advertising media, the vehicles which carry advertising messages to buyers. Just before that, we examined the process of building an advertisement. Now we are ready to look at what management does about designing complete advertising programs aimed at ultimate consumers.

If we think of the material covered thus far as involving advertising tactics, we are ready at this point to move up to advertising strategy. Formerly, we thought in terms of individual advertisements and separate types of media. Now we start thinking in broader terms, now we start looking at all consumer advertising a manufacturer runs during the course of a calendar year.

The traditional and classic responsibilities of management are to *plan*, to *organize*, to *control*. These apply just as much to *advertising* management as to other functional areas. Advertising management hopes to make those decisions which will result in the soundest, the most profitable advertising programs. Advertising management hopes to integrate these programs into the firm's *marketing* operations and into the firm's *total* operations.

The first chapter of this five-chapter section follows appropriately the preceding section on media by taking up the question of the *scheduling* of advertising. Three questions are basic here. (1) To which buyers should the advertiser communicate?

Advertising Management

(2) Through which media should he communicate? (3) How often should he communicate to those buyers? The compromises open to the advertiser are discussed.

The next chapter presents the concept of the *advertising campaign* addressed to ultimate consumers. The nature and the elements of these campaigns are examined. The three types of consumer campaign included are product-promoting, institutional, and horizontal cooperative.

The third chapter in this section describes how management achieves *coordination* between advertising and other activities of the firm. Major attention goes to the cooperation desired between advertising and personal selling, between advertising and sales promotion, and between advertising and public relations. Ways of achieving better coordination are suggested.

The fourth chapter of these five raises a most troublesome question: How large should a manufacturer's advertising *budget* be? Few companies indeed can defend themselves satisfactorily against the charge that they should spend 10% *more,* or against the charge that they should spend 10% *less.* The chapter offers some principles of sound managing of budgets.

The section's fifth and final chapter is devoted to what is by far and away the most universal and difficult problem in all advertising — *evaluation.* This problem is that of trying to determine just what a seller gets for the dollars he spends in advertising. So far as is known, *no* manufacturer can tell precisely what his advertising does to his profits, or even to his sales volume. Common approaches to this problem are described, including both pre-tests and post-tests.

Chapter 18

Scheduling

Scheduling as considered in this chapter is limited to the advertising done by a seller within any calendar or fiscal year. Our concern in this chapter is with the advertiser's problem of deciding what advertising to buy and run during the year.

The basic questions in scheduling are those of *whom* and *when;* to whom shall advertising be sent and according to what timing pattern; how large should the audience group be and how often should it be addressed. The first of these problems is one of *coverage;* the second is a dual problem of *frequency* and *continuity*. *Coverage* relates primarily to the selection of media because media are the primary determinant of the group exposed to the manufacturer's advertising. *Frequency* is the number of advertisements of the same size run by the seller during a given period of time. *Continuity* is a matter of regularity, involving the nature of the time intervals which separate the advertisements and the advertising run by the seller during the year.

Coverage, frequency, and continuity compete among themselves for the dollars which constitute the seller's advertising fund; each of the three is dependent on the other two. The compromises adopted by various sellers are as varied as they are inevitable, largely because so little is known for certain about these matters. The whole area of scheduling is one needing expanded and continuing research and experimentation; it is one of no established formulas and few if any hard-and-fast rules. Let's hope that the increasing use of computers in decisions involving media will result in better buying and in better selling of time and space. One complication to keep in mind throughout the chapter stems from the fact that advertising and individual advertisements have a quality all of their own. Outstanding excellence in advertisements can compensate somewhat for ineffective scheduling, and skilled scheduling can make mediocre advertising more productive.

COVERAGE

Selection of Media Types

In our media section, eight media types were included: newspapers, magazines, television, radio, outdoor, transit, point-of-purchase, and direct mail. Few manufacturers of any consequence can do a satisfactory advertising job using only one type of medium. An even smaller number uses all eight. No one medium type is superior to all others; each has its merits and its handicaps as were mentioned in the various "Features of the Medium" sections. The profitability of any one type varies from manufacturer to manufacturer even within a single product classification and can vary from year to year for a single manufacturer. Changes and shifts are about the only rule, making generalizations dangerous and any scientific selection of media types impossible.

An advertiser approaches the selection of media types by defining the typical buyer he intends to influence through his advertising. These buyers constitute his market; they are to receive his advertising message from and through the media he selects. The concept of coverage is of the advertiser's reaching the maximum number of these buyers — of these customers and prospective customers of his. Coverage, then, is limited to users of the advertiser's product and to persons who do not use it but should; coverage does not mean the maximum number of *all* consumers. Having defined his buyer, the advertiser then determines *how many* there are and *where* they are.

The remainder of the selection process involves how to send an effective advertising message economically to the group of buyers just defined. A major consideration here is the nature of the message; another is how often it needs to be delivered; still another involves the length of the campaign period. The advertiser must deliver this effective message at a cost which he can afford — at a figure which will make the advertising effort profitable.

As a manufacturer embarks on the task of selecting media types, he becomes aware immediately of several difficulties. A most serious one is that of audience measurement. The media chapters pointed out that media sell circulation or the opportunity to develop circulation. There is a *gross* aspect to circulation (how many copies of *Reader's Digest* were bought last month) and a *net* aspect (how many of those purchasers are prospects for the product, or, refined even further, how many prospects for the product saw an advertisement last month in *Reader's Digest*). Audience measurement in the broadcast media is not so precise as advertisers would prefer.

A second difficulty involves cost comparisons. There is a cost-per-thousand concept (or its counterpart) in every medium type — but the basic unit varies, sometimes being cost per thousand homes or thousand viewers, sometimes being cost per thousand passers-by, sometimes being cost per page per thousand copies sold. There is no sound, meaningful way to compare the value of a thousand pages in a publication with a thousand members of a broadcast audience. Just how does the reaction of a thousand housewives who read a food advertisement compare with that of a different thousand housewives who hear the same brand advertised over the air?

A third difficulty relates to the reliance a manufacturer should place on a type of medium. How much of his advertising effort should a food manufacturer place in magazines and how much in television — how much, if any, in outdoor or point-of-purchase? Which one type should be dominant and which ones supplementary?

Scheduling

Media costs, the costs of space and time, are the largest single expense item in most advertising budgets. The selection of media types to use is an undertaking which deserves, even demands, the very best thought and judgment of top management. What matters should get attention? *Availability* is obviously the first such matter if availability is a question; it is often of significance in the broadcast media, for example, or in connection with preferred space in publication and outdoor media. *Selectivity* is an important matter. The advertiser dreams of putting together an assortment of media which will reach every one of his customers and prospective customers — and no one else. A manufacturer's distribution is linked to this matter of selectivity because the nature and location of his market determine which media are acceptable and which are not. Regional markets, for example, can be of such limited extent that national circulation of magazines must not be used. Or, a product can have so thin a market that a medium such as radio would not be indicated for use. *Suitability* is a close kin to selectivity. Manufacturers of various personal products and distillers of alcoholic beverages, for instance, do not have the width of choice of media types that most other manufacturers have. If a manufacturer's circumstances are such that great flexibility is imperative, television and magazines may be ruled out of consideration. The essence of the copy is another matter of concern in many cases. Some big sales ideas demand visual presentation, others demand oral presentation; the urgency of some product messages demands immediate delivery; not so, for example, for most institutional copy. Radio cannot accommodate stories needing physical form, and outdoor advertising cannot accommodate long stories. Copy seeking direct action is different from copy seeking indirect action. Competition is a matter which the advertiser dares not ignore. A company may select media types *not* used by its competitors, counting on distinctiveness and domination to justify this choice. Or, it may elect to run with the pack, feeling that competitors must have found the media profitable, and that buyers will expect to find that company's advertisements in those media. If the company has some localized problems in certain markets because of the strength of competitors in those markets, the company may add local media such as newspapers, transit, outdoor, or spot broadcasts in those markets. Finally, as always, we return to the matter of *cost*.

Selection of Individual Media

Having finally decided to use magazines, for example, the advertiser's next job is to select *which* magazines should carry his advertising. This section takes up the topics of *circulation,* the *advertising schedule, duplication, left- versus right-hand page, services media offer to advertisers,* and *sources of media information.*

Circulation. As has been mentioned, what advertisers buy from media is *circulation* or, in the case of certain purchases from television and radio stations, the *opportunity to develop* circulation. Continuing our magazine thinking, the advertiser searches for magazines whose *quality* and *quantity* of circulation fit his needs. Alert magazines know much of a factual nature about their readers, information such as age, sex, income, size of family, and the like, which is made available to advertisers.

These reader characteristics plus the reading given to the magazine by readers cause the readers to be of high quality for one manufacturer, but of low quality for the maker of a quite different product. Visualize the various typical readers of *Fortune, Strength and Health, Dog News,* and *Parents Magazine!* When the typical reader of a certain magazine and the typical prospect of a certain manufacturer are the same individual, quality of circulation is excellent. Circulation of a medium in markets where the manufacturer does not have distribution reduces the quality of the medium for that manufacturer. The same is true of circulation made up of individuals who are not prospects for the manufacturer's product.

Quantity of circulation has already been discussed for each of the eight media comprising the media section. A manufacturer's market can be thought of as a specific number of individuals — with money, of course. Enough different media must be used so that the advertiser's message is delivered to at least whatever minimum percentage of this market is acceptable. Manufacturers study the circulation trend, upward or downward, of each medium under consideration, and, when circulation is increasing, manufacturers are interested in discovering why. If excellent editing and efficient marketing of a magazine explain its rising circulation, and if the renewal rate has continued high, well and good. If, however, the explanation is one of short-term subscriptions, premiums, cut-rate offers, combination offers of two or more magazines, or contests, then the increase in *quantity* was obtained at the price of a decline in *quality.*

The quality and quantity of a medium's circulation are meaningful only in terms of the medium's rates — and once again we return to the cost concept. This concept is one of cost per unit of circulation, cost per black-and-white page per thousand, you remember, for magazines. The only changes possible in this basic figure must reflect changes in page rate or amount of circulation, or both. A magazine raises its page rate in response to an increase in circulation (ability to retain the larger figure is assumed, as is the maintenance of circulation quality) or in concert with a rising price level. In other words, when the magazine starts selling more to advertisers, it charges them more; and, when its costs continue to rise, eventually it must raise its rates.

Comments on the quality, quantity, and cost of circulation would be incomplete without reference to some intangibles, to features which, continuing our magazine application, affect a magazine's ability to deliver a manufacturer's advertising message, but to features difficult or even impossible to measure. *Prestige* would certainly be such an intangible. Just what is prestige? Which magazines enjoy prestige? How much does this characteristic increase the performance of a seller's advertising? It is difficult to say. Excellence in putting together the editorial features which go into an issue contribute to a magazine's prestige; outstanding physical appearance makes a similar contribution. High advertising standards and patronage from a group of respected advertisers are evidences of prestige. *Influence* is also an intangible. Some magazines as carriers of advertising undoubtedly enjoy greater influence with retailers and with consumers than do other magazines. Manufacturers, of course, prefer those magazines with the greatest influence, but how do they identify them? Exceptional *readership* is another of these intangibles, eminently desirable, of varying quality, and most difficult to evaluate. More is needed than just personal statistics about the type of reader. How thoroughly is the magazine read? What is the intensity and the intentness of this reading? How much reader interest, reader loyalty, and reader confidence in the authority of the magazine are present in this reading?

Finally, however, the selection of individual media is essentially a matter of circulation. Certain statistical data are available, but all the information desired about a medium and its circulation is seldom to be had. A most challenging undertaking is to try to separate the quality inherent in an advertising medium from the quality of an advertisement carried by that medium. Selection cannot be an exact science; experience, skill, and judgment are invaluable.

The Advertising Schedule. The manufacturer's proposed advertising plans are consolidated into a schedule which contains this information:

> List of publications, broadcast stations, markets
> Dates of appearance of advertisements
> Sizes of advertisements (space or time)
> Costs of advertisements

What is the optimum schedule? Indeed, *is* there such? What is an adequate and acceptable schedule? Once again, there is no agreement, there is no formula. There is only judgment. The difficulty is easy to highlight: for the same amount of money an advertiser could add one more magazine to the list, or run larger advertisements, or run his advertisements more often. If the advertising fund is not to be enlarged, any increase in one of these three areas must cause a reduction in one or both of the other two. No advertiser, incidentally, knows exactly how much money he should spend in any one magazine, just as he did not know earlier what proportion of his total advertising fund should be spent in the magazine medium.

Do advertisers commit themselves to use too many individual media, or too few? Still continuing with our magazine adaptation, it appears that more advertisers make the mistake of using too many than the mistake of using too few. There are many prices which the advertiser must pay when his magazine list is long rather than short. He must run smaller advertisements, run them less frequently, or reduce his advertising's continuity as a result of shortening the advertising periods and, conversely, lengthening the periods during which no advertisements of his appear. In like manner, the advertiser sacrifices the benefits of concentration, repetition, and dominance. Because his advertisements must be smaller than were he using fewer magazines, their rates are high and their discounts very small if, indeed, they qualify for any discounts at all. The advertiser himself, being a small customer of each magazine, hardly is in line for any favored treatment, preferred position, or helpful services from each magazine. Long lists are more defensible when new products are being launched; concentration is the better policy for established products.

Sometimes a manufacturer will design not one schedule, but, instead, will set up two or three different schedules. Schedule A might be for all markets over 500,000 in population, schedule B for markets between 100,000 and 500,000, and schedule

Advertising Management

C for markets under 100,000 in size. In such an event, schedule A would be the one calling for the greatest number of dollars and the greatest amount of space or time. This variation would, of course, be reflected in local media (newspapers are an excellent example) rather than in national magazines.

Duplication. When the term *duplication* is used by an advertiser or a media representative it refers to a problem or a condition within a type of medium. Once again, magazines may give us our example. Suppose an automobile manufacturer runs the same advertisement in *Life* and in *Time* at about the same time, and the two advertisements are seen by a certain consumer; duplication has taken place. It is also a feature of television, of radio, and, to a lesser extent, of newspapers.

As we have seen, an advertiser must have coverage or else his message will not reach as many buyers as he *must* reach. As an advertiser adds magazine after magazine to his list in order to increase his coverage, he finds duplication inevitable. It is understandable that statistical duplication is greater than actual duplicated readership of the manufacturer's one advertisement. A household taking *Life* and *Time*, as in the example of the preceding paragraph, constitutes statistical duplication. Or, an individual living in that household who spent some time looking at those two copies would represent duplicated circulation. Despite these two possibilities of duplicated readership, however, it is entirely possible for no one person in that household to have read or even seen both advertisements. One way for the advertiser to have avoided duplication would have been to use only one of the magazines; another would have been to run a different advertisement in each of the two magazines.

Several arguments are heard against duplication. The most serious is that it limits an advertiser's coverage, and, it is true, duplication does just that. If a soft drink manufacturer, for example, wants to communicate with the maximum audience possible, if he feels no acute need of repeating the same stimulus to the same consumers, if he thinks that duplication is for products of high price, then his intent

Wrigley gum has poster schedules for two classes of market. (Courtesy: Wm. Wrigley Jr. Company)

Scheduling

to avoid duplication is understandable, perhaps even sound. So long as there is a large group of prospects not yet reached, duplication can be considered unwise. In television and radio, not much duplication is needed to cause a certain amount of viewer or listener irritation. Finally, duplicated circulation compounds a problem already most difficult — that of measuring the results of a manufacturer's advertising.

Points in favor of duplication are by now fairly obvious, the major ones being those of repetition and frequency. For shopping goods particularly, several exposures may be needed before the consumer acts, and duplication is a speedy method of making that necessary number of impressions in a short period of time. Then there is the fact that *advertisement* duplication is less than *statistical* duplication. There is economy in running the same advertisement in the two magazines. In summary, there does not seem to be much waste or damage which must be charged to duplication. By itself, it is neither good nor bad; each advertiser must discover whether it is good or bad *for him*.

Left- vs. Right-hand Page. No treatment of coverage dares omit reference to the question of whether left-hand pages are superior or inferior to right-hand pages. Although research findings are not in agreement, we are entitled to assume that there is no significant difference between the performances of the two. What is in the advertisement is more important than whether the advertisement is on a right-hand page or a left-hand page. After all, doesn't the magazine which sells both and, presumably, knows the worth of both, charge the same price for each?

Media Services to Advertisers. For manufacturers whose merchandise moves to the consumer through retailers, a consideration in selecting individual media is the number and nature of services offered by the various media under consideration. These services, these "extras," can be classified into two groups, the *research* group and the *merchandising* group. Research services consist of having or of getting information about the market in which the medium circulates, information which will benefit advertisers. Merchandising services are activities undertaken by a medium to help make manufacturers' advertising more productive, activities mainly involving work with retailers but some with wholesalers also. Newspapers are the most prominent type of medium offering these services to manufacturers. Magazines, television, radio, and some poster plants offer certain services. Advertising agencies encourage media to make these services available. As for the cost of the services, there are three possibilities. All may be "free," in which case all advertisers pay for the services although only some advertisers use them. Or, certain services can be offered "free" to manufacturers who buy not less than a stipulated minimum amount of space or time from the individual medium. Or, finally, any services beyond advice and consultation can be put on a fee basis, the fee usually equaling the actual cost of the job.

There are several common *research services*. A detailed breakdown of the market is one, showing current figures for population, income, retail sales, building permits, car loadings, consumption of utilities, bank debits, employment, and circulation — all broken down into market segments if practicable. Route lists for manufacturers'

Advertising Management

salesmen, particularly for products retailed through food stores, are another research service. Brand preference studies are an increasingly common service. These studies cover a limited group of consumer products of which drugs, food, soap, and appliances are examples. Brand preference studies show the rankings of the various brands for that limited group of consumer products; they list purchases consumers plan to make; they report on certain consumer buying habits. The rankings of brands are of particular interest to manufacturers whose products move through brokers, wholesalers, and then through retailers on their way to the ultimate consumer. A few media attempt to measure the retail sales of a small group of consumer goods in their respective markets. Some do this by checking the inventories and sales of certain product classifications in a sample of retail stores; some operate consumer purchase panels, groups of consumers who agree to keep a diary or record of their purchases of certain products, showing prices paid, brands bought, and type of retail store patronized. Some take pantry polls, checking the consumption of consumers somewhat as did those media which checked the inventories and sales of retailers. Local surveys and special market studies are a fifth and final type of research service, an example of which would be a medium's survey to determine which and how many retailers stock the product of a certain manufacturer.

From a manufacturer's point of view, there are three questions or problems about these media research services. First, do they reflect any bias? There is at least the possibility that the medium undertaking a particular market study is more concerned with getting promotional material to use in its own advertising and personal presentations than with determining facts in an impartial, unbiased manner. A manufacturer would be asking much of a medium if he expected it to publish findings which did not show the medium in a favorable light. Second, are the research studies sound or superficial, thorough or trivial? After all, a medium can afford to spend just so much on any one project, and potential advertisers have been accused of requesting quite sizable research jobs, for free, of course. Third, how can the manufacturer get the medium to do the study he wants done *before* his advertisements appear? Manufacturers can have changes of heart and plan even after the medium has gone to the trouble and expense of making the requested study. Media have had their fingers burned in just such a manner.

There are several common *merchandising services,* too. A medium may promise to send direct mailings to a manufacturer's wholesalers and retailers. The mailing may be a house organ or bulletin which tells about or, perhaps, also shows some of the advertisements the medium is scheduled to carry. The mailing could be a reprint of a manufacturer's advertising schedule accompanied by some proofs of some or all of the advertisements. The mailings could be promotional literature prepared and produced by the manufacturer himself. Instead of using direct mail, the medium might get in touch with the middlemen through the use of telephone calls or even personal calls. If an employee of a medium does call on a retailer, he would naturally tell the retailer about the forthcoming advertising and ask for good shelf space for the product in question. The employee might install window displays and build merchandise displays; he might solicit tie-in advertisements or cooperative advertising; he might check retail distribution of the manufacturer's product both before and after the manufacturer's advertising runs; he might even try to interest non-stocking retailers in handling the product.

Other possibilities of merchandising services are for the medium to supply speakers for wholesalers' sales meetings, to sponsor a meeting of retail dealers just prior to the start of a manufacturer's campaign, or to supply a manufacturer's salesmen with letters of introduction to individual dealers. Magazines can supply "As Advertised In _____" cards for retailers to use, newspapers can offer their mat services, and television and radio can mention the date and hour of a manufacturer's show. All in all, this merchandising of a manufacturer's advertising by the media carrying it increases the effectiveness of that advertising. Naturally, both advertisers and their advertising agencies are in favor of it.

Sources of Media Information. Advertisers and advertising agencies have found several sources of media information which are worth using before selecting individual media. The first source in the newspaper and magazine fields, naturally enough, is the medium itself. Examination of a copy of a newspaper or a magazine can be a revealing and informative step. In the broadcast media, certain stations have distinctive personalities which can be sensed by an analysis of the programs and the advertising carried. An individual medium is usually a member of a trade association which compiles information about that type of medium and supplies that information to advertisers. The Magazine Advertising Bureau and the Traffic Audit Bureau are examples.

A medium's own promotion is a second source of information. The advertising that a medium does for itself and the sales promotion literature it publishes contain basic, current, and helpful facts. Special studies, particularly those made for the medium by an able, independent, and respected commercial research firm, often give advertisers a more detailed, more accurate picture of the medium; such studies enable advertisers to make more intelligent decisions about what the medium involved offers and how it might perform. Rate cards summarize important statistical information needed by advertisers. But the most valuable type and amount of information about a medium to be found in the medium's promotion should be in the personal selling done in behalf of the medium. The presentations and the salesmanship referred to are those of the medium's own salesmen or those of the media representatives who present their clients' cases in person to manufacturers and their advertising agencies.

A widely used source of media information is the Standard Rate and Data Service. This service, published monthly by a private company, consists of sections which supply data about these media:

- Newspapers
- Business publications
- Network television and radio
- Transportation advertising
- Consumer magazines and farm publications
- Spot television
- Spot radio

Each section contains just about all the information, particularly the statistical rather than the intangible, needed by an advertiser using that particular medium.

Advertising Management

The information is current, accurate, and easily accessible, making the services a most handy and useful reference. The sections contain these types of information about individual media:

Address of medium	Medium's personnel
Name of medium's representative	Commissions and discounts
Rates	Mechanical requirements
Issuance and closing dates	Copy information
Circulation breakdowns	

A fourth source of media information consists of audit reports. The Audit Bureau of Circulations is a non-profit organization sponsored by publishers, advertisers, and advertising agencies. Management control rests with the *buyers* of space, the advertisers and their agencies, and *not* with the sellers of space. Most daily newspaper circulation and most consumer magazine circulation are audited by the ABC. The organization checks the accuracy of publishers' figures, certifies to *net paid circulation,* and issues standardized reports on circulation data. The ABC is keenly interested in the quantity, the distribution, and the quality of circulation, and in how circulation is built.

Finally, there are specialized commercial services (Starch, Nielsen, etc.), there are advertiser sponsored studies (Association of National Advertisers), and there is the Advertising Research Foundation.

FREQUENCY

Frequency is the number of advertisements of the same size appearing in or on an individual medium per day, per week, per month, or per campaign. Obviously, the per day type of frequency is possible only in television and radio. Because frequency is one of the big three areas of scheduling along with coverage and continuity, it affects those two and is, in turn, affected by them. The problem calling for frequency decisions is found *within* the continuing period. A manufacturer's decision to advertise in television for 39 out of 52 weeks and his implied decision to stay out of television for 13 weeks of the year are decisions involving continuity. The number of advertisements of the same length he will run during the 39 week period is a matter of frequency. But, this number is not meaningful until we know something about the nature of the time interval separating the second advertisement from the first, separating the third from the second, and so on; *that* is a matter of continuity.

As was true for coverage, and as will be true for continuity, there is no formula which will determine the ideal frequency; there *are,* however, some factors of considerable influence. A pair of factors which are completely, permanently, and universally dependent on each other are the size of the advertising fund and the size of advertisement to be run. If these are known, frequency can be derived. If broadcast shows identical in length cost $1,000 over a certain station and the advertiser has $39,000, frequency is 39 for the period; if it were magazine pages at $13,000 apiece, frequency would be 3. Another pair of factors closely related to each other are the number of media to be used and the length of the advertising period. As the number of media to be used increases, there is strong pressure to settle for a lower

Scheduling

frequency, or else to shorten the advertising period; other possibilities would be to enlarge the fund, or to reduce the size of advertisement. The nature of the product and the nature of the buyer are still another pair of influences. For example, new products, low-priced products, quickly used consumer products seem to call for relatively high frequencies; advertisements aimed at customers can be smaller *and hence more frequent* than those aimed at non-users of the product. The rates, discounts, and requirements of a medium affect the frequency of the advertisements it carries. The shorter the life of the advertising message (seconds for radio, hours for newspapers, days for magazines) and the more often a print medium is issued (365 versus 12), the greater seems the need for stepped-up frequency. Manufacturers cannot be unmindful of what competitors are doing in respect to frequency.

Some powerful reasons can be advanced for high frequency. One of them is the fact that, for any single advertisement, only a fraction of the medium's gross, poten-

THE DAILY PATTERN OF ADVERTISING
In Richmond Newspapers

One of the principal advantages of newspaper advertising is its flexibility. Space can be obtained in various sizes, on any given day or days, selected to maximize the sales impact.

For those interested in how others schedule their advertising from day to day, we have prepared the following table which shows the typical linage pattern of the Times-Dispatch and News Leader.

AVERAGE LINAGE PER DAY

Paper	Day	No. of Pages	Total	General	Auto-motive	Classi-fied	Dept. Store	Retail Food	Other Retail
Morning	Mon	30	45,528	4,214	1,036	13,734	17,374	616	8,554
	Tue	32	44,086	8,260	3,556	14,854	7,518	644	9,254
	Wed	38	57,204	12,278	6,118	15,736	11,970	322	10,780
	Thu	36	52,682	2,982	16,016	16,016	910	8,750
	Fri	48	79,884	18,732	3,052	16,800	15,680	13,286	12,334
	Sat	24	27,930	1,498	210	15,904	5,558	42	4,718
	Avg	34	51,220	8,032	2,826	15,507	12,353	2,637	9,065
Evening	Mon	34	49,588	10,808	3,164	13,244	4,088	2,856	15,428
	Tue	38	56,196	10,794	5,110	14,392	6,062	1,372	18,466
	Wed	42	66,066	11,382	5,586	15,050	6,678	3,066	24,304
	Thu	66	117,642	17,794	1,372	15,540	19,026	22,344	41,566
	Fri	40	61,390	3,990	1,358	16,352	10,472	182	29,036
	Sat	20	24,710	546	56	15,078	98	84	8,848
	Avg	40	62,600	9,219	2,775	14,943	7,737	4,984	22,942
Sunday	Sun	110	178,528	10,206	2,520	23,716	50,582	364	91,140

Newspaper advertising varies greatly during the week. Note retail food linage for each of the 7 days. (Courtesy: Research Department, Richmond Times Dispatch–Richmond News Leader)

tial circulation or audience sees it, reads it, or hears it. Advertisements are run in rapid succession as one means of increasing coverage. High frequency by itself seems capable of increasing the readership of each advertisement in the series. And, no one can deny that an advertiser's market can be described as a *parade* passing a given point (new faces or buyers as time passes) or as a *reservoir* whose fill pipe and drain are both busy. Each succeeding advertisement reaches new buyers. Another reason is that seldom does one advertisement get the ultimate results the advertiser is after. By speaking *often* to the buyer group, the advertiser is certain to speak to more buyers *who are just before buying*. Still another reason is the forgetting, the evaporating, the disappearing which takes place in consumer's minds. Memory loss has been found to be over 50 per cent during the first day after communication and about 80 per cent by the end of the third day. Because forgetting is greatest during the start of an advertising campaign, names, facts, and phrases need frequent repetition during that stage if they are to be remembered. The more often a message is repeated, the greater the proportion of it the consumer remembers.

Each advertiser needs to study his own circumstances and objectives to make the soundest frequency decisions possible. He needs to do research by medium type, by individual medium, and by entire campaign. He needs to determine whether more frequent, smaller advertisements are more profitable for him than less frequent, larger advertisements. He needs to remember that one of the greatest wastes in advertising is that caused by scheduling advertisements not frequently enough.

Size of Advertisement

One of the most important influences on frequency is size of advertisement, and its importance is great enough to justify a few more observations on this influence. We have recognized the possibility of *deriving* the number of uniform-sized advertisements to schedule for the advertising period. *Size* of advertisement, too, can be derived, if the advertiser sets the size of the advertising fund, decides the number of individual media to use, and settles on the number of advertisements to appear during the advertising period. Most of the factors which were mentioned as affecting frequency also affect size of advertisement, because what affects one inevitably affects the other. There are some influences not previously mentioned, however, which we should consider.

The policies of certain media influence size of advertisement even to the point of dictating it. A magazine may accept advertisements no smaller than one page, or advertisements in color no smaller than one-fourth page, or cover advertisements only of page size. There are standard sizes in the outdoor and transit media, and there are standard time units in the broadcast media. Then there is the matter of market potential; some manufacturers buy large space in large markets and smaller space in smaller markets. The purpose of the advertisement can be the strongest influence in determining the size of an advertisement; large space is used to announce, small space is used to remind. The amount of copy, the number of products included in one advertisement, and the illustration needs of the advertisement all help determine size. Finally, a company's salesmen and dealers may have strong opinions about how large advertisements should be.

Scheduling

Although advertising sizes cannot be evaluated apart from whatever excellence the contents of the advertisements possess, there are some plus points of large size — and some plus points of small size, too. *Large size* endows an advertisement with greater attention power and greater visibility, particularly in competition with other advertisements; this is desirable for new products and new campaigns. Large space gives the advertiser better display possibilities, gets him better position, and usually qualifies him for better discounts. The advertising message can be longer and more complete. Full-page advertisements look emphatic and important to retailers, perhaps important enough to be used as point-of-purchase advertising by many of those dealers. Manufacturers needing to enlarge their customer group know that as size of advertisement increases, the new readers added are mainly *non-users* of the product.

Small advertisements, however, have some points in their favor. Small space permits more coverage (additional media), more frequency (greater repetition), or more continuity (longer advertising periods). If there is considerable waste circulation in a medium for our advertiser, he cannot afford large space. If he wants to speak mainly to his customers, his best bet may be small space. Small advertisements make good teaser advertisements, good rateholders, and good off-season advertisements. They permit an advertiser to devote a complete advertisement to more of his products or more product uses. If he cares to, a manufacturer can schedule a group or "flight" of these small advertisements for a single copy of a newspaper or magazine. The composition of three flights actually used by three different advertisers was as follows: 10 advertisements totaling 480 lines; 9 advertisements totaling 800 lines; 6 advertisements totaling 480 lines. These flights are distinctive, they provide a type of repetition, they allow each advertisement to be tailored for the page on which it appears, and illustrations and humor can make the flight quite successful. Finally, one must remember that size of buyer-benefit is more important than size of space, that doubling the size of an advertisement does not guarantee a doubling of attention value, readership, or sales.

Comments on size of advertisement would be incomplete without reference to multiple-page insertions — three or more consecutive pages in a publication. Some of these feature the product or products of one manufacturer, some feature the related products of several different manufacturers. The cost in dollars, of course, runs high if the multi-page advertisement is that of just one advertiser. What does he get for this large figure? Large amounts of attention, dominance, impact, distinctiveness, story, illustration, and readership. These insertions have great merchandising potential, stimulating the enthusiasm of company salesmen and inviting the support of and use by retail dealers. They are good for introducing a manufacturer's new models, or for celebrating his anniversary, or for telling an institutional story. The advertisement itself is a natural for use as a direct mailing piece.

Color

Color is a factor which influences frequency in two ways. First, color influences size of advertisement, and size of advertisement is a major determinant of frequency. You recall that certain magazines, for example, do not permit color in advertise-

Advertising Management

ments smaller than one-fourth page. Second, color often commands a premium price. The minute a manufacturer decides, for example, to run a 4-color page rather than a black-and-white page, he must find the extra dollars color costs, or he must cut back in some other area — coverage, frequency, or continuity.

Rerun an Advertisement?

The question of whether an advertisement should ever be repeated without change is placed here in the section on frequency although it could have been classified as a *coverage* matter. Repetition has a considerable effect on advertising costs, and, as we saw in the preceding paragraph on color, anything affecting the cost of an advertisement affects its frequency.

What are the facts about the repeating of advertisements? Repetition is most common in the advertising done by mail-order sellers, in advertising that uses small space, in the broadcast media of television and radio, in outdoor, transit, and direct mail advertising. Repetition is *not* common for large publication advertisements seeking indirect action.

Why are so few large, indirect action advertisements repeated? Both the manufacturer and his advertising agency display reluctance to rerun. The manufacturer fears that readers will see the advertisement a second time, will assume immediately that there is no point in giving the advertisement any more notice, and will turn the page. Partial rebuttal for this feeling is the fact that no consumer reads the advertisement the first time it appeared with but a fraction of the thoroughness and intentness the advertiser himself gave it. In addition, the manufacturer fears that on its second appearance, the advertisement would not do so well as would a brand new advertisement. Finally, some manufacturers simply must accept rather than question a widespread custom of long standing. As for agency reluctance, it is based largely on the fears of being considered either lazy or sterile of imagination.

What is good about repeating a large, indirect action advertisement? First of all, no advertisement would be considered for rerun unless it had done well on its first appearance; rerun advertisements can be *proved* advertisements. Then, there are the savings in production costs, in engraving, typography, and electrotyping, and in art work too. Better art work can be justified, incidentally, if the cost is to be spread over a *number* of appearances. In addition, *new* readers are added whenever an advertisement is rerun; well under 100 per cent of the *potential* audience the advertiser wants to reach sees an advertisement, particularly a small one, the first time it appears. Still another point is the reinforcement of consumer memory, the penetration resulting from repetition of the same stimulus and from continuity of impression. Finally, if fewer different advertisements are to be built because the better ones will be repeated, more time and thought can go into the construction of each one; this should raise the quality of the advertisements.

The conclusion to which we seem forced is that more large, indirect action advertisements should be repeated. We are even entitled to wonder whether or not *every* campaign would be more productive if it contained some repeated advertisements. There is always the possibility, of course, of making a slight change or two in the rerun. In addition, it would be wise to consider separating the first run from the first rerun by one or more *different* advertisements.

CONTINUITY

Continuity now joins coverage and frequency to complete the "Big Three" of scheduling. Continuity reflects the nature of two time intervals: (a) the interval separating successive advertisements during an advertising campaign and (b) the interval of no advertising activity which separates one advertising period from the next advertising period. For example, suppose an advertiser is one of the many who curtail their advertising during the summer. Suppose further that he decides to buy 39 broadcasts shows during the September-May (inclusive) period, but to disappear from the air during June, July, and August. You recall that, by definition, frequency is 39 and applies to the September-May period. The (a) type of continuity relates to the time interval separating each of the first 38 shows from the show that follows. *Regular* continuity would make this interval *one week*, but it is possible, in theory at least, for the advertiser to schedule his 39 shows on 39 successive days if he preferred. The (b) type of continuity relates to the advertiser's division of the year; he has elected to advertise for 39 (not 26 or any other figure) weeks, then to do no advertising for 13 weeks, then to start another 39-week period of advertising, and so on.

It is easy to see that continuity is tied to coverage and to frequency. For example, if the advertiser in the last paragraph would go on for 26 and off for 26 (instead of on for 39 and off for 13), he could buy more stations during the 26-week period and thereby increase the size of the consumer group he covers. He would be getting more coverage at the cost of reduced continuity. Or, in respect to frequency, if the advertiser thinks that the weekly interval separating his 39 shows is too long, if he thinks he should schedule 3 a week, then he finds himself on for 13 weeks and off for 39. The (a) type of continuity, of course, amounts to what we commonly refer to as frequency. But, we decided originally to define frequency as a *number* — not as how often advertisements appear. So, we then think in terms of *two* types of continuity, the (a) and the (b) types described even though the (a) type can certainly be considered a matter of frequency.

Whether the concept of continuity applies to an advertiser's total program or to a single type of medium, it has connotations of consistency and of regularity. A high degree of continuity is desirable because it gives momentum to a manufacturer's advertising; it guarantees *past* advertising of recent date to which consumers can relate the *present* advertisement. Continuity causes the reader to feel an accumulating awareness of acquaintance with a manufacturer's product, his advertising, and even with the manufacturer himself. Communication by manufacturer to consumer is more satisfactory and successful when it is gradual rather than concentrated, when it is spread over a year rather than over a month. The longer the time period during which a seller is silent, either between advertisements within a campaign or between campaigns, the more formidable is his marketing problem once advertising is resumed.

Advertising Management

A manufacturer's decisions about continuity (and these decisions affect his decisions about coverage and frequency) must be made in the light of his own current conditions. He may cut his magazine list from twelve to six in order to step up both types of continuity — the recurrence rate of advertisements in a series and the speed with which one period of advertising follows the previous advertising period. He may think that he should schedule an advertisement every month in monthly magazines, and every fourth issue for weekly magazines. No two manufacturers make the same compromises, and one manufacturer's compromises of *this* year may not be the ones he will make *next* year. Whenever he is launching a new product on the market, or whenever he has a tremendous story to tell about an established product, he may be justified in sacrificing some of the (b) type of continuity in order to schedule larger advertisements more often in more media — for a shorter period. Undoubtedly, there is much guesswork involved in continuity decisions.

Timing

The timing of advertising campaigns is primarily a matter of continuity. The basic questions are these: when should a campaign *start,* and when should it *stop?* No one knows for certain. The seasonal angle is one to be considered. For seasonal products, as you know, the calendar year divides into one, two, or occasionally, three active buying periods; the rest of the year is a time of low or no buying. An extreme type of irregularity is that caused by special occasions such as Mother's Day or Valentine's Day. One advertising policy is to schedule heavy advertising just before and during the heavy buying season, to "strike while the iron is hot." Where there is very little of the seasonal in the consumption of a product (toothpaste, for example), scheduling can be more regular.

Mention of the seasonal question raises another consideration: can off-season advertising be used profitably to level out the sales curve or at least to raise the volume of consumption during the slack periods. In other words, can advertising get consumers to visit tourist areas in off-seasons or to drink coffee in the summer and tea in the winter? Would a furniture manufacturer be smart to schedule some advertising for the purpose of raising the extremely low level of production which had always been characteristic of the December-January period? Would a manufacturer of watches be well advised to try to sell more watches in other months than June and December or a pen manufacturer to bring his other months up to May, June, September, and December? Or, during the low months should he limit his advertising to small space and infrequent insertions — to institutional and reminder advertisements?

Another question is whether an advertiser should copy or violate the timing pattern of his competitors. If the other manufacturers of dog food practically discontinue their publication advertising during the summer months, does that encourage one manufacturer to splurge during the summer? Or, if a seller's competition observes the summer hiatus and drops out of television and radio during June, July, and August, should this seller do likewise? The broader question is: do consumers read and see and hear advertising in the summer? Many advertisers have found that they do. It may be well to mention at this point that an advertisement has about

A Christmas Prayer

Let us pray that strength and courage abundant be given to all who work for a world of reason and understanding ❖ that the good that lies in every man's heart may day by day be magnified ❖ that men will come to see more clearly not that which divides them, but that which unites them ❖ that each hour may bring us closer to a final victory, not of nation over nation, but of man over his own evils and weaknesses ❖ that the true spirit of this Christmas Season — its joy, its beauty, its hope, and above all its abiding faith — may live among us ❖ that the blessings of peace be ours — the peace to build and grow, to live in harmony and sympathy with others, and to plan for the future with confidence.

NEW YORK LIFE INSURANCE COMPANY

© 1963 New York Life Insurance Company

This seasonal advertisement was one-of-a-kind. It was not one of a series. (Courtesy: New York Life Insurance Co.)

Advertising Management

the same chances of success in a "thick" issue of a magazine that it has in the "thin" issues. This is true whether the advertisement lands in the front, the middle, or the back of the issue. As was true of left- and right-hand pages, the magazine charges the same for a page in a thick issue as for a page in a thin issue — the same for front, middle, and back with, of course, the exception of the covers.

Then there is a geographic consideration. In respect to seasons, growth, and temperature, the southern part of the country may be weeks ahead of the north.

The most important idea in timing is that there is an "ideal" amount to spend each day, week, and month. One approach to achieving this is to let the curve of scheduled advertising expenditure *conform to but lead* the annual sales forecast curve.

Questions and Problems

1. Toothpaste and bathroom tissue are consumed rather evenly throughout the year. Does this fact have scheduling implications?
2. List some types of consumer ads which are rerun without change.
3. Firms in the same industry often follow scheduling patterns which are dissimilar. Explain.
4. When a new product is being marketed, should its advertising appear in all media simultaneously?
5. What types of information does an advertiser need before selecting individual media?
6. In what ways is erratic, spasmodic, unscheduled advertising costly?
7. What developments within a firm can cause changes in its advertising schedule?
8. What are some major sources of information about advertising media?
9. Each year, figures become available showing the popularity of certain brands of certain product classifications in certain markets. A well-known branded food item might be the top brand in 4 markets, second in 6 markets, third in 3 markets, fourth in 1 market, and seventh in 1. In these 15 markets, this same brand's share-of-market may range all the way from 1% up to a high of 33%. A brand of electric appliance can show the same pattern. It can be first in 1 market, second in 4, third in 2, fourth in 2, fifth in 3, sixth in 1, and seventh in 2 markets. Its share-of-market can range from 5% to 18%. Relate this type of distribution pattern to a manufacturer's problem of scheduling his advertising.
10. The Basque Baking Company is an independent bakery which sells a variety of bread, rolls, and cakes over parts of a two-state area. Sales are made to food stores, restaurants, schools, and hospitals. Because Basque is a member of the Quality Bakers of America, it can call its baked goods Basque Sunbeam. Annual sales approximate $10,000,000, and the annual advertising budget is about $400,000. Sales show a slight seasonal rise during the summer months.

    Basque uses 20- and 60-second commercials on 4 TV stations in its market area. The bakery believes that over a 4-week period, September to May, its commercials reach 9 out of 10 TV homes an average of 8 times.

    Company policy is to reduce the TV schedule by 50% during June, July, and August because viewing drops off during the summer months. This reduction pattern is, of course, followed by many TV advertisers.

    What do you think of Basque's policy on scheduling?

Chapter 19

Manufacturers' Consumer Campaigns

The preceding chapter dealt with the scheduling of a manufacturer's advertising, with his concerns about coverage, frequency, and continuity. This chapter considers three types of campaign sponsored by manufacturers advertising to the ultimate consumer: the common *product-promoting* type of campaign, the *institutional, corporate,* or *strategic* campaign, and the *horizontal cooperative* campaign.

THE CAMPAIGN CONCEPT

Just what is an advertising *campaign?* It is an organized series of advertising messages. It is an orderly, planned effort consisting of related but self-contained and independent advertisements. The campaign has a single theme or keynote idea and a single objective or goal. The individual advertisements making up the campaign usually resemble each other, and this similarity is as intended as it is obvious. Thus, a unified theme or content provides *psychological* continuity throughout the campaign while visual and oral similarity provide *physical* continuity. In the short run, all campaigns want a predetermined psychological reaction; in the long run, practically all campaigns have sales goals. The campaign appears in one or more media.

The term *campaign* comes, of course, from the military, and its use by advertisers implies some similarity between operations in the two areas. There *is* some similarity. There is a need for information in each area before taking action; the military needs intelligence, the advertiser needs research. Each area demands sound planning, timing, and execution. A *series* of operations is usually needed in each before obstacles are removed and barriers overcome. The purposes of military and advertising efforts are to gain certain objectives or to destroy certain objectives. As has been made clear, the analogy cannot be complete — the advertiser and the buyers are *not* enemies; the only sound sales are those which benefit both buyer *and* seller.

Advertising Management

The advertiser's choices are clear. He can advertise in an erratic, spasmodic, opportunistic manner — or he can plan a concrete, detailed, sound advertising program; he can run some advertisements — or a campaign. The pressure to advertise in terms of campaigns is irresistible. Buyers forget. Buyers read advertisements casually or, sometimes, even carelessly. Some buyers are out of the market, not real prospects at the moment a particular advertisement appears. Far fewer than 100 per cent of an advertiser's current prospects see any one of the seller's advertisements. New prospects appear every day. Thinking and advertising in terms of campaigns practically forces the advertiser to study his past advertising efforts and activities with the intent of improving on them. Coordination, balance, timing, continuity, and performance all argue for campaign-type advertising.

Length

Campaigns vary in length. Some run for only a matter of days, some for weeks, some for a season, and some for an entire year. A range of three to six months includes many campaigns. Within the calendar year, some advertisers schedule two campaigns of six months each, some schedule two campaigns of four months each or, indeed, one campaign of ten months. Within the broadcast media, campaigns are often 13, 26, or 52 weeks in length. It is true, however, that an occasional advertiser makes no change whatever in his advertising for two or even for three years. What about the campaign concept in such a case? We are forced to consider such a two- or three-year advertising experience as consisting of two or three one-year campaigns. Because sales and profits must be computed for the calendar or fiscal year, advertising, too, must be limited to and considered a unit for the same calendar or fiscal year. Among the many factors influencing campaign length are competitors' advertising media policies, seasonal sales curve of the product involved, size of the advertising fund, campaign objectives, and the nature of the advertiser's marketing program.

Types

There are many bases on which advertising campaigns can be classified. Area covered is one such base; it can be one market, or a number of individual markets, or a region, or the entire country. When a manufacturer's distribution is limited, when his advertising fund is small, when his purpose is to test, or when he is trying to cope with a sectional problem, he is not seriously interested in sponsoring a national campaign. The nature, age, and position of the product in question provide bases for at least two types of campaigns. *Pioneering* campaigns are indicated for completely new types of products and for completely new uses for old products. *Competitive* campaigns stress competitive superiority in their efforts to hold on to present users, to increase the product's consumption by those users, and to encroach on competitors by taking some of their customers away from them. Then there is the media base, permitting one to think in terms of newspaper campaigns, for example, or direct-mail campaigns. A final base is the campaign's objective or purpose. Some are direct action, others indirect action; some are product-promoting, some are institutional.

PRODUCT-PROMOTING CAMPAIGNS

Theme

Every campaign needs a theme. This is the gist of the advertiser's message, a summary of his story, a point of focus for the campaign. In a word, the theme does for the campaign what the big sales idea did in Chapter 7 for an individual advertisement. A campaign's theme is often referred to as its keynote idea because it is the central, fundamental core of the campaign. The theme is expected to make the advertised product interesting and desirable to buyers; it is assumed to be the most influential story the advertiser can tell at that time. Because the campaign is organized around it and is concentrated on it, the theme must relate to and reflect campaign objectives.

In Chapter 7 we looked at buyer-benefits and recognized them as the satisfactions consumers experience and enjoy in their consumption of products and services. Campaign themes are distinctive, original expressions of those buyer-benefits; they reflect the benefits chosen earlier. Because they can be presented in many ways, each advertiser strives to express his product's benefits effectively and distinctively in a special, attractive manner. Many advertisers actually sell romance or the opportunity for romance, but each does so with his own individual theme. The benefit a manufacturer of toothpaste sells may be popularity, but his campaign theme will be "No Bad Breath When You Use Brand X."

The need for a campaign theme is not difficult to detect. Well-chosen themes attract and hold the interest of buyers; they encourage buyers to buy. A theme makes a series of advertisements more specific. Because it works for simplicity of story, a theme makes for advertising that is easy to read and helps the buyer translate and interpret the advertising message. Campaigns need unity and continuity of thought if they are to enjoy impact and penetration. Because the theme connects the individual advertisements and holds them together, it permits the campaign to concentrate on a single message, thereby achieving greater understanding and remembrance than would otherwise be possible.

For those who design advertising campaigns, a theme serves as a guide — a track on which the campaign should stay. One quickly discovers, of course, that the theme of many a campaign is not readily discernible. One possible explanation is that subtlety and camouflage have been used to mask the theme, although it is not clear as to just why this would be smart. Another explanation is that some advertisers schedule groups of advertisements without themes. This, too, is difficult to understand or defend.

Qualities. What characteristics make a theme good? Most important of all, it should be sound and effective psychologically, tied to the needs and wants of buyers and to the advertiser's product as the answer. Appeal and interest value recommend strongly that the theme promise a buyer-benefit to all consumers who should buy the product. Effective themes are true, believable, and convincing; their meaning is comprehended quickly and easily. Ideally, an advertiser would prefer a theme that is distinctive to the point of being unique, but he realizes that seldom can he promise a buyer-benefit which cannot also be promised by his competitors.

Advertising Management

For products which are totally new in type and in the case of totally new uses for established products, campaign themes benefit from shock value and education value. These themes must jolt the consumer and startle him; they must be dramatic as they inform, describe, and explain; they must be powerful if they are to succeed in changing the attitudes and actions of consumers, attitudes and actions which, in many cases, are of long standing. For established products, particularly those with keen competition from brands almost identical, the campaign theme needs some point of competitive superiority — over earlier and older models of the advertised brand as well as over current versions of competing brands. Outstanding themes for standardized products are so difficult to find that the advertiser must sometimes base his theme on a minor matter, perhaps the product's package.

Certain characteristics handicap an advertising theme for a campaign. Themes that are broad and general, and themes which do nothing more than make general claims of quality or superiority are weak. Certain bases for themes are of low or questionable effectiveness. Some themes, for example, use irrelevant bases; some use the company name of the advertiser; some emphasize a product feature or use which is of little significance and concern to buyers; some feature a buyer-benefit low in attraction, interest, and desire value. Some themes make the mistake of stressing a product-feature when they should stress a buyer-benefit. Never should an advertiser be content with a theme which offers consumers only what competing products deliver.

Examples. Here are some themes which advertisers have used:

Coca-Cola	refreshment; hospitality
Diamonds	"A diamond is forever"
Cigars	happiness; success
Southern Pacific	"Next time — try the train"
Ivory	That Ivory Look
Container Corporation	Great Ideas of Great Men
Allstate	You're in good hands with Allstate
Breck	Beautiful Hair
Longines	The world's most honored watch
Hunt	for the best
Society of American Florists	"Say It With Flowers"

Selecting a Theme. The selection or creation of a theme should be attempted only after the collection of all necessary information about buyers and about the product to be advertised. Particularly essential is knowledge about the attitudes and aspirations of those consumers who are genuine prospects for the product. The campaign's objective is also necessary information. Another influence is the number of benefits to be featured. As has been mentioned, one benefit can be stressed throughout the campaign; or, only one benefit can be included in an advertisement, but several benefits can be included in the campaign; or finally, two or more benefits can be included in a single advertisement in the series.

A strong case can be made for a single benefit as the campaign theme. The point being made is that a single idea is superior to a scattering of several ideas. The supporting claim is that if a prospect thinks brand A is clearly and impressively superior to B, C, and D *in one major respect,* he automatically and inevitably tends to think A superior on *all* points or certainly in a *net* way.

Another strong case can be made in certain situations, however, for a theme which combines *two* benefits. Colgate, for example, has claimed in the same advertisement that its toothpaste (a) rids the individual of bad breath and (b) fights tooth decay all day. Du Pont, too, has used the combination campaign theme as this excerpt reveals:

> A survey we recently made on cellulose sponges is one example of our use of research to develop a copy theme. We made a mail survey among members of a commercial "panel" who were familiar with cellulose sponges. We asked them what they used the sponge for; what they liked most about it; and what, in their own words, would they most likely say about the sponge if they were telling a friend about it.
>
> The results of the survey were most helpful in developing our copy approach. The answers to the first question confirmed our opinion as to the most popular uses for the sponge in the home. The replies to the second question showed us, as we expected, that people liked the sponge because it is easy to use. The answers to the third question developed a fact which we knew but did not consider too important — that the sponge is easy to clean after using.
>
> In other words, in analyzing the results of the survey, we found that when people were asked what they liked most about the sponge, they said, "It's easy to use." But when they were asked what they would be most likely to tell a friend about the sponge, they said, "It's easy to clean after using."
>
> In a previous campaign we had featured the fact that the sponge is handy and easy to use. We had made reference to the fact that it is easy to clean after using, but had not featured this point.
>
> As a result of the survey, we decided to give equal emphasis to the two points. So we developed this theme for our campaign:
>
> > So easy to *clean with*
> > So easy to *clean* after using[1]

Some advertisers have indicated their interest in themes which can be used over a considerable period of time — two or three years, or even five. These advertisers are undoubtedly aware of and impressed by the experience of other advertisers who have stayed with the same themes through months or even years. In addition, these advertisers are acutely conscious of the huge amount of money required to launch and establish a theme. So, some advertisers seek durable themes, versatile enough to be the basis of a succession of campaigns.

In a search for possible themes, advertisers can benefit from a study of prospects and a study of customers. The former group can reveal why they do not buy the product involved, whereas the customer group can indicate why they do. Within the customer group, a theme may develop based on the *type of user,* or on the *identity of certain individuals* who use the product, or on the *number of users.* An-

---

[1] From a letter to the author written by Mr. Gilbert M. Miller of the E. I. du Pont de Nemours & Company.

other source of theme ideas is, of course, the product itself. Perhaps its design, its package, its price, its materials, or its workmanship — all product features, to be sure — can supply an effective buyer-benefit to serve as the core of a theme. Still another source, most appropriate for institutional campaign themes, is the advertising company itself, its policies or background, for example, or its facilities.

Slogan

One of the questions facing an advertiser is whether or not to translate his campaign theme into a slogan; if he answers this in the affirmative, then he must decide just what uses he should make of the slogan. There are two types of slogan. The short-range type condenses the theme and crystallizes it; indeed, this slogan can be the campaign's theme. This type of slogan disappears when its campaign ends. The long-range type of slogan (Ivory's "It Floats") is not an expression of the theme of the current campaign; its origin, of course, may be the theme of an earlier campaign. Long-range slogans can stay on as one of a manufacturer's promotional items indefinitely.

Both types of slogan are deftly turned phrases or sentences intended to be repeated verbatim. The advertiser expects them to be remembered favorably by consumers. But, no matter how apt the wording, slogans seldom attain wide popularity overnight. All of them must have promotion to become established and then to stay alive. Incidentally, there is no method of isolating whatever inherent excellence or quality a slogan possesses from the time and promotion which have been put behind the slogan. Some of the best-known slogans are of poor basic construction.

The slogan is not a big feature of today's advertising. No slogan, regardless of how soundly phrased, is enough to insure advertising success. Many consumers easily overrate the slogan as an advertising device because they are familiar with and impressed by one or more popular slogans. Ignorance of the true nature of advertising contributes, no doubt, to this erroneous belief. Few advertisers make any serious attempt to establish their short-range slogans if, indeed, they bother to phrase such; few advertisements contain slogans; few copywriters ever sit down just to write a slogan. A product like chewing gum or cigarettes can make more and better use of a slogan than can an automobile or a sofa. The broadcast media are more appropriate for the transmission of slogans than are most other media.

One type of slogan is based on some product-feature, telling what the product does or is, how the product works, the product's best feature, what the product does *not* have to do, or how the product is made. Another type is, essentially, the promise or claim of a buyer-benefit. Still another type suggests or commands the use of the product or warns against the acceptance of substitutes. All slogans hope to fix firmly in the buyer's mind one clear important idea favorable to the product or to its advertiser.

Principles of Construction. Slogans need to be simple, clear and obvious, catchy and colorful. They should be built on a big sales idea, on self-interest, on a buyer-benefit because their substance is more important than their style. Even so, effective use can be made of such devices as the pun, the play on words, rhythm, balance, parallelism, and alliteration. These devices help make slogans easy to say and easy to remember. Brief slogans are preferred; four-word length is excellent, seven words should be maximum. Desirable features are that the slogan be unlike competitors' slogans and unadaptable by competitors. The buyer-benefit or buyer-problem should come before the brand name; the so-called Rule of Three recommends that a slogan identify the *type of product* involved, promise a *buyer-benefit,* and include the *brand name.* Certainly the brand name should be included because there is much mistaken and incorrect identification of slogans with their sponsors.

Dull slogans which merely claim quality or excellence for their products fail to register with consumers. Arrogant slogans offend. Subtle or irrelevant slogans are seldom understood. Be they ever so cute and clever, slogans which imitate other slogans cannot be defended.

Objectives

The assignments given to advertising have been suggested at various earlier points in this book. In summary, most advertising by far is asked to influence buyers so as to affect sales and profits favorably. Most advertising hopes to convert non-users of the advertised type of product into users of the advertised brand, to win some buyers away from competitors, and to increase the consumption of present customers. The consumption of present customers can be increased in several ways:

> More frequent use of the product
> More frequent replacement of the product
> Use of product for more purposes
> Consumption of more product at each time of use
> Extension of consumption period
> Purchase of higher price lines
> Purchase of accessory or related products of the advertiser

Consumer campaigns of the product-promoting type can be asked to stimulate *primary* demand (for *type* of product or service) or *selective* demand (for the advertiser's *brand*). They can make a bid for psychological reaction (attitude) or physical reaction (purchase). Many advertisers hope their consumer campaigns will have some success in respect to such secondary objectives as increased good will from customers and the general public, better company morale, and greater enthusiasm on the part of the retailers and company salesmen.

Here are typical objectives of product-promoting advertising campaigns aimed at consumers:

> To announce a new product or an improved product
> To hold consumer patronage against intensified competition
> To inform consumers about a new product use
> To teach consumers how to use the product
> To promote a contest or a premium offer
> To establish a new trade character
> To help solve a local or regional problem
> To obtain a prospect list

INSTITUTIONAL CAMPAIGNS

Advertising which promotes the company rather than the company's products or services has, for a long time, been called *institutional* advertising. More recently there has been some effort made to replace the adjective and call this type of advertising *corporate* advertising or *strategic* advertising. Institutional advertising is quite appropriate for products whose quality and value can be determined only after a long period of use or consumption — if they can be determined at all. It is also quite appropriate for companies selling services, many of which services, such as transportation or brokerage, do not compete against direct competition on a price basis. Almost all institutional advertising is indirect action in character.

The three types of institutional advertising were mentioned in an earlier chapter. *Patronage,* the largest of the three, intends to influence favorably consumer attitudes toward the advertising company. This is attempted by publicizing company policies, principles, facilities, services, personnel, integrity, leadership, age, reputation, and width of product assortment. *Public relations* campaigns are designed to build up good will in one or more of the advertiser's "publics." Plant city advertising, campaigns during strikes, and advertising intended to influence legislation are examples. *Public service* campaigns are run by manufacturers who feel an obligation to contribute to the public welfare and to carry out their social responsibilities. During a war, for example, a company might advertise to discourage hoarding, to support bond drives, or to promote greater security.

Objectives of Institutional Campaigns

Typical objectives of institutional campaigns are:

To create a corporate personality or image
To build company prestige
To keep the company name before the public
To emphasize company services and facilities
To explain the desirability of large companies
To enable company salesmen to see top executives consistently when making sales calls
To increase friendliness toward the company
To promote safer driving

HORIZONTAL COOPERATIVE ADVERTISING CAMPAIGN

There are two basic types of horizontal cooperative advertising campaigns, one sponsored by competitors, the other by non-competitors; the first type is by far the more important. In the first type of horizontal cooperative campaign, a group of competing manufacturers, a group of competing retailers, a group of sellers of services, or, indeed, a group of competing growers or producers decides to sponsor a common advertising effort. The meat packers, the florists, the life insurance companies, and the dairy farmers are examples. Each of these groups uses advertising to promote its generic product or service, to promote it for the entire

A Time To Remember Who We Are

This is the time of year when Americans traditionally observe a day of thanksgiving for their blessings. It is good that we should do this.

But is it not also fitting that on this day—so reminiscent of our origins—we should be mindful of our heritage and the trust it imposes on us. The price the Pilgrims paid for survival. The bloody feet at Valley Forge. The thunder at the Alamo, Gettysburg, the Argonne, Midway, Bastogne and Pork Chop Hill.

Of the people we are and must continue to be. The people who fathered Washington, Jefferson, Franklin, Lincoln and Lee. The people who first united a continent with roads and railroads, produced the steamship, the telephone, the airplane and the greatest economy the world has ever known.

Yes, let us remember who we are. For a little pride is the wellspring of courage. Let us endure unflinchingly whatever sacrifices we are called upon to make to defend our free institutions from the night of communism, which is bent on undermining our faith in ourselves. Let us rely not only on the gold in our vaults, but the iron in our blood. And let us cling like ivy to the faith of our fathers until, in God's good time, all men are free.

INSURED SAVINGS AND LOAN ASSOCIATIONS

Sponsored by The Savings and Loan Foundation, Inc., 1111 "E" Street, N.W., Washington 4, D.C.

Original nine color wood engraving by Brussel-Smith

Institutional advertisement sponsored by a trade association. (Courtesy: The Savings and Loan Foundation, Inc., Washington, D.C.)

industry. Thus, a rather unusual feature of this type of cooperative campaign is the absence from the advertising of brand names. This emphasis on product type rather than on brand, on entire industry rather than on any firm or brand within the group means that horizontal cooperative advertising campaigns are institutional in character rather than product (brand) promoting. The advertisements intend to influence consumer attitudes about the industry, to create attitudes which encourage purchase of the industry's products or services.

This first type of campaign is usually handled through and by the group's trade association. Magazines and newspapers are the most popular media. Typically, the advertising attempts to achieve its objectives by informing, educating, describing, explaining, and justifying.

In the second type of horizontal cooperative advertising campaign, non-competing branded products or services get together to sponsor joint advertising. A simple example would be a one-page magazine advertisement featuring an airline and an automobile rental service, the advertisement paid for by the two companies. A more elaborate version might be based on the concept of an "All-American Breakfast." This could be a multi-page advertisement featuring such branded breakfast items as coffee, bacon, hot cake mix, butter, or syrup. A controlled and coordinated point-of-purchase program is also desirable even though difficult.

Stimuli to Horizontal Cooperative Campaigns

Several conditions or developments may cause an industry to consider planning a horizontal cooperative advertising campaign. If the sugar refiners learn that consumers think sugar too fattening, if the meat packers discover that consumers believe that meat eating causes high blood pressure, or if the Swiss watchmakers find that consumers are hostile toward foreign-made watches, thinking about cooperative advertising may be stimulated. Ignorance, disapproval, and opposition on the part of the public have led to this type of campaign.

The public's attitude toward certain products and services has at times reflected large amounts of inertia and apathy. This has been true of men's hats, for example, of paint, and of electric power. Cooperative campaigns have appeared for each of the three.

The appearance of a new type of competition may disturb, even frighten an old-line group into doing something about it, with advertising. The leather, the fuel, and the transportation industries are examples.

Finally, a group is sometimes shocked to realize the huge size of its potential market — and the picayune size of its actual market. If the shock is great enough, a horizontal cooperative advertising campaign may result. Such happened for plywood, tea, and citrus products.

Advertising Fund Plans

There are two basic methods of raising the dollars with which to finance this type of advertising. One is the solicitation of voluntary contributions from the members of the industry. This has worked for the life insurance group despite certain inherent defects in the plan. This technique offers no basis to a member for setting the amount he should give; it is not proportional; it is not conducive to continuity and permanence of program.

The other method makes a specific levy on each member. This could be based on last year's *production* of each member (per hundred-weight of edible meat) or on last year's *sales volume* of each member (gross revenue of railroads).

Problems of Horizontal Cooperative Advertising

There are several extremely difficult problems in the planning and executing of horizontal cooperative advertising. The first one, of course, is that of enlisting the support and enthusiasm of all firms in the industry. The company president who is a prima donna but does not understand advertising and the company which wants to hitch a free ride from its competitors are typical causes of this first difficulty. Once over this hurdle, then the problem becomes one of maintaining harmony, teamwork, and cooperation within the group. Another most serious problem is that of setting each company's share of the costs of the project. This may involve two types of firm within the industry (fur felt hatters versus straw hatters) and even firms outside the industry proper (manufacturers of hat ribbons or hat-making machinery). Sometimes there is a conflict within the industry about whether *dollar* sales or *unit* sales should be the base.

The advertisements themselves can be the source of disagreement. Selection of campaign theme, approval of copy, endorsement of the campaign schedule — each of these can and has caused serious difficulties.

Finally, year-after-year continuity is not easy to insure. Initial interest and enthusiasm can wane quickly. The lack of precise measurements of the advertising's performance, discouragement, a change in conditions, intensified competition among the industry's members — these help explain why some programs are abandoned.

Essentials of Horizontal Cooperative Advertising

If an advertising campaign by competitors is to succeed, certain prerequisites and conditions are necessary. First of all, there must be a clear cut problem or some other strong, specific stimulus for group advertising. Similarly, there must be a unified purpose and a common essential goal for the campaign. The goal must be one which cannot be reached by the individual and independent advertising of industry members. Next, a clear majority of the industry must participate, including by all means the dominant firm of the group. Then, an educational job is needed; members must be convinced of the value of the advertising project and must be persuaded to coordinate their respective advertising and personal selling activities with the group promotion. Members need to understand that *group* advertising is not a replacement nor substitute for *each firm's own* advertising program.

Continuing, the undertaking needs leadership — strong, competent, enlightened leadership. Often this is to be found in a small, working committee of industry firms. Finances must be sound. This calls for a strong financial plan — one which is adequate, fair, and long-range. Enough dollars should be committed by members before the first advertisement appears. Finally, these campaigns, like all others, demand effective themes. They must tell the consumer more, for example, than just to "Eat More Bread."

Advertising Management

Objectives of Horizontal Cooperative Advertising

Typical objectives of horizontal cooperative advertising campaigns are:

> To give the public a clearer concept of the service the group sells
> To stimulate good will for the industry
> To promote group aims
> To explain and defend group attitudes
> To correct false ideas
> To influence legislation

Questions and Problems

1. Contrast product-promoting advertising campaigns addressed to consumers with political campaigns.
2. What can a manufacturer do to develop the interest and cooperation of his retailers in his advertising campaigns?
3. Under what circumstances might a manufacturer have more than one advertising campaign running at the same time?
4. What factors influence the size (extent and intensity) of advertising campaigns?
5. What would an advertiser lose by running ads on just any topic instead of sticking to a single keynote idea?
6. List some marketing goals which may not be attainable within a calendar year.
7. Several noncompeting advertisers (coffee, bread, eggs, fruit juice) plan some joint advertising featuring an "All American Breakfast." What problems confront these sellers?
8. List some purposes of institutional campaigns.
9. The Tea Promotional Institute, a hypothetical 3-firm trade association for the last 10 years, has just announced that it is discontinuing its horizontal cooperative advertising effort to increase the public's consumption of tea. It is believed that this decision reflects the Institute's loss of one of its members, the National Tea Company, packer of National Tea. National is one of five large tea companies. Its departure from the institute leaves only two firms in the Institute. One rumor is that the two firms remaining in the association will cut back, dropping all consumer advertising in favor of a modest publicity and educational program. Comment.
10. The Magnolia Company is a manufacturer of a diversified group of consumer products including dentifrices, shampoos, shaving soaps and creams, detergents, toilet and household soaps. One of its biggest, best known, and most profitable brands of toilet soap, its Magnolia brand, is now encountering keen competition from a brand recently launched by one of Magnolia's competitors.
    Magnolia's advertising manager thinks that a big consumer contest is indicated. He has noted that contests, which are popular — then unpopular — then popular again, are more numerous than for some time. The manager is well aware of the fact that contests have increased sales for many sponsors.
    The advertising manager is thinking in terms of the tried and proved, "I like Magnolia soap because . . ." in 25 words. He favors a diversified prize list including cash and merchandise. As for length of contest, he recommends eight weeks. The contest would, of course, have to be promoted and merchandised heavily.
    What do you think of the contest idea?

Chapter 20

Coordination

The purpose of this chapter is to show what Advertising might be asked and expected to do for other departments it touches in the typical company, and what those departments, in turn, might be asked to do for Advertising. *There is nowhere included a complete enumeration of the duties or functions of any department.* Rather, the basic concept is one of interdepartmental, two-way relationships between the Advertising department and each of the other departments within the company with which Advertising has considerable contact. These other departments are Sales, Sales Promotion, Public Relations, Research, Production, and the Controller.

ADVERTISING AND PERSONAL SELLING

Once a manufacturer has produced merchandise, he finds that two main forces are available for his use in moving that merchandise to its market, *personal selling* and *advertising*. The functions of the Advertising department and the functions of the Sales department are two phases of a single activity, *selling*. Viewed in this light, advertising is selling to masses while personal selling is selling to individuals. Viewed in any light, advertising and selling have the same purpose, a purchase-and-sale transaction, an exchange; their difference is in method.

Seldom does advertising start a buyer out on the road to a purchase and propel him through all the steps including the act of buying. True, advertising *does* do the entire marketing job for the mail-order group of sellers. They sell their food, clothing, correspondence courses, novelties, and gifts through the use of only one of the marketing forces, *advertising*. These mail-order sellers, it must be remembered, are a small minority group. Probably a larger group than the mail-order sellers makes use of personal selling and of no advertising in marketing its wares. Unless a manufacturer is small, or unless he is operating under conditions that are at least somewhat uncommon, he probably will find that all personal selling and no

Note: In this chapter, such words as advertising, production, research, and sales promotion refer to *functions*. When capitalized (Advertising, Research, etc.), they refer to *departments*.

advertising is not the best answer to his marketing problems. By far the most common pattern for the typical manufacturer is one that combines advertising and personal selling.

It is difficult if not impossible to imagine any two activities between which coordination is as necessary as between advertising and selling. In one sense, some degree of coordination or at least of cooperation is no less than inevitable. For example, both operate in terms of the same geographical areas — sales territories. Both must work together in budgeting the advertising effort among the sales territories. Timing of activities is a problem common to both; the wholesalers and retailers called on by the company's salesmen want the company's advertising to be neither too soon nor too late. Both Advertising and Selling are interested in the effect of advertising on the cost of selling, and, at least to some degree, on the cost of production. Both use the same data and base their activities on the same forecasts. Both promote the same products and sell the same buyer-benefits and -satisfactions to the same buyers. Both must analyze the over-all sales problem before they can determine which jobs advertising can do better, faster, and cheaper.

Because advertising and selling constitute a major part of a marketing program they must be intermeshed and coordinated effectively or else the marketing program is not organized. When advertising and selling work as a team, they can accomplish their marketing job more profitably than when each works alone. Provision must be made for healthy liaison and cooperation if each is to make the other's operation of maximum effectiveness and efficiency.

What Advertising Does For Personal Selling

Pre-Sells the Consumer and the Middleman. The greatest service advertising does for personal selling is to pre-sell the company's products to the company's buying publics, consumers and middlemen. This result is achieved by the Advertising department's building and running effective, informative, and persuasive advertisements that influence buyers.

Advertising may start by locating new prospects and then go on to condition them for a salesman's call. By spotting prospects and acquainting them with the salesman's products, advertising makes the salesman's job easier. The product is endowed with certain amounts of prestige, quality, and desirability before the buyer ever sees it. The manufacturer becomes a more acceptable source of supply because the consumer or middleman is familiar with him.

Increases the Salesman's Salespower. Because of this pre-selling, buyers' receptions are more friendly than they would be if the salesman's company did not advertise. During his time face-to-face with buyers the salesman can concentrate and specialize in telling his story because he is talking to buyers who have a picture of the general proposition. His calls are featured by less resistance and opposition than if he were selling a product that is not advertised; this is because advertising has run some interference for the salesman.

Middlemen are more receptive to the salesman's story because the advertising of the salesman's company has made less difficult the middlemen's own selling job.

The pre-selling influence of advertising prepares the consumer, informs him, warms him up, and even partially persuades him for the retailer. In addition, the same helpful and informative copy in the consumer advertising of the manufacturer influences, impresses, and is useful to the selling personnel of both wholesalers and retailers.

Advertising increases the salesman's morale. One reason for healthier morale is the fact that Advertising instructs and informs salesmen about advertising in general and about the company's advertising in particular. In this undertaking, Advertising itself functions, and it calls in the company's advertising agency to contribute what the agency is in a better position to offer. It is not uncommon for Advertising to arrange for someone from the advertising agency to attend sales meetings and brief the sales force. A second reason for healthier morale is the additional measure of confidence cultivated in a salesman by his company's advertising. When he is selling a product that is advertised by a manufacturer who believes in and employs advertising effectively, a salesman has cause for pride both in his merchandise and in its maker. This pride in his relationships, this feeling of superiority, gives the salesman an optimistic outlook and attitude.

Advertising can make the salesman's presentation stronger and more successful. Advertising serves the salesman as a source of selling points and ideas; when the salesman stresses the same buyer-benefits and satisfactions his company is emphasizing in its advertisements, he finds his selling reinforced by the advertising. In addition to talking points, Advertising supplies salesmen with helpful material and visual aids which make selling more effective. Advertising prevents a salesman's being forgotten by buyers when the time interval between calls is long.

Expands Sales Volume. In creating, educating, and guiding demand, advertising works toward the goals of influencing, regulating, and increasing sales volume. In markets where the potential is inadequate to support salesmen, advertising usually takes on the entire job of promotion. Thus, *a* major if not *the* major service Advertising does for Sales is to help in the stimulation and direction of the flow of the manufacturer's goods to the consumer.

One of advertising's greatest influences on sales volume is through its effects on the good will of buyers. In the middleman area, Advertising helps Sales to open new markets and to get distribution by inviting and getting the good will of wholesalers and retailers. Once desirable and adequate distribution has been achieved, then advertising starts to work helping the manufacturer hold these accounts. As good will grows among the trade, so grows the amount of renewal and repeat business the manufacturer attracts. In addition, the manufacturer enjoys a lower dealer turnover and a higher degree of dealer support. In the consumer area, good will has the same beneficial results, support, loyalty, enthusiasm, and continued patronage. An incidental feature of this delightful state of affairs is that the manufacturer's job of attracting and holding the better salesmen is less difficult.

Advertising both increases and stabilizes sales volume by helping Sales achieve *balanced* sales. If the manufacturer has a family of products, he can use advertising to help keep each member of the family in its most profitable place in the family.

Advertising Management

If the problem of balance has to do with types of consumer or types of middleman, advertising will help achieve balance among buyers. If the problem is geographic, the same is true. Finally, if the manufacturer's chief worry is seasonal, advertising will help make selling less difficult in the "off" seasons. By timing its activities to make personal selling most effective, advertising helps maximize and stabilize sales by combating and smoothing out seasonal variation and fluctuations. The promotion of hot tea in winter and iced coffee in summer would be examples of this last type of balance.

What Personal Selling Does For Advertising

Keeps Advertising Sales-Minded. Probably the first favor Sales should do for Advertising is to keep the advertising manager and his staff sales-slanted and sales-minded. Perhaps the advertising manager is inclined to wander away from his prime responsibility. Perhaps someone near and dear to him encourages him to advocate advertising activities which, while they may be eminently commendable on civic or cultural grounds, do not result in increasing sales and profits. Perhaps even his advertising agency may be blinded momentarily to its paramount duty. Regardless of how or why the error may occur, the point here is that Sales, under pressure hour by hour and day after day to raise sales volume and profits, can and should keep Advertising on the only track it should operate on. That is the track that leads to the same objectives Sales is instructed and determined to gain.

Shares Departmental Information. Neither the advertising manager nor his department can function intelligently or effectively without a hard core of facts which can come only from Sales. Sales records are one type of such information. Unless Advertising knows how many sales were made where, it is not in a position to plan next season's or next year's advertising program. Sales records are basic data by which Advertising can steer. They reveal essential facts which simply must be taken into account by Advertising both in checking on the performance of past advertising and in shaping future campaigns.

Sales plans are another type of information Advertising must have and can get only from Sales. These plans originate with the sales manager's problems and needs which, incidentally, he benefits from discussing with the advertising manager. Then come the sales forecasts for the coming period, on which forecasts both Advertising and Sales must build their own plans and programs. Clearly, Advertising needs to be in on the determination of these final figures, because, after all, advertising causes sales. So, the sales manager must keep Advertising informed as these estimates begin to take shape. Until Advertising knows what products Sales will be selling, what the prospects are for sales volume and for profits, and, indeed, what the sales manager's preferences are in regard to advertising, until then Advertising cannot plan its activities.

Supplies Materials and Suggestions. The salesforce of a manufacturer is one source on which Advertising can draw for the raw materials out of which advertisements are made. Experiences of buyers usually become known to a company through its salesmen, and these experiences can give the salesmen ideas worth relaying to Advertising. Or, the experiences themselves may be excellent case histories for Advertising to publicize, or at least the foundations for testimonials. Product information or news about the trade often contain materials from which advertisements or even campaigns can be fashioned.

Sales personnel can supply valuable suggestions as well as material. They can contribute to Advertising their opinions and recommendations about such matters as motivation, message, and media. Their views on timing, a matter of common interest, should be invited. Before any proposed advertising program is adopted as *the* program for the coming period, it should be submitted by Advertising to Sales for criticism and comment. Sales does Advertising a favor by checking the content and construction of these programs on the point of their selling effectiveness.

As a sidelight on this matter of suggestions from Sales about the company's advertising, it may be well to remember that Advertising is really doing *two* desirable things when it invites such suggestions. One, Advertising just may get an idea or two worth using. Two, Advertising's request is accepted by the salesmen as a compliment and a courtesy; it pleases the salesmen and, hence, encourages them to be cooperative.

Reports on Market Conditions. Although they might be reluctant or even embarrassed to admit it, salesmen serve as excellent eyes and ears for Advertising. Often salesmen are the only company employees in touch with the company's customers, both trade and ultimate. Typically, it is to the salesmen that wholesalers and retailers talk freely and frankly about products and prices — policies and promotions. It is not uncommon for a company, including its Advertising department, to acquire information of this sort through its salesmen when the same facts would not be obtained through any other channel or company activity.

Salesmen can keep Advertising posted continuously on the picture of and the conditions in each market. This picture includes what the salesman's company is doing and how it is making out in respect to advertising and sales and, in addition, the identity, the ranking, the marketing activities, and the apparent degree of success of each competitor in each market. Significant changes in any market should be made known to Advertising almost as promptly as to Sales. If such changes demand counter measures of the company's sales force or revisions of the company's sales plans, Advertising should certainly be notified at once because it, too, may want to make adjustments in its plans.

In the preceding section, the value of salesmen's ideas and suggestions was noted. In somewhat the same fashion, thoughts and suggestions from individuals in the markets can be extremely helpful. Advertising is properly curious about the reactions of people to the company advertisements, especially about any reactions that are in any way extreme. By learning as much as it can about the response to its advertisements, both critical and favorable, Advertising helps ready itself to do a better job.

When maximum use is made of salesmen as reporters of market conditions, a more snugly tailored advertising program can be fitted to a manufacturer's markets.

Advertising Management

Advertising learns from the salesmen of problems in various spots where advertising can be a partial or even the complete solution. Advertising learns, in addition, of opportunities where advertising would stand an excellent chance of being magnificently successful. And, for each of those particular markets, salesmen can describe the local point of view, the local attitudes, and the local preferences. In transmitting these to Advertising, in interpreting each market for Advertising, salesmen help tailor the company advertising to each market and guide in localizing the advertising activities to the needs and preferences of each.

Works For Dealer Support. In point of time sequence, salesmen do Advertising the great and absolutely essential service of stocking wholesalers and retailers with merchandise before the advertising program breaks. This is not always an easy undertaking, because one of the retailer's favorite stalls or objections is, "Your product and your promotion plans seem fine — but I'd better hold off stocking your merchandise until I begin to get calls for it." The salesman's maneuver, of course, is to convince middlemen that their profits can be maximized only if they have the items in stock and ready for customers when, in response to advertising, those customers ask for or even about the products. Before each advertising campaign opens, there should, there *must,* be a minimum amount of distribution if the campaign is to be of greatest effectiveness. Advertising must thank the salesforce for this distribution.

It is the salesman who, in the main, "sells" wholesalers and retailers on the advertising activities of his company. Once the middlemen, particularly the retailers, know and approve of the manufacturer's advertising program, they are urged to cooperate by coordinating their promotion activities with those of the salesman's company. The salesman asks them to synchronize their advertising, their display, and their personal selling with the manufacturer's promotion.

ADVERTISING AND SALES PROMOTION

There has never been a clear-cut, generally accepted definition of the sales promotion function. To some manufacturers, advertising is the force that pulls buyers toward the product, while sales promotion joins personal selling in pushing the product toward buyers. To other manufacturers, advertising is in direct contact with consumers, while sales promotion reaches those same consumers indirectly through the manufacturer's salesmen and through middlemen. Still another concept of sales promotion is that sales promotion starts, gets under way, carries on, and follows through where mass advertising stops. These three concepts point up the fact that a gap exists between advertising and personal selling; the advertising message generally talks impersonally to large groups of consumers, never seeing individual consumers nor the retailers who serve them, while the company's salesmen generally see and sell only to wholesalers or retailers. Sales promotion's assignment is to do something about this gap.

This section is based on the assumption that the sales promotion activity should include certain activities between manufacturer and ultimate consumer, certain relations between manufacturer and his middlemen, and certain liaison jobs between

Coordination

the Advertising department and the Sales department. There is no assumption whatever that the sales promotion manager should coordinate advertising and personal selling through line authority over the advertising manager and the sales manager; it is felt that he should *not* be in such an organizational relationship to them. The sales promotion manager should be on a par with the two other managers, not over them, and his duty is to assist and to intermesh the two functions, not to coordinate them from a position superior to both.

What Advertising Does For Sales Promotion

Gives Information. One of the greatest services Advertising can do for Sales Promotion is to keep the latter posted in areas of mutual concern. If Advertising informs Sales Promotion well in advance of its plans and schedules and something of the reasoning behind them, then Sales Promotion can do a better job as it works with the company's salesmen and middlemen. Advertising should make known the advertising theme or keynote idea it plans to feature, the individual media it is to use, the size of each advertisement and its date of appearance, and the

Although store displays such as this may be the responsibility of Sales Promotion, Advertising and Personal Selling, too, were probably involved. (Courtesy: General Mills, Inc.)

Advertising Management

specific products to be featured. Sales Promotion can plan effectively only if it knows what Advertising will be doing.

Offers Guidance and Aid. Sales Promotion naturally looks to and depends on Advertising for advice and even for assistance in some undertakings. Two of Sales Promotion's specific assignments, for example, are to see that the company is well represented at fairs, and to see that a good stage is set for the company's sales conventions. Sales Promotion can describe and explain the fairs and conventions to Advertising, and, if Advertising agrees or recommends, the two departments can work together to put together appropriate advertising exhibits. Another duty commonly assigned to Sales Promotion is that of training the company salesmen, and here, too, Sales Promotion needs to be guided and aided by Advertising. Promotion programs for dealers, also a Sales Promotion responsibility, cannot be harmonized with the manufacturer's program to the degree desired unless Sales Promotion is assisted by Advertising. It is neither improper nor surprising for Advertising to let *assistance* merge into actual *execution,* with, for instance, Advertising's actually writing a bit of copy now and then for Sales Promotion.

Supplies Materials. Advertising is one source of materials on which Sales Promotion draws. The portfolios Sales Promotion assembles for the company salesmen and the kits Sales Promotion prepares for wholesalers and retailers must contain certain items which practically can come from no source but Advertising. Too, when Sales calls on Sales Promotion for some special presentation to use in converting a prospect into a customer, it is quite likely that Sales Promotion will, in turn, draw some materials from Advertising. It is unusual if Advertising does not supply some of the materials Sales Promotion uses in constructing exhibits for trade shows.

Does Promotion Work. Sales Promotion would have to lower its sights considerably and even then be resigned to less effective operation if advertising were not available for use as a promotion force. Advertising's outstanding contribution in this respect is that of publicizing certain elements of the sales promotion program. It is the right of Sales Promotion, of course, to construct whatever programs it deems best. Once those programs have been shaped, however, it becomes Advertising's duty to help "sell" them. For example, Sales Promotion decides *whether* there is to be a consumer contest, and, if so, decides all details about its nature. Then Sales Promotion and Advertising get together on planning how the contest should be publicized. Or, Sales Promotion selects a premium and constructs a premium offer that Advertising helps promote. In addition to contests and premiums, other elements in sales promotion programs that make profitable use of advertising include sampling, advertising specialties, demonstrations in retail stores, and the consumer-education activity.

A milder degree of advertising cooperation is found when Advertising includes in advertisements the offer of Sales Promotion items, asking readers to write in for catalogues, color cards, price lists, instructional manuals, or booklets. Similarly, advertising may include the names and addresses of selected retailers in local advertisements and, sometimes, even in national advertisements.

Coordination

What Sales Promotion Does For Advertising

Teaches Salesmen About Advertising. Few conditions are more desirable, perhaps it is not too strong to use the word *essential,* than that a company's salesmen know what advertising is all about. Sales Promotion undertakes to inform and to educate salesmen about advertising as a marketing force, about what advertising can and should do, and about what it must not be asked to do. Having explained the potentials and the limitations of advertising, Sales Promotion then shows the salesmen how and why advertising is their ally and not their competitor.

Sales Promotion shows the salesmen first of all that the company's advertising does not displace salesmen or reduce their earnings, and, in the thinking of certain salesmen, these appear as real dangers. Following this, Sales Promotion convinces the salesman that it is possible for him to be more successful by engaging in some non-selling activities in connection with advertising along with his selling work. For example, Sales Promotion shows the salesman why it is profitable, hence smart, to help retailers construct more efficient advertising programs of their own within their own promotion programs.

Once advertising in general has been explained, Sales Promotion can then undertake the job usually termed "merchandising the company's advertising" to the salesforce. Sales Promotion describes the company's philosophy and convictions as regards its use of advertising. The future advertising efforts the company plans to make are studied. Sales Promotion posts the salesmen in advance on the objectives of each campaign, the appeals or keynote ideas to be used, and the schedules to be followed. The reasoning behind the proposed techniques and activities is presented. How the company arrived at its decisions about future policies and program is explained. Any changes in current advertising involving, perhaps, media, or timing, or techniques are justified. Sales Promotion hopes to leave the company's salesmen proud of the advertising their company plans to do.

Merchandising the company's advertising to the sales force also involves showing each salesman how he can sell the program he just bought — how to sell it to the middlemen he'll be seeing. Although the salesman is somewhat concerned with wholesalers as a group, his predominating interest is in the retailers who stock and sell his goods. How a manufacturer makes out can be influenced greatly by how his retailers feel and act about being, in effect, the manufacturer's local representative. Indeed, in some cases, manufacturers are considerably at the mercy of their retailers. In these circumstances, it is highly desirable for manufacturers to acquire and cultivate the good will and cooperation of their retail dealers, and then to strive for enthusiastic support from as many of them as possible. One channel through which to move toward this objective of dealer support is established by the manufacturer's advertising policies and programs. Sales Promotion endeavors to teach the salesmen how to present their company's advertising most forcibly and dramatically. Used in this manner, his company's advertising becomes for the salesman a powerful sales point. This advertising can be presented to retail prospects as reason for beginning to handle the line, and to established customers as reason for increased patronage. Salesmen are quick to recognize their company's advertising as one more strong reason for some of a middleman's business. Salesmen are

Advertising Management

quick to see that it is to their advantage to synchronize the story they tell with the story their advertising is telling.

Assembles Salesman's Advertising Portfolios. One of the most persuasive selling tools a salesman can use is an impressive advertising portfolio. So highly do some companies regard them that they prepare a new advertising sample case for their salesmen each month. The portfolios are properly assembled by Sales Promotion and include two types of material, company advertisements and items for retail dealers. The company advertisements are the same ones shown to the salesforce by Sales Promotion when it was merchandising the company advertising to the salesmen. In addition to pre-prints of company advertisements that will be appearing and to descriptions, often rather elaborate, of TV shows the company sponsors, there is usually accompanying information. Such information certainly should include schedules and media. The purpose of this company advertising material is to enable the salesman to merchandise his company's program to middlemen just as Sales Promotion merchandised it to him.

The second type of material in the salesman's advertising portfolio consists of items for use by retailers in their advertising. Typically, these items are constructed or selected with one hope in mind — that the retailer will find them so excellent and so convenient that he will use them to advertise the products of the salesman's company. In this group of items are suggested tie-in advertisements the retailer can run in his newspapers and suggested radio and TV announcements for his local stations. There will be samples of direct mail and other sales literature the retailer may order and use in a variety of ways. There will be small point-of-purchase items and pictures with descriptions of items too large to fit into the portfolio. Cuts and mats may be included, or they may be described so the retailer can order them. Pictures of displays show retailers possible treatments for window and interior display space, and diagrams indicate how product displays can be built to support the retailer's advertising activities.

Sales Promotion draws from Advertising all materials available from Advertising and does any preparation or processing necessary for use by the salesmen. Then Sales Promotion supplements this with items of its own design and construction, including any visual aids the salesmen will need in merchandising the company program to dealers.

Encourages Dealer Cooperation. One of the more significant responsibilities of the sales promotion manager is to enlist and guide the promotion cooperation of retailers. Sales Promotion keeps in touch with middlemen, both through its own personnel and through the company's salesmen; hence, it is the logical group to urge middlemen to go along with the manufacturer's advertising recommendations.

Advertising cooperation desired of dealers by the manufacturer can be of two possible types. First, the Sales Promotion department can suggest strongly that retailers use the advertising materials Sales Promotion has prepared for them — direct mail, point of purchase that includes dealer identification signs, ideas and suggestions about copy, and such. By making use of these aids according to the schedule set up and recommended by the manufacturer, the retailer steps up the effectiveness of the manufacturer's advertising in such media as magazines, radio, TV, and newspapers. When the retailer coordinates and synchronizes his advertising with the manufacturer's advertising, the over-all effect can easily be more helpful to each than should each follow his own personal dictates.

There is a second type of advertising cooperation possible between manufacturer and retailer. If the manufacturer follows a policy of sharing the cost of certain types of advertising done over the retailer's name, if he offers a vertical cooperative advertising program to his retailers, then Sales Promotion's interest is in getting retailers to participate in such programs.

In addition to the two types of advertising cooperation, Sales Promotion recommends that retailers cooperate in matters more strictly in the sales promotion province but most of which have advertising overtones or connections. Dealer contests are such a matter, because the greater the number of retailers who participate and the greater the enthusiasm of each, the more productive will be the manufacturer's advertising. Or, if a consumer contest is being run (and these are usually supported with heavy advertising), retailers may be asked to distribute entry blanks to contestants. Or, samples may be passed out to consumers in retail stores or premiums displayed or even distributed there.

Sales Promotion uses several techniques in trying to secure maximum cooperation from dealers. A representative to meet with dealers in person may be sent to dealer conventions and shows where next year's products and promotions are to be unveiled. Such a Sales Promotion representative may even be in charge of a company's booth or exhibit. Trade paper advertising both informs dealers of company plans and programs and urges dealer cooperation. Direct mail is used for the same purposes. Sales Promotion looks to its company's salesmen to point out to dealers why local advertising is needed to accompany national advertising and to explain fully why vertical cooperative advertising is a profitable promotion activity for dealers as well as for manufacturer.

Manages The Point-Of-Purchase Advertising. Point-of-purchase advertising, done on or in the retailer's place of business, should be a function of the Sales Promotion department. Because the Advertising department is responsible for the advertising done in a majority of the media manufacturers use, namely, newspapers, magazines, radio, TV, outdoor, and transportation, then it seems correct to say that Sales Promotion does a service for Advertising in being in complete charge of the point-of-purchase medium.

The manufacturer's major advertising efforts and advertising dollars are normally placed in the six media for which the Advertising department is responsible. This large part of the total advertising program is made much more effective if the same appeals, the same buying motives, and the same themes are seen by consumers at the point of purchase. Only the point-of-purchase medium can dramatize in retail stores the manufacturer's mass advertising. Because Sales Promotion works up the dealer program and then sells it to retailers through and by the manufacturer's salesmen, and because the point-of-purchase materials are an important part of the dealer

Size and impact characterize this floor display. Permission to erect may not have come easily. (Courtesy: Container Corporation of America)

program, it follows that Sales Promotion is shouldering no small task in undertaking to manage both the production and distribution of point-of-purchase advertising.

Manages the Direct-Mail Advertising. Sales Promotion is also in charge of direct mail. Many, if not all, of the company's departments will use direct mail for a variety of purposes, but, so far as direct-mail *advertising* is concerned, that activity should be lodged within the Sales Promotion department.

Two types of direct-mail advertising must be created by Sales Promotion. First, mailings to be sent to the manufacturer's wholesalers and retailers, mailings whose ultimate purpose is exactly that of all of the manufacturer's other advertising — increased profits through increased sales. As in the case of point-of-purchase advertising, this type of direct mail is so close to the dealer program and to dealer relations that its logical place is in Sales Promotion. The second type of direct-mail advertising is that created by Sales Promotion for use by the company's wholesalers and retailers. This clearly is a part of the dealer program and, hence, is properly handled by Sales Promotion. If middlemen are now using certain forms of direct-mail advertising and want an opinion or some advice about it, they should feel free to describe to Sales Promotion what they are doing and ask for criticisms and suggestions.

Handles Advertising Specialties. Sales Promotion is properly responsible for its firm's use (or non-use) of advertising specialties. What *is* an advertising specialty? It is a useful item given to a buyer by a seller; it usually carries an advertising message of some sort; it usually is imprinted with the seller's name, address, and telephone number; it is normally kept and used by the buyer. The advertising specialty field is both big and wide. Annual volume approximates $500,000,000, and the items range from address books and ash trays to yardsticks and yo-yo's.

These specialties are grouped into three classifications, one of which is termed *advertising novelties*. These are relatively inexpensive per unit and, consequently, can be distributed widely. Most carry the seller's identification, location, and brief promotional copy. Examples are ball point pens, pencils, key tags, blotters, combs, balloons, rulers, and bottle openers.

Executive gifts are a second type of advertising specialty. Because these are considerably more costly than advertising novelties, their distribution is limited to individuals whose influence and decisions are important. Although some executive gifts carry the seller's imprint and other gifts personalize the recipient's name, most carry neither. Desk sets, clocks, food, pen and pencil sets — these gifts have been described as reminders of someone's thoughtfulness.

Calendars, the third type of advertising specialty, account for about $135,000,000 of the $500,000,000 total and are the one most common specialty. Most calendars function as small "indoor posters," occupying free wall space or desk space at business or at home. Calendars are useful, they are looked at often, they have a long life, they require no upkeep.

Several features of advertising specialties deserve mention. Most do a repetitious type of communication, delivering their messages many times. They can be used before or after a sale; they can say "Please" or "Thank you." Most enjoy excellent positions, on wall, on desk, in pocket. The seller selects the group to receive the specialties, and he controls the distribution. Advertising specialties reach buyers by mail and by person, at home, or store, or office; they can be used to advantage with customers and with prospective customers.

Stimulates Consumers. In performing services for Advertising, Sales Promotion does not stop after working with salesmen and middlemen; there are contacts with and programs for the manufacturer's ultimate consumers. The main purpose of Sales Promotion's activities directed toward consumers is that of consumer stimulation. Prominent among these activities are contests, premiums, demonstrations, sampling, public fairs and exhibits, and consumer educational services and facilities. All phases of these activities from start to finish are under the management of Sales Promotion. They are listed here as a service Sales Promotion does for Advertising because such projects cause a manufacturer's prospects, customers, and the general public to be more favorably inclined to that manufacturer and his advertising.

Sales Promotion can be designated to receive all communications from consumers and to acknowledge receipt of them. If the communication is an inquiry that seems promising, Sales Promotion may follow up by mail or may turn the inquiry over to a company salesman or to one of the company's retailers for personal follow-up. If the letter is a complaint, Sales Promotion is the proper department to handle the matter. If the communications are in response to an offer or an invitation

Advertising Management

contained in advertisements, Sales Promotion can log the replies and collect information about advertising for the Advertising department.

ADVERTISING AND PUBLIC RELATIONS

The basic aim of a company's public relations is for the company to be and to be accepted as a good citizen. If this aim is to be achieved, a company must take three steps. First, the company must recognize that business and society share the same experience and fate, faring well or poorly together. Second, company policies and practices, decisions and actions must be in the public interest. Third, the various groups or "publics" who determine or even influence the success of a company must be informed about the company. Public relations, then, is fundamentally a point of view, an attitude, a frame of mind, or, indeed, a way of life.

The basis for public relations is the firm conviction that what people believe about a company and how they feel toward it and its merchandise are matters of major importance. Public relations wants to influence individuals' opinions; it wants the company to be understood and accepted; it wants approval and support for company policies, products, and personnel. Public relations invites and cultivates the favor and good will of all the company's "publics."

The essence of public relations is in formulating and executing sound policies and then in publicizing those policies-in-action by presenting them to the company's "publics." In this sense, public relations itself is a company *policy* rather than a company *department*. As a matter of fact, a manufacturer can get along without a Public Relations department — but not without a public relations *program*. Thus, public relations is not a function separate and apart from other departmental functions such as production or purchasing. It is, instead, all those activities a manufacturer engages in for the purpose of achieving a favorable attitude or feeling toward his company. Obviously, public relations is broader in scope than advertising.

Because public relations is a staff function of top management, its policies and objectives must be set by a company's management. Because Public Relations helps mold all company policies, the public relations function should report to top management and have its own budget. This arrangement, however logical, is far from universal, examination showing that the proper organizational slot for Public Relations is a matter for debate. When the Public Relations head does not report directly to top management, he may be found under the advertising manager or under the sales promotion manager.

Once the company is sound in management, products, and policies, Public Relations is ready to take up its various duties and to start employing its various tools and techniques. Public Relations depends on effective communication to achieve its objectives. Of its methods of communicating, *publicity* and *advertising,* as we have discussed in Chapter 2, are the most important. Both are an integral part of the Public Relations program.

Many secondary tools and techniques are available for use by Public Relations. One group includes books, booklets, reports, house organs, and literature of various sorts. Quite different, but quite effective, is personal contact. Public Relations may operate a speakers bureau or, in certain circumstances, it may supply only the speeches. Visits to and tours of the plant by outsiders can be handled in such a way as to further good public relations. Movies, exhibits, displays, and teaching aids for classroom use by instructors are other possibilities.

What Advertising Does For Public Relations

Provides a Channel to the "Publics." Advertising is the most obvious method of influencing public opinion, and, it must be recalled, the job of Public Relations is just that. One cannot influence, one cannot affect or persuade, unless one makes his point of view and the reasoning behind it known. For years advertising has been used to influence two of a manufacturer's "publics," his prospects and his customers, about the manufacturer's *merchandise*. What is more natural than for Public Relations to use this same form of communication to sell *ideas* to various "publics"? Indeed, how else does advertising sell products except through the selling of ideas? Public Relations finds in advertising, then, one means whereby company policies can be explained to the groups concerned and company ends and objectives can be achieved. For Public Relations even as for the marketing personnel, advertising is a voice. In addition, through the use of advertising, Public Relations can pinpoint its individual "publics" simply by making intelligent choices among individual media. Whether the manufacturer needs to reach the masses that compose his general public, or just the smallest segment of his "publics," advertising can accommodate him.

Builds Institutional Advertisements. Institutional advertising has been correctly described as a basic tool of Public Relations. An initial and fundamental question is whether the Public Relations people should produce their advertisements or whether the advertising staff should execute these advertisements for Public Relations. It would hardly seem wise to ask Public Relations to construct advertisements when there are specialized advertising experts in the company organization. The arrangement that seems best calls for Public Relations to place its problems in the hands of Advertising, together with ideas, information, and even recommendations, and for Advertising then to put the advertisements together — copy, layout, and such. This allows Public Relations to designate *what* is to featured and Advertising to decide *how*. Such a division of labor seems quite sound when one recalls that Public Relations is close to company actions and policies, even to the extent of having helped shape them, and Advertising specializes in advertising techniques and methods. Should Public Relations build its institutional advertisements, there would be grave danger of their "talking to themselves."

Creates a Favorable Atmosphere. The very fact that a company advertises usually results in an environment friendly toward that company, and, hence, one in which Public Relations can operate more successfully. If the advertising has been sound, then Public Relations is working with and for a company that is not only known but known favorably. Advertising all by itself makes an impression on all of a

Advertising Management

manufacturer's "publics," and, when that advertising is well planned and executed, one result is that the "publics" are conditioned to think highly of the company. The "publics" are allies because of the advertising.

What Public Relations Does For Advertising

Insists on Company Soundness. If a company is to operate so as to be liked by all groups it touches, and that, of course, is the heart of good public relations, then that company must be sound throughout. Sound companies are characterized by sound personnel, sound products, and sound policies; their internal affairs are in a state of good health; their merchandise is promoted as intelligently as it is produced. Where any segment or area of a company is unsound, there is always the real possibility that some unfavorable publicity will wipe out overnight many years and many dollars of advertising. Any concept of Public Relations is too narrow that sees the area as involving nothing more than the publicizing of company policies and good deeds. Public Relations has a basic and undeniable concern in policy formulation and determination in addition to its interest in policy execution and communication. Public Relations helps insure a climate of soundness in which and with which advertising functions, and this contributes to the performance of that advertising.

Places Publicity Releases. Where Public Relations handles publicity effectively and with good judgment, Advertising stands to benefit. Specifically, Public Relations can get publicity for the manufacturer's advertising program from the editors of media; this is quite desirable because of the greater reader-respect enjoyed by the editorial sections of a medium over the advertising sections. News releases can be constructed which will support and complement the current messages in the advertisements. Publicity can be both planned and timed so as to benefit Advertising. An excellent example of this sort of synchronization would be the preparation and distribution of news releases at the time Advertising and Sales are launching a new product on a broad scale. By exercising good judgment, Public Relations invites the good will of media and this, of course, can do Advertising no harm.

Helps Improve Advertising. Public Relations is always available to give advice and suggestions to Advertising as to how its advertising might be improved, and, in certain instances, Public Relations may even collaborate in the building of individual advertisements. It is from Public Relations that Advertising learns what the company's policies and attitudes are, and Advertising must know them before it can observe and respect them. It is also from Public Relations that Advertising learns how the various "publics" feel toward the company and its advertising. Sometimes unfavorable or hostile attitudes indicate conditions that can be changed, partially, at least, through advertising. It is not uncommon for the initial concept, the early planning, and the basic theme of certain institutional advertising undertakings to be blocked out by Public Relations. Always, Public Relations should examine the entire advertising program to see that it pictures the company accurately. Individual advertisements, promotional as well as institutional, should be checked for their effect on public relations, because a good advertisement builds good public relations just as surely as bad advertisement destroys accumulated good will. To the extent that Public Relations makes friends of a manufacturer's "publics," it makes advertising more effective because of the better reception advertising gets.

ADVERTISING AND RESEARCH

What Advertising Does For Research

Because of the nature of their respective activities, Advertising's position is one characterized by much more receiving than giving in so far as Research is concerned. It appears that Advertising's role in research is one principally of participation, both before and during the execution of the research project. In the "before" state, Advertising can join Research upon invitation to explore and decide various issues and questions about future research. Or, acting on its own initiative, Advertising can discuss with Research ideas, questions, convictions, or suggestions about research that Advertising thinks might be desirable, particularly about product and promotion matter. Another possibility in this pre-execution stage is for Advertising to make available to Research whatever records or other data which could serve as the raw materials for research. For example, Advertising may have valuable information about response to certain past advertisements and advertising, or the advertising manager may have received some research findings from media, findings Research needs but does not know exist.

What Research Does For Advertising

The research staff is a group of curious individuals, curious about why things work out as they do and about what will happen if certain moves are made or actions taken. As a matter of fact, this group is interested in identifying problems as well as in discovering solutions.

By answering questions and by keeping Advertising posted on developments that affect such factors as, for example, distribution channels, competitors, and new media, Research contributes to the reduction of waste in effort, in time, and in dollars. Research aids Advertising in its determination to avoid the repetition of mistakes. By helping before, during, and after any advertising effort, Research helps guide the planning, the execution, and the evaluating of those efforts.

Advertising decisions can be based on hunch, on guesswork, on prejudices and preferences, on personal opinions and reactions of the advertising manager or of a higher executive — or they can be based on *facts*. The fundamental relationship of Research to Advertising is that of supply, the supplying of facts that should be analyzed and interpreted before Advertising shapes its plans. Research, then, precedes advertising and is a prelude to planning. Research provides information for Advertising to use as a basis of operation and as a foundation for policies and practices.

Supplies Product Data. It is Research's responsibility to keep Advertising informed about products, including their packages and their prices, and including both com-

Advertising Management

pany products and competitors' products. In a general sense, Research's service is that of helping guide Advertising to the soundest decisions about product promotion. When today's products are changed, or when a new product is added, Advertising needs to be briefed by Research.

When Research discovers new uses for the company's products, this means new markets and the need for a review of promotion plans, including advertising. This posting of Advertising by Research should be done as promptly as possible. In the automobile industry, for example, Research may be able to give Advertising information about sales features of coming models as long as one year in advance.

Supplies Data About Buyers. Research tells Advertising many facts Advertising needs to know about its real boss, the buyer, be he an individual consumer or a business buyer. Research locates markets for the company's products, measures them to determine the potential volume of sales to be had from each, and keeps Advertising posted on a continuing basis about forecasts and estimates. In order to perform this service, Research must know who the company's prospects are, what their needs and wants are, how their motivation operates, what their buying habits are, what they do with the company's type of product, and their authority and their ability to buy. Advertising particularly needs information about the attitudes of buyers toward the advertiser and his products, and toward competitors and their products. Buyer's preferences are allies, or they are influences that Advertising must help change. Research tells Advertising which media reach various groups of buyers and under what circumstances.

Supplies Data About Advertising. The entire area of promotion is a proper province within which Research should function. Research helps the company management set up and assign duties to the Sales department, the Sales Promotion department, and the Advertising department — the "big three" in promotion. Advertising is correctly interested in and affected by what both Sales and Sales Promotion are doing, and what they do should be determined greatly by research findings. However, the great favor done Advertising by Research in the promotion area is the help given in respect to advertisements, campaigns, and programs.

Research helps Advertising decide *where, when, what, to whom, how much, how* — or, indeed, *whether* — to advertise. Particularly does Research supply valuable information about what products to advertise, what to say about them, in what media, on what schedule, and in what size and type of advertisement. Unless a powerful, persuasive theme is selected and unless this message is delivered in the most suitable media, the success of an advertising campaign is in serious doubt.

ADVERTISING AND PRODUCTION

What Advertising Does For Production

Works Toward Standardization Production. Advertising joins Production in preferring standardized products. Because Advertising customarily speaks to large groups when addressing messages to ultimate consumers, it must deliver a message that is largely standardized. The individual consumers to whom the advertising message is directed must be characterized by some degree of homogeneity, and, hence, can be described as being somewhat standardized. So, Advertising typically works to produce a standardized desire in standardized consumers for standardized products.

Of course, product quality must be acceptable if a profitable sales volume is to be obtained, and Advertising has something to say to Production about that quality. The advertising manager is qualified to express his views on this matter because he is in such a sensitive spot in seeing and sensing what consumers like and dislike. In all probability, the advertising manager (and, obviously, the sales manager, too) learns what consumers adore and what they abhor about the company's products sooner than does the production manager, and it is both the privilege and the duty of the advertising manager to pass back such information promptly.

Because Advertising is severely handicapped competitively if its product is inferior, and because Advertising is ever on the prowl for new themes and keynote ideas, the advertising manager constantly spurs Production in the direction of improved product quality. The whole area of packaging is, clearly, included in this concept of product quality. If Production can come forth with a new product or if it increases the quality of current products, then the effect is that Advertising can convert the superior product features into action compelling buyer-benefits more effectively.

Influences Morale Favorably. While it is true that *all* employees in *all* the company's departments are affected by the company's advertising, it may not be unlikely that the workers who produce the automobiles, the soaps, or the flour are the most significant group in this respect. Since Advertising is somewhat responsible for the jobs held by those individuals, they have an obvious reason for feeling kindly toward it. Then, Public Relations can take the company's advertising program and translate it into more cause for greater pride in affiliation and for healthier morale on the part of the labor force. Where such high morale is present, it should work to mitigate the seriousness of the problem of attracting the better workers.

Helps Reduce Production Costs. One of the greatest justifications for advertising and, incidentally, a favor that delights Sales as well as Production is lower production costs. Advertising can be correctly described as a major cause of mass distribution, and mass distribution permits mass production, and, in the vast majority of cases, mass production results in lower per unit production costs than does production on a lesser scale.

Advertising also reduces production costs by helping to smooth out the production curve. If the condition commonly referred to as overproduction exists, advertising may be increased to help relieve such a condition. If a manufacturer adds to his family of products in the hopes that diversification will reduce the range of seasonal fluctuations, Advertising will aid in developing markets for the additions. In those rare cases where production volume is smaller than what the market wants, Advertising can at least explain the situation to buyers.

Advertising Management

What Production Does For Advertising

Informs Advertising of Production Plans. Ideally, a company's marketing activities and its productive activities would match each other exactly; the amount of goods Production manufactured would be precisely the quantity demanded by buyers as a result of the company's promotion program. The fact that this perfect balance is seldom achieved reduces not one bit the pressure on a manufacturer to work constantly toward it. If market potential is underestimated, a vigorous advertising campaign increases the volume of back-orders, puts buyers on an allotment or quota basis, and, in general, irritates everybody concerned. This is unfortunate both as regards consumers and in respect to wholesalers and retailers. If the mistake is in the other direction, then the marketing division finds it impossible to move the amount of merchandise Production has made at the prices originally scheduled.

In the light of these contingencies, Production performs a valuable service by keeping Advertising adequately posted on Production's current operations and plans for the future. The proper start in such communication would be for Advertising to be kept informed about plant capacity and current output so that the advertising effort can be kept in line. Then, Production can apprise Advertising about its production schedules, indicating *how much* is expected to be ready for sale and *when*. This lets Advertising time its advertisements, adapt its message, and adjust the extension and the intension of the advertising program. When the manufacturing process is begun early enough, there is no difficulty in having the merchandise on retailer's shelves at the moment heavy promotion starts for such events as the World Series, for example, or Christmas. Whatever the production manager can do to avoid shutdowns and slowdowns makes the schedules he files with the advertising manager more certain of attainment.

In certain situations, information about the present and future rates of production is nothing less than a stark necessity. A change in product would cause one such situation, one where Advertising would need almost daily reports on the progress of the change. Change in the product's package would call for the same prompt and continuing communication. Package inserts can cause a third such situation when the message they carry can easily become out-of-date. For example, if the inserts publicize a contest or recommend the current TV show, then those inserts are working against eventual dates after which the insert messages must be changed.

Produces What Buyers Want. Well-advised production managers are not just willing to hear about the motivation of buyers, they are anxious to know and understand it in the same sense as the sales manager and the advertising manager. Such understanding invariably results in a product that will satisfy the desires of buyers, a product of uniform, controlled quality. When the time comes that product changes are needed, Production is willing to make beneficial changes and is not hostile, because the production manager realizes that improved products mean improved advertising and that the better the product is, the better the story Advertising can tell. Outstanding advertising cannot for long make an inferior product succeed, nor can an outstanding product achieve its maximum potential growth without effective advertising.

Offers Copy Assistance. Production can make a contribution to the excellence of the copy Advertising places in its advertisements. Talking points found in the product such as design, raw materials, workmanship, or the package can be suggested to Advertising. One of these or one like these might well serve effectively as an advertising theme. Production can supply technical information about products. Proposed advertisements can be submitted to Production for the scrutiny and verification of copy claims.

ADVERTISING AND THE CONTROLLER

What Advertising Does For the Controller

If the advertising manager wants seriously to contribute to the controller's happiness and efficient operation, then the first thing he should do is to adopt a cooperative, sympathetic attitude toward the controller's program and goals. The advertising manager should think in terms of improved operations and balanced budgets; he should strive to do his bit toward assuring and then maximizing profits. He should go out of his way to establish rapport with the controller, making himself easy to do business with and realizing that their relationship is one of cost and control. If the advertising manager succeeds in these endeavors, he will have little or no trouble teaching the controller what the possibilities and the limitations of advertising are.

What the Controller Does For Advertising

Keeps Records. The controller does the complete and official record-keeping for Advertising. Basically, these records are concerned with two matters: the dollar figures budgeted for the advertising activities, and the amounts actually spent for those activities. The controller's office keeps cumulative records on advertising expenditures (because it writes the checks for them) and, so, can tell the advertising manager at any time how and where he stands. Upon the advertising manager's request, the controller can get cost breakdowns and details as, for example, advertising expenditures by market, by medium, by product, by unit of time, by expense classification, and by type of campaign. Just as the advertising manager drafts reports for the controller, in similar fashion the controller reports to the advertising manager. Of course, general data on sales, costs, and profits, absolutely essential to the advertising manager, come from the controller.

Exercises Control. The controller exerts an influence on the advertising manager in the direction of sound budgets and adherence thereto. The controller reviews the first draft of the advertising budget with the advertising manager and then, probably after some changes, fits it into the company's over-all budget. The controller has ideas and suggestions about how certain advertising costs should be prorated, as, for example, the breakdown and allocation of the cost of institutional advertising. The controller is a party to budget review and budget revision. He compares actual performance with budgeted performance and reports discrepancies to the advertising manager for analysis and explanation.

AIDS TOWARD COORDINATION

Sound Management Decisions. If the advertising function is to be coordinated effectively with the other activities within the company with which it comes in contact, sound managerial decisions are necessary. In certain types of situations, no method of coordination is so appropriate and indicated as a selection, a determination, a designation — a decision by top management. Perhaps Advertising and Selling cannot agree on the duties of an advertising nature that should be assigned to the salesmen. Perhaps Advertising and Research do not see eye to eye on the extent to which advertisements should be used for research purposes. Or, perhaps the advertising manager and the controller are not able to iron out all differences of opinion about the advertising budget. In these instances, a clear-cut decision by management seems called for so that coordination may be enjoyed.

Organizational Structure. The organization of a company can work as a strong force in the direction of intra-company coordination. Indeed, smooth and profitable operation is difficult or even impossible to attain unless the enterprise is well organized. At the top of the company there is an individual or a group of top executives in whom final authority and responsibility reside. Whether this involves a president or, perhaps, a president plus his vice presidents, the individual or the group is, in a sense, the coordination as well as the coordinator. All activities can be coordinated because they all are under the direction of the one person or the one group.

Down one step are found various organizational units, and the head of each unit is in a position from which he can see to the coordination of the activities assigned to his unit. For example, as indicated in the preceding paragraph, a group might be the top management of a company and such a group might well include, among others, the president, the vice president in charge of marketing, the vice president in charge of manufacturing, and the treasurer. The two vice presidents and the treasurer would be on the same organizational level. Then, under the vice president in charge of marketing and reporting to him might be the advertising manager, the sales manager, and the sales promotion manager, all three on the organizational level just below the two vice presidents and the treasurer. Advertising, Sales, and Sales Promotion can be coordinated by the vice president in charge of marketing.

Organizational patterns will vary from company to company. In many companies the advertising manager will report to the sales manager; in many other companies the two of them are of equal executive status and report to a vice president in charge of sales. Some companies merge Sales Promotion into Advertising, while others combine it with Sales. Small companies may not have a Sales Promotion department, but, instead, divide the normal sales promotion duties between Advertising and Sales. Regardless of pattern, the organizational structure should contribute in significant amount to intra-departmental coordination.

Policies. When management decides which policies it will subscribe to and observe, it is affecting the internal climate in which cooperation and coordination will or will not thrive. Every phase of company operation is susceptible to control by policies the company has established. Indeed, every aid to cooperation in this section is a matter on which the company should have clear and definite policies.

If it is company policy to make no package change except after approval by a committee that includes the heads of all departments affected, then a certain amount of coordination has been insured. If it is company policy for the advertising budget to have been discussed and endorsed by the advertising manager, the sales manager, the sales promotion manager, and the controller, then a measure of coordination is certain. If it is company policy to give new salesmen an understanding of advertising and then to expect them to work with retailers on their advertising problems and solutions, this policy will result in coordination. Finally, if a new product is not launched until after all department heads have been informed and their recommendations heard, such a policy is a coordinating technique.

Procedures or System. Procedures or system refer to day-to-day, standard ways of doing things; as such, they can be used to achieve certain coordination. It is somewhat permissible to think of procedures as remotely kin to but clearly of less significance than major policies, and as helping translate those major policies into routine operation.

System might dictate that the scheduling of all advertising efforts be done far enough in advance so that the planning can be careful and thorough and so that all groups concerned can cooperate fully. The physical instrument here might well be a complete timetable for all the steps that should be included in each promotion. Or, it might be standing operating procedure for Production to notify Advertising of all changes in the production schedules. This would permit speedy revision of advertising plans if such would be desirable. Or, Research may be instructed to send the advertising manager a copy of all laboratory reports issued. A final example would be the designation by the advertising manager of one member of his staff to be the controller's contact in the advertising department. This person would be the one to deal with the controller's office in matters of budgets, invoices, financial reports, and the like.

Knowledge and Understanding. All persons of executive status in the company should be encouraged first to learn and then to probe for the reasoning behind why the company feels and acts as it does. Each major executive should, as a start, inform himself about the objectives, the methods, and the time schedules of departments related to his. These matters of *what, how,* and *when* are obviously fundamental. Immediately, then, the executive can seek to know as much about the question of *why* as is practicable.

The advertising manager, for example, should know just what duties are assigned to Sales, what facilities Research has, what the functions and responsibilities of Sales Promotion are, which of the controller's activities affect and are affected by advertising, and how Public Relations expects to make use of advertising in carrying out its assignments. He must without fail learn his company's answers to the questions raised in this chapter, namely, just what does Advertising do for others in the company and just what do others do for Advertising. Fortunate, indeed, is the ad-

Advertising Management

vertising manager who finds company policies and procedures reduced to clear writing and included in a company handbook for executives. Fortunate is he, too, if he can get into salesmen's territories and make calls with salesmen on retailers. Such experience in the field cannot be simulated; it has no substitute.

Communication. If others in the company are to know what the advertising department is doing, and if those others are to contribute ideas and suggestions which will benefit the advertising program, then there must be effective two-way communication. Free and healthy interchanges of facts and opinions make it possible for individuals to cooperate with others and to coordinate their respective operations. If Advertising keeps other departments informed in advance of its plan, those other departments can adapt their own plans so as to harmonize all activities. This merging of several departmental programs into a single, coordinated program for the company is impossible without communication.

Communications can be written or oral, formal or informal. Salesmen in the field get mailings from Sales Promotion telling of advertising plans; the advertising manager writes a letter to his company's advertising agency and sends a carbon to the Sales and the Sales Promotion managers; memos, bulletins, reports, minutes of meetings, and conferences, all result in communication. Two persons meet in the corridor or over coffee and exchange some ideas and engage in a bit of discussion — important communication may well have taken place. The advertising manager should make use of all types of communication to keep others informed about his day-to-day operations and also about his plans.

Committees. The committee is a device for coordination that needs little comment. For some proposed marketing programs, it is not difficult to visualize the analyzing and discussing that might be done in a committee composed of the heads of Advertising, Research, Production, Sales, and Sales Promotion. Some companies have gone so far as to designate a "coordinating committee." Such could be merely advisory — or it could be authorized to make final decisions that would affect, for example, Advertising and Selling. A special committee might be constituted to deal with big problems or big programs.

Conferences. Conferences are somewhat similar to committee meetings in respect to their being useful for purposes of coordination. Indeed, the regular, periodic gathering of top level department heads resembles nothing so much as a committee meeting. Often when an executive is convinced that there should be a rather drastic change within his department, the next step should be the scheduling of a conference to explore the matter. Even if only the advertising staff gets together each month to report on and discuss the plans for the company's future advertising, it will probably result in some contribution to the more effective coordination of company operations.

Incidentally, if the advertising manager can get invitations to certain conferences designed particularly for other departments of the company, then he has an opportunity to "sell" his plans and to urge coordination. By attending all related conferences and by expressing himself in the discussions, the advertising manager avails himself of one more channel of communication. When he is asked to take part in the conference program, the advertising manager should make every effort to do so. Of all the conferences a company schedules, the ones the advertising manager should try hardest to attend are those conducted by Sales. At the very least, the advertising department should be represented at all Sales meetings.

Physical Layout and Arrangement. Companies do well not to overlook any step, no matter how modest, in their determination to achieve the most profitable degree of coordination. One such move is to locate desks and offices so as to encourage chats, discussions, and questions between, for example, advertising manager and sales manager or advertising manager and the controller. Placing executives close together physically encourages their getting together on company matters and in company activities. Proximity begets communication. Impromptu visits in each other's office permit an exchange of ideas and information which, though informal, can be every bit as valuable as the most formal meetings.

Personal Relationships. A powerful defense can be made of the claim that the coordination of the advertising function starts with the personal relations between the advertising manager and the company's other officials. In other words, good personal relations have no substitute as a force favoring coordination. Personal relations are of great importance as between the advertising manager and the salesforce, between the sales manager and the advertising department personnel, and between the sales promotion manager and the advertising staff. Particularly on the executive level must personalities be so nicely integrated that they neither rub nor clash. If the advertising manager is an individual of keen sensibilities, if he is an understanding person, then he will respect his fellow executives and their respective areas of authority; by so doing, he makes a strong bid for retaliation in kind. Where one officer (vice president in charge of Public Relations, for example) is a man who formerly headed another unit (he was advertising manager for a period of time), there is apt to be a minimum of formality and reserve and a maximum of cooperation.

Budgetary Control. The advertising budget is one of the departmental budgets which must be fused into a single, over-all company budget. The company budget is both a plan and a control; it details the various departmental objectives and assignments. It is the company program which each of the executives accepts and agrees to support. That the company budget has coordinating implications is as obvious as it is that the matter of budgeting deserves and demands a treatment all its own.

Questions and Problems

1. Identify some of the coordination problems which bother manufacturers who offer new models of their products each year.

Advertising Management

2. What actions by competitors can complicate a manufacturer's problem of coordination?
3. What is the advertising department's interest in the company's distribution channels and channel policies?
4. What coordinating problems plague a company when a major change is made in the product's package?
5. What are some of the advertising department's interests in the firm's products and product policies?
6. Why is the advertising department interested in its company's pricing practices and policies?
7. What coordination problems are present when a company is doing both promotional *and* institutional advertising?
8. Before a manufacturer's display appears in many retail windows simultaneously, what previous coordination probably functioned?
9. What factors influence how much "pull" (advertising) and how much "push" (personal selling) a manufacturer should use in promoting his products?
10. On October 1, a leading TV network proposed to a manufacturer of cosmetics that he sponsor the "Bowl" football game that network would broadcast on next New Year's day. In a very few years, this manufacturer had achieved respectable distribution and sales volume in 60 major markets. He sold to a selected number of chains, wholesalers, department stores, and drug stores. The manufacturer was a heavy advertiser; he did cooperative advertising with his retailers; he supplied outstanding P-O-P materials to his retailers.

    The firm had a president, a vice president who was the top financial executive, and five department heads — Market Research, Production, Sales, Advertising, and Legal. The five department heads reported to the president.

    The president's first reaction was that he and his firm would not have enough time to get the most out of such sponsorship. The game would be broadcast in 75 major markets; in 60 of these the cosmetics firm had its own salesmen. On October 15, after discussions with key retailers, his own salesmen, and his department heads, the president decided to accept the proposal.

    What coordinating jobs do you see?

Chapter 21

Budgeting

The advertiser's search for the optimum advertising fund never ends, and, even more discouraging, he can never prove how right or how wrong his final figure was. The worst mistakes are: at one extreme, gross inadequacy; at the other, wanton extravagance. The very nature of budgeting protects the advertiser from these two errors. He is compelled to consider how much he will spend on each of his products; in each market; in each medium; by day, week, and month; by campaign; and by expense classification. Budgeting helps arrive at sounder prices for the various phases which constitute the advertising program, thereby making the total figure sounder.

Chapter 20 stressed the necessity of coordinated marketing and ended by hinting at the significance of budgeting in achieving such coordination. Only through budgeting can a manufacturer determine most profitably the responsibilities, the activities, and the schedules of personal selling, advertising, and sales promotion. Only through budgeting can he search successfully for the combination of sales-producing forces which will maximize profits. And coordination is not limited to just the marketing area. Production and purchasing, to cite just two examples, are activities which must be budgeted, and their budgets must be tied to the marketing budgets.

Because an advertising budget is a plan for the company's future advertising, the budget can make a major contribution to more profitable operation. It provides management with a program, with a unified and systematic proposal of activities. In a sense, there *must* be one best assortment of types of advertising to undertake, and, similarly, there *must* be one best timetable for them. The advertising budget has the opportunity to present the best schedule of operations.

In addition to being a plan, the budget also serves as a control to be observed and obeyed. It is a guide governing the manufacturer's expenditures for advertising, a standard against which performance can be measured. Periodic checks of *actual* advertising against *planned* advertising indicate what progress is being made, week by week and month by month, toward budgeted goals. If accomplishments are not according to schedule, if the advertiser has drifted off his plotted course, the

Advertising Management

findings discovered on these check dates are helpful to management in deciding what action seems indicated. As a plan, the budget tells management what to do; as a control, the budget tells how management is doing.

PLACE OF THE ADVERTISING BUDGET

The sales-income budget is the manufacturer's most important budget to all management and all budgeting, not just to the sales manager. Sales are the sole producer of revenue, and, unless there is revenue, there will be no operations. Thus, income from sales is the base necessary for all operating budgets. The production-, purchasing-, labor-, and marketing-expense budgets all depend on the sales budget and are tied to it. Of course, to the extent that advertising causes sales, the sales budget is also dependent on and influenced by the advertising budget.

Whether or not a manufacturer's operations are profitable depends on the number of units he sells, his production cost and selling price of each unit, his marketing costs, and his other costs. A well-known equation is worth recalling in this connection. For a business doing no advertising, the equation reads: Cost of goods sold plus selling expenses plus administrative expenses plus profit equals selling price.

The prime question is: What happens when advertising expense is added to the equation? In other words, what does advertising do to sales volume, production costs, selling costs, administrative costs, and profit? Or, more simply but just as defiant of simple answer, where advertising and personal selling are both used, what does advertising do to sales and to profits?

The advertising budget is set against this background. It is considered a part of the sales-expense budget by some manufacturers, while others deem it a separate, parallel budget. Clearly, the proper amount to spend on advertising is so interrelated with sales volume and with gross margin that the advertising plan of necessity becomes part of the over-all plan. Hence, the advertising budget is not just an intradepartmental matter; instead, it is a top management function.

SOME BUDGET CONSIDERATIONS

Instead of describing methods of setting advertising budgets, this treatment will limit itself to a consideration of the most important budget considerations. Management should analyze and weight those considerations that are involved in its advertising planning and then arrive at whatever budget it considers proper. It is felt that to offer here any so-called methods of setting the advertising budget would be grossly misleading. There is no scientific way to determine the size of any advertising budget; indeed, there is no *simple* way to set up a budget. Arbitrary, customary, conventional practices can be followed, but these do not constitute budgeting. To say in a textbook that an advertiser does or should use the "task" method to determine his budget might be interpreted by students as implying that advertising's task, cost, and results can be easily or even accurately defined, priced, and determined. Such is not the case. So, this section deals with budget factors, not budget methods. Two major considerations are examined first, the per cent-of-sales

Budgeting

concept and the advertising task or objective. The per cent-of-sales concept owes the amount of space given it here to its popularity rather than to any inherent excellence.

Per Cent-of-Sales Concept

When a manufacturer is described as using a percentage of sales to determine how much he will spend in advertising, he does one of two things. The first possibility, by far the more common, is that he selects a factor or multiplier, such as 2 or 7 per cent, multiplies his dollar sales figure by the percentage, and the sum resulting is the number of dollars he spends in advertising. If sales are $300,000 and the per cent is 4, $12,000 worth of advertising is bought. The $300,000 can be gross sales or net, past sales or future. The 4 per cent is the manufacturer's answer to the question, "What part of my sales dollar should be spent for advertising?"

The other possibility is for the manufacturer to select a fixed sum he regards as the proper advertising charge to levy against each unit of product he sells. This might be 7 cents for a box of oranges or $30 for an automobile. Then, using unit sales instead of dollar sales, the manufacturer or grower multiplies the number of units sold by the fixed sum and has the size of his advertising fund. If a manufacturer plans to sell 500,000 automobiles and thinks $40 is the proper fixed sum, then he will plan to spend $20,000,000 in advertising.

Past or Future Sales. When past sales are used, the manufacturer may use last year's figure or an average of figures of the last few years. Two advantages are usually claimed for past sales. The advertiser is using a base figure that is certain and concrete. Second, the procedure is termed "safe and conservative." There are several disadvantages, however. The procedure is guilty of making advertising follow and dependent on past sales. This puts cart before horse and has management in the position of contending that sales cause advertising. A second defect is that if either the base (last) year or the following year (budget year) is unusual because of business fluctuations, then the advertising figure is out of line. Finally, the needs of the future do not necessarily reflect the experiences of the past. Using past sales prevents any relationship between size of advertising fund and size of job needed done by advertising.

Future sales are a more logical base than are past sales in setting the size of advertising efforts. The major reason for this superiority is the fact that future sales keep the expenditures better in line with needs. This procedure relates advertising effort to future conditions, to the climate in which the advertising will be working, not to the past. These conditions include not only general trends or developments, but also specific developments or movements for those products which do not conform to the general pattern. It recognizes that next year's advertising dollars are to help obtain the sales volume forecast. It realizes that advertising *precedes* sales, and, hence, should be related to the sales volume it is to help produce.

The manufacturer's plans in this process rest on the correctness of the sales forecast which can be, of course, only an estimate. And, there are always unexpected developments that will cause estimates to be off. This is the basic problem involved

Advertising Management

in using future sales as a base. To be sure, if the sales, market research, and statistical departments are sound in their forecasts, then the manufacturer does have more to go on than just a sales manager's rosy hope. Even here, though, revisions will be necessary — often frequent, always prompt.

The Percentage Figure. The major problem as regards the percentage figure is its determination. The range in current use by various manufacturers runs from less than one-tenth of 1 per cent for some mining companies to over 40 per cent for some proprietary medicines. The figure varies from industry to industry, from company to company, and even from product to product within a company. In the absence of a formula that will identify the magic multiplier, a manufacturer must use a competitor's figure, all his competitors' figure (the "common" figure for his group), or select what he thinks is best and then adjust it in the light of his own experience.

Unit Sales and the Fixed Sum. As was indicated, a manufacturer may prefer not to use dollar sales and a percentage multiplier in aiming at the amount to spend in advertising. He may, instead, ask each unit of his output to contribute a set or fixed amount into what will be the advertising fund. This fixed-sum-per-unit of product is very much like the percentage-of-dollar-sales. Its use implies that a specific amount of advertising is needed in marketing each unit produced. Its soundness depends on selecting the sum that will do what advertising is to do. Like the percentage figure, it too can be adjusted, but revisions are quite infrequent. One point of superiority is that the manufacturer knows in advance how much the advertising cost of each unit of product will be; this is a firm figure.

The fixed sum seems to suit two groups in particular. The first group consists of manufacturers of one (or at most a few) specialty products of high unit price. Automobiles and washing machines are examples. The second group consists of cooperative marketing groups. Citrus products are examples. The fixed sum is least satisfactory for fashion products or where market conditions are uncertain.

Comments. Experience is largely responsible for the use of the percentage-of-sales approach. After a period of trial and error, experimentation and adjustment, management might conclude rather easily that advertising should run about 2 or 4 per cent of sales. Or, at least one firm is known to have looked back at its most profitable year, discovered that advertising for the year amounted to 2.73 per cent of net sales, and decreed that this figure would be used until a more prosperous year came along. The simplicity and concreteness of the technique make it easily understood. It seems reasonable and safe, earmarking only a small amount of the dollars which the advertiser receives as sales income. Its widespread use over a period of years has established it firmly as a practice of long standing.

The multiplier, both in the percentage-of-dollar-sales and in the fixed-sum-per-unit, is a problem, first in respect to original selection and then in respect to how long it should be used. In theory, the advertiser should be anxious to adjust the multiplier either upward or downward at the first signal recommending such action. Such adjustment is, of course, possible at any time. In practice, however, revision is infrequent. Inertia is one explanation. Too, perhaps the typical manufacturer using it feels that the right figure, once found, needs no changing — that changes in sales volume will be change enough. In some cases the advertiser would have no more, sometimes even less, confidence in the new multiplier than in the former one. And, if a manufacturer increases his product line from one to ten, should he use ten different multipliers?

The percentage-of-sales technique encourages an advertiser to spend the exact amount earmarked, even though his circumstances call for *more* or *less*. Those points in the business cycle at which business takes a decided turn for better or worse are clear examples of conditions which demand revision of plans. Any rigid adherence to a multiplier encourages inelastic thinking and, in some instances, hands the responsibility for and the formulation of policy over to competitors. This, certainly, is unfortunate preparation for new conditions and new problems. Such adherence, indeed, denies or at least ignores a basic fact of life, namely, that no two years are alike.

Certain blind spots appear in the percentage-of-sales area. Advertising cost per unit of output normally declines as sales volume increases. This development is discouraged or even made impossible by the way some advertisers worship their magic multipliers. What is the new company to use as a base, or what base will an established company use for a new product? What shall followers of this approach do about institutional advertising, particularly during a period when product-promoting advertising has to be replaced by institutional advertising in certain lines? No constant relationship exists between current sales volume and the desirability of additional sales volume — the primary and immediate aim of advertising. Finally, there is not necessarily any correlation between changes in sales volume and changes in an advertiser's undertakings.

Advertising Task

Basic Operation. Budgeting through the use of the task approach has been defined as "financing the objective" and also as "estimating the task to be done." Perhaps it is well to go along with the group that uses the word "objective" to designate the advertiser's long-term marketing aims. This leaves the word "task" for short-term undertakings, usually next year's sales goal. Our primary concern is with the task, the advertiser's short-term undertakings.

The basic operation of the task technique breaks down into three steps, the first of which is to define the task. In most cases, the task will be a sales task which will be broader than and will include advertising. The manufacturer seeks to measure the size of the total potential market, and then he asks what portion of this market shall be his. His answer to this second question may be in terms of unit sales, dollar sales, or a percentage of the total market.

Occasionally, the advertiser will set up for himself a non-selling task. Immediate sales are not his goal. An example of such a non-selling task would be to build good will. Eventually, of course, the advertiser expects the achievement of non-selling goals to be reflected in profits through the eventual impact on sales. It is obviously easier to determine the success of an effort that was aimed at getting

Advertising Management

prospects to buy than that of an effort aimed at changing or reinforcing prospects' attitudes and beliefs.

To define a task is not easy. Much research should precede it, research involving prospects, buying motives and habits, products, advertising techniques and media, past experience, competitors, and the like. Despite extensive research it is not uncommon to find outstanding campaigns with their tasks worded in only general terms. The following examples of defined tasks are from successful campaigns:

>To increase trade awareness of a product and its promotion
>To interest business executives in group insurance plans
>To develop a long-term selling theme
>To acquaint a market with a brand name
>To overcome consumer objection to using a modern style
>To introduce a new product
>To educate the public about the banking business
>To secure substantial distribution through wholesalers

The second of the three steps in the task process is to outline advertising's role in the accomplishment of the task. The manufacturer must designate what promotional efforts will be employed to attain his goal and how much dependence will be placed on each. The proportion between personal selling on one hand and advertising and sales promotion on the other is fundamental.

Monthly advertising expenditures in general should reflect monthly sales quotas. (Courtesy: Small Business Administration)

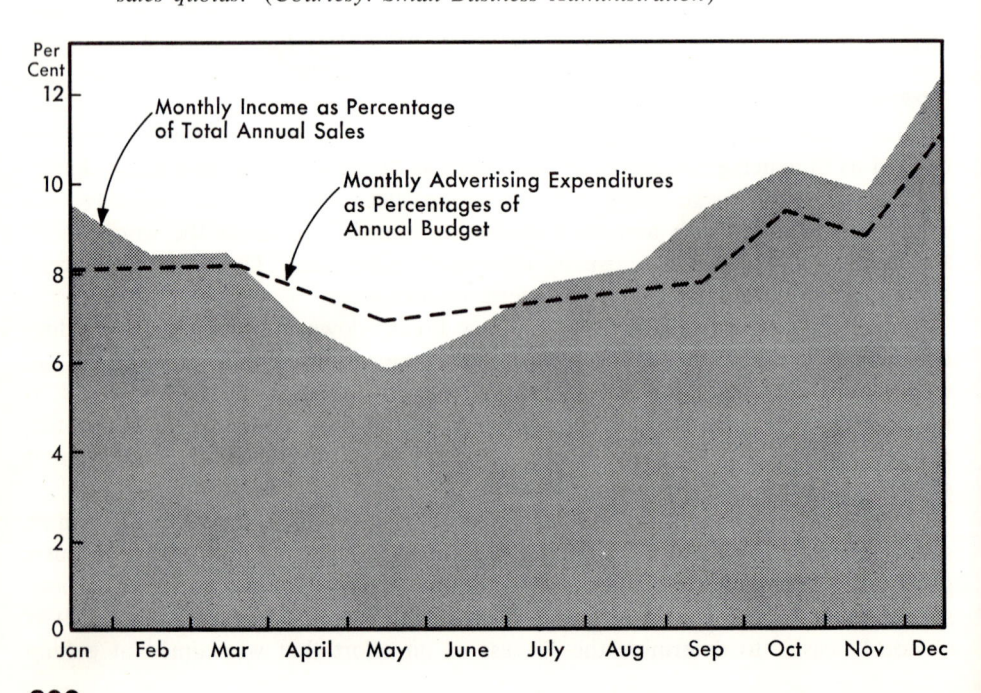

Budgeting

In essence, this second step is the determination of the amount and type of advertising needed if advertising is to carry out its assignment. This assignment will normally be to do what it can and should in helping the sales department accomplish its sales task. When one recalls how much difference there can be between an effective and a weak copy appeal or even between strong and weak headlines, one begins to realize how immense and challenging this second step is. Research, experience, and much judgment are all needed.

The third and last step is a costing process. The second step determined the amount and type of advertising needed; the third step prices that advertising. Usually the findings of the second step are general enough to permit the advertiser to choose a single advertising program from two or more alternates each of which seems capable of doing advertising's job. The cost of each possibility will be studied against the company's financial condition. The cost of the program chosen is the advertising budget and represents advertising's share in the cost of capturing our manufacturer's share of the total market.

Features. This task approach centers the manufacturer's attention and study on the assignment he gives to advertising rather than on some portion of sales. That assignment is what will determine the size of his budget; it matches dollars and job. The approach is not bound to or by the past. It does not worship any assumed statistical relations between advertising expenditure and sales volume, nor does it assume that past ratios will fit current problems. Rule-of-thumb, customary thinking, characteristic of much percentage-of-dollar-sales use, must be abandoned in favor of original, bold, and imaginative thinking. The task technique improves the quality of the manufacturer's forecasting by making poor estimating intolerable.

It recognizes all current factors and needs in their proper perspective and includes them in the budget-making process. In addition to the more specific, technical needs usually thought of in connection with the use of advertising, general needs too play a part. These might well include the need for more sales volume to cover higher costs of raw materials and labor, to provide for the payment of higher taxes, or to keep the plant operating at full capacity.

The task process is extremely difficult to apply and to establish in detail. It requires large amounts of research, and, even then, considerable amounts of sound judgment. Without doubt, the most bothersome feature of the task technique is encountered in the second step, which is to determine the *amount* and *type* of advertising necessary to do advertising's job. This feature is the impossibility of evaluating accurately the effectiveness or quality of advertising, either before it is run *or after*. There is no tougher problem in all advertising.

Comments. The principle of the task approach is clear and simple: the *needs* of each advertiser should determine the *size* of his advertising fund. And, equally clear and simple is the impossibility of denying the logic, the soundness of attempting this approach. Top management sets the company's objectives, usually in terms of dollar sales. Top management and marketing management decide on the company's dependence on personal selling, advertising, and sales promotion,

Advertising Management

respectively, in achieving those objectives. Then the best advertising program is sought within the ceiling placed on advertising.

The task technique is basically a "build-up" technique that arrives at an advertising budget through a pragmatic approach. It demands and rests on research. Some of this research will be quite scientific, some will amount to no more than crude calculations and rough estimation. In its finest form, the use of the procedure assumes that the advertiser has or will get more accurate information about various variables than is possible. The task procedure points up the great need for more accurate determination and evaluation of the results of advertising. It assumes that the significance of advertising in the manufacturer's marketing program has been clearly defined. This is not easy.

In the long run, the task technique is under the control of a maximum percentage of sales. Dollars the manufacturer spends must come from sales. If a manufacturer continually sets up tasks that are too ambitious, then he finds his cash position inadequate and the cost of additional sales greater than their worth to him. A limit is put on the amount of money that can be spent to get additional sales volume yet still leave a satisfactory profit.

The task technique must recognize the financial condition of the advertiser. If the minimum cost of the task first delineated seems high, several courses of action are open, the first of which, naturally, is the possibility of getting approval of the extra dollars needed. If this is not possible, then the duration of the advertising program may be shortened but the weekly or monthly volume of the program left intact. The other possibilities are to select more modest tasks and/or more modest programs. Finally, one or more objectives may be spread over a longer period of time or even postponed for the time being.

Even though the advertiser probably cannot avoid, in his thinking, translating a task-determined budget into a percentage-of-dollar-sales ratio, he is not entitled to adopt that percentage for future use. His only safe course is to delineate a new task for each new budget period.

Getting dollars approved for the task is rarely easy. If a task is soundly set up and soundly priced yet management says, "Too much!", then the effective determinant of the budget is the top amount management will approve — not the task. Still, the technique is winning approval from more and more advertisers as *the* right way to handle budgeting. Indeed, almost the only respectable answer offered or accepted when method of budgeting is being asked about is, "The task technique." This is the most rational approach to the budgeting of advertising yet developed, despite problems that are severe. The assumptions and revisions necessary are two of the most outstanding problems. The task approach is a desirable move toward sound budgeting. In principle it is the best way to attack the problem of budgeting.

Other Considerations

The "Minimum Job" Concept. To do a worthwhile job or to perform a task that was large enough to justify the manufacturer's undertaking it, a *minimum* amount of advertising is usually essential in order to make success possible. Perhaps a football analogy is appropriate. A team spends considerable energy, uses many plays, and makes several first downs in moving the ball from its own 20-yard line to its opponent's 10-yard line. However, ten more yards must be gained during that possession of the ball for the team to score six points. In somewhat similar fashion, a manufacturer's budget should always be at least large enough to do the smallest task worth doing. It is difficult if not impossible, for example, to think that a single advertisement in *Life* or *Look* would accomplish such a minimum task.

The various minima the advertiser should check include: consumer advertising; merchandising the consumer advertising; amount that the trade demands that he do; amount of vertical cooperative advertising that should be made available to dealers; and, if there is some joint advertising with competitors, the amount of horizontal cooperative advertising that should be done.

The Most the Advertiser Can and Will Approve. There is definitely a top limit on how much an advertiser can spend in advertising. In the short run, the number of dollars available is a limit, as is, though in a different way, the maximum capacity of the plant. In the long run, the gross margin in dollars is a maximum because it is the sole source of advertising dollars.

In the case of new companies or new products, management may spend in advertising as much as its financial condition will allow. All or practically all of net profit goes into advertising until company or product has elbowed its way into a place in the market. This tactic is not uncommon where the new company is small and will ask advertising to do much of the sales job during an initial period. For large companies whose products are entrenched or at least accepted, this all-out policy would be unwise. Soon the size of the budget would have grown beyond the point of profit maximization. Expansion of advertising beyond this point is sheer extravagance; it ignores the need for liquidity as well as market potential.

What an advertiser will approve as regards the size of his advertising fund is influenced by several factors. Hunch, competition, the bank balance, custom, observation, and experience are some of these factors. An additional influence of considerable moment is management's over-all attitude toward advertising. Too many executives are convinced that advertising is an expensive and totally unnecessary luxury, something to treat themselves to when sales and profits are lush. These executives are apt to be completely arbitrary in setting advertising funds, picking out of the air whatever lump sum they think right. They are apt to be erratic advertisers with no constant advertising policy; they are apt to spend too much or too little.

Other executives see advertising as a producer of sales and profits. Their faith in its ability to help increase profits usually stems from knowledge and experience. When an advertising manager proposes to these top managers that a certain soundly conceived, appropriate task be underwritten, these managers do not make a mockery of the task technique by arbitrarily instructing the advertising manager to trim down the task.

Competition. Each advertiser is rightly interested in what his competitors are doing in advertising. He probably watches one or two particular competitors quite closely, and then he watches what his industry or group, *all* his competitors, does as a unit. The individual advertiser hopes to find out how much competitors spend, both in terms of dollars and percentages, and, to the best of his ability, what the results of those advertising efforts are. While competitive statistics are not acceptable as standards to be adopted, they are useful in that they reflect long-term competitive thinking and policy. Too, in the short-run, what competitors start may call for our manufacturer to take those immediate countermeasures of a defensive nature he deems expedient.

Blind imitation is the course to avoid as regards competition. "Common" figures include strong companies and weak, with all kinds of policies, using their own individual expense account classifications, confronting different problems, in a variety of circumstances. Imitation lets budget decisions be made *for* the advertiser, not *by* him, and when competitors set a manufacturer's budget, they lead him into their mistakes. Paying too much attention to competition ignores the fact that advertising has quality in addition to quantity. It gives inadequate weight to the advertiser's own conditions and needs. Finally, a continuing policy of emulation discourages ingenuity and imagination, without which an advertiser cannot advertise effectively.

Advertising as a Capital Investment. If one agrees that a company's good will is a factor of real concern and has actual dollar-and-cents value in the market place, then one must argue that advertising has a dual character — that it is both expense *and* investment. "Expense" advertising is aimed at producing immediate sales; "investment" advertising is to create a capital asset, good will, then to increase the size of this asset, and, finally, to maintain it at the maximum size feasible.

If a manufacturer believes that good will is just as desirable as, even as *necessary* as, immediate sales, and a powerful defense of this position can be made, then he must earmark some dollars for "investment" advertising. Continuous use of this type of advertising has definite asset value in that it constantly replenishes the sum of good will the company owns and enjoys. Unless replenished and replaced, good will, like any other asset, will diminish or become depleted; it will simply evaporate. Despite the fact that "investment" advertising increases or maintains a capital asset, such advertising cannot be handled through the setting up of a reserve as is done for such a capital asset as a factory. Neither the revenue laws nor managerial thinking approves of capital charges of this nature.

So, advertising for the purpose of increasing good will or at least maintaining it in its current state of health must be treated as a current advertising expense. As such, it is part of the advertising budget. The difficult step is to estimate the number of dollars that should be spent during the coming budget period to keep good will at its present size or to increase it. The cause of this difficulty is the advertiser's inability to measure the return he gets on his advertising.

Net Profit. If a manufacturer prefers, he can use net profit as a base for his advertising expenditure, making the size of his advertising effort a function of net profit. This ties the advertising program to the result of the company's entire operations. Bankers are credited (or maligned) with recommending this policy as a conservative method of arriving at the size of the advertising program.

An intensive and extensive search reveals one good feature about the idea; it does consider the company's financial condition. Actually the policy is dangerous because it permits efficient advertising activities to be curtailed because of intracompany inefficiency in other departments. Furthermore, it makes no pretense of relating the advertising fund to the company's advertising needs, even to the extent of permitting the abandonment of advertising during a year of great need merely because last year's profit-and-loss figure was red. Profit as a base denies the dynamic character of markets and the fact that advertising causes sales. Even in economic theory, profit is a residual return; to use it as a cause instead of as an effect borders on nonsense.

Reserve Policy. If an advertiser considers it wise to set up a reserve within his budget, then the size of this reserve becomes a budget consideration. Such a reserve would enable the advertising manager to take prompt steps, if such were desirable, without having to wait for management to meet and act. Changes urging quick moves might be in cost of advertising, competitive activity, general business conditions, products, or market areas. The more uncertain the future, the stronger the case for a reserve, undisguised and instantly available, against the need for upward revisions of the budget.

Advertising Expense Classifications. One of the most obvious needs in the advertising field is for agreement on what should and what should not be charged to advertising expense. Clearly, if manufacturer A charges to advertising the Christmas gifts he sends to good customers or prospects, his advertising fund must be large enough to handle such gifts. More will be said about what is properly charged to advertising in the section on "Administering the Budget."

Advertiser's Past Experience. All the budget factors mentioned thus far are important, so important that they must not be ignored. Still, in one sense, we are entitled to speculate that the advertiser's own experience with advertising and what he thinks it did for him is probably the most influential guide in budget determination. This does not contradict nor preclude any of the principles mentioned thus far. The experience factor is present and influencing whether the manufacturer uses profit or sales as a base, whether he follows or ignores competition, or whether he favors last year's figures over next year's. Automatically, and even unconsciously, advertisers watch what happens as they advertise and wonder if, in the light of these happenings, some change might not have improved advertising's performance. Such wondering cannot be barred from future budget determination decisions.

BUDGET APPROACHES

Economic

In economics, the goal of profit maximization is reached by producing to that point where incremental cost equals incremental revenue. In other words, a

Advertising Management

manufacturer will produce to that point where the additional cost of producing the last unit would equal the additional revenue brought in by the last unit sold. For advertising, this principle would call for a manufacturer's increasing his advertising expenditure to the point where the last dollar spent for advertising is equaled by one dollar of net profit from the additional sales caused by that last dollar. The expenditure of that amount of money for advertising would maximize profits from advertising.

While this incremental approach to the proper size of the advertising budget may be interesting, it is extremely unrealistic. To apply it in practice would require far more accurate measurement than is now possible; therein lies its fundamental weakness. Not only is it impossible to measure precisely what advertising does to profits, it is, sad to admit, impossible to determine exactly what advertising does to sales volume. The mail-order sellers can come closest to finding out exactly what advertising does to sales, but even they must allow for such variables as weather, competition, business conditions, the day's headlines, quality of current advertising, continuing influence of past advertising, and the like.

Business

Where the economic approach asks a single question, the business approach asks many. Quite a few of the questions, furthermore, cannot be answered with anything resembling precision. Yet, the recommended procedure is for the advertiser to set the size of his advertising fund only after a serious attempt to answer these questions:

Who and where are the prospects for my product?
What do I need to know about these buyers, factors, for example, such as age, sex, purchasing power, buying habits, and buying motives?
How important a factor is brand name in the consumer's decision to buy?
How effective is advertising in influencing this decision?
What conclusions can be drawn from the previous advertising, if any, put behind my product?
Is the market for this type of product expanding, constant, or contracting?
What has been happening to my share of this market?
What is the nature of my product's present and anticipated competition?
What is the promotion picture for competing products?
Is my responsibility for creating demand for my product increasing?
How difficult is the job of pre-selling my product to its prospective buyers?
Should I advertise to any group other than my prospective customers?
How many dollars for marketing my product are anticipated out of gross margin?
What proportion of advertising seems indicated to help insure the most profitable marketing mix for me?
What ceiling on advertising expenditures is recommended by my present financial condition?
How much can I pay for possible increases in sales volume?
What is the relationship between the advertising I do and my break-even points?
What are the nature and the cost of appropriate advertising programs?

Build-up versus Breakdown

Another contrast in budget approaches is between the "build-up" and the "breakdown" schools of thought. A budget must be one type or the other; it cannot be both. The build-up budget is a product of assembly. The advertising efforts that will be needed are refined, priced, totaled, and there is the budget figure. This approach recognizes that advertising is only one cost of operation and not a separate, unrelated activity. It implies over-all managerial control. It is, in essence, a task approach because it puts company needs in control of the size of the budget.

The breakdown approach breaks down a lump-sum appropriation; it does not build up to a budget. It starts off with an amount that the company is going to spend, rather than arriving at the amount the company should spend. Because its fundamental issue is the size of the total advertising fund, the breakdown approach fits in snugly with blind observance of the percentage-of-dollar-sales technique.

Budget Period

Some manufacturers, mostly small, do not think of advertising in terms of specific time periods. Neither do those advertisers think in terms of exact sums to be spent in advertising. Their advertising is wholly opportunistic, being turned on only if management thinks that conditions, particularly the company's financial condition, are favorable.

For those advertisers who do budget, there is no one practice followed by all in respect to when the budget will be set up nor to the length of the budget period. About all that is permitted is the recognition that many large manufacturers set up annual budgets a few months before the start of the budget period. The fact that advertising accounting is interwoven so inextricably with other company accounting argues that advertising use the company fiscal period; this is usually one year.

When budget periods are short, and anything under twelve months must be considered short, continuity, that basic policy which is essential, is endangered. Furthermore, long-range advertising strategy and planning are virtually impossible where the budget is handled on a week-to-week or month-to-month basis. Even where the products are highly perishable or seasonal, few advertisers can ignore completely the off seasons. Probably the fashion goods area is where short budget periods are most nearly defensible.

Budget periods longer than a year can be criticized as being too long. There are too many variables and too much change. It is perfectly permissible, indeed, even desirable to think and plan in general terms for several years ahead, but a detailed budget for a complete three-year program would require so much revision as to make its construction unwise. It is true, however, that radio and television may demand that the advertiser commit himself for longer than twelve months for talent or time or both.

ADMINISTERING THE BUDGET

The immediate objective in administering the advertising budget is the achieving of the goals chosen. It is hoped, of course, that these goals will not have to be

Advertising Management

revised to any major degree and that the advertising efforts planned, too, will prove to be appropriate without substantial change.

For the long term, the administrator will want his experience gained in budgeting to contribute to better planning and policy formulation. He will want to insure continuity of profitable advertising. By learning how to spend advertising dollars more and more effectively, he increases his ability to demonstrate to top management that advertising is necessary and manageable.

Advertising Expense Classifications

If a manufacturer is to advertise profitably, he must provide adequate funds for all needed advertising activities of a legitimate nature; by the same token, he should not let illegitimate expenditures masquerade in the respectable cloak of "advertising." These two prerequisites of sound budget administration demand that a carefully constructed advertising expense classification be established that will include *all* and *only* proper advertising activities.[1]

What are proper advertising costs? There is no agreement. Some manufacturers include their catalogues as an approved charge against the advertising budget, while other manufacturers do not. The same is true of such items as publicity, trade shows, souvenirs, and even salesmen's cards. Perhaps substantial agreement exists on the acceptance of these four broad groupings:

Media	Production costs
Advertising department expense	Advertising research

Any additional groupings, such as a "miscellaneous" classification, are dangerous because they may become catch-alls, but some may be thought necessary.

A leading trade paper, *Printers' Ink,* has done a helpful service for advertisers by compiling three lists of charges. The *white* list contains charges that "belong in the advertising account." The charges in the *black* list "do not belong in the advertising account although all too frequently they are put there." The *gray* list contains "border line charges, sometimes belonging in the advertising account and sometimes in other accounts, depending on circumstances."

Distribution of the Budget

Budgeting consists of two steps, the *determination* of the budget and its *distribution.* The second step may result in apportionment in great detail or the earmarking may be done merely in terms of broad groupings. If a budget is truly and completely a built-up or assembled budget, if it is the result of studying and deciding about each product, each medium, each task, each market, and each day, week, or month, then the distribution will be identical with the build-up. In such cases, determination dictates distribution.

[1] Here is a list of the expenses charged to the advertising budget by the Wesson Oil & Snowdrift Sales Company: (1) all media including newspapers, magazines, radio, television, trade papers, and outdoor; (2) the production cost of all advertisements or commericals; (3) store material and other merchandising material; (4) the cost of national sales contests, of market research services, and of publicity.

What charges belong in the advertising account?

- Printers' Ink guide to allocation of the advertising appropriation
- Charges that belong in the advertising account: white list
- Charges that do not belong in the advertising account: black list
- Charges that are borderline: gray list

WHITE LIST

(These charges belong in the advertising account)

SPACE:
(Paid advertising in all recognized mediums, including:)
Newspapers
Magazines
Business papers
Farm papers
Class journals
Car cards
Theater programs
Outdoor
Point of purchase
Novelties
Booklets
Directories
Direct advertising
Cartons and labels (for advertising purposes, such as in window displays)
Catalogs
Package inserts (when used as advertising and not just as direction sheets)
House magazines to dealers or consumers
Motion pictures (including talking pictures) when used for advertising
Slides
Export advertising
Dealer helps
Reprints of advertisements used in mail or for display
Radio
Television
All other printed and lithographed material used directly for advertising purposes

ADMINISTRATION:
Salaries of advertising department executives and employees
Office supplies and fixtures used solely by advertising department
Commissions and fees to advertising agencies, special writers or advisers
Expenses incurred by salesmen when on work for advertising department
Traveling expenses of department employees engaged in departmental business
(Note: In some companies these go into special "Administration" account)

MECHANICAL:
Art work
Typography
Engraving
Mats
Electros
Photographs
Radio & TV production
Package design (advertising aspects only)
Etc.

MISCELLANEOUS:
Transportation of advertising material (to include postage and other carrying charges)
Fees to window display installation services
Other miscellaneous expenses connected with items on the White List

BLACK LIST

(These charges do not belong in the advertising account although too frequently they are put there:)

Free goods
Picnic and bazaar programs
Charitable, religious and fraternal donations
Other expenses for good-will purposes
Cartons
Labels
Instruction sheets
Package manufacture
Press agentry
Stationery used outside advertising department
Price lists
Salesmen's calling cards
Motion pictures for sales use only
House magazines going to factory employees
Bonuses to trade
Special rebates
Membership in trade associations
Entertaining customers or prospects
Annual reports
Showrooms
Demonstration stores
Sales convention expenses
Salesmen's samples (including photographs used in lieu of samples)
Welfare activities among employees
Such recreational activities as baseball teams, etc.
Sales expenses at conventions
Cost of salesmen's automobiles
Special editions which approach advertisers on good-will basis

GRAY LIST

(These are borderline charges, sometimes belonging in the advertising accounts and sometimes in other accounts, depending on circumstances:)

Samples
Demonstrations
Fairs
Canvassing
Rent
Light
Heat
Depreciation of equipment used by advertising department
Telephone and other overhead expenses, apportioned to advertising department
House magazines going to salesmen
Advertising automobiles
Premiums
Membership in associations or other organizations devoted to advertising
Testing bureaus
Advertising portfolios for salesmen
Contributions to special advertising funds of trade associations
Display signs on the factory or office building
Salesmen's catalogs
Research and market investigations
Advertising allowances to trade for co-operative effort

This chart is based on the principle that there are three types of expenses that generally are charged against the advertising appropriation.

The first charge is made up of expenses that are always justifiable under any scheme of accounting practice. These have been included in the white list of charges that belong in the advertising account.

A second type consists of those charges which cannot and should not under any system of accounting be justified as advertising expenses. These have been placed on the black list.

There is a third type of expense which can sometimes be justified under advertising and sometimes not. Frequently the justification for the charge depends upon the method used in carrying on a certain activity. These charges have been placed in a borderline gray list.

The chart is the result of the collaboration of the editors of PRINTERS' INK and several hundred advertisers. It has been revised for a third time for publication in this Annual, with the aid of advertising and accounting men. It may be considered, therefore, to represent sound, standard practice.

Printers' Ink *makes these recommendations about what should be charged to the advertising fund. (Copyright Printers' Ink Publishing Company, Inc., 205 East 42nd Street, New York 17, New York)*

No real budget exists until the advertiser has set up his schedule or plan in sufficient detail. Execution of plans and control of activities are not possible unless the advertising manager knows in what markets and media which products will be advertised when. He must also know the nature of the various advertising efforts scheduled and to what expense classifications the costs will be charged. Furthermore, intra-company coordination as described in Chapter 20 demands that the other departments know what to count on and expect.

By Market Area. Budgets are too general unless broken down in terms of market area. The advertising manager and the sales manager should work together on this job for obvious reasons. Indeed, the same technique may be used as was used in setting sales quotas. Many guides are available for this purpose. Some commonly used are: number of prospects, number of retailers, past sales, forecast sales, sales potential as measured by some "buying power index," and competitors' activities. Sales potential plus the advertiser's needs should be weighted heavily.

By Product. For the manufacturer with more than one product or even with more than one price line, there is the problem of distributing his advertising fund between or among the items or product lines he will advertise. Although many factors can be involved (relation of by-product to main line, optimum production volume, sales volumes, margins, competitive superiority, and the like), the overriding principle is to promote most actively that product or those products which will do the advertiser the most good. In general, the bulk of the advertising effort should be put behind the most popular products and prices. By so doing, the advertiser tells his public that he has what the public favors; he does not tell buyers what he thinks they should want.

By Medium. Because the selection of media types and of individual media was handled in the first two sections of Chapter 18 on scheduling, no more need be said about this form of distribution.

By Time Period. This breakdown of the budget was handled in Chapter 18 in the section entitled "Timing the Advertisements."

By Type of Advertising Effort. An advertiser may feel that he should know what portion of his total budget is being spent for each type of advertising effort planned. One possible breakdown is between product-selling efforts and institutional efforts. Another is among the various types of groups the advertiser hopes to influence, such as prospects, customers, professional groups, and middlemen. There are several "publics" to whom public relations advertising can be addressed.

By Expense Classification. Because the topic of advertising expense classifications was taken up earlier in this section, no further treatment of it will be made here.

Records and Reports

In the administration of his budget the advertising manager will make extensive use of records and reports. Some of these he will *request,* usually from the accounting department, and others he will *render,* usually to top management.

Essential reports the advertising manager will need include:

Advertising budget figures broken down as desired
Year-to-date expenditures; in addition to current figures, last year's figures may also be useful
Unspent balance remaining in each advertising expense classification
Sales broken down as desired
Profit-and-loss figures

The advertising manager will make periodic reports to top management on three major matters:

> Current advertising expenditures
> Explanation of deviations from the budget
> Estimated results of current advertising

The records and reports the advertising manager asks for will be used by him in guiding current advertising so as to achieve its objectives. He will check with them in order to keep track of how much he has spent; he will use them to help him stay within his budget. As a matter of fact, close scrutiny and analysis may reveal some possible savings in the budget. Particularly will the advertising manager watch those expense items of an indefinite amount, such as the cooperative advertising that retailers may or may not avail themselves of up to the top figure authorized. The records and reports will be asked to supply information only, not instructions as to what should be done.

Guarding against "Raids"

The possibility and the practice of raiding the advertising budget are aggravated by the absence of standardized accounting for advertising. As mentioned in the earlier sections on expense classifications, protection and control of the budget rest on the observance of a soundly constructed list of legitimate advertising charges. Advertising dollars should be spent only for advertising, and no other charges against the advertising budget should be approved. Yielding to the insidious whisper, "You *could* charge that to advertising," quickly dissipates the advertising fund. Especially difficult for advertising managers to turn down are such items as entertainment, contributions, gifts, plant athletic teams, and retail requests, particularly for free merchandise to give away as contest prizes.

Flexibility

Flexibility is essential to sound budgetary control and administration. Developments in several areas bar the advertiser from foretelling the state of business accurately for the usual budget period of twelve months. One area is competition. Here competing products or promotion, or both, can change. Second, the advertiser's own picture can change in respect to product, promotion, or market area. Third, media do not remain static. The advertiser may drop or add media, rates may change, or new media appear. Fourth and last, market potential shifts as sales opportunities go up or down.

Advertising Management

All these possible changes demand a mechanism for adjusting the advertising effort to new assignments and to new conditions. Such adjustment is indicated the moment the advertising manager concludes that his company would do well to spend more, or less, than the amount planned. In addition to size of budget, flexibility also includes timing, products featured, media, market area, and tactics.

Flexibility can be provided for through a "review and revise" mechanism or through a reserve. In the former, routine reviews of the budget are scheduled regularly and often. The maximum review interval acceptable is six months; this provides a review at the mid-point of the annual budget period. A preferred interval would call for a regular review every three months. Machinery should be available for getting special reviews executed on short notice. Once decided on, revision, either up or down, should be prompt. Automatic revision is found in some product lines, particularly where the fixed-sum-per-unit technique is used. Advertising funds are tied to sales volume or to the production schedule so that, for example, if the production estimates are revised downward, the advertising budget follows along. The other way to provide the advertising manager with flexibility is for a portion of the approved fund to be left unallocated, thus giving him an advertising reserve. How large this reserve should be depends on experience, present circumstances, and expected future conditions. If a balance should be in this reserve at the end of the budget period, it reverts to the company's general account.

Flexibility is as much a danger as it is a necessity because the manufacturer can so easily err in either direction. No pat rule is available or permissible. And, too much flexibility is just as costly as too little.

Too much flexibility is characteristic of the vacillating, erratic advertiser who actually has no advertising policy. The extremely worthwhile and cumulative results of the consistent employment of advertising are placed in serious jeopardy. Indeed, there is danger to the volume of current advertising that should be done. Management becomes as apt to cut the size of the budget because "business is so good" as because "business is so bad." So, either extreme, too little flexibility or too much, is to be avoided.

Continuity

In Chapter 18 on scheduling, the necessity for a minimum degree of month-to-month regularity in advertising was established. There is another type of continuity just as essential, year-after-year continuity. One can argue convincingly that the single most important advertising policy is consistency. It follows that no element of sound budget administration is more basic than a policy of year-after-year advertising continuity.

The arguments for advertising consistently year-after-year are overwhelming. The group to which advertisements are delivered is never composed of the same individuals, even in the short-run. Each day there are births, marriages, and deaths. Translate these facts into a three- or five-year period and the need for continuity is impressive.

Then, too, there is a momentum to advertising. This momentum decreases when advertising is turned off for a period of time, and the drop starts the very moment advertising is discontinued. Because of its cumulative operation, advertising works less efficiently when turned on and off at will, resulting in an expensive loss of momentum. Continuity is a multiplier of effectiveness and is just as profitable in advertising as it is in production.

The Predominant Manufacturer. Continuity is sometimes endangered when a manufacturer reaches a position of predominance in his industry or group. Just what ratio entitles him to consider his relationship as predominant is a matter of opinion. Some may feel that all he needs is to sell as much as all his competitors, while others may think he should sell two, three, or even five times as much. One might understandably claim that such an impressive portion of industry sales entitles a manufacturer to think of coasting along with only a minimum of reminder-type advertising.

Such a course of action would certainly be perilous, most probably fatal, for several reasons. There are still some prospects who should buy the manufacturer's products but do not, and this condition argues for continued advertising. The manufacturer wants to hold on to his present customers; if he lets them forget him, soon they will have drifted away because they become "unsold." In most cases, the per capita consumption of his customers can be increased, but not if advertising is curtailed. Of those who buy the manufacturer's product, wholesalers and retailers as well as consumers, some disappear each year and new ones appear; the new buyers need advertising. Should the manufacturer decide in the future to launch a new product or two or to enter and exploit some new market that appears, then he will be handicapped if he stops advertising now. Finally, discontinuance of advertising by him is an invitation to competitors.

The Oversold Manufacturer. Occasionally a manufacturer or an entire industry moves into an oversold condition. Because of war, scarcities, strikes, or floods, orders cannot be filled. Things are so reversed that buyers are entertaining and giving gifts to manufacturers' salesmen! Customers may be on an allotment basis, or, in case of war, they may be getting no consumer goods at all. In such a circumstance there is always the temptation to stop or to reduce sharply the advertising effort.

In addition to those points made against the predominant manufacturer's abandoning advertising, and some of them do apply here with equal validity, there are one or two additional reasons why continuity of advertising, year-after-year, should be maintained. These oversold conditions have always been temporary. The manufacturer must ask how much advertising he should be doing now to reduce buyer resistance in the buyer's market to come or to begin the cultivation of new or marginal markets he will enter when goods are again in abundance. The manufacturer should remember that the switch from a seller's market to a buyer's market can come overnight.

The capital asset of good will needs to be maintained year-after-year, and this can be done through adequate advertising. Consumers need an explanation of why they cannot get consumer products. They also need advice as to how to make their

Advertising Management

present products give satisfactory and continuing service until they can be replaced. Relations with wholesalers and retailers, both new and old, are jeopardized by a ruthless paring of the budget.

Competition argues for continued advertising. The manufacturer does not want to slip in relative standing if only he is oversold; he does not want his industry to seem so smug that newcomers will mushroom if the entire industry is oversold.

The oversold period is excellent for telling an institutional story to the various groups comprising the public relations area. This is harder to justify in normal times when competition for sales is fierce. The period can also be used for experimentation and for developing and testing long-range programs.

Advertising and the Business Cycle

Manufacturers generally spend heavy sums in advertising when business is good and light sums when business is off. This practice at first glance seems highly illogical. It reveals sellers using large quantities of a sales-producing force, advertising, when the getting of sales is an easy matter, when there is enough business for almost all sellers. Then, when buyers are few and hard to sell, when sellers need and scour the woods for even small orders, that same sales producing force is trimmed down drastically.

Why the paradox? Why spend much when little help is needed and not much when the need is painfully acute?

> Deep down in their hearts, the top management of many companies considers advertising to be primarily an expense. When times are bad, management cuts expenses to the bone.
>
> Immediate reductions of certain expense items (wages and rent are examples) may not be possible because of contracts. Expenses that *can* be cut are almost certain *to be* cut.
>
> Management likes to get the maximum return on each dollar it spends or invests. Potential response per advertising dollar is much lower in bad times than in good, suggesting to management that depression advertising would most probably not be profitable.
>
> When sales volume falls off, fewer dollars come in, and this means less gross margin whence advertising dollars come.
>
> The influence of percentage-of-dollar-sales thinking encourages large advertising funds in good times and vice versa.
>
> The attitudes and expectations of consumers are a deterrent to advertising in depressed periods. Consumers are not prone to buy, expecting lower prices as well as lower earnings.
>
> Government tax policy discourages manufacturers from accumulating large reserves in good times to spend for advertising in bad times. The Internal Revenue Service allows advertisers to deduct, as an expense, all current product-selling advertising and most good will and public policy advertising. However, a reserve set up this year to be used for advertising in some future year cannot be charged as an expense against this year's operations.

Budgeting

Is the cyclical advertising policy followed by practically all advertisers sound? This is a hard question. Because so many outstanding advertisers have followed this pattern for so long, it is unlikely that all of that number have been wrong. Yet, it is equally clear that an advertiser is well advised to spend advertising dollars today, even though his profit-and-loss figure is red, if by so doing his long-term profit is increased. It is practically impossible to imagine an advertiser who should discontinue all advertising during depressions.

If a manufacturer is ready to launch a new product with some extremely attractive feature, or an old product that has been improved to an amazing degree, or if the manufacturer is in an industry whose trend is strongly upward, then, when general business falls off, these specific manufacturers will have justification for continued vigorous advertising.

As for advertising's controlling the business cycle, that is simply not the case; there are too many other factors more potent. It is quite possible that advertising has had the effect, of unknown strength, of compounding the cycle by widening the gap between a cycle's peak and trough. More influential factors are actions by the government, international developments, the dollars the consumer has in his pocket to spend, and the frame of mind of the consumer.

SOME OBSERVATIONS ABOUT BUDGETING

Many advertisers set up no formal budgets nor do they plan in advance how much they will spend in advertising. Quite a few of these actually have no advertising policy, perhaps overspending in good times and doing little or no advertising when times are bad.

Because of the nature of the advertising budget, there is no scientific way to set it. If there were, then the $5,000,000 budget or the $50,000 budget reported in the press might become $4,987,000 or $50,500. This inability to set budgets scientifically stems from the impossibility of forecasting accurately what advertising will do to *sales* or to *buyers*. Against such a background, advertisers are torn between techniques that are simple and techniques that are sound. Soundness demands an analysis of such factors as the time lag between advertisements and response; the quality of advertising; the purchasing power, buying habits, and motivation of consumers; and changes in prices, products, competition, channels, and promotional efforts. Such analyses are not simple.

Advertising budgets must be related to sales volume. Sales income is the source of the budget; the immediate purpose of advertising is to increase sales volume. This relationship is obvious when the advertising promotes products; it is equally true of institutional advertising because patronage motivation will eventually be reflected in sales. There is no standard, universal relationship between advertising budget and sales volume. That will vary from industry to industry, from company to company, from product to product, from market to market, and from date to date. It is clear, however, that the ratio of advertising to sales is higher if the product is new, or has keen competition, or is a consumer product rather than an industrial product,

Advertising Management

if the product is highly responsive to advertising, or if the company is either small or new.

Budgets should be adequate. Enough dollars should be spent so that the effort will not be wasteful because stunted. So much should *not* be spent that dollar profits are actually smaller than would have been the case had the advertiser not been so active and ambitious. By all means, the advertiser's budget and his advertising goals should be in balance at the start of the budget period.

Budgets should be tailored. Each manufacturer should work toward the budget that suits him. His circumstances and problems are not like those of any other company, nor like those of his entire industry or group. The dollars he has available both now and in the future for advertising are an individualistic factor, too.

Where a manufacturer has and advertises two or more products, it is sounder for him to study and work up a budget for each than to pick a total figure and divide it. Not only will the amounts fit each more snugly, but also will there be less disturbance to the advertising of items B, C, and D should something happen to item A. Subsequent transfer of funds from one product's budget to that of another product is not an approved practice.

There is little reason to think that advertisers will, at an early date, change the cyclical pattern of their budgeting. Necessity and convenience products should continue to show more resistance to budget slashing in bad times than luxury and postponable products. This is because of the shorter lag between the consumer's receiving the advertiser's message and the consumer's date of next purchase. Continuity continues to be desirable. If an advertiser completely abandons advertising during depressions, he will be hurt badly in three ways. Old customers will forget, and new customers won't know him. Middlemen will cease to consider him a desirable supplier. Turning advertising on and off like an electric light is more expensive than some continuous use.

Setting the advertising budget for a new product is extremely difficult and arbitrary. If the company too is new, the condition is compounded; if the new product is joining a well-known, well-liked family of products, the condition is mitigated. Expenditures per unit of sale will be heavier during the initial period than after the product has been accepted; in fact, they may be so heavy as to use up more than the gross margin on sales during the starting period. The advertising used to launch a new product is an investment of capital, just as are dollars spent for plant or equipment. The amount earmarked for that advertising must be the arbitrary result of managerial judgment because the two basic figures it depends on, sales and gross margin in dollars, are not known.

The size of the budget must be determined in the light of what the advertiser needs accomplished by advertising. Heavy expenditures just because the current tax structure permits their deduction, or light expenditures just because competitors are spending little, to use just two misleading guides as examples, are not wise. Letting *needs* dictate calls for the task or build-up approach, the best approach known yet the most difficult.

There is urgent need for a standard classification, for an official list of advertising expenses. No standard budgeting practice is possible for advertising until there is

Budgeting

agreement on what constitutes advertising expense, until a standard list of approved charges has been accepted and established. Until that time, company-to-company or company-to-industry comparisons will continue to be meaningless.

Similarly, there is an urgent need for performance standards against which advertisements and advertising efforts can be measured. The greater the part played by advertising in his marketing program, and the larger the sum of money an advertiser elects to spend in advertising, the greater is his need for standards. Attempts are being made to arrive at some standards, including advertising cost per dollar of net sales, advertising cost per sale, and advertising cost per dollar of profit. The task approach itself is a step toward the setting of standards. It seems probable that the more detailed expense standards desired must be tailored and built up by each advertiser individually from within his own operations. All standards will be benefited by greater accuracy in measuring the effects of advertising.

An open mind and an experimental attitude are essential to sound budgeting because change is endless. No advertiser can assume that a budget setting process can be perfected that will be best for him indefinitely. Each season, each market, each campaign is different in some regard. For this reason, each advertiser should ask without prejudice or pre-conception each year, "How much should I spend for advertising next year?"

Much research is needed if the budgeting of advertising efforts is to be well managed. One area in which study is promising is that of the determination of market potential. Effective advertising presupposes that the seller can foretell the size of the market of which he hopes to capture a profitable part. A second area is concerned with what a seller can expect his advertising to do for him or what assignments should be given to advertising. In a third area is found the problem of grading, in advance, the quality of advertising; this is the problem of predicting what certain advertising efforts will do. A fourth and final area contains that most challenging undertaking, the determination of the effects of advertising. One set of effects is that of advertising on sales. The basic question is: Just how many sales does advertising cause? Immediately, the advertiser must divide these effects, in his thinking, into current effects and cumulative effects. He also sees at once that if he tries to isolate what *advertising* does to sales, he must also attempt similar isolation for *each* sales-producing force. That is extremely difficult. A second set of effects is that on costs. The basic question here is: Just what does advertising do to production costs and to personal selling costs? For example, if a manufacturer increases his advertising budget by 25 per cent what will that do to his sales expense budget? No advertiser can say. A final set of effects is on profits. The basic question is: Just what are the current and the cumulative effects of advertising on the net profit figure?

Questions and Problems

1. Why can't advertising funds be set by formula?
2. Why might a manufacturer spend less in advertising than the amount budgeted?

Advertising Management

3. What developments or events outside a company can change the company's sales forecast?
4. What can you say about the relationship of advertising to the business cycle?
5. How is a manufacturer's advertising unlike a family budget?
6. Is an advertiser ever encouraged to think in terms of a budget period of less than a year?
7. When should a firm start preparing its ad budget for next year? When should the final budget draft be approved?
8. Two manufacturers, units in the same industry, compute advertising-to-net-sales ratios and find considerable difference between the two figures. Suggest explanations for this difference.
9. Many advertisers exasperate many media by spending less than ¼ of their annual advertising budgets during the summer quarter, during June, July, and August. How do you explain this budgeting pattern?
10. An established manufacturer of a complete line of writing pens and pencils lost money last year and cut his advertising budget for this present year. It is now August. There is every indication that this year will be a red-ink year as was last year. Should money be budgeted for advertising for next year?

Chapter 22

Evaluation

The fact that there is profitable advertising and unprofitable advertising, that there are successful advertisements and unsuccessful ones is common knowledge. The fact that some advertising is less effective than some other advertising suggests that an advertiser cannot predict with precision just what effects a contemplated campaign or, indeed, a proposed advertisement will have. An even more disturbing fact is that the performance of the great bulk of all advertising cannot be measured with precision *even after the advertising has appeared.*

Some of the contrasts to be found in the experience of advertisers almost defy belief. Advertisements in the same campaign and costing the same produce inquiries at a cost of a few cents each — and at a cost of many dollars each. One advertisement of a mail-order seller sells more than fifteen times as many products as does another advertisement — same seller, same product, same cost of advertisement. In the same issue of a general consumer magazine one full-page, 4-color advertisement gets one reader per dollar of space cost while another full-page, 4-color advertisement gets forty-five readers per dollar.

This chapter deals with certain phases of advertising research. It describes what advertisers do in an effort to avoid advertising that would prove to be weak and how advertisers try to determine as accurately as possible the results of the advertising they do run. Evaluation is done mainly by three types of firm. *Advertisers* themselves do some of the work they need done in this area. *Advertising agencies* are active in testing and evaluating; they need to determine what to recommend to clients, and they need to be able to take credit for those recommendations (or to defend them) after the advertising effort has terminated. Finally, *commercial firms* do various types of advertising research.

EVALUATION AND GOALS

The over-all purpose of advertising research, of testing and evaluating, is to see how well advertising achieves the goals assigned to it. One view is that advertising must (1) achieve awareness, (2) affect attitudes, and (3) actuate action. Another

Advertising Management

view sees advertising's goals involving information and ideas, feelings and convictions, and then response and reaction. Still a third concept is that advertising's goals are *changes* — that advertising is to bring about changes in knowledge, opinions, and behavior as they relate to the act of buying.

Advertising goals are narrower than and must be distinguished from *marketing* goals. The top marketing executive thinks in such terms as dollar sales volume, unit sales volume, number of customers, size of sales force, and, of course, dollar profits. Although the top advertising executive has an interest in all these, he checks advertising performance against goals which are narrower, more immediate, and more easily checked. This top advertising executive sees his assignment to be essentially that of *communication*. His advertisements are expected to reach and to get through to a certain percentage of a certain homogeneous buyer-group in a certain period of time.

Because the first goal of all advertisements is a psychological goal, advertising research must rest heavily on psychological measures. It must measure accurately and reliably what it claims to measure. The purposes of testing and evaluating are best served by methods which are speedy, simple, and inexpensive.

TIMING ADVERTISING RESEARCH

Advertising research can be done *before* the campaign begins, *during* the running of the campaign, or *after* the campaign is over. Research prior to the start of the campaign is similar to product research prior to the marketing of a new product; the idea is to "get all the bugs out" before spending serious money. The big advertising effort often costs well into the millions, even the tens of millions, and this magnitude demands that the effort be sound and productive at the time it starts. Pre-testing can work the same in advertising as it does in marketing research; 5 cents of the dollar spent in pre-testing can result in the advertiser's getting more advertising performance out of the remaining 95 cents than had he spent the entire dollar for advertising without any pre-testing. The advertiser must be certain, of course, that the answers he gets in the pre-test period are still accurate and correct during the campaign period.

Each advertiser should do what he can about evaluating campaign performance while the campaign is running. In many instances, something can be done to improve and strengthen a campaign which, very soon after it starts, shows clearly that its effectiveness is less than expected. For example, if the theme turns out to be weaker than was thought, emphasis can be shifted or new elements can be added within a matter of weeks to improve performance. Coincidental research is, of course, best known in the broadcast media.

Post-mortems are essential. The curtain has been rung down on the campaign or on the entire program, the advertising fund has been spent, there must be an accounting. So, even though it is most difficult and even though it cannot be done with satisfactory accuracy, the job of evaluating the performance of advertising must be attempted.

THE CHECK-LIST

One method of pre-testing an advertisement is to examine its features and elements against a list of features and elements essential in the typical advertisement. Execution of this test is sometimes referred to as *psychological scoring*. This type of check-list can be a number of desirable values (memory value, attention value, etc.) or a number of questions (clear? believable? etc.). The check-list, thus, is a sort of master inventory of the selling elements or characteristics usually wanted in advertisements.

The creator of a check-list assigns whatever weight he thinks proper to each item. He may give *attention* value two times as much weight as he gives *action* value. Once the list has been drafted and weights assigned, the list's creator is ready to inspect an advertisement, check it against his list, and score how well the advertisement includes the elements or values which constitute the check-list.

Another type of check-list is concerned with readability or hearability. These lists are used to check copy for word length and difficulty, sentence length, and the number of "personal" words and sentences included. Personal pronouns, masculine words, and feminine words are examples of personal words; quotations, questions asked the reader, and commands given the reader are examples of personal sentences.

Merits Claimed

The greatest contribution of the check-list is in preventing the omission from advertisements of important elements — values which are basic and fundamental ingredients of most effective advertisements. The emphasis it places on essential values and superior techniques makes the check-list particularly helpful to advertising beginners. The execution of this technique takes place before large sums are spent, and the operation is simple and speedy. The cost is reasonable in that the advertiser buys *minutes of one person's time,* the analyst. There is excellent control of conditions and variables. Always implicit is the question, *"Why* does this advertisement score less than 100?"

Criticisms Heard

A major limitation of the check-list is the amount of dependence the advertiser places on the list's creator. That individual constructed the list, assigned the weights, and scores the advertisements as he sees them. As a result, the accuracy of the rating of an advertisement rests on the correctness and personal judgment of one person, a person, obviously, who has difficulty in being objective. He also has difficulty in preventing his reaction to the entire advertisement from reflecting in his scoring of the individual items which are on his list. Two judges of supposedly equal competence can rate the same advertisement against the same list — and come up with greatly different scores. Another major handicap is that no one list can be suitable in all instances. Copy format varies, situations vary, advertising objectives vary; teaser advertisements, for example, *must* omit identification, and institutional advertisements *must* contain less urge-to-action value than advertisements of mail-order sellers. The check-list does not tell for certain how effective an

Advertising Management

advertisement will be. It is resented by those creative individuals who consider it to be a strait jacket.

Comments on Check-Lists

The check-list is a *check* and not a test. It need not curb a copywriter because it need not stunt his creativity. Indeed, many experienced copywriters go through this type of analysis automatically and regularly even if informally. If there is to be a formal checking of advertisements against a list, that job should be assigned to someone other than the builder of the advertisements. Readability tests have made a contribution by putting a spotlight on important aspects of communication.

THE CONSUMER JURY

This technique which makes use of a group of judges, a so-called *consumer jury*, is also known as Control Opinion Ratings. It is based on the assumption that a group of typical prospects can and will identify the effective advertisements in an assortment of proposed advertisements more accurately than can advertising practitioners; the assumption is that "There is one wiser than *anybody*, and that is *everybody*." When the advertisements under consideration are submitted to the jury of consumers, questions such as these are asked:

Which of these advertisements would do the best job of attracting your attention?
Which would you be most inclined to read?
Which gives you the most information?
Which is most convincing about the product's desirability?
Which most probably would get you to try the product?

The opinions and reactions of the jurors as reflected in their answers and ratings are assumed to be typical of the consumers who constitute the advertiser's market.

Jury size ranges from twenty to several thousand; a group of about 200 is not uncommon. The research can be done by mail or by personal interview, and it can involve entire advertisements or elements of advertisements. Of the two basic patterns for judging, one asks the juror to consider two advertisements at a time and to identify the better one. The other basic pattern asks the juror to arrange a group of advertisements in order of their merit, from the strongest one down to the weakest one. Within the assortment of advertisements submitted to the jury the advertiser may include an old advertisement or two which he has actually run earlier; these can be thought of as "control" advertisements because their actual performance has been measured in some manner.

The broadcast media of television and radio employ an adaptation of the consumer jury. A group of typical consumers is gathered and asked to be the audience for a broadcast — shows, commercials, or both. During the broadcast of a show, each juror expresses his feelings about each portion of the show as he receives it. In one version, he can press one electrically wired button while he is pleased or approving, and he can move his finger to a second button to register his displeasure or disapproval. His indifference is indicated by not pressing either button. In an-

Evaluation

other version, the juror accomplishes about the same job by checking his reactions frequently on a score sheet. In both versions, a composite group reaction is charted on a graph to make a profile for the broadcast. At the close, there is a discussion period during which the jurors are questioned about their likes and dislikes.

Merits Claimed

The consumer jury technique is speedy because it can be executed in ten to fourteen days. It is not an expensive procedure; there are no space nor time costs, and the use of photostats of rough layouts keeps production costs low. It is both easy to administer and versatile. Whatever is learned from the test becomes known before major expenditures are made for the major advertising effort. Simplicity and control are features of this test in that the advertisements are the sole factor involved; there are no editorial features to adjust for, no other advertisements, no question of position. And, the basic philosophy is most sound, let the advertiser's customers and prospective customers rather than advertising people separate the good from the bad.

Criticisms Heard

The most serious defect of the consumer jury technique is its questionable validity. It is impossible for the juror to remain a normal consumer; he unavoidably becomes an advertising expert and tries to outguess the real buyers. Some jurors vote for "clever" advertisements, or for advertisements similar to some they have seen, or for advertisements they feel they *should* like. Some jurors try to cast those votes which will be most pleasing to the advertiser. Seeing advertisements out of context and ranking them is far from normal, natural, every-day exposure and reaction to advertising. It is most difficult, furthermore, for a consumer to spot an advertisement which will get that consumer's dollars. What the juror *says* he would most probably do and what he *actually* would do may be quite different. There are jurors who would be reluctant to admit the attraction power of a sexy illustration or the urge-to-action power of a negative or embarrassing keynote idea.

Comments on Consumer Juries

Juries seem to be in greater agreement about which advertisements are weak than about which are strong. They do a better job testing attention, interest, and layout than they do testing selling power, conviction, belief, and understanding. They measure the *relative* interest of different advertisements to consumers, not the *absolute* interest. Without doubt, each juror should be a genuine prospect for or an actual user of the product being advertised. College students are good jurors for soap and cigarettes; they are not acceptable for pianos and cash registers.

TEST MARKET TESTS

The procedure of testing some actual advertising in actual test markets is also referred to as Sales Area Tests and as Local Area Sales Tests. The basic idea is this: before spending a big sum on a big campaign, try the campaign idea on a small scale to determine whether any changes should be made before going all out in the advertiser's entire market. Test market tests can be used to learn about such matters as which benefit to feature, size of advertisement, type of illustration, or frequency of advertisement. The majority of products involved in such tests move to the ultimate consumer through food or drug stores.

In executing the tests, the advertiser designates a group of *test* markets, perhaps three, four, or five, and an equal number of *control* markets. Suppose, for example, the item to be tested is a new campaign theme based on a benefit which, up to now, the advertiser has never featured. Suppose, further, that the advertiser sets up a group of three test markets and a group of three control markets. Suppose, still further, that the item is a packaged food product. In each of the six markets, the advertiser will need to choose (and very carefully, too) a panel or sample of food stores; these samples should be typical for their respective markets and should be composed in observance of the best principles of marketing research. Not less than six stores should be included in each sample, and every merchant in a sample should be paid to cooperate in the test. For a period of time before the test, a period ranging from one to three months, sales of the food product involved and its competing brands are checked to get some idea of what is "normal" at that time. Then comes the test period. During it, advertising featuring the new theme is run in the three test markets, but no change whatever is made in the control markets; our seller continues his advertising there as in the past, or he continues to do no advertising in those control markets. This test period during which the proposed advertising is run in the test markets must be long enough for the effects of the advertising to show; the absolutely minimum test period is six months, and a full year's test or more is preferred. During this test period, the sales checks continue in all six markets. After the advertising stops, sales should be checked for at least two more months. The sales checks will show the food product's share of the market as well as absolute sales volume for the periods before, during, and after the advertising.

If the advertiser prefers to substitute consumer purchases for retail sales as a reflection of the effectiveness of the test advertising, he can set up a *consumer* purchase panel in each of the six markets instead of a sample of food stores. The consumers constituting a panel are expected to be representative of the market in which they live. They are paid to keep a record of purchases of certain food products, including, of course, the food product involved. Purchase data are date of purchase, brand, size, quantity bought, price paid, and store at which purchase was made. The panel members may or may not be asked to log their reading, viewing, and listening activities.

Test Market Characteristics

Which markets make good test markets? The characteristics of good test markets, of course, are also the characteristics of good control markets because the two groups should be as identical as possible. A test market ideally should be of economical and manageable size. (This is not always the case, however.) It and its retail trading area should be a natural marketing unit, isolated geographically from the influence of huge cities, independent economically, and self-contained within narrow boundaries. The test market should be representative of the advertiser's total market in respect to income, population, spending patterns, and growth. Diversification of income, stability, and the balance among agriculture, industry, and commerce should be typical of the entire market. The wholesale and retail structures should be adequate, equalized, and normally competitive; no one store or chain should dominate the market. Finally, the media set up must be favorable and coverage should be balanced. Each market should be self-sufficient as regards media, and if there is only one newspaper in each market, so much the better. The advertiser needs media which are able, cooperative, and comparable among the markets to be used. Grand Rapids, Davenport, Los Angeles, Syracuse, Minneapolis-St. Paul, Spokane, and Roanoke are popular test cities.

Merits Claimed

In principle, test market testing is the soundest technique; it reflects and measures the sales power of actual advertising. It is realistic and true-to-life; it tests television advertising in actual broadcasts and newspaper advertising in actual newspapers. Conditions are not artificial. The tests precede the big, the expensive advertising effort. Finally, there is increased income from the sale of additional merchandise.

Criticisms Heard

Control is a most difficult problem in test market testing because of the multitude and the magnitude of the variables present. Weather may cooperate in most of the markets but be unreasonable in a few. Local marketing conditions are ever changing, but the changes in one market are not identical with those in another market. In the ideal test, the personal selling and promotion of the retailers in the test and control markets would continue unchanged, yet this may not be the case. Price changes in one market but not in the others exasperate the advertiser in addition to distorting his findings. Retail controls must be rigid and retail inventory audits must be accurate and complete if the test is to be valid. Many retailers can and do buy from numerous sources, complicating the problem of control of purchases. Test market testing is a complex undertaking beset with many possible hazards and unforeseen events. It demands adjustments and allowances; it calls for most skillful interpretation.

A second major difficulty is the selection of test markets and control markets. The advertiser hopes, he even assumes, that the test markets are and will remain identical throughout his period of interest in them, that the control markets will do likewise, and that all markets, test and control, are similar. Almost invariably his attention will be attracted to differences he did not note at first, differences involving media, perhaps, or retailers.

Finally, test market testing is not suitable for all types of products and services. It is limited to local media. It takes much over-all time and many dollars. It tips competitors off to what the advertiser is up to, alerting them so they can adopt and adapt the winning technique — or counter it. Indeed, competitors *have* been accused of concurrent and extraordinary promotional activities in test markets or control markets undertaken just to confuse the advertiser doing the testing.

Advertising Management

Comments on Test Market Testing

Test market testing works best for products which are quickly consumed and repurchased by a large proportion of the consumers in a market. Advertising should have an important influence on the purchase of the products, and quick consumer response to advertising should be natural. Whatever the product, the advertising period should be long enough (and the volume of the test advertising great enough) for consumer reaction to be clear and undeniable. Test market testing is inappropriate for indirect action advertising; it much prefers advertising of the direct action type or at least advertising which will stimulate consumer reaction in a matter of days. The technique is obviously awkward for testing seasonal benefits; in some of the longer tests, adjustment is necessary for the seasonal element in the sales curve. Particular care should be taken to see that merchandising aid from media and company promotional efforts are frozen as completely as possible; they can make certain markets non-typical. The selection of popular test and control markets insures the use of proved markets; the danger of this selection is that other tests may be in progress at the same time, tests which could complicate the picture. Advertisers should try to make test campaigns as similar to the big, subsequent campaign as possible; they must also remember that conditions can change between test time and subsequent campaign time.

INQUIRIES

In this test, two or more advertisements are run containing one variable — perhaps the benefit or the headline, perhaps the layout or the medium. Each advertisement contains (a) an offer or an invitation to the consumer to respond to the advertisement, and (b) a key to identify the advertisement and the medium. The offer, for example, could be of a sample or a booklet; the key could be a number (street, department, post-office box), a name, initials, or a symbol in the corner of the coupon or order blank. The number of replies or inquiries produced by each advertisement is totaled, and then conclusions are drawn. This technique is used regularly by mail-order sellers. The assumption for advertisements seeking inquiries is that the best advertisement will produce the most inquiries; for advertisements seeking to influence buyers and future buying decisions, the assumption is that what produces inquiries will produce sales — that inquiries are a reliable indication of purchases.

The inquiry technique is used in newspapers and magazines, in direct mail, and in the broadcast media of television and radio. It gives the advertiser a relative measurement of one advertisement against another, of one medium against another, of one benefit against another. Typically, the advertiser divides the cost of each advertisement by the number of inquiries it produces to get cost-per-inquiry figures. Certain advertisers such as sellers of correspondence courses go one step further and compute cost-per-sale for each advertisement.

Type of Offer

The *coupon* is one of three methods of making the offer. This method, bold and obvious, encourages a large response. The coupon also lets the advertiser ask for

Evaluation

specific information about the person replying. Mail-order sellers and advertisers wanting large quantities of inquiries favor the use of the coupon. It is also appropriate in a newspaper or magazine with a small circulation. Some consumers will send in coupons without having read the body copy of the advertisement.

A second possibility is the *featured offer* without coupon. In prominent type, perhaps even in the headlines, the advertiser makes his offer, often underlining the word *FREE*. The featured offer, like the coupon, may be necessary in class media if enough inquiries to be meaningful are to be forthcoming.

The third way to make an offer or issue an invitation is to hide it — to bury it as the next-to-last sentence in the last (or next to last) paragraph of the body copy. The *hidden offer* does nothing to call attention to itself or even suggest its presence. It is particularly effective in mass publications in checking the readership of the text, in screening children's inquiries, in limiting total response, and in holding down costs.

Merits Claimed

The use of inquiries is both old and popular. The inquiry itself is evidence of advertising's power to provoke consumer reaction, and *physical* reaction, too. The test is versatile in that it can be used for benefit, body copy, headline, position, size of advertisement, color, and medium. The nature of the test permits its execution prior to the big, expensive advertising effort.

Criticisms Heard

Most advertisements inviting inquiries also have another objective, that of influencing the reader favorably toward the product or service being advertised. This makes them double-goal advertisements, one goal involving indirect, future action and the other involving direct, immediate action. Double-goal advertisements hope to sell the consumer on the product or service *and* on sending in an inquiry. Inquiries measure the success of the second undertaking but not the success of the first one; the consumer's attitude toward the offer or the invitation need not be the same as his attitude toward the product. So, inquiries need not be a measure of the selling effectiveness of an advertisement. Inquiries can be a time-consuming technique, particularly bothersome to seasonal advertisers. Those from advertisements in monthly magazines drift in over a period of seven months, and those from advertisements in weekly magazines over a period of seven weeks. And what is to be concluded about those consumers who do not make inquiries? Then there is the problem of low- or no-quality inquiries. These are sent in by children, competitors, mail-order sellers searching for new techniques, curiosity seekers, greedy sample seekers, and marketing students. Hiding the offer and charging for what is offered can help somewhat in this regard. Finally, control of variables (weather, news, position in medium) is never easy and is often unsatisfactory.

Comments on Inquiries

The number of inquiries an advertisement produces depends on the nature of the offer and how much emphasis is given to it. This number is more likely to measure

Advertising Management

reader interest than sales power; it is best for testing advertisement "A" against advertisement "B"; it is best as a relative measure of response rather than as an absolute measure. Inquiries reflect both the quality of the medium and the effectiveness of the offer *in a single measurement*. Because variables cannot be frozen, there is the problem of making proper allowance for them. The closer the advertisements are to direct action in nature, and the further away they are from indirect action in nature, the sounder are inquiries as a measure.

SPLIT-RUN TESTS

The split-run test, available in some newspapers and some magazines, is a refinement of the inquiry test. A simplified version of split-run testing might be as follows: A manufacturer takes 2 advertisements, "A" and "B", to a magazine offering split-run facilities; the two advertisements differ only in one respect — benefit, layout, illustration, premium offer, or headline. The magazine prints advertisement "A" in one-half of its issue and advertisement "B" in the other half, and then sees that one-half of the readers in every market get copies containing "A" and one-half get copies containing "B". Each advertisement offers the reader a booklet, the same booklet; each advertisement is keyed. Suppose the only difference between the two is that advertisement "A" featured safety and "B" featured sex. If "B" pulls four times as many inquiries as does "A", then it is obvious that "B" contains more power or value than does "A". Mail-order sellers can count the purchases produced by each advertisement rather than counting the requests for a booklet.

Some newspapers offer an every-other-copy split; some offer a rural-urban split. A magazine may be able to send advertisement "A" to the fourteen Southern states and "B" to the rest of the country. Another magazine may offer an East-West split. In addition to every-other-copy, some offer an every-third-copy split. Every-other-name is a common split in the use of mailing lists in the direct-mail medium.

Merits Claimed

Without any doubt, the great merit of split-run testing is the advertiser's practically complete control, the freezing of all variables except the one being tested. Normally, all other conditions are identical. The date is the same, the page, the position on the page, the other advertisements and the editorial material on the page, the weather, competitors' activities, the morning's headlines, the magazine's cover — all are held constant in every-other-copy splits, making the test quite scientific. Because advertisements "A" and "B" appear simultaneously, neither can affect the performance of the other. In addition, random sampling is automatic in the cases of every-other-copy. Because conditions are natural, the reader's reaction is normal; he or she does not know of the other advertisement or of the test. The fact that two or more advertisements can be run at the same time makes for speed in obtaining the results.

Criticisms Heard

Not much can be said against the split-run technique as a method of judging based on inquiries. Some media make a charge for the service, and some specify

Evaluation

the minimum size of advertisement accepted. Competitors may be tipped off as to what an advertiser is doing and planning to do. If monthly magazines are used, six months or even more may elapse for results to be clear. Finally, these test facilities are available from only a limited number of media.

Comments on Split-Run Tests

Split-run tests are excellent for mail-order sellers and for the testing of benefits to feature. For strictly testing purposes, the every-other-copy or the every-third-copy splits are preferable to the sectional splits. In the newspaper medium, the big circulation papers in our largest markets may be more accurate than smaller papers because of the heavy response they are able to produce. Because distribution of an issue may not be even, it is desirable to allow for a margin of error of about 15 per cent. In this respect an advertiser *can* split run the same advertisement, "A" and "B" are identical in every respect except their respective keys; if the medium's distribution is even, each advertisement should draw the same number of inquiries.

RECOGNITION TESTS

There are two types of readership evaluation, *recognition* and *recall;* recognition is treated in this section, recall in the next. Although the recognition technique is not the exclusive property of any one researcher, Daniel Starch and Staff and the Starch Advertisement Readership Service first come to mind when one hears the recognition technique mentioned. So, let us look at how Starch operates in the magazine field.

In the Starch Readership Service research, Starch interviewers make between 100 and 200 interviews for each sex for such a general magazine as *Life*. An individual is considered a reader and is interviewed if he or she claims to have read part of a copy of the magazine being checked. If the person is still in doubt about his reading after looking at the cover, he is allowed to look inside. Then the interviewer takes the consumer through the copy page by page, asking the consumer to point out all the advertisements of one-half page size or larger which he remembers. The headline, the subheads, the text, the illustration, and the logotype are asked about individually. Readers are eligible for three classifications:

Noted: The reader says he remembers seeing the advertisement in that issue of that magazine.

Seen-Associated: The reader says he saw enough of the advertisement to know what the product was or who the advertiser was.

Read-Most: The reader says he read 50 per cent or more of the written material in the advertisement.

Computations are then made. The number of individuals in each of the three classifications *per dollar of advertisement costs* is determined. Cost ratios are figured for each of the three classifications. For example, if a certain advertiser's cost per 100 "noters" is only one-half of the average cost for that issue, his cost ratio for the "Noted" classification would be 200 per cent, meaning that his advertisement did twice as well as the average advertisement in that issue of the publication.

Advertising Management

Then, the advertisements are ranked from top to bottom, from first to last according to those cost ratios. The advertisement getting the greatest number of "noters" in terms of cost of advertisement would rank first for the "Noted" classification. In other words, the advertisements are ranked from best to poorest in terms of dollars spent to get "Noters." The same is done for the two other classifications.

Merits Claimed

It is claimed that recognition tests establish the attention power of advertisements, measure the impression made by brand name or company name, and identify the advertisements which got and held readers' interest. The underlying assumption is that unless it is seen and read, an advertisement cannot influence buyers — that purchases will rise as reading does. The test shows whether a campaign is gaining or losing in reader interest, and it shows an advertiser how his competitors' advertising is faring. Inferences can be made about reader preferences in respect to layout, format, illustrations, benefits, and color for *all* advertisements. Scores are available rather quickly.

Criticisms Heard

Validity of these tests rests on the memory and the honesty of the reader. Most consumers don't read many advertisements carefully; they may have seen a similar advertisement earlier, or another advertisement from the same campaign; they may have seen the advertisement in another publication. Dishonest consumers will not admit to reading certain advertisements they may have devoured avidly. The test leaves much unknown about the quality of the reading, about the understanding, the acceptance, the belief, and the influence of the advertising message. Much remains unknown, too, about the quality of the reader; the advertiser wants to reach interested prospects, not everybody. Questions are raised about the soundness of the sampling procedure, about the quality of the interviewing, and about interviewer bias. Worship of high Starch figures may postpone the adoption of a new advertising pattern even though such a move is otherwise indicated. These tests are more expensive than certain other tests.

Comments on Recognition Tests

The more readership an advertisement enjoys, the greater its opportunity to influence readers. If there were no other variables, the remembered advertisement should usually be more effective than the one not remembered. Instead of attaching much significance to any *one* recognition figure, the wise advertiser realizes that a better use of recognition scores is on a trend or continuing basis, both for his own advertising and for that of competitors. A consumer tires as the interview continues, and this favors the advertisements checked early; Starch recognizes this and does randomize the starting page so as to equalize this fatigue element. Control procedures have been developed to measure the amount of consumer confusion which causes a reader to say he saw an advertisement when he could not possibly have seen it; there is no way to adjust for the reverse type of confusion. Probably the most important conclusion is somewhat of a warning. There are known ways to

What is the Bell System?

The Bell System is cables and radio relay and laboratories and manufacturing plants and local operating companies and millions of telephones in every part of the country.

The Bell System is people... hundreds of thousands of employees and more than two million men and women who have invested their savings in the business.

It is more than that.
The Bell System is an idea.

It is an idea that starts with the policy of providing you with the best possible communications services at the lowest possible price. But desire is not enough. Bright dreams and high hopes need to be brought to earth and made to work.

You could have all the equipment and still not have the service you know today.

You could have all the separate parts of the Bell System and not have the benefits of all those parts fitted together in a nationwide whole.

It's the time-proved combination of research, manufacturing and operations in one organization — with close teamwork between all three

that results in good service, low cost, and constant improvements in the scope and usefulness of your telephone.

No matter whether it is one of the many tasks of everyday operation — or the special skills needed to invent the transistor, the solar battery, or, with Telstar, to pioneer space communication — the Bell System has the will and the way to get it done.

And a spirit of courtesy and service which has come to be a most important part of the Bell System idea.

BELL TELEPHONE SYSTEM

American Telephone & Telegraph Company · Bell Telephone Laboratories · Western Electric Company · New England Telephone & Telegraph Company · The Southern New England Telephone Company · New York Telephone Company · New Jersey Bell Telephone Company · The Bell Telephone Company of Pennsylvania · The Diamond State Telephone Company · The Chesapeake & Potomac Telephone Companies Southern Bell Telephone & Telegraph Company · The Ohio Bell Telephone Company · The Cincinnati & Suburban Bell Telephone Company Michigan Bell Telephone Company · Indiana Bell Telephone Company · Wisconsin Telephone Company · Illinois Bell Telephone Company Northwestern Bell Telephone Company · Southwestern Bell Telephone Company · The Mountain States Telephone & Telegraph Company · The Pacific Telephone & Telegraph Company · Bell Telephone Company of Nevada · Pacific Northwest Bell Telephone Company

Can you suggest how the Bell Telephone System might try to determine how much good this advertisement did for them? (Courtesy: American Telephone & Telegraph Company)

Advertising Management

force up recognition scores; advertisements can be built so as to get high ratings. But, what the advertiser must have eventually are *sales;* higher scores *may* be obtained only at a foolish reduction of the sales power in the advertising. This is particularly dangerous for a product with a thin market, for example, a hearing aid.

AIDED RECALL TESTS

We have mentioned that readership tests are either *recognition* tests or *recall* tests. Both are memory-type tests. Recall tests are by far the more difficult of the two.

Recall interviews are held only with qualified individuals, with persons who prove that they have read in the magazine being checked by describing some material, article, or feature contained in that issue. The researcher shows the cover of the magazine to the individual being qualified and may be allowed to mention items from the table of contents to prompt him or her. Then the interviewer asks the reader to name the advertisements he recalls having seen in the magazine. The interviewer next shows the reader some cards on which are listed the brand names or the advertisers' names appearing in full-page or double-page advertisements in the issue, and he asks the reader to identify those he remembers. For those he remembers, the reader is asked to tell what each advertisement looked like and what each said. This response, this "playback," is the core of the testing technique. The last step finds the interviewer opening the magazine for the first time in the test, turning to the advertisements the reader said he remembered, and asking the reader if each is the advertisement the reader had in mind.

Merits Claimed

This aided recall test tells which advertisements were remembered without their being shown to the consumer; it measures the permanence or lasting quality of the advertisement's impression. In addition, the consumer reveals what the advertisement meant to him. The impact of the message and his understanding of it are reflected in what the consumer "plays back."

Criticisms Heard

Test findings are completely dependent on reader's memories, and this results in distorted, sketchy samples because so few readers remember so few advertisements. The test puts too much emphasis on the attention power of advertisements and not enough emphasis on their persuasion power and their influence. The reader's playback does not give a complete picture of what the advertisement did to the reader; indeed, he might play the message back in its entirety, yet be hostile, incredulous, or indifferent.

Comments on Aided Recall Tests

The ability to recall indicates both penetration and association. Advertisements can get high scores as "Noted" without having much impact; irrelevant illustrations, for example, are much noted. Advertisements are designed and written to influence buyers rather than to be remembered by buyers.

Triple Associates Test

Mention should be made of the *triple associates* test before leaving the subject of aided recall. In this test, no advertisements or publications are shown and no brand names are mentioned. Indeed, a brand name (and the *right* one, too) is the answer to the test. The three elements involved are a product classification (cigarettes, beer, automobiles), a campaign theme or slogan, and a brand name. The consumer is given the first two and is asked to supply the third. For example, the researcher can ask a motorist, "What gasoline is stressing that it contains no lead?" If the motorist answers, "Esso," his answer is wrong — he should have said, "Amoco."

An advertiser wants buyers to think of *his* brand when buyers think of that type of product and when they feel a need for that type of product. He hopes further that the big sales idea, the campaign's keynote idea on which he is spending his advertising dollars is registering and is becoming established. These circumstances recommend that the triple associates test be a *campaign* test and that it be repeated several times in order to show changes in consumers' awareness of campaign theme. Findings tell nothing about belief of message nor about the message's sales power. The test is not suitable in product classifications dominated by a single brand. For example, can *you* name two brands of yeast?

CAMPAIGN EVALUATION

Product-Promotion Campaigns

As has been observed several times, product-promotion campaigns are either *direct* action or *indirect* action in nature. For the former, the success of the campaign is measured by the number of sales made. There is no difficulty in computing the gross margin on this volume, in subtracting administrative and overhead costs, and in arriving at a net profit figure. Although the productivity of the advertising can, in a sense, be determined with precision, the seller's net profit figure is dependent on other factors such as product, price, and management matters. Even so, it is the *indirect* advertising campaign which causes the more difficulty in respect to evaluation.

How can a manufacturer determine what he got for the dollars he spent on an indirect advertising campaign? There are no simple, scientific ways at all, and one can argue with vigor that there is not even any satisfactory way. There is no difficulty in posing the basic questions to which the manufacturer needs answers:

> What did the campaign cost?
> What did it do to sales volume?
> What did it do to profits?

The first question can be answered without much trouble, but the other two are rough.

One cause of the difficulty is the multitude of factors which influence sales volume yet defy measurement. The basic, inherent merit of the product in question is one such factor. Any changes in product, package, or price are three factors which affect sales volume. Any change in channels of distribution or in geographic mar-

Advertising Management

keting area can hardly fail to influence sales. Any change in company promotion, such as an expansion of the sales force or an increase in the size of the advertising fund, will most probably cause a change in sales. Any changes in these areas made by competitors are likely to be felt. Then the consumer is a variable, too. His buying power may change, his tastes and preferences may change, even his number may change. Finally, many types of change are possible in the operations of wholesalers and retailers handling the product. Promotions, price changes, and inventory changes at wholesale or retail levels are reflected in the manufacturer's sales volume. A final thought about sales is that the total performance of a campaign need not be limited to *current* sales volume, especially in the case of high-priced, infrequently bought products.

If the problem of measuring the effects of advertising on sales volume is all that difficult, and it is, the magnitude of the task of attempting to find what advertising does to profits is easily appreciated. Related to this question and provoked by it are other questions. Could the same achievement have been realized at *less* cost? How could greater achievement have been realized at the *same* cost? How much change of consumer attitude is worth how many dollars?

What do manufacturers do in attempting answers to the question about what advertising does to sales volume and profits? They watch their own sales volume figures, and they watch their respective shares of the market for their type of product. They listen to the opinions and observe the reactions of wholesalers, retailers, and their own salesmen. Finally, they draw general conclusions which are based on judgment as well as on facts.

Institutional Campaigns

The assignment given practically all institutional campaigns is to change individuals' attitudes. Of course, product institutional or patronage advertising is expected to be reflected *at some future date* in purchases. But, no matter what the type of institutional advertising, the manufacturer cannot in any worthwhile way measure its effect on sales volume. He will, it is true, be sensitive to the reactions of his sales force and his middlemen; he will note correspondence which comes in from ultimate consumers relative to the campaign; he may make periodic surveys within the group he is addressing to detect changes in attitude. Despite these, the advertiser must rely for the most part on his own judgment.

CONCLUSIONS ON TESTING AND EVALUATING

There are no universally accepted methods of measuring the effectiveness of an indirect action advertisement. Almost every technique has advocates who swear by it — and critics who swear at it. Recognition scores sometimes agree with inquiries, and sometimes the two measurements disagree. Indeed, no copy testing technique measures copy effectiveness with precision.

The problems of testing and evaluating are most complicated. Because human attitudes and behavior are involved, because human reactions to stimuli are involved, our measurements of what advertising does to consumers are crude. Because most advertising is indirect action in nature, because advertising is just one element in the marketing mix, and because the effectiveness of media, too, is impossible to isolate, accuracy of measurement is far less than that desired.

Soundness of test and soundness of testing are prerequisite to sound findings. Testing and evaluation methods must observe all the principles of sound marketing research if results are to be valid. Always to be remembered is the advertiser's continuing query: how much greater were my sales and profits because of my advertising? Attention power, playback power, memory power, power to attract reading, viewing, and listening — these are desirable, but they may not reflect sales power.

The ideal technique is one which would measure what advertising will do, and then did do, to buyers; it would give absolute measurements as well as relative or comparative measurements. It is for this reason that test market testing with its avoidance of artificial conditions is so respected. Less-than-ideal techniques deal with the *advertising* rather than with the *buyers;* they count how many impressions of what sort advertising transmitted; they are comparative and not absolute.

Any measurements must be made against the goals or objectives assigned to advertising, but, you recall, those goals and objectives are subject to other, changing, unmeasurable influences. Increased sales volume is the most common type of goal; additional wholesale and retail customers are another type; good will is still another type. The goals of direct action advertising make it easier to measure than indirect action advertising. But, even mail-order sellers and retailers, who can tell better than other advertisers what advertising does to sales and profits, must make adjustments and allowances for many factors.

It is probable that advertisers rely to a greater extent on experience, feel, and judgment than on testing. Faulty interpretation has damaged the reputations of copy testing and of campaign evaluation. Sometimes the scores are so close as to be irritating. For example, suppose one advertisement scores 45 and another 43, what can you conclude? Or, how many inquiries must come in before you are entitled to consider the volume adequate? Because results are of uncertain validity, because findings still require interpretation, because *no* findings tell the advertiser what to do, advertisers rely heavily on what they hope is good common sense.

Finally, the only true measure of advertising effectiveness is of (a) its influence on purchases — immediate purchases, short-run purchases, eventual purchases, and (b) its contribution to net profits. Most advertisers know that advertising has force and that a reduction in this force causes a reduction in sales volume. But their knowledge is based on faith instead of facts. There is a great and continuing need in advertising for a method of determining what advertising does to the motives and memory, to the attitudes and actions of consumers — and to the sales and profits of advertisers.

Questions and Problems

1. What are some of the problems basic to copy testing?
2. What are some common uses of the findings from advertising tests?

Advertising Management

3. Comment on competitions in which individual ads are submitted and the "best" ones are selected by a board of judges composed of advertising practitioners.
4. What are some of the variable factors which add to the difficulties of advertisers using the test-market testing technique?
5. What complications plague an advertiser when he tries to measure the effects of his advertising on his sales?
6. Last year a manufacturer did some advertising but made no effort to measure its performance. How might he defend his actions?
7. Just what types of variables is an advertiser interested in testing?
8. What are some of the major difficulties in measuring the results of advertising campaigns?
9. Upon graduation, assume you go to work for a small advertising agency and almost immediately find yourself writing copy. The ads you are to turn out are regular, typical, product-promoting newspaper ads. They are not out-of-the-ordinary in any way. You feel that a 10-point check list might reduce the number of "beginner's" mistakes you will make. What might be your list of ten values your ads should contain?
10. One of the large companies in the aluminum industry celebrated a major anniversary and, of course, tried to capitalize on the event in various ways. The biggest single feature of the promotion program was the sponsorship of a television special, an adaptation of one of the plays of Shakespeare. The costs of this ran to a large figure. How might the manufacturer try to conclude whether he got his money's worth?

PART SEVEN

Advertising Organizations and Institutions

The time has come to bring this text to an end. We have reviewed the features of the marketplace; we have seen a seller get ready to advertise; we examined an advertisement and the media which carry it; we have looked at advertising campaigns and programs. What remains?

The *advertising agency* demands some attention. These specialized firms produce a large proportion of each year's advertising. They are unique in their relationships and in their blending of the business with the professional. Their future offers interesting speculation.

Advertising departments must be studied. The advertising manager (director of advertising in some firms) is a key individual and his department plays a key role in the advertising industry. The dealings between advertiser and advertising agency are quite interesting.

Up to this point, our interest has been almost completely in consumer advertising done by manufacturers. Before closing shop, we do need to glance at other types of advertising.

Advertising Organizations and Institutions

Chapter 25 describes two types of *business advertising*. The first is industrial advertising. It is used by those who sell goods and services to those who buy for the use of industry, for institutions, for government. Thus, it is addressed to purchasing agents. The second is trade advertising. As the term suggests, this is addressed to "the trade," to the wholesalers and retailers who move products to the ultimate consumer. Industrial and trade advertising are similar, yet they are different.

The final chapter is devoted to retail advertising. Its inclusion is justified on three counts. Its dollar volume is significant. Some students enter retailing. All students do and will buy from retailers.

Chapter 23

The Advertising Agency

An advertising agency is a group of advertising specialists plus marketing, merchandising, communication, and allied personnel. It is a creative business and a service business. Customers who buy its creativity and its services are referred to as accounts or clients. The great bulk of general or national advertising is created by agencies and is placed in media from which the agencies buy space and time. It has been said that the successful advertising agency is a combination of creative ability (to prepare advertisements), selling ability (to sell its services to clients), and business ability (to make money for itself).

In respect to *advertising* service, and that will be the agency service referred to unless otherwise noted, the agency first studies the advertiser's promotion problems. Then it plans an advertising program for that client, a program which consists of one or more advertising campaigns. The agency builds the individual advertisements, places them in the most appropriate media, and then pays media for the space and time occupied.

The advertising agency interprets the advantages, the satisfactions, the benefits of a product or a service to those who should buy it. The agency's undertaking is to prepare advertising which will induce buyers to prefer certain brands, advertising which will stimulate purchases of clients' products. The ultimate goal of the agency is to create a "consumer franchise" for each client; this goal has been achieved when a client's brand has become soundly established in the market and is preferred and bought repeatedly by a delightfully large number of consumers.

The agency offers clients an assortment of specialists and experts few clients could afford to have as company employees. It offers imagination and creative ability. It offers a breadth of experience no one client can match, experience with different products, media, markets, channels, conditions, problems, and solutions to problems. Finally, the advertising agency offers the client objectivity; its point of view is from outside, its perspective is fresh.

Advertising Organizations and Institutions

BASIC INFORMATION

Agency Development

The earliest advertising agencies were brokers and wholesalers of space. Their major asset was a list of periodicals scattered all over the country; the Audit Bureau of Circulations and the Standard Rate & Data Service were still many years in the future. Later, the agencies became selling agents for media, working on a commission granted by media. Agencies learned quickly that advertisements must be effective if sellers are to continue to advertise. At the same time, advertisers learned that publishers, running advertisements for competing brands, could not give each seller the advertising help he needed. So, it was only natural for agencies to become interested in what went into the space they sold and for advertisers to ask their agencies to help in the building of advertisements. Agencies probably learned, too, that *advertisements* are easier to sell than *space*.

Thus, advertising agencies gradually changed from *sellers* of space to *buyers* of space. But, even after the agency began buying space for clients, it continued to get its income in the form of commissions from publications. The advertising agency worked for and was responsible to the advertiser, not to media; its most important persons were its clients.

Today's advertising agency may consist of one person and a helper — or of 3,000 or 4,000 employees. It may serve one or two clients — or one or two hundred. Size of agency is customarily measured in *billings,* the amount it bills its clients for during the calendar year. Most large agencies are in large cities, and many of these have branches, both domestic and foreign. Agency clients are classified as consumer or general, industrial, financial, and export or international. Some agencies elect to specialize; this may be on the basis of media, functions, type of client served, size of client served, or geographical area covered.

A.A.A.A.

Several hundred advertising agencies, including most of the larger ones, belong to the American Association of Advertising Agencies, usually referred to as the "4A's." This organization has three main aims: (1) to protect, strengthen, and improve the advertising agency business; (2) to further the cause of advertising as a whole; and (3) to help its members operate more efficiently and profitably, doing for them either what they cannot do or what they cannot do so effectively or economically.

Advertising Agency Networks

More than 200 advertising agencies belong to seven national *networks,* a word which, in this usage, has absolutely nothing to do with the broadcast media of television and radio. The 7 networks are:

>Affiliated Advertising Agencies Network
>Continental Advertising Agency Network
>First Advertising Agency Group
>Mutual Advertising Agency Network

The Advertising Agency

National Advertising Agency Network
National Federation of Advertising Agencies
Trans-America Advertising Agency Network

Each of these networks consists of a number of agencies of small or medium size. Members are independent and largely non-competitive, and each must meet the membership standards established by the group.

The agencies in a network cooperate in a variety of ways. They work toward a strong organization and toward uniform operation in the hopes of serving large national accounts. They pool their brains and efforts in attacking common problems. They meet and exchange advertising ideas, experiences, market information, methods, policies, and procedures. They discuss matters relating to agency management, operations, costs, and services to clients. They offer their facilities (research, contact, merchandising) in all network markets to the clients of each member agency, acting somewhat as branch offices for each other. The main purpose of this cooperation is to help members compete more successfully against the larger advertising agencies.

ADVERTISING AGENCY FUNCTIONS

There is considerable variation from agency to agency in respect to the number of functions performed and in the emphasis placed on each. As will develop later in the chapter, this is an area of great current interest and change. The functions now to be mentioned are the most common ones. There have been entire chapters earlier on some of these activities and topics — on copy, layout, production, and media. So, the length of treatment here does *not* indicate the importance of the function; little need be said about *copy,* for example, but much needs to be said about *merchandising.*

New Business

Selecting Prospects. A planned, organized program for obtaining new clients, and such is absolutely essential for every agency, starts with defining or describing the type of new client the agency wants. Agencies want clients with able management, efficient operations, and products or services which are sound values. They want clients with whom the agencies see eye to eye on basic policies, on standards, on advertising, on marketing, and on agency-client relations and responsibilities. The advertiser's financial picture is a most important matter because the agency's credit relationship to a client is that of creditor to debtor. Some agencies solicit only within product classifications or within industry types which they know, with which they have had prior experience; many an advertiser wants his advertising agency "to have had experience in *my* field." Agencies may establish the size of the minimum advertising fund in which they will take an interest; some handle no accounts billing less than $100,000, others set this minimum figure at $50,000, still others set it much lower. In addition to these characteristics, advertising agencies want growth companies as clients and want them to be located nearby. If an advertiser's

"less"

Joshua Logan tells of Director Garson Kanin's struggle with an actor who, because of nervousness and misplaced zeal, was inclined to overact.

Before the first-night curtain, Kanin sent him a message with just one four-letter word: *"less."*

This is a one-word slogan which many advertising men might tack on their pinup boards.

We're satisfied that many ads, and certainly many television commercials, fail because of straining too hard to sock. Readers are driven right off the page, and viewers are flogged out of the room because of the excess energy in text or audio.

We believe Burnett ads are noted for simplicity; at least we know we believe in it more than in excessive strain for sledge-hammer virility.

Whistler once said it takes two men to produce a good picture—one to paint it, and another to beat him over the head and make him quit.

In other words, *"less."*

HERE ARE THE PEOPLE WE WORK FOR: ALLSTATE INSURANCE COMPANIES • AMERICAN MINERAL SPIRITS CO. ATCHISON, TOPEKA AND SANTA FE RAILWAY COMPANY • BROWN SHOE COMPANY • CAMPBELL SOUP COMPANY • COMMONWEALTH EDISON COMPANY AND PUBLIC SERVICE COMPANY • THE ELECTRIC ASSOCIATION (Chicago) • DOW CORNING CORPORATION • GREAT BOOKS OF THE WESTERN WORLD • GREEN GIANT COMPANY • HARRIS TRUST AND SAVINGS BANK • THE HOOVER COMPANY • KELLOGG COMPANY • KROEHLER MFG. CO. • THE MAYTAG COMPANY • PHILIP MORRIS INC. • MOTOROLA INC. • THE PARKER PEN COMPANY • CHAS. PFIZER & CO., INC. • THE PILLSBURY COMPANY • THE PROCTER & GAMBLE COMPANY • THE PURE OIL COMPANY • THE PURE FUEL OIL COMPANY • REPUBLICAN NATIONAL COMMITTEE • JOS. SCHLITZ BREWING COMPANY • STAR-KIST FOODS, INC. • SUNKIST GROWERS, INC. • SWIFT & COMPANY • UNION CARBIDE CONSUMER PRODUCTS COMPANY • VICK CHEMICAL COMPANY

LEO BURNETT CO., INC.

CHICAGO, Prudential Plaza • NEW YORK • HOLLYWOOD • TORONTO • MONTREAL

This is how one advertising agency advertises its own strengths and capabilities. (Courtesy: Leo Burnett Co., Inc.)

sales have been falling or if his advertising has been getting low ratings, maybe he will be more receptive to the idea of changing agencies.

Agencies seldom go after prospects who compete directly with present clients; the agency handling the Ford account would hardly think of trying for the Chevrolet account. In some product classifications, the highest priced brand and the lowest priced brand may not be considered directly competitive. Too, a New York beer and a West Coast beer would not be competitive. But it would be unthinkable for one agency to service both Schlitz and Miller at the same time to the satisfaction of both. For one reason, the agency-client relationship is too intimate and confidential. An agency may, of course, drop a *small* cigarette account in order to acquire a *large* cigarette account.

Techniques. How does an advertising agency go after new clients? Once in a long while, the first move is made by someone else. An advertiser may, for instance, mail an exploratory, screening questionnaire to a number of agencies — then brace for pursuit by the pack. Or, one agency may be recommended to an advertiser who is making a change by another agency which cannot handle the account. Tips may come from media or from media representatives, and from news stories in trade publications. Finally, an account executive may approach an agency about a job, promising to bring some clients along with him.

Another technique to get new clients, naturally enough, is for the advertising agency to advertise. Direct mail is a most suitable medium because it is selective, confidential, and economical, yet it still gives the agency the opportunity to demonstrate its advertising capabilities. Trade papers, although less used, are the other appropriate medium. Some agencies seem too busy with clients' advertising to find time for advertising themselves. Probably some feel that they are professional and that, consequently, they should not advertise.

By far and away the major technique used by agencies in getting new business is that of personal contact and solicitation. Contacts are made with prospects in clubs, business groups, professional societies, alumni groups, meetings, and associations. Aggressive personal selling is done by the top brass — the agency owners, principals, partners, and officers. These individuals have broad and detailed knowledge of their agency's operation; their prestige is impressive in calls on the top management of advertisers. One executive may be put in charge of new business although that would not be his sole assignment. Or, a committee of five or six executives could be assigned the responsibility of getting new business; such a committee would be free to enlist the help of other persons and even of entire departments in the agency. Some agencies set up a separate new business department consisting, in medium-sized agencies, of one man, a secretary, and a fat expense account. Able men to head such an operation are scarce; they may demand the title and the salary of a vice president; their expenses will run high. And, a possible complication is the solicited advertiser who wants the new man to service his account.

The agency sales story stresses profitable creativity, service, and ability to contribute to sales volume and profits. To back up such claims, agencies point to their growth, to their clients, to their clients' growth, to the length of time they have served those clients, and to case histories of outstanding successes.

Southern Pacific Company, advertised through Foote, Cone & Belding, leads all other Western railroads in total revenue

FOOTE, CONE & BELDING, ADVERTISING: NEW YORK, CHICAGO, HOUSTON, LOS ANGELES, SAN FRANCISCO, HOLLYWOOD; LONDON, ENGLAND

House advertisements of advertising agencies frequently feature their clients. (Courtesy: Foote, Cone & Belding)

The Advertising Agency

Speculative Presentations. As part of its attempt to get an account, an agency may make a speculative presentation. This consists of submitting suggested copy, art work, illustrations, complete advertisements, detailed schedules, or the findings of market surveys — all "free." It is not difficult at all for a speculative presentation to represent costs in excess of $25,000. And, there are cases on record of an advertiser's demanding that each agency desiring consideration make a speculative presentation. There are also agencies on record which refuse as a matter of policy to make this type of presentation.

There are strong reasons why an agency should be hostile to the idea of making a speculative presentation. Strongest of all is the undeniable fact that the agency cannot do a really good job; it lacks too much information about the advertiser's business, his product or service, his personnel, and his problems. Indeed, an agency looks far from good when it knowingly undertakes a job without the facts it would have to have to do a good job. Another argument against the speculative presentation is the fact that the advertiser is giving away what he does and should get paid for, his stock in trade. The advertiser being solicited may get the idea that the agency can be talked into doing extra jobs free. Brains, dollars, and time used in constructing a speculative presentation obviously cannot be used in serving present clients. Finally, no one can quarrel with the contention that an advertiser can make a most unfortunate selection when he chooses an agency because its speculative presentation strikes his fancy.

The Account Executive

Once a new client has been signed up, the question arises as to who will actually serve the account and be responsible for it. This assignment goes to an individual known by such designations as *account executive, account representative,* or *contact man.* The account executive studies his client's circumstances and problems, discusses them with the client, plans an advertising program he thinks appropriate, and submits this program and its individual advertisements for client approval. His major and continuing duty is to plan advertising which will keep the client happy — or at least keep the client.

There is much conferring between account executive and client, by telephone, by mail, in person. In these contacts, the agency man tries to grasp the client's attitudes and preferences and the thinking responsible for them. He represents his agency to the client, interpreting its attitudes and reasoning. He stands ready to help the advertising manager of the client company sell the proposed advertising program to client management. He anticipates problems; he adjusts difficulties.

The account executive applies the facilities and abilities of his agency to his client's advertising problems, sometimes even to his marketing problems. It is the account executive's obligation to get the best possible for his client from the agency. He directs the advertising agency's work on his client's advertising.

In agencies of medium and small size, the principals, partners, and officers typically serve as account executives. It is not uncommon for this type of account executive to write some copy. In the larger agencies, there are officers who are account executives, but there is also an employee type; he may be on salary or on

433

Advertising Organizations and Institutions

commission. An account executive may have one client or several, he may or may not have an assistant account executive, he may or may not be expected to spend some time in a search for new business.

Because of the key and difficult role he plays, an account executive needs several qualities and talents. He benefits from being a man of broad experience much of which, preferably, he acquired outside the agency. His knowledge, too, needs breadth; he must be informed about his client's business, about his own advertising agency, about advertising, and about the broader field of marketing. Personally, he must be a man of tact and diplomacy, able and willing to work in harmony with his client. Respect and confidence must be mutual between his client and him. The account executive must be both intelligent and enthusiastic; he must achieve close, frank, and friendly relations with his client; he must have the courage to defend his convictions and the integrity to say "No" when the occasion demands. The ideal account executive is exceptional as a salesman, as an administrator, as a business man. No wonder good ones are hard to find.

Copy

The three most basic functions of an advertising agency are *copy, art,* and *media.* As was indicated in the chapter on the topic, copy is the heart of all advertising. The copy activity within an agency is usually headed by a copy director, preferably an art-minded individual because the copy staff works more closely with the art staff than with any other group in the agency. The copy staff also works closely with the account executives; it may make much use of the research department's copy research.

A copy writer may write copy for all media — or specialize in one. He or she must be able to think and to write effectively. Writers need to be sales-minded; experience in personal selling or in reporting is considered helpful by some. While they need imagination and contribute some ideas, writers typically are more often known for their skill with words than for their ideas.

Art

Art directors should be copy-minded for the same reason that copy directors need to be art-minded. Copy and art make the advertisement; copy and art *are* the advertisement. A feeling of equality, cooperation, and understanding should characterize the relationship between copy and art.

The art staff works mainly with space advertising. It visualizes printed advertisements, prepares layouts, and does or buys the finished artwork or photography which illustrates the advertisements. Because more artwork is bought than done within the agency, the art director stays informed about the local artists and their talents.

Media

Copy and art are joined by media to complete the trio of core functions of advertising agencies. The media director and his staff study media and collect and analyze media information. Next, they select the media to carry the advertising of each client and make up schedules of which advertisement is to appear where and on what date. Cost estimates are arrived at for these schedules. Upon client approval, the media staff contracts to buy space for the client's advertising. Broadcast time may be bought by the media department or by the television and radio department or departments. Sometimes the media staff checks the appearance of newspaper and magazine advertisements, sometimes the accounting department does this checking.

The two prominent assignments given the media director involve evaluation and selection. In addition, the department contributes to the over-all media strategy for each client. It also attempts to concentrate agency-media contacts in the media department, hoping thereby to minimize the amount of account executives' time taken up by media representatives and salesmen.

Television-Radio

Because the broadcast media, you recall, are basically different from other media, some agencies have a separate department for television and radio. In a few instances, indeed, *each* is a separate department. A vice president sometimes heads the combined activity, having a television director and a radio director reporting to him. Motion picture production may be found in combined departments.

The broadcast staff is responsible for program production and supervision. Commercials may be done by this staff or by the copy staff. The agency can produce a client's program, or it can buy a complete packaged show for him, or it can buy time for him on a participation show. The broadcast department sometimes buys television and radio time, the media department sometimes does this buying.

Research

The research director and his staff help the agency get clients, serve clients, and hold clients. Research can help the new-business-getters make stronger presentations to more desirable clients. Research can help the creative personnel, particularly copy and art, build better advertising for clients. Research can help the contact man convince his client that his last advertising program *was* productive, too.

Agencies study buyers, both consumers and middlemen, paying particular attention to buying motives and buying habits. Agencies study markets and their characteristics. Agency analysis of products includes such features as design, styling, package, label, price, and competitive strength and weakness. Within the area of advertising, the research personnel research just about every element but concentrate on copy and media. Media research is done more often by the research department than by the media department. Some agencies have a library as part of the research department.

Large agencies are buying much of the research they need rather than doing it themselves. Bought research is often cheaper, more objective and therefore more sound, and more impressive prestige-wise with clients.

Who pays for the research the agency does or buys? As with other agency services, there is no clear pattern or policy here. If the research is for the specific use and benefit of a particular client, he probably pays for it. If it is primarily for agency benefit, even when used to help plan a certain campaign for a client, probably the agency pays.

Mechanical Production

The manager of this department is asked to transform copy, illustrations, and layout into a satisfactory printed advertisement. Obviously, he works closely with the copy director and the art director. He uses various commercial firms: typesetters to put copy into type, photoengravers for engravings, electrotypers for duplicate plates to be sent to publications, and commercial printers for printing.

Traffic

In an advertising agency, traffic is a matter of scheduling and control. The traffic manager sets up a work schedule and a routing sequence for each advertisement and then supervises the advertisement's movement through all its stages and departments in the agency. Once the advertisement has been prepared, then it is forwarded in good time to the media which will be carrying it. Only if copy, illustration, mechanical production, and client approval are on schedule can this essential goal or target date be achieved. If deadlines are to be made, if panics and work peaks are to be minimized, if the work flow is to be relatively even rather than spasmodic, if cooperation and coordination are to be assured, then there must be sound traffic supervision. Where there is no separate traffic department, the duty is assigned to the production manager or to the account executives.

Accounting

The agency accounting department strongly resembles any accounting department, and its personnel are more in the nature of accountants than advertising men. Common assignments are these: to check on the appearance of advertisements in media, to check media invoices against orders, to pay media bills, to bill clients and collect from them, to look after such matters as records, bookkeeping, and office routine. The accounting department is often headed by the treasurer or the comptroller.

Public Relations

Many of the larger agencies now have a public relations and publicity operation. The fundamental objective of public relations, you remember, is to build and then maintain good will with various "publics." The fundamental tools used in communicating with these publics are institutional or corporate advertising and publicity. The big job of an agency's public relations department is to build stronger relations between clients and their publics — customers, employees, middlemen, stockholders, plant cities. A smaller job is to do a public relations job for the agency itself with two publics, prospective clients and present clients. If the agency prefers, it can set its public relations activity up as a separate but subsidiary corporation, the clients of which may be but need not be advertising clients of the agency.

The specific activities or projects of the public relations unit cover a wide range. The staff may edit house organs for clients, or one for the agency. It may plan and stage press conferences for clients and for the agency. It counsels with clients on public relations matters. It may draft speeches, annual reports, employee handbooks, news stories, and dealer newsletters for clients.

THE COURSE OF AN ADVERTISEMENT IN PRODUCTION FOR PRINT MEDIA

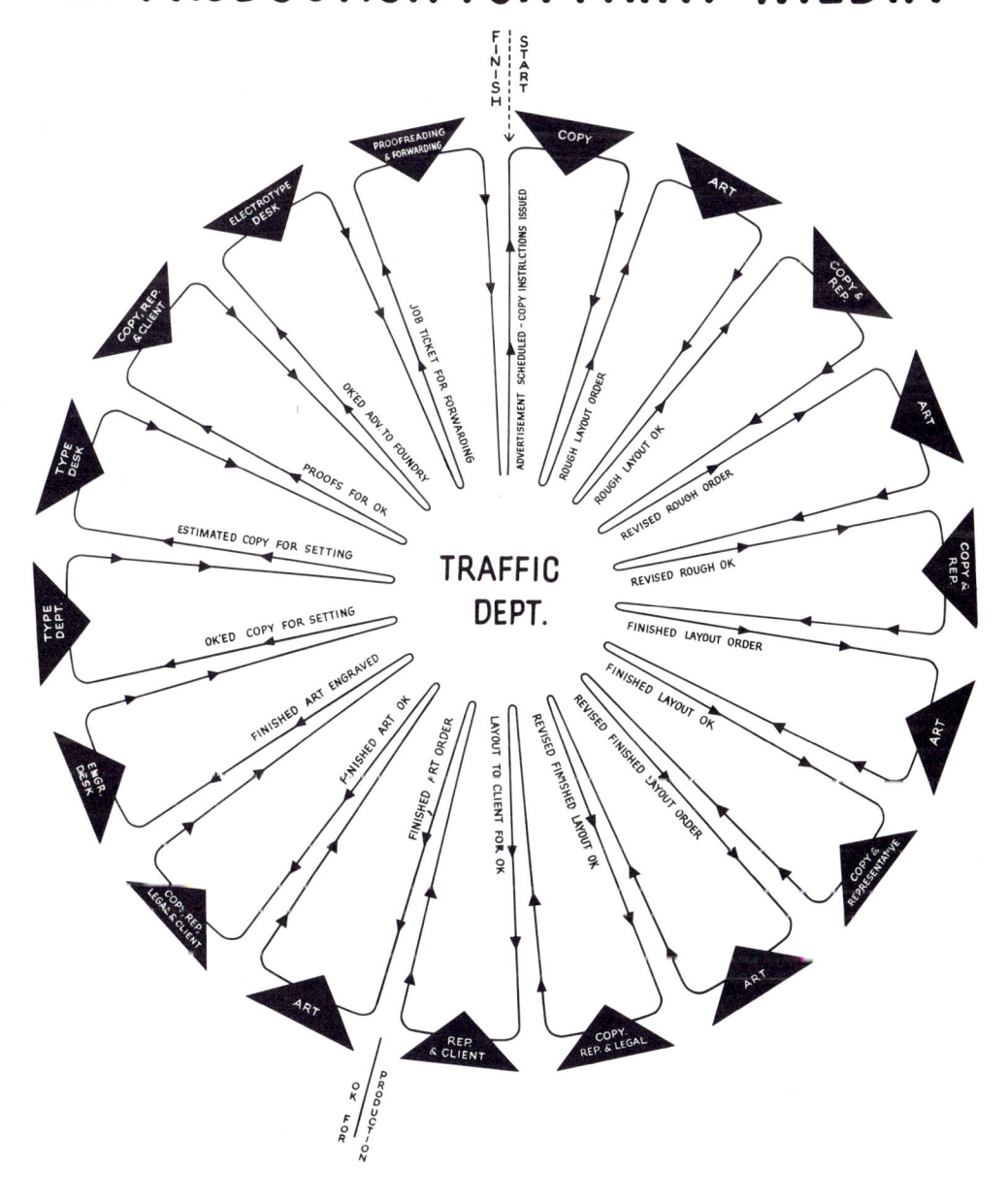

Traffic flow chart not uncommon in large advertising agencies. (Courtesy: J. Walter Thompson Company)

Advertising Organizations and Institutions

Merchandising — Sales Promotion

Emphasis on merchandizing and sales promotion varies among advertising agencies. Even the organization varies; there may or may not be a separate department, the activities may be merged with those of a marketing department, a merchandising department has in some cases been converted into a marketing department, or merchandising and sales promotion can be found housed in the research department. Like direct mail, merchandising activities do not appear so troublesome and unprofitable to agencies as they once did. It has been discovered, however, that adding a merchandising and sales promotion facility calls for adding merchandising and sales promotion specialists; the work cannot be done satisfactorily by the agency's copy and art personnel.

Like the public relations staff, the merchandising staff works with other departments of the client's organization (with Sales and with Sales Promotion particularly) in addition to the advertising department. The director of merchandising is anxious that a client's over-all marketing program contributes to the success of his advertising program, that advertising not be handicapped by such an unfavorable marketing element, for example, as a poor package. The director is keenly aware of the basic goal of good merchandising, namely, that of marketing the right products at the right prices in the right places at the right times in the right quantities and with the right services and atmosphere. He knows that effective promotion at the point of purchase makes the client's advertising in other media all the more effective.

The following groupings indicate possible interests and activities of an advertising agency's merchandising department:

Consumer matters
Contests, premiums, sampling, demonstrators, coupons, consumer education, consumer services.
Marketing matters
Product and package development, product identification, labels, inserts, pricing, channels, competitors' activities, marketing trends.
Dealer matters
Direct mail to middlemen, point-of-purchase advertising, retail promotions, advertising portfolios for retailers, catalogues, vertical cooperative advertising, merchandising clients' advertising to dealers.
Personal Selling matters
Trade shows, displays and exhibits at sales conventions, salesmen's portfolios and selling aids, sales training and stimulation, sales meetings, sales literature, merchandising clients' advertising to clients' salesmen.

ORGANIZATION AND MANAGEMENT

There are two basic types or patterns of organization within an advertising agency, the *group* type and the *department* type. Several adaptations and variations can be found for each. That both patterns can work well is proved by the fact that there are large and successful agencies of each type. Size, functions performed for clients, and personnel are among the determinants of agency organization.

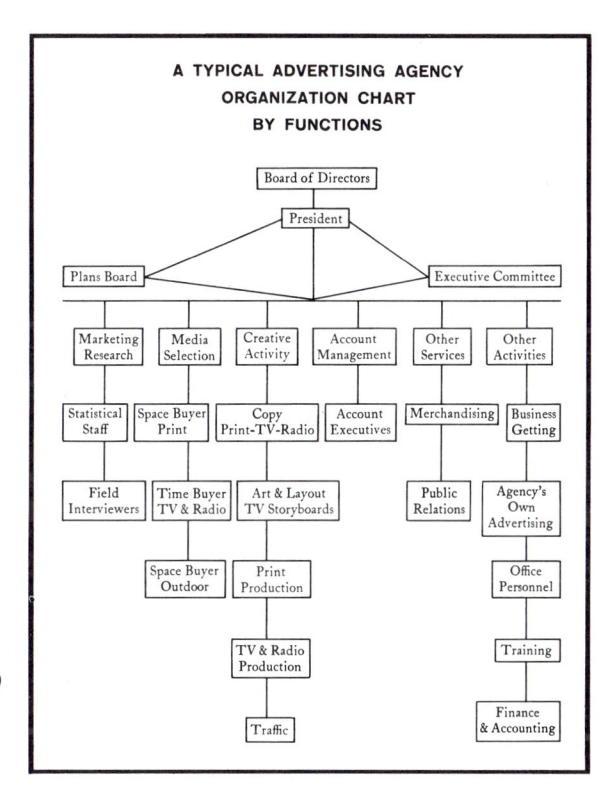

```
                    A TYPICAL ADVERTISING AGENCY
                        ORGANIZATION CHART
                           BY FUNCTIONS

                          Board of Directors
                               President
        Plans Board                              Executive Committee

   Marketing   Media      Creative    Account    Other      Other
   Research    Selection  Activity    Management Services   Activities

   Statistical Space Buyer Copy           Account    Merchandising Business
   Staff       Print       Print-TV-Radio Executives               Getting

   Field       Time Buyer  Art & Layout              Public       Agency's
   Interviewers TV & Radio TV Storyboards            Relations    Own
                                                                  Advertising

               Space Buyer  Print                                 Office
               Outdoor      Production                            Personnel

                            TV & Radio                            Training
                            Production

                            Traffic                               Finance
                                                                  & Accounting
```

(*Courtesy:* Advertising Age)

Group Organization

In this type of agency, each client has a team or group of individuals servicing his account. The idea is to tailor a group for each client and then to let those same persons work as a unit on the same problems. The group, sort of a little advertising agency all its own, does just the contact and creative work for a client; it calls on and uses such central units in the agency as media, research, mechanical production, and accounting as it needs them. Some groups serve several clients. Each group reports to an account executive or to a group head and clears its plans through agency executives. Although all groups do not include just the same talents, the core of practically all groups consists of the account executive, a copy writer, and a layout artist from the art staff. New groups can be set up as new clients are added.

Group organization is usually found only in the larger advertising agencies. It is inappropriate for small agencies. A *very* small agency is itself a group — its one and only group.

Common in group-type agencies is the *plans board*. This board is made up of senior executives with broad experience. It would not be unusual to find a plans board composed of the account executive plus the heads of these units: copy, art, media, research, and mechanical production. Duties assigned to plans boards include the selection of campaign themes, the design of campaigns, the drafting of advertising programs for clients, and the supervision of advertising strategy. It is logical for groups to clear their plans with a plans board.

Advertising Organizations and Institutions

Department Organization

In this second type of agency, there is a separate department for each major advertising agency function; each is headed by a specialist in that particular field, often a vice president of the agency. Each department serves the advertising clients; each client is served by the various departments of the agency rather than by a small group. In contrast to the group-type organization, a copy writer in the department-type organization might work with four or five different account executives and write copy for four or five different products. The personnel of each department are responsible to the department head; they are not supervised directly by account executives. Department organization is more common than group organization. Plans boards can and do function in agencies organized on the department basis.

Management

The top management in an advertising agency may consist of the chief executive, usually the president, plus an executive or advisory committee. Heads of major departments are often a part of top management. Sometimes the partners constitute management. Sometimes it is the plans board.

Management has several major concerns. One is financial because the agency is liable for the space and time it buys for use by its clients. Creativity is another because that essentially is what the agency has for sale. Growth is a responsibility of management; agencies grow by getting present clients to appropriate larger advertising funds, by getting additional products or patronage from present clients, by adding new clients, or by expanding and selling new services. Management supervises the agency's account executives, those key individuals who serve and hold on to clients. Management here as elsewhere determines policies and supervises operations. Management is particularly watchful over agency personnel; able individuals are an agency's greatest asset, and salaries take about two-thirds of agency income.

AGENCY RECOGNITION

For an understanding of agency recognition and the media commission system for which recognition serves as a base, we are well advised to recall the early days of advertising agencies and media. The aspect of this early period which interests us at the moment is that of agency-media relations, with particular emphasis on media's needs and the services advertising agencies are considered to have rendered.

During their early years, advertising agencies in a real sense functioned as salesmen for media, salesmen just as entitled to a commission on sales as any salesman. Agencies worked to convert non-advertisers into advertisers, and small advertisers into large advertisers. The result was greater revenue for media. In addition, the agencies did a service for media by assuming certain jobs of a technical nature. They submitted finished, complete advertisements to media, advertisements the agencies had built out of their copy, their illustrations, their layouts. They cut mechanical costs by sending plates to media. They drafted schedules for their clients, relieving media of this tedious job. In addition, agencies assumed the credit function, centralizing credit management and making it more simple and economical for media. All the while, agencies worked continuously for better, more effective advertising.

Against this background, it is easy to understand how the procedure of recognition developed. Media recognized that sound agency operation was of great benefit to media, that it was worth money to them. So, media began to recognize agencies satisfactory to do business with by giving them a discount from card rates, a discount referred to as a commission.

Recognition entitled an advertising agency to media commissions; recognition was necessary before an agency was given commissions by media. Thus, media began to recognize advertising agencies. The commission was 15 per cent except for outdoor advertising with a commission of 16⅔ per cent. Prior to the consent decree of 1956 which we discuss later in this chapter, media recognized few agencies which failed on any of these requirements:

> The agency must be staffed by personnel with the experience and the ability to do a good job for its clients.
> It must be sound financially, able to pay media.
> It should retain all commissions and not do any rebating to clients.
> It should not be controlled by an advertiser.

The following shows how recognition and commissions worked: Suppose a magazine page was quoted on the rate card at $10,000. This is the amount a manufacturer would have to pay if he bought direct from the magazine because advertisers were not entitled to the agency commission. A recognized agency, however, was quoted a price of $10,000 less 15 per cent — or $8,500. The typical cash discount of 2 per cent when earned by the agency was passed on to the advertiser when he paid the agency promptly enough to be entitled to it. In our illustration, this cash discount would be 2 per cent of $8,500 — or $170. So, the advertising agency owed the magazine $8,330 when the cash discount had been deducted from the $8,500. The agency billed the advertiser for $10,000 but relayed the $170 to him for prompt payment. The agency paid the magazine $8,330, the advertiser paid the agency $9,830 ($10,000 less $170), and the agency grossed $1,500 which, of course, is 15 per cent of $10,000.

In this transaction, the advertising agency was an independent contractor and not an agent of the advertiser in the legal sense. It contracted with the magazine in its own name and must pay the magazine even though the advertiser fails to pay the agency. The magazine cannot look to the advertiser for payment in case the agency fails to pay for the space.

AGENCY COMPENSATION

Media commissions have been for decades the largest single source of revenue for recognized advertising agencies.

A second type of compensation consists of *service charges*. These are added to the cost of materials and services bought by agencies for clients. Artwork, photography, typography, plates, mats, printing, these are examples of advertising ingredients to the cost of which agencies add 15 or 17.65 per cent. Suppose an artist's fees total $1,000. If an agency adds 17.65 per cent to this, it bills the client for $1,176.50. The service charge of $176.50 is 15 per cent of $1,176.50.

Fees represent a third type of agency compensation; they are based on the time and skill required in the performance of certain creative undertakings. One example is the agency's creation of non-commissionable advertising, catalogues and window displays, for instance. Another example is the fee added when media commissions are too small to pay the agency for the job of preparing the advertisements. A $100 advertisement in a business paper, for instance, does not earn a fair return in commission for the agency which prepared it. Agencies serving retail accounts and agencies serving some industrial and some financial accounts charge fees according to the amount of service rendered.

The fee pattern is neither standardized nor uniform. Some advertisers get billed by agencies for a service other advertisers get "free." Services are one more basis on which advertising agencies compete and clients can negotiate and bargain. In between the "free" services and those with fees which return the agency a profit are those services billed to clients at cost.

In addition to the basic three of media commissions, service charges, and fees, variations and combinations are sometimes used. These include: fee with commissions credited against it; fee plus commission; cost; cost plus a percentage; cost plus a fee; flat fee per job; retainer fee.

Prior to the 1950's, the commission system was considered very practicable, firmly established, and well understood. Even so, use and acceptance of the system were based more on tradition, custom, and length of operation than on logic; it is odd for an advertising agency to be hired by, to represent, to work for the advertiser — yet be paid by media.

If certain advertisers continue to want and use other services (than pure advertising service) from their advertising agencies, then the 15% media commission will decline in significance; fees and charges will increase in significance. Package design, public relations, and the research and development of new products are three examples. If agencies are to make such services available, then some sort of a fee arrangement is most logical, perhaps unavoidable. Also probable is a greater tailoring and individualizing of compensation plans between an agency and each of its clients. Of course, a complete abandonment of the media commission system and its replacement by a fee system *could* encourage a price war among agencies. That would not be good.

THE CONSENT DECREE

Basic Facts

In the middle 1950's the antitrust division of the Department of Justice filed suits against six associations in the advertising field, charging them with combination and conspiracy in restraint of trade. The six associations were these:

> American Association of Advertising Agencies
> American Newspaper Publishers Association

Periodical Publishers Association
Associated Business Publications
Agricultural Publishers Association
Publishers Association of New York

The two main issues in respect to the one agency association and the five media associations were (1) the recognition system and (2) the standard 15 per cent commission. The Justice Department complained to the American Association of Advertising Agencies about these three:

Agreement in concert not to rebate or split commissions with clients.
Agreement that the commission to 4-A members be fixed at 15%.
Agreement not to compete through the use of speculative presentations.

The American Association of Advertising Agencies entered into a consent decree with the Justice Department on February 1, 1956. The association agreed *not* to:

Participate directly in the recognition of advertising agencies.
Participate directly in fixing or maintaining a commission system of advertising agency compensation.
Continue its stand against speculative presentations by advertising agencies.
Urge advertising agencies to refrain from splitting commissions with clients.

Immediate Results

After February 1, 1956, *individual* advertising agencies could continue operating as before if they so desired. This was because individual agencies were not barred from engaging in any or all of the actions the 4-A's agreed not to do. An individual medium, likewise, could offer any commission it wanted to offer to any advertising agency the medium wanted to do business with. It was *collective action by associations* which the decrees banned.

But, nothing much happened immediately. Media did not rush to cut their commissions, nor did they start selling space at net prices to advertisers who wanted to place their advertising direct at card rates less 15 per cent. The 15 per cent commission continued to agencies; it was not offered to advertisers.

The formation of many "house" agencies, agencies set up, owned, and operated by advertisers for the purpose of capturing media commissions, had been predicted by some persons. Few appeared. There was no great increase in the employment of speculative presentations in competing for new business; agencies continued to do as they individually thought best about this selling tactic.

There was probably some increase in clients' demands for rebates and concessions. These had been present in the advertising business, of course, for decades. And, as for decades, "free" service continued to be one answer to such demands. Rebating probably increased some, too.

THE A. N. A. STUDY

Basic Facts

For a period of years prior to the consent decree of 1956, there had been some dissatisfaction among the ranks of the large national advertisers with the commission system of agency compensation. This dissatisfaction grew during the 1950's as a direct result of the agency practice of getting a 15 per cent commission on packaged television shows bought by agencies for their clients. Many large advertisers in television felt that an advertising agency was grossly overpaid when it collected a 15 per cent talent commission on a series of shows which it did not produce. Just on one series, this commission sometimes ran as high as $250,000 or $300,000 a year. So, this dissatisfaction of long standing plus the consent decree plus larger expenditures in television for packaged shows were three major explanations of a study the Association of National Advertisers approved in 1956.

Recognizing that compensation should reflect performance, the ANA planned to study first the functions and services advertising agencies performed for clients, and then to explore the area of agency compensation. Obviously, media could not be omitted from such an undertaking, so the project turned out to be a study of the advertising industry — advertisers, agencies, media.

To insure sound and objective findings, the ANA retained Professors A.W. Frey and K. R. Davis of Dartmouth to do the study. These men used mail questionnaires, personal interviews, and an examination of the literature in the field in collecting their facts. They obtained information from the presidents of companies which advertise and from their advertising managers, from presidents of advertising agencies, and from media. They issued their preliminary report late in 1957 and their full report in 1958.

The purposes of the study were:

> To determine and analyze the functions of advertising agencies in the marketing system.
> To get information on advertising agency organization, policies, services, and methods of compensation.
> To get information on the structure of the advertising agency field.
> To report on interesting differences in the working relations among advertisers, advertising agencies, and media.
> To get the attitudes of each group toward the other two.
> To reveal how advertising agencies are compensated and to describe suggested changes in current methods.

Findings

The findings of the ANA study were not startling. Significant segments of all three groups, advertisers, advertising agencies, and media, predicted changes in the methods of agency compensation. Advertisers and media, naturally, registered more dissatisfaction with the 15 per cent commission than did advertising agencies, and advertisers were more unhappy than were media. Advertisers and media were more favorably inclined toward changes in the compensation pattern than were advertising agencies. Many advertising managers felt that the 15 per cent was the most practical technique at the moment and that it would continue dominant for years despite changes. Over one-third of the advertising managers were in favor of abolition of the media commission and in favor of substituting for it a fee which

The Advertising Agency

the advertiser would pay to his agency for its services; these men wanted to be able to buy space and time at the rates formerly available only to recognized advertising agencies.

There was considerable discontent among advertisers with the rigidity and the inflexibility of the commission system. Advertisers felt, too, that the agency's relations to clients and to media had changed since the agency's early days but that the compensation pattern was outmoded because it had not kept pace with those changes. One point made was that advertising agency income was determined largely by how much space and time clients used — not by how much agency service an advertiser used. Another point made was that advertising agencies may not still be making the contribution to media operations agencies once made, yet the commission was still 15 per cent.

Comments

It seems clear that had the advertising industry undertaken to devise an agency compensation pattern from scratch in 1958, the industry would not have adopted the 15 per cent media commission. Even so, at the time of the ANA study, the 15 per cent media commission method seemed likely to continue as the primary form of agency revenue for a number of years.

Because clients' needs for agency service and their use of agency service vary, 15 per cent sometimes results in overpayment to the agency, often results in underpayment. A prediction at the time of the study was that overpayment and underpayment would tend to disappear. The reason for this was because agencies were learning how to determine the cost of their creative efforts more accurately and were beginning to charge more for services formerly underpriced. Better cost accounting in agencies and accurate profit-and-loss data on each project as well as on each account were recognized as essential. This points toward conferences between an advertiser and his agency, a determination of the services the advertiser should buy from his agency, and negotiation leading to agreement between the two about agency compensation on that account. This means a closer correlation between revenue and cost-of-service for each account. Advertisers will learn, incidentally, that trying to buy creativity and imagination at "cut-rate" prices is doomed to failure and, hence, foolhardy.

It seems most likely that the proportion of agency revenue from fees and from cost-plus arrangements will continue to increase — the proportion from media commissions to decline. Agencies, thus, will be getting more of their dollars from clients, fewer of their dollars from media.

There is no reason to believe that the time is here when advertising will be *bought* in adequate amount by manufacturers. Advertising, like practically everything else commercial, will have to be *sold,* and it cannot be sold satisfactorily except by salesmen who know much about it — maybe even how to build profitable advertisements.

In the wake of the ANA study, transition in the areas of agency services and agency compensation seemed inevitable but gradual, evolutionary rather than revolutionary.

Advertising Organizations and Institutions

THE MARKETING AGENCY

One hears much talk about the *marketing concept*. One notes that more and more top executives in large companies have titles which include the word *marketing*. There is wider and wider recognition of the dependence of our economy and our standard of living on the marketing operation. The need for coordinated marketing, for integrated marketing grows.

Clients have been requesting a broader range of services from their advertising agencies. Another pressure for the same development is the competition among advertising agencies for new business. These two activities combined to create something of a profit squeeze for the agencies. Interestingly, this squeeze was becoming progressively tighter at the time of the ANA study and during a period when agency compensation was attracting much attention.

The result has been an expansion in the operations of advertising agencies of such magnitude as to alter the nature of these firms. Essentially, advertising agencies have moved into the two broad fields of marketing and communication. Agencies still plan, produce, and place advertising; but they do much more, too. Included in these added services and activities are these:

Public Relations	Merchandising
Market Research	Sales Promotion
Motivation Research	New Product Development
Product and Package Design	Direct Mail
Point-of-Purchase Items	Brand Names
Marketing Counsel	Trade Marks
Specialized Literature	Trade Characters
Dealer Relations	Sales Development

One possibility is for the advertising agency to set up an affiliated firm to operate in a specific area. An agency, for example, might have a subsidiary corporation to do marketing consultation work. Or, it might have a separate unit to do market research work. Or, it might have a corporation to function in public relations and publicity. Advertising agencies perhaps are becoming holding companies, controlling one unit which does advertising for consumer goods, another unit to do industrial advertising, one for public relations and publicity, one for point of purchase, one for direct advertising, one for research, one to work in the general area of sales management, and one for marketing and management counsel.

A big question involved here is that of just where the advertiser should get the specialized services he needs. Which should he do for himself? Which should he buy? Which should he buy from his advertising agency? Which should he buy from specialized firms *not* advertising agencies?

No one can deny that advertising, marketing, public relations, sales promotion, and such are basic responsibilities of client company management; these duties are not to be delegated. But, no one can deny the advertising agency's legitimate interest in the factors other than advertising which can affect sales and profits by affecting advertising effectiveness. Agency interest in the client's profit-and-loss showing, not just in his sales volume, is increasing. Clients want more than just advertising from their advertising agencies. They do and will pay for these additional services. So, it seems reasonable to expect that advertising agencies will continue to move into clients' marketing and communications operations. Agencies will continue to increase their understanding of clients' over-all objectives and their support of clients' over-all programs.

The International Agency

More and more advertising agencies are now operating in foreign countries. This international expansion accompanied and reflects the growth of foreign markets and the increases in international manufacturing and marketing. Sometimes the case was one of an agency going overseas with and when a client did. In some instances, the domestic agency bought or bought into a foreign agency; in some instances, the domestic agency affiliated with a foreign agency; occasionally, the domestic agency simply established a wholly owned subsidiary.

Questions and Problems

1. On what grounds may advertising agencies resign accounts?
2. What points would you make if you were arguing that advertising agencies are necessary?
3. What do media get for the discounts they grant to advertising agencies?
4. What types of specialization are found among advertising agencies?
5. What selling points can a small advertising agency stress when soliciting a manufacturer's advertising account?
6. What pressures have been felt by advertising agencies to become marketing agencies?
7. Why are there so few retailers among the clients of advertising agencies?
8. Suggest some possible friction points between advertising agencies and media.
9. Every now and then you see a news story in an advertising business publication reporting the merger of two advertising agencies. Just what do the agencies achieve or get when they merge?
10. You and two of your friends decide to start an advertising agency. Among the three of you there is some capital, some experience, and some connections. What are some of the dangers or risks you must watch closely?

Chapter 24

The Advertising Department

As an introduction to this chapter, let's look briefly at the sizes, the internal organizations, and the locations of manufacturers' advertising departments.

Some advertising departments consist of one or two individuals, some contain several hundred. Neither sales volume nor amount spent in advertising dictates size of advertising staff. Why? The needs of firms are often not the same. Their markets can be quite different. There is great variation from firm to firm as regards products, brands, and product lines. Amounts and types of advertising done vary. Company A makes assignments to its advertising department unlike those Company B makes; this difference may reflect differences in top management's knowledge of and attitude toward advertising as a promotional force. So the range in size is great. As for internal organization, five patterns are not uncommon. (1) The department can be set up along advertising sub-functions — copy, media, etc. (2) The staff can be broken down by media — direct mail, business magazines, etc. (3) Individuals can be assigned to one of the product lines — automobiles, appliances, etc. (4) Organization can be by type of buyer or end user — consumers, purchasing agents, etc. (5) The breakdown can be geographic — domestic, foreign, etc.

As for location on the company organization chart, there are three patterns for single-division firms and three for multi-division firms. In the former, the Advertising Manager or the Director of Advertising (these are the two most common titles) can report (1) to the top executive in the firm, (2) to the top marketing executive, or (3) to the top sales executive. In multi-division firms, the advertising department can operate as a centralized unit in the home office. Or, it can be decentralized with each division having its own advertising unit. Or, there can be these divisional operating units *plus* a central advertising unit at the home office.

FUNCTIONS OF THE ADVERTISING DEPARTMENT

The range of functions performed by advertising departments varies greatly. If a company has no sales promotion department, it will probably ask its advertising

The Advertising Department

department to assume some activities which, in other companies, are handled by sales promotion. Or, if a company does not choose to employ an advertising agency, then its advertising department will normally be asked to do more jobs than were an agency employed. Third, even within the group of manufacturers using advertising agencies, each company must decide for itself which tasks it will do and which it will delegate to the advertising agency. Finally, the marketing problems and techniques for consumer products differ considerably from those of industrial products; it is only natural for these differences to be reflected in operating differences between the two types of advertising department.

The following list of functions of the advertising department seems short. It must be recognized that the list is limited to the major duties of advertising departments in large companies with sales promotion and public relations departments.

Most advertising departments will *create some advertising,* either from preference or necessity, in fulfilling their obligation to the sales department and to the company as a whole. This obligation is to assist the salesforce in selling, primarily by promoting the company's products and secondarily by promoting the company itself. In other words, the advertising department should work ahead of and with the sales department in creating and then in filling consumer-wants. Hence, it is almost inevitable that a manufacturer's advertising staff actually create some advertising, or at least some advertisements. In getting ready to do this, the staff collects promotion material on each product, visualizing the various benefits and advantages each product can deliver to buyers. Where a manufacturer has no advertising agency, or where he uses media which do not grant any commissions to advertising agencies (direct mail, point of purchase, and some technical publications are examples of such media), then clearly the advertiser has only two options — he can take care of the copy, the art, and the media jobs, or he can, for a fee, hire a commercial firm to do those jobs for him.

Another activity that concerns the advertising department is that of *market research.* An advertiser has some choice when deciding what he should do about arranging to get the market research findings he will need. One possibility, followed by many companies, is to assign the market research function to the advertising department. This seems to make too broad a demand of an advertising department, that is, if the advertiser is to obtain all the information he needs; market research includes sales management problems, distribution channel policies, and pricing decisions. These seem quite foreign to the operation of a manufacturer's advertising department. A second possibility is for the manufacturer to put a vice-president of marketing in charge of the sales, advertising, sales promotion, and market research departments. One of the virtues of this arrangement is that the advertising department is neither asked nor allowed to be the sole evaluator of its own performance. A third possibility is to employ commercial research firms to get the information needed. These three courses of action are not mutually exclusive because, for example, the advertising department will need to do pre-testing of campaign elements; then, the market research staff will do, for example, experimental work with package changes; and, finally, outside firms may well be employed to report, for example, on readership and listenership. All the while, the manufacturer's advertising agency will be researching in its client's interests.

Regardless of who does the actual market research work, certain areas are particularly significant to the advertising department. One topic of fundamental importance involves products; here the advertising department is quite interested in product-improvement and in the items added to or dropped from the company line. The department needs current and adequate pictures of the manufacturer's prospects and customers, with particular emphasis on their buying motives and buying habits. Forecasting and market potentials are research projects that must be undertaken before any final advertising plan can be drafted. In this connection, one can argue soundly that research is a prerequisite to the identification of the specific problems advertising can solve or help solve. Then, of course, the advertising department wants to improve its advertising techniques. This calls for a study of the entire field of promotion, with particular emphasis on the promotion of competitors. It also calls for more accurate methods of evaluating the results of advertising and more realistic standards for use in administering the advertising activity. Such standards might be sought in terms of advertising cost per unit sold, advertising cost per sale, number of new prospects or number of new purchasers obtained per advertising dollar, or dollars of net sales per advertising dollar.

The market research that a manufacturer does and has done for him has one purpose — that of increasing profits through eliminating waste and mistakes, through avoiding advertising that is ineffective and inappropriate.

A third activity, in addition to the creation of advertising and market research, is *record-keeping*. There were no universal rules as to just what advertising the department should do or just which research projects it should execute. There is, likewise, no general agreement as to which advertising records should be kept in and by the advertising department and which should be kept in the accounting department and elsewhere in the company. As a result, each company divides and assigns the record-keeping activity as it thinks best. Regardless of who keeps what records, three facts are clear. First, the advertising department has the responsibility for supervising the accounting done for advertising. Second, there must be adequate records, and they must be current. Third, the main purpose of record-keeping is to place in the advertising manager's hands information which will permit him better to control the amount, the nature, and the timing of advertising expenditures.

Another job of the advertising department is to *check and approve*. The department checks on the advertising ordered by and for the company and then approves payment for it. If 4-color advertisements are scheduled to appear in a magazine, the advertising department should check to see that they were run in the issues specified and in satisfactory positions, and that the advertisements looked as they were supposed to look. Then when invoices come in for space, art work, typography, and the like, the department audits those invoices and authorizes payment.

A final obligation of the advertising department involves *outside contacts*. One group of contacts involves media and their representatives. If the advertising department "sees" all salesmen of media, several benefits result. The department learns about new media as they appear. It also learns about changes, trends, and

The Advertising Department

developments in the media field. It keeps posted on the goals and the editorial slant of individual media. The good will of media can be cultivated. A second group of contacts is with the company's middlemen and consumers, and the purpose here is to keep in touch. A third group of contacts is with commercial firms, such as those who sell advertising research services. Finally, members of the advertising department will be dealing with individuals in the company's advertising agency.

There are other duties assigned to their advertising departments by some companies. The position taken in this text is that the sales promotion department in companies manufacturing consumer goods should be responsible for these:

Catalogues	Instruction manuals
Specification sheets	Point-of-purchase
Salesmen's portfolios and visual aids	Advertising service for middlemen
Sales training	Merchandising the advertising
Direct mail	House organ for middlemen
Trade advertisements	

Exhibits and displays at business shows, fairs, and conventions

It is also recommended that the public relations department be responsible for the following:

Publicity	Mail inquiries
House organ for consumers	Reports to stockholders
Signs and painted bulletins on factory premises	Plant city advertising

THE ADVERTISING MANAGER

One of the first and most basic advertising questions a company must answer is that of how important the advertising manager should be in the company's operations. In some companies the person with the title of advertising manager is a promotion strategist, a marketing expert, and a full-fledged executive who functions on the top management level. In other companies that same title belongs to a glorified clerk who rubber stamps the preferences and prejudices of his boss and runs errands for his company's advertising agency.

The strong recommendation here is for an advertiser to insist that his advertising manager be a top-level executive because, for the typical firm, the importance of advertising as a company activity is such as to demand it. The advertising manager should be a member of the group of officers who head major departments. He should be an active participant in management meetings and discussions where company projects and programs are planned. He must be big enough to coordinate advertising with the company's other activities. He should not be *told* what the thinking of top management is, he should have had a *part* in that thinking.

The advertising manager should keep informed. He should know the industry of which his company is one unit. Industry-wide conditions, problems, developments, and trends cannot fail to affect his company's marketing, and through this channel, affect the advertising manager's work. A second matter is the advertising manager's company itself. Needed here is a knowledge of the organization of the enterprise,

451

of the duties and functions of each department or division. Especially will the advertising manager want to grasp the interdependence and the interdepartmental obligations of the various departments as the company's circumstances change. Third, there are the company's products. Their technical features must be understood before they can be translated into buyer benefits and advantages. Finally, and in a sense the most important matter of all, the prospects and customers of the company must be known intimately by the advertising manager if his advertising is to persuade them to start and to continue buying. The advertising manager must know their buying motives and their buying habits and how to reach them most effectively.

There is no accepted, clear-cut list of the duties of the advertising manager. There *cannot* be so long as there is no accepted, clear-cut list of the activities that comprise advertising. Obviously, before defining the duties of its *manager,* one must define what *advertising* includes. The assignments given by advertisers to their advertising managers vary greatly. The advertising manager and his department work on the same problems and have the same ambitions; they just work on different levels. Somewhat arbitrarily the advertising manager's functions may be divided into *advertising* and *managerial* duties.

Advertising Functions

The advertising manager should be the most influential executive in determining *advertising policy.* He should recommend to top management those activities which advertising should include. He should indicate what he thinks his company ought to do about more specific areas within advertising; what company policy should be regarding copy, media, the use of advertising through the various phases of the business cycle, evaluation of the results of advertising, and such. It should be a basic policy of the advertising manager to see that company policies are clearly expressed and that company philosophy is accurately reflected in all company advertising.

The advertising manager is properly charged with outlining the company's *advertising strategy.* This function is mainly one of planning, and, one can stoutly claim, no contribution the advertising manager can make to the company's operation is of greater value than sound, shrewd planning. The immediate objective of such planning is to obtain, to retain, and to increase the purchase and consumption of the company's products. Over-all concerns of strategy are the methods of interpreting both products and company to buyers through advertising so as to increase sales and to reduce costs. The advertising manager should clear strategy decisions with top management; he himself should have authority to make tactical decisions.

The advertising manager should design his company's *advertising effort.* He should be responsible for the composition of the total advertising effort for the year. Decisions of major import must be made in this connection. How much of the year's effort should be product-promotional in character and how much should be institutional? How much of the advertising fund should be spent for consumer advertising and how much for advertising to the trade, or to professional groups? What will be the optimum balance between advertising that is national in nature and advertising that is localized? What advertising allowances are legal, and, of those, which are defensible? There are no pat answers to such questions. In the long run, the advertising manager thinks and plans in terms of, perhaps, a three-year, or even a five-year program. It is he who ascertains the long-range advertising needs of his company and, then, directs the preparation and supervises the execution of such programs.

It is the stern and continuing duty of the advertising manager to push ever forward in the direction of more accurate, more precise *evaluation* of the results of advertising. The strongest pressure in this area stems from the advertising manager's annual conference with top management to request an advertising fund for next year's proposed advertising activities. An early question voiced by management, of course, is, "Well, what did we get for our advertising dollars you spent *last* year?" In addition to its usefulness in explaining and justifying past actions, sound evaluation can be used by the advertising manager to improve future advertising efforts. Still another use of performance data concerns the two broad and basic questions each company must decide for itself: *how much* should we advertise — and *how?* In this endeavor to evaluate, most advertising managers will find that there are no satisfactory substitutes for travel and contacts out in the advertiser's markets. By getting out of his office and into the field, regularly and often, perhaps with company salesmen, the advertising manager can get a fresh outlook as well as information about the response to his advertising.

Advertising managers are obligated to keep posted on *advertising developments*. This demands extensive knowledge of competing products, each with its strong and weak points. It also demands considerable acquaintance with the advertiser's various markets, each with its unique features. Then, of course, advertising managers must be currently informed about the area of promotion, with particular emphasis on advertising. Today's advertising changes must be identified *before* trends can be detected. When new advertising fashions appear, when innovations are introduced in some company's advertising, the advertising manager must not only know *what* is going on — he must try to determine *why*. Because such changes referred to can take place in competitors' advertising, there is a compelling reason for the advertising manager to develop his sensitivity and his power of detection.

The last on this list of advertising functions for advertising managers is that of *creative thinking* — an activity in which all advertising managers must indulge. An advertising manager is somewhat less than outstanding if he fails to search for new keynote ideas and if he does not bother to dream up new advertising tactics. He is not a good advertising man unless he wonders and asks questions. He should let not a single day pass without hoping and trying to have a new idea or to think a bold, new thought. All advertising managers must supervise the advertising their departments are responsible for, and most advertising managers, occasionally if not regularly, create some advertisements themselves. An imagination that has been well exercised is an asset in both undertakings.

Managerial Functions

As the executive in charge of a department in the company, the advertising manager *administers* the advertising department. He is responsible for staffing and

Cost Comparisons: Regional, National Editions of Representative Magazines

Prepared by Leber, Katz & Paccione

	Guaranteed Circulation	Black/White Page Rate	Cost per Thousand	Premium for Regional Editions
READER'S DIGEST (effective January, 1962)				
National	13,300,000	$43,250.00	$3.25	—
Northeast	2,300,000	9,080.00	3.95	22%
Metropolitan N. Y.	1,150,000	5,500.00	4.78	47%
Great Lakes	2,650,000	10,530.00	3.97	22%
Southern	1,450,000	6,825.00	4.71	45%
North Central	1,350,000	7,040.00	5.21	60%
Southwest	1,000,000	5,190.00	5.19	60%
Pacific	1,365,000	5,850.00	4.29	32%
Metropolitan L. A.	735,000	3,350.00	4.56	40%
Pacific-Metro L. A.	2,100,000	8,832.00	4.21	30%
TIME (effective March 2, 1962)				
National	2,700,000	$15,365.00	$5.69	—
Eastern	1,000,000	6,830.00	6.83	20%
Central	750,000	5,125.00	6.83	20%
Western	600,000	4,100.00	6.83	20%
Southern	350,000	2,390.00	6.83	20%
LOOK (effective March 13, 1962)				
National	7,000,000	$32,020.00	$4.57	—
New England	500,000	3,127.00	6.25	37%
Middle Atlantic	1,390,000	7,540.00	5.42	19%
Southeast	715,000	4,198.00	5.87	28%
East Central	1,250,000	6,850.00	5.48	20%
West Central	900,000	5,119.00	5.69	25%
Southwest	525,000	3,252.00	6.19	35%
Pacific	1,035,000	5,790.00	5.59	22%
Central	570,000	3,476.00	6.10	33%
SPORTS ILLUSTRATED (effective January 8, 1962)				
National	1,000,000	$ 6,665.00	$6.67	—
Eastern	340,000	2,720.00	8.00	20%
Midwest	235,000	1,895.00	8.06	21%
Western	210,000	1,725.00	8.21	23%
Southern	130,000	1,185.00	9.12	37%
ESQUIRE (effective January, 1962)				
National	850,000	$ 6,500.00	$7.65	—
Eastern	290,000	2,540.00	8.76	15%
Midwestern	175,000	1,600.00	9.14	19%
Western	150,000	1,440.00	9.60	25%
Central-Southern	75,000	950.00	12.67	66%
BETTER HOMES & GARDENS (effective March, 1962)				
National	5,700,000	$25,745.00	$4.52	—
New England	265,000	2,281.00	8.61	90%
Middle Atlantic	920,000	5,470.00	5.95	32%
East Central	1,170,000	6,688.00	5.72	27%
West Central	785,000	4,813.00	6.13	36%
Central	530,000	3,571.00	6.74	49%
Southeast	545,000	3,644.00	6.69	48%
Southwest	420,000	3,035.00	7.23	60%
Pacific	930,000	5,519.00	5.93	31%

The quantity discount principle operates for regional magazine circulation. Advertising managers must decide whether the premium prices should be paid. (Courtesy: Leber, Katz & Paccione)

The Advertising Department

organizing his unit. He establishes departmental routine, setting up the pattern of work to be observed and coordinating the department internally. Because he is accountable for the operations of his group, it logically follows that he must be given authority that is commensurate. Here as elsewhere, responsibility and authority must go hand in hand. It is especially desirable, indeed, it is essential, that the advertising manager be in effective control of his department and its work because advertising, as an activity, is so fascinating, so unscientific, and so packed with prestige. Literally all the other executives are prone to feel that they are as competent in identifying good advertising from bad as the advertising manager is. The inescapable conclusion is that if the advertising manager is to direct his unit in fact and not just in fancy, if he is to interpret and execute company policy, and if he is to be able to demand that advertising policies be followed, he must enjoy an effective control of his department.

The advertising manager must have an influential voice in the setting of *advertising goals*. The goals, or objectives, will be the product of many minds and much discussion — probably the result of considerable compromise. In an overly simplified observation, management, including the advertising manager, will decide what part of the marketing job and what part of the public relations job will be assigned to advertising. There may well be a short-run aspect and a long-run aspect to each of these jobs. In any event, those assignments are the ends advertising is to gain.

The advertising manager must have much to say and do about the *advertising fund*. Briefly, the advertising manager drafts his proposed advertising plan and his request for dollars to finance it. The plan will indicate what and how much advertising will be needed if advertising is to carry out its assignments. The advertising manager's proposals are submitted to whatever, in his company, constitutes the budget authority. Once this authority has decided on the size of the advertising fund, it charges the advertising manager with the duty of allocating the dollars and administering the fund. A running comparison of actual expenditures against the planned expenditures helps in keeping costs under control. The advertising manager himself should stand ready to initiate any reduction of the advertising activity that seems desirable. By the same token, he will oppose to the best of his ability any ruthless cutting of the advertising fund.

It is the responsibility of the advertising manager to see that his company's top management has a correct and complete *understanding of advertising*. In a distressingly large number of cases, management seems to consider advertising to be far more of an expense than a sales- and profit-increasing expense. Such management is inclined to use advertising mainly or even solely as a defensive resort, not as an offensive technique for preselling buyers and for keeping customers sold. Advertising managers in these circumstances must "sell" the potentials of advertising to top management. They must convince management that brand acquaintance and brand preference are significant factors in the buying done by consumers. The manager's best approach is to prove, as exactly as he can, that advertising promotes both sales and profits. Among the types of proof that may be available and convincing are: statistics on sales volume and on production costs, reports from middlemen handling the line, reports from the company's salesmen, and the reactions of competitors. Advertising managers will undoubtedly want to "sell" themselves and their recommendations to top management at the same time they "sell" advertising as a marketing force. Success here gets, for the advertising manager, the right and the authority to run his own department, the acceptance of himself as a major executive, and the confidence and respect of top management.

One of the most challenging activities of established and accepted advertising managers is *participation in company management.* The advertising manager joins the sales manager and the sales promotion manager to form the company's team of promotion executives and to take part in drafting marketing plans. This trio recommends marketing goals or quotas to top management and then suggests the promotion program most suitable for the achieving of those goals. The trio, after research and analysis, indicates to management what seems to be the most profitable marketing mix — how many parts of advertising, how many of personal selling, and how many of sales promotion. The trio determines how much "pull" (advertising) and how much "push" (personal selling) shall be apportioned to which products. The three managers integrate the company's advertising into the over-all operation and coordinate it with the company's other marketing activities. In addition to the sales manager and the sales promotion manager, there will be company problems that bring the production manager, the research director, and the controller together with the advertising manager.

A marketing activity that must not be omitted is *merchandising the advertising.* This job consists, in the main, of telling the company's sales force and the company's middlemen about the advertising planned for the immediate future, and then following through by getting those two groups excited about and proud of those plans. In Chapter 20 the position was taken that merchandising the advertising, insofar as product-promoting advertising is concerned, should be assigned to the sales promotion manager. The public relations department should be responsible for "selling" the company's advertising to the company's employees as a whole. Despite these assignments, it seems desirable to mention here that the job of merchandising the advertising is a vital one and that, regardless of whether the advertising manager or the sales promotion manager draws the task, the advertising manager is certain to be involved. He either does the merchandising of the advertising, or he must insist that someone else do this job and do it well. Where he himself does not *do* the job, he will always need to *help* in the undertaking.

Most advertising managers sooner or later will be expected to *represent their companies.* In some cases, the advertising manager will be the advertising spokesman for his company, as when he speaks to college classes in advertising. In other cases, he will affiliate with a group of advertising persons, as in the local advertising club, the Association of National Advertisers, or the National Industrial Advertisers Association. Representation of these types can benefit not only the company but also the manager himself.

One of the most important areas in which advertising managers work is that involving *relations with advertising agencies.* We now turn to a discussion of the advertiser and his agency.

The Advertising Department

WHY MANUFACTURERS USE ADVERTISING AGENCIES

Many small manufacturers of consumer goods and some large makers of industrial goods do not employ advertising agencies, either because they do not care to or because advertising agencies do not care to handle such accounts. As for medium- and large-size companies making products for the consumer market, normally they will employ one or more advertising agencies. The explanation for this latter course of action is to be found in two areas, one involving what manufacturers get from advertising agencies and the other involving cost.

What Manufacturers Get From Agencies

The main contribution advertising agencies make to the more profitable operation of a manufacturer is that of expert, tailored advertising. It will be recalled that an advertising agency is essentially an assortment of advertising specialists with excellent advertising facilities; it may include on its staff specialists in other marketing areas and even in other management areas. The outstanding skill of these specialists is that of influencing buyers through constructing and running advertisements that challenge and persuade. Advertising involves such a variety of activities and such detailed activities that these outside specialists are the ones who can do the most effective job.

The advertising agency offers the manufacturer objective, competent advice. The agency is in continuous touch with numerous sources of essential information and, as a result, keeps posted better than does the manufacturer. For example, the scope and frequency of agency-media contacts or of agency-research firms contacts permit agencies to stay better informed in those two areas than manufacturers can. Too, the diversification and breadth of the agency's own experience increases its ability to give sound counsel to advertisers. The agency has done business with many advertisers whose varied problems have involved an assortment of products advertised in all media during all seasons to buyers in all markets. This wealth of experience entitles the agency to give manufacturers general marketing advice — to suggest product improvements or new products, or changes in package, price, or even channels.

What Agencies Cost Advertisers

Economy is the basis of the relationship between advertiser and advertising agency. To start with, the advertiser is going to have to pay the full rate to media regardless of whether or not he employs an advertising agency. If he does not use an agency, he must add to the cost of media the expense involved in creating his advertising. Patently, it would be all but impossible for advertiser-through-agency to cost as much as advertiser-plus-complete-advertising-facilities. The high salaries of the agency's specialists can be paid because the agency works for *several* clients. No one advertiser could afford those specialists because the media do not grant him commissions. The net result of all this is that, in effect, media pay agencies to create advertising for advertisers.

Relationship Is Complementary

The relationship between an advertising department and the advertising agency is one of rapport, not rivalry; the two do not compete with each other, they cooperate. Typically, an advertiser does *not* choose between having an advertising department *or* employing an advertising agency. What he wants is to harness together his agency with its specialized facilities, imagination, knowledge gained from experience, and technical services *and* his advertising department with its information and abilities. When advertiser and agency join forces, it is the linking of two specialists; the advertiser is a specialist in producing products, and the advertising agency is a specialist in producing buyers.

The "House" Agency

A perennial question asks why large advertisers do not set up their own advertising agencies, put a salaried manager in charge, and, through this maneuver, qualify for the agency commissions granted by media to agencies. The outstanding argument for such a move is, of course, financial. A minor argument is that a manufacturer would disclose more confidential information to his own people than he would to an outsider, thus placing the "house" agency in a position to do a better advertising job.

Only a very, *very* few advertisers have set up their own agencies, and the reasons for this decision are many. Such an organization would not have the scope of problems and experience that independent advertising agencies have. The point of view would be inside and limited, not outside and broad. There would be a serious problem of inbreeding and its accompanying danger of a decline in bold, virile thinking. The dollars available for staffing and equipping would be fewer than those of the larger independent agencies. The unit would have less incentive to do outstanding work because of the absence of keen competition. The advertiser would have less freedom of decision and less flexibility of action because his own unit could not be abolished so easily or so promptly as an outside agency can be replaced. Because the "house" agency could be subjected to pressure for the purpose of influencing it, independence and objectivity could hardly be expected of it. The financial attraction of the "house" agency is counterbalanced, to a degree, by the ability of large advertisers to get "free" services, particularly research, from independent agencies. Finally, there is the question of whether media would grant recognition (and commissions) to an agency owned and controlled by an advertiser.

IMPORTANCE OF THE SELECTION OF AN ADVERTISING AGENCY

The relationship between an advertiser and his agency has been aptly compared to marriage. In both cases, the union should not be undertaken lightly; it should be entered with eyes open. Each party should explore the field and make a thorough investigation before making his final choice. The single objective of each should be a working partnership for the long run; a permanence that can be had only if each assumes that the relationship is forever and only if each is determined to make it last. Each must know and approve (or at least be able to live with) the ideals, the philosophy, the beliefs, and the principles of the other. Each must be willing to compromise up to a point because the partnership must be one of give and take. Each must grow with and on the other toward a better understanding of the other. As in marriage, the advertiser-agency relationship feels the strongest pressure to dissolve during the second year. In both areas, change is costly.

The two parties, advertiser and agency, form a volatile combination, one that uses up many dollars and much imagination in activities the results of which cannot be determined with precision. Both advertiser and agency depend on each other, they find close collaboration essential, and they soon discover that their relationship is both intimate and confidential. There must be, then, an atmosphere of mutuality and reciprocity. Each must know and respect the capabilities and the limitations of the other. Ideas and viewpoints must be exchanged with tact and discretion. And these opinions and interests do not stay meekly confined to the area of advertising; instead, they break out in many directions and involve products, packages, prices, distribution channels, public relations, and promotion. The obvious conclusion is — that the advertiser and his advertising agency must be compatible.

FACTORS IN SELECTING AGENCIES

Suitability

One of the first screening procedures an advertiser executes is to eliminate from consideration all advertising agencies which, for some cause, are not appropriate. Four basic factors here are competing accounts, location, policies, and size; a fifth factor can be referred to as "connections."

Obviously, an advertiser will not care to place his advertising with an agency that would, simultaneously, be creating the advertising for one of the advertiser's *competitors.* As for *location,* most advertisers want an advertising agency whose home office, or at least a major branch office, is located where the advertiser's marketing executives are. The basis for this preference is the desire for convenience.

An agency's *policies* can affect its suitability insofar as any one advertiser is concerned. If it is the policy of an agency, for example, not to handle accounts below a minimum size, obviously that agency is not available to small advertisers. Or, if the agency observes policies about charging for services or about contract stipulations which do not suit certain advertisers, then those advertisers find the agency unacceptable. Or, as a final example, if an agency has specialized within certain service classifications, or product classifications, or media (banking and other financial services, or products that reach the consumer mainly through department stores, or direct mail), its greater knowledge of the marketing practices and problems in those areas could make it most suitable for certain advertisers.

The criterion of *size* is a bit involved. In simplified form, the manufacturer thinks in terms of large agencies and small. The virtues claimed for the *large* agency include its completeness, its wider range of skills, and its more numerous facilities and services. Its talents are considered superior because large agencies can pay more money for talent. Its experience is wider. Its size permits it to absorb a new client smoothly into its over-all operation. On the other hand, the *small* agency is considered to be more ambitious and eager, more receptive and enthusiastic than its larger competitor. Contact is claimed to be closer and service to be more personalized. The advertiser's account will get concentrated attention and handling from the agency's principals. Small agencies, to survive profitably, must be shrewd and ingenious in emphasizing their particular strengths, and, clearly, imagination is not a function of size. So, should an advertiser select a *large* or a *small* agency? One can't say categorically because there are other considerations. Every advertiser should want an agency which will value, even cherish his account. This desire is most likely to be realized if the account is of some significance to the agency. The desire helps explain why small advertisers prefer small advertising agencies and large advertisers prefer large ones.

Sometimes suitability is determined by quite different considerations that can be referred to as "connections." There are claims that certain investment banking firms have close relations with certain leading advertising agencies; if so, customers of the bank might be asked, or expected, to place their advertising accounts with agencies which work closely with the banks. Another version of "connections" is kinship, either by blood or marriage. Past friendship, stemming from business, social, or educational association, is still another version.

Facilities

Quite similar to the matter of suitability is that of the facilities found in advertising agencies. In comparing agencies with respect to their facilities, the dominant criterion is, of course, the needs of the advertiser. It was he who decided what role advertising should play in his total operation, and, in like fashion, it is he who must decide what services he will ask his advertising agency to supply. Thus, the advertiser checks first to see whether or not the various agencies are organized to deliver those services. The advertiser then makes a second check to determine how strong those departments are and whether or not they can take on another account, his own, and service it satisfactorily.

Imagination

Perhaps one is entitled to describe effective advertising as the offspring of profit-slanted imagination. It should hardly need saying that unless there is present in an agency a competent ability to create productive advertising, then such an organization has nothing to sell; it is bankrupt because ideas, new and profitable, are an agency's only stock in trade. Imagination enables an agency to develop a program for learning the marketing problems of advertisers, next to grasp those problems, and then to sense what advertising might contribute toward solutions. Sound imagination will reflect in, or be absent from, the initial and preliminary proposals the agency advances as possible courses of action for the company's advertising.

Record

Much is revealed about an advertising agency by its record. In one sense, an agency's record is one of the clients it has and has had, of their problems and what the agency did about them. Any advertiser is interested in the present clients of an agency, who they are, how large they are, when they came to the agency, and why. The same advertiser wants to know what the agency has accomplished for these current customers. Then he wants to know, too, about the advertisers who used to be but are not now clients of the agency, who they are and why they left.

Mention of an agency's record invariably raises the question of whether an agency should have had experience with the advertiser's type of product. The affirmative side claims that such experience will mean fewer mistakes, less uncertainty, little or no trial-and-error experimentation, quicker results, and sound decisions based on sound judgment. The negative side retorts that such experience often causes dull, tired, and flat advertising. Both sides favor *some* experience; they disagree about type and quantity.

Reputation

An enlightened advertiser is understandably concerned with the reputation of the organization that will be creating his advertising. He realizes that ethical standards and character are as essential in his advertising agency as they are in the research firms, the legal firms, and the accounting firms he retains. The raw tactics of the huckster, the sharp practice of the shyster, even copy that is borderline — all are to be condemned. Advertisers want the financial reputation of their agencies to be based on strength and stability. Such an agency can and does pay its bills promptly; it can make its moral strength felt by resisting pressure from clients; it can, indeed, resign an account and ride out the drop in billings. Sources of information about reputation include media, suppliers, clients, former clients, and an agency's competitors.

Management

A final selection factor which can, in a sense, be ranked most important of all is that of management. Management is largely a matter of personnel, its caliber and quality, its stability and background. The experience of the top executives is well ascertained in personal selling, in merchandising, and in sales promotion as well as in advertising proper. The records each made in earlier positions and in his present job are revealing. The turnover the agency has experienced in personnel is as valuable a bit of information as was the turnover in its accounts. Of particular interest to the advertiser are the identity and characteristics of the person or persons who would be placed in direct charge of the company's advertising. The advertiser must insist that they be able and personable.

The management of the agency finally chosen should be characterized by both strength and balance. Its basic attitudes and convictions about marketing and about all business should be sound; its concept of what advertising can and cannot do should be realistic. All of its decisions should be based on adequate information, logic, and objectivity.

USE OF MORE THAN ONE AGENCY

The circumstances of some companies are such as to present an option to each advertiser, the option of using a single advertising agency or of using two or more.

An advertiser may want a yardstick against which to compare the performance of his agency and feel that the best yardstick would be the accomplishments of a second agency. Or, an advertiser may feel that he insures greater competition and greater results if he divides his advertising between or among more than one agency. Or, further, he may be convinced that it is wise to have many brains thinking about his problems, more brains than are found in any one agency. In all cases, cost is not a significant consideration, because, in a broad sense, it costs no more to use two agencies than to use only one.

A multi-agency relationship can be established on several bases. A *product* basis was mentioned in the preceding paragraph. Of course, the products do not have to be competitive; a meat packer could place certain food lines with one agency but give the advertising of his fertilizers to another one. The basis could be *geographic*. An eastern manufacturer might place his West Coast advertising with a West Coast agency, feeling that it would have more detailed information about and more localized experience in the West Coast states. *Media* supply a third basis. Direct mail and television are two media within which are found agencies particularly outstanding in each respective medium. A fourth possibility would be to break the advertising down according to *type of campaign*. A domestic-foreign breakdown and a product promotional-institutional division are two versions here. Finally, a manufacturer might assign his advertising to two or more agencies to take advantage of *agency specialization*. Such specialization could be in research, public relations, or merchandising.

There are two serious deterrents to an advertiser's splitting up his advertising. First, the dollar volume of his advertising with any one agency is less than it otherwise would be, and this means he is a less important client than he would be if he concentrated all his advertising in one agency. Second, evaluation of the performance of his advertising is obviously more complicated.

THE ADVERTISER-AGENCY AGREEMENT

Some agreements between advertisers and their advertising agencies are oral and informal, others are spelled out in written detail. Where the advertiser uses two or more agencies, written understandings are practically unavoidable. But, then, there is heavy pressure on *all* advertisers (not to mention the agencies themselves) to have written agreements. There will be fewer disagreements if the features of the relationship have been reduced to writing as the rights and obligations, the authority and responsibility of each party will be matters of record. Another pressure stems from the fact that each client selects the tailored combination of services it wants its advertising agency to supply, and this fact argues for each advertiser to have, in writing, a statement of what the agency's commitments are. Some dealings other than for space and time between advertiser and agency can involve relatively large sums, research, for instance; this is another reason for written agreements. Finally, personnel changes can take place with less disturbance to the relationship if its provisions are written.

The Advertising Department

There are certain key matters which, if not completely clear to both advertiser and agency, can lead to expensive but avoidable controversy. One such matter involves the portion of the manufacturer's advertising which is to be done by the agency. Another involves the jobs or duties for which each party will be responsible. A third matter is the duration of the relationship, which raises the question of the conditions for the continuation of the association. Then there is the vital, most basic matter of what the agency will bill to the advertiser, how those amounts shall be determined, and on what terms. Where there is advertiser-agency friction, there is often dissatisfaction on the part of the advertiser over some phase or feature of the agency's billing procedure. Fifth, the two parties should have the same understanding about what the agency can and cannot do without specific authorization by the advertiser. Finally, there must be agreement about how the relationship can be terminated. Involved here are cancellation provisions, disposition to be made of unfinished work, handling of uncompleted commitments, and the financial obligations of each party.

ADVERTISING MANAGER-AGENCY RELATIONS

In his dealings with his company's advertising agency, the advertising manager is mainly concerned with the matters of *contact, communication, collaboration* and *control*.

As for *contact*, it is the advertising manager's responsibility to draft a pattern of channels and establish the procedure for all contacts between company and agency, regardless of which side initiates any contact. The advertising manager himself should be the official and sole contact in the handling of day-to-day matters. Contact of agency by advertiser at the managerial level should be by the advertising manager only except in extraordinary instances. The advertising manager should be kept informed of all company-agency contacts. If the account representative needs to see such company officials as the sales manager, the sales promotion manager, or the research director, this should be handled by and through the advertising manager. In this manner the advertising agency respects the advertising manager's authority and position by going neither over his head nor around him.

In the area of *communication*, the advertising manager functions in both directions. Company-to-agency communication depends on the advertising manager's informing the agency about the company organization, its products, its markets, and its problems. Research findings and records that bear on the agency's assignments should be made available to the agency by the advertising manager. It is he who describes the company's marketing goals to the agency as he talks about sales forecasts and specific objectives for advertising. He also transmits raw materials from which advertisements can be built. Agency-to-company communication consists largely of interpreting the agency's thinking and its proposals to his company's management.

Collaboration starts when the advertising manager and the agency begin to plan an advertising effort for the advertiser. Topics worked on together include budgeting and research, media and scheduling. They together dream up copy ideas and

Advertising Organizations and Institutions

build advertisements. The advertising manager coordinates the work of the agency with that of his department.

Finally, the advertising manager must *control* the advertiser-agency relations and activities. His first step here is to divide the advertising job into that part for which his department will be responsible and the part which will be assigned to the advertising agency. In this process, the advertising manager learns just what the agency's capabilities are and then decides which of the agency's talents to use. He takes care to see that the advertiser is given the time and attention he deserves from the agency. He keeps the agency sales- and profit-minded, preventing the creation of advertising intended primarily to appeal to the personal preferences of the advertising manager's boss. This, of course, requires both courage and diplomacy. Advertising created by the agency is received and, if approved, is processed, usually by being routed to the sales manager. Control cannot avoid leading to an evaluation of the work of the agency. In exercising control, the advertising manager looks on the agency as a partner, not just a vendor of services; as an equal, not as an inferior.

COSTS OF SWITCHING AGENCIES

When an advertiser remains with his current advertising agency a relatively short time, loss to the advertiser may result. While the over-all turnover rate must be considered high, the larger advertisers switch from agency to agency *less* often than do the smaller advertisers. When a change of agency is made, the advertiser suffers in two ways, one having to do with the old agency and one with the new.

When an advertiser leaves one agency to go to another, he is losing the old agency's experience with his problems and his operations. During its term of service, the old agency cannot avoid collecting a mass of marketing information bearing on the account, and this mass of data cannot be transferred with much success to the new agency. Not only does the old agency know and, at least to a degree, understand the advertiser, it also knows and understands something of his competitors, their products, their problems, and their promotion. The personnel of the two organizations have spent time with each other and have gone through the unavoidable and sometimes difficult stage during which each is trying hard to learn how to do business effectively with the other. If the relationship was quite brief, then the parting of the ways most probably occurred before the two, working as a team, reached the ripe, pay-off stage of their joint advertising undertaking. There is some justification for the claim that the quality of advertising improves with age of association.

There is cost involved, too, in moving to the new agency. Surveying the qualified agencies and then selecting one demands much time and many dollars. While this step is being taken, there does not have to be any interruption in the manufacturer's advertising, but it seems reasonable to assume that interruptions in planning, diversion of attention, and some diminution of marketing momentum will be unavoidable. Some of the advertising material prepared under the direction of the former agency may have to be discarded. The new agency must begin the study of the advertiser's products and problems, and this learning by the agency usually calls for some teaching by the advertiser. This is an expense. New personnel must be broken in, and this, too, is expensive. In one sense, new customers are not preferred customers, and, if the advertiser is somewhat of a drifter from agency to agency, he may never qualify for an agency's most preferential treatment. Certainly, for a while, the realistic advertiser must brace for less understanding, lower effectiveness, and less profitable advertising.

CAUSES OF ADVERTISER-AGENCY TURNOVER

There are many reasons why advertisers change agencies rather frequently. One is that the divorce can be executed so easily and quickly. Another is that neither party can prove conclusively how good or how bad a job the agency has been doing; evaluation is not that scientific or precise. If an account does not become profitable to the agency after a reasonable period of time, about the only course for the agency to take is to resign the account. If an agency has a small account and is offered a larger competitive account, it may resign the smaller one. If an advertiser decides to use a new medium with which his present agency prefers to have no dealings, or if he decides to begin securing from an agency some service which his agency does not supply, then, of course, that advertiser could justify a change. There are occasions when agency and client have honest, understandable differences of opinion about advertising strategy and tactics, differences so wide as to justify dissolution of the association. Sometimes it works out that the top individuals in the advertiser's company and the top persons in the agency simply cannot achieve the rapport necessary for them to work together satisfactorily. A few companies change their advertising agencies every so often solely for the sake of change, believing that there is merit just in the act of changing. Personnel changes in advertiser or in agency can lead to change in relationships. Weak planning on the part of either can have the same effect. If either client or agency finally concludes that the other is unreasonable and is going to remain unreasonable, then new arrangements may be inevitable. Loss of confidence in the competence or in the fairness of the other is the explanation in some cases. Finally, most agencies know that when a client becomes unhappy with the position of his brand in the market (rank or share of market), a shift to another agency is probable.

But, in addition to these more-or-less understandable explanations, there are two other sets of accusations that relate to this turnover of accounts, accusations that are somewhat bitter. The advertising agencies claim that politics, nepotism, and "connections" account for their loss of certain clients. They are convinced that often when the management of a company is replaced, the new managers brandish new brooms, flail about with equal parts of vigor and wildness, and fire the present advertising agency to demonstrate their administrative talents. Agencies also contend that their dismissal is often a diversionary bit of camouflage, the agency being the sacrificial scapegoat to cover up mistakes of the advertiser's making. In addition to these cases of advertiser-instigated change, there are resignations, too, that have more than just a flavor of pique. Here agencies say they had to give up an account because of too much direction, or too much supervision, even dictation, by the advertiser. Or, the resignation was caused by the advertiser's insistence on advertising that was freakish, unsound, or in violation of good public relations. Or, the agency found its hands tied so tightly that it could not do a good job. Finally, if an advertiser considers his advertising agency an outsider, and a *temporary* associate at that, he may refuse to let down his corporate hair in the presence of the agency and thereby refuse to supply information essential as a foundation for profitable advertising.

In similar fashion, advertisers hurl accusations at the advertising agencies. Many of the complaints can be grouped under the general heading of "poor" advertising. This charge is apt to be made when the advertiser's sales fall off, or when his advertisements get low "ratings." The wording of the charge may stress incompetence, ruts, staleness, ignorance, or lack of understanding on the agency's part. Then another charge is that of poor service. Here the advertiser finds fault either with the quality of the agency's service departments or with the careless, neglectful treatment received from the agency's top executives. A third charge is that the agency lets self-interest shape its budget recommendations and even then spends the dollars in a wasteful manner. Disputes over costs and fees, and the belief that advertising through a new advertising agency will be at least equally good but less costly are closely related to this third charge. It is probable that more changes result from the advertiser's dissatisfaction with his present agency than from persuasive selling by agencies wanting to obtain the account.

WHAT ADVERTISERS OWE TO AGENCIES

Because obligations are a reciprocal matter, it behooves an advertiser to determine and then to pay whatever dues he owes his agency. Among his smaller obligations is that of not employing an additional advertising agency without first clearing the move with his present agency. He must not blame the agency when media or suppliers of materials fail to deliver on their commitments. The advertising manager and the other top executives should be available to the agency personnel when needed. No advertiser should expect his advertising activities to be financed by his advertising agency.

A somewhat broader obligation is not to meddle in the work of the agency. Because he is paying the bill, and because evaluation of results is so difficult, an advertiser easily and often considers himself omniscient in the realm of advertising. That mistake must not be tolerated. No advertiser should assume that he (or his wife) can tell good advertising from bad, even the advertising agencies themselves have trouble doing that. When the advertiser meddles by rewriting copy, by rearranging layouts, or by revising the schedule of the agency's proposed advertising, usually his sole accomplishments are to mangle and mutilate good advertising.

Every advertiser owes to his agency a full, real partnership in the advertiser's business; otherwise, the agency cannot make its maximum potential contribution to the client's profitable operation. This clearly calls for an advertiser to supply his agency with confidential information, with figures about costs, margins, and volume. Companies are understandably hesitant about revealing such intimate facts

The Advertising Department

because, should the advertiser-agency association be dissolved, or should some agency personnel transfer to other companies, this confidential information could easily find its way into the hands of competitors. This obstacle is as real as is the obligation.

Every advertiser owes his agency a profitable account. Unless an agency makes money on an account, it feels strong pressure either to neglect the account or to resign it; either of these is expensive to the advertiser. For this reason, advertisers do well to think twice, even to deliberate, before making requests for many "free" services.

The advertiser owes his agency a huge amount of patience. About two years are needed for an agency to learn the products, the personnel, the policies, the problems, and the promotion of a new account. Incidentally, about the same length of time must elapse before the new account begins to show a profit for the agency. Unless the advertiser takes a fair and realistic position, he is apt to expect miracles long before they could possibly be wrought.

Finally, an advertiser should assure his agency of security, of tenure, if you will, so long as the agency does a good job. No agency can do its best, no agency can put its whole heart into its work on an account if that account may be whisked over to another agency on the advertiser's whim, or because the advertiser is childish, or because he wants to throw his weight around. If it knows the conditions for permanency of association, the agency is encouraged to spend its money, its personnel, and its efforts on the account. It can concentrate on selling the advertiser's products to consumers, and not always be having to sell itself to the client.

Questions and Problems

1. When might the manufacturer of a single product justify the use of more than one advertising agency?
2. Is the "house" agency a substitute for an advertising department?
3. What types of objectives can a manufacturer assign to his advertising?
4. One of the advertising manager's responsibilities is to achieve a coordinated advertising effort. What problems stand in his way?
5. List some types of business firms which make little or no use of advertising agencies.
6. How can an advertising manager keep posted on new trends in advertising?
7. An advertiser using a single advertising agency decides to divide his account between two agencies. What problems does he face?
8. Suggest some of the problems advertising managers have in their dealings with top management.
9. Credit managers, production managers, sales managers, personnel managers, advertising managers — all are *managers*. Can you draft a list of the basic skills, characteristics, or qualities one needs if he is to be a manager?
10. The Mann Drug Company is a medium-sized manufacturer of prescription-type products. For 30 years it has sold its line of ethical items to wholesalers, retailers, hospitals, and industrial accounts. Some time ago, the firm decided to expand by

developing some proprietary drug products. These would be sold without prescription over the counter. A poison-ivy remedy and a product providing relief from summer colds were typical of the branded consumer products Mann developed. For the first time, Mann needs an advertising agency to handle the advertising of its proprietary items. Draft a questionnaire for Mann to send to a group of agencies from which Mann expects to make a selection.

Chapter 25

Industrial and Trade Advertisers

Four types of business or vocational advertising can be distinguished: *industrial, trade, agricultural,* and *professional.* Because the rest of this chapter deals with industrial and trade advertising, perhaps a few words are called for here on each of the other types.

Agricultural advertising is addressed to the farmer *as a farmer* — as a producer, raiser, or grower. When a farmer buys a tractor, fertilizer, or seed, he buys as a business man. Indeed, his buying of products of that sort is very much like the buying done by a purchasing agent of a manufacturing firm. There are publications edited for farmers. These "farm papers" contain agricultural advertising *and* consumer advertising; the farmer and his family are consumers as well as producers.

Professional advertising is addressed to professional groups such as doctors, dentists, architects, engineers, and accountants. These are influential individuals because they can favor, recommend, or even prescribe the products of manufacturer A over the competing products of manufacturer B. For example, certain competing firms have great interest in an architect's answer when a client asks about electricity vs. gas or oil. Both Crest *and* Colgate want to be the darling of the dentists.

As we have said, this chapter is concerned with industrial advertising and trade advertising. It will stress how these differ from each other *and* how each differs from consumer advertising. The treatment of each will follow the organization and sequence of the book thus far. Most of the principles found sound for consumer advertising are equally sound here.

Purchasing agents work for business firms, for institutions, and for government. They buy goods and services for their employers to use in their operations. Wholesalers, retailers, and other middlemen buy goods and services for use in their operations. When, for example, a retailer buys furniture, typewriters, and floor coverings for use in his store, he buys as a purchasing agent. Wholesalers and retailers, in addition, buy merchandise for resale. When, for example, a retailer buys furniture, typewriters, and floor coverings for resale, he buys as a merchant.

Advertising Organizations and Institutions

PART I — INDUSTRIAL ADVERTISING

The Industrial Market

Both products and services are sold to the industrial market. Here is one classification:

> Plant (warehouse, mill, garage)
> Heavy equipment (elevator, locomotive, press)
> Light equipment (cash register, hand tool, employee locker)
> Raw material (wheat, wood, cotton)
> Processed material (steel, brick, leather)
> Fabricating material (zippers, auto tires, packages)
> Operating supply (soap, stationery, gasoline)
> Service (marketing research, transportation, advertising)

Industrial products either become components of the manufacturer's end product or they are used in the manufacturer's operation. They are not resold in their form at time of purchase. Industrial advertising thus promotes products and services used in making and marketing other products or services.

Certain features of the industrial market deserve recognition. The number of prospect-firms may be small, and those few may be concentrated geographically. Industrial demand fluctuates considerably, is often postponable, is a derived type of demand. Morton does not need blue packages unless housewives are buying Morton salt. Unit of purchase is larger and frequency of purchase is less, typically, than is true of consumer purchases. Some buying is on a "bid" basis, but other prices are negotiated by the buyer and the seller. Some buying is on the basis of the buyer's specifications, other is on the basis of performance. Buying by committees is common. In a single situation a seller may need to influence various types of person — individuals who will actually run or use the product, supervisors, advisers who will make recommendations, the person or persons who will decide to buy or not to buy, and purchasing personnel who may select the vendor.

Industrial Buying and Selling

Many of the products and services industrial buyers buy are quite technical. Turbines and transportation, for example, cannot be bought satisfactorily by just anyone. So, industrial buyers are technically trained buyers, able and smart, hard and price-conscious. Because they are professional buyers, because they spend the *firm's* money rather than *their own,* purchasing agents try to avoid making any emotional purchases. The purchasing agent is a salaried employee paid to buy what will benefit his company; only when he buys as a consumer can he treat himself to *personal* benefits.

Purchasing agents buy *increased profits*. An increase in profits can result only from (1) increased gross margin (typically from a greater sales volume) or from (2) a reduction in expenses. Traditionally, purchasing agents have been described as buying *quality, service,* and *price*. Quality must be uniform and appropriate, neither too high nor too low; service, particularly delivery service and repair service, must be adequate, prompt, and dependable; price must be reasonable or, even

Industrial and Trade Advertisers

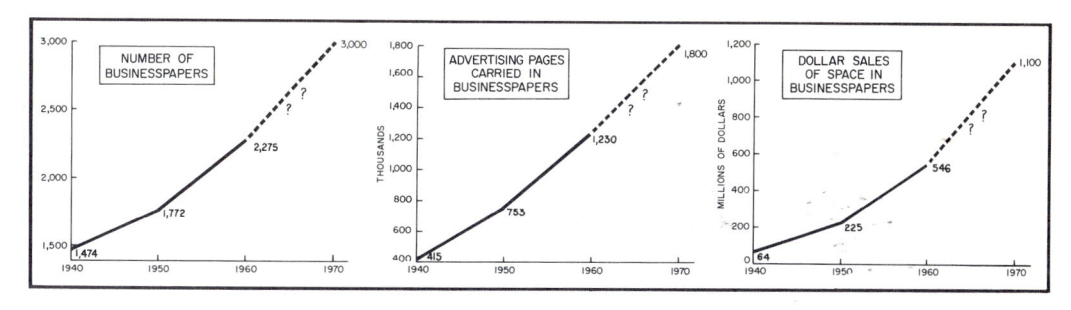

These charts reflect the growth going on in the business advertising area (Courtesy: Advertising Age. Charts by James B. Kobak of J. K. Lasser Co.)

better, low. If his firm goes in very much for reciprocity — if it has a policy of buying as much as it can from firms to which it sells — the purchasing agent probably feels that his authority to select suppliers is too limited.

Those who sell to purchasing agents must design promotional mixes just as do sellers-to-consumers. Clearly, personal selling is the dominant force in most of these mixes. All features of the industrial market and all aspects of buying and selling in that market suggest, even dictate, that advertising play a less significant role in industrial marketing than its role in consumer marketing. It is true, of course, that the cost of an industrial salesman's call goes up year after year. This trend strongly urges sellers to substitute advertising for as many salesmen's calls as is practicable.

Nature of Industrial Advertising

The advertising addressed to purchasing agents is basically similar to the advertising addressed to consumers. Most principles valid for consumer advertising are equally valid for industrial advertising. Promise benefits, write to the buyer and not to yourself, be clear, advertise continuously, don't advertise in too many media, define advertising goals as specifically as possible, integrate advertising into the total promotion program — these apply to both types of advertising. Industrial advertising is asked to pre-sell and to help sell far more often than it is asked to do the entire selling job.

Several features peculiar to industrial advertising deserve mention. Whereas consumers want various types of satisfaction, purchasing agents buy only for profit. Their rational buying calls for advertising which is less emotional and often more complicated than consumer advertising. Copy must frequently be written for half-a-dozen buying influences, no two of whom have identical interests in the advertised product or service. Buyers' responses are often slower than consumers' reactions. Few types of media are appropriate. Because advertising funds are relatively small, advertising agencies can seldom handle industrial accounts solely on the commissions granted by media.

Most industrial advertisers sponsor both indirect action advertising *and* direct action advertising. The manufacturer can stress his company or his brands. There

The ad that does double duty in TIME

When B. F. Goodrich wanted to broaden its company image *and* sell more products as well—a medium chosen to accomplish this dual job was TIME.

Says Marketing Vice President Don C. Miller: "We became aware, as the result of a national survey, that an important segment of our public thought of B. F. Goodrich as 'just another tire company.' This is far from the facts. B. F. Goodrich is a major, highly diversified corporation making a multitude of products for business and industry. The purpose of our present campaign in TIME is to establish this truth of B. F. Goodrich size, diversity and progressiveness—and at the same time to promote the sale of individual products.

"We chose TIME as a major medium for this dual job because TIME is read by the important segments of the dual audience we wanted to reach: customers and prospects *and* the informed general public."

Have these objectives been met? Assuredly. Tests of individual ads have indicated that this campaign is highly effective in accomplishing its dual objectives. It is transforming the businessman's view of B. F. Goodrich and bringing in inquiries of unusually high calibre.

A dual job—well done—in TIME.

TIME was used to carry an advertisement which had industrial and consumer objectives. (Courtesy: TIME)

is more product-promoting advertising than institutional. As with consumer advertising, good product-promoting advertising and a good product image can lead to a good corporate image.

Benefits Bought by Purchasing Agents

Just what do purchasing agents buy? Just what should industrial advertisements promise? One group of benefits is *product* based and contains satisfactions for the buyer such as these:

> New or improved product or service
> Product quality and superiority
> Low initial price
> Low installation, operating, and maintenance costs
> Versatility and adaptability of machine
> Greater productivity and efficiency
> Labor-saving potential
> Increased salability of buyer's end product

Another group of benefits is *institutional* in nature, related to the advertising firm. Examples of these are:

> Aid in solving problems
> Technical service
> Standards
> Experience
> Dependability
> Completeness of product line

What about the so-called *emotional* appeals? We have noted the pressure on purchasing agents to spend their firms' money in a rational, hard-headed, common-sense manner. Two facts, however, must be recognized. One, every purchasing agent is a human being with all the characteristics of one. Two, in many instances, the rational aspects are equalized. Sellers A, B, and C offer identical products at identical prices with essentially identical service. In such cases, the purchasing agent may make his choice on emotional bases. Typically, he is an ambitious man who wants to be or at least feel important. He wants recognition. Fear, pride, imitation, friendship, competitive feeling — these can and do play a role in some industrial purchases. Incidentally, it would be interesting to know how many planes and yachts have been bought by companies partially because of emotional motivation.

In selecting benefits to feature in his advertising, a manufacturer is well advised to study the *editorial* features of the business publications read by his prospects and customers. They identify, they contain the types of information readers expect to find in a publication's editorial columns *and* in its advertisements.

Illustrating Industrial Advertisements

Photographs seem to be superior to other types of illustration, and large photographs (50 per cent or more of advertising space) seem more effective than small

Advertising Organizations and Institutions

ones. A large photograph, one showing the product in use, including persons, and placed at the top or in the middle of the space is often the best choice.

Industrial Advertising Copy

Industrial copy is addressed to readers who are concerned about *their* business, *their* problems, *their* budgets, *their* quotas. A purchasing agent's mood is different from a consumer's mood. To repeat, the industrial buyer spends *company* money, not *personal* money. He is expected and even paid to read advertisements; he reads them seriously, intently, thoroughly. The capturing of attention, thus, is not a major problem.

Purchasing agents want advertising to provide helpful information about products and product applications. They want engineering data, construction details, physical and chemical features of products, and explanations of how buyers can use products and services profitably. Facts must be technically correct because buyers are technically competent. Often, only a technical expert can write acceptable copy.

Factual headlines including the name of the product or of the advertiser do well. Generous amounts of specific, concrete, detailed information do well. Case histories are well received. Long copy does not frighten away the purchasing agent provided the copy is of value and help to him. And even rational, "reason-why" copy can be interesting and imaginative; it need not be dull. Many industrial advertisements cannot include prices because the price eventually quoted to each buyer depends on so many variables.

Bleed advertisements seem to be worth their cost. So does color if it is used to do certain worthwhile jobs — to emphasize key words, to tie body copy to headline or illustration, to direct attention to product features and buyer benefits, and such.

Media Used by Industrial Advertisers

The industrial advertiser has a narrower choice in selecting media than does the manufacturer who advertises to consumers. Business publications rank first on the basis of dollars spent by advertisers, direct mail ranks second, and general consumer magazines rank third. Business publications are magazines or newspapers edited for specific industries, trades, professions, institutions, or vocational or executive groups. *Fortune* and *Business Week* are *general* business publications. Examples of *specialized* business publications of the industrial type are *National Petroleum News, Factory,* and *Electrical World.*

Specialized industrial publications contain strong, sound editorial content which provides a favorable atmosphere for advertising addressed to purchasing agents. Because of highly selective editing, circulation is small and there is a minimum of waste circulation. Page rates are low. These publications are read for *business information,* not for entertainment nor for relaxation. Reading interest is strong. When mailed to company addresses, these publications reach purchasing agents and other buying influences where and while those individuals are doing their jobs, part of which is to read advertising. Approximately three persons read each copy of business publications going to a company address.

YOU
INSPECT IT! COMPARE IT!

Then you'll know why Armco is your best building buy

To help you with your building decision, we'll arrange to show you Armco Buildings in service in **your** area. You'll see the combination of building advantages that has influenced businessmen throughout the world to build with the Armco system.

Armco makes the building with the famous STEELOX® Panel wall construction. This wall system gives you a building that is rugged, weathertight and handsome. The sculptured configuration of the panels provides a classic look that your architect may use with a variety of other materials.

Panel wall construction is easy to finish inside. You can finish with our own insulated steel liner panels or with any conventional materials. Thus you can get all-weather comfort — with the appearance you want.

Write us for complete Armco Building data, plus details about our complete dealer construction service. Or use the handy coupon. **Metal Products Division (formerly Armco Drainage & Metal Products, Inc.), Armco Steel Corporation, 7352 Curtis St., Middletown, O.**

Metal Products Division, Armco Steel Corporation
7352 Curtis Street, Middletown, Ohio

Please arrange for me to inspect Armco Buildings in my area. I am interested in a building for the following use:_____

NAME_____
TITLE_____
COMPANY_____
STREET_____
CITY_____ ZONE_____ STATE_____
TELEPHONE NUMBER_____

ARMCO Metal Products Division

This industrial advertisement uses a coupon in making a bid for direct action. (Courtesy: Armco Steel Corporation)

Advertising Organizations and Institutions

The nature of the industrial market and the nature of industrial buying and selling recommend direct mail as an advertising medium. Typical uses of direct mail are:

>To build a corporate image
>To lead and to follow up salesmen's calls
>To announce new products or services
>To substitute for salesmen's calls

The third medium mentioned is the general consumer magazine such as *Life* and *Look*. The major attraction of such media is the fact that these reach just about all buying influences (top management, directors, foremen) the seller needs to reach, buying influences whose identity may not even be known. If the item is a branded one which *consumers,* too, buy (sparkplugs, typewriters, zippers), then advertising in general consumer magazines can influence retailers and consumers in addition to purchasing agents. Many copies of consumer magazines are read at home where buyers and buying influences have leisure time at their disposal. Once in a while, this type of advertising locates a market of which the advertiser did not know. Good will and prestige are considerations, although minor. The great disadvantage, of course, is the tremendous amount of waste circulation.

Scheduling in Business Publications

The industrial advertiser using business publications approaches the job of scheduling his advertising in this manner. He starts by identifying and locating as accurately as possible the buyers and buying influences he hopes to influence. One of his major hopes at this point is to reach this group of individuals at the lowest cost per communication per person. Next, the advertiser identifies the industrial magazines edited for these individuals; he looks for magazines whose circulation covers or matches his market. He checks into the editorial content and quality of these publications; he notes the advertisers who buy space in them. He asks: Who reads each? Why? How are they served and benefited by reading? What do they think of each? The advertiser's competitors and a magazine's prestige can be influences.

Should the advertiser run large advertisements (1 page or more) or small advertisements (½-page or less)? The clear preference is to run large advertisements, although small advertisements are used when indicated. Large advertisements are particularly appropriate to announce new products, if market potential is great, if copy must contain technical information and detailed explanation. And, remember, page rates are low. Competitors can influence the size of advertisement just as they can the choice of magazine.

A high degree of frequency is desirable in scheduling. Heavy schedules are the rule even though this may force the advertiser to use fewer publications. Regularity is necessary because the buying decision process often starts long before the actual purchase is made. A buying decision can be the result of months of analysis, discussion, and deliberation. There is, to be sure, seasonal fluctuation in the advertising programs of many sellers. Seasonal fluctuation in *sales* volumes is one explanation. Special advertising programs and the dates of trade shows and conventions are other explanations. During its first year, a new product may get more advertising than the amount it gets the second year. If a manufacturer wants to dominate an issue of a magazine, he may use a 2-, 4-, 6-, or even 8-page insert, perhaps in color.

Good industrial advertisements do well when repeated even three or four times. On its first appearance, it captures only a portion of the issue's readers. When repeated, it is usually seen and read by an equal number of new readers or readers who do not recall seeing it. The time interval between repeats (one month — one year) does not affect readership.

Industrial Campaign Goals

Sellers of industrial goods and services sponsor product-promoting advertising *and* institutional advertising. Here are some common campaign goals:

> To increase sales or to hold present share-of-market.
> To launch new products or to find and develop new markets for present products.
> To aid the sales force by pre-selling buyers and by permitting salesmen to make fewer calls.
> To identify prospects by inviting inquiries from them. Follow-up can be by mail, by telephone, or by salesmen.
> To communicate to buyers and buying influences who won't see salesmen or to those unknown to the seller.
> To create a favorable corporate image or a favorable brand image.

How Advertising Aids Industrial Salesmen

Advertising and personal selling cooperate in industrial marketing as well as in consumer-goods marketing. Advertising helps locate prospects for salesmen. It works to get salesmen received, seen, and heard. It gives identity to the salesman, to his firm, to what he is selling. It endows the salesman with confidence. Through advertising, his company can communicate immediately with all of a salesman's buyers and most all of his buying influences when that is needed. One purpose of such communication is to arouse interest in what the salesman can offer. Another purpose is to urge buyers to take some specific action favorable to salesmen.

Salesmen sometimes fail to see as many as 40% of the buying influences in a firm. This fact helps explain why a great majority of manufacturers "sell" their advertising to their salesmen. These manufacturers describe their advertising programs to their salesmen, they tell what they want their advertising to accomplish, they give some idea of the thinking back of each program. Preprints or reprints of advertisements go to the salesmen. Sales meetings are frequently used as a presentation vehicle for the advertising story.

Industrial Catalogs

The industrial catalog is not an advertising medium. It is correctly considered to be a sales promotion item because of its similarity to direct mail advertising. Thus, it is kin to advertising *and* related to personal selling. This is no place for a comprehensive treatment of catalogs, but a brief reference does seem indicated. It is not uncommon for an industrial manufacturer to spend 13%, 15%, 18%, and even 25% of his *advertising* budget on catalogs.

What Catalogs Are. The typical catalog is an illustrated listing of products. The *general sales* catalog includes a seller's complete line. It is used by salesmen when making sales presentations. The *specialized* catalog is edited for one homogeneous buyer-group to whom a manufacturer sells; each of these types of catalog contains only those products of interest to its own group of buyers. Prices usually are an integral part of a catalog or are printed on separate price lists.

A catalog has a relatively long life because revision is slow, difficult, and costly. Mistakes are difficult to correct; changes are difficult to make. These features argue for careful planning and sound design.

A manufacturer may notify buyers that he is sending catalogs to them or his salesmen may deliver them in person.

Features of Good Catalogs. The good catalog speeds up buying and selling. It is organized into self-contained sections each of which follows the preceding one in logical sequence. It is of a size easy to file. If lengthy, it is indexed. A most essential feature is that buyers must be able to locate product information quickly and easily. And that information must be complete enough to answer just about every question to which buyers want answers.

Copy must be descriptive, detailed, accurate, and still persuasive. It should include all the facts, technical data, and specifications buyers want. It must be easy to read and easy to understand. From the copy, buyers should be able to compare products, particularly to tell differences between two similar but not identical products. Illustrations need to be simple, realistic, and clear.

Uses of Catalogs. *Sellers* look on catalogs as tools which enable and encourage buyers to consider, to recommend, to request, and to approve purchase of the seller's products. In this role, the catalog is one of a manufacturer's "silent salesmen." Real salesmen use their catalogs when selling. Sellers hope their catalogs will be seen by all buying influences in a firm. Once in a while, as many as *thirty* individuals have a voice in the buying decision. Sellers also hope that catalogs will stimulate some requests for additional information — literature, prices, or a salesman's call.

Buyers refer to catalogs; they buy from them. They consult catalogs when looking for possible sources of supply. Catalogs permit buyers to compare products and prices, to requisition a particular brand.

The Industrial Advertising Budget

Budget setting in the industrial area is dominated by two approaches. The *task* approach features the job a manufacturer needs to do to hold or increase his share-of-market. The *percentage of sales* approach needs no elaboration; a popular per cent is the industry average. A few advertising managers grumble that their budgets are residual-determined — that they get what is left after every other budget is approved. The ratio of industrial advertising expense to net sales varies greatly. The center range is 1%–3%, and the average is 1.5%.

Here are the items most often paid for out of the industrial advertising budget:

>Business publication advertising
> (space plus production costs)
>Catalogs
>Direct Mail
>Trade shows and exhibits
>Sales aids for industrial distributors
>Promotional literature
>Advertising department expense

The largest item is business publications advertising. So, the typical industrial advertising budget is small because page rates are so low in business publications and because their circulations are so small.

Evaluation of Industrial Advertising

Attempting to measure the performance of advertising is more difficult in the industrial area than in the consumer area. Contrast the marketing of a cake of soap with the marketing of a locomotive, a can of soup with a group-insurance contract. It is true that *occasionally* a certain volume of sales can be traced directly to advertising. Far more often the truth is that the industrial advertiser cannot determine what effect his advertising had on his sales volume. As for pre-testing, very little is done. Pre-testing cost is high in relation to the cost of an advertisement.

Studies of *readership* constitute the leading post-evaluation technique. This is followed closely by the use of *inquiries*. Recognition studies and recall studies are two other techniques. Some advertisers survey a sample of buyers by telephone or by mail to determine what they know, think, read, and prefer — company preference as well as brand preference. Here are typical questions:

>What companies make packaging materials?
>List them in order of preference.
>Which of their advertising do you recall?
>What products do you associate with the Able Manufacturing Company?
>Do you consider Monarch values excellent, good, or fair?

Sometimes the advertiser asks buyers to report any specific response they made, any action they took after reading an advertisement. Here are examples of such responses:

>Request more information from advertiser
>File advertisement for reference
>Order the product or service advertised
>Investigate the advertised item
>Plan to buy
>Discuss with fellow employees
>Refer advertisements to someone else
>Get in touch with advertiser's salesman

Advertising Organizations and Institutions

Some advertisers use a version of test-market testing in an attempt to evaluate past advertising. Two groups are questioned, perhaps by telephone; one group was exposed to the advertising, the other was not. Finally, some advertisers question their salesmen about buyers' reactions to the advertising.

Industrial Agencies and Departments

The use of advertising agencies by industrial advertisers is common. Often an agency does the complete job of building clients' advertisements. Almost as often, agency and client collaborate on this job; the more technical the copy, the greater the role the client plays. The advertiser can place his account with an agency which specializes in industrial advertising, or he can go to an agency which does both consumer *and* industrial advertising.

Some industrial sellers do not use an agency. The products or services may be so specialized and technical that copywriters with adequate backgrounds simply cannot be found in agencies. Then, if the advertiser's own staff is going to do his catalogs, his direct mail, his promotional literature and materials, why not do the advertising, too?

The big problem confronting the agency is the relationship between agency costs and media commissions, granted, incidentally, by most but not all business publications. When *Life* had a circulation of 7,000,000 and a page rate of $33,860, *Textile World* had a circulation of 26,000 and a page rate of $590. Contrast 15% of those dollar figures! Establishing a satisfactory system of fees and charges is not easy.

Industrial advertising departments are small; many have no internal organization; many are asked to handle inquiries, to do the direct mail and the catalogs; some do public relations, publicity, sales promotion, exhibits, even market research.

Industrial advertising managers enjoy less pay and less recognition than managers in consumer advertising. Many report to their sales managers. Industrial advertising and its managers suffer in status and salary because of (1) the difficulty of tracing sales directly to advertising, and (2) the proportion of top management with backgrounds of production, engineering, and finance.

A study made by the author indicates that when manufacturers pick an agency, they check:

>Talent of individuals to handle the account
>General reputation of the agency
>Experience with industrial accounts

Manufacturers change agencies mainly because of:

>Need for fresh copy approach
>Need for additional services
>General dissatisfaction

Manufacturers expressed over-all satisfaction with the work of their agencies.

PART II — TRADE ADVERTISING[1]

Our second type of business advertising is *trade* advertising. Manufacturers of consumer products which reach consumers through middlemen have a selling job to do on *two* types of buyers. (1) *Ultimate consumers* must buy, try, and repurchase if the manufacturing firm is to survive. (2) *Middlemen* must buy, stock, and make the merchandise available if consumers are to buy it. In our brief treatment, we concentrate on one type of middleman — the retailer.

Just as these manufacturers had to design promotion mixes which would "sell" ultimate consumers, they similarly must have promotion which will influence the attitudes and actions of retailers when those retailers buy and sell as merchants.

The retailer occupies a strong position when buying merchandise for resale. He can choose what to buy from a large group of national brands in most lines. Often he will have his own private brands on certain products; this makes the selling of a national brand to him even more difficult. Seldom does a retailer *have* to carry the brand of any one manufacturer. Almost without exception, the retailer refuses *each week* to take on an additional line or brand for the first time. Why? He simply does not have anywhere to put it. If he adds something, he has to drop something else now handled. So, the retailer cannot stock all merchandise offered to him.

The manufacturer wants retailers to stock, to promote, to favor *his* products. He can use trade advertising to help achieve these goals, to help convince retailers that they should buy and sell *his* brands.

What Retailers Buy

The one great objective of the retailer is profit; that is why he became a retailer. So his basic question when considering a purchase of merchandise for resale is: *Will it sell — at a profit?* Retailers buy (and trade advertising features) product salability, sales volume, gross margin, quality-to-price relationship, terms of sale, relations with suppliers, and promotional help directed by manufacturers to ultimate consumers. All these are profit determinants.

Selling to Retailers for Resale

The big sales story manufacturers tell retailers runs something like this:

"Mr. Retailer, consumers in your market will buy and like my products. If you stock my products, you will like them. You will like dealing with me. You, Mr. Retailer, will increase your sales and profits by stocking and pushing my lines."

This story can be told by salesmen when they call on retailers, or it can be told in trade advertisements. If a manufacturer, his market, his resources, and his advertising fund are small, then trade advertising may be the only form of advertising he can consider doing. A very few manufacturers sponsor *consumer*

---

[1] Much of the material in this section comes from a comprehensive study of trade advertising made by W. F. Halcomb, Phillip Pedlow, and W. B. Seale when they were graduate students at the University of North Carolina.

Advertising Organizations and Institutions

advertising powerful enough to generate strong consumer preference and emotional motivation. They feel little need for trade advertising because enough retailers feel forced to carry those particular brands. For the great majority of brands, however, retailers have so much to say about selecting their stock for consumers and then selling to consumers that manufacturers feel pressure to do trade advertising.

Nature of Trade Advertising

The substance of trade advertising has been suggested. It is run by manufacturers of consumer products sold through retail stores. It is addressed to retailers who handle the advertiser's products or to retailers he wants to start handling them. The advertiser hopes retailers will stock and sell, display and advertise, even prefer personally the advertiser's brand.

Most trade advertisers use their advertising for immediate response purposes *and* for the institutional purposes of building stronger patronage motivation and better public relations.

Building Trade Advertisements

Here are some of the benefits promised in trade advertisements:

> Potential sales and profit volume
> Markup and gross margin
> Acceptance and popularity of brand name
> Outstanding sales features of product
> Package superiority
> Higher turnover and lower inventory
> Low cost of handling
> Speedy reorder filling
> Manufacturer's consumer advertising

As is true of all copy, trade advertising needs to be informative, direct, simple, clear. The specific is superior to the general. Strength and believability are essential. Testimonials and case histories are good formats. So is a preview of a forthcoming *consumer* advertisement with names of the media it will appear in and with dates of appearance.

Media for Trade Advertising

Where the industrial advertiser concentrated in industrial publications and direct mail, the trade advertiser concentrates in *merchandising* publications, often called trade papers, and direct mail. Unlike the industrial advertiser, the trade advertiser cannot give serious consideration to the use of general consumer magazines.

There are regional, there are even metropolitan trade papers. There are state trade papers and association-sponsored trade papers. There are wholesale publications as well as retail. Great use is made of national merchandising publications. Examples are *Chain Store Age, Women's Wear Daily, National Furniture Review, Hardware Retailer.*

Scheduling

The trade advertising of the typical manufacturer seems to be *more* regular (rather than *less*) during the year than his consumer advertising. A time lag is often present. The trade schedule is heavy *earlier,* it peaks *before* the consumer advertising effort. This permits retailers to order and receive merchandise, to plan in-store promotion, to prepare tie-in advertisements of their own. A manufacturer of a popular Christmas gift to children spends 60% of his trade advertising budget in September, but 50% of his consumer advertising budget in December. Trade advertising for swim suits may lead consumer advertising by six months.

As was suggested, trade advertising is scheduled on a rather regular basis. There is a preference for large advertisements, usually full page, and regular schedules, but not necessarily an advertisement in every issue of a merchandising publication. This scheduling pattern is common even though it forces an advertiser to advertise in fewer publications.

Campaign Objectives

In the research project mentioned in a footnote earlier, the three researchers were told that trade advertising goals rank in this descending order of use:

Number of Mentions	Objective
43	To announce new products or programs
29	To get dealers to stock and to promote product
24	To announce specific deals or "specials"
23	To keep name before dealers
21	To "sell" advertising and promotion programs
19	To inform dealers of consumer advertising
17	To supplement efforts of salesmen
13	To acquaint dealers with features of a line
12	To inform and to help dealers
10	To impress dealers and their salesmen
9	To interest new dealers in the line
8	To help distributors "sell" their dealers
7	To stress patronage benefits such as service
6	To announce and to explain changes
5	To interest advertiser's own salesmen
4	To build dealer enthusiasm at market time
3	To promise dealers more profits

We must recognize the manufacturer's great need to tell retailers about his own promotion plans (consumer advertising and point-of-purchase, particularly) and to whip up retail enthusiasm for those future programs. Essentially, this is "merchandising" his promotion to his retail dealers. And the manufacturer's consumer advertising *must* be sold, especially to that group of merchants who would prefer advertising allowances or greater margins. The advertiser frequently builds into his own program a promotional role he hopes his retailers will play. Examples of this, each of which must be "sold" to retailers are: special merchandise displays,

Advertising Organizations and Institutions

tie-in advertisements, use of manufacturer's point-of-purchase and other sales promotional materials, and suggestion selling by retail salespersons.

Coordinated Trade Advertising

Manufacturers should, can, and do "merchandise" their *trade* advertising to their salesmen when "merchandising" their *other* advertising and promotion. We need not go through that again. We do, however, need to refer to the integrating of his trade advertising into a manufacturer's retail dealer program.

Dealer programs vary in construction and content. Manufacturers' needs vary as regards dealer programs. Our job at the moment is to glance at the more common elements in dealer programs, elements with which trade advertising must be coordinated.

Promotional materials for retailers to use are a prominent element in many dealer programs. Manufacturers may supply retail advertisements — actual posters and car cards, suggested commercials for broadcast use, and newspaper advertisements. These newspaper advertisements are usually in the form of mats — tough papier-mâché moulds in which metal printing plates can be cast. The retailer can insert his own name and prices. Indeed, if he wants to, he can use just part of the mat, the illustration, the brand name, or the copy. Point-of-purchase items are one type of these promotional materials. Direct mail for retailers to send to consumers is another type.

Another common element is the *advertising allowance*. Typically, the retailer does not contribute to this promotion fund, the manufacturer supplies all. The retailer is expected to use these dollars to promote the manufacturer's brands. He may do this with displays, in handbills, in his own advertisements, in his own special promotions. Allowances are sometimes quoted as so much money per case or per gross of the retailer's purchases. Some retailers look on these as additional discounts, not to be earned.

A third common element is the *vertical cooperative advertising program*. It is treated in the next chapter.

Fourth, some manufacturers edit an external-type of *house organ* for retailers. In some respects, this reminds one of an advertising medium.

Finally, the dealer program often offers *management counsel* to the manufacturer's retailers, particularly counsel on personal selling, on advertising, on sales promotion.

Budgeting Trade Advertising

When setting up the trade advertising fund, manufacturers favor the task approach. They think the size of the budget should reflect the job to be done. Typically, the *trade* advertising budget is not a fixed per cent of the *total* advertising budget. Manufacturers told the three researchers that the amounts they spend for trade advertising usually range from .1% to .5% of net sales, from 5% to 10% of the total amount spent for advertising.

30 LEADING BUSINESSPAPER ADVERTISERS — 1962

(Millions of Dollars)

1.	General Electric Company	$4,500.0
2.	American Cyanamid Company	4,033.0
3.	United States Steel Company	3,158.3*
4.	General Motors Corporation	2,944.9*
5.	Merck & Company, Inc.	2,851.9*
6.	E. I. Du Pont De Nemours & Company, Inc.	2,700.0
7.	Abbott Laboratories	2,467.3*
8.	Minnesota Mining & Manufacturing Company	2,370.2*
9.	Minneapolis-Honeywell Regulator Company	2,300.0
10.	Allis-Chalmers Manufacturing Company	2,195.2*
11.	Eastman Kodak Company	2,000.0
12.	Bendix Corporation	1,950.0
13.	Standard Oil Company of New Jersey	1,894.2*
14.	Westinghouse Electric Corporation	1,700.0
15.	Union Carbide Corporation	1,600.0
16.	United States Rubber Company	1,523.8*
17.	Allied Chemical & Dye Corporation	1,481.0*
18.	Eli Lily & Company	1,460.0
19.	Republic Steel Corporation	1,458.7*
20.	Caterpillar Tractor Company	1,454.2*
21.	B. F. Goodrich Company	1,448.4*
22.	Colorado Fuel & Iron Corporation	1,380.2
23.	General Telephone & Electronics Corporation	1,366.6
24.	Ciba Pharmaceutical Company	1,300.0
25.	Goodyear Tire & Rubber Company, Inc.	1,251.0*
26.	Westinghouse Air Brake Company	1,246.8*
27.	A. H. Robins Company	1,200.0
28.	Bethlehem Steel Company	1,182.7*
29.	Monsanto Chemical Company	1,178.5
30.	American Home Products Corporation	1,177.3*

* Estimated

This list consists of smaller sums than these firms spend in consumer advertising. (Source: Associated Business Publications)

Evaluating Trade Advertising

There is almost no testing or evaluation of trade advertisements. Why? Advertisers feel that there are no sound techniques, that elaborate testing would not be worth doing because space in merchandising publications is so low in price.

Managing Trade Advertising

There are many patterns and there is much variety in the management of trade advertising. Most manufacturers work through advertising agencies, and, certainly for large trade advertisers, agencies build most of their advertisements. A manufacturer's advertising department can have a trade advertising sub-section which may do *some* advertisements. Agencies are paid by media commissions, by commissions plus a supplement, or on a cost-plus-17.65% basis.

Advertising Organizations and Institutions

Questions and Problems

1. Why are brand names less common and less important for industrial products than for consumer products?
2. Why are trade characters more helpful in selling products to consumers than in selling the same products to purchasing agents?
3. Justify the placing of industrial ads in consumer magazines.
4. Industrial advertisers in the same industry often follow scheduling patterns which are dissimilar. Explain.
5. Comment on the advertising manager of a manufacturer of industrial goods versus his counterpart in a firm making consumer goods.
6. One of the largest firms in the steel industry checked up on its public relations with the general public and discovered, to its dismay and disappointment, that its corporate image was not the best. Consumers, when referring to the corporation, used such terms as "monopoly," "too powerful," "administered prices," even "gyp the public." Two relevant questions ask: Just what is a corporate image? How was it determined?
7. A manufacturer of machine tools has operated satisfactorily for 55 years. During this time, the great part of his promotion job has been done by an able sales force. There *has* been some use of direct mail advertising. Last year for the first time the manufacturer sponsored an advertising campaign in business publications, terminating in December. No publication advertising was scheduled for this year and none has been run. It is now July, and the manufacturer is convinced that last year's publication advertising was a waste of money. Comment.
8. What can you say about testing consumer ads versus testing trade ads?
9. Why do advertising campaigns addressed to consumers need to be "merchandised" to the trade?
10. Picture a manufacturer of proprietary drug products (headache remedies, tonics, foot preparations) who relies heavily on consumer advertising. The manufacturer also sponsors trade advertising, one objective of which is to encourage retail support of the manufacturer's brands. Specifically, how can retailers make difficult the achievement of the goals of this manufacturer's *consumer* advertising?

Chapter 26

The Retail Advertiser

As was stated in Chapter 3, this is primarily a book about manufacturers' advertising. A text designed for the beginning course *must* look at advertising from the manufacturer's point of view for reasons mentioned in that chapter. At the same time, however, it seems desirable to include at least one chapter on the advertising done by retailers, even though many observations and principles from the area of manufacturers' advertising are equally sound in the case of retail advertising. The dollar volume of retail advertising is impressive; interest in retail advertising is considerable; the amount of literature on retail advertising is small. For these reasons, this chapter is included. Its general approach is to point up the similarities and the differences between advertising done by the retailer and advertising done by the manufacturer.

BACKGROUND

Advertising functions as a marketing force to increase sales and profits for retailers just as it does for manufacturers. Where the manufacturer advertises to promote and establish his *brand*, the retailer advertises to promote and establish his *store*. The manufacturer urges, "Buy *my* brand — at *any* store," whereas the retailer urges "Buy *any* brand — at *my* store." Most retailers combine advertising with some personal selling and with some sales promotion activities. Retail advertisers, their customers, and their media are the groups involved; there is no middleman problem as faced by manufacturers, and the role of the advertising agency is small. Some retail advertising is institutional in character, but the great bulk is product promoting; retailers generally want a quicker response from buyers than that wanted by manufacturers. Retail advertising demands the same favorable climate as manufacturers' advertising. The product and its price must be right because advertising is not a substitute for markdowns. If customers are responsive and financially able to buy, the advertising will be more productive. The store's location, its services, its facilities, and its other promotion should contribute to the advertising's effectiveness.

487

Advertising Organizations and Institutions

Types of Retail Firms

Because there are many types of retail firms, generalizations about the retail group are subject to many exceptions. Even so, a classification seems worthwhile.

There is a type of store which must be described as *non-promotional*. These stores handle the finest quality merchandise and appeal to customers in the top income brackets. These stores can be counted on to have the latest fashions first. Their prices are matched by each store's prestige as a style and taste authority. This type of store does some regular price advertising and, perhaps, some institutional advertising; its advertising-to-sales ratio is low. Tiffany & Co. and Abercrombie & Fitch are typical.

At the other extreme is the *promotional* store with its aggressive promotion and with its reputation for reduced prices and bargains. Services are fewer, and regular patronage less than for the non-promotional firms. These merchants run much advertising of a highly promotional character but little if any institutional advertising. The advertising-to-sales ratio is high for promotional stores. Discount houses and cut-rate liquor or drug stores are examples.

In between the non-promotional and the promotional groups is, of course, the *semi-promotional retailer*. He does a healthy amount of promotional advertising (regular prices, special events, store-wide promotions) and some occasional institutional advertising. His advertising-to-sales ratio is medium. The average department store is typical of this group.

Retail Advertising Goals

The *product-promoting advertising* of retailers may be designed to increase the immediate sale of merchandise at regular prices. Or, the advertising may be put behind a special promotion at reduced prices, a promotion involving a single product, or a department, or the entire store. Or, the advertising may be designed to clear out certain merchandise at sharply reduced prices. In all these instances, the merchant's most urgent interest is in creating store traffic, in attracting consumers to his store to see and buy the advertised items and also to see and buy other merchandise. In a few instances, the merchant's goals are consumer purchases by telephone or by mail, but in the vast majority of cases, he is happy if his advertisements produce traffic on the floor and in the aisles. The retailer joins the manufacturer in expecting his advertising to help (a) hold present customers by keeping their interest between purchases and by encouraging the habit of going to the retailer's store, (b) get a larger share of each customer's business as a result of more concentrated buying, and (c) acquire new customers. The retailer's hope is to improve his profit showing by selecting the "right" merchandise to feature and then by advertising it at the "right" time with advertising that is "right." Greater profit may reflect greater sales volume achieved without a corresponding increase in total expenses; it may reflect a sales volume more evenly distributed over the selling days of the month and week; it may reflect greater sales with no increase in inventory.

The *institutional advertising* of retailers is designed to build prestige and reputation for the store and for its merchandise as a whole. Its goal is to create a per-

488

Example of an advertisement run by a non-promotional store. (Courtesy: Tiffany & Co.)

Advertising Organizations and Institutions

sonality or corporate image for the firm. Consumer good will is invited by informing consumers about the store's policies, facilities, services, personnel, and competence as the purchasing agent of consumers. Or the store could stress such matters as convenience; merchandise assortment, variety, and quality; a philosophy of low prices; courtesy of sales staff; or store integrity.

Marketing Research for Retailers

The retailer's need for market information and data is the same as any seller's need for facts of this sort. It is a continuing need just as it was for manufacturers. Small retailers can themselves engage in only the more informal, the more inexpensive forms of research such as observation or chats with customers and salespeople. Some research is done for and supplied to retailers, particularly to the smaller ones, by suppliers and resources from whom they buy and from media, particularly from newspapers and the broadcast media. Retailers can and should know more about their markets and their competitors than do manufacturers; their markets are more homogeneous, and their competitors are, for the most part, local.

There are many types of questions to which retailers need answers. Questions about the *market* include these:

What are the attitudes of my customers toward me, my merchandise, my prices, and my services?
What local tastes and preferences are significant features of my market?
What members of the family take part in the decisions to buy my types of merchandise?
How many customers do I lose and gain each year? Why?
How many inactive accounts do I have, and why are they inactive?
What is the composition of my market in respect to age, income, race, occupation, buying habits?

Questions about *sales patterns* include these:

What are my most important product lines by dollar sales volume?
What are my most important product lines measured by gross margin in dollars?
What does a chart of sales-by-month and sales-by-season show?
What are my heaviest selling hours of the day?
How much of my weekly sales volume is done on each day in the week?
What portion of my sales represents planned purchases and what portion represents impulse purchases?

Examples of *promotion* questions are these:

Which merchandise deserves advertising support?
What do customers and potential customers like and dislike about my advertising? Just what do they want from it?
How does my advertising compare with that done by my competitors in respect to products featured and benefits stressed?
Which media should I be using, and according to what schedule?
How much should I spend for advertising, and how can I arrive at that figure?

The Retail Advertiser

IDENTIFICATION

For those retailers who handle only *manufacturers'* brands, the identification job is that of making the *store* known as the home of those brands. Some retailers, usually mass retailers or prestige firms, do have their own private or house brands. As for identification, *these* retailers have the same naming, packaging, and promotion problems as do manufacturers who put their own brands on their products; they adopt many of the same solutions, too.

Because of their continuous use of advertising, and also because they concentrate the great bulk of their advertising in local newspapers, larger retailers are in a position to achieve *advertising* identity more quickly and more certainly than can manufacturers. The goal of many a retail merchant is for consumers to be able to identify his advertising even with the name and address of the store masked. This goal is understandable when one realizes that readership rises as more and more consumers recognize instantly who the advertising retailer is. This desire for advertising identity can lead to advertisements which have a single, consistent personality, an unmistakable, distinctive individuality of their own. Care must be exercised, of course, in fitting the type and character of the advertising to the store to the end that advertising and store have the same personality.

Either substance or style can be employed to achieve advertising identity. Among the style elements used are layout, artwork, typography, copy format, and logotype. His logotype, incidentally, is a retailer's trade mark and, for this reason, deserves to be designed with the thought and attention a manufacturer gives to his trade mark. Far too many retail logotypes are commonplace instead of distinctive.

In the case of trade characters as in the case of brand names, some retailers make worthwhile use of manufacturers' trade characters, some create their own. The Planters chain's Mr. Peanut is a good example. It seems that every retailer should explore the possibility of designing and making effective use of his own trade character.

BUILDING RETAIL ADVERTISEMENTS

Benefits

Retailers advertise to the same individuals and confront the same consumer motivation as do manufacturers. Retailers, like manufacturers, know the attention-interest-desire-conviction-action sequence. Getting the attention and interest of possible customers is often an easier job for retailers than for manufacturers. The retailer's merchandise is greater in variety and in number than is the manufacturer's. Many consumers know the store and its personnel. Many consumers look regularly and intentionally for the advertisements of certain stores, perhaps because they are interested in or even attached to the store, or because they are contemplating the purchase of some specific product, or perhaps they just want to keep posted on what is new. Most retailers are quite happy if their advertisements create consumer desire to see the advertised merchandise and result in visits to the store. Few retail advertisements attempt to achieve conviction, much less to consummate a sale.

In one respect, the retailer's job of influencing the ultimate consumer is a greater challenge than is that job for manufacturers. For any given manufacturer, no other brand is exactly similar to *his* brand, and he is the sole source of that brand. Almost every retailer, on the other hand, sees other and competing retailers handling most of the same identical products and brands *he* handles. Because of this, the retailer has a dual job — to stimulate a desire for the product, and then to sell himself to the consumer as the most desirable source of supply.

Retailers probably must be more vigilant than manufacturers in their efforts to play up buyer benefits and to play down product features. Because attention and interest are often achieved easily, the retailer can devote a relatively large amount of space to product features. He can and does use a higher proportion of product features to buyer benefits than do manufacturers. Even so, the retailer must take care to see that he places more emphasis on benefits than on features. Like the manufacturer, the retailer searches for the most persuasive benefits of his major products or product lines. All retailers recognize the key role of price.

Copy

Retail copy has, in general, the same goals as manufacturers' copy, but the emphasis is different. We saw earlier that manufacturers favor *indirect action* advertising; we now see that retailers stress *direct action* objectives, with the most common reaction desired being a visit to the advertiser's store. Only a minor portion of retail advertising is designed to build mental associations over the long run in consumers' minds. The two types of copy are alike in that each is predominantly promotional rather than institutional.

Headlines. Because most retail advertising is placed in newspapers and because newspaper advertising benefits from being newsworthy, headlines in retail advertisements should, if possible, contain news. Price reductions, a revision of store hours, and the arrival of new merchandise are examples of such news. When a big sales idea is included in a news type headline, the advertiser stands an excellent chance of alerting a satisfactory number of prospects and of inducing a satisfactory amount of readership. Retail headlines should supply information which the reader cannot get from the illustrations. Label headlines and those composed of product specifications are usually weak.

Body Copy. Retailers use body copy to enlarge on and develop the information in the illustration and headline or to supplement those two elements with additional, new information. The entire advertisement and its body copy may be promoting regular merchandise at regular or at reduced prices, or special merchandise, or, if institutional, the store itself.

Institutional advertising gets a small percentage of retail advertising funds; it gets literally none of the advertising dollars of many retailers. Because merchandise and prices are so nearly identical among so many stores, there *is* a place for retail institutional advertising. Some retailers use it effectively to identify proudly the

The Retail Advertiser

national brands they stock; to tell about the store's reputation as a source of outstanding values; to brag about variety and assortment, size and age, or personnel and services; and to explain policies, shortages, and interruptions. Retail institutional advertising can be but need not be dull material.

Retail body copy is considerably shorter than is manufacturers' body copy. There is less need to organize retail body copy and less use of a lead paragraph. Many consumers in the market know the store, many know and use the products retailers advertise. The copywriter's goal, as has been mentioned, is a visit, considerably less than a purchase.

There are other differences between the body copy of retailers and that of manufacturers. Retail copy can be more friendly and warm, more personal, than manufacturers' copy because it can be localized. It is less sensational and less spectacular for two reasons: one disappointed, vocal customer can do a store considerable damage for a long period of time; also, the Better Business Bureaus in larger markets take a close and continuing look at local advertising. Retail copy is probably more factual and informative than is manufacturers' copy; retail copywriters, in constant touch with store buyers and with the store's customers, usually have much detailed knowledge of the merchandise about which they write.

The smaller retailers can get copy assistance from three sources. Advertising services such as Metro Associated Service and Meyer Both Company supply mats of complete retail advertisements. Some manufacturers do likewise or at least supply copy material and suggestions. Finally, media write copy for their retail advertisers.

Price. The retailer has less option than the manufacturer has about the inclusion of price in his advertising. Most retailers must include their prices; most retailers, furthermore, can do this much more satisfactorily than can manufacturers. Price is of major importance in the advertisements of promotional retailers; it is equally significant in clearance advertisements and even in special promotion advertising. Where merchandise, services, personnel, and location are about the same, price is a natural basis for competition among retailers. In quoting prices, a multiple-unit price should be included if feasible ("pint $2 — quart $3.75;" "1 for $2.95 — 3 for $8.25").

The greater the bargain, the larger the type should be. If prices have been reduced, the former figure, too, should be included. The use of *comparative* prices ("Was $10 — now $6.95") can be powerful and profitable, but it can also be abused. Because comparative prices have been abused by some, certain retailers have adopted a policy of never quoting them.

The Close. Because they seek specific and immediate response, most retail advertisements do and should close with an urge to act — quickly. These can be strong, making use of such imperatives as *go, see, telephone, come,* and *ask*. These give memory value as well as action value to body copy. The close should give the reader all the facts needed to carry out his purchase. Some of these are the name of store, address, telephone number, department or floor, whether telephone and mail orders can be placed, and store hours.

Advertising Organizations and Institutions

Layout and Typography

In respect to layout and typography, the qualities and features desired in retail advertising are just about the same as those in manufacturers' advertising. Layouts should be attractive and inviting, sound and simple. They should make use of balance, movement, proportion, contrast, and unity. There is the same pressing need for illustrations to carry heavy responsibility, ably supported by headlines and body copy. The retailer is under greater pressure to picture the product itself than is the manufacturer; indeed, many manufacturers try to avoid letting their products dominate their advertising illustrations. Retailers must learn how best to picture certain items: clothes (hats, dresses) should be displayed on persons rather than on hangers; accessories (shoes, belts) should be pictured alone. Many retailers do what few manufacturers dare do when they put the advertiser's name at the *top* of a newspaper advertisement in order to help consumers find it.

MEDIA

Newspapers

Retail advertisers spend more money in newspapers than in any other medium for reasons which are obvious. The newspaper is the medium which covers snugly the retail trading area of its market. It is an economical medium in many ways for many retailers; only the small retailers find the circulation in the city zone too wasteful. Newspapers get quick response from shoppers who depend on them as guides. Each day's issue has fresh appeal. Color facilities are both expanding and improving.

Some retailers prefer to use a "truline" rate in analyzing newspapers rather than the milline rate described in Chapter 11. These two rates differ in this respect: where the milline rate uses total circulation as its denominator, the truline rate uses circulation within the retail trading area only; this is because the "All other" circulation is practically worthless to retailers. The truline formula is this:

$$\frac{\text{retail line rate} \times 1{,}000{,}000}{\text{circulation in retail trading area}}$$

Magazines

Because they usually cover such an extensive geographic area, most magazines are unsuitable for retail advertising. But there are exceptions, of course, to this generalization. Certain mass retailers, be they chain stores, department stores, specialty stores, or mail-order firms, do advertise in certain consumer magazines. Woolworth, Marshall Field, Bergdorf Goodman, and Sears are examples. Some of this advertising appears quite understandably in the individual or local newspaper magazines, such as the New York Times Magazine. Equally understandable is the advertisement of a New York retailer in the city edition of *The New Yorker*. The increasing fragmentation of magazine circulation works, of course, in the direction of making certain geographically concentrated editions (a metropolitan edition, for example) more attractive to certain retailers.

The Retail Advertiser

Somewhat less obvious is the reasoning of an independent retail advertiser who schedules advertising in general consumer magazines with national circulation. Why does he do this? One explanation may be that the retailer is promoting mail-order purchases. Another explanation, less strong, may be the retailer's intent to impress his most valuable customers and his most desirable prospects in his retail trading area or consumers throughout the country who will be visiting the retailer's city. Other possible explanations are the advertising's effects on suppliers and on store employees, and the use of reprints as point-of-purchase material or direct mail.

Television and Radio

Retailers use both broadcast media, but not to any great extent. Both product-promoting advertising and institutional advertising appear in each medium. Both regular shows and announcements are bought. Among sponsored shows are these types: weather, local news, and mistress of ceremonies programs. Considerable use is made of announcements on disc jockey shows. Stores with wide distribution are in a position to buy network time as well as local time. Department stores, largely self-sufficient in other media, often employ outsiders to help design their television advertising or else buy packaged programs. It is quite possible that retailers still have much to learn about the profitable use of the broadcast media.

Outdoor and Transit

These two media are of limited use to most retailers because of the type of circulation in each and because of the copy handicaps in each which limit the amount and the freshness of the advertising message. Large department stores and chains can use posters regularly, and other stores, jewelry, for example, can use them seasonally. For most retail advertisers, painted walls and bulletins are more appropriate than are posters, particularly if the retailer must buy his own individual posters in small quantities. The great majority of retailers are more concerned with store-site signs than with general outdoor advertising.

Point of Purchase

You will recall that all of Chapter 16 was devoted to the point-of-purchase activity. The importance of this type of retail promotion is indicated by the fact that many retailers credit one-third to one-half of their sales volume to their window displays. If a merchant wants to maximize the sale of the merchandise he advertises in newspapers or in the broadcast media, he gives those products window and interior display. There may be compelling reasons at times for giving some of that display space to non-advertised products.

Direct Mail

Of all the media, direct mail is probably the one which can be used profitably by the largest number of retailers. It is the only medium in which the smaller stores can control satisfactorily both cost and circulation. Many manufacturers supply direct-mail materials for retailers to use. Retailers with credit facilities and those who accept orders by telephone or mail have excellent mailing lists supplied to them automatically. Two popular uses of direct mail are to revive inactive accounts and to give charge-account customers advance notice of sales.

SCHEDULING RETAIL ADVERTISING

Coverage

Media Types. In selecting the types of media to use, retailers share manufacturers' interest in *availability* in respect to store and in respect to merchandise to be advertised, *selectivity,* and *cost*. Retailers hope to reach the greatest number of prospects and customers through media most appropriate for the products in question and with a minimum of waste circulation. One sees quickly that the retailer has a narrower choice than has the manufacturer; the smaller the retailer and the smaller the advertising fund, the narrower this choice is.

As has been mentioned, newspapers are the most popular media type, getting about three-fourths to four-fifths of the retail advertising dollars spent for space and time. Direct advertising, largely handbills and direct mail, and broadcast advertising follow newspapers but at a considerable distance back. In the larger markets, the larger retailers must use newspapers; the smaller retailers cannot afford to use them.

The question of the use of national media by retail advertisers has been raised in connection with magazines and with network broadcasting. As a retailer's geographic extent of operation enlarges, as he grows marketwise, the amount of waste circulation in national media decreases. The high degree of mobility of our population recommends that such a retailer consider national media. The in-store promotions of national chains can benefit from this type of advertising. Occasionally, the use of national media is essentially a defensive move — the adoption of the tactics of competitors.

Individual Media. As for any one newspaper or broadcast station, the retail advertiser is interested in quality of circulation, quantity of circulation, and cost. He checks on its reputation, its advertising standards, and the number and identity of other advertisers using it. He tries to determine its relative effectiveness among other local media in the light of the merchandise to be advertised, the copy and art work contemplated, the size, timing, and position of the advertisement.

Retailers are interested in the services available from media to a much greater degree than are manufacturers. Mention was made in the paragraph on marketing research of the practice of media, particularly newspapers, television, and radio, of supplying research findings to retailers. More important than research to the smaller retailer is the assistance media give in the area of advertising management. Newspapers, for instance, chart a retailer's seasonal sales pattern, help the retailer to arrive at the amount he will spend in advertising, recommend what merchandise should be promoted when, and go so far as to help plan entire promotions. Media serve as the advertising departments for small retailers, usually drawing on the mat services to which they subscribe for art work and also for copy and layout ideas. Large newspapers have copy service departments and even artists; on small newspapers, the advertising solicitors are responsible for seeing that advertisements are built for their retail accounts.

Frequency

A retailer's advertising needs to be featured by high frequency, by a large number of advertisements per year, per season, and per month. For most retailers, frequency should be achieved even at the price of a reduction in size of advertisement. One of the most common mistakes of small retailers is that of advertising too infrequently. Among all retailers, the largest department stores usually advertise the most often and usually run the largest advertisements.

On the *minus* side, retailers find their small advertisements buried on the newspaper page, often on a less desirable page, and weak because of their small size. On the *plus* side, small advertisements are appropriate for low traffic days, for reminder use, and for testing; their return per dollar of cost is good for most products; they permit greater consistency and continuity.

Continuity

Because retailers do not advertise in terms of campaigns in the same sense as do manufacturers, there is no problem of determining how much time should separate one campaign from the campaign to follow. There is, however, a common problem — that of the nature of the time period separating one advertisement from the next. The advertisements of a retailer are scheduled closer together than are those of a manufacturer. Retailers make heavy advertising expenditures just *before* and *during* peak buying periods; they don't dare wait until the active period actually starts because research has established the fact that women start thinking about a buying season *days* before that season arrives.

Wednesday, Thursday, and Friday are heavy advertising days within the week. Sunday, too, is a heavy day. That leaves Monday, Tuesday, and Saturday the light days; on these days, a retail advertiser has a good opportunity to get better position in newspapers.

There is a general principle in most buying which recommends that a buyer avoid spreading his volume of purchases over too large a number of sellers. That principle is a most sound one when a buyer is buying advertising, and is particularly to be observed when that buyer is a retailer of medium or small size. Concentration can add much to the effectiveness of the advertising; in addition, it works to make the retailer a preferred customer of the medium. Of all advertisers, retailers must guard vigilantly against frittering away their advertising funds in the many odd, irregular media which can often make strong solicitations to retailers. Any dollars given to most of these media should be charged to contributions or to public relations — not to advertising.

COORDINATION

Retail advertising needs to be coordinated with the store's personal selling and with its display. No matter how much persuasion is built into an advertisement and

Advertising Organizations and Institutions

no matter how expertly the advertisement is scheduled, its performance will be increased by support from the retail salespersons and from the store's display facilities, particularly the windows.

One of the universal and chronic problems of retailers is that of how to get a store's selling employees to read the store's advertising. Salespeople certainly cannot recommend, support, and be enthusiastic about the advertised merchandise unless they read the advertisements. How to try to get them to read the store's advertising? Some merchants circulate the advertisements and instruct each salesperson to read and initial. Some offer rewards for finding a mistake in any advertisement. But a satisfactory solution is yet to be found.

THE ADVERTISING FUND

Chapter 21 was devoted exclusively to the question of how much an advertiser should spend in advertising, and it is only natural that practically every idea in that chapter applies to the retail advertiser. In light of this fact, the advertising fund gets extremely brief handling here. An advertising retailer, like all other sellers using advertising, spends a specific number of dollars for advertising. Like all other sellers, he can relate each of his expenses to net sales and arrive at percentages. Wages and salaries may be 14 per cent, rent may be 3 per cent, advertising may work out to be $1/20$ of 1 per cent — or $4\frac{1}{2}$ per cent of net sales. It is common for a retailer to check his various expense percentages against those of the entire group of which he is a member. He knows that those common figures are averages and are subject to all the limitations which apply to averages. He knows further that there are circumstances which simply demand that his figure be higher, or lower, than the common figure. Even so, he finds the comparison both desirable and inevitable.

Many influences affect the size of the retail advertising fund. Advertising programs have short-range objectives and long-range objectives. The need for advertising varies among a group of stores; variety stores, for example, need advertising less acutely than do department stores, and stores with a liberal offering of services (credit, delivery, adjustment) need more than the stores with few services. The age, size, and location of the store are three influences; the media to be used are another; the type of customer desired is still another. Business conditions and the promotional activities of competitors affect the size of the retail advertising fund in the same manner as they affect the size of a manufacturer's advertising fund. A conclusion in Chapter 21 equally true here is that the retailer's experience with and in advertising is usually the most powerful influence in the determination of the size of the advertising fund.

Retailers distribute their advertising over just about the same bases manufacturers use. They spread their dollars over products and departments, and among the media selected for use. They budget their expenditures by time periods, by season, by month, by week, by day. They earmark certain amounts for special events and other amounts for special promotions. They distribute the total figure over the various expense classifications which have been approved as advertising activities.

The Retail Advertiser

Few retailers need to apportion dollars over geographical territories as the large manufacturers must do.

When sales volume drops below the forecast, retailers join most other advertisers in cutting down the amount of their advertising. They are well advised, however, not to reduce advertising as severely as sales drop.

"Co-op" Advertising

A treatment of the retail advertising fund must be followed by a reference to vertical cooperative advertising. Just what is "co-op"? When a retailer runs a local advertisement over his own name featuring a manufacturer's brand and the two share the cost, the advertisement is referred to as "co-op" and the advertising as vertical cooperative advertising. This type of advertising is found in such retailing fields as hardware, department, drug, shoe, appliance, clothing, and food. Exclusive distribution (only one retail dealer in a market) and selective distribution (only a chosen few retail dealers in a market) fit in with cooperative advertising more satisfactorily than does the intensive or unlimited distribution characteristic of cigarettes, chewing gum, aspirin, soft drinks, and the like. The co-op advertisement when properly handled saves money for both manufacturer and retailer; they share the cost, and the cost is based on the retail rate rather than on the general rate which the manufacturer would have to pay. The basis of sharing varies; the manufacturer may even pay 100 per cent of the cost — or, he may pay considerably less than 50 per cent. Probably the 50-50 per cent split is most common.

In most cooperative advertising arrangements, the manufacturer sets a limit on the number of dollars he will contribute. This maximum may be 2 per cent or 5 per cent, for example, of the dollar value of a retailer's purchases for last year; or, it may be a type of advertising allowance — 50 cents per unit or 28 cents per case bought by the retailer.

Most co-op dollars go into newspaper advertising. Many manufacturers, in fact, restrict their cooperative advertising funds to this medium. Co-op advertisements, however, are also found in television, radio, outdoor, transit, point-of-purchase, and direct-mail advertising. Manufacturers may or may not ask retailers to get pre-approval for co-op advertisements or to submit proof of cooperative advertising run. In some cases, it appears that the retailer is paying one-half the cost of a *manufacturer's* advertisement; in other cases, the manufacturer appears to be paying one-half the cost of a *retailer's* advertisement.

Advantages Claimed for Manufacturers. Cooperative advertising is attractive to manufacturers on several counts. The retail rate is considerably lower than the general rate. As a generalization, retailers' advertisements get better position in media than is given to manufacturers' advertising. The fact that a manufacturer offers retailers a cooperative plan can be helpful in signing up additional and especially wanted dealers. It can also be helpful in getting present retail customers to stock his merchandise in quantity and to display it. The offer can stimulate retail interest in the manufacturer's products and make a bid for retail good will. The availability of co-op dollars encourages some retailers to advertise; it causes other retailers to

Advertising Organizations and Institutions

advertise the manufacturer's brands more than they would otherwise. Cooperative advertising ties the manufacturer's brand to a local store, giving the brand a local home and telling the consumer where to buy. Manufacturers launching a new product stand to benefit particularly if the cooperating retailer's prestige is outstanding in his community.

Manufacturers' Problems. One of the most serious problems in a manufacturer's use of vertical cooperative advertising involves rates and charges. There are several versions of abuse and sharp practice in this area. In one version which requires a friendly medium, the retailer pays the local rate, but gets another invoice — one figured on the general rate — to send to the manufacturer. If the split was 50–50, and if the general rate is twice as high as the retail rate, the retailer would be getting the advertising at no cost to himself. In another version, the retailer may qualify for a large discount off the open (retail) rate because of the large amount of space he buys during the year — but bill the manufacturer at the full open rate. A few large retailers actually broker local time and space to manufacturers, making a calculated and intended profit on the co-op advertisements. Dishonest retailers have discovered several ingenious ways to defraud manufacturers. One of their techniques, for instance, is to split-run two or more different advertisements, then bill each manufacturer as though his advertisement appeared in the newspaper's entire circulation.

What can the manufacturer do? One course of action, drastic to be sure, is to abolish his vertical cooperative advertising program. Another possibility is for the manufacturer to build outstanding advertisements for his retailers and then to pay only for them. Some manufacturers set a fixed line rate for each city and pay only in terms of it. Better administration of the program, particularly more checking up on the advertisements for which retailers request dollars, is indicated in some cases.

That leads to a second problem, namely, that of administering the program. These programs are costly to supervise, manage, and control. There is much bookkeeping, clerical work, and correspondence if the manufacturer tries to check on rates, copy, schedules, prices, and media. For this reason, some manufacturers make no effort to get proof of retailers' advertising, feeling that too much detail and expense are involved.

A third problem, related to the second one, consists of the differences, the disagreements, the possible causes of friction between a manufacturer and his retailers. A real danger is that the retail group will ask a manufacturer for more and more in the way of advertising assistance. If the manufacturer goes along and grants some of the requests, his cooperative advertising program can easily become too large a part of his total advertising. And, once started, these programs are most difficult to discontinue. Even if only one-sixth of a manufacturer's retailers run any cooperative advertising, they may account for 30, 40, or even 50 per cent of his sales volume. Another possibility, a real and present problem to some unfortunate manufacturers, is that some retailers will run more advertising than they are entitled to run — and expect the manufacturer to participate. Some retailers have been known to run a full-page advertisement of which one-eighth was given to a manufacturer's product — yet the manufacturer was asked by the retailer to pay one-half the cost of the page. Sometimes retailers include competing products in the same advertisement, or rewrite the copy supplied and stipulated by the manufacturer, or schedule the advertising for poor days, or use a co-op advertisement when in need of a rate holder. These and other similar possibilities can cause trouble for the manufacturer.

A final problem is the legal risk of offering promotional aid to retailers. Sections 2d and 2e of the Robinson-Patman Act can trip any manufacturer who discriminates illegally among or between competing retailers.

Advantages for Retailers. Cooperative advertising reduces the amount of money a retailer would otherwise spend for advertising, or it permits him to do more advertising with the same number of dollars. Often the advertisements supplied by a manufacturer are superior to advertisements created locally. In certain cases, the retailer acquires some prestige from identifying himself in his advertising with certain manufacturers and their brands.

Retailers Problems. It is easy and natural for retailers to feel that manufacturers go too far in telling a retailer what he can and cannot do. It is easy and natural for retailers to resent the manufacturer's emphasis on *his* identity and brand. Retailers must avoid running advertisements that have too much of a "canned" look or too much of a non-local appearance. Retailers must resist trying to live off manufacturers' cooperative dollars for promotion. Sometimes a brand is advertised mainly because co-op funds are available even though that selection was not sound, even though it denied promotion to a brand which deserved it. Retailers complain that some manufacturers reimburse too slowly.

TESTING AND EVALUATING

Retailers have the same interest in maximizing and then measuring the performance of their advertising dollars that manufacturers have. Most of the techniques already mentioned can be adapted and used by retailers wanting to do so. Ideally, the retailer would like to be able to determine (a) the dollar volume of purchases caused by each advertisement and (b) the number of consumers who visit his store as a result of each advertisement. These goals are too precise to be realistic.

Although the pulling power of any one advertisement other than mail order cannot be measured with complete accuracy, a check of the cash register does reflect consumer response fairly satisfactorily. Because his advertising is so direct-action in nature and because he does not have to attempt campaign appraisals, the merchant can do a more accurate job of advertising evaluation than can the manufacturer.

The more systematic retailers keep a detailed record of their advertising. This record includes date of advertisement and weather on the selling day, the day on which the response to the advertisement can be expected; for advertisements in Thursday's afternoon newspapers and for those in Friday's morning newspapers, Friday is the selling day. The product advertised and its price are noted. The size of the advertisement, its cost, and the medium in which the advertisement appears

Advertising Organizations and Institutions

are recorded. If practicable, a normal sales volume for the selling day is approximated. Actual sales volume of the advertised product on the selling day is recorded, and the ratio of advertising cost to this sales volume is computed. Then, promotional stores may keep a record of sales for one or two days after the selling day, non-promotional stores for four or five subsequent days.

Some retailers try to arrive at desirable ratios between selling-day-sales-volume-in-dollars and advertising-cost-in-dollars. For example, a promotional retailer may hope this ratio to be 5-to-1 for regular-priced items, 10-to-1 for special promotions. A non-promotional retailer, in like manner, might hope these two ratios for him would be 2-to-1 and 4-to-1.

THE RETAIL ADVERTISING DEPARTMENT

In Small Stores

There is no formal advertising department in small stores; indeed, there is no departmentalization for the advertising activity and rarely is there a single full-time advertising employee. The owner or manager is, in effect, the advertising manager just as he is the credit manager, the personnel manager, the sales manager, and so on. Because of his limitations in respect to both talent and time, the typical small merchant does not have a planned program of advertising. Instead, he is most likely to advertise whenever he feels like it or in response to some successful selling by a representative from a local medium.

Advertising assistance for the small retailer from his local media was mentioned in the section on scheduling. Trade papers and national trade associations also offer advertising help. Certain manufacturers who market their brands through selective distribution channels have advertising service facilities on which their retail dealers can draw for advertising advice and materials. The more progressive of the small merchants study the advertising done by the large, mass retailers who use advertising successfully, and then adapt, or even adopt. Finally, certain small retailers make some use of the services of local specialized advertising firms and of free-lance specialists.

In Large Stores

In the larger store, there may be one junior employee who looks after the firm's advertising, or one executive and a clerk, or a complete, competent advertising department staffed by a dozen or two specialists in media buying, copy, proofreading, art work, layout, and typography. The large departments plan and then prepare the store's advertising, seldom being forced to go outside the firm for any advertising services. Seldom do these large departments make use of manufacturers' copy or art work, of mat services, or of media assistance. Such staffs are at all times close to the store's customers, to the store's merchandising executives, and to the merchandise bought.

The head of the advertising staff in the large stores has a counterpart and complement in the person in charge of the store's display. The organization chart might look like this:

502

The Retail Advertiser

```
                    Sales Promotion Manager
                             or
                      Publicity Director
                              |
    ————————————————————————————————————————————————
    |                                              |
Advertising Manager                         Display Director
    |                                              |
  • Copy                                        • Window
  • Art                                         • Interior
  • Production
```

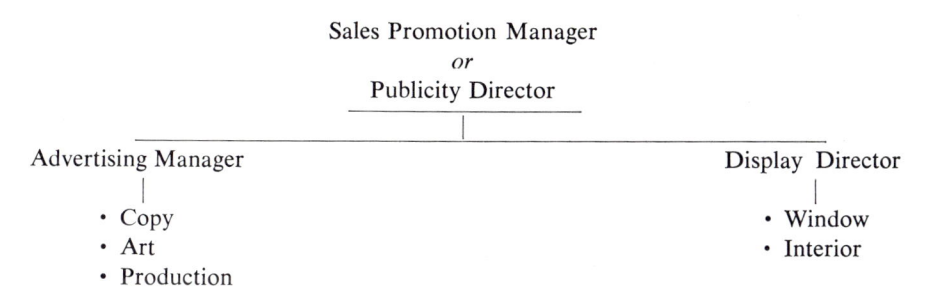

Use of Advertising Agencies

There are two prominent features of retail advertising which argue against the use of advertising agencies by retail advertisers. One is the use of the retail rate by media when billing retailers; this rate, you recall, is considerably lower than the general rate, and advertising billed as retail is not commissionable. Because of this fact, any use of advertising agencies by retailers in the preparation and placing of local advertising must be on a fee basis, a fee paid by the retailer to the agency. The other discouraging influence is the frequent need to make last minute changes in a retailer's advertising. A stock of merchandise sells out, a price is changed, a special purchase is made unexpectedly, competitors act and cause immediate reaction, the weather departs from its forecast, or expected merchandise fails to arrive on time. Because these developments do occur, and because much retail advertising is *news*, to go through an advertising agency would take too much time.

Despite these conditions, some medium-sized stores do find satisfactory the use of agencies to handle retail clients. In such instances, the agency is somewhat of a substitute for a modest advertising department. The medium-sized stores may choose to supplement the work of the agency with the services of free lance advertising specialists or, indeed, to hire those specialists rather than an agency.

Even some of the largest retailers work through advertising agencies on occasion. They may employ an agency to handle the advertising in a specific medium, magazines or television, for instance. Or, they may assign to an agency the responsibility for advertising some special event or project or for the firm's institutional advertising.

THE RETAIL ADVERTISING PLAN

A great advertising need of a great number of advertising retailers is for more and better planning. Most small retailers do not plan their advertising; instead, they advertise when they feel like it, or feel that they can afford to, or feel that a medium's salesman is correct in claiming that the store should run an advertisement or two. Media sales forces, incidentally, could do nicely with additional genuine and able salesmen who analyze a retailer's business and then design an appropriate advertising program; they already contain enough individuals who sell one advertisement at a time.

Before a retailer starts drafting an advertising plan, his first responsibility is to check his operations to see that they are sound, that he is ready and entitled to invite

Advertising Organizations and Institutions

the public to visit his store. In this pre-advertising stage, he will check to see that his merchandise is right, that his prices are right, that he offers the services his customers want, that his physical store and its premises meet with the approval of those customers, and that his personnel are ready, even anxious and expert if such can be achieved, to serve customers as customers prefer to be served.

Building the Plan

The first step toward an *advertising* plan is the drafting of the *sales* plan, a sales forecast of the merchandise the merchant intends to sell during the coming calendar year. These merchandise budget figures need to be available month by month and department by department.

Step two is to plan tentatively the number of dollars which must be spent in advertising in order for the firm to attain the sales goals set in step one. Then, this figure should be allotted to the departments by months according to each department's monthly sales quota. Adjustment, however, will be necessary. The date on which Easter falls changes, for example, calling for a recognition of this fact in making up monthly plans; or, if a new line of merchandise or, indeed, a new department is scheduled for a certain time next year, need for advertising dollars will be greater then than in previous years. The importance of advertising varies from department to department with the result that the advertising-to-sales ratios vary. Cameras and candy, to cite two examples, may draw advertising amounts which approximate 1 per cent of their sales quotas, whereas for summer furniture and house dresses, to cite two examples, the ratio may work out to be 4.7 per cent. Be that as it may, each department winds up with two figures for each month of next year — a sales quota and an advertising allotment. If a department expects to do 15 per cent of next year's sales during the month of September, then its September advertising allotment would be 15 per cent of its advertising allotment for the year.

The retail advertising plan is set up in this manner because of the regularity of a store's sales pattern year after year. Department stores, for example, can count on their dollar sales volume to follow a pattern closely. Within the department store, however, individual departments would vary from any over-all total pattern.

The sales-and-purchase patterns tend to repeat year after year because consumers buy according to patterns which change very little from year to year. These patterns can and should be used by retailers in timing their advertising but usually with some minor adjustment. Retailers probably should spend less percentage-wise for December advertising and a little more in January, in February, and in the summer months than each month's sales volume would dictate. Retailers should not, of course, attempt to level out completely or even to modify drastically their seasonal sales curves.

Within each month, the most effective advertising schedule observes the same principle just examined — heavy advertising for big selling days, and light advertising for days when traffic is naturally light. As has been mentioned, advertisements in Thursday afternoon newspapers and advertisements in Friday morning newspapers "work" on Friday, their "selling" day, and it is the selling day rather than the publication day which is important. Thursday is the biggest problem day of the week. It is too far along to benefit much from the previous Sunday's advertising or from first-of-the-week buying, yet it, in consumer thinking, is before and not a part of the weekend. Many merchants are aided in their scheduling by a sales promotional calendar published annually by the Domestic Distribution Department of the Chamber of Commerce of the United States entitled, "Special Days, Weeks, and Months."

To summarize, the retail advertising plan should be thought of as being based on these concepts:

(1) Sales forecast broken down by months and by departments.
(2) Advertising budget broken down by months and by departments.
(3) Media to be used scheduled by days and by departments.
(4) Schedule of advertisements to be run — by size, by medium, by days, by departments.
(5) Advertising costs in dollars and as a per cent of sales.

The one remaining matter — what merchandise to advertise — is the subject of our next section.

What to Advertise

What to advertise is a big problem for the typical retailer because he stocks hundreds of items; there are, however, some principles and some guides available to him. Research is indicated in some situations; a large retailer can stock a small, trial quantity of a certain product, observe and conclude from the response it gets, and, if the product sells quickly and impressively, he can reorder in volume and advertise it. Another guide, clearly and unquestionably proved, is the principle of placing the bulk of an advertising fund behind the most popular items in the fastest selling price lines. This is the principle of advertising those products which would sell best if the firm did no advertising. Some advertising dollars *are* used to clear out slow-moving merchandise; price reductions and aggressive personal selling are also used for this purpose. Another sound principle, one closely related to the one recommending the popular products, is to advertise *timely* merchandise, items the consumer has reason for wanting *today*. Just what products are timely? Those about which there is legitimate news are timely. Those related to events of the day (school opening, weather, holidays, local pay day) are timely. Seasonal products are timely just before the peaks of their heaviest buying seasons. Timely products for a retailer to put tie-in advertising behind are those being promoted vigorously at the moment by their manufacturers. Sources of supply will advise a retail customer what to feature; media will also give advice. Multi-product advertisements benefit from the inclusion of one or more traffic-building items, products bought frequently such as sugar or coffee in the grocery area or loss leaders which are outstanding values. The profit potential of a product is a consideration; what competitors are advertising is another. Some small retailers feature the national brands they carry, whereas the mass retailers feature their own brands. An ever present influence is the retailer's experience in selecting merchandise to be advertised. His own sales records tell what sold well at the same time *last* year. The Bureau of Advertising of the American Newspaper Publishers Association reports on the items which, in general,

Advertising Organizations and Institutions

BEST SELLERS FOR DECEMBER

Commodities which in December received 8.3% or more of the year's total sales.

Woolen Yard Goods	11.0	Men's Clothing	15.4
Linens and Towels	15.1	Men's Furnishings and Hats	27.2
Blankets, Comforters and Spreads	12.6	Boys' Wear	18.2
Women's and Misses's Coats	12.2	Men's and Boys' Shoes and Slippers	17.1
Juniors' Coats, Suits and Dresses	13.1	Draperies, Curtains, Upholstery and Awnings	9.5
Girls' Wear	16.2	Lamps and Shades	14.0
Blouses, Skirts and Sportswear	15.4	China and Glassware	17.7
Aprons, Housedresses and Uniforms	9.8	Housewares (Including Small Appliances)	15.8
Furs	19.8	Radios, Phonographs and Television Sets	19.4
Handkerchiefs	28.6	Toys and Games	39.9
Neckwear and Scarfs	18.6	Sporting Goods and Cameras	25.4
Women's and Children's Gloves	25.5	Luggage	19.5
Corsets and Brassieres	10.2		
Infants' Wear (Including Infants' Furniture)	15.9		
Handbags and Small Leather Goods	20.6		

When selecting what to advertise, retailers are attracted to items popular that month. (Courtesy: Bureau of Advertising; Source: Federal Reserve Board Sales Report)

were heavily advertised at the same time last year. This Bureau also identifies the months in which certain products sell better than average, months in which sales are greater than 8.3% of total annual volume.

Administration

The larger stores arrive at a total figure for the advertising fund and then earmark two portions of it. A reserve of about 10 per cent is set aside against future needs. These dollars are available to advertise new products, new services, or special purchases — needs and opportunities whose exact natures and dates are not known now. A second portion of about 10 per cent is set aside for two uses, institutional advertising, and storewide promotions such as an Anniversary Sale, a Dollar Day, or End-of-Month Sales. The remainder of the fund, about 80 per cent of the total figure, is used in day-to-day advertising, including departmental promotions such as Travel Week, Housewares Sale, or the August Fur Sale. Some of the larger stores prepare charts to show the relation of next year's plans month by month and department by department to this year's performance.

A well-kept scrapbook, current and complete, can be used to advantage in increasing the effectiveness of a store's advertising. In it is filed a copy of each advertisement run with comments and suggestions about each. Essentially, the scrapbook shows what the store did, tells how the store made out, summarizes why the advertising performance was what it was, and recommends what should be done next year. The scrapbook can be extremely helpful in determining how much to spend

The Retail Advertiser

in advertising, in selecting the merchandise to advertise, in writing better copy and in making better layouts, in choosing media more wisely, and in scheduling advertising more profitably.

Benefits of Planning

The benefits of planned retail advertising are overwhelming. Planning leads to an awareness of past and present advertising, an awareness which logically leads to study, analysis, and improvement, to a repetition of what was profitable and an avoidance of what was unprofitable. Planned advertising prevents hit-or-miss, haphazard, day-to-day advertising decisions, encouraging, instead, an advertising policy characterized by unity and continuity. Only by planning can the retailer insure the proper amount of advertising to each product line, to each department, and to each promotion; each gets equitable and appropriate treatment. Planning helps maximize the effectiveness of each advertising dollar by making for the most productive advertising schedules. Thus are avoided advertising feasts — and famines. There is more and more efficient coordination where there is planning, coordination all the way from buying to delivery of customers' purchases. Finally, when a store's policy is to plan its advertising one month in advance (with an absolute minimum of one week for an advertisement and with major promotions planned six months in advance), enough time will be budgeted for the preparation and the execution of sound, profitable advertising.

Questions and Problems

1. How do you account for the unethical advertising run by a few retailers?
2. What differences may be found between retailers' advertising copy and manufacturers' advertising copy?
3. What differences do you see between the marketing research needs of retailers and those of manufacturers?
4. When might it be smart for a retailer to feature a manufacturer's brand name or trade name in a window display?
5. How might a retailer go about compiling a mailing list of his cash customers?
6. How may displays designed by top-quality department and specialty stores differ from displays supplied by manufacturers?
7. What features of vertical cooperative advertising appeal to retailers?
8. What differences do you see between retailers' scheduling and that done by manufacturers?
9. A high quality, high prestige jewelry store in a large city is understandably concerned with the personality attributed to it by prospective customers. Suggest some features for the store's newspaper advertising if the store is to acquire and maintain the image it desires.
10. The Monarch Organ Company makes a line of electric organs for the home. It is a closely held corporation; the founder's son was president and chief executive officer for 25 years, retiring last year. A grandson of the founder became the firm's third president. He immediately began to question every policy and practice of the

Advertising Organizations and Institutions

firm, including cooperative advertising. The new president thought these dollars should be spent in magazine advertising.

Monarch sold through a small number of retail dealers, granting franchises for exclusive distribution except in the very largest markets. Monarch's total advertising fund averaged about 3% of net sales; about one-half of the fund was spent on the cooperative advertising program. Monarch matched its retailers dollar-for-dollar on newspaper advertising featuring Monarch organs, this matching going up to 5% of a dealer's purchases. Analysis showed that one-sixth of Monarch's retailers used up to the limit of the cooperative dollars available; this one-sixth accounted for two-fifths of Monarch's dollar sales volume. One-third of the Monarch dealers did not participate in the coop program.

Comment.

Index

A

A.A.A.A., 428
Account executive, 433
Acquired wants, 122
Advertisement's goals, 115–117
Advertising:
  as communication, 109–114
  direct, 19, 308
  industrial, 469–480
  nature of, 32–47
  retail, 487–507
  social and economic aspects, 48–68
  trade, 481–485
  vs. public relations, 28
  vs. publicity, 26
Advertising agencies, 427–447
  A.A.A.A., 428
  accounting, 436
  A.N.A. study, 443–445
  account executive, 433
  art, 434
  as marketing agencies, 446
  compensation, 441
  consent decree, 442
  copy, 434
  development, 428
  functions, 429–438
  in industrial advertising, 480
  international, 447
  mechanical production, 436
  media, 434
  merchandising, 438
  networks, 428
  new business, 429–433
  organization, 438
  public relations, 436
  recognition of, 440
  research, 435
  relations with clients, 457
  selection of, 458
  traffic, 436
Advertising budget (*see* Budgeting)
Advertising Council, 65

Advertising departments, 448–467
  advertising managers, 451–456
  functions of, 448–451
  industrial, 480
  relations with agencies, 457
  retail, 502
  selection of agencies, 458
Advertising managers, 451–456
  advertising functions, 452
  managerial functions, 453–456
Advertising research (*see* Evaluation)
Advertising specialties:
  advertising novelties, 369
  calendars, 369
  executive gifts, 369
Aided recall tests, 420
A.N.A. study, 443–445
Appeals, positive vs. negative, 124–126

B

Basic wants, 122
Believability, 181
Benefits which appeal to buyers, 115–135
Booklets, 311
Brand names, 70–85
  desirable characteristics, 77–80
  generic, 82–84
  types of, 73–76
  undesirable characteristics, 80–82
Broadsides, 312
Budgeting, 383–405
  and the business cycle, 402
  approaches to, 393–395
  budget administration, 395–403
  budget distribution, 396
  budget period, 395
  considerations, 384–393
  continuity, 400
  flexibility, 399
  for industrial advertising, 478
  observations about, 403–405
  place of budget, 2, 384
  "raids" on budgets, 399

509

Index

Business magazines, 221
Buyer benefits, 15, 117
Buying decisions, 162

C

Calendars, 369
Campaigns:
   consumer, 345–356
   evaluation of, 421
   horizontal cooperative, 352–356
   institutional, 352
Catalogs, 312
Catalogs, industrial, 477
Channels, marketing, 21–25
Check lists, 409
Circulars, 311
Classified advertising, 210
Classified display advertising, 211
Color, 198–202, 339
   and media, 201
   limitations of, 201
   psychology of, 199
   qualities of, 198
   reproduction, 199
   uses of, 200
Communication, 107–114, 380
   advertising as, 109–114
   construction, 109
   objectives, 109
   reception, 111
   response, 112
   symbols, 108
   transmittal, 110
Consumer:
   juries, 410
   motivation, 119
   Movement, 65–68
   services, 21
Consumer campaigns, 345–356
   campaign concept, 345
   horizontal cooperative, 352–356
   institutional, 352
   objectives, 351, 352, 356
   product promoting, 347–351
   slogans, 350
   themes, 347–350
Consumers, 3, 4
Consumers, what they buy, 3–12
   images, 8

   price, 9
   product satisfaction, 5
   seller-supplied services, 7
Contests, 21
Continuity in scheduling, 341–344
Controller, coordination with advertising, 377
"Co-op" advertising, 499–501
Coordination, 357–381
   advertising and personal selling, 357–362
   advertising and production, 374–377
   advertising and public relations, 370–373
   advertising and research, 373
   advertising and sales promotion, 362–370
   advertising and the controller, 377
   aids toward, 378–381
Copy, 158–183
   considerations, 180–182
   format, 165
   headlines, 166
   length of, 179
   objectives of, 163–165
   principles, 160–162
   retail, 492
   subheads, 174
   text or body, 174–179
Coverage in scheduling, 327–336

D

Davis, K. R., 444
Demand stimulation:
   primary, 40
   selective, 43
Direct advertising, 19
Direct mail advertising, 308–324
   as sales promotion, 368
   circulation, 316–318
   features of, 313
   forms of, 309–313
   letters, 318–321
   techniques, 322
   testing, 323
   timing, 322
   uses of, 314–316
Duplicated circulation, 332

E

Engravings:
  half-tone, 194
  line, 193
Evaluation, 407–423
  aided recall tests, 420
  check lists, 409
  conclusions on, 422
  consumer juries, 410
  inquiries, 414–416
  of campaigns, 421
  of retail advertising, 501
  recognition tests, 417–420
  split-run tests, 416
  test market tests, 411–414
  timing the research, 408

F

Folders, 311
Formal balance, 150
Frequency in scheduling, 336–341
Frey, A. W., 444

G

Gaze motion, 148
General display advertising, 209
Generic brand names, 82–84
Gifts, 313
Guardians of the consumer, 60–65

H

Halcomb, W. F., 481
Headlines, 158
Horizontal cooperative campaigns, 352–356
House organs, 313

I

Identification, retail, 491
Illustrations, 152–157
Images:
  of brand, 8
  of seller, 9
Industrial advertising, 469–480
  budgets, 478
  campaign goals, 477
  catalogs, 477
  construction of, 473
  evaluation of, 479

  media for, 474
  nature of, 471
  scheduling of, 476
Industrial campaign objectives, 477
Industrial catalogs, 477
Industrial and trade advertising, 469–486
Informal balance, 151
Inquiries, 414–416
Institutional advertising, 36, 371, 488
Institutional campaigns, 352

L

Labeling:
  grade, 103
  informative, 103
Landes, Dean J. D., 210
Lanham Act, 84
Layout, 136–157
  balance, 150–152
  characteristics desired, 139
  contrast, 145
  gaze motion, 148
  illustrations, 152–157
  movement, 147–150
  nature of, 137–139
  optical center, 143
  proportion, 146
  requisites of good, 144–152
  structural motion, 148
  types, 138
  unity, 144
  visualization, 136
  weight, 143
Letters, 310, 318–321
Local area sales tests, 411–414

M

Magazines, 219–234
  business, 221
  circulation, 226–230
  cost comparisons, 233
  features, 223
  general consumer, 219
  newspaper type, 222
  rate structure, 230–233
  women's, 221
Mail order selling, 308
Mailing cards, 309
Mailing lists, 316–318

Index

Manufacturers' consumer campaigns, 345–356
Marketing channels, 21–25
  changes in, 25
  consumer products, 23
  determinants of, 24
  distribution intensity, 22
  industrial products, 23
  structure, 22
Marketing research, 28–30
  information sources, 29
  limitations of, 30
  need for continuity, 30
  typical projects, 29
  what, 28
  why, 29
Media:
  for industrial advertising, 474
  for retail advertising, 494
  for trade advertising, 482
Merchandising the advertising program, 365–370, 456, 484
Milline rate, 217
Motivation of consumers, 119
Motivation, emotional vs. rational, 123
Motivation research, 129–135
  conclusions, 134
  definition of, 131
  techniques, 131–133

N

Networks, advertising agency, 428
Newspaper magazines, 222
Newspapers, 205–218
  circulation, 212
  classification of, 205–207
  cost comparisons, 217
  features of, 208
  position, 214–216
  rate structure, 212–214
  types of advertising, 209–211

O

Optical center, 143
Outdoor advertising, 271–279
  circulation, 277
  copy, 278
  design, 279
  features of, 274
  painted displays, 272
  posters, 271
  rate structure, 276
  spectaculars, 273
Outside envelopes, 310

P

Package inserts, 104
Package qualities, 93
Packaging, 93–105
  copy, 98
  decisions, 99–103
  design, 97
  grade labeling, 103
  informative labeling, 103
  package inserts, 104
  what consumers want, 96
  what manufacturers want, 94
  what retailers want, 95
Painted displays, 272
Pedlow, P., 481
Percent-of-sales concept, 385–387
Personal selling:
  coordination with advertising, 357–362
  creative selling, 14
  data salesmen need, 15
  job of selling, 14
  salesmanship, 14
  selling process, 17
  service selling, 14
Point-of-purchase promotion, 19, 291–307
  as sales promotion, 367
  classification, 291
  display essentials, 297–299
  distribution methods, 299
  features of, 292–298
  management of, 305
  payment for, 301–303
  retailers' selection of, 300
  uses of, 298
  waste in, 303–305
Posters, 271
Premiums, 21
Price, 9
Prices in general advertising, 182
Pricing:
  cost plus, 11
  market minus, 11

Primary demand, 40, 123
Printing processes, 196
Product advertising, 36, 488
Product features, 15, 117
Product-promoting campaigns, 347–351
Production, 193–197
  Ben Day, 196
  coordination with advertising, 374–377
  engravings, 193–196
  printing processes, 196
Products, consumer:
  convenience, 5
  shopping, 5
  specialty, 6
Promotion mix, 2
Public relations, 27
  coordination with advertising, 370–373
  phases, 28
  programs, 28
  vs. advertising, 28
Public relations activities, 451
Publicity, 25–27, 372
  forms of, 26
  media relations, 26
  planning of, 27
  vs. advertising, 26

R

Radio, 235–269
  circulation, 248
  commercials, 266–268
  composition and classification, 236
  features of, 240–242
  programs, 260
  rate structure, 251
  scheduling, 260–261
  spot, 254
Rationalization, 128
Reading notices, 211
Recall tests, 420
Recognition tests, 417–420
Research, advertising (*see* Evaluation)
Research, coordination with advertising, 373
Retail advertising, 487–507
  background of, 487–490
  budgeting, 498
  construction of, 491–494
  "co-op," 499–501
  evaluation, 501
  planning of, 503–507
  scheduling, 496
Retail display advertising, 210

S

Sales area tests, 411–414
Sales management, 17
Sales promotion:
  activities, 451
  advertising specialties, 368
  consumer stimulation, 19
  coordination with advertising, 362–370
  direct advertising, 19
  direct mail advertising, 368
  intra-firm services, 18
  merchandising the advertising program, 365–370
  point-of-purchase promotion, 19, 367
  retail relationships, 18
Sampling, 21
Scheduling, 327–344
  color, 339
  continuity, 341–344
  coverage, 327–336
  duplication, 332
  frequency, 336–341
  left- vs. right-hand page, 333
  media services, 333
  of trade advertising, 483
  reruns of ads, 340
  size of ad, 338
  the advertising schedule, 331
  timing, 342–344
Scale, W. B., 481
Selective demand, 43, 123
Self-mailers, 311
Sellers, how they sell, 13–30
Slogans, 350
Social and economic effects, 48–68
  on consumer prices, 55
  on consumers, 48–52, 58
  on costs, 54, 59
  on prices, 59
  on products, 52, 59
  on the economy, 56, 59
Social stratification, 120–122
Spectaculars, 273
Speculative presentations, 433

513

Index

Split-run tests, 416
Structural motion, 148

T

Task approach to budgeting, 387
Television, 235–269
    audience measurement, 242–245
    circulation, 246–248
    commercials, 262–266
    composition and classification, 235
    features of, 238–240
    merchandising the show, 268
    network, 254–256
    programs, 256–259
    rate structure, 248–251
    scheduling, 260
    spot, 253
Test market tests, 411–414
Trade advertising, 481–485
    campaign objectives, 483
    construction of, 482
    media for, 482
    nature of, 482
    scheduling of, 483
Trade characters, 85–91
Trade marks, 70–85
    desirable characteristics, 77–80
    undesirable characteristics, 80–82
Transit advertising, 280–290
    circulation, 284
    copy, 289
    features of, 285–288
    inside space, 280–282
    outside space, 282
    station posters, 283
Triple associates tests, 421
"Truline" rate, 494
Typography, 184–193
    anatomy of type, 184
    selection of face, 188
    suggestions, 190–193
    type groups, 185–188
    type measurement, 185

V

Visualization, 136